P9-DES-987

Tudor Royal Proclamations

1

Tudor Royal Proclamations

Volume 1

The Early Tudors (1485-1553)

edited by

Paul L. Hughes and James F. Larkin, c.s.v.

New Haven and London: Yale University Press, 1964

Designed by John O. C. McCrillis,
set in Granjon type,
and printed in the United States of America by
the Vail-Ballou Press, Incorporated,
Binghamton, New York.

Library of Congress catalog card number: 63-13965

Contents

List of Illustrations

Introduction

IF THE Tudor period of English history has left behind a large number of unsolved constitutional problems, it has also bequeathed a rich legacy of original documents to aid scholars in their search both for the actual Tudor conditions and for the precedents essential to an adequate understanding of modern times. Of special importance among surviving source materials for the clarification of many of these problems, and perhaps for the eventual solution of some of them, are the royal proclamations of the Tudor monarchs. Until the present time, however, most of the Tudor royal proclamations have been unavailable in print.[1] The result has been that these official crown documents remain virtually unexplored in modern research over a complex period of English history.[2]

1. Royal proclamations as yet have received little consideration in the standard collections of Tudor constitutional documents. For the period covered in this volume, there is one (17, below) in Geoffrey R. Elton's *The Tudor Constitution: Documents and Commentary* (Cambridge, 1960); one (218) in Richard H. Tawney and Eileen Power, eds., *Tudor Economic Documents* (London, 1924); one (129) in Carl Stephenson and Frederick Marcham, eds., *Sources of English Constitutional History* (New York, 1937); one (17) in Joseph R. Tanner, ed., *Tudor Constitutional Documents, A.D. 1485–1603* (2d ed. Cambridge, 1930); none in George B. Adams and Henry M. Stephens, eds., *Select Documents of English Constitutional History* (New York, 1901).

Among the earliest collectors of state papers relating to Tudor history, John Foxe, in his *Acts and Monuments,* ed. George Townshend (London, 1843–49), includes six proclamations (85, 122, 129, 200, 272, 287). David Wilkins, ed., *Concilia Magnae Britanniae et Hiberniae* (4 vols. London, 1732–37), gives the texts of 14 of Henry VIII's proclamations (85, 122, 129, 130, 155, 158, 186, 188, 191, 200, 203, 214, 248, 272) and seven of Edward VI's (287, 296, 297, 299, 300, 313, 383). Edward Rymer's *Foedera, conventiones, literae et cujuscunque generis acta publica . . .* (London, 1703–35) prints six from the reign of Henry VII (3, 5, 6, 20, 28, 55), four from that of Henry VIII (72, 89, 90, 91), and one (275), from the reign of Edward VI. John Strype, ed., *Ecclesiastical Memorials* (London, 1721), prints one proclamation of Henry VIII (191), ten of Edward VI's (276, 277, 280, 296, 299, 301, 309, 338, 348, 382), and a number of other excerpts and summaries. Seven Edwardian proclamations (287, 296, 297, 299, 303, 313, 352) are included in Edward Cardwell's *Documentary Annals of the Reformed Church of England* (2 vols. Oxford, 1844). Georg Schanz prints ten (144, 181, 184, 189, 199, 228, 233, 234, 238, 242) in his *Englische Handelspolitik gegen Ende des Mittelalters* (2 vols. Leipzig, 1881).

2. Geoffrey R. Elton has made the observation: "Proclamations remain a subject to be studied; we do not even yet possess a complete list, since R. R. Steele's well-known catalogue has gaps, nor has anyone yet attempted a systematic analysis of their content, enforcement, and general significance." See his "State Planning in Early Tudor England," *Economic History Review,* 2d series, *13* (1959–60), 434. The present work provides complete texts for such analysis. See Robert Steele, *Bibliography of Royal Proclamations of the Tudor and Stuart Sovereigns. . . . With an Historical Essay on their Origin and Use,* Vol. 5, *Bibliotheca Lindesiana* (Oxford, 1910). With its brief summaries of texts, this calendar has heretofore served, for the most part, in place of the documents themselves.

As the first edition of all extant early Tudor royal proclamations, the present volume attempts to fill part of this editorial gap. It presents modern English transcripts of 388 proclamations by Henry VII (1485–1509), Henry VIII (1509–1547), and Edward VI (1547–1553). Of these historic documents,[3] 238 (or just under two thirds) appear here in printed form for the first time; the others exist for the most part only in rare editions dating from their original issue.[4] A second volume, containing the royal proclamations of the later Tudors, Mary I (1553–1558) and Elizabeth I (1558–1603), now in preparation for the press, will complete the first collected edition of Tudor royal proclamations.

Most students of history are agreed that the years from the accession of Henry VII to the death of Elizabeth I represent a significant phase in the emergence of the modern English constitution. Many are convinced that this constitution, though based on custom and precedent, has outgrown the medieval concept of natural law and the national concept of common law as the people's chief defense against concentration of political power in the body politic. In any case, England's modern constitution received a rugged shaping in the political struggles, social and economic frictions, and intellectual and religious conflicts which developed early in the Tudor age. In these grave issues, the Tudor sovereigns made perhaps their most characteristic contribution in the form of frequent royal proclamations.

A final definition of the Tudor royal proclamation must await further study of their historical antecedents. Such investigation will have to take into account, among other sources, Anglo-Saxon laws[5] and writs[6] and medieval

3. This edition contains only proclamations by the Tudor monarchs. Non-royal proclamations, i.e. by the King's Council, commissioners, sheriffs, justices of the peace, mayors, and proclamations of parliamentary acts are thus excluded.

4. Each of these original editions is descriptively identified and located in the *Short-Title Catalogue of Books Printed in England, Scotland and Ireland, and of English Books Printed Abroad, 1475–1640,* ed. Alfred W. Pollard, G. R. Redgrave, et al. (London, 1926). There are two other important collections. In a volume covering the years 1547–50, Richard Grafton, Edward VI's printer, published a collective edition, *All Suche Proclamacions as Haue Been Sette Furth by the Kynges Maiestie . . .* (London, 1550), *STC* 7758. And there are lithographic reproductions of some 40 early Tudor royal proclamations in *Tudor Proclamations: Facsimiles of Proclamations of Henry VII, Henry VIII, Edward VI, and Philip and Mary* (London, Society of Antiquaries, 1897), an edition limited to 24 copies.

5. For Anglo-Saxon legislation by King and council in terms of royal command, see *Die Gesetz der Angelsachsen,* ed. Felix Liebermann (Halle, 1903–16): for Alfred, *1,* 46; for Aethelstan, *1,* 147; for Edmund, *1,* 187; for Eadgar, *1,* 195, 206; for William, *1,* 483. See also two useful collections, with revealing titles: *The Laws of the Earliest English Kings,* ed. and trans. F. L. Attenborough (Cambridge, 1922); and *The Laws of the Kings of England from Edmund to Henry I,* ed. and trans. A. J. Robertson (Cambridge, 1925). The latter gives modern translations of two royal proclamations by King Canute, in 1020 and 1027 (pp. 140, 166).

6. A list of royal writs serving the purpose of proclamations appears in *Anglo-Saxon Writs,* ed. Florence E. Harmer (Manchester, 1952), p. 19. For the resemblance of these writs to Frankish royal edicts, see pp. 30–31.

charters prior to the establishment of the House of Commons as a legislative body.[7] Steele's bibliography includes a preliminary handlist of pre-Tudor royal proclamations between 1204 and 1485.[8] A final definition must also await further study of the processes of Tudor administration. Heretofore, emphasis on statutes of the realm [9] passed in parliament, which eventually emerged with full sovereignty,[10] has perhaps obscured the historical importance of the Tudor monarch as the source of English law, the source not only of statutes enacted by the King with the consent of parliament but also of proclamations issued by the King with, at most, the consent of his council.[11]

For the purpose of this edition, however, and on the basis of the primary source materials which it presents, the early Tudor royal proclamation can be defined as: a public ordinance issued by the King, in virtue of his royal prerogative, with the advice of his council, under the Great Seal, and by royal writ.

Each element in this definition reveals a successive stage in the emergence of the proclamation as a legal document. The proclamation calls attention first of all, and throughout, to its origin in the royal prerogative. It embodies the strict order and command of "our sovereign lord the King." It carries the King's validating signature, or sign manual.[12] It is dated by the King's regnal year, and usually from his palace [13] or chancery.[14] It is promulgated by the King's writ.[15] Violators or breakers of his proclamation will incur

7. William Stubbs, ed., *Select Charters and Other Illustrations of English Constitutional History* (Oxford, 1913), p. 54. This collection includes the Middle English text of Henry III's proclamation pledging adherence to the Provisions of Oxford in 1258 (p. 387).

8. Steele, pp. CLVII–CLXVII.

9. *Statutes of the Realm*, eds. Alexander Luders et al. (London, 1810–28), is the source of all references to acts of parliament in the present edition.

10. For documentation of this development, see Paul L. Hughes and Robert F. Fries, eds., *Crown and Parliament in Tudor-Stuart England: A Documentary Constitutional History, 1485–1714* (New York, 1959).

11. Professor Holdsworth erroneously reads into the Statute of Proclamations (31 Henry VIII, c. 8, 1539, *SR 3,* 726) the necessity of Council consent for the validity of a Tudor royal proclamation (William S. Holdsworth, *History of English Law*, Boston, 1922–27, *4,* 103). For the text of the statute, which stipulates only the council's advice, see Appendix 1, p. 545. In his own royal proclamations Henry VIII records his council's advice 44 times, its consent three times.

12. For the sign manual of Henry VIII, see Plate 2, p. 84; for that of Edward VI, see Plate 4, p. 484.

13. An Edwardian draft mustering support for Somerset (351) is dated at Hampton Court on 1 October, 3 Edward VI: see Plate 4, p. 484. (The present edition supplies the year A.D. in every case: here, 1549.)

14. For a signed but undated proclamation bill (61), registered in the Westminster chancery on 20 November and filed with other Chancery Warrants during November, 1 Henry VIII, see Plate 2, p. 84.

15. For a printed Latin proclamation writ by Henry VII, ordering the sheriffs of Norfolk and Suffolk to proclaim the accompanying schedule of an ordinance regulating coin (57), see Plate 1, p. 60. For a similar directive in English, prefacing a proclamation by Henry VIII, see Plate 2, p. 84.

the King's indignation and must suffer penalties at his discretion. The general protocol of the document thus reveals it as a public ordinance having its origin in the King's prerogative.

Secondly, the early Tudor proclamation involves, at least in principle, the advice of the King's council.[16] Where evidence survives (and only excerpts from official acts of the Tudor councils are available before 1542), the council normally deals with proclamation drafts (5, 365, 376) and issues orders for proclamation to be made (13, 195, 276, 357, 373). In follow-up action, the council may order continued execution of an ordinance (33, 43, 357, 380), grant exemptions from its command (365), or set a penalty on violation (378).

Passage under the Great Seal is the third validating step in the emergence of a Tudor proclamation. Evidence of this action must be sought in a Chancery Warrant[17] for affixing the Great Seal to the signed proclamation bill. This Warrant, usually a rectangular parchment sheet, regularly records (1) the King's sign manual; (2) his writ of proclamation; (3) the schedule, or text, of the proclamation; and (4) evidence of the King's Privy Seal. The sign manual, i.e. the King's elaborate personal signature or initial, entered at the upper left-hand corner, identifies the document as an authentic crown instrument and serves as a warrant for the Privy Seal. Normally below the sign manual appears the King's writ, a formal written order to the proper crown official, ordering publication throughout his area of jurisdiction of the proclamation schedule which follows. This schedule is the legal text of the royal proclamation, the actual public ordinance by the King. It is, in other words, the Tudor royal proclamation as commonly understood and as presented in the documents which make up the present edition. Evidence of the Privy Seal on the Chancery Warrant now appears only in the small sharp slits originally made in the folded document for closure by the Privy Seal. These slits indicate that the document, having passed under the Privy Seal, warrants passage under the King's Great Seal.[18] By affixation of the Great Seal, the Tudor royal proclamation carries the full authority of the King's Letters Patent.

The Patent Rolls[19] provide a fourth official criterion of the proclama-

16. The assenting signatures of council members on a proclamation bill carrying Henry VIII's sign manual appear on Plate 2, p. 84. For Acts of the King's Council during the period covered by this edition, see Charles G. Bayne and William H. Dunham, Jr., eds., *Select Cases in the Council of Henry VII* (London, 1958); Huntington Library MSS Ellesmere; Nicholas H. Nicolas, ed., *Proceedings and Ordinances of the Privy Council of England, 1386–1542* (London, 1837); and John R. Dasent et al., eds., *Acts of the Privy Council of England, 1452–1628* (London, 1890–1907).

17. Chancery Warrants are classified under C82 in the Public Record Office of Great Britain. For a reproduction of a CW proclamation, see Plate 2, p. 84.

18. The Great Seal remains attached to one proclamation schedule (358) preserved in PRO (SP 13/Eliz./Case H).

19. The Patent Rolls are preserved in PRO, under C66. See Plate 3, p. 132.

tion. These parchment sheets, sewn together to make up rolls of permanent public record, contain true copies of the original Warrants. Proclamations usually appear on the Patent Roll's reverse side, or *dorsa* (hereafter, *d*). As a rule, the Patent Rolls confirm the evidence found in the earlier Chancery Warrants to which they correspond. More significantly for the completeness of this edition, they have preserved a number of texts for which the separately filed Chancery Warrants have disappeared. Once on the Patent Rolls, the proclamation is in the public domain.

There remains the dispatch of a proclamation writ ordering the proper crown official to proclaim publicly throughout his jurisdiction the attached proclamation schedule. Usually directed in the first instance to one officer (9, 127, 253, 359), this writ may be addressed to a number of sheriffs in proclamations affecting more than one section of the realm (18, 45, 63, 110, 266) or, as in the case of distraint of knighthood, to sheriffs throughout the land (9, 48, 49). Less formal than the Latin writ, Letters Patent may instead direct the promulgation and execution of proclamations involving numerous and varied officials (82, 168, 243, 301). Writs of proclamation are lacking for a number of the texts in this edition. Their absence is especially felt in the case of important proclamation drafts abolishing enclosures (75, 113, 309, 327), revaluing the coinage (180), and limiting the performance of plays and interludes (240).

Headnotes to the separate texts in this edition record all available validating evidence: of supporting actions by the King's Council, of the King's own signature, of Warrants for use of the Great Seal, of Patent Enrollments, and of writs of proclamation. These headnotes also include evidence of actual proclaiming found in editions by the King's printer, local public records, and contemporary diaries and chronicles.

From the preceding definition of early Tudor royal proclamations in terms of their textual provenance, it should be sufficiently clear that these public records are legal crown documents. As such they have the same constitutional validity as any other official instrument of Tudor government, including the statutes of the realm. Heretofore, it must be repeated, the problem has been that of their weight in the scale of English constitutional values. The traditional view, as set forth by Steele[20] and Holdsworth,[21] would limit the legal effects of Tudor proclamations to (1) publication or enforcement of an existing statutory or common law, (2) formal announcement of a royal act, (3) enforcement of crown rights in feudal contracts, and (4) temporary regulation or injunction based on a recognized crown prerogative. Of the 388 proclamations of the first three Tudors, 41 (or about 10 per cent), as indicated by their titles in the table of contents, directly enforce existing statutes. The statutory index at the end of this volume reveals, moreover, that 118 proclamations (or about one third) cite 167 statutes of the realm in the body of the

20. Steele, Introduction, pp. IX–XXIV, LXXV–XCI.

21. Holdsworth, *4*, 99 ff; *5*, 303 ff.

texts. To this extent, therefore, it is true that the early Tudor proclamations implement and supplement, rather than supplant, statutory law.

At the same time, however, massive evidence in the proclamations reveals that their authority was original rather than appellate and that there is serious need of a more adequate analysis of their legislative nature. Indications of firm legislative purpose appear even in the structure of these documents, a literary form psychologically gauged to elicit from the subject an obedient response, favorable to the will and interests of the crown. Lacking parliamentary authority, the early Tudor proclamations frequently conceal their legislative intent beneath what one scholar has aptly termed an "uncanny skill in presentment" [22] of the crown's case to the immediate interests of both the English subject and the English commonwealth. The establishment of the crown's actual purpose may involve as many as five distinct and successive steps, coordinated with legal and literary skill. These steps appear, as a rule, in the following sequence:

1. *Authorization.* The introductory element of an early Tudor proclamation frequently appeals to some source of civil authority other than the King's royal prerogative. This may be the law of God (63, 371), ancient custom (6), the advice or consent of lords and commons in parliament (15, 17, 80), the "advice of the lord chancellor of England and all the justices of either bench" (270), the statutes of the realm (122), or, specifically, the authority vested in the crown by the Statute of Proclamations (205, 211, 231, 271).[23] Edward's earliest proclamations appeal to both parliament and his royal predecessor (278, 279, 280, 283). By late spring of his first regnal year, however, the boy King's ordinances begin to stress the "advice of our dear uncle Edward, Duke of Somerset, protector . . . and the rest of our Privy Council" (284), a formal attribution persisting until Somerset's fall and Northumberland's ascendancy in the council. To achieve the royal purpose, the proclamation tends, in its first step, to direct public attention toward an established sanction for the present legislative order.

2. *Rationalization.* Carefully constructed to insure broad popular acceptance of this order, the second section of a Tudor proclamation focuses public attention on a definite need of the commonwealth and, thereby, on the virtue of the royal ordinance as a remedy. To protect English subjects, especially

22. John Craig, *The Mint* (Cambridge, 1953), p. 106.

23. 31 Henry VIII, c. 8, 1539, *SR 3,* 726. See Appendix I, p. 545. Relying on Steele, who failed to note this element in the proclamations, Professor Holdsworth was led into another error: "The passage of this statute may have been a very remarkable constitutional phenomenon; but a reading of the Tudor proclamations gives us no hint of its appearance" (*History of English Law, 4,* 296). For a recent analysis of this statute, reviewing the extensive bibliography, see Geoffrey R. Elton, "Henry VIII's Act of Proclamations," *English Historical Review, 75* (1960), 208–22. The texts of this act, the act modifying it (34 & 35 Henry VIII, c. 23, 1542, *SR 3,* 923), and the pertinent portion of the act repealing it—1 Edward VI, c. 12, 1547, *SR 4(1),* 19—are reprinted in Appendix I, pp. 545–52.

the poor, against fraud, Irish coins are henceforth outlawed (25). Because the export of grain is causing great dearth and scarcity at home, no one may henceforth export grain without the King's "special license, sealed under his Great Seal" (26). Inasmuch as English miners can no longer sell their ore at a profit, it will be necessary to establish a Staple of Mines (27). To frustrate the French King's diabolical plan to destroy Christian unity, a war subsidy must be collected (65). The flight of gold to the Continent can be halted only by raising its price, (i.e. lowering the gold content of English coins) at home (111). Because many inconveniences arise from interludes, common players will be imprisoned unless they can show the King's special license (371). Commonly occurring in this section of the proclamation is an expression of the King's zeal for his subjects' wealth, property, and security, the enjoyment of which, however, is likely to be limited by the present ordinance.

3. *Order.* This royal command, following the carefully laid groundwork of authorization and rationalization, is the heart of the proclamation. Previously alluded to as a need, for reasons often developed at length, the order is now directly issued. Ordinarily the central section of the document, the royal order is forthright in expression, precise and logical in structure. The obligation which it enjoins or the action which it prohibits is, so far as the King's talent and his council's advice can make it, unmistakable to all. Yet, despite its strict charge, the King's command is, if possible, not stated as a new limitation on the subject's liberty or so as to suggest that the crown's action is legislative in a statutory sense.

4. *Enforcement.* The 1539 Statute of Proclamations stipulates that proclamation violators are to be tried by a committee of the King's Council "in the Star Chamber or elsewhere."[24] We have already seen that the council, which originally gave advice on a proclamation, followed through in some cases with its enforcement. Indeed, the Ellesmere extracts from now-lost original Acts of Henry VIII's council[25] indicate that that body spent considerable time, even before enactment of the statute, trying violations of proclamations in the Star Chamber (66, 122, 129, 225). But the enforcement clause of a Tudor proclamation seldom makes any reference to the Star Chamber. One mentions it in a threat against regraters of grain (118); another as the place in which informers may claim their moiety of forfeiture for reporting unlicensed export of commodities (365). Possibly to receive delegation of responsibility for enforcement of particular legislative orders, all royal commissioners (109) and all justices of the peace (305) present in

24. Appendix I, p. 545.

25. Huntington Library MSS Ellesmere 436, 438, 439, 2654, 2655, 2758. These extracts from the Acts of the Council of Henry VIII were made late in the reign of Elizabeth I. With other related source materials they were made apparently to document both the antiquity and continuity of the Star Chamber and the royal prerogative of issuing binding proclamations. See William H. Dunham, Jr., "The Ellesmere Extracts from the *Acta Concilia* of Henry VIII," *English Historical Review, 58* (1943), 301–18.

London at the time are ordered to appear in the Chamber on given dates. Otherwise, the early Tudor proclamations mention it only as one of several courts for which barristers must obtain a special license (270).

Outside of the council, the enforcement clause of the proclamation may specify a commission of oyer and terminer (78) or special commissions, as in the case of enclosures (113, 114, 132, 338), peace (63), tithes (140, 148), and pensions (307). For the better enforcement of statutes, proclamations may give directions to quarter session (63, 108) and assize courts (183, 294). More regularly, however, the texts which make up this edition place the burden of executing and enforcing proclamations on local officials[26] already charged with executing parliamentary statutes.[27] The cases in which the early Tudor proclamations authorize these officials to act for the King are impressive: suppression of rebels (19, 333), trial of unlicensed printers of books (122, 161, 273, 371), punishment of heresy (85, 122, 299), discovery of persons evading distraint of knighthood (9, 48, 49), punishment of rumor mongers (11, 371), protection of patents and monopolies (27), apprehension of vagabonds and beggars (16, 30, 128, 204, 371), search of private premises for hoarded goods and commodities (242, 366), punishment of rumor mongers for passing tales concerning coin debasement (378), arrest of unlicensed fishermen (215) and military deserters (244), prohibition of meat in Lent (367), and exclusion of pirates from English ports (362). Sheriffs are ordered to observe and report back to the King and council the failure of bishops to execute royal proclamations on religion (158).

This de facto delegation of broad authority for the enforcement of royal proclamations to local officials again illustrates the necessity of consulting the documents themselves in order to understand the actual roles of central and local institutions in Tudor government. The enforcement clause of the proclamations points to increasing use of and control over local officials to insure the execution of legislative orders. It also suggests a manifest purpose on the part of the Tudor sovereigns to see their proclamations enjoy the same authority as parliamentary statutes within the jurisdiction of the common law.

5. *Penalty.* The final division of the Tudor proclamation prescribes punishment for the non-fulfillment or violation of its charge. Nowhere in the document is there clearer evidence of coercive purpose. Fines, forfeitures, and imprisonment are common penalties imposed.[28] Subjects may be offered re-

26. Fifteen of Henry VII's 59 proclamations directly charge local officials with enforcement. Henry VIII gives a similar charge in 73 of his 216. Edward does the same in 40 of his 113 proclamations.

27. 4 Henry VII, c. 12, 1488, *SR* 2, 537. This statute embodies a proclamation (17) ordering justices of the peace to execute all statutes and commands them to repeat the same proclamation four times each year.

28. Fines or forfeitures are indicated in 23 of Henry VII's proclamations, in 49 of Henry VIII's, and in 26 of Edward VI's; imprisonment in 19 of Henry VII's, 108 of Henry VIII's, and 38 of Edward's.

wards for informing on violators (133, 134, 357, 358), or may incur identical guilt by not preventing or by not informing on violations (11, 374, 378). Arbitrary penalties include the pillory (30, 63, 183, 377), corporal punishment (128, 204), mutilation (378), and galley service (329).

Contrary to a formal proviso in the Statute of Proclamations, intended to protect the rights of subjects under the common law,[29] an unexpected number of early Tudor royal proclamations carry the death penalty. In his first proclamation, uncalendared by Steele, Henry VII orders the execution of anyone breaking the peace begun by the death of Richard III (1). A year later he issues the same penalty for recrimination, robbery, and even for failure to pay prices legally established for victuals (13). Henry VIII commands the execution of disobedient soldiers and of any subject aiding the King of France (71). In 1535 all persons holding or teaching Anabaptist doctrines "shall within twelve days next after this present proclamation depart out of this his realm on pain of death" (155). Anyone disputing on the Holy Eucharist, other than a scholar, may be put to death (186). For homicide committed in street frays, as for slaying the King's officers, the penalty is death (179). In 1539 Henry decrees capital punishment for unlicensed shippers (190). Proclamations of Edward VI carry the death penalty for rioting over enclosures (334, 341), aiding pirates (323), and importing counterfeit coin (326). This incidence of capital punishment and the variety of offenses for which it is invoked raise their own questions of actual relationship of the common law and statutory penalties to Tudor proclamation penalties. But, mild or severe, statutory or arbitrary, within the royal prerogative or outside the common law, the penalty is there, a final, coercive reminder that subjects must obey the legislative orders of their King.

In summary: the structural pattern of the early Tudor proclamations reveals them as stressing the King's sovereign authority, issuing unmistakable public commands on grounds of the common good, and enforcing these legislative orders by means of penalties which include fine, forfeiture, imprisonment, corporal punishment, mutilation, and death. All this adds up to the presence in these documents of determined legislative intent on the part of the crown. Their immediate consequences in vital areas of English life make it difficult to avoid the conclusion that these documents have the full

29. "Provided always that the words, meaning, and intent of this act be not understood, interpreted, construed, or extended, that by virtue of it any of the King's liege people, of what estate, degree, or condition soever he or they be, bodies politic or corporate, their heirs or successors, should have any of his or their inheritances, lawful possessions, offices, liberties, privileges, franchises, goods, or chattels taken from them or any of them, nor by virtue of the said act suffer any pains of death other than shall be hereafter in this act declared, nor that by any proclamation to be made by virtue of this act, any acts, common laws standing at this present time in strength and force, not yet any lawful or laudable customs of this realm or other his dominions nor any of them, shall be infringed, broken, or subverted . . ." (Appendix 1, p. 546).

effects of law as well. It is by proclamation, rather than by parliamentary statute, that the early Tudor monarchs claim sovereignty (5, 208, 275). By proclamation they pronounce treasons (8, 41, 161, 339) and forfeitures of land and goods (41, 59, 339).[30] They proclaim war (52, 71, 220), truce (3, 76, 104, 120), peace (29, 51, 105, 268, 354), and alliances with foreign powers (23, 52, 71, 120, 147). At home, as we shall see, by royal proclamations more effectively than by statutes, they regulate coinage and commerce, grant licenses and patents, control the wool trade, profit from enclosures, and exercise crown supremacy in the church.

Nowhere in the national life do the early Tudors more effectively exercise the royal prerogative than in their ordinances affecting the coinage of the realm. Henry VII issues seven proclamations ordering acceptance of English coins (25, 38, 44), including "thin and old pence" (42) and coins admittedly "small and light in weight" (43).[31] Against a growing practice of clipping coins, he issues two ordinances regulating their acceptance and remelting (54, 57). Henry VIII intervenes in mint activities in 1522 with the first of a series of proclamations setting new values on foreign gold coins (88, 95, 102, 103). In 1526 he raises the value of English gold coins (111); at the same time he introduces the heavier Troy pound to replace the Tower pound on which existing coinage was based, and a new lighter crown standard, 22 carats, to replace the ancient standard of 23 carats (112), with a corresponding reduction in the sterling content of new silver coins. Again exercising his prerogative in 1544, during a period of war with France, Henry further reduces the carat and sterling content of English coins (228). Immediate effects of these measures are a rise in commodity prices (230, 231, 232, 235) and the unwillingness of producers to bring their goods to market (242). After several attempts to counteract the previous debasement of the currency (302, 321, 332), Edward VI resumes the coinage policies evident in his father's proclamations. In 1551 he lowers the value of the shilling, first to 9*d.* (372) and then to 6*d.* (379). The proclamations illustrate graphically the inevitable effects of early Tudor manipulations of the country's coin.[32]

30. For Henry VII's early development of an effective nonstatutory procedure for enriching the crown with forfeited lands, goods, and offices, see Charles H. Williams, "The Rebellion of Humphrey Stafford in 1486," *English Historical Review, 43* (1928), 181–89; also Walter Richardson, "The Surveyor of the King's Prerogative," *English Historical Review, 56* (1941), 52–75.

31. Rogers Ruding, *Annals of the Coinage of Britain* . . . 2 (London, 1819), 59, suggests that these last two proclamations of Henry VII may represent the first Tudor currency debasement.

32. According to Frederick C. Dietz, *English Government Finance: 1485–1558* (Urbana, 1921), Henry VIII gained more than £363,000 by recoinage and debasement from May of 1544 until his death (p. 140), while Edward VI profited by more than £330,000 between 14 May 1547 and 1 January 1551, i.e. before the worst debasement of his reign (pp. 176–77). For a list of forty species of coin affected by the proclamations of the first three Tudors, see Glossary.

An immediate consequence of this debasement of the coin is a corresponding number of proclamations by Henry VIII and Edward VI attempting to stabilize the price of commodities, especially foods. These include a commission for citing regraters and forestallers of grain before the Star Chamber (118), penalties for hoarding commodities (125, 127, 151, 242), and embargoes on the export of grain in times of dearth (94, 295, 304). After ordering enforcement of a recent statute requiring butchers to lower the price of meat by selling it by the pound (139), Henry repeatedly suspends this by proclamation (144, 148, 154, 159, 162, 193, 196). In a final effort, in 1544, he sets a maximum price of ½*d.* per pound on beef (231). To halt a continuing rise in the price of wines, Henry rates the best imported Gascon: in 1534 at £4 per tun (149), in 1537 at £5 per tun (170), and in 1544 at £8 per tun (206). In 1545, at the end of hostilities with France, he fixes the best wine at £6 per tun (260). During the war, Henry had issued proclamations pricing sugar (218), longbows, and armor (213, 235). Inheriting his father's problem of rising prices, Edward VI prohibits the export of commodities (315, 319, 357, 361) and successfully lowers the price of Gascon wine (383). His 1549 ceiling of 48*s.* 4*d.* on the best oxen (336), however, yields to a higher law of currency debasement in 1551 and to a new ordinance pricing the same animals at 53*s.* 4*d.* (380).

Licenses and monopolies account for some of the most effective early Tudor proclamations. At the outset of his reign, Henry VII permits only licensed persons to engage in the valuable monopoly of money exchange (10). He grants monopolies of grain export (26) and trade in continental markets (31).[33] Through the establishment of a Staple of Mines at Southampton in 1492, he is able to control both smelting and customs of tin and lead (27). And he places a proposed free mart at Calais in control of the Staple already in operation there (56). In 1499 he licenses foreign travel (47). Licenses to collect alms are granted by both Henry VII (32) and his successor (82, 84).

Henry VIII's first licensing proclamation protects an earlier patent for the exclusive import and sale of French and Gascon wines (68). Patentees supplying Calais are threatened with loss of their "protections" for unsatisfactory performance (91, 96). Defining the privileges of the Staple at Calais (115), Henry threatens with ultimate peril their unlicensed competitors (190). After granting a patent for money exchange (173), he later revokes it by allowing all merchants the same privilege (181, 182). The rationalization is encouragement of commerce, but the revocation may at the same time have resulted in greater income for the crown. Printing is also licensed. In a 1538 proclamation, Henry VIII prohibits the printing of any English book with-

33. For a concise summary of export and import licenses granted by Henry VII and Henry VIII, see Geoffrey R. Elton, "State Planning in Early Tudor England," *Economic History Review,* 2d series, *13* (1959–60), 438.

out license of the King's deputies (186) and unless the book contains the names of author and printer and the date of printing (272). After authorizing Cromwell to approve one Bible in English (192), he gives a monopoly for printing it to Anthony Marler (210) and outlaws the translation of Tyndale (272). In 1545 Henry grants exclusive license for printing the authorized English *Primer*[34] to Richard Grafton and Edward Whitchurch (251).

Like his father, Edward VI makes extensive use of licensing proclamations. After first extending permission for grain export to all his subjects (280), he soon prohibits all such export "without his special license under his Great Seal of England" (295). He requires exporters of food products to obtain special licenses, under penalties ranging from forfeiture to imprisonment (285, 304, 315, 319).

The proclamations indicate that the wool industry is of no less concern to the early Tudor monarchs than it had been to their predecessors. Henry VII does not permit serious differences with Burgundy in 1496 to interfere with the English export trade (31). With peace restored three years later, he immediately issues a proclamation re-establishing the highest standards of grading and marking of wool for sale abroad, under the jurisdiction of the merchants of the Staple (45).

In 1534, Henry VIII issues a proclamation reinforcing earlier statutes on the true making of woolen cloth (152) under pain of forfeiture of the improperly made materials, and of fines. However, a contemporary statute[35] obliging weavers to install new machinery in order to raise the quality of English woolen cloth meets so much opposition between 1536 and 1541 that the King repeatedly exercises his royal prerogative to suspend its effects (166, 175, 198, 202, 207). In 1545 fraudulent packers are threatened with imprisonment for ten days after which they are to be pilloried in public with fleeces hung about their necks (258). A year later, Staple officials caught conniving in fraud are held to forfeit double the value of their attempted deceptions (264).

Edward VI, in his first year, reissues this last wool proclamation minus, however, the prescribed penalty (278). To prevent further frauds in dyeing, stretching, and filling out of cloth in manufacture, he commands city and local officials to visit weaving houses four times each year to execute present orders for true manufacture, and to cite offenders before his council. Illegal wool buyers, violating both the law of the King and the high standards of the Staple, are to be imprisoned, pending further knowledge of the King's pleasure (331). Staple officials conniving in wool frauds are to suffer not only double forfeiture but also loss of their offices (345). Edward's final wool

34. *STC* 16,034.
35. 27 Henry VIII, c. 12, 1535, *SR 3*, 544.

proclamation, in 1550, is an ordinance against allowing contamination of the fiber before shearing (359).

The enclosure of open and common fields for the purpose of raising sheep appears in the early Tudor proclamations as a grievous source of current social evils.[36] "So daily increasing," is this practice, according to a proclamation by Henry VII in 1493 that to it must be attributed much of the idleness, beggary, and vagabondage and many of the robberies and murders of the time (30). In this proclamation, the first Tudor orders enforcement of his statute of five years earlier penalizing the failure to restore husbandry.[37]

Henry VIII's enclosure proclamations reveal an increasing royal preoccupation with the problem. In a 1514 draft (75) coincidental with his own first two statutes on husbandry,[38] he orders the leveling of all hedges planted since the first year of his father's reign. In 1526 he again commands general destruction of enclosures and the restoration of tillage (110). He further orders all persons indicted on enclosure charges to appear in chancery (113) and to post recognizances or be fined 400 marks (114). In addition he invites the public in 1528 to bring to the chancery secret information of such enclosures (119). Henry VIII's final word in 1529 again orders all enclosures to be destroyed within one year under penalty of existing statutes (123).

The results of land enclosures become more obvious after Henry's death. In 1548 Edward's first proclamation on the subject, a moving document unrecorded by Steele, condemns covetous landholders for having caused "marvelous devastation" through the countryside and for having caused people to be "eaten up and devoured of brute beasts and driven from their houses by sheep and bullocks" (309). For remedy he authorizes a new commission to gather evidence for convenient and speedy reformation. One year later, a second and equally compelling instrument, recalling the original purpose of the enclosure statutes of Henry VII and Henry VIII, "that the commonwealth of this realm should have been renewed and restored to the ancient force and wealth it had in times past," threatens continued violations with severe penalties (327). Edward's last constructive proclamation against the evil is an itemized list of instructions to another royal commission for in-

36. Joan Thirsk, in *Tudor Enclosures* (London, 1959), p. 12, points out the error of blaming contemporary social evils on sheep culture alone: "Engrossing as a cause of depopulation was deplored in the proclamations of 1514 and 1528, the act of 1533, the proclamation of 1548, the enclosure commission of the same year, the proclamation of 1551. Indeed it is difficult to explain why historians in recent years have so often seemed to forget that engrossing and enclosure were regarded by contemporaries as twin evils in the countryside and equally injurious to the commonweal."

37. 4 Henry VII, c. 19, 1488, *SR 2,* 542. The penalty was set at one half the issues and profits of such lands as long as they remained enclosed.

38. 6 Henry VIII, c. 5, 1514, *SR 3,* 127 and 7 Henry VIII, c. 1, 1515, *SR 3,* 176. In these statutes the next higher lord is also entitled to make claim to one half the income from the lands enclosed contrary to 4 Henry VII, c. 19.

vestigating the extent and effects of enclosures since the first year of Henry VII (338).

On the other hand, five Edwardian proclamations in 1549 aim at repressing violent popular actions against enclosures. The first commands local officers "to prosecute by the sword" all such offenders "who have arrogantly and disloyally . . . taken upon them his majesty's authority, presumed to pluck his highness' sword out of his hand, and so gone about to chastise and correct whom they have thought good, in plucking down pales, hedges, and ditches at their will and pleasure" (333). The second, offering pardon for past rioting, orders justices of the peace to apprehend such offenders, "who are to suffer such pains of death, loss of lands, goods, and chattels as by the laws of the realm in such case is provided" (334). A third, dated 16 July 1549, commands those concerned to submit to the King's direction "upon pain of death presently to be suffered and executed by the authority and order of law martial" (340). Following the fall of Somerset, and following parliamentary reconfirmation[39] of the statutes of Merton and Westminster, Edward's two final proclamations indicate a repudiation of the fallen Protector's program for land reform. The first of these orders local officers to arrest enclosure rioters for immediate execution upon reception of orders from the Privy Council (342). In the other, after vaguely censuring all who contribute to the decay of husbandry, Edward declares that he will minister "the sharp terror of his sword" to all seeking illegal redress (373).

By repeating themselves, these early Tudor proclamations against land enclosure prove how difficult it was to accomplish their primary purpose, namely, to restore land to cultivation and to re-establish husbandry in England. But we are not permitted to ignore the fact that their penalty clauses, backed by statutes, produced considerable income for the crown.[40]

As documentary evidences of religious change in the early Tudor period, the royal proclamations are less significant for their number than for their effects. Invoking canon law, Henry VII officially reissues in English a papal bull recognizing, and commanding the English people to accept, Henry's claim to sovereignty, on the basis of public order, blood, inheritance, conquest, and the election of parliament (5). Reciprocally, he sets severe penalties against any subject desecrating churches or sacred vessels, or abusing

39. 3 & 4 Edward VI, c. 3, 1549, *SR 4(1)*, 102.

40. In a study of litigation over enclosure penalties, Eric Kerridge cites scores of cases pleading for the discontinuance of the statutory penalty of one half the annual profits from the land: "These pleas for the discontinuance of distraint were not heard with any dispatch and the cases might drag on three, four, six, or twenty years, the Crown meanwhile taking the half-profits." See his "Returns of the Inquisitions of Depopulation," *English Historical Review, 70* (1955), 219. On the other hand, according to Edward VI's proclamation (327) of 11 April, 1549, "the moiety of the yearly rent of the lands so increased . . . being rated after the old rent, is but a trifle in respect of the gains that they unlawfully take by decaying the houses and turning the lands from tilling to pasture."

religious women (13). Agreeable state-church relationships continue well into the reign of Henry VIII, who proclaims his purpose personally to invade France "for the succor, maintenance, and defense of [Pope Julius'] person, and of our mother Holy Church" (65). The same loyal motivation prefaces his 1513 ordinances of war, the first injunctions of which regulate the actions of soldiers toward church and clergy (73). In 1521 royal and local officials are commanded, at their uttermost peril, to aid the Bishop of Lincoln in suppressing and punishing heresy (85). A proclamation of 1529, containing a sharp attack against Martin Luther, suppresses 15 specified heretical books, orders immediate and diligent execution of former statutes against heresy, and directs ecclesiastical trial, with secular punishment, for relapsed and abjured heretics (122).

Compared with the anti-Roman parliamentary enactments between 1530 and 1537, Henry's proclamations for the extinction of papal authority in England, though fewer, are more sharply pointed. In 1533 he decrees that anyone who names, accepts, writes of, or obeys Catherine of Aragon as Queen, incurs thereby the penalties of the Statute of Praemunire (140).[41] In 1535, to enforce recent statutes abolishing papal authority in England, he orders sheriffs to cite uncooperative bishops before the council (158). He also orders the same officers, on pain of punishment, to spy out, judge, and forthwith confiscate any books containing matter opposed to the King's supremacy or the law of the land, especially a sermon by Bishop John Fisher (161). For full suppression of the Pilgrimage of Grace, animated mainly by the expropriation of monastic lands and the Act of Supremacy,[42] he declares the immediate readiness of his royal army to destroy the rebels, their wives, and children with fire and sword (169).

In the area of Scripture and the liturgy, Henry orders the clergy—in the spirit of perfect obedience "to the King's most excellent majesty, supreme head of the Church of England"—to instruct the laity in the "one true doctrine set forth by his majesty" and in the meaning of church ceremonies and the observance of religious festivals (188). A 1539 proclamation draft prohibiting religious disputes and urging instead the quiet and sincere reading of Holy Scripture, with alterations in Henry's own hand emphasizing his royal prerogative, appears to anticipate[43] the Statute of Proclamations, enacted later in the same year (191). In subsequent proclamations he delegates Thomas Cromwell to approve one English translation of the Bible (192),

41. 16 Richard II, c. 5, 1392, *SR 2,* 84.

42. 26 Henry VIII, c. 1, 1534, *SR 3,* 492.

43. One alteration in Henry's handwriting states that the proclamation is set forth "according to an authority of parliament already to his highness, successors, and council granted." The Act of Supremacy (26 Henry VIII, c. 1, 1534, *SR 3,* 492) does not include the council in its authorization of the King and his successors to reform errors, abuses, and enormities within the church.

orders a large Bible of the authorized translation, under penalties of fine and responsibility to the King, to be placed openly in every parish church (200), gives Anthony Marler a monopoly to print this Bible (210), and finally forbids possession or reading of William Tyndale's version, along with other prohibited books, under the penalty of "imprisonment and punishment of his body at the King's majesty's will and pleasure" (272). Henry's measures to suppress doctrinal opposition include a 1535 proclamation threatening capital punishment of foreign heretics who deny the doctrine of the real presence of Christ in the Eucharist (155). A later edict, identifying these persons as Anabaptists and Sacramentaries "which be lately come into this realm," is equally stringent and even more comprehensive (186).

Edward VI's proclamations consolidate the Tudor crown's authority in religious matters. Preachers must obtain faculties from the council as well as from the Archbishops of Canterbury or York (287). Justices of the peace are ordered to imprison unlicensed preachers along with the curates in whose pulpits they are allowed to appear (303). Finally, revoking all preaching licenses, Edward orders the regular sermons in the church service replaced by public reading from an official book of *Homilies,*[44] under pain of imprisonment (313). Failure to abstain from meat in Lent is also subject to imprisonment (297, 386) and fine (368).

The proclamations document increasing Edwardian control over pensions paid to late incumbents of religious houses. Changing a statutory provision[45] that these persons be paid by Court of Augmentations receivers, Edward, in September of his first year, orders future payments to be made instead by that Court's treasurer (289). Shortly thereafter he sends royal commissioners into the counties to arrange yet another procedure for future payments (307). This instrument is clarified five months later by a proclamation directing that such disbursement henceforth be delegated from the Court of Augmentations officers to county auditors, receivers, and surveyors (316).

The sacrament of the Eucharist is the subject of several important proclamations by Edward. In what is perhaps his most comprehensive statement on doctrine and devotion, adapted from an earlier proclamation of his father (186) and with special reference to earlier *Iniunctions*[46] issued "by the authority of . . . King Henry VIII," Edward in 1547 urges his subjects to receive often "the communion of the very body and blood of Christ" (287). In the same year, to halt religious controversy, he orders imprisonment of anyone refusing the common Eucharistic doctrine, namely "that the body and blood of Jesus Christ is there" (296). However, in the preface to his 1548 *Communion Order,* while enforcing a recent act of parliament ordering administration of Holy Communion under both forms, Edward announces his

44. *STC* 13,639.

45. 1 Edward VI, c. 14, 1547, *SR* 4(*1*), 24.

46. *STC* 10,085 and 10,086.

intention of proceeding with such reformation and godly orders "as may be most to God's glory, the edifying of our subjects, and for the advancement of true religion" (300). These orders appear in 1552 in his official interpretation of the rubric "that the communicants kneeling should receive the Holy Communion." "We do declare," the proclamation reads, "that it is not meant thereby that any adoration is done, or ought to be done either unto the sacramental bread or wine there bodily received, or unto any real or essential presence there being of Christ's natural flesh and blood" (385). This directive, the so-called Black Rubric, is not included in the text of the first 1552 edition of *The Boke of Common Prayer*[47] as authorized by parliament.[48] Interleaved in two other editions,[49] it finally appears as part of the printed text in the fourth edition, issued later in the same year.[50]

A review of the subjects with which the early Tudor proclamation writ deals—sovereignty, foreign and domestic affairs, money, prices, trade, agriculture, and religion—leads to the conclusion that the proclamations are source materials for a more complete and accurate history of the period. Embodying primary evidence, they offer new insight into and a new term of comparison for the solution of a number of Tudor questions which have remained unanswered. To what extent, for example, do the proclamations counterbalance their companion documents, the statutes of the realm? To what extent do they enable the Tudor crown to escape parliamentary control of royal income? When and where do they infringe established parliamentary rights? What precedents do they afford for later crown action? In what particulars do they illustrate Tudor administrative processes? What do they add to our understanding of the function of the King's council and Star Chamber, of economic problems such as inflation, of the Statute of Proclamations? What is their contribution to the secularization of the English parish organization? What is their relation to the burgeoning bureaucratic development of the period? What contribution do they make to division within the body politic and thus to the emergence of parliamentary sovereignty? What, finally, is their effect on the common law? These questions must be answered if we are to realize the actual conditions of the Tudor constitution and if we are to understand the precedents of the modern state. The early Tudor period is an important stage, in Western history, in the evolution of the concept of political sovereignty, from its condition of very real, if unclearly defined, limitations, to a modern reality of sovereignty which resists limitation. The early Tudor proclamations embody the position of the English crown in this struggle for power, which has ended finally in victory for the political state. As long as the rights of the individual con-

47. *STC* 16,279.
48. 5 & 6 Edward VI, c. 1, 1551, *SR* 4(*1*), 130.
49. *STC* 16,280 and 16,281.
50. *STC* 16,282.

tinue to come in conflict with the powers of a political state in which personal liberty tends more and more to be a permissive privilege, the Tudor royal proclamations will have significance.

The editorial method followed in preparing this edition deserves explanatory space. The point of departure in identifying and locating original sources has been Robert Steele's *Bibliography of Royal Proclamations of the Tudor and Stuart Sovereigns,*[51] the final revision and extension of Lord Crawford's bibliographical contribution to "one of the most valuable, though neglected, branches of the history of our country." [52] Cataloguing manuscript as well as printed sources, Steele's work is an indispensable reference work; in this edition it is cited in the headnote to each Tudor proclamation which it lists.

The Short-Title Catalogue (*STC*) published in 1926 provides a more nearly complete finding-list of printed proclamations. While in general it confirms the comprehensiveness and accuracy of Steele, it corrects and supplements the earlier list. William A. Jackson's willingness to share unpublished materials for a revision of *STC* has enabled the present editors to find still more printed sources. The headnotes to the texts in this edition thus carry both *STC* and *rev. STC* citations for editions of proclamations printed between 1485 and 1553; they also cite University Microfilms [53] of *STC* items when such exist.

Since the objective of this edition is to present in each case the proclamation schedule which, according to surviving criteria, represents that authorized by the crown, an order of precedence has had to be established among the varied sources of the texts.

Whenever available, the contemporary printed schedule, officially published by the King's printer, is used as the basic text for presentation. In many cases this text is unique (5, 32, 136, 200, 271, 303, 371). A first edition is preferred to a later one, even by the same printer (296, 299, 302, 336). Because of its actual public dissemination, it is preferred over Patent Roll (57), Chancery Warrant (189, 376), or local public record (263).

Second in textual authority, in this edition, are the Patent Rolls. Bearing witness to the passage of the document under the Great Seal of the realm, these rolls supply a number of unique proclamation schedules (e.g., 3, 20, 50, 63, 83, 91, 134). As Letters Patent of the King, PR schedules are considered more official than those in the Chancery Warrants (33, 40, 275, 379). Because

51. Steele, pp. 1–44.

52. James Ludovic Lindsay, Earl of Crawford, *Bibliotheca Lindesiana: Handlist of Proclamations, 1* (Aberdeen, 1893), *vii.* This three-volume catalogue and finding-list of British royal proclamations is a revision and enlargement of his original *Handlist of a Collection of Broadside Proclamations* (London, 1886), located in *Bibliotheca Lindesiana.*

53. University Microfilms, *English Books 1475–1640: Consolidated Cross Index by STC Numbers, Years 1–19* (Ann Arbor, 1956).

of their official character they are chosen over unregistered documents (89, 90).

Thirdly, Chancery Warrants for the use of the King's Great Seal are responsible for a number of unique texts in this edition (2, 4, 9, 58, 62, 95). Backed by the Privy Seal and sign manual, CW is considered more authoritative than local record (130) or other manuscript collection (308).

Next in value to the official Chancery records described above are those in local record offices, which may record the reception, actual proclaiming, and, indeed, the only surviving schedule of an early Tudor proclamation. The Corporation of London Journals (LJ) and Letter Books (LL), both MSS, contribute to this edition otherwise unknown proclamations: in LJ, prohibiting plays and interludes (240), decreeing death for assaulting officers (288), and ordering punishment for enclosures (327); in LL, regulating currency (180). In this edition, LJ claims precedence over other unregistered MSS (e.g., 80, 102, 152, 175). At the other end of the realm, the City of York House Books (YH) provide our only textual evidence of Henry VII's early proclamations seeking to establish peace in the dukedom of York (11, 12, 13).

Although Acts of the King's Council (AC) have survived chiefly in minutes, orders, and considerations, they nonetheless provide schedules of several proclamations by Henry VII for which no other criteria exist (7, 13).

Unavoidably, certain proclamations in this edition are based on other public records. (Two PRO Crown Precedent books—C193/3 and 30/26/116—containing MS copies of proclamations by Henry VIII and Edward VI came to light too late for notice in this edition.) For some proclamations, the only known schedule is that in the Close Rolls[54] (15, 18, 19), in State Papers Domestic[55] (64, 75), and in miscellaneous Exchequer of the Treasury Receipts[56] (219, 239). For others, reliance has had to be placed on quasi-public records, such as those in the Society of Antiquaries Library (Antiq), an extensive collection of English royal proclamations, some of which are official broadsides by the King's printer and others manuscript copies in late sixteenth-century handwriting, all mounted and bound chronologically into volumes the first three of which contain Tudor proclamations down to the end of Edward VI's reign. This collection points to Peter LeNeve, president of the Society of Antiquaries from 1707–24, a highly reputed antiquarian and himself a king of heralds. Antiq offers a number of proclamations otherwise unknown (250, 252, 266, 298, 386). Another such collection is the British Museum manuscript volume Harleian 442 (Harl 442) containing late sixteenth-century copies of royal proclamations by Edward IV, Henry VII, and

54. Close Rolls have the PRO class, C54.

55. State Papers Domestic are so classified in PRO.

56. Exchequer of the Treasury Receipts have the identifying PRO class, C34.

Henry VIII. According to Humphrey Wanley, Robert Harley purchased this volume from Peter LeNeve.[57] Both collections have calligraphy suggesting the same provenance as that of the Huntington Ellesmere MSS extracts of AC. Since both cover much the same textual ground, there is little to choose between them. Antiq may supply a writ (132), Harl 442 a date (114); the latter includes one unique proclamation (274). For other texts the present edition makes use of other British Museum MSS (10, 29, 52, 71, 157, 191, 292). Later printed editions are used only when a substantive text is unavailable (1, 85, 382) or incomplete (72, 122).

The next problem, after establishing texts of the proclamations, is deciding how best to present them in modern typography. Here the decision has been determined by the original purpose of the present edition: to supply a general need in the primary documentation of English history. A variorum edition of the Tudor royal proclamations exists in the realm of hope. To fill the present need, the decision has been as accurately as possible to transcribe each proclamation schedule in normalized modern English orthography, punctuation, capitalization, and paragraphing. For scholars who will want to consult the original sources of these texts, necessary bibliographical references are available in textual headnotes. Writs, Letters Patent, conventional greetings, and closing admonitions are omitted in this edition, except when required for an understanding of the text itself.

This edition attempts to present the early Tudor royal proclamations in their chronological order. For historical convenience it would be pleasant to be able to assign one definitive date for each proclamation. However, the provenance of these documents and gaps in evidence prohibit such simplification. The complete date of a standard Tudor proclamation would require precise knowledge of (1) place and date of council action, (2) place and date of proclamation writ, (3) place and date of the King's signed bill[58] and of its delivery to the chancery, (4) place and date indicated on Patent Rolls, (5) place and date of entry in local public records, (6) place and date of actual public proclamation by a herald or other crown officer, and (7) place and date of printing if the proclamation was published at the time. The date which this edition prefers is that of the King's authorization of the proclamation from his palace or chancery, by means of his royal writ. But because of the lack of some, and significant differences in other, of the above criteria, the present edition includes in each headnote all available evi-

57. Humphrey Wanley, *A Catalogue of the Harleian Collection of Manuscripts* (2 vols. London, 1759), 4T*v*. For Peter LeNeve, see *DNB, 33,* 36. For his activity in the Society of Antiquaries, see the MS Book of Society of Antiquary Minutes (Burlington House), especially pp. 63–64.

58. BM MS Royal 18.C.xxiv, Docquet-Book of Signed Bills Used as Warrants for the Great Seal, 1550–53, records the date on which Edward VI signed a number of proclamation bills during these years. See 367, 368, 377, 379, 381, 385.

dence of dating at each of the stages indicated above. Due regard has been maintained for the chronology of Steele, whose calendar provides the only suggested date for a number of the Tudor proclamations.

Action by the King's Council, ordinarily occurring first in the history of a proclamation (6, 56, 200, 367), may bear the later date of a printed copy (356, 372). Carrying the same date as a later stage however, council action may be recorded from another place (357). In one case the appearance of a proclamation predates by three days a council order for its issue (219).

Surviving proclamation writs provide the only precise dating information on so many of the texts that make up the present edition, that the place and date assigned to each title is that of the writ, unless otherwise indicated. From the Chancery Warrants we receive the only indicated date for a number of proclamations by both Henry VII (e.g., 2, 9, 18, 44) and Henry VIII (61, 94). There are two warrants for Henry VIII's first proclamation confirming Henry VII's final pardon (59), one dated 23 April 1509, the second 30 April. A proclamation adding "King of Ireland" to Henry VIII's royal style in 1539 (208) and carrying a Chancery Warrant date of 17 January was printed on 23 January and orally proclaimed in London on 6 February. The inclusion of all distinct dating phenomena in the present edition should clear up what might otherwise seem discrepancies.

Patent Rolls provide the unique date of a considerable number of texts in this edition. Usually bearing the same date as the Warrants on which they are based (e.g., 33, 55, 275, 375), they sometimes provide more specific dating information by including the day of the month (40, 56).

Local public records, which provide unique dating criteria in some cases (80, 86), may carry a date differing from that of other MSS (170, 197) or of a printed edition (54). One of the chief values of local record office dates lies in their fixing of the date of actual public proclamation. Thus, one of this edition's earliest proclamations (2), with a Chancery Warrant dated 24 October 1485, is recorded in the City of York House Books as having been proclaimed sixteen days earlier, on 8 October. Although one ordinance, ordering foreign artisans to register, is publicly proclaimed on the same day that it is registered in the London Guildhall (199), the act of proclaiming normally follows the schedule date by from one day (187, 194, 197) to a week (198, 224, 383) or more (12, 193). Raising the question of an acceptable date for one proclamation, LJ records the public proclaiming of an order by Henry VIII six years later than the date proposed by both Steele and *STC* (138).

In other cases proclamation dates can be learned only through the earliest printing (e.g., 32, 65, 81, 136, 201, 331). For a number of Edwardian proclamations 'which passed the print,' Grafton's collection of 1550 is the only surviving source we have for both date and schedule (e.g., 297, 304,

316, 339, 342); in other cases, it may give a date earlier (349) or later (359) than that in another source. Some proclamation dates can be inferred only from dated neighboring materials (240, 317) or from a later MS note (64). Finally, the editors have had to rely on the judgment of Steele for dating a number of proclamations (e.g., 29, 129, 191, 384).

In dating the early Tudor proclamations, this edition retains the Old Style references to days and months but gives years in the New Style throughout. To make the texts more useful, it includes a glossary of unfamiliar terms, which also supplies calendar dates of Saints' days and religious festivals; a bibliography; personal, topical, and statutory indexes; appendixes containing statutes pertinent to the execution of royal proclamations, and an additional proclamation; and a table of abbreviations.

There remains only the pleasant duty of acknowledging our debts. Unpublished Crown Copyright material in the Public Record Office has been reproduced by permission of the controller of Her Majesty's Stationery Office. For similar permission to reproduce other proclamation texts, both unpublished and printed, acknowledgement is here made: to the Trustees of the British Museum; to the Society of Antiquaries of London; to the Librarian of the Cambridge University Library, and to the Master and Fellows of Corpus Christi College, Cambridge; to the Bodleian Library and to Queen's College, Oxford; to the Exeter Cathedral Library; to the Lambeth Palace Library; to the Corporation of London Records Office; to Edmund Brudenell and the Northampton Record Society; and to the City of York Archives. At the outset, Lord Crawford encouraged publication of the proclamations, offering the hospitality of Balcarres for inspection of the Crawford Collection, which is now in the University Library, Cambridge.

In the United States, permission to use their resources was extended by the Folger Library, the Huntington Library, the Newberry Library, and by the university libraries of Chicago, Harvard, Williams, and Yale. De Paul University supported the project continuously with research grants, reduced teaching schedules, secretarial assistance, and a leave of absence to Father Larkin, who is also grateful to the Clerics of St. Viator for opportunity to work in the libraries and record offices of Great Britain. Virginia Schnare Hughes, while typing and retyping the manuscript, offered insights which otherwise would have escaped the editors. Leonard Conversi and Alice M. Miskimin saw the copy through the press.

Many scholars contributed valuable time and special knowledge to this edition: first and foremost, Stanley T. Bindoff, Professor of History, University of London; William H. Dunham, Jr., Professor of History, Yale University; Geoffrey R. Elton, Fellow of Clare College, Cambridge University; Pearl Hogrefe, Professor of English, Iowa State University; Robert S. Hoyt, Professor of History, University of Minnesota; William A. Jackson, Professor of Bibliography, Harvard University; Robert M. Kingdon,

Professor of History, University of Iowa; Dom David Knowles, Regius Professor of Modern History, Cambridge University; Bryce Lyon, Professor of History, University of California; Frederick G. Marcham, Professor of History Emeritus, Cornell University; George L. Mosse, Professor of History, University of Wisconsin; T. F. Reddaway, London historian; Walter C. Richardson, Professor of History, Louisiana State University; Peter L. Roberts; John J. Scarisbrick, History Reader, Queen Mary College; Goldwin Smith, Professor of History, Wayne State University; Lacey Baldwin Smith, Professor of History, Northwestern University; Craig R. Thompson, Librarian and Professor of Modern History, Haverford College; and Louis B. Wright, Director of the Shakespeare Folger Library. Other scholars to whom we are in debt are listed in our bibliography. Acknowledging our own responsibility for editorial judgments, we offer all of them heartfelt thanks.

Paul L. Hughes
James F. Larkin, C.S.V.

De Paul University
Michaelmas 1963

Abbreviations

See Bibliography for complete references

AC	Acts of the King's Council
Add.	BM MSS Additional
Antiq	Society of Antiquaries Library
Bayne	*Select Cases in the Council of Henry VII*
BD	Docquet-Book of Signed Bills
BM	British Museum Library
Calais	*Chronicle of Calais*
Campbell	*Materials for a History of the Reign of Henry VII*
Cardwell	*Documentary Annals*
Chapin	Chapin Library, Williams College
Cleo.	BM MS Cleopatra E. 5.
CR	Close Rolls, Public Record Office
CSPD	*Calendar of State Papers Domestic*
CSPForeign	*Calendar of State Papers Foreign*
CSPR	*Calendar of State Papers . . . Rome*
CSPSpanish	*Calendar of State Papers Spanish*
CSPVenetian	*Calendar of State Papers Venetian*
CW	Chancery Warrants, Public Record Office
d	*dorsa,* i.e., *verso*
Dasent	*Acts of the Privy Council of England*
DFo	Folger Shakespeare Library
Dibdin	*Typographical Antiquities*
DNB	*Dictionary of National Biography*
Drake	*Eboracum*
Edward VI	*Journal*
ETR	Exchequer of the Treasury Receipts, Public Record Office
Foxe	*Acts and Monuments*
Grafton	*All Suche Proclamacions*
Grey Friars	*Chronicle*
Hall	*Vnion . . . of Lancaster and York*
Harl	Harleian Collection of Manuscripts, British Museum Library
Herbert	*Typographical Antiquities*
HM Ellesmere	Huntington Library, MSS Ellesmere
Holinshed	*Chronicles*
ICN	Newberry Library

Lambeth	Lambeth Palace Library
L&P	*Letters and Papers . . . Henry VIII*
LJ	London, Journals (MSS)
LL	London, Letter Books (MSS)
Machyn	*Diary*
More	*Workes*
Nicolas	*Proceedings and Ordinances of the Privy Council*
NRO	Northampton Record Office
Pollard	*Reign of Henry VII*
PR	Patent Rolls, Public Record Office
PRO	Public Record Office of Great Britain
rev. STC	Jackson, William A., unpublished materials
Rymer	*Foedera*
Schanz	*Englische Handelspolitik*
SP	State Papers Domestic, Public Record Office
SR	*Statutes of the Realm*
STC	*Short-Title Catalogue*
Steele	*Bibliography of Royal Proclamations*
Stow	*Annales*
Strype	*Ecclesiastical Memorials*
Titus	BM MS Titus
TR	Treaty Rolls, Public Record Office
TRS	*Transcript of the Registers of the Company of Stationers*
ULC	University Library, Cambridge
UM	University Microfilms
Wilkins	*Concilia*
Wriothesley	*Chronicle*
YH	York House Books (MSS)

The Proclamations of Henry vii

1485-1509

1. Announcing the Death of Richard iii[1]

[York, 25 August 1485, 1 Henry VII]

Drake 122: date as above; writ to mayor and aldermen of York; payment to herald for proclaiming; schedule as below. YH 2, 169: Henry proclaimed King in York on 23 August. Halliwell *1*, 169. Pollard *1*, 111. Not in Steele. Text: Drake

HENRY, by the grace of God King of England and of France, Prince of Wales and lord of Ireland, strictly chargeth and commandeth, upon pain of death: that no manner of man rob nor spoil no manner of commons coming from the field, but suffer them to pass home to their countries and dwelling places, with their horses and harness; and moreover, that no manner of man take upon him to go to no gentleman's place, neither in the country nor within cities nor boroughs, nor pick no quarrels for old or for new matters, but keep the peace, upon pain of hanging.

And moreover, if there be any man afeared to be robbed and spoiled of his goods, let him come to Mr. Richard Borow, the King's sergeant here, and he shall have a warrant for his body and his goods, unto the time the King's pleasure be known.

And moreover, the King ascertaineth you that Richard, Duke of Gloucester, late called King Richard, was slain at a place called Sandford within the shire of Leicester, and brought dead off the field into the town of Leicester, and there laid openly, that every man might see and look upon him. And also there was slain upon the same field John, late Duke of Norfolk; John, late Earl of Lincoln; Thomas, late Earl of Surrey; Francis, Viscount Lovell; Sir Walter Deveres, Lord Ferrers; Richard Ratclyff, knight; Robert Brackenbury, knight; with many other knights, squires, and gentlemen. Of whose souls God have mercy.

2. Pardoning Northern Rebels

[Westminster, 11 October 1485, 1 Henry VII]

CW (C82/2): date of delivery as above; sign manual; schedule as below. YH 2, 172: proclaimed in York on 8 October. Steele 1. Text (MS): CW

FORASMUCH as many and divers persons of the north parts of this our land, knights, squires, gentlemen, and other, have done us now of late great

1. The bracketed place and date for each proclamation is derived from information given in the writ of proclamation unless otherwise indicated. Writs, letters patent, and closing admonitions are omitted except when essential to the meaning of a text.

displeasure, being against us in the field with the adversary of us, enemies of nature, of all public weal; which, as we be informed, repenting their defaults, desire to do us such pleasure and service as might reduce them unto our grace and favor;

We, moved as well of pity as for the great dangers, perils, losses of goods and lives, that the ancestors of the inhabitants of that country have borne and suffered for the quarrel and title of the most famous prince, and of blessed memory, King Henry VI, our uncle; and also for that, that they of those parts be necessary, and according to their duty must defend this land against the Scots: of our especial grace, pardon to all and to every person or persons of the estate and degree above named or under, of what condition they be of or be, what name or names they or any of them be called or named, within our counties of Nottingham, York, Northumberland, Cumberland, and Westmorland, our city of York and bishopric of Durham, all manner riots, murders, treasons, felonies, insurrections, confederations, conspiracies, against their allegiances done and committed; and all other offenses and trespasses, whatsoever they be, by them or any of them done against us before the 22nd day of September in the first year of our reign.

Except Sir Richard Ratclyff, Sir James Haryngton, Sir Robert Haryngton, Sir Thomas Pylkynton, Sir Thomas Broughton, Sir Robert Myddelton, Thomas Metcalve, and Miles Metcalve.

Wherefore we will and grant that all knights, esquires, gentlemen, and other thrifty commoners of our counties, city and the bishopric aforesaid, except above except, that will sue to have our pardon under our great seal, shall have expedition thereof of our Chancellor of England for the time being, so that they make their suit before the Feast of the Purification of Our Lady next coming after the date of these presents;

And all other persons of the counties, city, and bishopric abovesaid, as be not of power to sue in like form for our said pardon, that these presents be to them sufficient discharge against us in the law, concerning and touching the premises.

3. Announcing Truce with France

[Westminster, 12 October 1485, 1 Henry VII]

PR (C66/562/*17d*): date as above; writ to sheriffs of Surrey and Sussex; schedule as below. Campbell 1, 226: date, after 29 September; writs to Newcastle-upon-Tyne, Kingston-upon-Hull, Lincoln, Norfolk, and Suffolk. Pollard *3*, 1. Rymer *12*, 277. Steele 1a. Text (MS): PR

Forasmuch as certain appointments and conclusions of truce and abstinence of war be had, made, and concluded between the King our sovereign lord of the one party, and his most dearest cousin Charles of France of that other party, to begin the first day of this present month of October and to endure unto the last day of September next ensuing:

The King our said sovereign lord straightly chargeth and commandeth all and every his subjects and true liegemen that they nor none of them move nor cause to be moved any manner of war or hostility against his said cousin or any of his subjects by land, sea, nor fresh waters; but that they and every of them peaceably suffer the said subjects of his said cousin, as well merchants as other, to enter, come, pass and repass into and from any port or ports or other place or places within this his realm, there to charge and recharge, and to make free intercourse of merchandise from time to time, as oft as it shall please them, during the truce afore expressed, without any safe-conduct, license, or safeguard, and without any impediment, arrest, or grief otherwise than is according to his laws, upon pain of forfeiture of all that they may forfeit, and their bodies at the King's will.

4. Dismissing Forces Mustered in the North

[Westminster, 20 October 1485, 1 Henry VII]

CW (C82/354): date of delivery as above; sign manual; schedule as below. Steele 2. Text (MS): CW

Whereas the King our sovereign lord directed now late his Commissions of Array with other his high commandments in writing to his sheriffs and other gentlemen of this his realm, charging them by the same to see his faithful and true subjects to be put in array, and so to give their attendance upon his most royal person for the subduing of the malice of his rebels associate with his ancient enemies the Scots, intending the destruction of his said person and the subversion of his realm, it is now so that the foresaid rebels, understanding that our said sovereign lord hath made politic and mighty purveyance for the recounter and subduing of their said malice and rebellion, have withdrawn themselves and be severally departed, sore abashed and rebuked:

Wherefore his highness is content, and will that none of his true subjects be put to any further charge, pain, or labor at this season because of the premises, but that they be ready at all times hereafter, when it shall like his grace to call upon them; and for the readiness, towardness, and good disposition that they have now shewed to his singular pleasure, his said highness yieldeth them special thanks, and will have them in the more tender favor of his good grace, and see that none of them be oppressed nor wronged, but to live in good rest and peace under his laws.

5. Summarizing Papal Bull Recognizing Henry VII

[London, after 13 June 1486, 1 Henry VII]

AC (Bayne 8): date, 13 June; order for Bishop of Lincoln to translate and make copies of Bull. PRO (SC 7/23/5): original Bull of Innocent VIII, dated 27 March 1486; reprinted in Rymer *12*, 297. *STC* 14,096, Antiq 1, 7: printed by W. de Machlinia (London, 1486); schedule as below, imperfect Steele 3: date, April. Text (*STC*): Antiq

Our holy father the [Pope,] Innocent VIII, to the perpetual memory of this [event] to be had, by his proper motion, without procurement of our sovereign lord the King or [of any] other person, for conservation of the universal peace and eschewing of slanders an[d to en]gender the contrary of the same, understanding of the long and grievous variance, dissensions, and debates that hath been in this realm of England between the house of the Duchy of Lancaster [on the] o[n]e part and [the] house of the Duchy of York on the other part, willing all such divisions [therefrom] following to be p[ut a]part: by the counsel and consent of his college of cardinals, approveth, confi[rmeth], and establisheth the mat[ri]mony and conjunction made between our sovereign lord, King Henry VII of t[he house] of Lancaster of that one party and the noble Princess Elizabeth of the house of York of that other [party], with all their issue lawfully born between the same.

And in likewise His Holiness confirmeth, establisheth, and approveth the right and title to the crown of E[ngland] of the said our sovereign lord Henry VII, and the heirs of his body lawfully begotten to him [as ap]pertaining, as well by reason of his nighest and undoubted title of succession as by the right of his most noble [victory], and by election of the lords spiritual and temporal and other nobles of his realm, and by the [ordi]nance and authority of parliament made by the three estates of this land.[1]

Also our said Holy Father the Pope, of his proper motion, by high and holy commandment, c[hargeth and] requireth every inhabitant in this land and every subject in the same, of what degree, state, or condition [they be of], that none of them by occasion of any succession, or by any other color or cause within this realm, [by them]self or other mediate persons, attempt in word or deed against the said our sovereign lord, or th[e heirs of] his body lawfully begotten, contrary to the peace of him and his realm, upon the pain of his great curse [on every of] them; the which they and every of them that so attempteth falleth in forthright by that self deed d[one; from] the which curse and anathema no man hath power to assoil them but our Holy Father himself [or his speci]al deputy to the same.

1. See 1 Henry VII, *Preamble*, 1485, *SR* 2, 499.

Furthermore he approveth, confirmeth, and declareth that if it please God that the said Eli[zabeth], which God forbid, should decease without issue between our sovereign lord and her of their bodies bor[n and had], then such issue as between him and her whom after that God shall join him to shall be had and born [shall be] heritors to the same crown and realm of England; commanding that no man attempt the [contrary under] the pain of his great curse, which they and every of them so doing falleth in; in the self deed [done they] may not be assoiled but by him or his special deputy to the same.

Over this, the same our Holy Father giveth his blessing to all princes, nobles, and other inhab[itants] of this realm, or outward, that favoreth, aideth, and assisteth the said our sovereign lord and his heirs a[gainst his] or their rebels, giving them that die in his and their quarrel full and plenary pardon an[d remissi]on of all their sins.

Finally he commandeth all metropolitans and bishops, upon the pain of interdict of [all men of] the church, abbots, priors, archdeacons, parish priests, priors, and wardens of the friars an[d other] men of the church, exempt and not exempt, upon the pain of his great curse which they falleth in [if they do it] not to denounce and declare, or cause to be denounced and declared, all such contrary doers and rebels a[t every] such time as they to the same in the name of the said our sovereign lord shall be required; with aggrava[tion of the] same curse, if the case shall so require, so that if they for dread shall not move to publish the sam[e it be to] them lawful to curse their resistance to the same and to oppress them by power temporal, which [they may] call for their assistance to the same in the said our Holy Father's name.

And as touching the articles of this Bull, the Pope's holiness by this present Bull dero[gateth and] maketh void all manner grants, privileges, and exemptions made by hi[m or] his predecess[ors to] any person or place whereas they should or might be prejudicial to the execution of these presents, [and they are] all such as expressly revoked by this same as though they were written word by word withi[n these pre]sent Bulls, as by it undersaid here more largely doth appear.

6. Ordering Coast Guard against France and Empire

[Westminster, 10 June 1486, 1 Henry VII]

AC (Bayne 13): date, 7–9 June; order for proclamation to be made in towns by sea. PR (C66/563/19*d*): date as above; writ to sheriffs of Norfolk and Suffolk; schedule as below. Campbell *1*, 42. Rymer *13*, 106. Steele 4. Text (MS): PR

Forasmuch as the King our sovereign lord, Henry VII, by the grace of God King of England and of France and lord of Ireland, hath credible information that there is like to be open war had, moved, and stirred, as well by water as by land, between his cousin Charles of France on the one party, and his cousin the King of Romans on the other party; whereupon great navies of both parties be in rigging, ready to set unto the sea, wherethrough hurt and prejudice, by the riotous demeaning of the said navies, might suddenly grow unto this his realm and to his subjects of the same, if no remedy were in that behalf foreseen, ordained, and provided, which God defend:

Our said sovereign lord, not willing any such hurt or prejudice to ensue unto this his said realm nor unto any of his said subjects, willeth, chargeth, and straightly commandeth all and every of his said subjects that they and every of them keep watch and ward upon the coast of the sea where need should require; and that all beacons and other tokens upon the same coasts be made ready to be set on fire and to warn all his said subjects to be ready to come and defend this his said realm and his said subjects if need be, according to their duties in manner and form as in old time in like case hath been used and accustomed.

7. Ordering Port Courtesies to Army of Emperor

[Westminster, 16 July 1486, 1 Henry VII]

AC (Bayne 3): date as above; order for proclamation to be made in Cinque Ports and other havens; schedule as below. Not in Steele. Text: AC

Forasmuch as the right high and right mighty Prince Maximilian, Archduke of Austria and Duke of Burgundy, one of the friends and confederates of our sovereign lord King Henry VII, for the weal and surety of his countries, lordships and subjects and merchandise, intendeth to set an army of war unto the sea, there to abide for a certain season; the which be and shall be straightly charged by him to do no grief nor damage to the king our sovereign lord, his realm nor subjects, nor in any wise to do against such treaties and intelligences as have been taken between our said sovereign lord and him; promising over this that if any such grief or damage, which God forbid, should hap to be done, he will see for due recompense to be made for the same:

The King our sovereign lord, knowing and considering the premises, and by his cousin, King of Romans, thereunto desired, hath granted and ordained that if the men of war so set to the sea by the said King of Romans, during the army aforesaid, be by fortune of wind, tempest of the sea, or otherwise constrained to take lodging and rest within any port or haven in any place of this realm of England, that then they be suffered so to enter and come in to his ports and havens; and also that it be lawful to them, as oft as they shall need victualing, to send therefor to land, by one boat only, paying duly for the same victualing at their proper cost.

Wherefore our said sovereign lord chargeth and commandeth all and every his subjects dwelling on the sea coasts or any other places of this his realm, what estate, degree, or condition they be of, that between this and the first day of January next coming, they entreat the army of the said King of Romans with all courtesy and [regard] according to the premises, in suffering them of the said army which shall hap so to be by wind, tempest, or otherwise constrained to take port and enter the King's said haven, and to have victual as oft as the case shall require; and to send therefore one boat only, so that they truly pay for the same.

The which ordinance and commandment the King wills be kept in all points, to his said friend and confederate the King of Romans; and in likewise to all his other friends and confederates, whensoever their armies shall stand in like necessity during the truce betwixt our said sovereign lord and them: among whom the king remembereth especially his cousin of France; the Kings of Spain, Portugal, and Scotland; and the Duke of Brittany, and the [steads] of the [Hanse] in Almain. Provided always that by none of the armies anything prejudicial be attempted against the King our sovereign lord, his lands, nor subjects anywise.

8. Ordering Rebels to Surrender within Forty Days

[Westminster, 16 July 1486, 1 Henry VII]

PR (C66/564/3*d*): date as above; writ to sheriff of Northumberland; similar writs to sheriffs of York and Cumberland; schedule as below. Campbell *1*, 512. Pollard *1*, 43. Steele 5. Text (MS): PR

WHERE Thomas Broughton, knight; John Hodylston, knight; William A. Thorneburghe; William Ambrose and other of their coadherents, for their great rebellious and grievous offenses lately by them done and committed against the most royal person of our sovereign lord Henry VII, by the grace of God King of England and of France and lord of Ireland, keep them in huddle and secret place, and over that have disobeyed divers and many his letters and Privy Seals, to his great displeasure and disobeisance and to the great trouble and vexation of his true liegemen and subjects:

Our sovereign lord, willing the good rule, tranquillity, and restfulness of this his realm and of his subjects of the same, straightly chargeth and commandeth the said Thomas, John, William, and William, and their coadherents, that they and every of them, except Geffrey Frank, Edward Frank, John Ward, Thomas Oter, and Richard Middylton, otherwise called Dyk Middylton, personally appear before his highness, wheresoever he be, within 40 days next after this proclamation.

And if the said Thomas Broughton, John Hodylston, William, and William, and their said coadherents, or any of them, except before except, absent themself and of their obstinacy will not appear and come to our said sovereign lord as his true and obedient subjects, they and every of them so absenting themself be had, taken, and reputed as his great rebels, enemies, and traitors; and so forfeit their lives, lands, and goods at the pleasure of the same our sovereign lord.

9. Distraining Knighthood

[Westminster, 14 December 1486, 2 Henry VII]

CW (C82/19): date of delivery as above; sign manual; writ to sheriff of Middlesex; similar writs to sheriffs throughout England; schedule in Latin, translated below. Steele 5a. Text (MS): CW

ALL PERSONS having £40 per year in lands or revenue either in hand or to their use in fee, and who have so had during three years past, and who are not now knights, are commanded to appear in our presence on February fourth next, in order to receive the order of knighthood, at their uttermost perils; and all sheriffs diligently to seek out all persons having £40 in lands or revenue, as is aforesaid, and to make certification of their names in our chancery before the said fourth of February; neglecting not so to do, at their own perils.

10. Prohibiting Unlicensed Money Exchange

[ca. 15 June 1486, 2 Henry VII]

AC (Bayne 9): date 15 June; communication on the coin with mayor of London, but nothing ordered. BM MS Harl 442, 11: schedule as below. Steele 6: date as above. Text (MS): Harl

It is assented, accorded, and the King defendeth unto all people, merchants, clerks, and other as well strangers as denizens of soever estate or condition they be, upon pain of whatever they may forfeit, that none of them upon the said pain privily nor apertly send nor convey or do to be sent or conveyed out of the realm aforesaid any gold or silver in money, bullion, plate, vessel, nor for exchange to make, nor otherwise, whatsoever it be, saving for the wages of Calais and of other fortresses and castles of the King beyond sea; except prelates, lords, and others of the same realm unto whom it behooveth sometime necessary to make payment beyond sea, of the which payment only they may make exchange in England by good and sufficient merchants to pay beyond sea, and thereupon first to have especial *congé* and license of our sovereign lord the King, as well for the exchangers as for the person that shall make payment, showing expressly the sum that so shall be exchanged.

And also it is assented that the merchants that so shall make the said exchanges be diligently examined and sworn in their proper persons, as oftentimes as they shall have the said license, that they neither send nor convey beyond the sea any manner of gold nor silver under color of the same exchange; and if after the proclamation of this ordinance any person be thereof duly attaint that he hath sent or conveyed beyond sea any gold or silver contrary to this defense, statute, and ordinance, to forfeit unto the King the same sum so sent or conveyed.

And forasmuch as the King our sovereign lord, considering that there hath grown and daily groweth great displeasure to God, great hurt to his highness and to his realm, by and for the inordinate changes and rechanges that hath been of long time used and yet continueth within this his realm, without any authority obtained of our said sovereign lord to make any manner such changes or rechanges; which is not only contrary to his laws but also to his prerogative royal:

For remedy whereof, many noble statutes have been made by divers the progenitors of our said sovereign lord, whereof one especial statute made in the 25th year of King Edward III,[1] and also another special statute made in the fifth year of King Richard II,[2] with other divers statutes made for the same remedy in times of the reigns of the Kings Henry IV,[3] Henry V,[4] and Henry VI,[5] that all such statutes should be put in due execution from thenceforth, and that no men should make any exchange without the King's special license, nor make any exchange or rechange of money to be paid within this realm but only such as the King hath or shall depute thereunto to make and answer for such exchanges and rechanges, upon the special pains in the same several statutes of the said late noble progenitors of our said sovereign lord is contained; and that no person nor persons, whatsoever degree they be of, make any exchange, rechange, or expedition within the same his realm without his special license first for the same obtained, but only to and with such persons as he of late hath assigned and deputed by his letters patent to make such exchange, rechange, and expedition, and to give license to other persons to and for the same, and also to take such duties of and for the same as heretofore have been used and accustomed to be taken.

And our said sovereign lord straightly chargeth and commandeth that if any person or persons from henceforth make any exchange into any parts of beyond the sea contrary to this his proclamation, that then the same person and persons making the said exchange to forfeit unto our sovereign lord the King all and singular such penalties and forfeitures as in the same several statutes be contained.

11. Ordering Pillory for False News

[Windsor, 3 June 1487, 2 Henry VII]

LL L, 234*v*: writ to mayor and sheriffs of York; schedule as below. YH 6, 121*v*: date as above. Steele 7. Text (MS): LL

FORASMUCH as many of the King our sovereign lord's subjects be disposed daily to hear feigned, contrived, and forged tidings and tales; and the same tidings and tales, neither dreading God nor his highness, utter and tell

1. 25 Edward III, st. 5, c. 12, 1351, *SR 1*, 322.
2. 5 Richard II, st. 1, c. 2, 1381, *SR 2*, 17.
3. 2 Henry IV, c. 5, 6, 1400, *SR 2*, 122.
4. 4 Henry V, c. 6, 1415, *SR 2*, 195.
5. 2 Henry VI, c. 9, 1423, *SR 2*, 221.

again as though they were true, to the great hurt of divers of his subjects and to his grievous displeasure:

Therefore in eschewing of such untrue and forged tidings and tales, the King our sovereign lord straightly chargeth and commandeth that no manner person, whatsoever he be, utter nor tell any such tidings or tales but he bring forth the same person the which was author and teller of the said tidings or tales; upon pain to be set on the pillory, there to stand as long as it shall be thought convenient to the mayor, bailiff, or other officer of any city, borough, or town where it shall happen any such person to be taken and accused for any such telling or reporting of any such tidings or tales.

Furthermore the same our sovereign lord straightly chargeth and commandeth that all mayors, bailiffs, and other officers diligently search and inquire of all such persons, tellers of such tidings and tales not bringing forth the author of the same, and them set on the pillory as it is above said.

12. Providing Victual for Army in North

[Kenilworth, 5 June 1487, 2 Henry VII]

YH 6, 105*v:* date as above; order for proclamation to be made on 26 July; schedule as below. Not in Steele. Text (MS): YH

FORASMUCH as the King our sovereign lord, accompanied with great multitude of his nobility and subjects of this his realm, intendeth in short time to pass through these parts for the repressing and subduing of the malicious purpose of his great rebels and enemies; and for that his highness nor his said company in no wise should be destitute or wanting of victuals for man or horse:

He straightly chargeth and commandeth every victualer, and all other his subjects dwelling in every town or place where his said highness and his said company shall come, to provide and make ready plenty of bread and ale, and of other victuals, as well for horse as for man, at reasonable price in ready money therefor to them;

And every of them truly to be contented and paid, as they and every of them intend the weal of his most royal person and of this his realm, and to avoid his grievous displeasure.

13. Enforcing Public Order, Military Regulations

[Kenilworth, ca. 6 June 1487, 2 Henry VII]

AC (BM MS Julius B. 12, 26*v*): order for proclamation to be made; schedule as below. Steele 7a: date as above. Text (MS): Julius

THE KING our sovereign lord [doth] straightly charge and command that no manner of man, of whatsoever state, degree, or condition he be, rob nor spoil any church, nor take out of the same any ornament thereunto belonging, nor touch nor set hand on the pyx wherein the Blessed Sacrament is contained, nor yet rob nor spoil any manner man or woman, upon pain of death;

Also that no manner of person nor persons, whatsoever they be, make no quarrel to any man, nor seize nor vex nor trouble any man by body or goods for any offense or by color of any offense heretofore done or committed against the royal majesty of the King our said sovereign lord, without his authority and especial commandment given unto him or them that so do in that behalf, upon pain of death;

Also that no manner of person nor persons, whatsoever they be, ravish no religious woman, nor man's wife, daughter, maiden, nor no man's nor woman's servant, nor take nor presume to take any manner of victual, horse meat, or man's meat, without paying therefor the reasonable price thereof assized by the clerk of the market or other the king's officer therefore ordained, upon pain of death;

Also that no manner of person nor persons, whatsoever they be, take upon them to lodge themself nor take no manner of lodging nor harborage but such as shall be assigned unto him or them by the King's harbinger, nor dislodge no man, nor change no lodging after that he be assigned, without advice and assent of the said harbinger, upon pain of imprisonment and to be punished at the will of our said sovereign lord;

Also that no manner of man, whatsoever he be, make no quarrel with any other man, whatsoever he be, for no manner cause, old nor new, nor make no manner of fray within the host nor without, upon pain of imprisonment and to be punished according to their trespass and defaults; and if there happen any such quarrel or affray to be made by any evil-disposed persons, that then no manner of man, for any acquaintance or fellowship that they be of, take no part with no such misdoers in any such affrays or quarrels, upon pain of imprisonment and to be punished at the King's will; but that every man endeavor himself to take all such misdoers, and bring them to the marshal's ward to be punished according to their deserts;

Also that no manner of person, whatsoever he be, hurt, trouble, beat, nor let no manner of person, man, woman or child, bringing any victual unto the King's host, upon pain of imprisonment and his body to be at the King's will;

And over this, that every man being of the retinue of our said sovereign lord, at the first sound or blast of the trumpet, do saddle his horse; at the second, do bridle; and at the third, be ready on horseback to wait upon his highness upon pain of imprisonment;

Also that no manner of person, whatsoever he be, make no scries, shoutings, or blowing of horns in the King's host after the watch be set, upon pain of imprisonment and his body to be at the King's will;

Also that no vagabond, nor other, follow the King's host but such as be retained or have masters within the same, upon pain of imprisonment and to be punished in example for other;

And that no common woman follow the King's host, upon pain of imprisonment and openly to be punished in example of all other;

Also whensoever it shall please the King our sovereign lord to command any of his officers of arms to charge any thing in his name, by his high commandment or by the commandment of his constable or marshal, that it be observed and kept, upon pain of imprisonment and his body to be punished at the King's pleasure.

14. Ordering Aynesty Wapentake to Assist City of York

[Pomfret, 26 August 1487, 3 Henry VII]

YH 6, 109*v:* date as above; writ to mayor and council of York; schedule as below. Not in Steele. Text (MS): YH

Henry, by the grace of God King of England and of France, and lord of Ireland, to all knights, squires, gentlemen and other residents and inhabitants of and within the wapentake of Aynesty, adjoining unto our city of York, greeting:

Forasmuch as we be credibly informed that the said wapentake is within the precincts and bounds of the franchises of our said city, and every of you ought of right to be ready and obedient unto the mayor there, when he shall warn and call you to the assistance and defense of our city when the case shall require:

We therefore, tendering the weal and surety of the same, will and command that whensoever the said mayor and his brethren shall call upon you for your assistance in the defense and tuition of our said city, you be, according to your duty (setting apart all retainers and attendance upon other persons, and commandments of our wardens of our marches toward Scotland, and of our sheriffs of our county of York for the time being), helping, attending, obeying, and assisting in all things; as you will answer therefor unto us at your perils.

15. Ordering Keveston Outlaws to Surrender

[Knole, 23 December 1487, 3 Henry VII]

CR (C54/348/5*d*): date as above; writ to sheriffs of London; similar writ to sheriff of Salop; schedule as below. Campbell 2, 220. Not in Steele. Text (MS): CR

FORASMUCH as the King our sovereign lord, considering the great abomination as well of murders, robberies, and other great and inordinate offenses, as of contempts and disobedience of his high commandments, committed and done by Thomas Keveston, Humphrey Keveston, Oliver Keveston, and Richard Keveston, late of Shropshire, gentlemen, contrary to their allegiances and fidelity;

By the advice of his lords spiritual and temporal and his commons in parliament at Westminster, the 9th day of November last past begun and there holden assembled, and by the authority of the same hath been ordained and enacted [1] that after writs of proclamation made unto the sheriffs of London and Shropshire, that the said Thomas Keveston, Humphrey Keveston, Oliver Keveston, and Richard Keveston personally do appear afore his highness in his Court of Chancery the 15th day after the Feast of St. Hilary next coming, wheresoever it be, within this his realm of England, to answer to such things as there shall be shown against them;

And that if the said Thomas, Humphrey, Oliver, and Richard, or any such of the said persons Thomas, Humphrey, Oliver, and Richard Keveston appear not, as is aforesaid, then that person or persons of the said Thomas, Humphrey, Oliver, and Richard which do appear not, be reputed and taken as a person lawfully outlawed of felony; and forfeit life, goods, and land as he should forfeit it if he were lawfully outlawed of felony by the course of the common law.

1. 3 Henry VII, c. 1, 1487, *SR* 2, 509.

16. Prohibiting Weapons in Frays, Punishing Vagabonds

[23 December 1487, 3 Henry VII]

BM MS Harl 442, 14: schedule as below. Steele 8: MS note in Steele's personal copy (BM L.R.274.d.10), date as above. Text (MS): Harl

THE KING our sovereign lord, having a tender respect to the surety, peace, and restfulness of all his true subjects, for the conservation of his peace, by the advice of his council straightly chargeth and commandeth all his true liegemen and subjects, of what estate, degree, or condition they be of, that they nor any of them, in perturbing of his peace, bear or cause to be borne any manner bills, bows, arrows, swords long or short, bucklers, nor any other harness nor weapons invasive, in any town nor city within this his realm but at such times as they journey or ride (except sheriffs, mayors, bailiffs, constables, and other officers assigned for keeping of the peace and good rule of such towns and cities), upon pain of forfeiture of all such harness and weapons, and the bodies of the trespassers in that behalf to be imprisoned at the will of our said sovereign lord.

And over that, that no manner person, whatsoever he be, make any affray or quarrel with any other person for any matter or cause, old or new, otherwise than shall accord with his laws and peace, upon pain of imprisonment and further to be punished at the will of our said sovereign lord; and also that no vagabonds abide within any town or city, nor be resorting to the same after this proclamation made, upon pain of imprisonment and to be openly punished according to the statutes in that behalf made.

And furthermore his highness straightly chargeth and commandeth all mayors, bailiffs, sheriffs, constables, and all other ministers and officers of every such city and town, that they and every of them make due search in every suspect house or place in the same city and town for all such vagabonds and other suspect persons; and them to arrest, take, and put in ward, in sure keeping, from time to time, as often as the case shall require; and that every of the said subjects of our said sovereign lord be ready at every time to aid, assist, and support the said mayors, bailiffs, sheriffs, and other officers in executing of this his high commandment, as often as they or any of them shall be thereto required; as they and every of them will eschew his grievous displeasure, and answer therefor to his highness at their perils.

17. Enforcing Statute Requiring Justices of Peace to Execute All Statutes

[Westminster, after 13 January 1489, 4 Henry VII]

PRO (C65/126/14): date based on Parliamentary Roll, 4 Henry VII, here cited; statutory order for proclamation at all quarter sessions every year; schedule as below. For 1490 date see SR 2, 524. The statute and proclamation are included in Geoffrey R. Elton, *The Tudor Constitution* (Cambridge, 1960), p. 463. See 138. Steele 9. Text (MS): PRO

THE KING our sovereign lord considereth how daily within this realm his coin is traitorously counterfeited, murder, robberies, felonies be grievously committed and done, and also unlawful retainers, idleness, unlawful plays, extortions, misdemeanings of sheriffs, escheators, and many other enormities and unlawful demeanings daily groweth and increaseth within this his realm, to the great displeasure of God, hurt and impoverishing of his subjects, and to the subversion of the policy and good governance of this his realm; for by these said enormities and mischiefs, his peace is broken, his subjects troubled and inquieted and impoverished, the husbandry of this land decayed, whereby the Church of England is upholden, the service of God continued, every man thereby hath sustenance, every inheritor his rent for his land.

For the repressing and avoiding of the said mischiefs, sufficient laws and ordinances be made, by authority of many and divers parliaments holden within this realm, to the great cost of the King, his lords, and commons of the same, and lacketh nothing but that the said laws be not put in due execution, which laws ought to be put in execution by the justice of peace in every shire of this realm, to whom his grace hath put and given full authority so to do, since the beginning of his reign.

And now it is come to his knowledge that his subjects be little eased of the said mischiefs by the said justices, but many of them rather hurt than helped; and if his subjects complain to these justices of peace of any wrongs done to them, they have thereby no remedy, and the said mischiefs do increase, and [be] not subdued.

And his grace considereth that a great part of the wealth and prosperity of this his land standeth in that, that his subjects may live in surety under his peace in their bodies and goods, and that the husbandry of this land may increase and be upholden—which must be had by due execution of the said laws and ordinances—chargeth and commandeth all the justices of peace of this his shire to endeavor them to execute the tenor of their commission, the said laws and ordinances ordained for subduing of the premises, as they will stand in the love and favor of his grace, and in avoiding of the pains that be ordained if they do the contrary.

And over that, he chargeth and commandeth that every man, what degree or condition that he be of, that let them in word or deed to execute their said authority in any manner form abovesaid, that they show it to his grace; and if they do it not, and it come to his knowledge by other than by them, they shall not be in his favor, but taken as men out of credence and be put out of the commission forever.

And over this, he chargeth and commandeth all manner of men, as well the poor as the rich—which be to him all one in due ministration of justice—that is hurt or grieved in anything that the said justice of peace may hear or determine or execute in any wise, that he so grieved make his complaint to the justice of peace that next dwelleth unto him, or to any of his fellows, and desire a remedy;

And if he then have no remedy, if it be nigh such time as his justices of assize come into that shire, that then he so grieved show his complaint to the same justices; and if he then have no remedy, or if the complaint be made long afore the coming of the justices of assize, then he so grieved come to the King's highness, or to his chancellor for the time being, and show his grief. And his said highness shall then send for the said justices to know the cause why his said subjects be not eased, and his laws executed.

Whereupon, if he find any of them in default of executing of his laws in these premises, according to this his high commandment, he shall do him so offending to be put out of the commission, and furthermore to be punished according to his demerits.

And over that, his said highness shall not let, for any favor, affection, cost, charge, nor none other cause, but that he shall see his laws to have plain and true execution, and his subjects to live in surety of their lands, bodies and goods, according to his said laws, and the said mischiefs to be avoided, that his subjects may increase in wealth and prosperity, to the pleasure of God.

18. Renewing Trade with Austria and Burgundy

[Westminster, 5 April 1489, 4 Henry VII]

CR (C54/349/*6d*): date as above; writ to Henry Botefysshe, mayor of Calais; similar writs to sheriffs of London, Kent, Essex, Surrey, Southampton, Lincoln, Norfolk, Suffolk, Somerset, Dorset, York; schedule as below. Steele 10. Text (MS): CR

FORASMUCH as certain appointments, conventions, and conclusions of and upon a true, perfect, and perpetual amity, league, confederation, union, and customs of merchandise, have been commenced, treated, covenanted, served, contracted, determined, and concluded between the King our sovereign lord for his realm, lordships, countries, and other places, his subjects and liegemen of that one party; and his most dear cousins, Maximilian, King of Romans and Philip his son, Archduke of Austria and Duke of Burgundy, for their realms, lands, lordships, countries, and other places, subjects and liegemen of that other party; as in the letters patent interchangeably thereupon made more plainly is contained:

Therefore the King our said sovereign lord chargeth and commandeth all and every of his subjects and true liegemen that they nor none of them, of what estate, degree, or condition he or they be of, move nor cause to be moved any manner of war or hostility against his said cousins or any of their subjects by land, sea, nor fresh waters; but that they and every of them peaceably suffer the said subjects of his said cousins, as well merchants as other, to enter, come, pass, and repass into and from this his said realm, land, and lordship and other places, in every port and ports, and other places of the same, with their ships and vessels, there to discharge and recharge, and to make free intercourse of merchandise from time to time, as oft as it shall please them, during the said amity, league, confederation, and union, without any safe-conduct, license, or safeguard, and without any impediment, arrest, or grief, otherwise than is according to his laws; upon pain of forfeiture of all that they may forfeit, and their bodies at the King's will.

19. Ordering Suppression of Yorkshire Rebels

[Westminster, 10 May 1489, 4 Henry VII]

CR (C54/349/6*d*): date as above; writ to sheriff of York; schedule as below. *CSPVenetian 1*, 553: date, 9 May; Henry VII reported mustering troops against the murderers of Northumberland. Campbell *2*, 447. Pollard *1*, 71. Steele 11. Text (MS): CR

Forasmuch as the King our sovereign lord, for the defense of this his realm of England, and for repressing, punishment, and subduing of his great rebels and traitors of the north parts of Yorkshire (which of late in their rebellious and riotous assembly, seditiously and traitorously, against all humanity, cruelly murdered and destroyed his most dear cousin the Earl of Northumberland, a peer of this realm and of the King's most noble blood; and so yet continue their said riotous assembly, daily calling and assembling to them robbers, thieves, and all ill-disposed persons; and in maintenance of their treasons and murder intend not only the destruction of the King's most noble person and of all the nobles and lords of this realm but also the subversion of the politic weal of the same, and to rob, despoil, and destroy all the south parts of this his realm, and to subdue and bring to captivity all the people of the same) intendeth therefore, in his most royal person at his great costs and charges, with his lords and nobles accompanied, with a great army to go toward the said part and put himself in devoir to recounter and subdue them by God's grace of their malicious purpose and intent:

Our said sovereign lord the King, of his blessed mind and disposition, willing these parts now in his absence to be surely kept and defended as well from the invasions and assaults of his adversaries and enemies outward as from all other rebellious insurrections and unlawful assemblies of rioters, robbers, and vagabonds, straightly commandeth and chargeth all his true liegemen and subjects that they and every of them be at all times readied, in their best and defensible array, to be attendant unto the justices of the peace, the sheriff, and to other having there the King's authority; and them aid, assist, and obey in all things as appertaineth from time to time; and that all gentlemen residents within the said shire not appointed to go with the King in this voyage keep hospitality and be resident at their places to see the good rule of the country;

And also that all sheriffs, mayors, bailiffs, constables of towns and villages, and all other officers assigned for the conservation of the king's peace, put themself in devoir to repress, subdue, and make to cease all manner of insurrections, riots, routs, unlawful assemblies; and all other misdoers, vagabonds, finders, and makers of new rumors and tidings to attach, arrest, and imprison, and after their demerits to correct; and all other things to do that shall be for the conservation of the peace and good rule and government and defense of the said shire; and that they nor none of them fail this to do upon pain of forfeiture of all that they may forfeit, and their bodies at the King's will.

20. Mustering Forces for Brittany

[Windsor, 16 August 1489, 4 Henry VII]

PR (C66/569/29*d*): date as above; writ to sheriffs of London and Middlesex; schedule as below. Rymer *12,* 377. Steele 12. Text (MS): PR

FORASMUCH as the King our sovereign, for defense of this his realm of England and his subjects of the same, and for the repressing and resisting of the malice of his enemies, intendeth by God's grace in all goodly haste not only to reinforce his army now being in Brittany but also to put and send a mighty army upon the sea for the sure keeping thereof:

Our said sovereign lord the King therefore commandeth all his true liegemen and subjects, which for that intent will take upon them to go in any of the said armies for their competent wages to them to be paid in that behalf, that they and every of them, armed and arrayed in their best and defensible array, come unto our trusty and well-beloved Charles Somerset, knight; whom amongst others we have deputed and charged to go unto our city of London, there to take the musters of all such as be able and will go in any of the said armies, and to all them that he shall think able thereunto to give prests according, and further to do that shall be necessary and requisite in that behalf.

21. Announcing Peace Treaty with Denmark

[Canterbury, 15 April 1490, 5 Henry VII]

PR (C66/570/20*d*): date as above; writ to lieutenant of Calais; similar writs to sheriffs of Kent, Cinque Ports, Norfolk, Suffolk, Surrey, Sussex, Essex, Herts, Somerset, Dorset, Devon, Cornwall, Lincoln, Southampton, Northumberland, London, Middlesex, towns of Kingston-upon-Hull, Newcastle-upon-Tyne; schedule as below. Steele 13. Text (MS): PR

FORASMUCH as by the commissaries and orators as well of the King our sovereign lord as his dearest cousin [Hans] the King of Denmark certain appointments, conventions, and conclusions of truce, abstinence of war, increase of merchandise, and amities be had, made, covenanted, appointed, and concluded between the same our sovereign lord and his said cousin, their heirs and successors, realms, lands, countries, lordships, leagues, confederates, and adherents, whatsoever they be, perpetually to be observed and kept under such manner and form as in divers articles thereupon made and engrossed more plainly it doth appear:

Our said sovereign lord, willing the same appointments, conventions, and conclusions on his part inviolably to be observed and kept, straightly chargeth and commandeth all and every his subjects that they nor any of them, whatsoever estate, degree, or condition he or they be of, move nor stir, nor in any manner of wise cause to be moved or stirred, any manner of war or hostility against his said cousin nor any of his subjects, by land, sea, nor fresh waters; but that they and every of them suffer the subjects of his said cousin, if any of them by tempest of the sea, shipwreck, or otherwise, happen to be driven (or for any other reasonable cause in any of the said articles specified, to arrive or come) into any port or place of this his realm, or elsewhere under his obeisance, peaceably to arrive, sojourn, and depart at their liberties, with their goods and merchandises, according to the said appointments and conventions; nothing doing or attempting to them or any of them to the contrary, wherethrough the said truce and conventions should in anywise be violated, hurt, or broken; as they and every of them will eschew the grievous displeasure of our said sovereign lord and answer unto his highness at their uttermost perils.

22. Expelling Scottish Vagabonds from Northern Shires

[Westminster, 22 May 1490, 5 Henry VII]

PR (C66/570/21*d*): date as above; writ to Thomas, Earl of Surrey, for York, Northumberland, Cumberland, Westmorland, and the marches of the same against Scotland; schedule as below. Steele 14. Text (MS): PR

FORASMUCH as the King our sovereign lord hath perfect knowledge that great number of Scots and other strangers, being suspect and not well-disposed, applying themself to idleness and begging, leaving their occupations in their countries, forsaking and departing out of the same their natural countries, have resorted and yet daily do resort unto this his realm, and specially his shires of Northumberland, Westmorland, York, and Cumberland, and into his marches against Scotland, to the great hurt, inquietation, and often disturbance of his poor, true, and faithful subjects of the same, and to their likely impoverishing, except due remedy be therefor provided in this behalf: [1]

Wherefore his highness, most desirous to have his poor subjects to live in great peace and restfulness under his laws, and to avoid all manner enormities and jeopardies which daily groweth and is like to grow amongst them by reason of the misdemeaning of the said idle and suspect persons, straightly chargeth and commandeth all manner of such strangers, suspect, and idle persons abovesaid, which now be abiding within the said shires and marches or hereafter shall be, except such as be householders or menial servants with the King's subjects and known of good name and disposition and be sworn to the allegiance of our said sovereign lord, to avoid and depart out of the said shires and marches, and return into their said countries immediately after the proclaiming of this his high commandment, so that they nor any of them be not known from thenceforth abiding or tarrying within the same shires or marches; upon pain to be committed to prison, there to remain unto such time they will make before the rulers and guiders of the said shires and marches solemn oath immediately to depart.

1. See 7 Henry VII, c. 6, 1491, *SR* 2, 553.

23. Announcing Alliance with Empire and Spain against France

[Woking, 17 September 1490, 6 Henry VII]

PR (C66/571/11*d*): date as above; writ to sheriffs of London; similar writs to sheriffs of Kent, Essex, Herts, Surrey, Sussex, Southampton, Devon, Wilts, Norfolk, Suffolk, Lincoln, Cornwall, Somerset, Dorset, York, Northumberland, cities of Norwich, Bristol, Canterbury, Lincoln, York, towns of Newcastle-upon-Tyne, Kingston-upon-Hull, Southampton, Constable of Dover and warden of Cinque Ports, and Calais. Rymer *12*, 410. Steele 15. Text (MS): PR

FORASMUCH as betwixt the King our sovereign lord, King of England and of France and lord of Ireland, and the most high and mighty princes, the King of Romans and the King and Queen of Spain, there is a very firm and perfect amity, confederation, and intelligence for them, their heirs, and successors perpetually to endure, accorded, consented, and concluded; in the which confederation, amongst other things it is comprised that if Charles the French King invade, or do to be invaded, them or any of them or any of their subjects, or the Duchess of Brittany their ally, by sea or by land, then every of the said three Kings, of Romans, England, and Spain, shall declare himself enemy unto the said French King, and make actually war against him by sea and by land, to the best of his power, as soon as he thereunto shall be required by any of them for invasion done so unto him or to the said Duchess of Brittany; always foreseen that he of them that is so invaded, or for the invading of the said Duchess of Brittany, will incontinent upon his said request make like war on his behalf, as in the said letters thereupon engrossed and made more plainly it doth appear:

Wherefore our said sovereign lord chargeth and commandeth all his subjects to entreat, take, and accept the subjects of the said King of Romans and of the King and Queen of Spain as comprised in this amity and confederation; nothing attempting or doing nor yet suffering, as far as in them shall be, to be done to them or any of them that in any wise should be contrary to these premises, or any part thereof, upon pain of falling into the great displeasure of our said sovereign lord, his body to be committed to prison and further to be punished according to his demerits.

24. Ordering Punishment of Piracy against England's Allies

[Windsor, 17 November 1490, 6 Henry VII]

PR (C66/571/11*d*): date as above; writ to sheriff of York; similar writs to sheriffs of Norfolk, Suffolk, Essex, Sussex, Southampton, Somerset, Dorset, Devon, York, Lincoln, London, Calais, Cinque Ports; schedule as below. Steele 16. Text (MS): PR

WHEREAS divers leagues, confederations, and amities, as well between the King our sovereign liege lord and his most dear cousins (the most high and mighty princes, Maximilian, King of Romans, and Philip his son, Archduke of Austria; the most high and excellent princes, Ferdinand and Elizabeth,[1] King and Queen of Spain; and the most excellent prince John, King of Portugal; as the right noble and excellent Princess Anne, Duchess of Brittany) for our said sovereign lord and for the said princes, his said cousins, and his and their said lands, seigniories, countries, subjects, vassals, allies, confederates, and adherents, whatsoever they be, were lately covenanted, made, concorded, appointed, and concluded, perpetually to endure;

Which notwithstanding, divers and manifold spoliations and robberies be daily had, committed, and done upon the sea, unto the said subjects of the said most high and mighty princes, his most dear cousins, as well by their enemies as by other pirates and robbers which, as it is said, daily resort into divers ports and places of this his realm of England, and there be suffered to utter and sell their prizes, spoils, and pillages, unto the great comfort of the said misdoers, contrary to the laws and statutes of this land, in violation and in breach of the foresaid leagues, confederations, and amities, and in grievous contempt of our said sovereign lord, and to the importable damage of the foresaid subjects:

Our said sovereign lord the King, willing the said leagues, confederations, and amities firmly and entirely to be observed and kept, and the foresaid subjects truly and rightwisely to be entreated according to the purport and effect of the same, straightly chargeth and commandeth that no manner of person, of what estate, degree, or condition he be of, from henceforth comfort, take, nor receive in any of the said ports or other places of this his realm any of the said misdoers; nor any merchandises or goods by them spoiled or taken from any of the said subjects in any manner of wise, buy or otherwise receive; upon pain of forfeiture of the same merchandises or goods, in or to the value thereof, for restitution thereof to be made to the

1. Isabella.

parties grieved, and upon pain of imprisonment of their bodies and otherwise to be punished at the King's will.

25. Outlawing Irish Pence, Declaring English Pence Legal Tender

[Westminster, 15 April 1491, 6 Henry VII]

PR (C66/571/7*d*): date as above; writ to sheriffs of London and Middlesex; similar writs to sheriffs of Kent, Surrey, Sussex, Southampton, Somerset, Dorset, Cornwall, Warwick, Leceister, Norfolk, Suffolk, Devon, Bristol, London, Coventry; schedule as below. Steele 17. Text (MS): PR

WHEREAS our most dread sovereign lord the King, Henry by the grace of God King of England and of France and lord of Ireland, is certainly informed not only by the estates and nobles but also by divers inhabitants within his cities and boroughs and other his subjects of this his said realm, that forasmuch as certain pennies, and pennies of 2*d.*, coined in his said land of Ireland, without his authority or knowledge be to his high displeasure in great number brought into this his land by divers evil-disposed persons unknown unto our said sovereign lord, to the intent they might be put to course among his subjects; which money is of much less value, as well in fineness as weight, than the pieces of pence and pennies of 2*d.* coined at his tower of London and other places within this his said realm; and that also divers of his subjects, for fear and ignorance of the said Irish money, refuse to take and receive in payments the pennies and pennies of 2*d.* coined within this his realm, to the great annoyance, disturbance, and manifest hurt of his said subjects, specially the poor:

Our said sovereign lord, intending to provide for due remedy in this part, not willing in anywise his said subjects to be hurt or defrauded, nor the said Irish money for the cause above rehearsed to be current in this his said realm, but utterly to be refused and damped, and his pennies and pennies of 2*d.* of silver, lawfully within this his realm of England coined, to be among his subjects current, used, and accepted, as reason requireth, will and straightly chargeth and commandeth all and every of his subjects, of what estate, degree, or condition they be, that none of them from henceforth refuse to receive and take in payment any good and lawful penny or penny of 2*d.* made within this his said realm, upon pain of imprisonment of his body, and fine making at the will of our said sovereign lord;

And on the other part, that no manner person from henceforth convey or bring into this realm any of the said Irish pennies, or other money coined in his said land of Ireland, nor there in any manner wise utter or put forth and deliver in payment within the same realm; under pain of forfeiture of the same, the one moiety thereof to appertain to our sovereign lord, and the other moiety to the first finder and seizer of the same, and his body to be put in prison to abide punition and fine at the will of our said sovereign lord.

And over this, our said sovereign lord straightly chargeth and commandeth that no manner of person, high or low, bear or convey or carry near or towards his said land of Ireland any silver in coin, plate, or mass; upon pain of forfeiture of the same, and imprisonment of his body, and fine making at our sovereign lord's will with the half of the said forfeiture to appertain to [our] said sovereign lord, and the other half to the finder and seizer thereof; and also that every person that hereafter shall have knowledge of any such person that from henceforth beareth or conveyeth any gold or silver in coin, bullion, plate, or mass, into his said land of Ireland, or bring any coin coined in Ireland into this land, he put him in devoir to take the said person and to bring him to the King's next jail, there to remain till the King's pleasure be known for his deliverance; upon pain of imprisonment and further to be punished at the King's will.

26. Prohibiting Unlicensed Grain Export

[Westminster, 19 September 1491, 7 Henry VII]

PR (C66/572/3*d*): date as above; writ to sheriffs of Somerset, Dorset; similar writs to sheriffs of Devon, Cornwall, Wilts, Southampton, Surrey, Sussex, Kent, Essex, Norfolk, Suffolk, Lincoln, York, Northumberland, Cumberland; schedule as below. Steele 18. Text (MS): PR

FORASMUCH as the King our sovereign lord, Henry by the grace of God King of England and of France and lord of Ireland, considering that great dearth and scarcity of grain were the last year past, and specially by occasion of the carrying out over the sea of the same grains; considering also that his highness with God's grace intendeth with an army royal to pass in his person over the sea to resist the malice of his great enemy of France:

Our said sovereign lord the King therefore, tendering the policy and effectuously desiring the commonweal of this his said realm and of his subjects, and also the defense of the same, straightly chargeth and commandeth that no manner person, of what estate, degree, or condition he be of, from henceforth carry nor do to be carried any manner grain out of this his said realm unto any parts beyond the sea, without his special license sealed under his great seal; upon pain of forfeiture of the same and further to be punished at the King's pleasure.

27. Establishing Staple of Mines at Southampton

[Westminster, 24 June 1492, 7 Henry VII]

PR (C66/572/30*d*): date as above; letters patent to all sheriffs mayors, bailiffs, constables, and other officers, liegemen, and subjects; schedule as below. Steele 19. Text (MS): PR

FORASMUCH as the King our sovereign lord, considering that the mines within this realm of England and other countries adjoining bearing gold, silver, and tin, copper, lead, and other metals, for lack of diligent labor be left unsought and unwrought, and so the commodities and riches in the same mines turn no manner to profit:

His highness therefore hath granted and licensed an incorporation to be had, of a mayor and a certain fellowship of merchants of the Staple of all manner of metals, to the intent that they shall not only cause the said mines to be occupied and much idle people to be set over in work for the approvement of the commodities therein, but also shall cause all the metals hereafter to be found in the said mines to be uttered for a reasonable price, to the great wealth of his said highness and of his realm and of his subjects of the same; and thereupon hath ordained certain Staples of metals to be set and kept in divers places within this his said realm, that is to say, at Southampton, so that no tin nor lead, after the Feast of St. Michael the Archangel next coming, be shipped nor carried out of the said realm but it be first brought and stapled at one of the said Staples, and the customs and duties to his said highness thereof due be to him there contented and paid; upon pain of forfeiture of all such lead and tin, that one half thereof to his said highness and that other half to the finder of the same, according to the tenor of our said sovereign lord's letters patent thereupon made.

And over this, in eschewing of the great disdain and untruth that heretofore hath been used in false melting of tin, it is ordained that no manner of person or persons, from the said Feast of St. Michael, presume to take upon him to melt any tin ore, but if he be first admitted and sworn by the mayor, lieutenant, and constable of the said Staples, or their deputies, upon pain never after to occupy melting of tin; and also that all tins so molten within two months after the melting be brought unto the place or places of the old time accustomed, or to such other places as by the advice of the chancellor for the time being shall be assigned, there to be coined, upon pain of forfeiture of all such tin or the value thereof, the one half thereof to the use of our said sovereign lord and his heirs, and the other half to the finder.

And because the tin workers and specially poor men have been heretofore sore damaged forsomuch as they have sold in time past their tin beforehand, not taking therefore half the value, not being of ability to keep their tin unto the time of the tinnage, which was but two times of the year, that is to wit, Midsummer and Michaelmas: for redress whereof, and for relief of the said poor men, it is ordained four tinnages to be kept in the year, or more or fewer, as necessarily shall require for the profit and advantage of the said tin workers;

Also that at such time as the tin shall be coined at the places of the tinnages, the merchants of the said Staples be bound to buy all the said tin and restain it at the same places of the coinages, paying for every cwt. at the weight of coinages of old time used, of the best, 22*s.;* and hardy tin, black tin, and other, at the rate to be abased, of so much of the price as it is worth than other, in such manner and form as it hath been of old time used and accustomed; and that price, of 22*s.,* cwt. of the best, to continue besides the coinage forever, be it good-cheap or dear, in peace and war.

And because the King's highness, his heirs, nor none of his true liege people should be disdained by misconveying of tin otherwise than it ought to be, his highness therefore hath ordained, and by his said letters hath granted, that if any of his said subjects, at any time after the said Feast of St. Michael, find any tin or lead, by the land or fresh water, after the said day bought, not being at the melting places, the places of coinage or bowls or Staples, or not bought to be occupied within the realm, nor can be proved appertaining to any of the said merchants of the said Staple, that then the said tin and lead to be forfeited, the one half thereof to the King's highness and his heirs, and the other half to the finder.

And over this, his highness will and granteth that if there be any person or persons willing to be admitted a merchant of the said Staples and come or send to the said mayor or to his assignees between this and the last day of August next coming, [they] shall pay 40*s.* unto the said mayor, and they shall be admitted for merchants, and their names registered; and that as many merchants as shall come after the said last day of August, to be admitted merchants of the said Staples, shall pay for their entry as by the said merchants of the Staple shall be esteemed.

And forasmuch as the silver mines shall be continually set on work, it is ordained that every merchant of the said Staple shall spend every year at the least in the said silver mines £10, or else to be banished of the said Staple and taken for no merchant. Also forasmuch as it is said that the woods in Devonshire and Cornwall be little enough for the tin works, it is therefore ordained that all such lead ore bearing silver, and by the said merchants and their deputies labored and gotten out of the ground, shall be molten nowhere but in the said Staples or in a melting place therefore provided, but if it be for approof, upon pain of forfeiture specified in the letters patent;

And that no person or persons to dig or wash for gold or silver without knowledge given to the governors of the said Staples; upon pain of forfeiture of all the said silver, gold, ore, and other metals as they shall happen to find, the one half to our said sovereign lord and that other half to the finder. And if any person or persons having license or no license to dig or wash for gold or silver withdraw and bring not to the said Staples, to the intent the King's highness may thereof be ascertained and answered of his right and duty in that behalf, the mayor and constables of the same Staple have power to punish all those persons as withdraw gold or silver, as is abovesaid, according to their demerits.

And over this the King's highness will that if any of his subjects [are] willing further to be ascertained and to have perfect knowledge of all the ordinances, rules, statutes, and provisions of the foresaid Staples, [they] resort unto the mayor and constables of the said Staples which without contradiction or delay shall show unto them the King's letters patent, declaring all the foresaid ordinances, rules, statutes, and provisions more at large, so that the breakers and offenders of the same shall not excuse themselves by ignorance.

And moreover his highness straightly chargeth and commandeth all mayors, sheriffs, bailiffs, constables, and other his ministers, officers, and all other his true liegemen and subjects, as well within the franchises as without, that they and every of them unto the foresaid mayor and constables, merchants and other ministers of the said Staple, their factors and attorneys, in laboring of the said mines and all other things concerning the said Staples and in executing of all articles comprised in the said letters patent, be aiding, assisting, counciling, and obedient as appertaineth, in no manner of wise letting, impeaching, or disturbing them contrary to the tenor and effects of the said letters patent; upon pain of imprisonment and further to be punished at the King's will.

28. Mustering Forces in Kent

[Canterbury, 2 August 1492, 7 Henry VII]

PR (C66/572/31*d*): date as above; writ to sheriff of Kent; similar writs to sheriff of Sussex, mayor of Canterbury, constable of Dover and warden of Cinque Ports and his deputies; schedule as below. Rymer *12*, 482. Steele 20. Text (MS): PR

THE KING our sovereign lord, having a tender zeal to the wealth, surety, and defense of this his realm of England and of his subjects of the same, for divers great and believeful considerations him moving, straightly chargeth and commandeth all and every his subjects inhabited within this his shire of Kent, having harness of his own and being of ability in his person to serve his highness if need be, that they and every of them prepare themself and be ready in their said harness, upon an hour warning, to serve our said sovereign lord at his wages, in such manner and form as the case shall require.

And over that, his said highness chargeth and commandeth all the constables of every hundred within the said shire, that they and every of them make search within the hundred where he is constable, for all inhabitants of the same that be of ability and harnessed to serve his said highness, as is aforesaid; and thereupon to make certificate of their names and apparel unto his said highness without any delay, so that his grace may be ascertained of the number and apparel of his said subjects that so be able to serve him.

29. Announcing Peace Treaty with France

[12 December 1492, 8 Henry VII]

BM, MS Julius B. 1, 93*v:* schedule as below. *CSPVenetian 1,* 626: date as above; peace reported between England and France. Steele 21: date, December. Text (MS): Julius

THE KING our sovereign lord Henry, by the grace [of God] King of France and of England and lord of Ireland, doth you to understand that good, sure, and firm peace, union, and amity is made and concluded betwixt the King our said sovereign lord and the right high and mighty prince his cousin of France, their realms, countries, lordships, and subjects, during their life natural, and of either of them longer living, and by a year after the decease of him that last liveth; and that by this peace the subjects of the said realms, countries, and lordships, of what estate or condition they be, may haunt and be conversant by way of merchandise or otherwise, the one with the other, by land, by sea, and by rivers, without that they shall need safe-conduct, general or special; in the which peace and amity be comprised the allies of either party, if they will be comprised; for the surety and entertaining of which peace, be advised, accorded, and concluded, certain points and articles, declared at length in the treaties made by the ambassadors of the said princes, the which articles shall be by them ratified and confirmed.

30. Enforcing Statutes against Murder, Decay of Husbandry, Robberies, Vagabonds, Beggars, Unlawful Games

[Westminster, 18 February 1493, 8 Henry VII]

PR (C66/574/4*d*): date as above; writ to sheriffs of Norfolk and Suffolk; schedule as below. Steele 22. Text (MS): PR

THE KING our sovereign lord is informed that full heinous murders, robberies, thefts, decay of husbandry, and other enormities and inconveniences daily increase within this his realm, to the great offense unto God, displeasure to his highness, hurt and impoverishing, vexation, and trouble of his subjects by the means of idleness; and specially of vagabonds, beggars able to work, and by fautours, some excusing themself by color of pilgrimage, some excusing themself by that they were taken by the king's enemies upon the sea, some by that they be scholars of the one university or the other within this realm, some that they be hermits and so begging by color of feigned devotion and many other suspicious and vicious livings thus used in this realm; whereby if hasty remedy be not had, the said mischiefs and other more be like to ensue and increase, to the great noyance and hurt of his subjects; for repressing of the said mischiefs and inconveniences, divers full reasonable and notable statutes [1] and laws hath been made as well in his time as in the days of his noble progenitors to the great charge and cost of this his realm, but the due effect of them hath not ensued for all of their due execution:

But forasmuch as the death of man is to God above other offenses singularly displeasant, and also to the King most detestable, for there is nothing earthly that he desireth more than that his subjects may live in surety of their bodies according to his laws: he will therefore that the statute [2] made in his last parliament save one, which was ordained for hasty punishment of murders, be put in execution without favor or sparing of any persons, for the weal and surety of the lives of his subjects.

The effect of which statute is this, that if a murder be done in a town by day, the township is bound to arrest the murderer and his accessories, upon pain of grievous amercement; and if any man be stricken so that he is in peril of death, the party so offending to be arrested; and also the coroners to

1. 23 Edward III, c. 7, 1349, *SR 1*, 308; 34 Edward III, c. 1, 1360, *SR 1*, 364; 7 Richard II, c. 5, 1383, *SR 2*, 32; 12 Richard II, c. 7–9, 1388, *SR 2*, 58–59.

2. 3 Henry VII, c. 2, 1487, *SR 2*, 510.

exercise and do their office truly and inquire upon the body dead, as well as of the murderers and their accessories, as of the escapes of murderers if they escaped and were not taken. And in like wise, the justices of the peace have power to inquire of the said murders and escapes; and to the intent that murderers should be punished speedily, such as be indicted without delay to proceed to their deliverance within the year at the King's suit; and if they be at the King's suit acquit, they eftsoons to be put to answer in appeal sued against them for the same, the acquittal afore notwithstanding; and to the intent that the coroners should effectually and truly do their office, the coroners to have for every such inquiry of murder 13*s.* 4*d.* of the goods of the murderer, or of such fine as shall fall in his office; and if any coroner be negligent or remiss in doing his office in this part, he to forfeit for every default 100*s.*, as in the said statute it appears more at large.

And for avoiding of idleness by the mean of vagabonds, beggars, fautours, and other suspect persons afore rehearsed, it is ordained by a statute made in the days of King Richard II [3] that justices of peace, sheriffs, mayors, bailiffs, constables, and other governors of hundreds, cities, boroughs, and other places within this realm, to have power to examine all vagabonds and fautours of their misbehaving and evil deeds, and to compel them to find sufficient surety of their good living, and to answer to all defaults against them to be alleged; and if the same vagabonds find no such surety, then they to be committed to the next jail, there to abide till the next coming thither of the justice of the jail delivery; and the same justice of jail delivery then to do to them as shall seem most convenient according to the law.

But forasmuch as the King's grace most entirely desireth amongst all earthly things the prosperity and restfulness of this his land, and his subjects of the same to live quietly and surefully to the pleasure of God and according to his laws, willing and always of his pity intending to reduce them thereunto by softer means than by the extreme rigor thereof; considering also the great charges that should grow to his subjects for bringing of the said vagabonds to the jails and the long abiding of them therein, whereby by likelihood many of them should lose their lives in murdering:

Of the said statute, his highness hath ordained that where such misdoers should by the said examination be committed to the common jail, there to remain as is abovesaid, that the sheriffs, mayors, bailiffs, high constables, petty constables, and all other governors and officers of cities, boroughs, towns, townships, villages, and other places, immediately after, and upon the hearing of this proclamation, make due search and take or cause to be taken all such vagabonds, idle and suspect persons living suspiciously; and them so taken to set in stocks, there to remain by the space of three days and three nights and there to have none other sustenance but bread and water, and after the said three days and three nights to be had out and

3. 7 Richard II, c. 5, 1383, *SR* 2, 32.

set at large and then to be sworn to avoid the town; and if eftsoon he be taken in such default in the same town or township, then to be set in likewise in the stocks by the space of six days with like diet as is above rehearsed; and if any person or persons give other meat or drink to the said misdoers being in stocks in form aforesaid, or the same prisoners favor in their misdoing, then they to have like pain and imprisonment as is limited for the said misdoers.

Also his highness chargeth and commandeth that all manner of beggars not able to work, within six weeks next after this proclamation made, go, rest, and abide in his hundred where he last dwelled, or there where he is best known, or born, there to remain and abide, without begging out of the said hundred, upon pain to be punished as is abovesaid; and that no man be excused by that he is a clerk of the one university or the other, without he show the letters of the chancellor of the university from whence he saith he cometh; nor none other calling himself a soldier, shipman, or traveling man, without he bring a letter from his captain or from the town where he landed, and that he then to be sworn to go the straight highway into his country.

And over this it is ordained that if any mayor, sheriff, or other officer afore rehearsed execute not the premises as is abovesaid, of every vagabond, hermit, or beggar able to labor, or clerk, pilgrim or shipman, as oft as any such cometh in his sight, or that he hath thereof knowledge within the town where he hath authority, rule, or governance: that as oft as any such of the said misdoers departeth unexamined and unpunished as is abovesaid, for every misdoer so departed he to lose 20*d.;* and that the lord of every leet within this realm and the sheriff in his tourn have authority to inquire thereof in his leet and tourn, and the lord of the leet to have for every escape found as is abovesaid, 20*d.;* and the sheriff of every shire to inquire in his tourn of such escapes not found in the leet, and to have 20*d*. for every such escape found in his tourn; and the penalty limited by this ordinance to be forfeited by any officer or any other person for non-punishment of vagabonds and laborers and other misruled persons within every city where mayor or aldermen be, that the profit of every such penalty be unto the alderman of every ward where such forfeiture is had and made to his own use and profit.

Also he chargeth and commandeth that no sheriff, mayor, or other officer afore rehearsed suffer any man's knaves to play with dice or at tennis, under the pains of the statutes ordained for the same. And as for men living suspiciously in any city, borough, town, according to the Statute of Winchester [4] so examine all such persons so living, and compel them that harboreth and lodgeth any such to find surety to answer for the defaults of them that they so harbor; and all such as they find living suspiciously, to avoid them the town and not to tarry there over a day and a night.

4. 13 Edward I, c. 4 (Winchester), 1285, *SR 1*, 7.

31. Prohibiting Unlicensed Trade with Burgundy

[Westminster, 18 September 1493, 8 Henry VII]

CW (C82/124): date as above; sign manual; writ to warden of Cinque Ports; similar writs to sheriffs of London, Kent, Norfolk, Lincoln, Southampton, Northumberland, Westmorland, Cumberland, Surrey, Sussex, Wilts, Somerset, Dorset, Devon, Cornwall, city of York, towns of Kingston-upon-Hull, Southampton, Bristol; schedule as below. PR (C66/575/21*d*): writ to warden of Cinque Ports; similar writs as CW, plus Suffolk; schedule as below. Steele 23. Text (MS): PR

THE KING our sovereign lord, for divers great and urgent causes his highness specially moving, by the advice of his council straightly chargeth and commandeth that no manner of Englishman, denizen, nor yet any stranger, of what estate, degree, or condition he or they be, from henceforth carry or convey or cause to be carried or conveyed out of this his realm of England unto any of the parts and the obeisance of his cousin the Archduke of Austria and Duke of Burgundy, nor yet to any parts or countries nigh thereunto adjoining, by the mean whereof any intercourse of merchandise might ensue betwixt his subjects and the said strangers and the subjects of his said cousin, any manner of goods or merchandise grown or made within this his realm, wool and woolfells from the Staple of Calais except; nor that they nor any of them from henceforth buy, bring, nor cause to be bought or brought, out of any of the said parts into this his said realm, any manner of goods or merchandise there by them or any of them now bought, provided, or packed, or hereafter by them or any of them to be bought, provided, or packed, to be carried into this his said realm, without special license under his great seal; upon pain of forfeiture of all such goods and merchandise so bought, conveyed, or brought into this his realm or any other parts of his obeisance;

And if happen any manner vessel to pass out of any port or creek of this his said realm, or else to come into the same by way of merchandise to or from the obeisance of his said cousin contrary to this his proclamation, and be not therefore put under arrest by the customers, comptrollers, and other officers of the same port or creek where the said vessel shall so go from or come unto, that then all the said officers and also their deputies culpable therein lose their offices and forfeit their goods unto our said sovereign lord.

32. Granting Thomas Andrew License to Collect Alms

[Westminster, 8 February 1496, 11 Henry VII]

Rev.STC 7760.2, Antiq Lemon *Addenda* 1: printed by R. Pynson (London, 1496); date as above; schedule as below. Not in Steele. Text (*rev.STC*): Antiq

KNOW YE THAT OF LATE, by showing of our humble subject Thomas Andrew of the parish of Southmymes in the county of Middlesex, and also we be informed by faithful witness, that before the Feast of Christmas last past, the house, four stables, two barns, . . . and all other movable goods of the foresaid Thomas, through the misfortune of fire, were burned and wasted, whereby he is fallen into great and extreme poverty, having nothing left to succor and relieve himself, his wife, and his children; wherefore he humbly desired our license safely to go and come in all parts of this our realm of England to gather the alms [of] devotion and charitable gifts of Christian people.

To which petition we, being inclined favorably, have received the said Thomas, his men, servants, and goods unto our protection and defense: safely to go and come in all parts of this our realm [of] England for the cause abovesaid, to gather the almsdeeds and charitable gifts of Christian people.

And therefore we desire and pray all you prelates and other spiritual persons, when the said Thomas, his men, and servants shall come to your churches, chapels, or any other spiritual place, that you receive them freely, to desire and gather the alms and charitable gifts, and favorably suffer them therewith to depart.

And to all mayors, sheriffs, bailiffs, constables, and other our faithful ministers and subjects aforesaid, we charge and command: that ye maintain, protect, and defend the said Thomas, his men, servants, and goods, wheresoever they come, for the cause abovesaid, to desire and to gather the almsdeeds and charitable gifts, and therewith to return again; and that you shall do to them none injury, molestation, damage, violence, impediment, or grief, nor suffer the same to be done of any other person. And if any trespass or injury be done unto them, then you without delay shall see it duly corrected and reformed.

33. Announcing Peace Treaty with Austria and Burgundy

[Westminster, 28 February 1496, 11 Henry VII]

AC (Bayne 29): date, April 1496; communication to be had with mayor and aldermen for keeping the peace with Burgundy; CW (C82/145): date of delivery as above; sign manual; schedule as below. PR (C66/577/7*d*): date as above; writ to sheriffs of London and Middlesex; similar writs to sheriffs of Kent, Surrey, Sussex, Southampton, Wilts, Somerset, Dorset, Devon, Cornwall, Essex, Herts, Norfolk, Suffolk, Lincoln, York, Northumberland, Cumberland, Westmorland, towns of Bristol, Kingston-upon-Hull, Southampton; schedule as below. Steele 24. Text (MS): PR

FORASMUCH as betwixt the King our sovereign lord, Henry by the grace of God King of England and of France and lord of Ireland on the one party, and the right high and mighty prince, his right dear and well-beloved cousin Philip, by the same grace Archduke of Austria and Duke of Burgundy on the other party (for them, their heirs, lands, countries, and subjects, to the laud of God, the exaltation of their honors, and the commonweal of their said subjects) is taken, accorded, and concluded peace perpetual, union, amity, and intelligence, with sure intercommuning of merchants, intercourse of merchandise, and free passage by land and by waters on both sides in an ample and more large form, better surety and with as great liberties and privileges as of anciety have been accustomed by God's grace always to endure:

Our said sovereign lord, in consideration of the same, straightly chargeth and commandeth that no man from henceforth do or attempt anything by land or by waters against any of the subjects of his said cousin the Archduke contrary to the terms of the treaty of the said peace and intercourse, or whereby they might be troubled in body or goods, or letted freely to use and exercise the same.

And over this, where our said sovereign lord by the advice of his council, for reasonable cause him moving, by his proclamations heretofore in that behalf made, commanded that no manner of person should pass the sea into his said cousin's lands, his grace, in consideration of the said peace and intercourse, is now contented and pleased and giveth plain license and liberty to all manner of men, denizens and strangers, from henceforth at their pleasures and to their most advantages, to use, take, and enjoy the profit and benefit of the treaty of the said peace and intercourse, according to the tenor and effect of the same; any proclamation, defense, or restraint heretofore to the contrary notwithstanding.

34. Declaring War against Scotland

[Westminster, after 25 September 1496, 12 Henry VII]

CW (C82/331): sign manual; for 25 September date, and writ, see schedule; schedule as below. Steele 24a: date, Westminster. Text (MS): PR

WHEREAS THE KING our sovereign lord had heretofore concluded with the King of Scots a firm truce and alliance of war for themselves and for their realms and subjects, the same to have endured for seven years complete, whereof four whole years be yet to come;

And where also our said sovereign lord had of the King of Scots, for the better assurance thereof, his sign manual and Great Seal, ratified in the word of a King, like as our said sovereign lord made for his part:

Yet nonetheless the said King of Scots, of his wilful headiness, and without cause or occasion given by our said sovereign lord, hath entered with his person and with the power he could make, and with his banner displayed, some four miles within this realm, contrary to the truce and his sign manual, and contrary also to his seal and promise aforesaid, directly and expressly to his reproach and dishonor in that part.

And over that the said King of Scots hath done, within the bounds of the said four miles, great cruelty to man, woman, and child, cast down three or four little towers, besides burning, and other outrageous deeds by him committed within the same.

And as soon as the army of our said sovereign lord began to advance them towards the Scots out of the King's town and port of Newcastle, which was the 25th day of September last past, the King of Scots and his whole power returned and stole away into Scotland the self same day about midnight.

Wherefore the King our sovereign lord wills you [to] know that by this the King of Scots' entry and cruelty foresaid, the war between the King's highness and the said King of Scots is open and at large.[1]

And therefore, and to the intent you should set yourself out of the trust of the said truce, and to make war and to do from henceforth by land and by sea all the annoyance possible to the Scots that you can or may, the King notifieth this unto you by this his present writ of proclamation.

1. See 11 Henry VII, c. 65, 1495, *SR* 2, 635; 12 Henry VII, c. 12, 1496, *SR* 2, 642.

35. Pardoning Blackheath Rebels

[Westminster, 20 June 1497, 12 Henry VII]

CW (C82/163): date as above; sign manual; writ to sheriff of Cornwall; similar writs to sheriffs of Devon, Wilts, Somerset, Dorset, Southampton, Gloucester. PR (C66/580/24*d*): date as above; writ to sheriff of Cornwall; writs as CW; schedule as below. Steele 25. Text (MS) PR

WHEREAS it is openly understood and known as well within this the King's realm as in other realms and countries thereunto adjoining, to the great slander and infamy of this land, that divers and many of his subjects and liege people of his counties of Devonshire and Kent, and of divers other counties and places of this his realm, assembled in great number by the instigation, procurement, and setting on of divers seditious and ill-disposed persons, the King's rebels and traitors; intending the destruction of the King's most noble person and of all the nobles and true and substantial persons of this his said realm, and the grievous subversion of the same, and the retracting, stop, and let of his most noble voyage and royal army prepared toward the realm of Scotland, which was agreed and concluded in the last parliament by the three estates of this land, for the revenging of such open injuries and damages as have been done unto our said sovereign lord and this his realm by the king of the said realm of Scotland, to the inestimable and irrecoverable damage and dishonor as well of the King as of all his said land; and his subjects of the same have rebelliously made insurrection and for the same intent put themself in great number in harness and levied war with their banners in the field openly displayed, and so came through the counties of Somerset, Dorset, Wiltshire, Sussex, and Surrey, into the Blackheath beside Greenwich in the county of Kent, so that many of the King's subjects of the same counties to them resorted, repaired, and greatly increased their number, and by courage thereof set themself in battle there to fight against the King's highness unnaturally, contrary to the duty of their allegiance, and against his laws, dignity, and crown; where the King's grace in his person, with his banner displayed, well accompanied with his nobles and true subjects of his realm, knightly and courageously recountered, vanquished, and subdued them by the help and sufferance of almighty God:

Yet the King's highness, moved with pity in eschewing more effusion of Christian blood and most specially of his subjects, of his mere motion and abundant grace, putting apart all cruelty, rigor of justice, and the straightness of his laws (by the execution whereof should and ought to ensue not only great execution and pains of death of many of his said subjects and losses and forfeiture of lands and goods, but also desolation of the countries where they inhabit, which he in nowise of his mercy and pity will suffer, but rather at the reverence of almighty God, and of the good and tender zeal that he beareth to all his subjects of this his said realm), is contented to accept and admit them into his grace and favor, and to pardon not only them that have been actually offenders in the said insurrection and rebellion but also all such that have been councilors, aiders, or privy favorers unto them or any of them, the which will sue and submit themself unto his highness, and desire his grace, making their reasonable fines according to their haviors and demerits.

And for the execution and accomplishing of this his most blessed and gracious mind, his highness hath given full power and authority to his special commissioners on this behalf, to inquire, and do to be understood, the grounds and principal causes of the said rebellion and all other offenders and favorers in and of the same; and thereupon and upon their submission and suit made for grace to the said commissioners for their said great and natural offenses, they to receive the said subjects into the King's grace, favor, and protection; whereby they and every of them, so by the same commissioners accepted and received, shall move, obtain, and have the King's pardon, mercy, and grace of their lives, and grant of their land and goods, their offenses and demerits by the discretion of the commissioners always to be considered.

And over that, the King's highness straightly chargeth and commandeth that no manner of person, of what estate, degree, or condition he be of, rob or despoil any of the said offenders and misdoers, as they will eschew the King's high displeasure, and upon pain of imprisonment of their bodies, and further to be punished according to their offenses and demerits.

36. Mustering Forces against Scotland

[Westminster, 24 June 1497, 12 Henry VII]

PR (C66/580/12*d*): date as above; writ to sheriff of York; similar writs to sheriffs of Northumberland, Cumberland, Westmorland, Notts, Berks, Lincoln; schedule as below. Steele 26. Text (MS): PR

Forasmuch as the King our sovereign lord, for the honor and necessary defense of this his realm and his subjects of the same, intendeth in all goodly haste to make war against the malice of his ancient enemies, the Scots, and by God's grace to subdue them:

Therefore his highness straightly chargeth and commandeth all and every his true liegemen and subjects between the age of 60 and 16, able in their bodies to labor, to prepare and arready themself in their best and most defensible array, to serve his highness on this behalf, upon an hour's warning; and that they fail not so to do, as they intend their own weal and to do him pleasure and eschew his indignation.

37. Mustering Forces against Scottish Invasion

[Woodstock, 30 August 1497, 13 Henry VII]

PR (C66/581/6*d*): date, 30 August; writ to sheriff of Northumberland; similar writs to bishop of Durham and Thomas Lord Dacre, warden of western marches against Scotland; schedule as below. Steele 27: date, Woodstock. Text (MS): PR

FORASMUCH as the King our sovereign lord hath perfect understanding that his ancient enemies the Scots, continuing in their rooted malice against our said sovereign lord and this his realm and subjects of the same, intending with their power to invade this his said realm the seventh day of the month of September now next coming, proposing in their invasion to do to the subjects of our said sovereign lord, nigh inhabited the marches against Scotland, all the hurt and annoyance to them possible:

Our said sovereign lord, willing the said marches to be defended against the said Scots according to the ancient custom there used, straightly chargeth and commandeth all and every of his subjects inhabited within this his county of Northumberland being between the age of 60 and 16, that they and every of them prepare themself in their best and most defensible array, and to be ready to give their attendance under his right trusty and well beloved cousin, the Lord Neville, and such other captains as by the right reverend father in God, the Bishop of Durham, and the said Lord Neville, shall be assigned to make resistance and defense against the said Scots, and further to annoy them by all means possible, for the weal and surety of this his land, the marches, and subjects aforesaid.

38. Declaring Silver Pence Legal Tender

[Woodstock, 5 September 1497, 13 Henry VII]

PR (C66/581/6*d*): date as above; writ to bailiff of city of Worcester; schedule as below. Steele 28. Text (MS): PR

FORASMUCH as the King our sovereign lord hath certain understanding that great difficulties, ambiguities, and doubts be had among his subjects of this his realm of England, and specially within this his city of Worcester, of, for and upon the course, payment, and utterance of pennies coined within this his realm of England, to the great hurt and damage of his highness and of his subjects aforesaid:

His said highness, in avoiding of the said difficulties, ambiguities, and doubts, straightly chargeth and commandeth all and every of his said subjects that they nor any of them from henceforth refuse to take and receive for and in payment any manner pennies or other coins being silver and lawfully coined within this his said realm of England; upon pain of imprisonment and further to be punished at the pleasure of our said sovereign lord;

Provided always that, by color of this his high commandment and proclamation or otherwise, any manner of pennies or other money coined within his land and seigniory of Ireland in no wise have course nor be uttered in payment within this his realm, upon pain of forfeiting of the same.

39. Outlawing Imperial Groats and Pence

[Westminster, 27 February 1498, 13 Henry VII]

PR (C66/581/15*d*): date as above; writ to sheriffs of London and Middlesex; similar writs to sheriffs of Kent, Essex, Herts, Norfolk, Suffolk, Southampton, Lincoln, Somerset, Dorset, Devon, city of York, towns of Bristol, Newcastle-upon-Tyne, Southampton, Cinque Ports; schedule as below. Steele 30. Text (MS): PR

Forasmuch as the King our most dread sovereign lord, well understanding that divers counterfeit and new-forged strange coins, specially groats called Roman groats, and pennies of 2*d*. called Roman pence of 2*d*., far of less value than men take them for, be daily brought in great number and be uttered within this his realm, to the great deceit, damage, and loss of the King's highness and his true liegemen and subjects, and to the great hurt of the common and politic weal of this his said realm:

His [highness] therefore, in avoiding of the said deceit, damage, and loss, and effectually desiring the increase of the commonweal, straightly chargeth and commandeth that no person, of what estate, degree, or condition he be of, from henceforth receive, take, nor deliver in payment, nor otherwise but as bullion, any of the said Roman groats and pence of 2*d*., nor any other strange coins, but only such as hath been by the King's highness and his council heretofore approved and accepted; upon pain of forfeiture of the same and further to be punished at the King's pleasure.

40. Announcing Peace Treaty with France

[Westminster, 23 August 1498, 14 Henry VII]

CW (C82/332): date, uncertain; sign manual; writ to sheriffs of Middlesex, London; similar writs to sheriffs of Devon, Cornwall, Dorset, Wilts, Southampton, Surrey, Sussex, Kent, Essex, Herts, Lincoln, Norfolk, Suffolk, York, Northumberland, Westmorland, Cumberland, cities of Canterbury, Norwich, York, towns of Bristol, Kingston-upon-Hull, Newcastle-upon-Tyne, Southampton, mayor of Calais. PR (C66/582/15*d*): date as above; writs as CW, omitting Calais; schedule as below. LJ 10, 132*v*: date, 24 August; writ unspecified; schedule as below. Steele 31. Text (MS): PR

WHEREAS between the King our sovereign lord Henry by the grace of God, on the one party, and the right high and mighty prince his dearest cousin, King Charles of France, late deceased, on the other party, a sure peace, amity, confederation, and intercourse of merchandise was before this time agreed, covenanted, and concluded, to endure for the lives of them both and a year after the decease of him that soonest should fortune to die, as in the treaty [1] thereupon made, ratified, and confirmed, under either their Great Seals, whereof the party of the said late King remaineth in the treasury of our said sovereign lord, more plainly is contained; the which peace, amity, and intercourse of merchandise, and all articles contained and expressed in the said treaty, the right high and mighty prince and his dearest cousin, King Louis, now of France, hath under the Great Seal confirmed, approved, and ratified, in as large and ample form as they were before agreed and confirmed by the said King Charles, so to be observed and contained during the life of our said sovereign lord and of his said cousin King Louis, now of France, and a year after the decease of him that first of them both shall fortune to die; and for the sure and inviolable observance of the said peace, amity, and intercourse, the said King Louis hath bound himself by his letters patent, under his Great Seal, and by a solemn oath by him made upon the Holy Evangels, as in writing thereupon engrossed and subscribed with his hand plainly and expressly is specified and contained:

So it is therefore that all our said sovereign lord's subjects shall, without peril or jeopardy of their persons or goods surely to resort, pass and repass, to and from the realm of France, and to all parts and countries under the obeisance of his said cousin King Louis, by water and by land, without any safeguard or safe-conduct, with their ships, goods, and merchandise, there doing their feats of merchandise, or otherwise at their pleasure.

And moreover for the more sure observance and good continuance of the said peace and amity, it is concluded and determined between our said sovereign lord and his said cousin King Louis of France, that he shall not from henceforth receive, nor by any of his subjects shall suffer to be received, within the realm of France or into any place under his obeisance, any of

1. See 29.

the subjects of our said sovereign lord being rebels, traitors, or other suspect persons of treason, neither shall give nor suffer to be given any aid, favor, council, comfort, or other assistance to any such rebels, traitors, or other suspect persons; but at the desire and request of our said sovereign lord, his said cousin King Louis shall, within 20 days after he is by the King's letters required, do deliver or cause to be delivered the said rebels and traitors unto such person or persons as by the King our sovereign lord, for the receiving of them, shall be named and deputed. And in likewise, the King our sovereign lord is bound so to do to his said cousin, if any of his rebels and traitors, being his subjects, resort unto this realm of England or to any parts being under the obeisance of our said sovereign lord.

And forasmuch as many attempts have been committed and done afore this time upon the sea by the subjects of the late King Charles of France upon the subjects of our said sovereign lord the King, contrary to the said peace and amity (for the which despoils and robberies, little or no restitution has been made hitherto, but by means of long process and delaying of judgment by occasion of appeals and otherwise, the true and speedy execution of justice hath been always deferred and put apart), certain articles be now agreed and concluded between the King our sovereign lord and his cousin King Louis now in France, by the which all such delays and deferring of restitution of goods, so unlawfully taken, shall be from henceforth thoroughly put apart, and the parties so robbed and despoiled soon to have remedy for the wrongs and robberies so done unto them. For it is within those articles by our said sovereign lord and his said cousin of France determined and concluded, as in the same articles is comprised, that certain judges of good conscience and understanding shall be by both princes deputed in certain cities and towns near to the sea coasts most convenient, unto whom the suitors and complainers may have most easily their resort; the which judges shall be sufficiently authorized to determine and decide within right short time, the which time is specified and limited in the said articles, all manner causes to be pursued before them upon such despoils and robberies, and to cause restitution briefly to be made thereupon as the case shall require; all manner of appeals unto the Court of Parlement of Paris and all other long delays utterly set apart.

It is also provided and concluded that all manner of causes as be now in suit before the admiral or vice-admiral of France for such robberies and spoils as have been done upon the King's subjects in time past, and also all other like causes which shall hereafter be pursued in the court before the same admiral for like injuries, shall be determined by him or his deputy within six months at the furthest, all appeals utterly put apart. And in case that the said admiral or vice-admiral within the said time of six months do not finally determine the said causes, then may the parties grieved resort for remedy and justice unto the King's Great Council, where their causes shall be within other six months finally determined and decided, and thereupon the party indemnified to have restitution of his goods, or duly recompensed for them, as the case shall require.

And in avoiding of all such spoils and robberies hereafter to be done upon the sea, it is agreed, provided, and ordained that no ship shall pass out of any haven or creek of the realm of France or of other parts being in the said King's there obeisance unto such time that sufficient surety be found and made by them that shall pass in any such ship; that they shall not, nor any of them shall, take any ship or man of this realm of England, nor of any other place being under the obeisance of our said sovereign lord, but suffer them peaceably to pass without any injury or violence to be done unto them, as in the letters patent containing the said articles, sealed with the Seal of his said cousin of France, remaining in the treasury of our sovereign lord, more plainly it is expressed.

It shall be therefore right expedient to such of the King's subjects that findeth themself grieved by any such robberies or spoils to resort for the restitution of their goods, or recompense for the same, unto those judges deputed in the said cities and towns near to the sea coasts or else unto the admiral's court, as they shall think most behooveful for them; by which judges, justice with speedy process shall be ministered unto them, all delays and appeals put apart. And over that, all the King's subjects may hereafter safely resort with their ships and goods to the realm of France without peril or jeopardy either of person or of goods, there to occupy their feats of merchandise during the said peace and amity, and to be there lovingly and surely entreated, as appertaineth.

Our said sovereign lord therefore, willing effectuously the said peace and amity and all other premises firmly to be observed and kept, straightly chargeth and commandeth all and every of his subjects that they and every of them duly observe and keep all that is comprised in the said amity, and nothing to presume to do that might be to the violation thereof, or of any part of the same; upon pain to be punished at the King's will and forfeiture of all that they may forfeit.

41. Ordering Northumberland Truce-Breakers to Surrender

[Westminster, 26 November 1498, 14 Henry VII]

PR (C66/582/6*d*): date as above; writ to sheriff of Northumberland; schedule as below. Steele 32. Text (MS): PR

FORASMUCH as one William Hedley, otherwise called Weykspere; Hogge of Hedley, brother to the same William; Hob Rede; Crysty Mylbourne, the son of Cryspy of Heale; William Charleton, otherwise called Willy Charleton; Hob Charleton; Sandy Charleton; George Charleton; Thomas Charleton; Percival Charleton; William Charleton, the son of William Charleton; Robert Charleton; Cok Fenwyck, the maugh of Willy Charleton; George Robeson; Rob Robeson; Cok Crissop; Rob Hog; George Wilkynson; Cuthbert Wilkynson; Rowle Whelpden; and Thomas Rede, the son of Willy Rede; inhabitants of Ryddisdale and Tyndale within the county of Northumberland; for certain murders and slaughters now lately by them done upon certain Scottishmen, contrary to the truce and amity now being betwixt the King our sovereign lord Henry, by the grace of God King of England and of France and lord of Ireland on the one side, and the right excellent, right high and mighty Prince James, King of Scotland on the other side, and their realms and subjects; whereby after the laws and customs of the borders of the said realms, they have done and committed felony and treason, have oftentimes had sufficient warnings and commandments on the behalf of our said sovereign lord to have appeared in their persons at divers days of truce, to have answered to the said murders, the which to do they have always hitherto refused; and for the eschewing of the punition that in such case is requisite, have feloniously fled and withdrawn themself, so that no justice can be done upon them, to the high displeasure of our said sovereign lord and, as far as in them is, to the breach of the said truce:

Our said sovereign lord, considering the same, and willing justice always to be done and the said truce inviolably to be kept and observed, in the most straight wise chargeth and commandeth the said murderers that they and every of them, within three days next and immediately ensuing the making of this proclamation, be and personally appear within the town of Berwick, before Sir Thomas Darcy, knight, our said sovereign lord's lieutenant of his east and middle marches against Scotland; upon pain to be taken, immediately after the lapse of the said three days, the King's felons, traitors, outlaws, and banished men, and to forfeit life, land, and goods.

And also forasmuch as all the surnames of the said Charletons, Redes, Hedleys, Robesons, Mylbournes, Wilkynsons, Crissops, Dodds, Hogges, Hunters, Oblissous and Fenwyckes, inhabitants of the said Tyndale and Ryddisdale, bear favor, succor, and maintain the said murderers or some part of them; and so to bear favor, succor, maintain, and defend them against all them that would endeavor them to take them and bring them where they might stand to the King's laws, they be confederated, banded, and sworn together:

The King therefore our sovereign lord in likewise chargeth and commandeth that every of the said surnames, after the said three days be past, and that the said murderers or any of them make not their appearance before the said lieutenant as before is rehearsed, endeavor them to the best of their powers to take, and within five days next after the said three days indeed take, the said murderers and every of them failing the said appearance; and them bring and deliver to the said lieutenant, upon pain the said surnames and every of them inhabited within the said Tyndale and Ryddisdale, for the said confederacies, succor, favor, and maintenance giving to the said murderers, to be taken as the King's rebels, traitors, outlaws, and banished men; and that none of the King's liege people, of what condition soever he be, after the said three days receive, lodge, favor, or succor, in meat, drink, or lodging, any of the said murderers, nor after the said five days any of the said surnames, inhabitants of the said Tyndale and Ryddisdale; but that every man after the said days endeavor him to the best of his power for for the taking of them, upon pain to be taken in likewise as traitors and to forfeit to the King their lives, lands, and goods.

42. Declaring Clipped Pence Legal Tender

[Westminster, 12 December 1498, 14 Henry VII]

LJ 10, 143*v:* date, 12 December; schedule as below. Steele 33: date, Westminster. Text (MS): LJ

Forasmuch as the King our sovereign lord Henry, by the grace of God King of England and of France and lord of Ireland, understandeth the manifold inconveniences that daily ensue among his subjects for refusing of his coin, that is to say, of small, thin, and old pence, and that hereafter might ensue if due reformation were not provided and had in that behalf:

His highness therefore, willing in any wise his said subjects universally to take and receive his money current, straightly chargeth and commandeth all and every of his subjects foresaid, that no manner person from henceforth refuse to take and receive in payment all manner pennies of our said sovereign lord's coinage, so that they be silver and whole; and that upon pain of imprisonment of every person that so will refuse to take his said coinage, and to make fine therefor at our sovereign lord's pleasure.

43. Outlawing Irish Pence

[Knole, 16 January 1499, 14 Henry VII]

AC (Bayne 31): date, 11 February; order prohibiting further minting of pennies and calling for a new mold for Irish coin. PR (C66/582/15*d*): date as above; writ to sheriff of Kent; schedule as below. Steele 34. Text (MS): PR

Forasmuch as the King our sovereign lord considereth well that great difficulty, grudge, and trouble rest and daily grow among his subjects, for the course and payments of such small pence as be in the hands of his said subjects; for some men would have such pence as have been coined within his land of Ireland to have course here in England, and some men refuse to receive pence coined in England because they be so little and so small of weight:

His highness therefore, in avoiding and putting apart of all such doubts, difficulties, and grudges so resting and daily growing among his said subjects, straightly chargeth and commandeth all and every his said subjects, of what estate, degree, or condition they be, that they nor any of them from henceforth take not in payment any pence counterfeited or coined in Ireland; and also that no man refuse to take and receive in payments any manner of pence being silver and coined in any of his mints within this his realm of England; and that all manner such pence so being silver and coined as is aforesaid in England, though they be small and light in weight, be from henceforth admitted, reputed, and taken in payments and receipts among his said subjects as true and lawful current money, without any challenge, contradiction, or doubt to be made to or against any man in that behalf; upon pain to be punished at the King's pleasure.

44. Declaring All King's Pence Legal Tender

[Ford, 23 March 1499, 14 Henry VII]

CW (C82/188): date of delivery as above; sign manual; writ to all sheriffs; schedule as below. PR (C66/584/1*d*): date as above; writ to mayor of Canterbury; similar writs to sheriffs throughout England; schedule as below. Steele 36: date, 18 March. Text (MS): PR

THE KING our sovereign lord, Henry, by the grace of God King of England and of France and lord of Ireland, well understanding the great doubts now of late being among divers of his subjects within this his realm, for such manner of pence the which many men surmiseth to be coined within his land and lordship of Ireland, and so daily refuseth to take them in payment though they have been coined in divers mints within this his said realm:

His highness, for putting apart of all doubts and ambiguities among his said subjects in this behalf, by good deliberation and by the advice of his council, willeth, commandeth, and straightly chargeth that all manner pence being silver and having the print of his coin, have course and be current within this his realm, without any manner of refusal or contradiction, except only the penny bearing divers spurs or the mullet betwixt the bars of the cross; and that none of his said subjects refuse none of the said pennies before rehearsed but such as beareth the said print of the spurs or mullet, upon pain of imprisonment and further punishment at the King's pleasure; and that the said penny bearing print of the spurs or the mullet be current and shall have course but only for an half-penny. And he that thinketh or trusteth to have any better advantage by the same penny than above the value of an half-penny, he may at his liberty resort to the King's mint within the Tower of London, there to take the best advantage that he can.

45. Announcing Trade Treaty with Duke of Burgundy

[Westminster, 18 May 1499, 14 Henry VII]

PR (C66/584/2*d*): date as above; writ to sheriffs of London and Middlesex; similar writs to sheriffs of Norfolk, Suffolk, Southampton, Kent, Somerset, Dorset, Essex, Herts, Hereford, Lincoln, Oxford, Berks, Gloucester, Bedford, Bucks, city of York, towns of Kingston-upon-Hull, Newcastle-upon-Tyne, Southampton, Cinque Ports; schedule as below. Steele 37. Text (MS): PR

THE KING our sovereign lord, Henry, by the grace of God King of England and of France and lord of Ireland of that one party, and the right high and mighty Prince Philip, Archduke of Austria and Duke of Burgundy, etc., of that other party:

For the weal and restfulness of both their realms, lands, seigniories, and countries, and for the increase and profit of their subjects, divers and certain appointments and conclusions concerning the mutual conversation of merchants, the King's and his said cousin's subjects, and their intercourse of merchandise, by great advice and ripe deliberation have been of late treated, covenanted, appointed, and concluded, as well for the merchants of the Staple as for the merchant adventurers, and all other the King's subjects, in manner and form as followeth:

First for the merchants of the Staple, it is agreed and concluded that no packer of this his realm of England shall from henceforth occupy the office of a packer before he be admitted and abled thereunto before the mayors and constables of the Staple, and that his ability and cunning be approved by certain discreet merchants and packers sworn and thereto deputed and assigned by the said mayors and constables after the customs therein of old time used. And the same packer, so in manner and form aforesaid admitted and approved, shall make his oath before the same mayor and constables and other by the King's highness thereunto named, that he without fraud, collusion, or deceit, shall make his packing of wool truly, indifferently, and sufficiently, so that he shall not pack or wrap, or cause to be packed or wrapped, in the fleeces of the said wool, earth, stones, dung, or sand; and that every packer so admitted, approved, and sworn, shall truly name all manner of wools by him packed, of the country where they were grown, after the nature of the same wools, and not of any other country, in any manner of wise; and that the packer shall write, or cause to be written, with open, great letters upon every serpler, poke, or pocket of good wools: of March wools, these words, *Good March;* and upon the serplers of middle March wool shall write, or cause to be written, *Middle March;* and upon all serplers of good wool of Cotswold, *Good Cotswold;* and the same order to be observed of all wools of the growing of all countries in this his realm of England, to be conveyed from henceforth to the said Staple of Calais; and also the same packer shall write or cause to be written upon [all] and singular serplers aforesaid his own surname in such wise that the name of the wools nor the surname of the packer may not be put out without breaking of the said serplers, pokes, or pockets;

And if any packer presume to pack any wools contrary to the form of this present ordinance, that then he be put from his office of packing, and to be punished for his perjury at the King's pleasure; and if the said wool be wrong packed by the fraud and knowledge or consent of the merchant buyer thereof, contrary to the tenor of this ordinance, and thereupon the same merchant to be thereof convicted before the treasurer of England for the time being, by good, true, and indifferent men, that then the merchant or merchants so convicted shall forfeit for every sack so fraudulently packed, as often as he or they shall so offend, £20 sterling, whereof the King's highness shall have £15, and £5 shall be paid to him that detecteth the said false packing; which ordinance shall take effect after the first day of June next coming.

And the merchants and subjects of the said Archduke shall make their payments to the merchants of the Staple of Calais, and to their factors, in good sterling money after the rate of a table made, which remaineth in the hall of the said Staple, except it be otherwise agreed between the said parties. And it shall be lawful to the said merchants and their factors and other our said sovereign lord's subjects to receive of their debtors all manner of coins of gold and silver now having (or hereafter shall have) course within the lands and lordships of the said Archduke. Also it shall be lawful to the said merchants of the said Staple, and other of our said sovereign lord's subjects, that shall now receive all such moneys and buy all manner of plate and jewels, being gold or silver, made and wrought by the hands of an artificer to any certain or perfect shape, to convey or carry, or do to be conveyed or carried, by land, sea, and fresh waters, out of the lands and lordships of the said Archduke, without any manner of dread of forfeiture of the same, into his town of Calais, or into his realm of England, or to any other place at their pleasure, without let, trouble, vexation, or grief, of the said Archduke or of any of his subjects.

Also for the merchants adventurer and others the King's subjects, in like wise it is agreed, covenanted, and concluded betwixt the King and the said Archduke, that the same Archduke from henceforth shall release, amove and utterly put apart the *floren* and every part thereof, and all manner other imposition afore this time made and set upon the English cloths, so that all times hereafter [it] shall be lawful to all [and] every of our said sovereign lord's subjects to utter and sell their said cloths made within this his realm freely at their liberties, and that as well the King's said subjects as all other persons, of whatsoever nation they be, buying the said cloths, shall be quit and discharged of the said imposition and of all other impositions hereafter to be demanded of them or any of them for the selling or buying of any of the said English cloths;

And over that, that all manner of statutes, proclamations, ordinances and provisions made, ordained, and proclaimed within the lands and lordships of the said Archduke, that English cloths should be brought only to the towns of Antwerp and Bergen-op-Zoom and to none other place within the said Archduke's land, there and in the same two towns only to be uttered, be from henceforth void and of no force nor effect; and that it shall be lawful from henceforth to all and singular merchants of England, and to their factors, to convey and carry by land, sea, and fresh waters, all manner of English cloths to all places within the lands and lordships of the said Archduke, Flanders only except, and there the same cloths to sell and utter at their pleasure, without let, trouble or vexation of any persons; and also it shall be lawful to the subjects of the said Archduke to occupy and wear the same cloths in like manner and form as they have used and enjoyed, [in] the time of the noble progenitors of the said Archduke, and no brief and writing, commonly called *kynkernells,* or any other brief or writings of like nature, shall not be from henceforth granted by the said Archduke, to the hurt or fraud of the merchants of this land; and if any such brief or writing hereafter be granted, that they then to be taken as of no force nor effect; and also if any of the subjects of the said Archduke be condemned to any of the King's subjects in any sums of money, that the execution of the said judgment shall not be letted nor delayed by any brief called a *skepynbreef,* or any other writings, but that they shall have thereof plain execution without delay, the said brief notwithstanding.

And if it shall fortune any merchants of this land to come to any of the marts of Antwerp or Bergen-op-Zoom, or to any other place or countries of the said Archduke, it shall be lawful to them to buy all such merchandises as shall like them, for such prices as they may agree with the seller of the same, without that the master of the English merchants, commonly called the court master, shall first by himself or with other Englishmen set and limit a price upon such merchandises as shall be bought by the said English merchants; saving nevertheless all manner of privileges and liberties granted and given to the said English merchants;

Also if it fortune any of the said merchants of the Staple, their factors, or other subjects of England, to commit any offense within the lands or lordships of the said Archduke, for the which he ought to forfeit any goods or otherwise to be punished, that then the same offender, having goods in his possession belonging to other persons, shall forfeit none other but such as be his own proper goods; also that if any merchants or other subjects of our sovereign lord the King, or their factors, fortune to decease within the lands or lordships of the said Archduke, having goods and merchandises as well of their own as of other persons, shall not from henceforth be reputed and had as bastards and not legitimate, but that all such goods be retained and kept without diminution to the use of their executors or next kinsmen or other of his blood being English born, as in the said appointments and conclusions, with divers other articles in them contained and ratified, and also conserved under the Great Seal of our said sovereign lord and enrolled amongst the records of his chancery, more plainly and evidently it doth appear.

Our said sovereign lord, willing all the said appointments and conclusions, and every of them, firmly and inviolably to be observed and kept on his behalf, willeth, straightly chargeth, and commandeth all and every of his said subjects, of what estate, degree, or condition soever they be of, that they and every of them from henceforth truly observe and keep the said appointments and conclusions and every part thereof, nothing to attempt that may be in breech and violation of the same; upon pain of forfeiture of all that he may forfeit, and further to be punished at the pleasure of our said sovereign lord.

46. Forbidding Ships to Carry Unlicensed Passengers

[Charing, 20 August 1499, 14 Henry VII]

PR (C66/585/4*d*): date as above; writ to sheriff of Kent; similar writs to sheriffs of Norfolk, Suffolk, Essex, Cinque Ports; schedule as below. Steele 38. Text (MS): PR

Whereas the King our sovereign lord, well remembering that it hath been established and enacted in times past by his highness, and by the advice of his lords spiritual and temporal, that no ship or vessel should depart out of any port, leam, or creek belonging to the same, unto the parts beyond the sea, without he found sufficient surety that no hurt nor damage should be done by any, being within such ship or vessel, against the King's highness, his realm, nor his subjects, neither yet his friends or allies:

For divers considerations moving, now his grace commandeth and straightly chargeth that no ship nor boat pass, conveying any person or persons, over the sea without he so to be conveyed have a license under the King's seal or sign manual, or else that it be such a person and of such substance and truth that the township where he passeth will be chargeable for his demeaning against the King, his realm, and his subjects, as is aforesaid; and this to be observed and kept, under the pains comprised in the indentures before time by the said ports and creeks made, and also upon pain of forfeiture of their goods, and their bodies to be committed to prison, and further to be punished at the King's will and pleasure; nor yet suffer any vessels coming from beyond the sea, with any person to arrive within any port or creek within this his realm, and to have his liberty to depart where he will, but such as they shall think of true disposition toward the King, as they will answer to his grace at their great peril.

And moreover, his highness chargeth and straightly commandeth all manner of customers, comptrollers, searchers, and keepers of ports, that they nor any of them permit nor suffer any manner of person or persons to depart out of this his said realm without license, as is aforesaid; upon pain also of forfeiture of all that they may forfeit, and his body to be committed to prison, there to remain at the King's pleasure.

47. Permitting Merchants to Cross Sea

[Knole, 1 September 1499, 15 Henry VII]

CW (C82/332): date of delivery as above; sign manual; writ to sheriff of Kent also to sheriffs of Suffolk, Essex, Cinque Ports; schedule as below. PR (C66/585/14*d*): date as above; writs as CW, omitting Cinque Ports; schedule as below. Steele 39. Text (MS): PR

Whereas the King our sovereign lord now of late caused his proclamations to be made and published into certain places and shires within this his realm, that no ship or vessel should depart out of any port, leam, or creek belonging to the same unto the parts beyond the sea, without he found sufficient surety that no hurt nor damage should be done by any being within such ship or vessel against the King's highness, his realm, nor his subjects, nor yet his friends or allies:

Yet the King, of the tender favor and zeal that he beareth to his true subjects, intendeth not, nor yet will, that any of his said subjects, true and substantial merchants, intending to go to Bordeaux or other places for feat of merchandise, be in anywise restrained by force of the said proclamation, but that they have their free liberty in passing, as they ought and have been accustomed to have:

And over that, the King straightly chargeth and commandeth all his mayors, bailiffs, customers, comptrollers, and searchers, and other his officers upon the sea coasts, that they and every of them do make so good espial and search that no suspect person be suffered in any wise to pass over the sea in any ship, whithersoever she go, as they will answer unto the King thereof at their peril; and upon pain them to be committed to prison, and further to be punished according to the King's pleasure.

48. Distraining Knighthood

[Westminster, 9 March 1500, 15 Henry VII]

CR (C54/360/5*d*): date as above; writ and schedule as CW. CW (C82/332): date, March; sign manual; writ to sheriff of Kent; similar writs to sheriffs throughout England; schedule in Latin, translated below. Steele 40. Text (MS): CW

ALL THOSE HAVING £40 or more per year in land or revenue, either in hand or to their use in fee, and having so had during three years past, and who are not now knights, are to prepare themselves to receive the order of knighthood. And the names of all those within your bailiwick having the said £40 or more in land or revenue are to be certified into the hands of our chancellor no later than the day after the next coming Feast of the Ascension.

You will also serve all those within your bailiwick so having £40 or more with due summons to appear personally in our presence, on the Feast of St. Michael the Archangel, in order to receive the order of knighthood; under peril of the penalties they may incur.

49. Distraining Knighthood

[Woodstock, 7 December 1500, 16 Henry VII]

PR (C66/587/15*d*): date as above; writ to sheriff of Kent; similar writs to sheriffs throughout England; schedule in Latin, translated below. Steele 41. Text (MS): PR

ALL THOSE HAVING £40 per year or more in land or revenue, in hand or to their use in fee, and who have so had for three years past, and are not now knights, are commanded to appear in our presence on the day assigned, under their personal peril. And each sheriff is to certify to us and to our council without delay, before the day assigned, the names of all in his bailiwick so having £40 in land or revenue.

We already know the names of certain persons who for some time have had in hand the said £40 or more per year in land or revenue, from returns of the sheriff, and who has also certified to us certain other persons in his said bailiwick, similarly having land and revenue to the said value or above per year, who are not knights. But except for this return, he had not made these names altogether clear to us.

Wishing to know more exactly the names of all and singular such persons in the said county, we therefore straightly charge that, immediately upon receipt of these presents, you cause to be publicly proclaimed in all places, as well within as without the liberties of your bailiwick, wherever you think best, that all and singular persons having land and revenue of the said value appear personally in our presence before the next coming Feast of the Purification of the Blessed Virgin Mary; and that by due summons you notify them all to prepare themselves, as said before, to receive the order of knighthood; so that they be prepared to receive the order of knighthood on the said feast day, under the said peril.

50. Prohibiting Retainers

[Westminster, 10 March 1502, 17 Henry VII]

PR (C66/590/5*d*): date as above; writ to sheriff of Kent; similar writs to sheriff of Sussex, cities of Canterbury (date, 1 April), Rochester (date, 1 April), Sir Richard Guilford (date, 1 April), Thomas Iden, bailiff of Hundred of Milton and Marden in Kent; schedule as below. Steele 42. Text (MS): PR

THE KING our sovereign lord, Henry, by the grace of God King of England and of France and lord of Ireland, for the tender zeal and inward affection that he naturally beareth to his loving subjects within his county of Kent, reserved from the beginning of his reign the retainer to himself of all his subjects within his said county, in avoiding the divisions, enormities, and inconveniences that else percase might have ensued amongst them, to have inquietations and subversion of all good policies. And whereas it is come to the perfect knowledge of our said sovereign lord that retainers within his said county, as well by liveries, tokens, cognizances, promises, and badges, as otherwise, have now late been used and given there, and daily increase, contrary to his mind and laudable statutes in such case provided;[1] by the sufferance of which enormities, dissensions, debates, and other inconveniences be not unlike to ensue, to the universal annoyance, hurt, and damage of his

1. 13 Richard II, st. 3, 1389, *SR* 2, 74; 16 Richard II, c. 4, 1392, *SR* 2, 84; 20 Richard II, c. 2, 1396, *SR* 2, 93; 1 Henry IV, c. 7, 1399, *SR* 2, 113; 2 Henry IV, c. 21, 1400, *SR* 2, 129; 7 Henry IV, c. 14, 1405, *SR* 2, 155; 8 Edward IV, c. 2, 1468, *SR* 2, 426. See also 19 Henry VII, c. 14, 1503, *SR* 2, 658.

subjects, without speedy provision of convenable remedy be provided in this part:

His highness, having tender respect to the said governance of all his said subjects and intending his said statutes to be inviolably observed, chargeth therefore and expressly commandeth that none of his subjects within his said county presume or take upon them to use any retainers, or to be retained by livery, wages, cognizance, or promise; but to reserve them wholly to his person and to be ready to serve him like as they shall be commanded and appointed, when and as often as the case shall so require; and that not to fail to obey and fully execute this his solemn proclamation and pleasure, upon the penalties in his said statutes limited, and in avoiding his high displeasure and other dangers that may ensue for the contrary doing.

51. Announcing Peace Treaty with Scotland, Marriage Contract between James IV and Princess Margaret

[Westminster, 14 March 1502, 17 Henry VII]

PR (C66/590/11*d*): date as above; writ to sheriff of Kent; similar writs to sheriffs throughout England; schedule as below. *CSPVenetian 1*, 821: conclusion of marriage contract reported on 23 February. Steele 43. Text (MS): PR

THE KING our sovereign lord, Henry, by the grace of God King of England and of France and lord of Ireland, doth you to understand that, to the laud of God, the honor of our said sovereign lord, and the tranquility and great weal of his realm and subjects, there is taken, accorded, and concluded between his grace on the one party, and the right excellent, right high and mighty prince, his right dear and well-beloved brother and cousin James, King of Scots, on the other party, for them, their heirs and successors, realms, lands, countries, and places, whatsoever they be, their vassals, liegemen, and subjects, upon both sides, perpetual peace, firm and entire amity, league, and confederation, by land and by waters, to endure from the 24th day of January last past, forevermore and whilst the world shall endure, and also alliance by way of marriage made and contracted between the said King of Scots and the right excellent princess, the Lady Margaret, the eldest daughter of our said sovereign lord.

And amongst other great and notable matters, right honorable and profitable for our said sovereign lord, his realm and subjects, expressed in the treaty of the said perpetual peace, it is specially ordained, accorded, and concluded betwixt our said sovereign lord and the said King of Scots, that neither of them shall receive, succor, nor favor, nor suffer any of their subjects to receive, succor, or favor, none of their traitors nor rebels, of what estate, pre-eminence, or condition soever they be. And if it fortune any of the said traitors or rebels to come into the one or the other of the said realms of England or Scotland, they shall be taken, sent, and delivered to their sovereign lord, to whom they have done the treason or rebellion. And if any king or prince of any other realm or country, whatsoever he be, no prince nor person excepted, levy or make war against our said sovereign lord or the said King of Scots, either of them shall succor, help, and assist the other as faithfully, as effectually, diligently, and truly as he would do for himself in his own cause; any amity, league, covenant, or confederation before the said 24th day of January made with any other prince to the contrary notwithstanding.

It is also ordained, accorded, and concluded betwixt our said sovereign lord and the said King of Scots that the castle and town of Berwick, with all the inhabitants of the same, and the lands and bounds to them belonging, shall forevermore and as long as the world shall endure, have and enjoy and stand under the said perpetual peace; and the said King of Scots nor his heirs nor successors nor none of them shall nevermore from henceforth, during the world, levy or make war, assault, nor siege; nor no hurt, fraud, or damage, work nor imagine privily nor openly against the said castle nor town of Berwick, as in the said treaty of the said peace more plainly is contained.

All which treaty of peace and everything comprised in the same, our said sovereign lord straightly chargeth and commandeth all manner of persons, of what estate, degree, or condition they be of, firmly and inviolably to keep and observe, nothing doing nor presuming to do in violation or breach of the same; upon pain of forfeiture of all that they may forfeit, and their bodies at the King's will.

52. Announcing Alliance with Emperor Maximilian against Turks

[Westminster, 11 November 1502, 18 Henry VII]

BM MS Sloane 747, *62v:* date as above; writ to sheriffs of Bedford and Bucks; schedule as below. Steele 44. Text (MS): Sloane

THE KING our sovereign lord, Henry, by the grace of God King of England and of France and lord of Ireland, doth you to understand that to the laud of God, the advancement of the commonweal of our faith, the defense of the same against the Turks, and the honor and utility of this his realm and his subjects of the same, there is appointed, accorded, and concluded betwixt his highness, for him, his heirs and successors and for his realm, countries, seigniories, lands, jurisdictions, and all places being under his obeisance, and for all his vassals, liegemen, and subjects, on the one party; and the right excellent, right high and mighty prince, the King of Romans, for him, his heirs and successors, and for the whole empire and every city and place being under the obeisance of the same, and for all his realms, countries, seigniories, lands, jurisdictions, and all places being under his obeisance, and for all his vassals, liegemen, and subjects, on the other party: good, entire, and firm peace, amity, league, and confederation, with free and sure intercourse of merchandises by land and water, salt and fresh, from this day forward, perpetually and forevermore to endure.

It is also accorded and concluded betwixt the said kings that neither the said King of Romans, into nor within the said empire nor any other place under his obeisance, nor our said sovereign lord into nor within his realm nor into any place under his obeisance, shall receive, nor in any manner wise suffer or consent any other person or persons to receive, succor, favor, counsel, assist, or maintain, by word, deed, writing, or by any other mean, nor by color, fraud, or *mal engine,* privily or openly, nor with no ships, money, men of war, victuals, or with any other manner assistance, aid any of their rebels or traitors, or any other manner of person or persons that for rebellion or treason hath avoided or fled, or hereafter shall avoid or flee, out of the realms or obeisances, of what estate, degree, dignity, or pre-eminence soever he be; but that within ten days next after that the one of the kings hath opened to the other king that any of his rebels or traitors is within any of his realms or obeisances, he shall banish the same rebel or traitor, rebels or traitors, out of the same, upon pain of death. And if the same rebel or traitor, rebels or traitors, disobey or do contrary to the said banishment, and afterward be found within any of the same realms or places, he or they so disobeying, and so found, shall forthwith, without further delay or any excuse, be executed and put to death.

It is also accorded and concluded betwixt the said Kings of England and Romans that either of them shall immediately, after the said agreement and conclusion, banish out of the said realms and obeisances all such their rebels and traitors as now be within the same, upon pain of death. And if any of the said rebels, at any time after the said banishment be done, be found within their said realms or obeisances, they shall, within ten days after they be found and taken, be executed and put to death.

And the King our said sovereign lord, considering the said agreement and conclusion, straightly chargeth and upon pain of death commandeth that no manner of person, of what estate, degree, dignity, or pre-eminence he be, being rebel or traitor to the King of Romans, bide or remain within his realm or in any place being under his obeisance; but that he forthwith void and depart out of the same, and never return thereunto hereafter, upon pain to be executed and put to death immediately after he be taken;

And that this proclamation be sufficient advertisement, notice, and publication to every person that it toucheth, to the intent that from henceforth no person have cause to pretend ignorance in the same.

53. Distraining Knighthood

[Westminster, 14 December 1503, 19 Henry VII]

PR (C66/593/5*d*): date as above; writs to sheriffs throughout England; schedule in Latin, translated below. Steele 45. Text (MS): PR

ALL THOSE WITH £40 or more per year in land or revenue, in hand or to their use in fee, and not yet knighted, will prepare themselves to assume the order of knighthood:

Every sheriff to certify to our chancery the names of all those within his bailiwick having £40 or more per year in land or revenue; and further, that he serve due summons on all in his bailiwick having in this fashion £40 or more per year, as said before, to prepare themselves without delay; and that on the date specified in our letters they appear personally in our presence, prepared to receive the order of knighthood, under peril of the penalties into which they might fall.

And further, we charge each sheriff to make solemn proclamation in all places within his bailiwick, that all and singular persons so having land or revenue to the said yearly value, in hand or to their use in fee, being duly summoned according to the tenor of our said command, appear at once to assume in our presence the said order of knighthood.

And lest otherwise they fall into manifest contempt of our person and of our said command, we charge that in all places where it will be thought best to do so, both within and without the liberties of your bailiwick, you see that the following public proclamation is made:

That all and every person so having land or revenue to the said value or above, and not yet knights, are to appear without delay in our presence on the next coming Feast of the Purification of the Blessed Virgin Mary, and be then prepared to receive knighthood, under penalty of £200; and that without delay, and in accordance with this our present charge, you duly certify to our chancery the names of all and singular such persons, together with the total scutage from your bailiwick.

54. Regulating Clipped Coin

[Westminster, 5 July 1504, 19 Henry VII]

CW (C66/260): date as above; sign manual; writs to sheriffs of London and Middlesex; similar writs throughout England; schedule as below. *Rev.STC* 7760.4, Antiq 1, 9: printed by W. Faques (London, 1504): date as above; writ to sheriffs of Norfolk, Suffolk, etc.; schedule as below. Another edition, *rev.STC* 7760.6 LJ 10, 309*v:* date, 3 April; writ to sheriffs of London; schedule as below. Steele 46. Text (*rev.STC*): Antiq

THE KING our sovereign lord, calling to his remembrance that at his last parliament holden at Westminster it was ordained and enacted,[1] for the common weal of this his realm in avoiding the clipping and destruction of his coin and for the preservation of good money to be current within the same, that as well all manner groats of English coin, and of the coin of other lands then current within his said realm for groats or for 4*d*. being silver and not clipped, though the same were cracked or worn, should go and be current in all this his realm for the sum that they were coined for; and also that all groats, as well English coin as coin of other lands, that were clipped should not go nor be current in anywise within his said realm; forasmuch as it is common to the perfect knowledge of his highness, that many and great number of his subjects make themself ignorant in knowledge of English groats and double placks, whether they be clipped or not clipped, by mean whereof great trouble and vexation daily is had to his true and well-meaning subjects in making and receiving of their payments:

Wherefore, and in avoiding of such vexation of his said subjects, the King's highness, by good deliberation and advice of the lords spiritual and temporal, and other of his council, upon the sight of the same English groats and double placks, albeit that many English groats have by the coiners been misstricken, doth declare, decree, and adjudge all English groats and double placks, having the limits or marks as hereafter it is expressed, not to be clipped but to have course and to be current and not to be refused; that is to say, every English groat being silver, that hath three points of the cross whole on the side and the most part of the scripture whole on the other side, to go and be current and in no wise to be refused, though the same be not perfectly printed and coined; provided always that this proclamation be only extended to such groats as were coined before the making of the said act of parliament, and not to groats new coined sithen the making of the said act, which new groats shall not be current unless they have their full print on both sides according to the said act; and also that every double plack being silver which hath his scripture apparent on the one side or on the other side, to go and to be current and not to be refused.

Wherefore the King's highness willeth and straightly commandeth that

1. 19 Henry VII, c. 5, 1503, *SR 2*, 650.

Henricus dei gracia Rex Anglie et francie et dñs Hybernie. Uic. Norff. Suff. &c. Salutē Precipimus vobis firmiter iniūgentes q statim post receptionem presentiū in singulis locis infra balliuā vestrā tam infra libertates q̄ extra vbi magis expe diens videritis ex parte nostra publicas pclamationes fieri faciatis ī hec verba.

The kynge our souerayne lorde callynge to his remembraunce yͭ at his last parliament holden at westm̄ it was ordeyned & enacted for the comon wele of this his Realme in auoydynge yͤ clyppyng and dystruccyon of his coyne/ & for yͤ preseruacion of good money to be curraunt wyth yͤ same. That aswell all maner grotes of Englysshe coyne. & of yͤ coyne of other londes than curraunt wyth his sayd Realme for grotes or for. iiij pens beynge syluer & not clypped thoughe yͤ same were cracked or worne/ shold go & be curraūt in al this his realme for yͤ sōme yͭ they were coyned for. And also that all grotes aswell Englysshe coyne/ as coyne of other londes yͭ were clypped sholde not go nor be curraunt in ony wyse within his sayd realme. For asmoche as it is comen to the perfyte knowlege of his hyghnes/ yͭ many & grete nombre of his subgectꝭ make themself Ignorauͭ in knowlege of Englysshe grotes/ and double plakes whyder they be clypped/ or not clypped by meane wherof grete trouble & vexaciō dayly is had to his true & well meanynge subgectes in makynge & receyuynge of theyr paymentes. wherfore and in auoydynge of suche vexacion of his sayd subgectes. The kynges hyghnes by good deliberacion & aduyse of the lordes spūell & tēporell & other of his counceyll vpon the syght of the same Englysshe grotes & double plackes/ all be it that many englysshe grotes haue by yͤ Coyners ben mystryken dothe declare/ decre/ & adiuge all Englysshe grotꝭ & double plackes hauynge yͤ lymyttes or markes as herafter it is expressed not to be clypped but to haue cours & to be curraunt & not to be refused That is to saye. euery Englysshe grote beynge syluer yͭ hath thre poyntes of yͤ crosse hole on yͤ syde/ And the moste pte of yͤ scrypture hole on the other syde to goo & be curraūt & ī no wyse to be refused thoughe the same be not pfytely prynted & coyned. ¶ Prouyded alway yͭ this pclamacion be onely extēded to suche grotes as were coyned before yͤ makynge of yͤ sayd act of plyamēt/ & not to grotes newe coyned sythen the makynge of the sayd acte whiche newe grotes shall not be curraunt onles they haue theyr full prynte on bothe sydes accordynge to the sayde acte.

¶ And also yͭ euery double placke beynge syluer whiche hath his scrypture apparaūt on the one syde or on the other syde/ to goo and to be curraunt and not to be refused.

¶ wherfore yͤ kynges hyghnes wylleth and streytely cōmaundeth that as well all englysshe grotes as double plackes hauynge the markes or lymytes aboue sayd shalbe taken as well by his receyuours as all other psones in this his realme & not to be refused vpon payne of enprysonemēt & to make fyne at his pleasure. & all englysshe grotes & plackes beynge syluer not hauynge yͤ markes or lymytꝭ afore sayd to be reputed for clypped money/ & not to go nor to be curraūt for coyne.

¶ And the kyngꝭ grace for yͤ more ease & quyetnesse to be had amōge his sayd subgettes in this behalfe wylleth & cōmaundeth yͭ suche money as is aforesayd reputed for clypped money shall be taken in payment/ or in eschaūge for iij. s. & ij. d. the vnce at yͤ leeste & in lyke wyse the halfe vnce/ the quarter & yͤ halfe quarter of yͤ sayd clypped moneye after the rate of the same & no lesse to be gyuen for yͤ vnce the halfe vnce yͤ quarter & yͤ halfe quarter accordȳge to the sayd rate of suche money after this pclamacyō made in euery shyre by ony persone vpon payne of forfeyture by yͤ receyuour of the same money so receyued and vpon payne of enprysonement & fyne to be made at the kynges wyll.

¶ And that all and euery suche persoñ and psons as shall take or receyue clyppd money by waighte furthwith & imediatly in yͤ presens & sight of hym that shall so vttur yͤ same money the said taker and receyuer therof shall cut or cause to be cutte in sunder all the said clypped money in payne of forfetuñ of all yͤ said clipped money so receyued & taken & to haue imprisonement and make fyne & raunson at the kyngꝭ wyll:

¶ And ouer that the kyngꝭ hyghnesse straytely cōmaundeth that none of hys subgectes presume to vse weyghtes made of styckes endes comynly called of olde tyme awncell weyghtes vpon payne and punysshement afore expressed.

¶ And also the kyngꝭ hyghnesse cōmaundeth yͭ all Mayres/ baylyfs/ constables/ & all other hede offycers of cytees/ townes/ bourghs/ or vyllages to se the premysses duelye executed to the best of theyr powers vpon payne of enprysonement and to make fyne at the kyngꝭ wyll & pleasure vpon cōplaynt to his hyghnesse/ or to his counceyll/ or to ony Justyce of yͤ peas therof made & approued to be true yͭ they do not to be executed this the kynges pclamacyon & hyghe cōmaundemēt

¶ Et hoc sub periculo incūbenti nullatenus omittas Teste meipso apud westmonasteriū quinto die Julij Anno regni nostri Decimonono. Regius Impressor. Wyn seynt Elens Guillam.

Plate 1. Contemporary print of Proclamation 54, by Henry VII. Proclamation writ, to sheriffs of Norfolk, Suffolk, etc. Schedule, regulating clipped coin. Dated Westminster, 5 July, 19 Henry VII [1504]. Marginal illustrations of three coins, both sides. Printed by William [Faques], within St. Helen's [London]. *Rev.STC* 7760.4. Antiq 1, 9.

as well all English groats as double placks having the marks or limits abovesaid shall be taken as well by his receivers as all other persons in this his realm and not to be refused, upon pain of imprisonment and to make fine at his pleasure; and all English groats and placks being silver, not having the marks or limits aforesaid, to be reputed for clipped money, and not to go nor to be current for coin.

And the King's grace, for the more ease and quietness to be had among his said subjects in this behalf, willeth and commandeth that such money as is aforesaid reputed for clipped money shall be taken in payment or in exchange for 3*s.* 2*d.* the ounce at the least, and in likewise the half-ounce, the quarter and the half-quarter of the said clipped money after the rate of the same, and no less to be given for the ounce, the half-ounce, the quarter, and the half-quarter, according to the said rate of such money, after this proclamation made in every shire, by any person; upon pain of forfeiture by the receiver of the same money so received, and upon pain of imprisonment and fine to be made at the King's will; and that all and every such person and persons as shall take or receive clipped money by weight, forthwith and immediately in the presence and sight of him that shall so utter the same money, the said taker and acceptor thereof shall cut or cause to be cut in sunder all the said clipped money, in pain of forfeiture of all the said clipped money so received and taken and to have imprisonment and make fine and ransom at the King's will.

And over that, the King's highness straightly commandeth that none of his subjects presume to use weights made of sticks' ends, commonly called of old time auncel weights, upon pain and punishment afore expressed.

And also the King's highness commandeth that all mayors, bailiffs, constables, and all other head officers of cities, towns, boroughs or villages, to see the premises duly executed to the best of their powers; upon pain of imprisonment and to make fine at the King's will and pleasure, upon complaint, to his highness or to his council or to any justice of the peace thereof made, and approved to be true, that they do not to be executed this the King's proclamation and high commandment.

55. Proposing Payment of King's Debts

[Westminster, 19 August 1504, 19 Henry VII]

CW (C82/332): date uncertain Henry VII; sign manual; writ to sheriffs of London and Middlesex; similar writs to sheriffs throughout England, and chancellor of Duchy of Lancaster; schedule as below. PR (C66/594/27*d*): date as above; writs, as CW; schedule as below. Rymer *13,* 106. Steele 48. Text (MS): PR

FORASMUCH AS THE KING our sovereign lord, Henry, by the grace of God King of England and of France and lord of Ireland, amongst other his great and notable acts concerning the administration of justice, hath for the pleasure of God, the discharge of his conscience, and the tender zeal and fervent love that he beareth to his subjects, always had a special regard, mind, and desire, in no manner wise to do any wrong or to be indebted to any person or persons in any sum or sums of money, neither for loan nor prest that his highness hath had in times past, nor for any thing that his grace hath bought or that hath been delivered to the use of his honorable house or wardrobe, nor for any other cause or matter, nor to have any manors, lands, goods, nor chattels otherwise than good reason and conscience will require, or that by the due order and course of his laws hath been adjudged:

Our said sovereign lord therefore willeth and desireth, and for the discharge of his conscience chargeth, that if there be any person or persons that reasonably and truly can and may claim and demand of his highness any sum or sums of money for any loan or prest that he hath made, or for any thing that he hath bought or that hath been delivered to the use of his honorable house or wardrobe, or that can provably show and prove that our said sovereign lord hath done him any wrong, or hath had any of his lands, goods, or chattels, otherwise than by good reason and conscience or by the due order and course of his laws, that the same person or persons having reasonable complaint for any of the premises put their complaints in writing and deliver the same at any time at their pleasure betwixt this and Michaelmas, come two years, or at any time before in the term time, to the Bishop of Winchester, keeper of his Privy Seal; Sir John Fineux, Chief Justice of his bench; Sir Thomas Frowyck, Chief Justice of his common pleas; Sir Thomas Lovell, Treasurer of his house; Sir John Mordaunt, Chancellor of his duchy of Lancaster; Master Geffrey Symeon, Dean of his chapel; or Master Thomas Routhale, his secretary; or to any of them, the which his highness hath appointed to receive the said bills of complaint. And the complainants shall be by them, or four of them, favorably heard and so reasonably and specially answered, that of reason they shall have good cause to hold them satisfied and contented.

56. Establishing Calais as an English Free Mart

[Croydon, 15 January 1505, 20 Henry VII]

AC (Bayne 43): date, 16 November 1504; order for merchants to appear within ten days with articles drawn for the mart. CW (C82/330): date, January; schedule, illegible. PR (C66/595/12*d*): date as above; writ to mayor and sheriffs of London; schedule as below. Steele 49. Text (MS): PR

FORASMUCH AS THE KING'S SUBJECTS, as well merchants adventurer as others, pretending themself greatly grieved and damaged by new impositions of tolls and other exactions set upon them in the countries of the Archduke, contrary to the liberties and privileges heretofore granted unto them and the ancient customs hitherto by them used, to their importable charge, extreme hindrance, and damage, have most instantly and [in] right humble manner desired the King's highness, for their remedy in that behalf, to grant unto them liberty and free license from henceforth to resort unto his town of Calais, there to keep a free mart, as well for themself as for all other merchants stranger resorting to the same, and not to be compelled to resort to any mart to be holden hereafter within the said Archduke's countries:

The King therefore our sovereign lord, remembering their desire and petition in that behalf and greatly minding the commonweal of his land and the profit of his subjects, by the deliberate advice of his council both spiritual and temporal lately assembled in a great number for that purpose, is condescended and agreed that a free mart shall be holden and kept in his said town of Calais; the same to begin the first day of February next coming and endure by the space of 40 days immediately ensuing, so to continue yearly at four times of the year, quarterly from time to time in like form and manner as the marts heretofore have been accustomably used within the countries under the obeisance of the said Archduke.

And to encourage all merchants stranger the rather to resort thereunto for the exercise of their feats of merchandise there, the King's highness hath also ordained and determined the said mart to be as frank and free, and the merchants as well strangers as others repairing thereunto to have as great and as large or larger freedoms, liberties, and immunities there as they have had and enjoyed in the marts holden heretofore in the Archduke's countries, and as favorably there to be entertained and entreated with as great humanity and as kind and loving manner as they have been in any parts or countries where marts have been used and kept heretofore, as by the points and articles hereafter ensuing it shall more specially appear:

That is to say, that the said mart so to be holden at the King's said town of Calais be as frank and free as any mart holden in the towns and countries of the said Archduke have accustomed to be, and that all merchants, as well strangers as other resorting thereunto merchantly for the exercising of the feats of merchandise, there may have and enjoy as great privileges and liberties as merchants heretofore have customably had and enjoyed at any mart customably holden at Antwerp or in any parts or countries under the said Archduke's obeisance; provided always, inasmuch as the said town of Calais is a town of war, that no stranger enter the same with any harness or weapons, nor do or attempt anything contrary to the statutes and ordinances made and established for the sure keeping thereof.

And the King's highness willeth that all manner merchants, stranger and other, resorting to the said town and marches of Calais be and abide under the protection and surety and safeguard of his grace, both body and goods, thither to come and go, pass and repass, merchantly at all time at their liberty by land, sea, fresh waters, on horse or on foot, by chariot, cart, or with any other manner of carriage, with their factors, families, or servants, in the said town and marches; to be conversant and abide there to occupy and exercise the feats of merchandise in buying, selling, bartering, or distributing their goods and merchandises at all times at their liberty; without let, disturbance, arrest, vexation, trouble, or contradiction of the captain, deputy, lieutenant, treasurer, or comptroller of the said town of Calais, the mayor of the same town for the time being, or of any customer, comptroller, searcher, bailiff, water bailiff, toller, wardens of the passage, or of any officer or officers whatsoever for the time being, of the lieutenant or keeper of the castle of Calais, of the keeper or constable of the town of Rysbank for the time being, or of any other manner persons or person for them or any of them; and without paying of any head money, half-passage money, *sandgeld, wharfgeld,* the Flemish toll, or any other toll, whatsoever they be, except only such customs and tolls as the King's subjects have paid and be accustomed to pay at marts heretofore holden at Antwerp or in any other town or place under the said Duke's obeisance;

And also that it be lawful to the King's merchants adventurer and to all merchants stranger to ship their goods and merchandises from the said town and port of Calais in all manner ship or ships, of what nation soever they be, at their choice and liberty, without paying any half-passage, or any other exactions to be taken of them for their ships, goods, or merchandises, upon pain of imprisonment without bail or mainprize, and further fine and punishment at the King's pleasure.

Also that all the King's subjects merchant may peaceably and quietly resort and come to the said town and marches of Calais with their goods and merchandises and from thence pass and go at all times at their liberty, from the incalling of the said mart unto the end thereof, and not to be vexed, troubled, grieved, or arrested in body or goods, being at the said mart, for any debts or duty growing or rising upon or for any contract or bargain made out of the said town and marches, if the party grieved or arrested will require the freedom of the mart, except for contracts or bargains made within the same mart instant; provided always that every person the King's subject, or other claiming the freedom of the mart there, depart from thence, the same freedom denying, if wind and weather will serve; and that all merchants stranger be as free in bodies and goods within the town and marches of Calais as the King's subjects merchant be, owe to be, or pretend to be, in the Archduke's countries, during the freedom of the mart there holden, the provision before specified, made for the surety of that town, always saved.

And albeit that the said merchants stranger exercising the feats of merchandise at the marts heretofore holden in the countries under the obeisance of the Archduke have been accustomed to content and pay divers and many more tolls, charges, and customs, and more larger, for their goods and merchandises thither brought, than the King's subjects repairing to the same marts: yet the King's highness, of his grace especial, willing the said merchants stranger resorting to the said mart so to be holden at Calais favorably to be entreated within the same so that by means thereof they may be the better encouraged to repair to the said mart from time to time hereafter, hath of his singular grace and favor ordained and determined that all and every such merchants or merchant stranger pay for their goods and merchandises within the said town, port, and marches of Calais, coming or going from the said town and within the mart time or without, none other tolls, *gabels,* exactions, impositions, or customs, than the King's merchants subject have paid or owe to pay within the countries of the Archduke, in towns where the marts be holden as above; and in likewise all merchants the King's subjects to pay, for their goods and merchandises to be by them brought to the said mart to be holden at Calais, such customs and tolls as the same merchants the King's subjects have paid, owe to pay, or have been accustomed to pay, for the same in the said Archduke's countries and none other;

Also that no merchant stranger repairing to the said town and marches of Calais, or from thence going, be constrained within the said town, port, and marches, to pay any other toll, custom, *gabel,* or exactions for their goods and merchandises than be rated and extended upon the King's merchants subject in the privilege of Duke Philip of Burgundy, conserved by the towns of Antwerp and Bergen-op-Zoom, according to two tables thereupon to be made, whereof one to be set in the open market place of Calais and the other in the custom house there; and if any officer of the said town or marches presume to exact or levy any toll or custom above the rate expressed in the said tables, and thereof be found culpable, every such officer to be punished with imprisonment and other fines at the King's pleasure, like as is above specified. And in case the said merchants stranger or any of them, by covert concealing or not entering their goods and merchandises in the customer's books there to be appointed, bring in or convey out of the said town of Calais, in defrauding the King's highness of his said customs, then they to be mulcted and punished with like pain and forfeitures as the King's subjects for like offense and concealment have sustained and borne, or owe to sustain and bear, within the said Archduke's countries; and as for the King's subjects, if they or any of them, by concealment or not entering their goods and merchandises in the customer's books there to be appointed, bring in or convey the same out of the said town of Calais, in defrauding the King's highness of his said customs, then they and every of them, from time to time and as often as they shall so do, to pay the said toll and ten times as much;

Also that the governor or governors of the said merchants adventurer, or such a person as they shall choose to be their ruler for the time, may have and use like authority, power, and jurisdiction in the rule and governance of the said merchants as the governor or governors of the same merchants have had and used or ought to have and use in the said Archduke's countries; and that all actions of debt, trespass, or other variance to be moved or attained within the said town and marches by any merchant or merchants adventurer against any of the said merchants adventurer, stapler, or other, for any cause or matter concerning the feat of merchants adventurer or by any other person or persons against any of the said merchants adventurer for causes concerning their said feat, be commenced afore the governor or governors and fellowship of the same merchants, there examined, pursued, and finally determined by sentence definitive, without any further appeal, according and like as the grants be made unto them in the Archduke's countries;

And in likewise all actions of debt, trespass, or other variance to be moved or attained within the said towns and marches by any merchant or merchants of the Staple against any of the merchants' fellowship or servant of the said Staple, merchants adventurer or others, for any cause or matter concerning the feat of merchants of the Staple or by any other person or persons against any of the said merchants of the Staple, for cause or matter concerning their said feat, be commenced afore the mayor of the said Staple, there examined, pursued, and finally determined by sentence definitive, without any further appeal; the statute [1] and ordinance of that town provided for punition of malefactors and trespassers in criminal cases, violators and breakers of the King's peace or any of the ordinances within the same, always standing in their full strength, vigor, and effect;

And that also all and every merchant of the Staple using or exercising the said feat of the merchants adventurer, buying or bartering any of the merchandises belonging to the same feat, not only observe and keep the statutes and ordinances made or to be made and ordained from time to time by the said merchants adventurer but also be contributories unto them for the same, like as other merchants adventurer do or hereafter owe to do; and also that every merchant adventurer using or exercising the said feat of merchants of the Staple, buying or bartering any of the merchandises belonging to the same feat, not only observe and keep the statutes and ordinances made or to be made and ordained from time to time by the said merchants of the Staple, but also be contributories unto them for the same, like the other merchants of the Staple do or hereafter owe to do;

Also if any officer or officers within the said town, marches, or port of Calais, constrain or compel the King's merchants adventurer or stranger, to pay any toll, custom, *gabel,* or exactions for their goods and merchandises at the said town, marches, or port, inward or outward, either within or without

1. 19 Henry VII, c. 27, 1503, *SR* 2, 667.

the mart, or compel any merchants stranger to pay any other tolls, customs, or exactions, within the mart or without the mart, than by the effect of these articles and the said tables shall be rated and extended, that then the King's treasurer and comptroller of that town for the time being and the said governor or governors or ruler jointly, or two of them at the least, whereof the governor to be one, have power and authority to examine the causes and complaints of the merchants grieved in this party, and to levy of the officer or officers so offending six times the value of such exaction or exactions, besides imprisonment and other punishment of his body at the King's pleasure; whereof half to be paid to the King, and the other half to the party grieved;

Also that the said merchants adventurer may be corporate within the said town and marches as they be in the Archduke's countries; and that they may keep their courts and assemblies and make ordinances and statutes for their politic rule and governance; ordain and levy fines, forfeitures, and impositions; establish weights and measures; admit meters, insurers, employers and packers; order and extend peisage, cranage, carters, rollwains, in like manner and form as the said merchants have made, ordained, established, and used in the Archduke's countries; and this without interruption, let, impediment, or challenge, of the mayor, water bailiff, or any officer or officers within the said town, port, or marches, upon pain of imprisonment and fine to be assessed by the King's treasurer, comptroller, and the governor of the said merchants or his deputy, whereof half to be applied to the King and the other half to the party grieved;

Also that all merchants, both of the Staple and others, and all other persons for them, be restrained and inhibited to buy any goods or merchandises of the Archduke's countries, but only within the said town and marches of Calais; and if any of the said merchants, or any other for them, buy or do to be bought any goods or merchandises within the said Archduke's domination, but only in the said marts holden at Calais, every such merchant, or any other for them or in their name so buying or doing to be bought, forfeit and lose also the same goods and merchandises so by them bought, or the value thereof, to be divided in three parts; the first part thereof to go to our sovereign lord the King, the second part to the said merchants adventurer, and the third part thereof to remain to the finder: gold and silver wrought and unwrought, victuals, horses and harness, only except;

Also that all the King's subjects merchant shall ship and convey their goods and merchandises only into the said town of Calais, and to no place of the Archduke's countries, upon pain of forfeiture and loss of all such goods and merchandises as shall be thither conveyed into any part of the said countries, or the value thereof, to be divided in three parts and to remain to the persons aforesaid; provided always that if it fortune the said merchants or any of them, by violence of wind, storm, or tempest, to be driven by force with their ships and merchandises into any part of the Archduke's countries, that they therefore fall not into any forfeiture of goods, so that they deliver no goods nor merchandises out of their said ship or ships, nor break no bulk there, but return with the same goods and merchandises wholly and entirely to the said town and marts of Calais or unto the realm of England, upon pain of forfeiture of the same;

Also that tin, leather, butter, cheese, tallow, and lead, called Staple ware, and in likewise Newcastle wool and fells usually accustomed to be sold by merchants adventurer in the Archduke's countries and other places, be conveyed and uttered at the marts of Calais foresaid, without any let, impediment, contradiction, or disturbance of the mart and fellowship of the Staple of Calais, or any other officer there for the time being; and to be in occupying of the said feat under the rule and governance of the governor of the fellowship of the said merchants adventurer, in like manner and form as they have been accustomed in the said Archduke's lands; provided always that the said wool and fells be searched by such the officer and searcher as shall be appointed and assigned by the King's highness; also that all persons having showhouses or packhouses within the said town or marches shall let to serve the same houses to the merchants adventurer for reasonable prices; and if the owners of such houses be unreasonable in that part, that then the ruler or governor of the said fellowship, and the King's deputy and treasurer there, have power to choose four merchants adventurer and four persons indifferent, inhabitants of the same town, the same persons or more part of them to rate, assess, and extend the farm of every such showhouse or packhouse after a reasonable price, so as the merchant and the owner may have cause to be contented.

And also it is ordained and established by the King's highness that all merchants of the Hanse, France, Spain, Portugal, and all other merchants comprised in league and amity made by their princes and heads with the King's grace, and also Florentines, Genoans, Venetians, Luccans, Boulognese, Milanese, Italians, with all other merchants which now be here, or shall be here, under the King's safe-conduct, shall not convey nor do to be conveyed, by themself nor by any other for them, by fraud, color, or *mal engine,* into any parts or place under the Archduke's obeisance, any woolen cloths or other of the King's commodities, upon pain of forfeiture of all such goods and merchandises, or the value of the same goods and merchandises; two parts of the said forfeiture to belong unto the King's highness and the third part to the finder;

Also in likewise that none of the said merchants stranger either of the Hanse or Italy, or any other country aforenamed, nor any other for them, bring or do to be brought into this the King's realm to the mart to be holden at Calais, or other countries under the King's obeisance, any goods, wares, or merchandises bought within the Archduke's countries, under pain of forfeiting the same, unless they buy the said wares and merchandises at the marts to be holden at Calais foresaid or in England.

Nevertheless, if the said merchants of the Hanse, Italians, or others, intend to convey cloths or other merchandises of the commodities of the King's realm into their own countries through the Archduke's countries, the King's highness is contented that they shall so do, and bring the commodities of their own countries or of any other country, the commodities of the Archduke's countries only excepted, through the said Archduke's lands into his realm or to the town of Calais; provided always that before they ship the said commodities of this realm to be conveyed into their own countries as above, they make sufficient sureties and bonds before the King's comptroller and customers of such town and port where the said goods and merchandises shall be shipped, in the custom house there, that they shall not break no bulk, open no pack for making sale, bartering, commutation, or dressing of any part of the said merchandises within the obeisance of the Archduke's countries, but only to be dried if necessity so require;

And in likewise that none of the same merchants of the Hanse, or any other for them, bring or do to be brought into this the King's realm, or into any other place under his obeisance any goods, wares, or merchandises of the commodities of the said Archduke's countries, or bought in the same countries, unless they buy the same at the mart at Calais.

Also the King's highness is contented that all such goods and merchandises as were bought, as well by merchants adventurer as by Easterlings and other strangers within the obeisance of the Archduke's countries, at any mart before the first day of January last past, may be brought into this his realm without jeopardy or danger of loss of any of their said goods and merchandises, any commandment or restraint heretofore passed to the contrary notwithstanding, so that the same be brought into the King's realm within six weeks after the day of this proclamation made; provided always that under color of this license and privilege they bring into the King's said realm none other merchandises but such as were by them bought before the first day of January last past, and none other, without color, craft, or *mal engine,* upon pain of forfeiture of all such goods and merchandises so to be brought by them into this the King's realm.

And to the intent that all merchants, as well strangers as other, may have perfect knowledge and notice of every point and article comprised in this proclamation, the King therefore our sovereign lord hath ordained that the same shall with all speed and diligence be imprinted, so that therein no man shall nor may pretend ignorance.

57. Regulating Clipped Coin

[Westminster, after 27 April 1505, 20 Henry VII]

AC (Bayne 42): date, Saturday, 23 November 1504; order for proclamation to be made on Monday next. CW (C82/330): date, Westminster, 27 April 1505; sign manual; writ to sheriff of Kent; schedule as below (Section I); Steele 49a. CW, loc. cit.: another warrant, under same date; sign manual; writ to sheriff of Kent; schedule as below (Sections I and II); Steele 50. PR (C66/595/33*d*): date, Westminster, 27 April; writ to sheriff of Kent; schedule as below (Sections I and II); Steele 50. *STC* 7761 (UM 517, *2359), ULC 7072: printed by W. Faques (London, 1505); date, based on additional content, after 27 April; schedule as below (Sections I, II, and III) imperfect. Steele 51. Text (*STC*): ULC, emended from PR

[I]

WHERE THE KING our sovereign lord, by good deliberation and advice of his lords spiritual and temporal and other of his council, in avoiding of such vexation and trouble as were among his subjects, making them ignorant in knowledge of English groats and double placks, whether they be clipped or not clipped, and refusing of them contrary to the true meaning and intent of the act of parliament[1] thereof made, directed his several straight commandments and proclamations[2] to all mayors, sheriffs, constables, and bailiffs and all other head officers, commanding them upon a great pain and fine therein limited duly to execute the same; whereby was explained and openly declared all such groats and double placks as were and should be current, reputed, and taken for good groats and double placks, not clipped, with their limits and marks contained in the same proclamations more at large;

And this notwithstanding, the King our sovereign lord, having perfect knowledge that the same proclamations, according to the tenor and effect thereof, be not duly put in execution in default and negligence of the said mayors and other head officers, and of such willful persons as without cause reasonable refuseth to take in payments and receipts such good groats and placks as be not clipped, but by the coiners misstricken, and ought to be current by the said act and proclamations, to the great hurt, trouble, and inquietness of his well-disposed subjects and his grievous displeasure, to the great danger of the offenders in that behalf;

Wherefore in eschewing of such further vexations and troubles of his subjects, and that the good laws and order of the amendment and reformation of the coin, made by the assent of his lords spiritual and temporal, and the commons of this his realm, for the politic weal of his subjects, should be duly kept and observed; and for that there is now of late many

1. 19 Henry VII, c. 5, 1503, *SR* 2, 650.
2. See 38, 39, 42, 44, 54.

subtle crafts and inventions daily found and used in minishing and impairing of the said coin to the great hurt, damage, and impoverishing of all his subjects:

The King our sovereign lord straightly chargeth and commandeth that no manner of persons clip, mash, batter, boil, or otherwise minish or impair any coin, upon pain of death.

And furthermore his highness straightly chargeth that every person, what degree or condition he be of, upon pain of imprisonment without bail or mainprize and fine to be made at the King's will and pleasure, shall receive, and in no wise refuse to take in payments and receipts any English groats being silver, having three staves of the cross whole, and also all English groats that have but only two staves of the cross whole, though the other two staves be not whole and seemeth to be clipped or otherwise minished; nevertheless if the whole or yet the half of the scripture on the other side foragainst the staves so seeming to be clipped or minished do show and appear, then the same groats to be current in payments and receipts without any refusal, upon like pain; and over that every double plack being silver having the more part of the scripture apparent on the one side or on the other to be taken in payments and receipts; and that all pence and pence of 2*d.* being silver be also current and taken in receipts and payments upon pain aforesaid; except pence having the spur or the mullet within the staves of the cross side, and the same pence to go and be current for ½*d.* and none otherwise;

And that all such groats and placks as have not the limits and marks afore rehearsed be reputed for clipped money, and none otherwise to be current, but taken in payments or in exchange by weight after 3*s.* 2*d.* the ounce; and in likewise the half-ounce, the quarter, the half-quarter, after the rate of the same, and no less to be given therefor, so that they pass not in every such ounce of groats and placks together the fifth part of the ounce in placks, and in likewise in the half-ounce, the quarter, and half-quarter not in every such ounce of groats and placks together the fifth part of the ounce in placks, and in likewise for the rate in the half-ounce, the quarter and half-quarter as above; and that every such person as shall take or receive such clipped money by weight do forthwith and immediately, in the presence and sight of him that it so shall utter, cut in sunder to the half or thereabouts, or cause to be cut, all the said clipped money so received and taken, upon pain of forfeiture thereof, and to have imprisonment and to make fine at the King's will and pleasure.

[II]

And forasmuch as the King our sovereign lord considereth the great hurt, trouble, vexation, and damage that in many sundry wise doth and [might] ensue to his subjects for lack of short and speedy exchange of such money as is clipped and not current, but by weight as is afore[said; and for the] weal, profit, and quietness of them, and also in eschewing the great loss and charge that they bear and sustain for and about such making [of exchange,] and of necessity given for their speed to depart with such clipped money under the said value and rate; and also long abide and tarrying at the [King's mint] for the new coining of the same, for the great quantity of bullion and clipped money [that] is daily brought to the same mints to be coined[: of his mere] motion, great providence, and blessed disposition, and also the tender love and especial favor to his subjects and the commonweal [of this his realm, at] his own proper costs and charges, full graciously hath ordained and appointed exchanges to be had, at Leaden Hall within the city of [London, of good] and current coin according to his proclamation. Therefore every of his subjects that to that place will repair and deliver such clipped [money, not] current by this proclamation, by weight after 3*s.* 2*d.* the ounce, the half-ounce, the quarter, and half-quarter, and so ratably as aforesaid;

[To] the intent that under color of this exchange, which the King's highness of his gracious disposition hath ordained of his own proper goodness [and] substance for the relief and succor of his subjects, no clipped groats, nor other money before declared not to be current, should be uttered either by the keepers of the said exchange or by any of the King's subjects, which perchance would affirm that they had received the same clipped, not current, or damned groats at the exchange aforesaid: his highness therefore, of his high providence and singular zeal that he beareth to the weal and restfulness of his said subjects, hath provided and ordained that at the said exchange, there shall none other money be given or paid to the King's subjects, nor to any other person by the keepers thereof for clipped groats or other money thither to be brought by way of exchange, but only gold pence of 2*d.* and 1*d.;* whereby it may evidently appear to all the King's said subjects and other, that no clipped groats nor any other money not current is paid or shall be paid at the said exchange, but only good and lawful money like as is before specified.

And to the intent the said clipped money so delivered and received shall no more be current to the hurt and vexation of his subjects or that they thereby in any wise be deceived or inquieted, the King's most noble grace straightly chargeth and commandeth every person keeping the said exchange, that taketh or receiveth such clipped money by weight, as well in the presence and sight of him that it shall so deliver as of them that the same shall receive, to cut or do to be cut in sunder the same clipped money to the midst or half thereof, and the deliverers of all such money before that done not to depart; the said exchange and course of clipped money by weight, ounce or otherwise, no longer to endure than to the Feast of the Purification of Our Lady next after the making of this proclamation; and after the same feast, all such clipped money not current as aforesaid, found in the hands of any person or persons, not cut in sunder or broken, to be forfeited, the one half thereof to the King our sovereign lord and the other half to the finder.

And also the King's highness straightly chargeth and commandeth that all mayors, sheriffs, constables, bailiffs, wardens of fellowships, and all other head officers of cities, towns, boroughs, and villages, to see the premises according to the tenor and effect thereof duly executed to the best of their powers; upon pain of imprisonment without bail or mainprize, and to make fine at the King's will and pleasure for their unfitting disobeisance and non-executing of this proclamation and the King's most high, dread commandment in this behalf.

[III]

And over this, forasmuch as the King our sovereign lord, by credible information and report, hath now of late understood that divers and many indisposed persons (interpreting his proclamation otherwise than the letter thereof soundeth or ought to be understood) refuse to take and receive such groats, placks, pence of 2*d.* and pence having the marks, limits, points, tokens, or scripture declared in the foresaid proclamation to be current, under pretense and color that the same money so declared to have course and passage in the form therein contained should no longer be current than unto the Feast of the Purification of Our Lady next ensuing; by reason whereof great refusal is made of the King's foresaid coin and money, so determined to be current, not only against his commandment, mind, and pleasure, but also to the great inquietness, loss, and damage of his said subjects:

The King therefore, our sovereign lord, considering the premises and bearing tender zeal, love, and especial favor to the quietness of his subjects and commonweal of this his realm (willing also and intending to amove and put apart all manner ambiguities, darkness, and difficulties sinister interpreters be pretended and made [of] his said proclamation, though the same of itself be clear, plain, and open to men, substantially and groundly regarding, and nothing the same), expressly signifieth unto all and singular his subjects and others by these presents, declaring that the clause contained above in his proclamation, specifying the same no longer to endure than to the Feast of the Purification of Our Lady aforesaid, is to be understood in this wise following:

That is to say, that the exchange and course of clipped money, not having the limits, marks, points, tokens, or scriptures specified, to be uttered for only payments by weight or ounce, shall no longer endure than to the said Feast of the Purification of Our Lady next coming; but that after the same feast all such clipped money, not determined to be current, found in the hands of any person or persons, not cut in sunder nor broken, to be taken as forfeited, the one half to the King's highness and the other half to the finder thereof;

And that all other groats, placks, pence of 2*d.*, and pence having the limits, marks, points, tokens, or scriptures contained above, in this the King's proclamation, to have course and passage, without any difficulty or contradiction, as well after the Feast of the Purification next coming as also from thence forward, like as they had or ought to have had heretofore and hitherto; upon pain of the penalties and forfeitures before contained and specified in this proclamation;

And that every person or persons that find them grieved in refusal of any money, contrary to the tenor and effect of this proclamation, come to the mayor, the King's lieutenant, sheriffs, wardens of fellowships, or such other of this his city and chamber of London, bringing with them sufficient proof of such refusal; and they shall have due reformation and punishment against the offenders in that behalf.

58. Reserving Wrecks at Calais for King's Use

[1509, 24 Henry VII]

CW (C82/331): date, uncertain month, 24 Henry VII; sign manual; writ to lieutenant and council of Calais; schedule as below. Steele 52: date as above. Text (MS): CW

FORASMUCH as the King our sovereign lord perfectly understandeth that where by sudden great storms and other misfortunes and adventures, divers and many ships, crayers, and other vessels, happen ofttimes to perish and to be wrecked within the scunage and other places of this his marches of Calais and of havens herebefore, as well by his subjects, soldiers and inhabitants of this his said town, as his subjects and farmers within the said marches, have been suddenly as well by day as by night despoiled, taken, carried away, devoured, so that his highness nor any other person having any title unto them might or could not by his treasurer and controller here sufficiently be answered as right would:

The King our said sovereign lord chargeth and straightly commandeth that no manner of person nor persons, of what degree or condition he or they be of, from henceforth, when any such wreck or waif or any other casual profit or forfeiture shall happen to fall within the said scunage or haven of Calais by any such fortune (as God defend), take, carry, or lead away any part of any such wreck, waif, or forfeiture, nor intermeddle nor in any wise deal with the same, but such persons as by his treasurer and controller here, or their deputies, shall be assigned; upon pain of forfeiture of double the value of such goods that so shall be taken, carried, or conveyed, and imprisonment of the bodies of him or them that so offendeth by the discretion of his said treasurer and controller.

The Proclamations of Henry viii

1509-47

59. Confirming Final Pardon by Henry VII

[Tower of London, 23 April 1509, 1 Henry VIII]

AC (HM Ellesmere 2655, 7): date 11 October; council petitions King to declare all non-record court decisions void. CW (C82/335): date as above; sign manual; schedule partly legible. Ibid., a second warrant: date, Tower of London, 30 April; sign manual; writ to Chancellor; schedule in Latin, partly legible. PRO (SP 1/1/2): schedule as below. *Rev.STC* 7761.3 and 7761.7; (BM, Microfilm A.424, 4) ULC: fragments, printed by R. Pynson (London, ?1509). LJ 11, 64: date, 24 April; schedule as below. Holinshed *3*, 799: proclaimed on 25 April. Steele 53: date, 30 April. Text (MS): LJ

THE KING our sovereign lord, Henry, by the grace of God King of England and of France, and lord [of] Ireland, of this name the eighth, doth you to understand that forasmuch as the King his father of most noble memory, whose soul God pardon, of his blessed disposition and for the surety and comfort of his loving subjects in his lifetime, gave and granted to all and every of them a general pardon of misprisions, felonies, trespasses, forfeitures, outlawries, certain recognizances, and divers and many other offenses done and committed before the tenth day of April last past, as more plainly appeareth by the same:

The King our sovereign lord that now is, King Henry VIII, considering that the said pardon is by the death of his said father expired, amortized, and of none effect, his grace, for the tender zeal and entire love that he beareth to his said subjects, and to put them in good quietness of mind and out of all doubt and fear to be troubled or vexed in their bodies or goods by him or his officers for any offenses done and committed in the King his said father's days, or before the day of his reign, of his special grace and mere motion, free will and good heart, hath given and granted to all his said subjects, of what estate, condition, or degree soever they be, a general pardon of all manner offenses, trespasses, outlawries, forfeitures, and all other matters, debts and accounts only excepted, which is much more ample, gracious, and beneficial than was the said pardon granted by the King his said father, every of his said subjects to have his said pardon under his Great Seal at any time that they shall list to sue for it to his Chancellor of England.

Also our said sovereign lord commandeth and ordaineth that all such persons as were authorized by the King his father's commissions to be sheriff or justices of the peace within this shire, they altogether for the whole shire, and every of them apart in the quarter where they dwell, have a special regard to the keeping of the King's peace, putting themself to the best of their powers in full devoir, and diligence for the effecting of the same. And if anything fortune to be attempted by any misruled person or persons, to the breach of the King's peace, or the commotion of his people, that then and in that case the said sheriff and justices and every of them in their quarters put them forthwith in their like endeavor to repress and subdue the same and to commit all such misdoers to ward within the next jail, there to remain without bail or mainprize till our said sovereign lord be thereof advised and his pleasure known in that behalf. And for the better accomplishment of this our said sovereign lord's commandment, his highness will that if the case so require, and that it be thought good and expedient so to be done, that then the said sheriff and justices, by the warning and calling of the said sheriff, assemble themself together in some convenient place or places as often and when it shall be thought good to devise, treat, commune, and conclude for the better performance and execution of this our said sovereign lord's commandment; and that they and every of them lay apart all other business for the season and give their attendance and do their true diligence in and about the premises as if they and every of them stood all this time in such authority, commission, and power as they did in the life of the King's said father, and as they will deserve to be put hereafter to semblable authority, and as they altogether for the whole shire and every of them for his quarter will answer to our said sovereign lord at their perils. And our said sovereign lord, as soon as goodly may be done, shall send them his commissions whereby they may be more perfectly authorized for the executing of the premises.

And over this, our said sovereign lord of his more abundant grace will and straightly chargeth and commandeth that his said chancellor of England, the justices of both the benches, the treasurers and barons of his exchequer, the justices of assizes, the justices of the peace, sheriffs, mayors, and escheators, and all other his officers and ministers of justice, from henceforth do and minister justice, and in every cause and matter do and execute their offices freely, rightwisely, and indifferently to every of his subjects, after the laws of his land, good conscience, charity, and discretion, as well where his highness is the one party as also betwixt party and party; not letting so to do, neither for fear nor displeasure of our said sovereign lord, nor for his letters if it shall fortune any such to be written to them in time to come to the contrary, nor for no speech, writing, monition, or charge to be given to any of them to the contrary by any of his council, whatsoever he be; and in likewise that none of his subjects forbear nor make no doubt nor difficulty in all cases lawful to make their traverses, for his highness willeth and straightly chargeth his said chancellor, treasurer, and barons that they not only admit such traverses and also grant the forms where the case shall so require, according to the old true course of his letters.

Also his highness, for the advancement of the commonweal of his realm and the universal weal and profit of his subjects, will that all manner of merchants, denizen and stranger, clothiers, artificers, and folks of all manner of mysteries and occupations do exercise, occupy their feats, mysteries, occupations, crafts, and merchandises, freely, quietly, and peaceably, and without any fear of forfeiture by reason of any light and untrue informations or wrong surmises of customers, comptrollers, or searchers, or of any persons calling themself promoters or by reason of any statutes or ordinances made of long time past, given, put in ure, use, or execution, till now of late time. And his grace shall provide for the reformation of the great extremity and rigor wherewith his said subjects have been grievously vexed and troubled in time past, so that they shall now freely, quietly, and surely, without fear of any such wrongs, hereafter occupy their feats of merchandise, clothmaking, and all other mysteries and occupations.

And over this, our said sovereign lord willeth and straightly chargeth and commandeth that no manner of person, of what estate, degree, or conditions soever he be, for any occasion, cause, or quarrel of time past, revenge his own or any other person's cause or quarrel by way of fight at his own hand, but that every person keep the King's peace, every of them against other, without any riots, routs, affrays, quarrels, unlawful assemblies, or commotions making of the King's people, whereby his peace may be in anywise broken or troubled, upon the uttermost peril and pain that may thereupon ensue, and that every man that findeth him grieved or wronged sue for his remedy at the common law or to the King's grace and his council by bill of complaint, and they shall have justice ministered at reasonable speed and lawful favor.

60. Henry viii's Accession Pardon

[Westminster, 25 April 1509, 1 Henry VIII]

AC (HM Ellesmere 2655,8): date, 14 November: King consents that prisoners be released on making bond. *STC* 7762 (UM 2,3,309), ULC: printed by R. Pynson (London, 1509); schedule as below. Another edition, *rev.STC* 7762.5: printed by R. Pynson (London, ?1509). Holinshed *3*, 799: pardon granted on 25 April. Steele 54: date, Westminster, May. Text (*STC*): ULC

These be the articles following, the which the King's grace has pardoned:

First, high treason, petty treason, murder, and all other manner of felonies.

All judgments, executions, and outlawries of and for the same; and the issues, profits, goods, and chattels forfeited by reason of the same.

All escapes of every of the same, both willful and negligent, of all prisoners attainted, convict or otherwise.

All rebellion done, insurrections, and misprisions.

All trespasses, riots, conspiracies, forcible entries, embracery, perjury, maintenance, and extortion.

Misuse noyous, and usurpation of liberties and franchises and profits taken for the same.

All misdemeanor of sheriffs, escheators, stewards, mayors, bailiffs, constables, all justices and commoners, and all forfeitures and penalties by reason of the same.

For hunting in forests, parks and chases, or elsewhere, and felling wood in the same.

All offenses touching sewers, weighers, etc., and all penalties and judgments for the same.

All payments of gold or bullion, etc., to strangers.

Alienations into mortmain without the King's license, or to any other to that use, for the issues and profits of the same, deodands, treasure trove, wreck, waifs, and strays.

Praemunires and suits in spiritual courts in derogation of the King's crown, and penalties for the same.

All intrusions and entries and alienations without the King's license, with the issues and profits of the same.

Ravishment of wards and entries into their lands, and the valor of the marriage of the same wards being married, and marriage of the King's widows and of heirs female without license, and the issues and profits for the same.

All wastes of lands of heirs within age, and that to the King should belong by reason of the same.

Benevolences, fifteenths, subsidies, tenths, and aids.

The seizing of idiots, lunatics, and of the issues of their lands.

Buying and selling of alum.

Usuries, corrupt bargains, unlawful making of cloth, loaning for days to strangers, chevisance and unlawful exchanges, and all other forfeitures concerning merchants or merchandises by reason of any statute or otherwise, and all penalties of the same.

Forestalling and regrating, using of false weights and measures.

Concealments and withdrawing of customs and subsidies, and wrongful entries of merchandises.

All debts and forfeitures by reason of any recognizances, mainprize, *mucianas,* obligations to the King or to any other to his use, made alonely for keeping of his peace, for good abearing, allegiance, and appearance.

All manner outlawries: goods and chattels, issues and profits, forfeit for the same.

All forfeitures for misusing of apparel statute; laborers for all unlawful games.

All unlawful retainers.

Casting and letting down of houses against the statute.

Building of towers and embattling.

Fines and amercements of cities, boroughs, and towns.

And over all this, the King of his most abundant grace hath pardoned the breaking and violation of all statutes, restraints, and ordinances, and all condemnations, judgments, executions, debts, and penalties that should or might grow by reason of the same. And all these premises have relation to the 23rd day of April, the first year of the reign of our sovereign lord, King Henry VIII.

And by the same pardon, his grace hath granted that it shall be interpreted and declared and taken [fav]orably, graciously, and beneficially to all his subjects.

61. Mustering Forces for Defense

[Westminster, 20 November 1509, 1 Henry VIII]

CW (C82/342): date of delivery as above; sign manual; writ to Chancellor; schedule as below. Not in Steele. Text (MS): CW

The King our sovereign lord, Henry, by the grace of God King of England and of France and lord of Ireland, having a tender zeal and entire love to the wealth, surety, and defense of this his realm of England, and of his subjects of the same, according to the providence and wisdom of all princes, willing in time of peace to provide and foresee for the wars and other chances that by mutability of fortune may happen, and hereafter ensue;

Forasmuch as is supposed that by reason of the peace which, blessed be Jesus, hath long continued in this his realm, his subjects be not so well appointed and provided with horse, harness, and weapon convenient for the war, as they have been in time past:

Therefore, and for other divers great and necessary considerations him moving, straightly chargeth and commandeth all and every his subjects inhabited within this his shire of ———— being able in person and goods to serve his highness in time of war, to prepare and ordain for himself alone, or two, three, or more (according to his degree, power, and substance, and the laws and customs of the land in such case used and provided), horse and harness competent, and weapons convenient, for the war;

And that every other his subjects inhabited within the said shire, being of good power in substance and goods, and not able in his own person by reason of sickness, age, or otherwise, to serve his highness, prepare and ordain one or two men or more, according to his degree, power, and substance, appointed and armed with horse, harness, and weapons convenient as above, to serve his highness for him and in his place, in time of war.

And over that his highness chargeth and commandeth that all manner sheriffs, bailiffs, and constables of cities, towns, and boroughs, and the constable of every hundred within the said shire, charge and warn every city, town, borough, village, and hamlet within their said offices that they and every of them prepare and ordain one or more able men harnessed and weaponed as above, according to their power and substance, and in such number as they have been heretofore used and accustomed to do;

And that every man so appointed with horse, harness, and weapon, put himself betwixt this and Candlemas in full readiness, as before is said, to appear and muster afore the commissioner or commissioners by his highness to be appointed for that purpose, in manner and form as heretofore hath been used and accustomed, at such time and place as shall be to them by the said commissioners appointed and assigned.

62. Prohibiting Retainers

[Westminster, 3 July 1511, 3 Henry VIII]

CW (C82/380): date of delivery as above; sign manual; schedule as below. Not in Steele. Text (MS): CW

WHEREAS THE KING our sovereign lord, Henry, by the grace King of England and of France, and lord of Ireland, for the defense of his most noble person, his realm, and his subjects, hath now lately, by the advice of his council, by his letters under his signet and sign manual, commanded as well all the lords as also the substance of all the nobles of this his realm forthwith to prepare such and as many able men for the war, sufficiently harnessed, as they can and may prepare of their own servants and other inhabitants within their offices and rooms, and none other, as in the said letters is more plainly expressed and specified:

Our said sovereign lord is now informed, to his great displeasure if it so be, that divers and many of the said lords and nobles, as well by color of the said letters as of other his former and older letters and placards, prepare for the war divers and many persons not being their own tenants nor inhabited within their offices and rooms, contrary to the King's said letters, but also retain divers persons, wheresoever they may get them, some by promises and some by badges and cognizances, and some otherwise, contrary to the mind of our said sovereign lord and his laws in that case provided.

Wherefore his highness straightly chargeth and commandeth that no manner of man, of what degree or condition he be, make no retainers otherwise than his laws [1] will suffer, upon the dangers and peril of the same

1. 13 Richard II, st. 3, 1389, *SR* 2, 74; 16 Richard II, c. 4, 1392, *SR* 2, 84; 20 Richard II, c. 2, 1396, *SR* 2, 93; 1 Henry IV, c. 7, 1399, *SR* 2, 113; 2 Henry IV, c. 21, 1400, *SR* 2, 129; 7 Henry IV, c. 14, 1405, *SR* 2, 155; 8 Edward IV, c. 2, 1468, *SR* 2, 426. See also 19 Henry VII, c. 14, 1503, *SR* 2, 658.

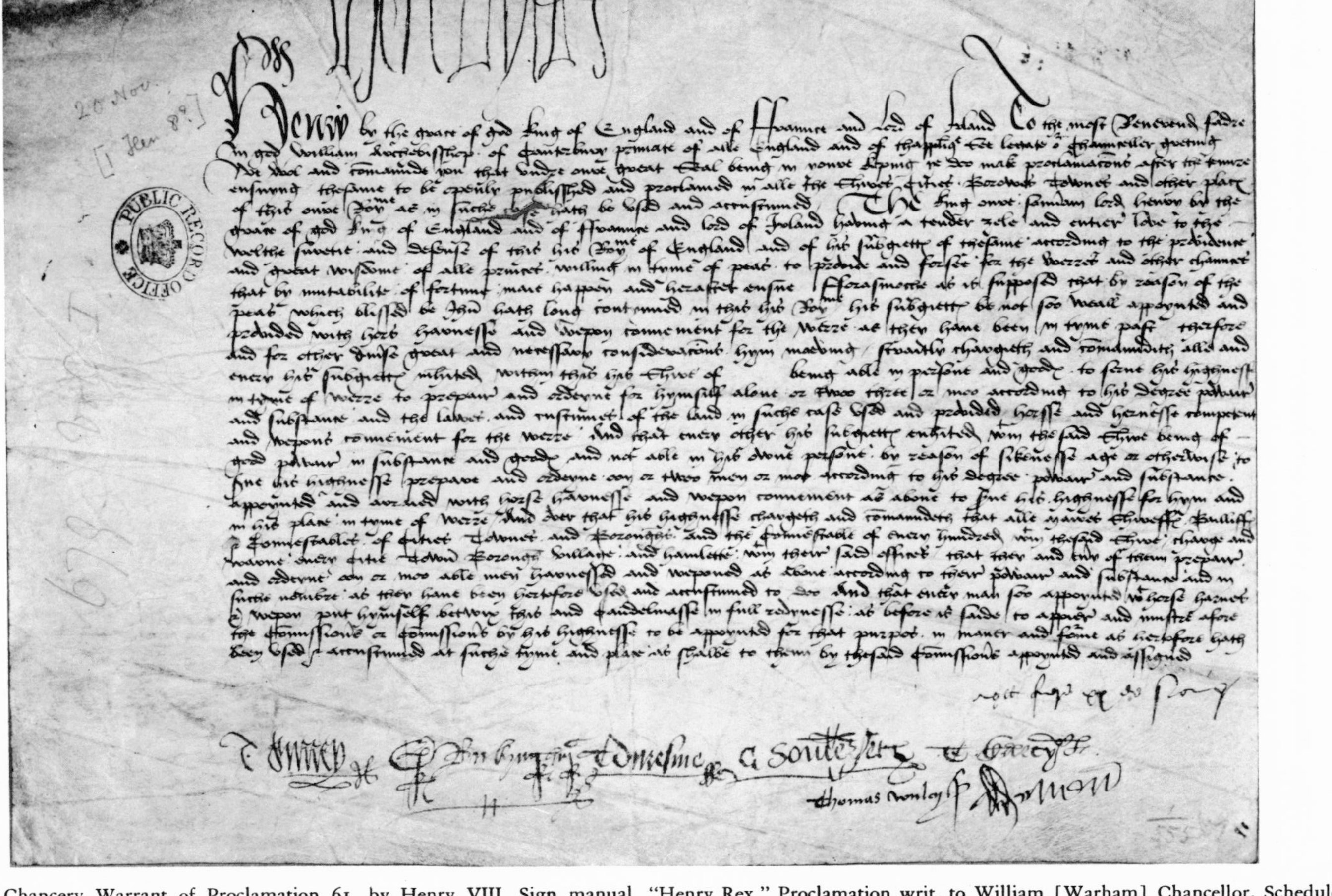

Plate 2. Chancery Warrant of Proclamation 61, by Henry VIII. Sign manual, "Henry Rex." Proclamation writ, to William [Warham] Chancellor. Schedule, mustering forces for defense. Dated Chancery, 20 November [I Henry VIII, 1509]. Countersigned by Privy Council members: E[dward Stafford, Duke of] Buckingham, T[homas Ruthall, Bishop of] Durham, C[harles] Somerset, T[homas] Darcy, Thomas Wulcy [Wolsey], Sir D. Owen. PRO (C82/342), 20 November.

laws; nor no man bear or wear any man's badge or cognizance otherwise than the law will, upon the same peril; nor prepare no man for the war but only such as be his own servants or inhabited within his office or rooms, according to the said letters;

And that every man that hath otherwise ordered or demeaned him in that behalf forthwith purvey the remedy, so that his highness hereafter have no complaint thereof, at his uttermost peril, and upon the King's great indignation and displeasure.

And as for the said former and older letters and placards, of what date and nature soever they be, or to whom or for what cause soever they were granted, the King's highness declareth them now to be void and of none effect, but utterly derogate by this his last letters, which, his highness will, stand in force and effect, and none other.

63. Enforcing Statute of Winchester

[Westminster, 5 July 1511, 3 Henry VIII]

AC (HM Ellesmere 2655, 9*v*): date, Star Chamber, 28 January 1512; order to mayor and sheriffs of London to set and post prices for fowl and fish. PR (C66/615/7*d*): date as above; writ to sheriffs of London; similar writs to sheriffs, mayors, and bailiffs throughout England; schedule as below. Steele 56. Text (MS): PR

FORASMUCH as the King our sovereign lord, Henry, by the grace of God King of England and of France and lord of Ireland, by credible information right well understanding how the great decay and ruin of this his realm of England hath continued many years by means of heinous murders, felonies, robberies, riots, unlawful assemblies, and other great and inordinate offenses daily within this his said realm, committed and done to the high displeasure of God, great danger and peril of this his said realm, inquietness and destruction of many of his true subjects of the same, to his great displeasure; the which to avoid, above all things earthly his grace desireth, and to reduce in his days the same his realm of England into the ancient weal, honor, and prosperity; considering also the occasion thereof as evidently appeareth that most necessary statutes heretofore in such case provided, and especially the Statute of Winchester [1] and other statutes which hereafter ensueth, have not been duly executed as appertaineth:

Our said sovereign lord the King therefore, and for the tender zeal that his highness beareth to his most loving subjects, intending especially the perfect redressing and reformation of such murders, robberies, and other enormities, so that his said true and loving subjects may henceforth live in

1. 13 Edward I (Statute of Winchester), 1285, *SR 1*, 96.

sure rest and perfect tranquility, which his highness most especially desireth, [by] the advice of the lords of his most honorable council, to the intent that none of his said subjects shall pretend ignorance or lack of understanding of the said Statute of Winchester, amongst the other good and necessary statutes for the commonweal which hereafter ensueth, hath caused the same statutes to be translated out of French into vulgar tongue of English; willing and straightly commanding all and every his subjects for their havior, degree, and authority to put as well the said Statute of Winchester as all the other behooveful laws and statutes hereafter following, heretofore made for the reformation, punishment, and eschewing of the premises, in due and full observance and execution, and the same statutes inviolably from henceforth to observe, keep, and execute, as they and every of them intend to avoid the penalties and punishments for the offenders in such case provided, and also as they intend to avoid the King's high displeasure if they or any of them be hereafter found faulty, negligent, or remiss in the premises or any of these the tenors of which statutes be hereto annexed.

First, the Statute of Winchester [2] made the 13th year of the reign of the King's noble progenitor King Edward I as ensueth. Forasmuch as daily robberies, murders, and burnings be more often and commonly done within this our realm than ever was heretofore, and that felons hath not been therefor attainted by the oath of the jurors, which rather willfully suffer felonies to be done to strange persons and to pass without punishment of indictment of the said misdoers, whereof great part of the said misdoers be of the people of the same country, or at the least if the said misdoers be of another country, the receiptors be of the neighbors of the same country, and the said jurors do not regard nor fear their oaths where the said felonies be done; and as to the restitution of them that were damaged and hurted before time, no pain was purveyed for the concealment or misbehavior of the said countries or jurors where such offenses were done;

The King our sovereign lord, for to eschew and abate the power of felons, hath established a pain in this case: so that for fear of the same pain rather than for fear and dread of their oaths, and that no persons from henceforth offending shall not escape nor no felonies be concealed, the King our said sovereign lord commandeth that a cry and proclamation be solemnly made in all shires, hundreds, markets, fairs, and all other places where great assembly of people shall be, so that by ignorance no person shall excuse him, that every country from henceforth be kept so that forthwith after any robberies and felonies be done, fresh suit be made from town to town and country to country;

And also if need be, that inquests be made in town or towns by him or them that is sovereign of the town or towns, and after in hundred and in franchises, and in the county or counties and sometime in two, three, or

2. *Ibid.*

four shires in case when felonies be done in marches of the same shire or shires, so that the said misdoers may be attainted according to their demerits. And if the country or countries do not take the body or bodies of such misdoers, their punishment and pain shall be such, that is to say, every of the people in the country abiding there shall answer of the robberies and damages done there, so that the hundred or hundreds whereas the robbery or robberies shall be done within the franchise or franchises within the said hundred or hundreds shall answer of the said robbery or robberies; and if the said robbery be done in the ends or the dividing of two hundreds then shall both the hundreds with the franchise within them answer for the said misdeeds and offenses done; and the country or countries shall have no longer term after the robbery or robberies, felony, or felonies done, but 40 days within which time the said country or countries shall make agreement or recompense of the said robbery or robberies and misdeeds, or else answer the body or bodies of such misdoers.

And furthermore the King's highness for the further surety of his subjects chargeth and commandeth that all the gates in every great walled town or towns be shut at the sun setting, and not open before the sun rising. And that no person shall be lodged nor harbored in the suburbs nor in the foreigns of any such town but by daytime, nor yet by daytime but if the host will answer for him. And the bailiffs of town or towns every week or every 15 days shall make inquiry of the people harbored and lodged in the suburbs or foreigns of town or towns; and if they find any man that harboreth or do lodge any person suspect, or do against the King's peace or contrary to the premises, the said bailiff shall do them right and punish them according to the laws.

And from henceforth it is ordained and commanded by the King's said highness that watch be made as of old time it hath been used and accustomed: that is to say, from the Day of the Ascension unto the Feast of St. Michael the Archangel, that in every city in the night six men at every gate; in every borough, 12 men; and every uplanded town, six men or four, after the number of the people there dwelling. And they shall make watch continually from sunset to sun rising. And if any stranger pass by them, they shall arrest him or them and keep him or them till the morrow: and if no suspicions be found in him or them, then he or they to be delivered and set at his liberty; and if suspicion be found in him or them, he or they to be delivered to the custody of the sheriff, which shall receive and keep him without any difficulty till he be in due manner delivered; and if such suspicious persons will not obey the rest that them pursue, and cry be made upon them from town to town unto the time they be taken and delivered to the sheriff according as afore is said. And for the taking and detaining of the said persons no body shall be hurt or damaged.

It is also commanded that the highways leading and going from merchant towns to merchant towns shall be from henceforth enlarged in such places where there is woods, hedges, or ditches; so that there shall be no ditches, wood, underwood, or bushes whereby a man may escape to do any hurt; and the said way shall have 200 foot clearly in every side of the same, so that this statute extend not to great oaks nor other great wood, so that the said ground be clear under the great wood. And if there be any default in the lord of the said wood, that he will not fell his underwood, bushes, and cast any his ditches in manner and form before rehearsed, and robberies and felonies be there done, the lord of the said grounds shall answer for the same; and if it be murder, he shall be ransomed at the King's will. And if the lord be not able to cleanse the way and cut down the said wood, the country shall help him thereunto. And the King's highness will that in his own demesne, lands, and woods, within his forests and without, that his ways be enlarged in form before rehearsed. And in case any park be near the highway, then it behooveth the lord of the same park to diminish his park till at the least there be 200 feet next to the highway, as before is said, or that he make such a wall, ditch, or hedge that the misdoers may not pass nor return, to do contrary to the tenor of this statute.

Also it is commanded that every man have in his house armor for keeping of the peace, according to his havior and substance as they have been and shall be ordered by the commissioners after the old assize.

And also it is ordained and enacted by the statute [3] made the third year of the reign of King Henry VII that if any person be slain or murdered in the day, and the murderer escape untaken, that the township where the said deed is done be amerced for the said escape, and that the coroner have authority to inquire thereof upon the view of the body dead, and also justice of peace have power to inquire of such escapes and that to certify afore the King in his bench; and after that the felony found, the coroners deliver their inquisitions afore the justices of the next jail delivery in the shire where inquisition is taken, the same justices to proceed against such murderers if they be in the jail, and else the same justices to put the same inquisitions afore the King in his bench.

The Preamble for the Proclamation of the Statute for Vagabonds and Unlawful Games [4]

Moreover, whereas the King our sovereign lord is credibly informed that his subjects, and in especial servants of husbandry and servants of artificers, do daily incline themself to unlawful games, as to carding, dicing, and other unlawful games heretofore by divers statutes prohibited, whereby the said servants fall to robberies and oftentimes to robbing of their masters, to the undoing as well of themself as of their masters; and by the use of such

3. 3 Henry VII, c. 2, 1487, *SR 2*, 510.
4. 12 Richard II, c. 6, 1388, *SR 2*, 57.

unlawful games, shooting, which is and ever hath been the most sure and natural feat of war for his said subjects in and for the defense of their persons and of this his realm, is greatly decayed and out of exercise; his most noble grace, for the tender zeal that he hath to his subjects, and for their surety and quietness, intending specially the avoiding and eschewing of such robberies and other mischiefs which ensue upon the use of such unlawful games; and to the intent that that most defensible and natural feat of shooting should in no wise decay but increase; and whereas they, evil-disposed persons being of sufficient ability and power in body, will not put themself to labor, but delight to live in idleness, untruly feigning themself to be sick and diseased, whereas indeed they be not so, of the which idleness and untruly feigned sickness ensue all vices and enormities to the high displeasure of God and disturbance of the King's peace and his subjects, and to the great hindrance of husbands and artificers which cannot get laborers for their money:

The King's grace therefore, especially desiring that his subjects should above all things eschew the said idleness and feigned occasions, mother and cause of all vices, to the honor and strength of this his realm, hath commanded the statutes which do prohibit such unlawful games and idleness to be published and proclaimed, to the intent that none of his subjects shall pretend ignorance of the same; charging and straightly commanding all and every his said subjects for their degree, havior, and authority, to put the said statutes from henceforth in due and perfect observance and execution, as they will avoid his most high and grievous displeasure and the penalties and punishments for the offenders in such case ordained and provided, the tenor, etc.

It is ordained, established, and enacted that where such misdoers should be by examination committed to the common jail, there to remain as is aforesaid, that the sheriffs, mayors, bailiffs, constables, petty constables, and all other governors and officers of cities, boroughs, and towns, townships, villages and other places, three days after this act now proclaimed, make due search and take or cause to be taken all such vagabonds, idle people, and suspect persons living suspiciously, and them so taken to set in stocks, there to remain by the space of one day and one night, and there to have none other sustenance but bread and water; and after the said day and night passed, to be had out and set at large, and then to avoid the town or place where they be taken, into such city, town, place, or hundred where they were born, or else to the place where they last dwelt or made their abode by the space of three years, and that as hastily as they conveniently may, and there remain and abide. And if eftsoons they be taken with such default in the same town or townships, then to be set likewise in stocks by the space of three days and three nights with like diet as is before rehearsed; and if any person or persons give any other meat or drink to the said misdoers so being in stocks, in form aforesaid, or the same prisoners favor in their misdoing, or them receive or harbor over one night, that then they forfeit for every time so doing 12*d*.

And also it is ordained by the said authority that all manner of beggars not able to work, within six weeks next after proclamation of this act, go rest and abide in his city, town, or hundred where they were born, or else to the place where they last made their abode by the space of three years, there to remain or abide, without begging out of the said city, town, hundred, or place, upon pain to be punished as is aforesaid; and that no man harbor or keep any such beggar in his house over one night, upon the same pain; and that no man be excused by that he is a clerk of the university from whence he saith he cometh, without a letter of vice-chancellor of the university from whence he cometh; nor none calling himself a soldier, shipman, or travelling man, without he bring a letter from his captain or from the town where he landed, and that he then be commanded to go the straight highway into his country. And if he depart not according to such commandment in that behalf to him given, that then he be taken, reputed, and punished as a vagabond. And he that harboreth any such person shall forfeit for every one such person that he harboreth over one night, 12*d*.

And over this, it is ordained by the said authority if any sheriff or other officer before rehearsed execute not the premises, as is abovesaid, of every vagabond, hermit, or beggar able to labor, or clerk, pilgrim, or shipman, as often as any such cometh in his sight, or that he hath thereof any knowledge, within the town or place where he hath authority, rule, or governance, and that as often as any such of the said misdoers abiding thereabout one day and one night depart unexamined and unpunished as is abovesaid, for every misdoer he to lose 3*s*. 4*d*.; and that the lord of every leet within this realm and the sheriff in his tourn have authority to inquire thereof and of all the said defaults and misdemeanors in his leet and tourn, and the lord of the leet to have for every default found as is abovesaid, the forfeiture above limited, and the sheriff to inquire in his return of such escapes within the jurisdictions of his tourn and to have 3*s*. 4*d*. for every such default found in his tourn; and that this penalty limited by this ordinance to be forfeited by any other officer or any other person for non-punishment of vagabonds and other misruled persons within every city where mayor and aldermen be, that the profit of every such penalty be unto the aldermen of every ward where such forfeiture is had or made to his own use and profit. And also it is ordained and enacted by the said authority that it shall be lawful to every man entitled to have the said penalty to distrain for it, in likewise as the lord of any leet may do for amercement and fines had and assessed in the same leet.

And for this, be it enacted by the said authority, that the Chancellor of England or Keeper of the King's Great Seal, the Treasurer of England, the two Chief Judges, the Barons of the King's Exchequer for the time being, and also the justices of assize within their circuit, and every of them, shall have within the shire or shires where they or any of them shall fortune to be, full power and authority to call before them and every of them the sheriffs, mayors, constables, and all other officers of or within the same shire or shires which have to put the statute in execution, and them and every of them to examine of the execution of this statute; and if it can be found by such examination that the said officers or any of them be defaulted in due execution thereof, that then the said officers and every of them so found defective shall have and suffer like pain and punishment as if the said officer or officers had been thereof duly convicted by the due process and course of the King's laws.

And over this, be it enacted that the steward, treasurer, and comptroller of the King's most honorable household for the time shall have full power and authority [to] examine, correct, and punish as is afore rehearsed, being within the precinct and liberty of the verge. Also the mayor and aldermen of the city of London, that is to say, every alderman within his ward and the mayor throughout the whole city, have like power and authority to examine, correct, and punish the said offenders within the said city and liberties of the same, in manner and form abovesaid.

And furthermore it is ordained and enacted by the said authority that none apprentice nor servant at husbandry, laborer, nor servant artificer play at the tables from henceforth, nor at the tennis, closh, dice, cards, bowls, nor any other unlawful games in no wise, out of the 12 days at Christmas; and then to play only in the dwelling house of his master or where the master of the said servant is present, upon pain of imprisonment by the space of one day in the stocks openly; and that the household where dicing, carding, tennis, playing bowls, closh, or any other unlawful games afore rehearsed shall be used otherwise than is afore rehearsed, and then lawfully be presented afore justices of peace, mayor, sheriff in his tourn, and steward in his leet, or by examination had before the said justices of peace, that process be made upon the same as upon indictment of trespass against the King's peace; and that the said misdoer be admitted to no fine under the sum of 6*s.* 7*d.*

And that it be lawful to two of the justices of peace, whereof one shall be of the quorum, within their authority to reject and put away common ale-selling in towns and places where they shall think convenient, and to take surety of the keepers of alehouses of their good behaving by the discretion of the said justices, and in the same to be advised and agreed at the time of their sessions.

Provided always that diminution of punishment of vagabonds and beggars aforesaid may and shall be for wives great with child, and men and women in great sickness, and persons being impotent and above the age of 60 years, by the discretion of him that hath authority to do the said punishment, this act notwithstanding.

Furthermore be it enacted by the said authority that the justices of peace or two of them at the least within their shires, and every shire-sheriff and bailiff within their cities, towns, or boroughs, shall have full power and authority to make four times in the year, that is to say, every quarter once or oftener as by their discretion shall be thought reasonable, through all their shire, a due and diligent secret search, and if they or any of them can find by the reason of the said search any of the said misruled persons, the said misruled persons so found to have like punishment and correction as is aforesaid.

The Preamble of the Statutes of Victuals [5]

And over this, whereas all the King's subjects are daily greatly grieved with the excess of the price of victuals, and in especial his poor subjects laborer which by occasion of such excess cannot live with such convenient wages as hath heretofore been to them taxed by divers statutes therefor provided, to the great costs and hindrance of the King's subjects, and the enhancement of the said wages, contrary to the statutes in such case ordained: the King's grace, of his blessed disposition intending especially the observance of his laws to the best policy and least charge and costs of his subjects, the occasion of the contrary utterly to be avoided and eschewed, hath caused the statute concerning victuals to be published and proclaimed to the intent and charging, etc.

The Statute of Victuals

Also for the common profit of the people it is accorded that [the] minister or officer in city or borough which by reason of his office should [have] the assize of wine and victuals, during the time of his office use no merchandise or wine nor victuals in gross nor by retail; and if any so do, and thereof be attainted, the merchandise whereof he shall be attainted be forfeited to the King, and the third part thereof be delivered as of the King's gift to him at whose suit the trespasser shall be so attainted; and in that case every man shall be received to sue in that behalf.

Victualers

Also fishmongers, butlers, ostlers, brewers, bakers, and all other sellers of victuals, whatsoever they be, shall sell for a reasonable price, having consideration to the price and according to the distance of the places from whence the said victuals [came], shall upon pain of forfeiture of the double value of thing [or] things sold to him that is grieved; and if he will not sue therefor, other shall have the suit that will. And mayors and bailiffs of cities, boroughs, and market towns, and of other towns and places of the sea, have power to inquire of the premises, and to execute and levy the

5. 12 Edward II, c. 6, 1318, *SR 1*, 178.

pains aforesaid. And justices of peace have power to inquire of the defaults of mayors and bailiffs at the suit of the party or of him that will sue; and if they be convict, they shall yield triple damage, and shall make fine unto the King.

The chancellor and treasurer and other of the King's council may make ordinance for prices of wines and fishes.

Also foreigners and aliens may sell fish and victuals to retail in London and elsewhere.

Also he that disturbs a foreigner or an alien for to sell fish in London or any other place, by great or by retail, shall forfeit 40*s.;* and he that will sue shall have the half of the forfeiture.

64. Granting English Citizenship at Calais

[Calais, 8 March 1512, 3 Henry VIII]

PRO (SP 1/2/39*a*): date, MS note, proclaimed at Calais on 8 March; schedule as below. Not in Steele. Text (MS): SP

FORASMUCH as the old ordinances and decrees of this town and marches of Calais concerning mere Englishmen born within this town, whereby many persons were in dread to inhabit themselves, and purchase any lands within the same town and marches,

Wherefore our sovereign lord, King Henry VIII, of his blessed disposition and abundant grace, and also for the tender zeal that his highness beareth towards this town and marches of Calais, for the increase and continuance of Englishmen to be inhabitants within the same, hath granted, and by the advice of his most noble council, is agreed, in manner and form following:

That is to say, it shall be lawful to any man or woman mere English to intermarry, without any license, with any man or woman born within the said town and marches of Calais; and that issue of them to be reputed, had, and taken as mere Englishmen; and [if] any of them or of their issue depart out of the said town and marches and inhabit themselves in any other country out of the King's obeisance, that then they and every of them so departed, to forfeit unto the King their lands wholly, and the quint of their moveable goods, according to the old ordinance thereupon made and provided, and they to be reputed and taken afterwards as strangers;

And that it may be lawful to every man or woman born within the said town and marches of Calais to intermarry, without license, at their pleasure, with any other man or woman born within the said town and marches, and that issue of them may be reputed and taken as good English; and if they or any of their issue depart out of the said town and marches and inhabit themselves in any other country out of the King's obeisance, that then they and every of them so departed, to forfeit unto the King his lands wholly, and the quint of his moveable goods, according to the old ordinance thereupon made and provided; and they to be reputed and taken afterward as strangers forever, any statute, decree, ordinance, or proclamation lately made or passed to the contrary notwithstanding.

65. Commissioning Levy for War against France

[Westminster, 4 November 1512, 4 Henry VIII]

STC 7763 (UM 1,4,280), BM K.T.C. 115.a.4, 4: printed by R. Pynson (London, 1513); schedule as below. Steele 59: date as above. Text (*STC*): BM

FORASMUCH as it is openly and notoriously known unto all persons of Christ's religion that Louis the French King, adversary unto our most dread sovereign and natural liege lord, King Henry VIII, and to this his realm of England, hath moved and stirred, and daily moveth and stirreth by all the subtle means to his power to set and bring schism, variance, and as much as in him lieth, studieth the mean of continual error to be had in the Church of Christ, taking of late upon him, against the wit and mind of our holy father the Pope, the whole court of Rome, and Holy Church, to summon and call a council to be holden at Pisa, whereunto among other of his arrogant presumptions he letted not by plain declaration of his said malicious pretense to summon our holy father the Pope to have there appeared in his proper person, and in the same council presumptuously, contrary to the laws of God and all Holy Church, proceeded, and in the same toward the further execution of his evil malice, and to the intent to have the whole rule and governance of all Holy Church under his dominion and commandment; and that the schism and error should in such manner be sown that it should be right hard to be redressed or withsaid; and without ground, cause, or authority, in the same council caused to be decreed that our said Holy Father should from thenceforth be sequestered of and from all such direction and administration papal, as by the same more at large doth appear;

And howbeit our said Holy Father, for the charitable reformation of the said French King, willing the health of the soul of the said French King, hath for his said presumptions and divers other his manifold offenses, as is before declared and published, the whole realm of France and all territories under the dominion and governance of the said French King to be interdicted; and so under that interdiction yet remain; the said French

King, that not regarding, but always abiding in his said indurate and pervert opinions and erroneous mind, and the decree of the interdiction despising, will not thereby reform himself, but always erroneously defending and maintaining his said obstinate opinions against the voice of Holy Church; and also hath moved, and daily moveth and maintaineth, war and battle against our said Holy Father and the universal Christ's Church in such manner that our said Holy Father, for the succor, maintenance, and defense of his person and of our mother, Holy Church, and for the ceasing of the said schism and errors, hath written and sent for aid and assistance unto our said sovereign lord and to many other Christian princes; which schismatic demeanor of the said French King is and hath been perilous and terrible example to all Christian faith:

For reformation whereof, our said sovereign lord the King, of his blessed and godly disposition for the true faith that his highness beareth unto Almighty God and to our mother, Holy Church, as well for resisting the said purposed malice and errors of his said adversary, by the same adversary against our said Holy Father the Pope and Holy Church borne and maintained, as for that his said adversary hath of late attempted divers enterprises of war as well by sea as by land against his highness and his subjects of this his realm of England, hath prepared and ordained, and purposeth in all hasty speed to prepare and make ready, as well by land as by water, divers and sundry great armies and navies for the intents and defenses beforesaid.

And if in case the said schism and other the premises cannot be by that mean or otherwise reformed, his highness, of his most virtuous and blessed disposition, purposeth by the grace of Almighty God in his most royal person to take his voyage for and about the same which armies and navies and voyages, as is beforesaid. For the same defenses cannot be supported, maintained, and borne without right great costs and charges.

In consideration whereof, and also for that our said sovereign lord in any of the divers and great charges for defense of this his realm in divers sundry wise of late hath borne and sustained; and for the goodness, bounteousness, [. . .], pity, favor, and tender zeal by his highness shewed to his said commons, as evidently is known: the same loving commons, in this present parliament assembled, with the assent of the lords spiritual and temporal in the same parliament in like manner assembled, have granted to our said sovereign lord the King one whole fifteenth and tenth to be had, taken, perceived, and levied of goods, movables, chattels, and other things to such fifteenth and tenth usually contributory and chargeable, within counties, cities, boroughs, and towns and other places of this realm of England in manner and form aforetime used. Except the sum of £6000 thereof fully to be deducted in relief, comfort, and discharge of the port towns, cities, and boroughs of this realm of England, wasted, desolate, and destroyed, or over greatly impoverished, or else to such fifteenth and tenth over greatly charged; the sum of £6000 of the said fifteenth and tenth, after such rate as was before this time made to every shire, to be divided and in such manner and form as in and upon one whole fifteenth and tenth of the last grant of two whole fifteenths and tenths unto our said sovereign lord in this present parliament before the prorogation of the same was had and divided. Except also the lay people and inhabitants within the shire of the city of Lincoln, suburbs and precinct thereof; the lay people and inhabitants within the town of Great Yarmouth, in the shire of Northumberland; and the lay people and inhabitants within the borough of New Shor[ham] in the county of Sussex, now greatly wasted by the sea, and every of them or any of them; for the goods and chattels and other things of the said inhabitants of the said shire, of the said city of Lincoln, suburbs and precinct thereof, or within the town of Great Yarmouth and precinct thereof, or within the said borough of New Shor[ham] to the payment of the said whole fifteenth and tenth, or any part thereof, be not exacted nor compelled, but that they and every of them, in the form abovesaid of this grant, and every parcel thereof, be utterly quit and discharged.

And also provided that this present grant extend not, nor in any wise be prejudicial to the mayor, bailiffs, and commonalty of the town of Cambridge, neither to their successors, as to or for any other charge for any fifteenth or tenth, as is beforesaid, but after such rate as was set by one act made by authority of one parliament holden in the third year of the reign of King Edward IV. That is to say, £15 to the grant of every whole fifteenth and tenth; but that they of any greater charge than in the said act is specified be and stand utterly quit and discharged, this present grant of fifteenth and tenth notwithstanding. The said fifteenth and tenth, the exceptions and deductions aforesaid thereupon had, to be paid in the fifteenth of Easter which shall be in the year of Our Lord 1514.

And over this, be it ordained by authority of this present parliament that the knights elected and returned of and for every shire within this realm for this present parliament, citizens of cities and burgesses of boroughs and towns where collectors have been used to be named or appointed for the collection of any fifteenth or tenth before this time granted, shall name and appoint sufficient and able persons for the collection of the said fifteenth and tenth in every of the said shires, cities, boroughs, and towns, and the names and surnames of every of the said collectors for the said fifteenth and tenth, the said knights, citizens, and burgesses for the shire, city, or borough that they so be for, shall certify before the king in his chancery at this side the Feast of St. Catherine, which shall be in the year of Our Lord 1513. The which said collectors and every of them shall have like allowance upon their account of fees, wages, and reward for the collection of the said fifteenth and tenth, in as large manner and form as any collector or collectors of the fifteenth and tenth have had at any season in time past.

And further be it enacted by the said authority that if any of the said collectors, or any of their deputies or other in their name deputed, or any of them, refuse to allow any deduction or abatement beforetime allowed and made to any town, borough, manor, or other place; ask, require, or take more or greater sum, or in other manner and according to this grant ought to be asked, required, or taken, in or upon any town, borough, manor, or other place: that then two justices of the peace, whereof one shall be of the quorum of every shire or other place where such injury or wrong shall happen to be committed or come in question and variance, at the complaint of the parties or persons so grieved, and every of them, or of the constable or other officer of the said town, borough, or other place, in the name of any party so grieved or wronged, have full power to hear and determine such complaint as well by examination as by bill or otherwise, and therein to do as by the same justices shall be thought convenient and reasonable for the direction, reformation, and ordering thereof, and for the punishment, by their discretion, of the offender in that behalf.

And for the said fifteenth and tenth, as is beforesaid granted, extendeth but unto a small sum toward the said great charge, the said loving commons after, to their powers willing a greater sum toward the said charges to the use of our said sovereign lord, as well in shorter time as in more easy, universal, and indifferent manner to be levied, than such common tare of fifteenth and tenth hath or can be according to the ancient use thereof; willing also the great estates, peers, and nobles of this realm, toward the payment of that greater sum in such easy manner to be charged, that the same estates, peers, and nobles shall have benevolent courage to charge themself in their preparation for them and their retinues or companies toward and for the said defenses: have by the assent of the lords spiritual and temporal in the parliament assembled, granted unto our said sovereign lord one subsidy to be taken and paid of every person underwritten within this realm of England, in manner and form as followeth. That is to say:

Of every duke, £6 13*s*. 4*d*.

Of every marquis, earl, marquess, or countess, £4.

Of every baron, baronet, and baroness, 40*s*.

Of every other knight not being lord of the parliament, 30*s*.

Of every person, man or woman, having lands, tenements, or rents, freehold, copyhold, or ancient demesne, fees, offices, annuities, or corodies, to his own use or other person or persons to his use, to the yearly value of £40 or above, 20*s*.

Of every person, man or woman, having lands, tenements, or rents, freehold, copyhold, or ancient demesne, fees, offices, annuities, or corodies, to his own use or other person or persons to his own use, to the yearly value of £20 or above, and under the yearly value of £40, 10*s*.

Of every like person having lands, tenements, or rents, freehold, copyhold, or ancient demesne, fees, offices, annuities, or corodies, to his own use or other person or persons to his use, to the yearly value of £10 as above, and under the yearly value of £20, 5*s.*

Of every such person having lands, tenements, or rents, freehold, copyhold, or ancient demesne, fees, offices, annuities, or corodies, to his own use or other person or persons to his use, to the yearly value of 40*s.* or above, and under the value of £10 yearly, 2*s.*

Of every such person having lands, tenements, or rents, freehold, copyhold, or ancient demesne, fees, offices, annuities, or corodies, to his own use or other person or persons to his use, to any yearly value under the yearly value of 40*s.*, 12*d.*

Of every person, man or woman born under the King's obedience having goods or chattels movable to the value of £800 or above, 53*s.* 4*d.*

Of every such person having goods or chattels movable to the value of £400 or above, and under the said value of £800, 40*s.*

Of every such person having goods or chattels movable to the value of £200 or above, and under the said value of £400, 26*s.* 4*d.*

Of every such person having goods or chattels movable to the value of £100 or above, and under the value of £200, 13*s.* 4*d.*

Of every such person having goods or chattels to the value of £40 or above, and under the value of £100, 6*s.* 8*d.*

Of every such person having goods or chattels movable to the value of £20 as above, and under the value of the said £40, 40*d.*

Of every such person having goods or chattels movable to the value of £10 or above, and under the value of £20, 20*d.*

Of every such person having goods or chattels movable to the value of 40*s.* or above, and under the value of £10, 12*d.*

Of every alien born, made denizen, having like substance in lands, rents, or other possessions as is beforesaid, or goods or chattels as in any of the rates beforesaid, like sum of money to be taxed as of him that is born under the King's allegiance, and no otherwise.

And of every alien and stranger, not born under the King's allegiance and not made denizen, having any lands, tenements, or other real possession, or goods or chattels movable to any manner of value as is beforesaid, to be charged with and in the double in money, after and in every rate beforesaid, as the person of like value born under the King's obedience is before taxed. And so to pay the same double sum.

Of every laborer, journeyman, artificer, handicraftman, and servant, as well men as women, above the age of 15 years, taking wages or other profits for wages to the value of 40*s.* by year, or above, and being born under the King's allegiance, except women covert-baron, 12*d.*

Of every laborer, journeyman, artificer, handicraftman, and servant, as well men as women, above the said age of 15 years, taking wage or other profit for wage to the yearly value of 20*s.* by year, or above, and under the value of 40*s.*, being born under the King's obedience, women covert-baron except, 6*d.*

66. Prohibiting Grain Forestalling and Unlicensed Provisioning of Army

[Westminster, 15 December 1512, 4 Henry VIII]

PR (C66/619/9*d*): date as above; writ to sheriff of York; schedule as below. Steele 60. Text (MS): PR

FORASMUCH as the King our sovereign lord, by the advice of his council, for the sure keeping of the sea and for the defense of his realm against the enemies of the same, and the letting of the landing of them in any part of his said realm, hath appointed a great number of ships sufficiently apparelled, rigged, and furnished with mariners, soldiers, artillery, and all other things expedient or necessary for the same, to be set in the sea in the beginning of the month of March next coming and to continue upon the same unto the time of winter; and forasmuch as the said army shall require great plenty of victual: our said sovereign lord the King by his commissions, as well under his Great Seal as otherwise, hath assigned divers his trusty servants to purvey and buy for his money, at reasonable price, wheat and other victuals necessary to be had within the said shire of York for the same.

His highness therefore, by the advice aforesaid, straightly chargeth and commandeth that no manner of person of what estate, degree, nation, or condition he be of, by himself or any other, from henceforth engross, forestall or regrate within the said shire of York, or carry and convey out of the said shire of York or any parts of the same into any parts beyond the sea or on this side the sea within this realm of England, any manner of wheat or victuals foresaid, except only the said persons assigned and to be assigned by our said sovereign lord the King by virtue of his commissions under his Great Seal or otherwise, for the victualing of the said army, upon pain of forfeiture of all such wheat and necessary victual, or the value of the same, and further to be punished at the King's will; the one half of the said forfeiture to be taken to the use of our said sovereign lord, and the other half to the use of him or them that shall find, seize, or prove the same. And that no customer, comptroller, searcher, or other officer within any port within the said shire, suffer any such wheat or necessary victual to be conveyed out of the port where any of them be officers, into any part beyond the sea or on this side, upon pain of losing of his office, and further to be punished at the King's pleasure.

67. Providing Victual for Fleet at Southampton and Portsmouth

[Westminster, 15 December 1512, 4 Henry VIII]

PR (C66/619/9*d*): date as above; writ to sheriff of Wilts; similar writs to sheriffs of Sussex, Southampton, Berks, Dorset, Lincoln; schedule as below. *L&P 1*, 1524, 30: writs to York, Hants. Steele 61. Text (MS): PR

FORASMUCH as the King our sovereign lord, by the advice of his council, for the sure keeping of the sea and for the defense of this realm against the enemies of the same and the letting of the landing of them in any part of this his said realm, hath appointed a great number of ships sufficiently apparelled, rigged, and furnished with mariners, soldiers, artillery, and all other things expedient or necessary for the same, to be set to the sea in the beginning of the month of March next coming and to continue upon the same unto the time of winter; and forasmuch also that the said army must for the more part of the said time be victualed in the ports of Southampton and Portsmouth, which cannot be done of the victuals coming and growing of the county of Southampton only, but that it shall be necessary also to take a great part of the said victuals in divers shires nigh adjoining to the same shire: his highness therefore by the said advice hath ordained that the said victuals shall be taken not only within the said shire of Southampton, but also in the shires of Sussex, Southampton, Berks, and Dorset.

Wherefore his highness straightly chargeth and commandeth that no manner of person of what estate, degree, nation, or condition he be of, from henceforth carry or convey, or do to be carried or conveyed, out of this his shire of Wilts into any part beyond the sea or on this side the sea within the realm of England but only into the said ports of Southampton and Portsmouth, any manner of wheat, malt or oats; which grains be very necessary for the said victualing, upon pain of forfeiture of all such wheat, malt, and oats, or the value of the same, and further to be punished at the King's will; the one half of the said forfeiture to be taken to the use of our said sovereign lord, and the other half to go to him or them that shall find, seize, or prove the same. And no customer, comptroller, searcher, or other officer within any part within the said shire suffer any such wheat, malt, or oats to be conveyed out of the port where any of them be officers, into any part beyond the sea or on this side, save only unto the said ports of

Southampton and Portsmouth, upon pain of losing of his office and further to be punished at the King's pleasure.

68. Prohibiting Unlicensed Import of Gascon Wine

[Westminster, 17 December 1512, 4 Henry VIII]

PR (C66/619/9*d*): date as above; writ to sheriffs of London; schedule as below. Steele 62. Text (MS): PR

THE KING our sovereign lord, Henry, by the grace of God King of England and of France and lord of Ireland, for certain great and urgent causes moving him and his council, hath by the advice of the same ordained that no manner of man shall bring nor cause to be brought into this his realm of England any wine of Gascony in no manner of vessel nor bottom whatsoever it be, English or other, upon pain of forfeiture thereof.

Wherefore his highness chargeth and straightly commandeth that no person nor persons whatsoever they be, English or other, in any wise attempt the contrary, upon pain and forfeiture foresaid, except it be by his license expressly obtained in that behalf.

69. Ordering Muster against French Invasion

[Westminster, 28 January 1513, 4 Henry VIII]

PR (C66/619/9*d*): date as above; writ to sheriff of Kent; similar writs to Earl of Oxford for Norfolk and Suffolk, Earl of Oxford and Lord Fitzwater for Essex, Edward Willoughby, Sir John Arundel, and Sir Piers Eggecombe for Cornwall, Lord Brooke for Devon and Dorset, Earl of Arundel for Sussex, Sir John Lisle and Sir William Sandys for Wilts; schedule as below. Steele 63. Text (MS): PR

THE KING our sovereign lord, Henry, by the grace of God King of England and of France and lord of Ireland, having a tender zeal to the wealth, surety, and defense of this his realm of England and of his subjects of the same; and considering that now of late by credible report it is come to his knowledge for certain that his ancient enemy the French King, continuing in his perverse and malicious purpose, hath prepared and put in readiness a great and a strong navy, furnished with men of war, to invade and enter this [the] King our said sovereign lord's realm of England in the month of

February now next ensuing, intending to burn, slay, and destroy all that they may overcome in their most cruel manner.

In consideration whereof, our said sovereign lord the King hath deputed certain captains, knights, and other gentlemen within this his realm in the shires and counties nigh adjoining to the seacoast; and specially within this shire of Kent, the Lord of Abergavenny to conduct and lead the whole power of the shires whither they so be appointed, with the assistance of the sheriffs of the said shires; willing and commanding them and every of them to put themself with their uttermost powers and the powers of the same shires in readiness with all possible diligence to resist the said enemies.

Wherefore our said sovereign lord the King by the advice of his council ordaineth, chargeth, and straightly commandeth that every man being of the age between 60 and 16 within this his shire prepare, and defensible make himself ready in harness to the uttermost of his power, to come and resort unto the said captains, knights, and gentlemen at every place and places as they shall assign them, upon one hour's warning, for the surety of this realm and themself; and that they fail not thus to do, upon their allegiance and the peril that may thereof ensue.

And over that, his said highness straightly chargeth and commandeth that all manner of beacons, watches, and especially in places within this his shire accustomed for the [same, so] our knowledge of the coming and arriving of the said enemies, and knowledge and warning to be given to the country, be had, prepared, ordained, and duly kept, so that hurts and perils that might ensue of the contrary, for lack of the same, be utterly avoided.

70. Providing Victual for London

[Charing, 11 March 1513, 4 Henry VIII]

PR (C66/619/10*d*): date as above; letters patent to the admiral of the navy, all captains, soldiers, victualers, purveyors, commissioners, sheriffs, bailiffs, comptrollers, searchers, officers, ministers, and subjects; schedule as below. Steele 65. Text (MS): PR

FORASMUCH as it is necessarily requisite and behooveful that our city of London be at all times sufficiently furnished and served of victuals, we therefore by these presents will and command you and every of you, that whensoever or in what place within this our realm, or beyond the sea of our army, (the shires of Hampshire, Sussex, Dorset, Wiltshire and Berkshire county excepted), the said victualers, citizens, and purveyors or any other persons assigned for our said city, have bought or shall buy or provide any wheat, malt, or other grains for the use and behoof of our said city, or to be sold in our said city, you permit and suffer them and every of them to have, keep, carry, or convey to our said city for their provision, as well by water as by land, all and singular such victual, from time to time so bought and provided or to be bought and provided for their moneys; without demanding, let, taking, stopping, or keeping, by you or any of you, from them, any of the said victual or any parcel thereof at any time hereafter, neither for the expenses of our said household or for the victualing of our said army nor otherwise, any commissions, letters, placards, proclamations, or other commandment by us in any wise passed or to be passed, to the contrary hereof notwithstanding.

Granting by these presents license to the mayor, aldermen, citizens, and other officers of our said city or other providing for the same, to take and provide for their moneys or wares, from time to time, all such wheat, malt, or other grains as they shall buy, bargain, or purvey for their moneys or wares to the use of the same city, or there to be sold; and the said victual, to keep, carry, convey, and use for the victualing of our said city, as is abovesaid. And that you our said admiral, captains, victualers, soldiers, mariners, commissioners, and purveyors as well for our household as for our army, and all other our said officers and ministers, nor any of you, take nor purvey, for our said household or army or otherwise anywhere, malt or grains that shall be bought within the river of Thames to be sold in our said city.

71. Announcing Alliance with Spain

[Westminster, 20 April 1513, 4 Henry VIII]

BM MS Arundel 26, 54*v:* date as above; writ to sheriffs of London and Middlesex: schedule as below. *CSPSpanish 2,* 97: league against France reported on 5 April. Steele 66. Text (MS): Arundel

THE KING our sovereign lord, Henry VIII, by the grace of God King of England and of France and lord of Ireland, doth you to understand that, to the laud of God, the defense of Christ's Church, and for the tranquillity and peace of the Christian religion, and recovery and obtaining of the inheritance of our said sovereign lord the King, and of other Christian princes to them rightwisely belonging and appertaining; and by Louis the French King and his adherents with force and violence and against right and equity usurped, detained, and withholden: there is appointed, accorded, and concluded betwixt his highness and the most high and mighty Christian princes, the Emperor and the King of Aragon, as well for himself as for the most excellent lady, the Queen of Castile, and their heirs and successors and all their realms, countries, lands and seigniories, their vassals, subjects, allies and confederates spiritual and temporal, an entire, firm, faithful, and perpetual amity, league, confederation, and peace, by land and water, to endure forevermore.

And amongst other great and notable matters right goodly, honorable, and profitable for our said sovereign lord the King, and of this his realm and of his subjects of the same, and for the other princes before rehearsed and of their realms and subjects expressed in the treaty of the said league, amity, and confederation, it is specially ordained, accorded, and concluded by the ambassadors of every party before expressed, sufficiently authorized in that behalf, that for the intent afore specified our said sovereign lord the King and the other high and mighty Christian princes before named, within 30 days from the date of the said treaty or league, amity, and confederation, next and immediately to be accomplished, by their proclamations shall openly declare, and every of them shall declare himself, enemy to the foresaid Louis the French King; and that they and every of them, within a certain time now shortly following, at their costs and expenses, by themself or their sufficient captain or captains, against the said French King, in divers and sundry places of the realm of France and the countries obeisant unto the said French King, shall make battle invasive with effect to the most annoyance of their foresaid common enemy the French King, with potential armies, mightily and well apparelled, as well on foot as on horseback, with artillery and other instruments of war in such case necessary and requisite. And also that neither our said sovereign lord the King nor none of the said high and mighty Christian princes in the said league confederate shall suffer any of their subjects to serve their said enemy the French King in battle and to take wages of their said enemy, but that our said sovereign lord the King and the other Christian princes before named, and every of them, solemnly and openly shall forbid, prohibit, and command, at time of publication of the said league, amity, and confederation, that none of their subjects, upon pain of their lives and forfeiture of all their goods, so to do or attempt the same; and if the said subjects do not obey their said prince's commandment as is aforesaid, that they to suffer death without pardon or remission for the same, as in the said treaty of league, amity, and confederation more plainly is contained.

The King's highness, ensuing the said agreements and conclusions, and graciously minded to execute and to accomplish that to his highness appertaineth, publisheth, and openly declareth himself, by this his present proclamation, enemy unto the said Louis the French King, and thereof giveth to all his subjects perfect knowledge and understanding: willing and commanding all his said subjects to accept and take, and in every behalf ordain and prepare themself accordingly. And over that, the King's highness straightly forbiddeth, chargeth, and commandeth all and every of his subjects, upon pain of death and loss of all their goods, that none of them do serve his said common enemy the French King, his heirs or his successors, in battle, or take wages of the same; and for disobeying of this the King's commandment, to suffer the same as before is specified, without any pardon or remission to be obtained in that behalf. And the King's pleasure is that this proclamation be sufficient advertisement now, and publication to every person that it toucheth, to the intent that no person have cause to pretend ignorance in the same.

72. Limiting Transport of Army to France

[Knole, 17 May 1513, 5 Henry VIII]

TR (C76/194/7): date as above; writ to constable of Dover and warden of Cinque Ports; similar writs to sheriffs of Sussex, Southampton, and to king of arms; schedule as below. Rymer *13*, 369. Steele 67. Text (MS): TR

Forasmuch as the King our sovereign lord, Henry, by the grace of God King of England and of France and lord of Ireland, hath now by God's grace decreed and fully determined in his own most noble person to pass over the sea with his armies royal against his ancient enemy, Louis the French King and his adherents, his highness by the advice of his council, for the sure conveyance of his most loving subjects prepared to pass in our said sovereign lord the King's armies in form aforesaid, hath ordained, constituted, and assigned by his sufficient commission under his Great Seal, his right trusty and well-beloved the Lord Mountjoy, and his well-beloved servants William Atclyffe and Miles Gerrard, to survey, appoint, limit, and assign to all and singular captains and other his well-beloved subjects of the said armies, and other their retinues in the ports of Dover, Sandwich, Winchelsea, Hastings, and Rye, and in other ports, creeks, and places whatsoever they be within the realm of England where the said captains and other the King's subjects of the said armies shall happen to take passage, such and as many ships and other vessels for their sure passage over the sea as the said commissioners by their discretions shall and may perceive and think necessary, requisite, and behooveful, according to such instructions as the same commissioners have by the King's commandment to them delivered.

* Wherefore our said sovereign lord the King willeth and straightly chargeth and commandeth by these presents all and every person and persons of what estate, degree, or condition he or they be of, that none of them presume to enter or ship themself, their baggage, or their horses or any other their goods in any manner ship or ships or other vessel concerning the said passage, but they to the said ships or vessels by the King's said commissioners, by their writings apparent in that behalf, be first appointed

and assigned; and that no captain nor any other person or persons disobey the said commissioners or any of them in executing the premises, or presume to the contrary in this the King's high proclamation upon pain of the King's most grievous displeasure; and over that to be committed to ward, there to remain without bail or mainprize unto such time as they and every of them so offending have made fine and ransom at the King's will and pleasure.

And over that our said sovereign lord the King straightly chargeth and commandeth by this his present proclamation all and singular his true, faithful, and loving subjects that they and every of them be unto his said commissioners, in the premises, from time to time, assistant, helping and attendant as appertaineth, upon pain of our said sovereign lord the King's most grievous displeasure.

73. Proclaiming Statutes and Ordinances of War for Calais

[London, ca. 15 May 1513, 5 Henry VIII]

STC 9333 (UM 11,62,1489), HM 9333: printed by R. Pynson (London, 1513); schedule as below. Another edition, *STC* 9334: printed by T. Berthelet (London, 1544). *L&P* 2(2), 144: payment to R. Pynson for printing. Hall 23*v:* 8,000 men at Calais about the middle of May. Rymer 13, 369. Not in Steele. Text (*STC*): HM

Forasmuch as it is often seen that man's reason, whereby he should discern the good from the evil and the right from the wrong, is many times by seduction of the Devil, worldly, covetous, and sensual appetites, repressed and vanquished; whereupon commonly ensues discords, murders, robberies, divisions, disobeisance to sovereigns, subversion of realms, and destruction of people, so that where these reign, victory in time of war and justice in time of peace be utterly damped and exiled: therefore emperors, princes and governors of time past, for refraining of such inordinate appetites, and punishment of those folks which rather eschew to offend for fear of bodily pain or losses of goods than for the love of God or justice, full wisely and politicly ordained divers laws serving to the same purpose as well in time of war as peace.

Semblably our sovereign lord Henry, of this name the VIII, by the grace of God King of England and of France and lord of Ireland, intending by the same grace with all goodly speed to pass over the sea in his own person with an army and host royal for the repressing the great tyranny of the French King now lately committed and done, as well in usurping upon

Christ's Church and the patrimony of the same and in raising, nourishing, and maintaining a detestable schism in the said Church, to the great inquietation of all Christendom, as also in detaining by violence realms, lands, seigniories, and dominions of divers and many Christian princes, disturbing, and inquieting by such seditious, ambitious, and contentious means the state's tranquillities and restfulness of all Christian regions, to the manifest danger of his highness and this his realm of England and subjects of the same, unless the inordinate appetite of the said French King be speedily with might and power repressed and resisted. And inasmuch as for the honor of his grace, surety of his host, and for the achieving of his most noble purpose, it appertaineth and behooveth as well toward his folk of the war in justice by the ministers of the law as to arraign them in battle by the chieftains of his army; his highness by the advice of such lords of his blood, captains of his army, and other folk as be of his council, hath made, ordained, and established certain statutes and ordinances hereafter ensuing.

First, that all manner men of the King's host, of what nation, estate, or condition soever they be, be obeisant unto the King our sovereign lord, upon pain of drawing, hanging, and quartering. And over that, that every man aforesaid, the King's lieutenant, the chief captains of the foreward and rearward for the time being only except, which lieutenant and chief captains for their persons be reserved only to the obeisance of the King's highness and to his lieutenant in his absence, shall be obeisant unto the marshal of the host for the time being, upon pain of death. And that also he and they obey and duly keep all such proclamations, ordinances, and statutes as now be or hereafter shall be on the behalf of our said sovereign lord made and proclaimed, upon the pains within the said proclamations, ordinances, and statutes, or any of them, comprehended.

For Holy Church

Also that no man be so hardy irreverently to touch either the holy sacrament of God's Body, or the box or the vessel which the same is in, upon pain to be drawn and hanged therefore.

Also that no man be so hardy to rob nor to pill Holy Church of any good or ornament that belongeth thereunto, nor to slay nor to take prisoner any man or woman of Holy Church, religious or other, but if he be armed; or else that he or she aid, abet, or support the King's enemies with goods, victual, armor, artillery, or other thing defensible, after the King's proclamation made to the contrary; nor to enforce any woman, religious or other, upon pain of death. And if any person of the church so aiding, abetting, or supporting the King's enemies be taken for the same or for suspicion thereof, the King will that he be brought afore the captain of the taker, and by the captain to the King or the marshal of the host, upon pain of imprisonment and further to be punished as it shall please the King; the said taker to be rewarded after the havior and demeanor of the prisoner.

Also that no manner man without sufficient authority or commandment take from any house of religion, or of St. Anthony, though they have not the King's safeguard, nor of any other place, person, town, or country, having safeguard of the King, any manner goods or victuals without the agreement and will of the wardens of the same places or persons, upon pain to be imprisoned and his life at the King's will.

For harborage

Also that no man be so hardy to go before the battle, but that every man keep himself in due order under the banner or pennant of his lord, master, or captain, except harboragers, the names of whom shall be delivered and taken to the marshal by their said lords, masters, or captains, upon this pain: he that in this offendeth shall be put from his horse and harness both, to be committed unto the ward of the marshal unto the time he hath made such fine as shall be cessed by the marshal to the King's use, and found surety that he shall no more offend.

Also that no lord nor captain, nor lords nor captains harborager, take no lodging without deliverance of the marshal of the lodgings, or his deputy or deputies having his authority; and that no soldier take no lodging without it be delivered by his lord or captain's harborager, upon pain of imprisonment and to make fine at the King's pleasure. And that after time that the harborage is assigned and delivered, that no man be so hardy himself to dislodge, nor to disarray, for any thing that may fall, without commandment of him that hath power: upon pain of horse and harness to be put in arrest of the marshal to the time he have made fine with him to the King's use as above, and moreover their bodies at the King's will.

For musters

Also when it shall like the King to command musters to be taken of his host, it is ordained that no captain be so hardy to have or to show other men in his musters than those that be with himself retained, and withhold for the same voyage without fraud: upon pain to be holden false and reproved, and his body to be imprisoned and punished at the King's will. And if he be the second time thereupon convict and found faulty, then to die for it. And that in likewise no man come nor appear at any muster under any captain, except he be as afore is said retained with him for that voyage, upon pain of imprisonment at the King's will.

Also the commissioners, when they take the musters, shall make captains and petty captains with their retinues to be sworn that they shall be good and true to the King our sovereign lord, and that they shall to their powers keep his cries and ordinances, and serve him truly against all his enemies, no person reserved.

Also they shall swear whether that the horse and harness that they have at that season be their own or their master's or captain's or any, and that they shall not without license of their captains depart the company.

Also that the said commissioners shall diligently inquire and see that every man coming unto the musters have all his harness necessary and as appertaineth for him without any guile or subtlety. And in especial at the first muster, that every archer have his bow and arrows whole; that is to wit, in arrows 30, or 23 headed and whole in a sheaf at the least. And for the more surety in this case, the said commissioners to cause every soldier to swear that his harness, bow and arrows be his own, or his master's or captain's.

And also that no man that once mustered and was admitted for an archer alter or change himself into any other condition without the King's especial license, upon pain of imprisonment at the King's will.

That captains make payment to
their soldiers of their wages

Also it is ordained that every captain, petty captain, and all other having under them retinue of any soldier or soldiers at the King's wages, shall pay to their retinue of soldier or soldiers the wages rateably as is allowed unto them by the King our sovereign lord or the treasurer of his wars, without lessing or withdrawing of any part thereof and for as long time as they shall receive wages for him; except only such servants as be at the household wages and finding of the said captains, whose wages the said captains may retain to their own uses for their said finding. This payment to be made unto the said retinues by their captains or petty captains of soldier or soldiers always within six days next and immediately after, as the said captains, petty captains, and other shall have received their wages of the King or of the treasurer of the wars or of their lords and masters. Upon the penalty that which offendeth therein shall forfeit to the King all his goods and chattels and his body to prison at the King's will, except he be reasonably letted in that behalf; whereof he shall within the same six days duly certify the said treasurer of the wars.

And also it shall be lawful to every man finding him grieved in this behalf to complain him unto the treasurer of the wars, where as he shall find his sufficient remedy in this case.

For departing from the host
without license

Also that no man depart the stall without leave or license of his lord or master, upon the pain that he that otherwise departeth to be arrested and to be in the ward of the marshal, and at the King's will his life; and also to lose all his winning of that day, reserved to his lord or master the thirds of his winning, and to the lord of the stall the surplus of the same winning the same day. Also that no lord nor captain license any servant of his to depart from the stall without knowledge and license of the chief captain of the stall.

For them that make themselves captains to withdraw men from the host

Also that no man by raising of banner or pennant of any arms, images, or other token, or any otherwise assemble people to withdraw them out of the host to go to any other place without the King's authority, upon pain to be drawn, hanged, and quartered. And that no man follow nor ensue any such person upon the pain to be hanged. And as well the raisers of the said banner or pennant and assembler of people as the followers to be reputed as traitors and to forfeit to the King all their lands, goods, and chattels forever.

Also that no man make any unlawful assemblies of the King's people or make any bonds, conspiracies, routs, or conventicles, or raise or engender murmurs or grudges against the King or any person of his host, whereby might ensue murder, division, dissension, sedition, exhortation, stirring, or commotion of the people in the host, to parts taking or bonds making upon the same pain; and that every man be sworn to detect the same conspiracies.

For keeping of watch and ward

Also that every man be obeisant to his captain, and under his captain keep his watch and his ward, stall and foray, and to do all that belongeth to a soldier to do, upon pain his horse and harness to be put in the ward of the marshal unto the time that he that so offendeth hath agreed with his captain after the ward of the court.

Also that every captain keep duly his watch, ward, stall, and foray with as many men of arms and archers as to him shall be assigned, but if he have a cause reasonable first allowed before the marshal; and to abide upon his ward, watch, and stall the term to him limited without departing from it no way, but if it be by the assignment or license of him by the which the said watch, ward, and stall is made: upon pain his body to be imprisoned and to stand at the King's will. Also that every captain have day and night watch within his lodging, upon pain of losing four days wages.

That no man disarray him in the battle for no scry that cometh in the host

Also that no tidings nor for no manner of scry that may come in the host, no man move him in disarray out of the battle if they ride or go, but by leave of the chieftain: upon pain that he that so offendeth shall be put from his horse and harness to the ward of the marshal unto the time he have made his fine with him to the King's use, and found surety that he shall no more so offend; and at the second time his body to stand at the King's will.

For unlawful scries

Also that none unreasonable nor outrageous scry be in the host by day nor night, upon pain that he that is found the beginner thereof to die therefor, and the remnant to be imprisoned and their bodies to be punished at the King's will. And he that certifieth who is the beginner shall have 40*s*. for his labor of the marshal.

Also that every captain keeping the host that shall fortune to have soldier of his retinue to be discharged or to depart out of his company or to be dead, be it naturally or by murder or slaughter, within 10 days next and immediately ensuing his said discharge, departing, or death, certify by bill his name, with the day of his discharge, departing, or death, unto the treasurer of the wars. And if the same captain be with any retinue in garrison or elsewhere out of the host by the King's commandment, that then he make the said certificate in all goodly haste, upon pain to forfeit to the King all his goods and chattels and his body to prison at the King's will. And that no captain nor petty captain, into the place of any of his soldier or soldiers as above is said discharged, departed, or dead, in any wise take another, except it be by the sight and allowance of the treasurer of the wars, upon pain of imprisonment of his body and further punishment at the King's will.

For scries made by enemies in the host

Also if any scry fall in the host by enemies after the army be lodged, that every captain of the King's ward draw him to the King, and captains of the other wards draw them to the chieftain of the ward where he is lodged, leaving his lodging sufficiently kept, except the enemies fall in that side where he is lodged; and then in this case the said captain shall abide there himself and all his men, and to send word to the chief captain of the ward, upon pain of imprisonment and further to be punished at the King's will.

For robbing of merchants coming to the market and ravishing of women and also murder

Also that no man rob no victualer nor merchant nor none other person coming unto the market with victual or other merchandises for the refreshing of the host, or returning from the same, upon pain of death. Nor that no man of the King's host rob any other of the same of horse meat or man's meat, upon pain of imprisonment, and his body to be punished at the King's will; nor of any other goods, upon pain of death; nor also no man murder nor rob no manner of person, except he be the King's enemy, upon pain of death; nor ravish no woman, upon the said pain.

For the resisting of justice

Also if any man be judged to the death by the King's marshal or any other judge ordinary or any other officer lawful, no manner man be so hardy, be it by setting hand on the condemned or otherwise, to resist the execution of the judgment: upon pain that if the said condemned be a traitor, he that is the chief to have the same death that unto him belongeth; and all they that be participant or consenting to have their heads stricken off. And if it be any other cause criminal, the causer of the resisting to have the same death that the said judged should have, and the remnant at the King's will.

For them that break the King's arrest

Also that every man obey unto the King's sergeants, porters of places, and all other officers having authority to arrest, made by the King or the marshal or by any other officers of authority; and that no man be so hardy to break their arrest, upon pain of imprisonment and his body at the King's will. And if the prisoner disobeying the said arrest maim any of the said officers, then to die therefor; and if he grievously hurt or wound any of them, then to be imprisoned and his body at the King's will.

For good rule to be kept

Also that every lord, captain, and petty captain, having any retinue great or small, see for the good rule and guiding of his people at his parcel and charge, as he will answer for them to the King.

Also that after the watch shall be set, unto the time it be relieved in the morning, no manner of man make no shouting, blowing of horns, nor none other whistling or great noise, but if it be trumpets by a special commandment, upon pain of imprisonment and further to be punished at the discretion of the marshal.

Also that no man take upon him to bear no new arms other than he is born to of blood, without the advice of officers of arms, where through strife and contention might fall in the host, upon pain to be punished at the King's pleasure and to be reproached for the same.

Also that no captain, having any carriage, appoint for the attendance upon his carriage any more soldiers of the King's wages but such and as many as shall be requisite for making of his lodging and setting up of his tents, halls, or pavilions, upon pain the captain to lose his month's wages and the soldier imprisoned at the King's will.

Also that every horseman at the first blast of the trumpet do saddle his horse, at the second to bridle, at the third to leap on his horse's back to wait on the King or his lord or captain. And that every man wait upon the standard of his own lord and captain, and not to depart therefrom, nor to meddle with none other companies in riding nor going, but such as be commanded, as harboragers and other carriers, as is above rehearsed in the article of harborage. Upon pain of imprisonment and further to [be] punished at the King's will.

For dicing, carding, and all manner of games

Also that no man play at dice, cards, tables, closh, handout, nor at none other game whereby they shall waste their money or cause debates to arise by the same. And if any so be found playing at any of these games, that for the first time he or they shall be committed to ward, there to remain eight days and to lose all such money as they or any of them play for; the one half to the provost of the marshal and the other half to him that so findeth them playing. And if any of the said army be found twice playing, he shall be committed to the provost's ward, there to remain a month and to forfeit a month's wages; the one half to the King and the other half to the finder. Provided always that he that so findeth any of them warn the treasurer of the wars incontinent after he hath so found them, or as soon as he may, or else to take no profit of that part of the said wages. And if any so be found the third time playing he to be committed to ward, there to abide the King's pleasure and to have such further punition as shall please the King.

For bordel keeping in the host

Also that no man bring with him any manner of woman over the sea, upon pain of forfeiture of their goods to the marshal and their bodies to be imprisoned, there to remain at the King's will. And that no man hold no woman within his lodging beyond the sea, upon pain of imprisonment and loss of a month's wages. And that no common woman presume to come within the King's host, nor nigh the same by the space of three miles, upon pain if any so be taken to be burned upon the right cheek at the first time. And if any be taken with the host, or within three miles of the same, after she or they have be so burned, then she or they to be put into ward of the provost marshal, there to remain in prison as long as shall please the marshal and to have further punition as by him shall be thought convenient.

For debate making

Also that no man make debate, strife, nor contention, for any hatred or malice of time passed nor for time to come, whereby any man be slain: upon pain of him or them that is or shall be raisers of the said debate, strife, or contention, or causers or partners of the murder, to be hanged therefor. Or if it happen any man scry his own name or his captain's, lord, or master to make arising of the people, by the which any affray do fall in the host, he that in such wise scrieth shall be drawn and hanged therefor. And he or they that shall make such scry, though no affray fall thereof, to be committed to the ward of the marshal and to have punition at the King's pleasure.

For barretors

Also that no man debate for arms, prisoners, lodging, for none old cause or quarrel or other thing whereby any riot, contention, or debate may grow in the host, upon pain of imprisonment and further punition at the King's pleasure. Nor that no man take part in any affray, but utterly apply him to appease the same, upon the pain aforesaid. And if any man find him grieved for any matter, cause old or new, let him shew his grievance to his captain, and his captain to the marshal, and right shall be to him ministered.

For them that give men reproach

Also that no man give no reproach to none other by cause of the country that he is of; that is to say, be he French, English, Northern, Welsh or Irish, or of any other country whence soever he be of. Nor that no man say no villainy to none other for no cause, through the which villainy-saying may fall sudden manslaughter, raising of the people, dissension, debate, or division in the host; upon pain all such barretors to be imprisoned for as long as it shall please the King.

For them that cry havoc

Also that no man be so hardy to cry havoc, upon pain of him that is found beginner to die therefor, and the remnant to be imprisoned and their bodies to be punished at the King's will.

For burning

Also that no man without commandment special of the King or of his head officer burn willfully any town or house, upon pain of death, except the King's enemies be within it and can be none otherwise taken.

For burying of carrion

Also the King straightly chargeth and commandeth that if it happen that his host tarry by the space of three days or above in one place or ground, be it at siege or otherwise, that then every man keep clean his lodging, not suffering any carrion, filth, or any other unwholesome or infective stinking air to be in or near the same his lodging, but forthwith to bury the same deep in the earth upon pain to be punished after the discretion of the marshal.

For wasters of victual

Also if any man find wine or other victual, that he take himself as much as he needeth and that he save the remnant to other of the host without any destruction, upon pain to be imprisoned for as long as it shall please the King. And that no man of the host use forestalling or regrating of any victual within the host or brought towards the same, upon pain of forfeiture of all his goods and chattels and his body to be imprisoned and further to be punished at the King's will.

For them that take horse or oxen from men going to the plow in countries won or patised

Also that no man take no horses nor oxen in country won or patised, from any man going to plow, or any other laborer, but if the provost and his company and the purveyors of the ordnance which shall have sufficient commission in that behalf, upon pain of death. And that the said provost company and purveyors of the said ordnance see true contentation according to the cessing and seizing of the provost marshal had in that behalf. Upon pain for his or their first default to be committed to ward, and forfeit to the King his or their month's wages; and the second time to forfeit to the King his other movable goods, and their bodies to be in prison during the King's pleasure if the default be found in any of them. And if the default be found in any other person that owe to pay and discharge the said provost company and purveyors against the said countries and people so won and patised, then they that so offend to have like punishment that the provost's company and purveyors of the ordnance should have had in that behalf. And that it be lawful to the master of the ordnance to send for pioneers into what country won or patised where he shall think necessary; and that the purveyors certify the provost marshal what number of horse or oxen will serve him, and that by his advice the said purveyor draw to such quarter as shall be well understand most necessary by the said provost, taking of him his bill to the intent that he send none other men into the quarter that the said purveyors shall take his horse and oxen in.

For keeping of the country

And also if any country or lordship be won, either by free will offered unto the King's obeisance or otherwise, that no man be so hardy to rob nor pill, or take them prisoners after the peace is proclaimed, upon pain of death. And if any man, of what degree soever he be, come unto the King's obeisance, that no man take him, rob him, or pill him, upon the same pain: so that he or they that thus will obey bear a Cross of St. George.

For justice to be kept within
the retinue of the ordnance

And if any of the said retinue of the ordnance rob or slay any of their own company or make any debate or affray or have any demand or question among themselves, that then it be reformed, judged, and punished by the master of the ordnance and such as he shall call to him. Always provided if any man find himself grieved after any final sentence, that he be at his appeal afore the marshal at all seasons and for all causes made between any of them and any other person of the army. That then, they or any of them abide the judgment of the marshal and his court.

For taking of prisoners

Also it is ordained and enacted that all Kings and King's sons, Dukes and Duke's sons, Lieutenants General, Great Constables, or any of the Chief Marshals of France, or of any other regions or provinces, or any of the blood royal, bearing arms royal, that shall happen to be taken by any person of the King's army, shall stand only prisoner to the King our sovereign lord. And that no man take upon him to deliver or put to ransom any such King, Prince, or any other personage in this act afore rehearsed, upon pain of death; and that the taker of any such person bring him immediately to the King or his lieutenant, and he shall have for his taking such sufficient reward as shall accord with reason.

Also be it at battle, deed of arms, or other place where prisoners may lawfully be taken, he that first may have his faith shall have him for his prisoner, so he take from him his weapon or some token, and shall not need to abide upon him to the end of the journey; and none other shall mowe take him for his prisoner, but if so be that the said prisoner be found with weapon ready to inbard, in which case his ransom shall equally be dealt between them, the keeping of the prisoner always reserved to the last taker finding surety for the safe-keeping of the same prisoner.

Also if any manner deed of arms be done whereby any enemy is borne to the earth, he that first hath borne him to earth shall have him prisoner, but if so be that after he be relieved and found standing at his defense another cometh and taketh the faith of the said prisoner; then the smiter down shall have the one half and the taker of the faith the other half, with the keeping of the said prisoner making surety to his partner for the other half.

Also if any man have taken a prisoner and the victory had upon their enemies in battle, skirmish, chase, or otherwise, [and] any other man for any cause kill the said prisoner, he that so doth shall die for it.

For them that ransom their prisoners and sell
them without leave of their lords or captains

Also that no man be so hardy to ransom or sell his prisoner without special license of his captain that indenteth with the King under his license and seal, upon pain to forfeit his part in the prisoner unto his captain and he to be under arrest of the marshal unto the time he have agreed with his captain. In likewise that no captain ransom or sell his prisoner without license of the King or his treasurer of the wars, upon pain of forfeiture of the same prisoner unto the King; and that no man buy no such prisoners upon pain to lose the gold and money that he payeth for him, and the prisoner to be arrested to the captain aforesaid.

Also the captain, upon notice had of the said prisoner and license asked by his soldier, shall not, without cause reasonable shewed unto the marshal, let the said soldier to take his best advantage of the said prisoner; howbeit that if the captain will give as much for the said prisoner as another, he shall have the prisoner and preferment.

Also if any man take any enemy the which hath been sworn and had billet, or any man which oweth legiance unto our liege lord the King; that is to wit, English, Welsh, Irish, or any other of such condition; that then as soon as he is come into the host or elsewhere, he be brought by the taker into the ward of the marshal, upon pain to have the same death that the same traitor or enemy shall have. And he that any such bringeth in shall have 100*s*. of the King or of the marshal for his travail at the King's charge.

Also if any man take any prisoner forthwith as he cometh into the host, he bring his prisoner unto his captain or master, upon pain of losing of his part to his foresaid captain or master; and then that his said captain, if he be within the host, certify the marshal within two days. And if he be out of the host in garrison or elsewhere, that he certify the said marshal as soon as he conveniently may, and declare his name and havior by bill as nigh as he can after his knowledge, so that he be not led none other way, upon pain to lose his part to him that shall give first to the marshal knowledge thereof, and his body to be imprisoned and punished at the King's will. And that every man do keep or do to be kept his prisoner, that he ride not nor go at large in the host nor in lodgings but if ward be had upon him, upon pain of losing of the same prisoner. Reserving to his lord or master his thirds of the whole, if he be not party of the default; and the second part to him that first shall accuse him, and the third part to the marshal; and also moreover his body in arrest at the King's will. Also that he suffer not his prisoner to go out of the host for his ransom nor for none other cause without safe-conduct of the King, his lieutenant, or the marshal, upon the pain aforesaid.

Also that every captain, in likewise, present and show his prisoner unto the treasurer of the wars, to the intent the King may be answered of his part, upon pain of forfeiture of the same prisoner unto the King.

Also that the marshal from eight days to eight, during the King's army, do certify the treasurer of the wars of all such certificates as shall be brought in by the captains or any other unto him, as well of his own as of other, all manner prisoners taken by any man in the host certified unto him, upon pain of running in the King's indignation and to forfeit the double of the value to the King of the said prisoner or prisoners so concealed. And like as every captain and soldier is bound to bring in and certify his prisoner under the form above rehearsed, so in the same wise and under semblable penalties they and every of them shall bring in and certify all other prizes, goods, and chattels by them won by the war.

For paying of thirds

Also that every man pay his thirds to his captain, lord, and master of all manner winnings by war, and that as well those that be not in fold but lodging or hosting under the banner or pennant of their captain, upon pain to lose his part of his foresaid winning to his captain, and his body to be in ward of the marshal unto the time he have agreed with his foresaid master. And also that every captain pay unto the King as well the third part of his own winnings of the war as the third of the thirds whereof each of his retinue shall be answering unto him, of which thirds and thirds of thirds every captain shall be accountable before the treasurer of the King's wars, upon pain of forfeiture of the said winnings unto the King.

For giving of safe-conducts or *congés*
and for breaking of them

Also that no man give no safe-conduct to prisoner nor to no other, nor license no enemy to come nor to go out of the host nor into the host, upon pain of forfeiture all his goods to the King and his body to be imprisoned at the King's will, except the King his lieutenant, or the marshal if he have special commission so to do. And that no man be so hardy to break the King's safe-conduct, his lieutenant or his said marshal having such authority, upon pain to be hanged and drawn and his goods and inheritances to be forfeited to the King.

For giving of safeguards

Also that no man grant no safeguard by writing nor otherwise to no noble person nor for the apatising of any country except the King, upon pain of imprisonment and his body to be punished at the King's will. Nor that no man grant no safeguard to no victualer except the marshal and provost of the King's host, upon pain abovesaid.

For them that bear not a bond
or a Cross of St. George

Also that every man going in action or battle, of what estate, condition, or nation he be, of the King's party and host, except he be a bishop or officer of arms, bear a Cross of St. George sufficient and large, upon the pain that if he be wounded or slain, in the default thereof he that so woundeth or slayeth him shall bear no pain therefore. And if he for any cause pass the bonds of the field, that then he bear openly a Cross of St. George with his captain's cognizance, upon pain to be imprisoned and punished at the King's will. And that no soldier bear no cognizance but the King's and his captain's, upon pain of death. And that none enemy bear the said sign of St. George but if he be prisoner and in ward of his master, upon pain of death.

For making of raids

Also that no man make no raids by day nor by night but by license and knowledge of the King or of the chieftains of the wards, so that the chieftains may know what way they draw them, to the intent they may have succor and help if need be, upon pain of them that herein offend, their bodies and goods to be at the King's will.

For assault making without license

Also that none assault be made to castle, town, strength, or fortress by archers nor by none other commoners without the will and presence of a captain thereunto appointed by the King or his lieutenant, upon pain of imprisonment. And if any assault be made by chance or adventure, then as soon as the King, his lieutenant, or the marshal send for to cease to the said assault, that then no man be so hardy to assault after. And if any man do it, he shall be corrected by imprisonment of his body and lose all the goods gotten at the said assault.

For the withdrawing of men's servants from their masters

Also that no man be so hardy to take or withdraw servant from other, the which is in covenant with him for the voyage, as well soldier, man of arms, archer, groom, or page, after time he is known or challenged by his master. Upon pain his body to be imprisoned to the time he have agreed with the party complainant after the ward of the court.

For women that lie in childbed

Also that no man be so hardy to go into no chamber or lodging where that any woman lieth in childbed, her to rob nor pill of no goods, the which [be]longeth unto her refreshing, nor for to make none affray wherethrough she and her child might be in any disease or despair: upon pain he that in such wise offendeth shall lose all his goods, half to him that accuseth, and half to the marshal; and himself to be dead, but if the King give him grace and pardon.

For children within the age of 14 years

Also that no man be so hardy to take no children within the age of 14 years but if he be a lord's son or else a worshipful gentleman's or rich man's son or a captain's. And that as soon as he hath brought him into the host or into the garrison where he is abiding, he bring him to his lord, master, or captain, upon pain of losing horse and harness and his part of the same child; reserving to his lord, master, or captain his duty, so that they be not consentant unto the said default. And also that the said lord, master, or captain bring him unto the King within eight days.

Also forasmuch as our said sovereign lord, for the inward love, tender zeal, and entire affection which he beareth naturally to his subjects being of his said host and army, would be loathest and most displeasant to see or understand any of them to do the offense whereby he should deserve the least punishment by the said ordinances provided: his highness therefore desireth and tenderly prayeth his said subjects to consider and understand that his good speed in his said journey, the honor of his realm, and the weal and surety of the same his subjects, standeth upon the observation of the said statutes. Wherefore though it be to the greatest heinousness and displeasure, yet must he of necessity, when the case it requireth, see the said statutes executed, and the offenders punished.

In consideration whereof he willeth and straightly chargeth his said subjects to have themself in so good a way that in no wise they offend the said statutes. And to the intent they have no cause to excuse them of their offenses by pretense of ignorance of the said ordinances, his highness hath, over and above the open proclamation of the said statutes, commanded and ordained by way of imprint divers and many several books containing the same statutes to be made and delivered to the captains of his host, charging them as they will avoid his great displeasure to cause the same twice, or once at the least, in every week wholly to be read in the presence of their retinue.

Here endeth certain statutes and ordinances of war made, ordained, enacted, and established by the most noble, victorious, and most Christian prince, our most dread sovereign lord, King Henry VIII, King of England and of France, and lord of Ireland, by the advice of his noble and discreet council, for the weal, surety, good rule, and safeguard of his honorable lords, captains, and other his humble subjects; and also for such of them of his said realm of France that hereafter will become his true subjects, being in his most royal host against his ancient enemies of France.

74. Regulating Thérouanne Camp

[Thérouanne, ca. 4 August 1513, 5 Henry VIII]

BM MS Arundel 26, 56: schedule as below. Hall 28: date, 4 August; siege of Thérouanne. Steele 68: date, Thérouanne, ?August. Text (MS): Arundel

Concerning cleanliness in the camp area

THE KING our sovereign lord chargeth and expressly commandeth that every man keep clean his lodging, not suffering any carrion, filth, or any other unwholesome, infective, or stinking air to be in it, or near to the same lodging, but incontinent to bury it or to cause it to be buried deep in the earth. And if any person will ease himself, to go out of the compass and precinct of the field, or else to bury it in the earth, upon pain of imprisonment after the discretion of the marshal.

Concerning relations between English and German soldiers

The King our sovereign lord straightly chargeth and commandeth that no Englishmen intermeddle or lodge themself within the ground assigned to the Almains for their lodgings, or to give them any reproach or unfitting language or words by the which noise or debate might ensue, upon pain of imprisonment, and further to be punished as the case shall require. And in like wise, if that any Almain give any reproach or unfitting language to any Englishmen, that then the Englishmen to complain them to the captains of the Almains, which shall see and provide for remedy in that behalf.

And over that, the King's highness commandeth that all Englishmen and other of his army friendly and courteously do treat the said Almains after like manner as though they were his proper subjects.

For observation of all military laws

The King our sovereign lord straightly chargeth and commandeth that all manner of men, of what estate or condition soever they be, now being retained in his army royal, keep and observe all his statutes and ordinances of war which of late were openly read, published, and declared unto them from article to article, and from point to point, upon the pains contained in the said statutes and ordinances. And his highness willeth and commandeth my lord marshal and other his officers having authority of the same duly and diligently to execute the said statutes upon pain of his high displeasure.

Also if there be any manner of person that findeth themself grieved in any thing that toucheth the office of my lord marshal, let them resort Monday, Wednesday, and Friday unto the lord marshal's court kept here within this town and city during the time that it shall please the King's highness here to tarry and abide; and that all such persons as be in the army do resort unto such place as is appointed by my said lord marshal to keep his court in there where they shall be heard, and equity and justice shall be duly done and administered unto them.

75. Prohibiting Enclosure and Engrossing of Farms

[?1514, 6 Henry VIII]

AC (HM Ellesmere 2655,10): date, Star Chamber, 2 May 1515; King's consent to plan reforming enormities in the realm, by use of power, if necessary. PRO (SP 1/9/432): date, MS note, as above; schedule as below. Leadam *1*, 7. Not in Steele. Text (MS): SP

THE KING our sovereign lord, like a virtuous and gracious person, daily travailing about the increase of the commonwealth of this his realm and his true and faithful subjects of the same, as well by the lamentable complaint of his said subjects as by the credible report of his justices of the peace and commissioners of every shire within his said realm, perceiveth and graciously considereth that the long continued scarcity, as well of grain as of other victuals within this realm, to the great detriment of his said loving subjects, hath been and yet is not only by converting arable ground unto pasture but also by engrossing of many farms and tenements of husbandry unto the hands and possession of a few covetous persons, which for their own particular lucre neglecteth tillage and, only applying the land belonging to the said farms unto pasturage and feeding of cattle, suffereth the houses of the said farms and tenements to decay and fall into ruin, unneth keeping as many persons upon all the said farms or tenements as in every of them severally were wont to be kept before the said engrossing and decay of husbandry; by occasion whereof not only all manner of corn and grain hath been in a great quantity minished, poultry and other victual necessary for man's sustenance decayed, which were wont to be bred in the said farms and tenements when they were inhabited, but also an infinite number of the King's subjects, for lack of occupation, hath fallen and daily do fall unto idleness and consequently unto thefts and robberies; and finally by the rigor of the laws of this realm, many of them have been put to the execution of death, to the great depopulation and weakening of this noble realm, and the lamentable remembrance and great heaviness unto the King's highness.

His grace therefore, for the zeal that he hath to the commonweal, desiring to encounter with the uncharitable and covetous appetites as well of them which converteth arable ground into pasture as of the said engrossers of farms and tenements of husbandry, reputing them as enemies of the commonwealth of this his realm of England, straightly chargeth and commandeth all and every his subjects, spiritual and temporal, of what estate, degree, or condition he or they be, which now hath or hereafter shall have any more farms or tenements of husbandry than one, and mindeth to keep them in his or their own hands, or that any other person or persons hath to his use, that they and every of them do till or cause to be tilled, by the Feast of St. Michael the Archangel next coming, all such lands lying or appertaining to all and every of their said farms and tenements of husbandry as was occupied and used in tillage at any time before the first year of the reign of the most noble prince of famous memory, King Henry VII; and the said lands being tilled as is before said continually to exercise and use it in tillage accordingly.

Semblably that the said engrossers immediately do cause all and every of the said houses of husbandry yet standing, whereunto the said lands to be put in tillage as is beforesaid do appertain or belong, to be inhabited and dwelt in by husbandmen or laborers according as it was before the engrossing of the said houses. And that they fail not thus to do, upon such grievous pain as will ensue, and as they will avoid the King's highness' indignation and displeasure.

76. Announcing Truce with France

[Otford, 10 August 1514, 6 Henry VIII]

CW (C82/409): date of delivery, as above; sign manual; schedule as below. PR (C66/623/7*d*): date as above; writ to mayor of Calais; similar writs to mayor and sheriffs of London, mayor of Southampton, constable of Dover and warden of Cinque Ports; schedule as below. *L&P* 2(2), 3298: proclaimed in London on 11 August. Stow 828: proclaimed on 13 August. Steele 69: date, Oxford, 1 August. Text (MS): PR

HENRY, by the grace of God King of England and of France and lord of Ireland, doth you to understand that to the laud of God, the exaltation of our faith, the defense of the same and the advancement of the commonweal of this his realm and subjects, there is taken, accorded, and concluded betwixt his highness, for him, his realms, lands, countries, and all places being in his possession or under his obeisance on this side, or beyond the sea, in and for all his confederates and subjects on the one part, and the right excellent, high, and mighty prince, King Louis of France, for him, his realm, lands, countries, and all places being in his possession or under his obeisance, and for all his confederates and subjects on the other part, good, entire, and firm peace, amity, league, confederation, and alliance by way of marriage, with free and sure intercourse and merchandises and conversation of the subjects on both sides, by land and water, fresh and salt, without any license or safe-conduct to be given, the seventh day of this present month of August and to endure during the lives of the said two kings, and one year after.

Wherefore our said sovereign lord willeth and straightly chargeth that all his officers, true liegemen, and subjects inviolably keep and observe the said peace, league, and amity, upon the utter peril that thereupon may ensue, signifying unto you that all his subjects may from henceforth freely and liberally use intercourse and feats of merchandise, by land and water, with the subjects of the said realm of France, and freely pass, remain, and repass to and from the same, in their liberty.

77. Enforcing Statutes against Liveries

[Westminster, 12 October 1514, 6 Henry VIII]

STC 7768 (BM Microfilm A.122, 11), BM K.T.C. 115.a.4, 1: printed by R. Pynson (London, ?1514); schedule as below. LJ 11, 199*v:* date as above; writ to sheriffs of London and Middlesex; schedule as below. Steele 70. Text (*STC*): BM

FORASMUCH as in the times of the noble progenitors of the King our sovereign lord divers statutes [1] have been made and established for punishment of such persons that give or receive liveries, or that retain any person or persons, or be retained with any person or persons, by oath, promise, livery, writing, token, badge, or otherwise, upon divers pains and forfeitures in such statutes contained; that notwithstanding divers and many persons have taken upon them, some to give and some to receive, liveries, and to retain and be retained contrary to the form of the said statutes, and little or nothing is or hath been done for the punishment of the offenders in that behalf; by reason whereof many murders, riots, routs, unlawful assemblies, maintenances, embraceries, and other great inconveniences have ensued and daily do ensue to the disturbance and inquietation of the King's subjects, and to the let of the execution of the laws:

The King our most dread sovereign lord, having tender zeal, love, and affection to the commonweal, rest, and quietness of this his realm and his subjects of the same, by the advice of his council willeth, straightly chargeth, and commandeth all his true and faithful subjects and liegemen of what degree, state, or condition soever he or they be, that they and every of them from henceforth observe, keep, and perform all and singular statutes and ordinances and every part of the same aforetime had or made

1. 13 Richard II, st. 3, 1389, *SR 2,* 74; 16 Richard II, c. 4, 1392, *SR 2,* 84; 20 Richard II, c. 2, 1396, *SR 2,* 93; 1 Henry IV, c. 7, 1399, *SR 2,* 113; 2 Henry IV, c. 21, 1400, *SR 2,* 129; 7 Henry IV, c. 14, 1405, *SR 2,* 155; 8 Edward IV, c. 2, 1468, *SR 2,* 426; 19 Henry VII, c. 14, 1503, *SR 2,* 658.

against such as made unlawful retainers, and such as be so retained or that give or receive liveries contrary to the form and effect of the same statutes and ordinances; and that no person nor persons from henceforth do retain nor be retained contrary to the said statutes; nor that any person or persons heretofore in any wise retained by the King's letters missive, placard, patent, or otherwise, from henceforth use or wear any livery, badge, token, or otherwise call himself servant to any such person to whom he or they have been so retained; upon such pains and forfeitures as been contained in the same statutes, without any manner hope, trust, or confidence of any pardon or release to be obtained of our said sovereign lord for any such unlawful demeanor; any commandment, letters missive, placards, commissions, or letters patent under the King's Great Seal to the contrary made in any wise notwithstanding. All which commandments, letters missive, placards, commissions, and letters patent, of whatever date or nature soever they be, or to whom or for what cause soever they were granted, the King's highness utterly hath revoked and by this proclamation clearly declareth them now and from henceforth to be void and of no force, strength, nor effect. . . .

78. Appointing Commissioners to Reform York Disorders

[Westminster, 23 November 1514, 6 Henry VIII]

PR (C66/623/4*d*): date as above; writ to sheriff of city of York; similar writs to sheriffs of county of York; schedule as below. Not in Steele. Text (MS): PR

WHEREAS the King our most dread sovereign lord, Henry, by the grace of God King of England and of France, and lord of Ireland, by the advice of the lords of his most honorable council, for reformation of many great and urgent causes and enormities now lately committed and done within his city of York, the suburbs and county of the same, and also within the whole county of the same, to his great displeasure, subversion of his laws and inquietness of his true and loving subjects, inhabitants of the same, hath now lately directed his commissions of oyer and terminer under his Great Seal in due form made to his right dear cousin the Earl of Northumberland and other his trusty councilors to hear and determine the same as well at the suit of his highness as of other his subjects in that behalf grieved or wronged, as by the same commissions more at large doth appear;

And where also as our said sovereign lord, for the singular affection, love, and favor which his highness beareth always toward his faithful and loving subjects, and for the ease, quietness, and surety of his subjects, hath straightly charged and commanded his said right dear cousin the Earl of Northumberland and the other his councilors, commissioners in that behalf appointed to sit and inquire in such place and places, and at such time as they by their discretions shall think most convenient and necessary, and then and there to hear and determine for due reformation of the premises according to the laws and customs of this his realm of England:

His highness therefore willeth and straightly [chargeth] and commandeth all and singular persons as hath cause to complain or in any manner of wise find himself grieved or wronged by any person or persons, of what estate, degree, or condition soever he or they be, to assemble before the said commissioners at such time and in such place as the said commissioners shall appoint, and there to show and declare as to them shall appertain. And the King's pleasure is that indifferent justice and right shall be to them ministered, according to his laws.

79. Announcing Peace Treaty with France

[Otford, 16 April 1515, 6 Henry VIII]

PR (C66/623/30*d*): date as above; writ to mayor and sheriffs of London; similar writs to sheriffs of Devon, Cumberland, Bristol and Southampton, constable of Dover and warden of Cinque Ports; schedule as below. *CSPVenetian 2,* 586: signing of treaty reported on 9 March. Steele 73: date, Oxford. Text (MS): PR

THE KING our sovereign lord, Henry, by the grace of God King of England and of France and lord of Ireland, doth you to understand that to the laud of God, the exaltation of our faith, the defense of the same, and the advancement of the commonweal of this his realm and subjects, there is taken, accorded, and concluded betwixt his highness for him, his realm, lands, countries, and all places being in his possession or under his obeisance on this side or beyond the sea, and for all his confederates and subjects on the one part, and the right excellent, high, and mighty prince, King Francis of France, for him, his realm, lands, countries, and all places being in his possession or under his obeisance, and for all his confederates and subjects on the other part, good, entire, and firm peace, amity, league, and confederation, with free and sure intercourse of merchandises and communication of the subjects on both sides by land and water, fresh and salt, without any license and safe-conduct, to begin the fifth day of this present month of April and to endure during the lives of the said two kings and one year after.

Wherefore our said sovereign lord willeth and straightly chargeth that all his officers, true liegemen, and subjects inviolably keep and observe the said peace, league, and amity, upon the uttermost peril that may thereupon ensue; signifying unto you that all his subjects may from henceforth freely and surely use intercourse and feats of merchandise by land and water with the subjects of the said realm of France, and freely pass, remain, and repass to and from the same at their liberty.

80. Enforcing Statutes on Apparel, Vagabonds, Laborers

[Westminster, 19 February 1517, 8 Henry VIII]

AC (HM Ellesmere 2655, 11): date, Star Chamber, 20 February; order for prices to be set on wool. Ibid., 2655, 12*v:* date, Star Chamber, 29 January 1518; order for judges to confer on statutes of apparel and vagabonds. LL N, 33: date as above; writ embodied in schedule; schedule as below. Steele 74. Text (MS): LL

To THE MAYORS, aldermen, and sheriffs of our city of London, greeting.

Whereas divers and many statutes, acts, and ordinances, as well in the times of our noble progenitors, late Kings of this realm of England, as in the time of our reign, by authority of parliament, for the good and politic order, rule, and governance of this our said realm have been made; that is to say, amongst many other, the Statute of Winchester,[1] the acts of apparel,[2] vagabonds,[3] and laborers:[4] We willing and desiring the prosperity of our faithful and natural subjects and for the tender zeal and affection which we continually do bear unto the same, will and command you to make immediately, upon the sight hereof, open proclamations in such places as you shall think most expedient (as well within liberties as without) for the full, effectuous, and inviolable observing of the same according to the tenor, purport, and effect thereof, and that you fail not hereof as you tender our pleasure.

1. 13 Edward I, c. 4 (Winchester), 1285, *SR 1,* 97.

2. 11 Edward III, c. 2, 1337, *SR 1,* 280; 37 Edward III, c. 8–14, 1363, *SR 1,* 380–81; 3 Edward IV, c. 5, 1463, *SR 2,* 399.

3. 13 Edward I, c. 1–6 (Winchester), 1285, *SR 1,* 96–98; 13 Edward I (London), 1285, *SR 1,* 102; 5 Edward III, c. 14, 1331, *SR 1,* 268; 23 Edward III, c. 7, 1349, *SR 1,* 308; 7 Richard II, c. 5, 1383, *SR 2,* 32; 12 Richard II, c. 3, 4, 1388, *SR 2,* 56, 57; 12 Richard II, c. 7–9, 1388, *SR 2,* 58; 11 Henry VII, c. 2, 1495, *SR 2,* 569; 19 Henry VII, c. 12, 1503, *SR 2,* 656.

4. 23 Edward III, st. 2, c. 1–4, 1349, *SR 1,* 311; 34 Edward III, c. 10, 11, 1360, *SR 1,* 367; 42 Edward III, c. 6, 1368, *SR 1,* 388; 6 Henry VI, c. 3, 1427, *SR 2,* 233; 8 Henry VI, c. 8, 1429, *SR 2,* 244.

81. Sumptuary Regulations

[London, 31 May 1517, 8 Henry VIII]

STC 7768 (UM 1,4,289), BM K.T.C.115.a.4, 3: printed by R. Pynson (London, 1517): date as above; schedule as below. Steele 75. Text (*STC*): BM

Provision made by the King's highness and his council putting apart the excessive fare, and reducing the same to such moderation as followingly ensueth, the observance whereof to begin the last day of May, the ninth year of the King now our sovereign lord, Henry VIII:

First, that a cardinal may have nine dishes at his own mess at one meal, besides potages to be served in courses at his pleasure.

Item, an archbishop and a duke may have seven dishes at their own messes at a meal, besides potages to be served in courses at their own pleasure.

Item, marquises, earls, and bishops may have seven dishes at their own messes at a meal, besides potages to be served in courses at their pleasure.

Item, all lords temporal under the degree of an earl, abbots being lords of the parliament, mayors of the city of London for the time being, Knights of the Garter, to have six dishes at their own messes at a meal, besides potages to be served in courses at their pleasure.

Item, judges, the chief baron of the exchequer, the King's council, the sheriffs of the said city for the time being, and all other both spiritual and temporal that may dispend in land or fees to the yearly value of £200 may have five dishes at their own mess at a meal, besides potages to be served as they will.

Item, all persons spiritual and temporal that may dispend £100 by year, and not £200, may have four dishes at their own mess at a meal, besides potages.

Item, all persons spiritual and temporal that may dispend £40 by year, and not £100, may have three dishes at their own mess at a meal, besides potages.

Item, all persons spiritual and temporal having goods to the value of £2000 may have like dishes as he that may dispend in lands to the value of £200 by year.

Item, all persons spiritual and temporal having goods to the value of £1000 may have as many dishes as he that may dispend £100 by the year.

Item, all persons spiritual and temporal having goods to the value of £500 may have as many dishes as he that may dispend £40 by the year.

Item, if two meats of one kind be diversely dressed, or two meats of divers kinds be served in a dish, every of them shall stand for one dish, after the rate abovesaid.

Item, cranes, swan, bustard, peacock, and all other fowls of like greatness, but one dish.

Item, partridge, plovers, woodcocks, and all other wildfowl of like greatness, but six in a dish for a cardinal only, and four in a dish for all other lords.

Item, quails, dotterels, snites, and all other fowls of like greatness, but eight in a dish.

Item, pheasants, gulls, and all other fowls of like greatness, but two in a dish.

Item, larks and all other fowls of like greatness, but 12 in a dish.

Item, all persons aforesaid may have less dishes at their pleasure, but no more at one meal than is afore limited, nor otherwise than is afore rehearsed.

Provided always, that at the day of marriage of any person, he or she, after their degrees, above the said rate may have three dishes more at a meal than is above limited after the rate.

Provided also, that brawn and other entrails of beasts and purtenances of beasts and fowls, oysters, cockles, mussels, all white meats not altered out of their kind, shall not be taken for any dish.

Item, three saltfish of any kind to be accounted for one dish; and having any more kind of saltfish, every of them to be accounted for one dish.

Item, at the receiving and feasting of ambassadors and noblemen of outward parts, every man to be at his liberty, the rate before taxed notwithstanding; and in semblable manner, the Knights of the Garter to be at their liberties on St. George's Day only.

Item, it is ordered that in case any of the estates or other before rehearsed shall fortune to dine or sup with any other of a lower degree, it shall be lawful to the person or persons with whom the said estates or other shall so dine or sup to serve them and every of them according to their degrees, after the rates before specified.

Finally, it is determined that if any person or persons shall otherwise order themself than is contained in the foresaid rate and provision, and so following their sensual appetite shall violate the same, he or they so doing shall not only be reputed and taken as a man of evil order contemptuously disobeying the direction of the King's highness and his council, but also to be sent for, to be corrected and punished at the King's pleasure to the example of other that shall enterprise any such follies and sensual appetites hereafter.

82. Authorizing Collections for Ransom of John Sargy

[Westminster, 26 October 1518, 10 Henry VIII]

STC 15,476 (UM 25,149,1708), BM C.18.e.2, 8: printed by R. Pynson (London, 1518); date as above; letters patent under Great Seal; schedule as below (following an English summary of bull by Pope Leo X, dated 12 June 1516). Steele 76. Text (*STC*): BM

It hath pleased the King's most noble grace, not only moved with pity and compassion toward the redemption and deliverance of the abovenamed prisoners from the servitude and thralldom of the abovesaid Turks, enemies to the name and religion of Christ, but also right entirely exhorted and required unto the same by the Pope's Holiness, hath accepted and taken the forenamed John Sargy, protector for him and his said brethren, his servants and goods, into his most royal and gracious protection and defense, wheresoever he or they shall come within this realm; requiring all bishops, abbots, priors, parsons, vicars, and other spiritual personages, in whose churches the said John or his deputies shall come, thankfully to accept and admit them in that behalf. And also straightly commandeth all his sheriffs, mayors, and other his officers and subjects temporal, that they shall maintain, defend, and aid the said John, his deputies and servants and goods, wheresoever they shall come, for alleving and gathering of alms and charitable gifts of Christian people in this behalf; and that his said officers and subjects shall not do unto them any injury, hurt, molestation, trouble, or grief, but shall let the same to be done by any other. And if any such malicious demeanor be committed against him, his said deputies, or servants, then they shall see it speedily and without delay duly corrected, as more plainly it is expressed in his most gracious letters patent under his Great Seal thereupon made, dated at his palace of Westminster the 26th day of October in the 10th year of his reign; which letters of his said most royal and gracious protection his highness will that after one whole year next ensuing the date hereof shall be void and of none effect.

83. Announcing Acceptance of Claims against Piracy

[Westminster, 12 July 1519, 11 Henry VIII]

PR (C66/633/9*d*): date as above; writ to sheriffs of London; similar writs to towns of Bristol, Southampton, Kingston-upon-Hull, and to counties of Bedford and Bucks, Cambridge and Hunts, Notts and Derby, Oxford and Berks, Warwick and Leicester, Somerset and Dorset, Norfolk and Suffolk, Surrey and Sussex, Essex and Herts, Gloucester, Southampton, Stafford, Lincoln, Salop, Northumberland, Cumberland, Westmorland, York, Worcester, Hereford, Wilts, Cornwall, Devon, Northampton, and Cinque Ports; schedule as below. Steele 77. Text (MS): PR

WHEREAS divers English merchants repairing unto Guienne were despoiled by a Frenchman called Guillam de la Fountaine in September and October last past, and requisition hath been made by the King our sovereign lord and his council to the French King for due restitution to be made, the French King upon the said requisition is contented that, after the certificate of the value of the goods of all them that were despoiled shall be made unto him by the Lord Cardinal and Legate, the said value by him so to be certified shall be sent unto the hands of the said Lord Cardinal and Legate, to the intent to restore to every man as the price of his restitution shall amount unto.

Therefore if any English merchants were despoiled by Guillam de la Fountaine or any other Frenchman in the said two months of September and October last past, let him bring in his proof before the said Lord Cardinal and Legate, or before the Master of the Rolls and Master Christopher Middleton, deputies to the said Lord Cardinal, before the first day of November next coming; and their said proofs shall be received, and certificate made thereupon to the French King for their restitution accordingly; signifying unto them that if they bring not their proofs before the first day of November, then after the said first day shall be past, they shall not be further heard in demanding of their restitution.

84. Authorizing Collections for Ransom of John Pyllet

[before 1521]

STC 7769, BM C.18.e.2, 49: printed by R. Pynson (London, before 1521); letters patent under great seal; schedule as below, imperfect. Steele 79: date as above. Text (*STC*): BM

BE IT KNOWN to all Christian people that Sir John Pyllet, e[squire], Knight of the Holy Sepulcher of Christ, coming from Jerusalem w[as held by the] Moors and infidels, cruel enemies unto Christ's faith, and by them th[rough] their great torments and threatenings of death was compelled either to [abjure Christ's] faith and to follow and observe their most damnable sect and laws o[r promise] unto them many millions of ducats of gold. And because the said kn[ight preferred] to lose the goods of this world than he would deny the faith of Ch[rist and lose] the joy of everlasting life, hath bound himself in the sum of 2,000 [ducats to cer]tain Venetians, which did pay the said sum of 2,000 ducats out of hand to the s[aid Moo]rs and infidels for the deliverance of the said knight from their prison and torments; [in payment whereof the] foresaid knight is bound by the oath of his religion and by laudable ordinances and sta[tutes either] to come in his own person or by some sufficient man for him, not without his great costs. [Yet he be bound to] his great master, now and for the time being, as often as he shall be called, to fight for h[im and for the] Christian faith against the said infidels, cruel enemies unto Christian religion. And whereas [it is unlaw]ful to the said knight to come contrary to his oath and profession; and it is honest[ly thought that the mer]chants of Venice should be recompensed and satisfied of their duty, the which can not b[e done by the said] knight except he should sell such lands and goods [which belong to him, his master, and order, and which although they] were sold [would be insuf]ficient for the contentation of the said 2,000 ducats. And also the said knight by such necessary sale, to the honor of that religion and knights of the same, should be compelled to beg for h[is living. In the] tender consideration whereof that the said knight might be somewhat relieved, and that Chris[tians might] be the more glad to put to their helping hands to the premises in as much as by such [charitable acts] they may trust to obtain the health of their souls, our Holy Father, Pope Leo that now [is, being of him]self not sufficient to succor all such persons that be oppressed and cometh to Rome for [aid in such cases], by the mercy of almighty God and by the authority of Saints Peter and Paul, to every man and w[oman being] truly penitent and confessed, which by himself or by any other man shall put to their hel[ping hands] and give their

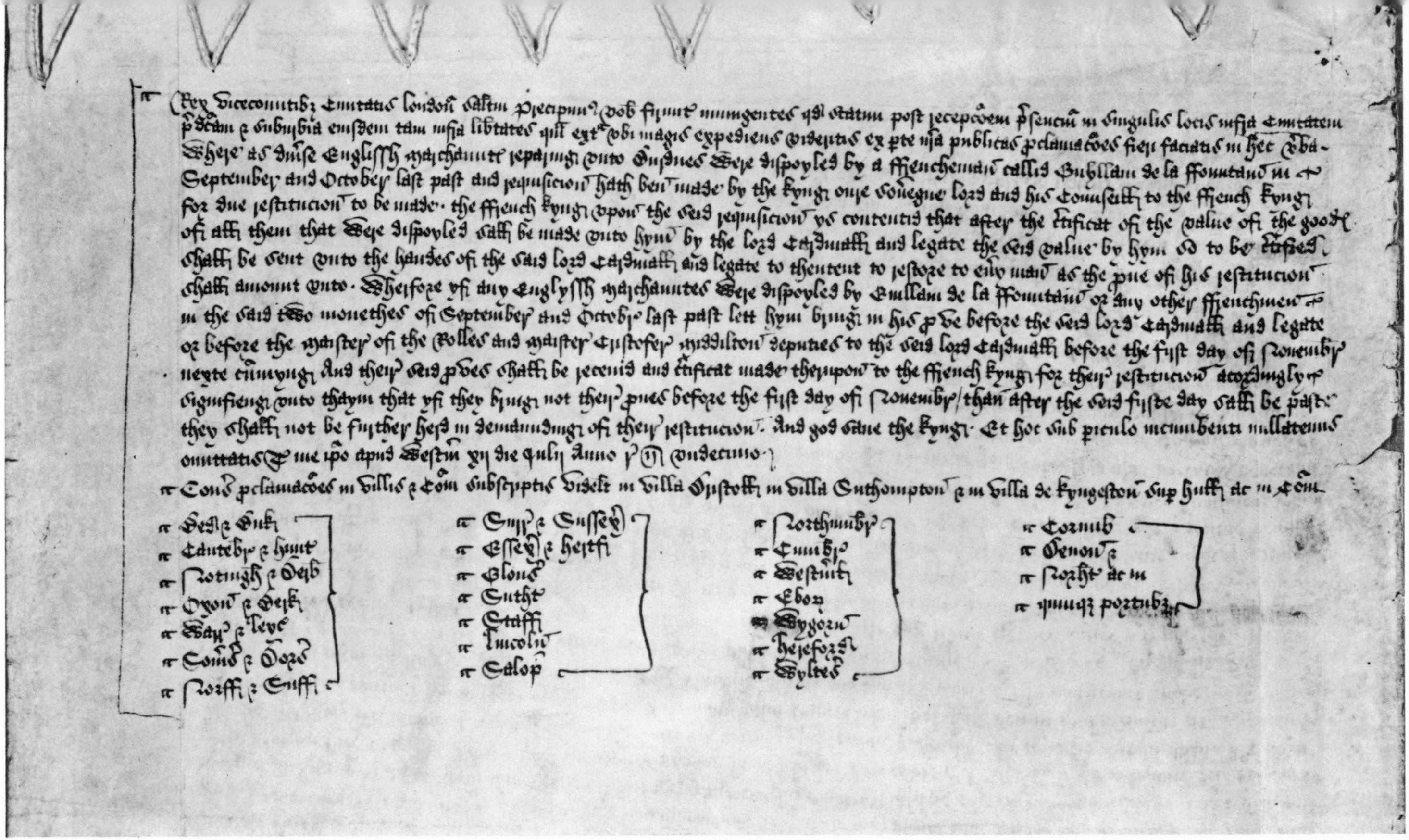

Plate 3. Patent Roll text of Proclamation 83, by Henry VIII. Proclamation writ, to the sheriffs of London; similar writs, to towns and counties listed below. Schedule, announcing acceptance of claims against piracy. Dated Westminster, 12 July, 11 Henry VIII [1519]. Note stitching of membranes to form roll of Letters Patent. PR (C66/633/9*d*).

alms unto the foresaid John, Knight of the Holy Sepulcher, or to his d[eputy, alms in] payment of the said sum of 2,000 ducats, hath released, as often as they shall do it, 15 ye[ars and as ma]ny lents of penance enjoined. And in like manner for these considerations above said, 12 car[dinals have] granted 1,200 days of pardon for every time so doing. Also my lord Archbishop, [of Canterbu]ry, Primate of England, hath granted 40 days of pardon.

Also my lord Bishop of Linc[oln hath gran]ted 40 days of pardon.

Also my lord Bishop of Rochester hath granted 40 days of [pardon. Also] my lord Bishop of Chester hath granted of his special grace, 40 days of pardon.

Al[so my lord Bishop of] Salisbury hath granted 40 days of pardon.

The sum of the whole indulgence is 7,5[00 days of pardon.]

Also our sovereign lord King Henry VIII hath given out his letters patent u[nder his Great] Seal requiring and praying to all them that be his true lovers and subjects favorably to [receive this knight's] messengers; furthermore, hath straightly charged and commanded to all singular head officers, the [justices of peace], mayors, bailiffs, and constables of every city, borough, and town, as well within the libertie[s as without, that] they to [*sic*] gather the alms deeds of every charitable and well-disposed person, and it so gathere[d to forward] to the said collectors, and they to have for their good deed God's blessing and ou[r thanks].

85. Ordering Aid to Bishop of Lincoln against Heretics

[Westminster, 20 October 1521, 13 Henry VIII]

Foxe *4*, 241: date as above; schedule as below. Wilkins *3*, 241: schedule as below. Not in Steele. Text: Foxe

To ALL MAYORS, sheriffs, bailiffs, and constables, and to all other our officers, ministers, and subjects these our letters hearing or seeing, and to every of them, greeting:

Forasmuch as the right reverend father in God, our trusty and right well-beloved councilor, the Bishop of Lincoln, hath now within his diocese no small number of heretics, as it is thought, to his no little discomfort and heaviness, we therefore, being in will and mind safely to provide for the said right reverend father in God and his officers, that they nor any of them shall bodily be hurt or damaged by any of the said heretics or their fautors, in the executing and ministering of justice unto the said heretics according to the laws of Holy Church, do straightly charge and command you and every of you, as you tender our high displeasure, to be aiding, helping, and assisting to the said right reverend father in God and his said officers, in the executing of justice in the premises, as they or any of them shall require you so to: not failing to accomplish our commandment and pleasure in the premises, as you intend to please us, and will answer to the contrary at your utmost perils.

86. Providing Victual for London

[Westminster, 26 January 1522, 13 Henry VIII]

LJ 12, 158: date as above; writ to sheriffs of Cambridge and Hunts; similar writs to Bedford, Bucks, Essex, Herts, Norfolk, Suffolk, Hants, Surrey, Sussex, Warwick, Leicester, Notts, Derby, Oxford, Berks, Lincoln; MS note, delivered to mayor on 6 February; schedule as below. Steele 80. Text (MS): LJ

THE KING our sovereign lord, for many great and divers considerations his grace specially moving, willing his city and chamber of London to be substantially furnished and provided of wheat, malt, rye, and all other grain, as well for the benefit and commodity of the noblemen of this his realm and all other repairing to the same city as of the citizens and inhabitants of the same, giveth full power, license, and authority to all and every person and persons within this his county, as well within liberties as without, that will repair to the said city with any wheat, malt, rye, or other grain for the victualing of the same; may at all times from henceforth at their liberties freely, quietly, and peaceably without any let or interruption of any person or persons lade, carry, and convey the same to the said city, as well by land as by water.

And further his highness willeth and giveth straightly in commandment to all justices of peace, sheriffs, mayors, bailiffs, constables, customers, comptrollers, searchers, and their deputies, and all other ministers and officers as well within liberties as without, to whom [it] shall appertain within this his county, that they and every of them permit and suffer all and every such person and persons freely and quietly and also peaceably, without let or interruption of them or any of them, to lade, carry, and convey all such wheat, malt, rye, or other grain to the said city for the victualing of the same. As they will avoid the King's highness' displeasure, any act, proclamation, restraint, commandment, or provision henceforth had, made, or granted to the contrary, under his Great Seal or otherwise, in any wise notwithstanding.

Foreseen and provided that the customers, comptrollers, searchers, or any of them at every port, haven, or creek where any such wheat, malt, rye, or other grain or victual shall be loaded to be conveyed to the said city, shall take sufficient bonds of the owners or conveyors of the said wheat, malt, rye, or other grain, that they and every of them shall truly convey the same to the said city of London to and for the victualing of the same, and to none other place, not failing hereof as they will avoid the King's highness' displeasure.

87. Requisitioning Empty Wine Casks

[Greenwich, 23 February 1522, 13 Henry VIII]

Antiq 1, 18: date as above; letters patent to all subjects and strangers; schedule as below; proclaimed in London on 10 March. BM MS Harl 442, 18: date, MS note, 13 March. Steele 81. Text (MS): Antiq

THE KING our sovereign lord, Henry VIII, by the grace of God King of England and of France, defender of the faith, and lord of Ireland, for certain causes and considerations his highness moving, in most straight manner chargeth and commandeth all and every his subjects and strangers of whatsoever estate, pre-eminence, or condition soever they be, none excepted, as well spiritual as temporal, that they and every of them within two days after the publication of this proclamation openly in the streets, set out before their houses and dwelling places all and every such casks and void vessels.

That is to say, tuns, pipes, hogsheads, tierces, butts, and all manner other void wine foists or vessels, to the intent that the King's purveyors, appointed for the taking of such vessels, may forthwith have the same at price reasonable. Not failing this to do under the pain of 100*s*. to be forfeited to the King's grace by the owners for every such void foist if, contrary to this proclamation, and search to be made thereupon after the expiring of the said two days made, they reserve the same vessels secret in their houses without setting out of the same as above; besides imprisonment of them and every of them which contrary to this proclamation shall conceal and reserve secret the same foists, considering the great necessity that now is for the speedy purveyance of the said foists and vessels.

88. Revaluing Coinage

[Canterbury, 25 May 1522, 14 Henry VIII]

LL N, 203: date as above; writ to mayor and sheriffs of London; schedule as below. *L&P 3,* 2357: printed copy delivered for proclamation in Winchester and Southampton. Steele 82. Text (MS): LL

THE KING our sovereign lord, for divers and great urgent considerations and respects, by the advice of council, straightly chargeth and commandeth that from henceforth these moneys of gold and silver here expressed and not clipped shall be current and have course within all places throughout this his realm of England, Ireland, Wales, Calais, and the marches of the same; to be taken, paid, repaid by change, rechange, and all other payments, as well betwixt his subjects as between his subjects and all others, whatsoever they be, at the rate and value hereafter following.

That is to say, every ducat, large, of gold at 4*s*. 6*d*. sterling; every crown *soleil,* named crown of the sun, not clipped, at 4*s*. 4*d*. sterling; and every crown of gold, not *soleil,* nor clipped, at 4*s*. sterling; and all manner groats, half groats, and pence of the King's coin, and all other groats and half groats not being the King's coin, having [course] and being current within this his realm, not clipped nor fully broken albeit they shall be much cracked, to be taken, received and paid throughout this his said realm without any manner refusal or denial.

And moreover the King's highness straightly chargeth and expressly commandeth all mayors, sheriffs, bailiffs, constables, and other his faithful officers and subjects, that if any person or persons of what estate, degree, or condition he be, refuse or deny to take and receive the said moneys of gold and silver in manner and form aforesaid, be it for merchandises, change or rechange, or other cause whatsoever, forthwith to take and arrest the same person or persons so making refusal or denial, and to put him in ward and prison, there to remain and further to be punished at the King's pleasure.

89. Ordering Muster against French Invasion

[Winchester, 24 June 1522, 14 Henry VIII]

PR (C66/641/21*d*): date as above; writ to justices of peace and sheriffs of Norfolk; similar writs to sheriffs of Suffolk, Essex, Kent, Sussex, Southampton, Somerset, Dorset, Devon, Cornwall, Lincoln, York, Northumberland, the constable of Dover and warden of Cinque Ports; schedule as below. BM MS Harl 442, 20: date, 14 June; writs as PR; schedule as below. Rymer *13*, 770. Steele 83. Text (MS): PR

FORASMUCH as the King's highness hath perfect intelligence and knowledge that his ancient enemies the Frenchmen, of their perverse and most cruel purpose, intend to invade and enter the seacoasts of this his realm, and not only to burn, destroy, and consume all that they may overcome, but also to steal, spoil, and rob his subjects and people, inhabitants of the same.

For resistance and repressing whereof, for the tender zeal and love his highness beareth to his said subjects, specially regarding the defense, safeguard, and tutelage of his said coasts and subjects, by the advice of his said council, straightly chargeth and commandeth all and singular his subjects of every estate, degree, and condition, betwixt the ages of 60 and 16, dwellers and adjoinanted to the said seacoasts, that they from henceforth upon one hour's warning be in a readiness, ably armed with weapons defensive, apt and meet for the wars, to resist, withstand, repress, and impugn his said enemies.

And furthermore expressly chargeth and commandeth his said subjects to devise, ordain, prepare, and put in a readiness, from time to time, beacons, signs, and tokens in places heretofore accustomed and therefor convenient, and also to keep watches daily and hourly, as well near the said seacoasts as also in other places, so that by warnings, signs, and tokens of the said beacons and watches, the King's said subjects may be in a readiness forthwith to resist, withstand, repress, and impugn his said enemies, in case they shall or will purpose or attempt any invasion or enterprise upon the said seacoasts or his said subjects in any behalf.

90. Ordering Muster against Scottish Invasion

[Westminster, 14 August 1522, 14 Henry VIII]

PR (C66/641/21*d*): date as above; writ to sheriff of Staffordshire; similar writs to sheriffs of Salop, Notts, Derby, York, Northumberland, Westmorland, Lancaster, Chester, Durham; schedule as below. BM MS Harl 442, 21: date, August; commission to Earl of Shrewsbury on 30 July; writ to sheriff of Northumberland; schedule as below. Rymer *13*, 773. Steele 84. Text (MS): PR

FORASMUCH as the King's highness our sovereign lord hath sure and certain knowledge that his ancient enemies the Scots, by the exhorting and instigation of his notorious and cruel enemy the French King, in the beginning of this next month of September, or before, intend to invade this his realm of England, and not only to burn and consume all that they may overcome, but also to steal, spoil, and rob his subjects and people of the north parts and marches near adjoinant unto the same Scots:

His grace therefore, as well for resistance and repressing of the malignities of the said Scots, for the tender zeal and love his highness beareth to his subjects, specially regarding the defense, safeguard, and weal of his said north parts and marches and his subjects of the same, by the advice of his council, straightly chargeth and commandeth all and singular his subjects of whatsoever estate, degree, and condition they be, betwixt the ages of 60 and 16, inhabitants within the county of ―――――― that from henceforth they upon one hour's warning be in areadiness, defensibly arrayed with harness and weapons apt and meet for the wars, to attend and set forward with his right dear and well-beloved cousin and councilor, the Earl of Shrewsbury, Steward of his Household and Knight of his Order of the Garter, his Lieutenant General of all the north parts for against Scotland, upon monition and warnings given or to be given to them and every of them by the King's said Lieutenant, to resist, withstand, repress, and impugn the malicious purposes of his said enemies; not failing thus to do as they tender and love the King's honor, the safeguard of his royal person, and the wealth, defense, and surety of this his realm and his subjects of the same.

91. Providing Victual for Calais

[Westminster, 24 August 1522, 14 Henry VIII]

PR (C66/641/21*d*): writ to sheriffs of London; similar writs to sheriffs of Salop, Notts, Derby, York, Northumberland, Cumberland, Westmorland, Lancaster, Chester, Durham; schedule as below. BM MS Harl 442, 22: date 24 August. Rymer *13*, 773. Steele 85: date, Westminster. Text (MS): PR

FORASMUCH as the King our sovereign lord hath now at Calais a puissant army lying, for the victualing whereof necessary it is that provision from time to time be made, the King's pleasure therefore is that all such persons as have protections by reason whereof they ought to provide victuals for the said town, shall immediately provide bread, beer, and other victuals for the same, and send them thither upon pain of forfeiture of their said protections. And all other the King's subjects who will send thither any manner of like provision of bread, beer, and other victuals, shall for the time of the abode of the King's army there be discharged from payment of any manner of customs of all the said victuals thither by them to be sent or brought. And also [by] the King's council there being shall, for all such victuals, [be] well entreated, without exaction of any toll or custom there to be taken or exacted for the same; and that they shall have for their victuals such price given unto them as they may have reasonable gain.

92. Ordering Watch in Kent

[Westminster, 24 October 1522, 14 Henry VIII]

CW (C82/524): date as above; sign manual; writ to sheriff of Kent; similar writs to counties, cities, and towns throughout England; schedule as below, imperfect. BM MS Harl 442, 23: date as above; writ to sheriff of Kent; schedule as below. Steele 86. Text (MS): Harl

THE KING our sovereign lord, for certain causes and considerations moving his highness, by the advice of his council, straightly chargeth and commandeth all and singular his subjects, dwellers and inhabitants within all and every hundred, city, borough, town, and village within the county of Kent, not only adjoining to the seacoasts but also in all the places distant from the seacoasts, as well within liberties as without:

That they from henceforth, as they will answer to the King at their uttermost perils, from time to time, both by day and by night, keep good and substantial watches by all highways, and specially in places suspect; so that all the King's subjects and others may safely and surely pass and repass at all times and hours, by day and by night, without any robberies, felonies, or any other damages or perils to ensue unto the same the King's subjects or to any of them.

93. Ordering Arrest of French Persons and Goods

[Westminster, 24 November 1522, 14 Henry VIII]

CW (C82/524): sign manual; date as above; letters patent to subjects in all counties, cities, and towns throughout England; schedule as below. Not in Steele. Text (MS): CW

For certain causes we, and our council moving, will and straightly charge and command you that forthwith and immediately upon receipt of these our letters you not only put all and singular those persons and goods, as well of Frenchmen, Bretons, and all other the French King's subjects, under arrest and sure custody, in whose hands or possession the said goods shall be found; and also restrain and let that none of them [go] out of this our realm to any outward parts, either in person or with their goods, letters, or writings, whatsoever they be; but safely and surely cause the same to be kept till you shall be advised of our further pleasure, ascertaining us and our said council by your writing what you shall do in the premises from time to time. Fail you not with diligence to execute this our pleasure and commandment, as you will answer to us at your uttermost peril.

And moreover we will and command all and every our mayors, sheriffs, constables, wardens of our ports, customers, controllers, searchers, and all other our officers and faithful subjects, whatsoever they be, that in the executing these premises they be duly aiding, helping, and assisting, as they shall answer at their perils.

94. Prohibiting Grain Export

[Westminster, 24 November 1522, 14 Henry VIII]

CW (C82/524): date as above; sign manual; writ to sheriff of Dorsetshire; similar writs to sheriffs of Wilts, Berks, Sussex; schedule as below, imperfect. *L&P 3*, 2685: schedule summary. Steele 87. Text (MS): CW

The King our sovereign lord, upon certain special cause, straightly chargeth and commandeth that no manner person, of whatsoever estate, degree, and condition, that they nor any of them convey or do to be conveyed out of the county of Dorset into any other shire or county any manner of grains, that is to say, wheat, rye, barley, oats . . . but send them to Southampton and Portsmouth for such victualing as his highness shall appoint and assign there . . .

95. Revaluing Coinage

[Westminster, 24 November 1522, 14 Henry VIII]

CW (C82/524): date as above; sign manual; schedule as below. Steele 88. Text (MS): CW

THE KING our sovereign lord, for divers great and urgent considerations, by the advice of his council [straightly chargeth and commandeth that from henceforth these] moneys of gold and silver here expressed shall be current and have course within all places throughout this his realm of England, Ireland, Wales, Calais, and the marches of the same, to be taken, paid, repaid by change, rechange, and all other payments as well betwixt his subjects [as between his subjects and all others, whatsoever they be, at the rate and value] hereafter following, that is to say: every ducat of gold and weight, at 4*s.* 6*d.;* every crown *soleil* (named crown of the sun) of weight, 4*s.* 4*d.;* and every crown of gold of weight (not *soleil*), at 4*s.* sterling; every piece of fine gold [named a carolus keeping weight, 6*s.* 10*d.;* pieces of base gold named florins, 3*s.* 3*d.;* pieces of base gold, also named florins, 2*s.* 1*d.;*] and all manner of groats, half-groats, and pence of the King's coin, and all other groats and half-groats not being of the King's coin, having course and being current within this his said realm [and not clipped nor fully broken, to be taken, received and paid] throughout his said realm without any manner refusal or denial.

And moreover, the King's highness straightly chargeth and expressly commandeth all mayors, sheriffs, bailiffs, constables, and others his faithful officers and subjects that if any person or persons, of what estate, [degree, or condition he be, refuse or deny to take and receive the said moneys of gold and silver in manner and form aforesaid, be it for merchandise], victuals, change, or rechange [or other cause] whatsoever, forthwith to take and arrest the same person or persons so making refusal or denial, and to put him in ward and prison, there to remain and further to be punished at the King's pleasure.

96. Providing Victual for Calais

[Hampton Court, 21 August 1523, 15 Henry VIII]

LJ 12, 243*v:* date as above; writ to mayor and sheriffs of London; schedule as below. Steele 89. Text (MS): LJ

FORASMUCH as the King our sovereign lord doth at this time send to Calais a puissant army, for the victualing whereof necessary it is that provision from time to time be made, the King's pleasure therefore is that all such persons as have protections by reason whereof they ought to provide victuals for his said town shall immediately provide bread, beer, and other victuals for the same and send them thither, upon pain of forfeiture of their protections. And all other the King's subjects which will send thither any manner of like provision of bread, beer, or other victual, shall for the time of their abode there and in those parts of beyond the sea, be discharged for payment of any manner of custom of all the said victuals thither by them to be sent or brought. And also the King's council there being shall, for all such victualers well entreated, without exaction of any toll or custom there to be taken or exacted for the same; and that they shall have for their said victuals such price given unto them as they may have reasonable gain.

97. Ordering Muster against Scottish Invasion

[Hampton Court, 10 October 1523, 15 Henry VIII]

BM MS Harl 442, 25: date as above; writ to sheriff of Staffordshire; smiliar writs to sheriffs of Notts, Derby, Salop; schedule as below. Steele 90. Text (MS): Harl

THE KING our sovereign lord, being certainly advised that the Duke of Albany is of late descended and arrived in Scotland having great number and provision of men of war, Scots and others, with artillery and ordnance, intending to invade this the King's realm the morrow after St. Luke's Day next coming, straightly chargeth and commandeth all and singular his subjects of every estate, degree, and condition within the said county of Stafford, being heretofore appointed or warned by the King's letters or the letters of the Earl of Surrey, the King's Lieutenant General in the north parts against the Scots, that they forthwith put themselves in such assured and perfect areadiness as, upon one day's warning to be sent to them by the King's said Lieutenant, they may (all excuses and delays utterly set apart) proceed and set forth with all diligence toward such places as they shall be appointed unto for the service of war to be done against the King's said enemies the Scots and others. And that they fail not this to do as they tender and regard the wealth and service of the King's highness and the defense of this his realm and subjects of the same, and will avoid his highness' indignation and displeasure at their uttermost perils.

98. Appointing Commission on Crimes in Yorkshire

[Westminster, 16 July 1524, 16 Henry VIII]

BM MS Harl 442, 26: date as above; writ to sheriff of York; schedule as below. Steele 91. Text (MS): Harl

The King our sovereign lord (having tender respect and inward zeal unto the tranquillity and quietness of his subjects, willing every of the same to have justice equally to be ministered unto them and every of them, so that none of his said subjects by unlawful maintenance, oppression, embraceries or other misbehaviors, be wronged, damaged, or inquieted) of his benign grace and most godly disposition and goodness, hath at this time sent into those parts his right dear and well-beloved cousin and councilor, Thomas, Duke of Norfolk, Treasurer of England; Raphe Swillington, his General Attorney; and John Porte: his commissioners authorized by his letters patent under his Great Seal to examine, view, correct, reform, and reduce to good any such misbehaviors and enormities as shall come to the knowledge of the same commissioners or any of them.

Wherefore the King's highness willeth and commandeth and also straightly chargeth and commandeth that if any of his said subjects by oppressions, unlawful maintenances, embraceries, bearings, or any other manner wise be wronged, oppressed, or damaged by any person of what degree, condition, or estate soever he be, that he or they so being damaged or wronged come to our said commissioners unto the city of York, the 30th day of this instant month of July, bring their complaints and their witnesses and proofs with them unto the said commissioners or to any of them. And the same party grieved shall not only be favorably heard, but also due redress shall be made as to good justice and equity shall appertain, without regard of any person of what degree soever he be.

99. Appointing Commission on Crimes in Northumberland

[Westminster, 16 July 1524, 16 Henry VIII]

BM MS Harl 442, 26*v:* date as above; writ to sheriff of Northumberland; schedule as below. Steele 92. Text (MS): Harl

The King our sovereign lord *ut supra* [98] hath at this time sent into these parts his right dear and well-beloved cousin and councilor, Thomas, Duke of Norfolk, Treasurer of England; Thomas, Lord Devon and Graystork; Raphe Swillington, his General Attorney; John Porte; Milton Bulmer, knight; and Thomas Tempest, knight: his commissioners authorized *ut supra* [98] come to our said commissioners unto Newcastle-upon-Tyne by the tenth day of August next coming, and bring their complaints and their witnesses and proofs with *ut supra* [98].

100. Regulating Coinage

[St. Albans, 1 October 1524, 16 Henry VIII]

LJ *12,* 290*v:* date as above; writ to sheriffs of London; proclaimed in London on 2 November; schedule as below. Steele 93. Text (MS): LJ

The King our sovereign lord, Henry VIII, by the grace of God King of England and of France, defender of the faith, and lord of Ireland, remembering that at the parliament holden at London the 15th day of April in the 15th year of his reign, it was enacted,[1] ordained, and provided by authority of the same that all manner of coins should go and be current throughout this his realm unto the Feast of St. Michael the Archangel last past, at such value and prices as in an act thereupon made more plainly appeareth: straightly chargeth, willeth, and commandeth that no manner of person or persons of what estate, degree, or condition he or they be of, within this his realm, from henceforth do refuse to take and receive in payment all such coins at such values and prices as they be expressed in the said act, upon pain of imprisonment, and further to be punished at his pleasure.

1. 14 & 15 Henry VIII, c. 12, 1523, *SR 3,* 218.

101. Prohibiting Weapons in Westminster

[Westminster, 18 October 1524, 16 Henry VII]

BM MS Harl 442, 28: date as above; schedule as below. Steele 94. Text (MS): Harl

THE KING our sovereign lord straightly chargeth and commandeth that no manner of person, of whatsoever estate, degree, or condition he be, except the sheriff of Middlesex, the warden of the fleet and his officers, bear or wear any manner of weapon, that is to say, bills, swords, bucklers, wood knives, daggers, or other weapons, within his palace or hall of Westminster or the precincts of the same, upon pain of forfeiture of the same weapon, and his body to be committed to ward and to be further punished at his pleasure.

102. Revaluing Coinage

[Westminster, 6 July 1525, 17 Henry VIII]

LL N, 289: date as above; writ to mayor and sheriffs of London; schedule as below. Steele 95. Text (MS): LL

THE KING our sovereign lord, for divers great and urgent considerations and respects, by the advice of his council, straightly chargeth and commandeth that from henceforth these moneys of gold and silver here expressed shall be current and have course within all places throughout this his realm of England, Ireland, Wales, Calais, and the marches of the same, to be taken, paid, repaid by change, rechange, and all other payments, as well betwixt his subjects as betwixt his subjects and all others whatsoever they be, at the rate and value hereafter following.

That is to say: every ducat large of gold and weight, at 4*s*. 6*d*. sterling; every crown *soleil,* named crowns of the sun, of weight, 4*s*. 4*d*. sterling; and every crown of gold of weight not *soleil,* at 4*s*. sterling; every piece of fine gold named a carolus keeping weight, at 6*s*. 10*d*. sterling; every piece of base gold named a florin keeping weight, at 3*s*. 3*d*. sterling; every piece of base gold of less quantity named also a florin keeping weight, at 2*s*. 1*d*. sterling; and all manner of groats, half-groats, and pence of the King's coin, and all other groats and half-groats not being of the King's coin, having course and being current within this his said realm, not clipped nor fully broken, albeit they shall be much cracked, to be taken, received, and paid throughout his said realm without any manner refusal or denial.

And moreover the King's highness straightly chargeth and expressly commandeth all mayors, sheriffs, bailiffs, constables, and other of his faithful subjects that if any person or persons of what estate, degree, or condition he or they be, refuse or deny to take or receive the said moneys of gold and silver in manner and form aforesaid, be it for merchandises, victuals, change or rechange, or other cause whatsoever, forthwith to take and arrest the same person or persons making refusal or denial, and to put him in ward and prison, there to remain and further to be punished at the King's pleasure.

103. Revaluing Gold and Silver Coins

[Westminster, 8 July 1525, 17 Henry VIII]

BM MS Harl 442, 31: date as above; writ to Earl of Shrewsbury, steward, and to treasurer and comptroller of the household; schedule as below. Steele 96. Text (MS): Harl

THE KING our sovereign lord, for divers great and urgent considerations and respects, by the advice of his council, straightly chargeth and commandeth that from henceforth these moneys of gold and silver here expressed shall be current and have course within all places throughout this his realm of England, Ireland, Wales, Calais, and the marches of the same, to be taken, paid, and repaid by change, rechange, and all other payments as well betwixt his subjects as betwixt his subjects and all other whatsoever they be, at the rate and value hereafter following.

That is to say, every ducat, large of gold and weight, at 4*s.* 6*d.* sterling; and all crowns *soleil* named crowns of the sun, of weight, and other crowns named porpentines, and all other crowns being of like fineness of weight as the crowns of the sun be, at 4*s.* 4*d.* sterling; and all other crowns of gold not being of like fineness and weight as crowns of the sun, be at 4*s.* sterling; every piece of fine gold named a carolus, keeping weight, at 6*s.* 10*d.* sterling; every piece of base gold named a florin, keeping weight, at 3*s.* 3*d.* sterling; every piece of base gold of less quantity named also a florin, keeping weight, at 2*s.* 1*d.* sterling; and all manner groats, half-groats, and pence of the King's coin, and all other groats and half-groats not being of the King's coin having course and being current within this his realm, not clipped nor fully broken (albeit they shall be much cracked) to be taken, received, and paid throughout his said realm without any manner refusal or denial.

And moreover the King's highness straightly chargeth and expressly commandeth all mayors, sheriffs, bailiffs, constables, and others his faithful officers and subjects, that if any person or persons of what estate, degree, or condition he be, refuse or deny to take and receive the said moneys of gold and silver in manner and form aforesaid, be it for merchandises, victuals, change or rechange, or other cause whatsoever, forthwith to take and arrest the same person or persons so making refusal or denial, and to put him in ward and prison, there to remain and further to be punished at the King's pleasure. Fail not this to do as you tender our pleasure and will eschew the contrary.

104. Announcing Truce with France

[More, 15 August 1525, 17 Henry VIII]

LJ *12*, 300: date as above; writ to mayor and sheriffs of London; proclaimed in London on 21 August; schedule as below. Steele 97. Text (MS): LJ

FORASMUCH as the Lady Regent of France, mother unto the French King, by consent of the peers and princes of the *sang royal,* and other of the council within the same, hath on the behalf of the French King and of the three estates of the realm of France, sent unto the King's highness honorable ambassadors sufficiently authorized to pursue, require, and labor for peace, and the same under honorable conditions and offers to conclude with the King's highness, if it so shall stand with his gracious pleasure; and that the Lady Margaret, Archduchess of Austria, Duchess and Countess of Burgundy, for and in the name of the Emperor for his Low Countries of Brabant, Holland, Zeeland, Flanders, Hainaut, and other adjacents thereunto, hath now of late concluded and taken a truce and abstinence of war with the said Lady Regent of France, which is passed, published, agreed, and proclaimed;

The King's highness therefore, being no less inclined to the restfulness and tranquillity of Christendom and the furtherance of peace for the weal of this his realm and his loving subjects of the same than other princes, his confederates, be; and to the intent that the peace desired, pursued, and required by the said ambassadors of France may, God willing, the more facilely and commodiously be in brief time concluded and brought to good effect: hath by deliberate advice of his council, by his commissioners sufficiently authorized for that purpose, to the laud and pleasure of Almighty God and the comfort of all Christendom, concluded and taken with the said ambassadors of France, authorized for the realm of France as is aforesaid, a good, sure, sincere, and faithful truce and abstinence of war. That is to say, between the realms of England and France and all other the countries, lands, dominions, castles, cities, territories, ports, and towns to the King's highness or to the French King or to either of them belonging; for all manner their subjects, dwellers, and vassals of the same, as well spiritual as temporal, of what estate, dignity, degree, or condition soever they be; the same truce to begin and be accounted from the 14th day of this present month of August and to endure unto the first day of December next ensuing: so as by and during all the said time of truce and abstinence, it shall be lawful to the subjects of either of the said Kings quietly, surely, and peaceably, as well by sea as by land, ports, havens, creeks, and fresh waters, to have mutual communication and intercourse the one with the other; all feats of merchandise and other arts not prohibited by the laws of the realms to use and exercise; and from the one realm to the other to pass thereto, sojourn, remain, and abide about their lawful errands at their pleasure, and through the same to depart into any further countries or from or by the same to return into their own, without offense, license, or safe-conduct to be impetrate for the same, and without molestation, disturbance, or interruption; and semblably, to fish on the sea as well herring as all other manner of fish, to repair into any havens, ports, or creeks, and from the same again to depart safely, surely, and quietly; and generally to pass and repass with their goods, wares, and merchandises and all other lawful necessaries in as ample manner and form as before the time of the wars, and in season of peace they might or were accustomed to do.

And over this, that all ambassadors, orators, heralds at arms, messengers, couriers, and bearers of letters, as well of the said kings as of their ambassadors, shall pass either unto other and through the other realms, seigniories, and countries, and in the same remain at their pleasure, with their letters, fardels, goods, carriages, and other their baggages, utensils, and necessaries, without search, molestation, or impediment, so that they practice nor attempt anything to the prejudice of the said princes, their realms, seigniories or countries, as quietly, freely, and liberally as they might have done in time of peace.

Wherefore the King's highness willeth and commandeth all and singular his officers, ministers, and subjects of what estate, dignity, or degree soever they be, duly and inviolably to accomplish, obey, and fulfill the effect of the said truce for their parts accordingly, without doing anything contrary unto the same, at their perils.

105. Announcing Peace Treaty with France

[More, 6 September 1525, 17 Henry VIII]

LJ *12*, 305: date as above; writ to mayor and sheriffs of London; proclaimed in London on 9 September; schedule as below. Hall 145: proclaimed in London on 8 September. Steele 98. Text (MS): LJ

THE KING our sovereign lord, by the great and deliberate advice of his council, having always most tender remorse and regard unto the restfulness and tranquillity of Christendom, and namely to the weal, quiet, and increase of this his realm and his loving subjects of the same; considering also that on the behalf of the French King, the lady his mother Regent in France, by consent of the peers and princes of the *sang royal* with other of the council there, and also of the three estates of the same, hath sent unto his highness honorable ambassadors sufficiently authorized to pursue and labor for peace, and the same under conditions both honorable and profitable to conclude to the laud and praise of Almighty God, the honor, utility, benefit, profit, and great quietness of this his realm and his loving subjects of the same: hath taken, passed, accorded, and concluded a good, perfect, sincere, firm, and assured peace, intelligence, confederation, union, and amity between his most excellent highness on the one part, and the right high and mighty prince, the King Francis of France on the other part; for them, their realms, countries, cities, towns, lands, dominions, territories, and seigniories, places, castles, vassals, and subjects, by sea, land, fresh water, and elsewhere.

By the which peace it is provided and ordained that from henceforth all hostility and war shall cease on either part and the said princes, with all their vassals and subjects to live together in peace, amity, intelligence, concord, love, unity, and friendship; and that it shall be lawful to all and singular the subjects of either of them of what estate, degree, or condition soever they be, freely, quietly, peaceably, and at liberty and without any safe-conduct or license to enter into other realm, there to remain, demur, haunt, frequent, be conversant, dwell, sojourn, abide, or through the same to pass at their pleasure; and all feats of merchandise, intercourse, exchange, buying, selling, or other business whatsoever it be, not prohibited or defended by the laws of the realm to use, occupy, do, and exercise; and from the same to pass and repass with their goods, merchandises, ships, carts, carriages, horses, armors, and other things whatsoever they be, not prohibited, without arrest, stop, molestation, contradiction, or impediment; and generally all other things to do, use, and exercise as freely, quietly, and liberally as ever they have done in any time of peace taken between the realms of England and France heretofore. In which peace be comprehended not only the Emperor and the Lady Margaret, Duchess of Savoy, and all their subjects, lands, and countries, but also all other the King's old and ancient friends, confederates, and allies. And no manner thing touching love or amity with them or any of them, nor any intercourse of merchandises or other thing is by this present peace violated, broken, impaired, diminished, or hindered, but all remaining in the same strength and virtue as firmly, wholly, entirely, and perfectly as they were before.

It is furthermore provided for the weal of the King's subjects that all injuries, depredations, attempts, and wrongs, done or committed unto any of them by the French King's subjects before the publication of the last wars, shall in speedy manner and without trait, delay, or long process be reformed, recompensed, restored, and amended, by the order of the Bishop of London for the party of England, and the chief President of Rouen for the party of France, who be deputed judges for the speedy redress of all attempts and wrongs that be past. And likewise any injury which shall fortune hereafter to be committed or done to any of the King's subjects shall be semblably redressed after such brief and speedy manner as the like hath not been seen at any time heretofore. And all prisoners of both parties under the degree of an earl to be freely and frankly delivered without any manner fine or ransom.

Wherefore the King's highness straightly chargeth and commandeth all and every his said subjects, of what estate, dignity, or degree or condition soever they be, duly to accomplish, fully perform, and obey, everyone for their part, the tenor and effect of the said peace accordingly.

106. Ordering Arrest of Coventry Rebels

[More, 6 November 1525, 17 Henry VIII]

BM MS Harl 442, 37: date as above; writ to mayor and sheriff of Coventry; schedule as below. Steele 99. Text (MS): Harl

WHEREAS of late divers riotous and evil-disposed persons, not dreading nor fearing our sovereign lord the King nor his laws, riotously assembled themselves in great routs and unlawful numbers within this the King's city of Coventry, against the mayor, aldermen, burgesses, and other well-ruled and disposed inhabitants thereof, to the great trouble, fear, and inquietation of the said inhabitants if due punishment and correction had not been done and had in that behalf; and albeit that divers and many of the said riotous persons, as well by imprisonment and banishment as otherwise, within the same city and elsewhere, have been punished and corrected for their said misdemeanors, yet that notwithstanding, as the King's grace is credibly informed, divers evil-disposed persons, yet continuing in their perverse and malicious purposes, have not only of late eftsoons privily renewed their said combinations and unlawful confederations but also they have caused seditious bills and writings to be made against certain well-disposed aldermen and burgesses of this the King's city, to their no little inquietation and trouble and the emboldening of evil-disposed persons:

For remedy, punishment, and reformation whereof, the King our sovereign lord, by the advice of his council, straightly chargeth and commandeth all and singular persons of what estate, degree, or condition soever they be, from henceforth that they not only desist, forbear, and cease their said confederations and combinations, but also that as soon as any of them shall know or hear any such conspirators, combiners, makers, devisers, or consenters of such seditious bills or writings, that they forthwith attach them or cause them to be attached and arrested; or else to show or give knowledge thereof to the said mayor, aldermen, and sheriffs of the said city, to the intent they may be by them attached, taken, and imprisoned; and so there to remain unto such time as the King's highness and his council may be ascertained thereof, and thereupon to be punished by fine and ransom, and furthermore their bodies to be at the King's highness' pleasure.

107. Enforcing Act against Crossbows and Handguns in London

[Westminster, 10 April 1526, 17 Henry VIII]

LL N, 319*v:* date as above; writ to mayor and sheriffs of London; schedule as below. BM MS Harl 442, 38: date, 11 April; schedule as below; MS note, like proclamations, *mutatis mutandis,* sent into other countries. Steele 100. Text (MS): LL

WHEREAS by an act of parliament[1] made and established in the 11th year of the reign of the late King our father of most famous memory, King Henry VII, whose soul God pardon, amongst other was enacted that no man from the Feast of Pasch then next following should bear any hawk of the breed of England called an eyas, goshawk, tercel, lanner, lanneret, or falcon, upon pain of forfeiture of the said hawk, as in the said act more plainly appeareth; and where at a parliament holden at London the 25th day of April, the 14th year of the reign of our sovereign lord the King that now is, it was enacted[2] and by authority of the same established that every person or persons having lands, tenements, fees, annuities, or other yearly profits in his own right or in his wife's, to the yearly value of £100, from henceforth may lawfully use and shoot in crossbows and handguns and every of them; and that every person or persons not having in use or possession lands, tenements, fees, annuities, or other yearly profits to the yearly value of £100 as is aforesaid, offending contrary to the said act, shall forfeit for every time that he shall so offend but only 40*s.*, and the crossbows and handguns to be had, recovered, seized, and levied according to the said act as in the said act more plainly appeareth:

The King our sovereign lord, by the advice of his council, straightly chargeth and commandeth all and singular person and persons of what estate or condition soever they be, resident and inhabiting within the said city, do firmly and inviolably from henceforth observe and keep the whole

1. 11 Henry VII, c. 17, 1495, *SR 2,* 581.
2. 14 & 15 Henry VIII, c. 7, 1523, *SR 3,* 215.

contents and effect of the said act in every point, as they will avoid the penalties and dangers contained in the same.

And furthermore his highness straightly chargeth and commandeth the said mayor and sheriffs and all justices of peace within the said city, that they and every of them diligently at all times do see the effect of the said act to be duly and effectually put in execution, as they tender his pleasure and will eschew the contrary. And in case the King's highness do perceive or understand the said mayor and sheriffs and justices of peace to be negligent, slack, or remiss in seeing the premises to be duly and effectually executed, his grace will not fail but will see them punished in example of all other.

108. Enforcing Statutes against Unlawful Games, and for Archery

[Westminster, 5 May 1526, 18 Henry VIII]

LL N, 320: date as above; writ to mayor and sheriffs of London, sheriff of Middlesex; schedule as below. Steele 101. Text (MS): LL

FORASMUCH as in the times of the noble progenitors of our most dread sovereign lord, divers and many laudable acts, statutes, and provisions in sundry parliaments have been made not only for punishing and laying down of bowling, closh, quoiting, loggatting, playing at tennis, dice, cards, and tables, and other unlawful games; [1] but also like laudable acts and statutes have been made for maintenance and exercising of longbows and the archery of this realm; [2] which good acts and provisions for longbows and archery notwithstanding, the said unlawful games be so continually used and exercised within this realm, and no due punishment had in that behalf according to the said provisions and statutes against the said unlawful games, that the exercising of longbows and archery of this realm is almost utterly set apart and extremely decayed; which is to the high displeasure of our said sovereign lord:

For remedy whereof his highness, by the advice of his council, straightly chargeth and commandeth that from henceforth no person within this his realm of what estate, degree, or condition he or they be, do play or use the said unlawful games nor any of them, nor householder suffer them within

1. 11 Henry IV, c. 4, 1409, *SR 2*, 163; 17 Edward IV, c. 3, 1477, *SR 2*, 462; 11 Henry VII, c. 2, 1495, *SR 2*, 569.

2. 13 Edward I, c. 6 (Winchester), 1285, *SR 1*, 97; 12 Richard II, c. 6, 1388, *SR 2*, 57; 22 Edward IV, c. 4, 1482, *SR 2*, 472; 3 Henry VIII, c. 3, 1511, *SR 3*, 25.

their houses, upon pain of forfeiture of the penalties contained in the said acts, statutes, and provisions, without any manner favor, redemption, or pardon in that behalf.

And furthermore his grace, considering the said decay of longbows and archery to be within this realm, straightly chargeth and commandeth all and singular his justices of assize, justices of peace, mayors, sheriffs, bailiffs, constables, headboroughs, stewards, and officers within liberties and places franchised, and all other his faithful officers in all cities and places within their rooms, authorities, and offices within the several shires and places within this his said realm, that they and every of them from henceforth with all effectual diligence do not only see and cause to be quickly and diligently executed all acts, provisions, and statutes made for the maintenance of longbows and archery within this realm, in the time of assizes, sessions, sheriffs' tourns, leets, and other courts, by inquiry, privy search, and other knowledge, using all the good ways and means for maintenance of longbows and archery within this his realm within every shire and shires of the same according to the said acts and statutes; but that also they practice, use, and devise all the good, lawful, and discreet ways and means they can or may possibly for repressing and correcting the uses and exercises of the said unlawful games; so that no negligence be found in the said justices or the said officers, as they will answer to his highness at their uttermost perils. And that the said justices and other officers from time to time give special charge and commandment also to all manner householders, having special regard to them that they, their children, and servants at all times hereafter have in their houses bows and arrows, exercising and using the same accordingly, upon the pains contained in the same statutes. And that as well the said justices and other officers as also the same householders not observing this high pleasure and commandment, further to be extremely punished as is aforesaid, without favor or any manner redemption, and to be in our said sovereign lord's indignation and high displeasure.

109. Ordering All Commissioners in London to Appear in Star Chamber

[Westminster, 2 July 1526, 18 Henry VIII]

BM MS Harl 442, 41: date, MS note, proclaimed in Court of Chancery on 2 July; schedule as below. Steele 102. Text (MS): Harl

THE KING our sovereign lord, upon certain urgent respects and great considerations, by the advice of his council chargeth and commandeth all and singular his subjects being commissioners of his peace within any part or shire within this his realm, or commissioners of the subsidy or anticipation of the same, or commissioners of sewers, or being authorized in any other his commission or commissions, now being or that shall be within the city of London or the suburbs of the same, or Westminster, before Thursday next coming, that they and every of them personally appear before the most reverend father in God, the Lord Thomas, Cardinal and Legate *de latere,* his chancellor, and other his council in the Star Chamber the same Thursday, and not to fail thereof upon pain of his high displeasure.

110. Ordering Enclosures Destroyed, and Tillage Restored

[Westminster, 14 July 1526, 18 Henry VIII]

BM MS Harl 442, 42: date as above; writ to Sir Robert Brudenell and Sir Richard Broke, judges of assize for Norfolk, Suffolk, Cambridge, Hunts, Bedford, Bucks, and the city of Norwich, to all jailers in their counties, and to all justices of peace; schedule as below. Steele 103. Text (MS): Harl

FORASMUCH as the King our sovereign lord and his council well and evidently perceive the great and manifold inconveniences, damages, and hurt that be arisen and come to this his realm of England and to all his subjects of the same, where in few years by the willful waste, destroying, and pulling down of towns, villages, and hamlets and other houses of husbandry within the same, in no small number; and the grounds and lands to them lying converted from tillage unto pasture, and with hedges, ditches, pales, and otherwise, enclosed and kept several; by occasion whereof the same grounds and lands be brought to great sterility and barrenness, whereby not only the honor and service of God greatly is diminished but also thereby is engendered dearth and scarceness of every kind and manner of victuals through this realm; and by the same occasion idleness, the mother of all vices, sin, and mischief increased; and not only the living of innumerable tillers and husbandmen extinct and taken away, but also of other artificers, merchants, chapmen, and victualers in cities and borough towns (who take and have their livings by the said multitude and number of tillers and husbandmen) so extincted, whereby many of those cities, boroughs, and market towns of this his realm be brought to desolation, ruin, and decay, the service of God there withdrawn and taken away, and his people in number inestimably diminished as well to the high displeasure of Almighty God, as also in manifold and sundry wise to the great derogation of his most noble person, crown, and dignity royal.

Wherefore his grace, the premises considering, having tender zeal and respect above and before all other things to the honor of Almighty God, and the advancement of the commonwealth of this his realm, hath not only in his own person travailed by sundry businesses and devices, but also by the industry and diligence of his most dear and entirely beloved councilor, Thomas, Lord Cardinal Archbishop of York, Legate *de latere* of the See Apostolic and Chancellor of this his said realm, with other lords of his council, to reform, remove, and repress the foresaid great enormities and inconveniences and to cause and devise speedy reformation thereof; which notwithstanding, very little reformation thereof as yet is had or made, as evidently doth appear, to his no little grief and displeasure.

Wherefore his high majesty eftsoons determinably minding and intending to see the assured reformation of the premises, straightly chargeth and commandeth all the actors and offenders in the premises, of what estate, degree, and condition soever they be of, and also all the owners of every such towns, villages, hamlets, or other houses of husbandry decayed, brought to desolation and ruin, as is aforesaid, and the grounds and lands lying to them enclosed with hedges, ditches, pales, and other enclosure, and unlawfully brought from tillage into several pastures at any time sith the first year of the reign of his most dearest father of famous memory, King Henry VII, within this shire, whereof any inquisition or office is found and remaineth of record: that they and every of them, before the 15th of Michaelmas next coming, take away, destroy, cut, and cast down the hedges, pales, and other enclosures thereof, and fill the ditches and make the grounds plain as they were before the enclosures thereof had and made, as they and every of them at their uttermost perils will avoid his high displeasure, and upon such pain and danger as may further ensue to them and every of them. Except the owners of the same grounds so enclosed justify and sufficiently prove by good, true, and unfeigned allegations and approved reasons, to be made before the King our sovereign lord in his said high court of chancery at the said 15th of St. Michael, that the continuance and standing still of their hedges, pales, and other enclosures be not prejudicial, hurtful, nor to the annoyance of the King's subjects, nor contrary to the laws and commonwealth of his realm.

Further his grace willeth and commandeth that the said offenders and owners of the said grounds and lands so enclosed and perverted and turned from tillage unto pasture as before is expressed, and every of them of what estate or degree soever they be, that they, before the said Feast of St. Michael next ensuing, reduce into tillage so much ground and lands of the same pastures as were eared and tilled at any time in one year when it was exercised in tillage and husbandry by the tillers or husbandmen that manured and occupied the same grounds and lands at the time of the decaying of the same town, village, hamlet, or other house decayed as is beforesaid; or at any time seven years before the decay thereof; or in like manner and form as tillers and husbandmen of other towns next adjoining to the same town so decayed do exercise and use their grounds and lands in tillage and husbandry. And that this be done without fraud or color by the said Feast of St. Michael next coming, upon like penalty as is afore expressed.

111. Revaluing Coinage

[Hampton Court, 22 August 1526, 18 Henry VIII]

BM MS Harl 442, 45: date as above; writ to sheriff of Kent; schedule as below. Schanz *2*, 630: date 24 July; warrant authorizing Wolsey to take all necessary means. Stow *1*, 56: proclaimed in London on 6 September. Steele 104. Text (MS): Harl

Forasmuch as now of late in outward parts beyond the sea, as well in Flanders as in France, the price of money and gold, not only coined in those countries but also gold of the King our sovereign lord's coin of this realm, is so much enhanced in the valuation thereof that not only strange golds, as crowns and ducats, but also the gold of this realm, as nobles, half nobles, and royals, by merchants as well strangers resorting hither as the King's subjects repairing into those parts, for the great gain and lucre that they find thereby daily, be transported and carried out of this realm to no little impoverishing thereof, and finally to the total exhausting and drawing out of all the coins out of the same, unless speedy remedy be provided in that behalf; and albeit the King our sovereign lord hath given straight charge and commandment to all and singular his customers, comptrollers, and guardians of his ports to put all such good acts and statutes in execution as heretofore hath been made for conservation of the King's coin within this his realm, yet nevertheless, for the great gain and advantage thereof rising by reason of the high price of money beyond the sea, the King's coin is daily, by secret means such as cannot be espied nor deprehended, still carried over; and further where the King our sovereign lord, by his ambassadors resident with outward princes, have instantly required that the money of this his realm should not go so high in those parts to the intent that the price thereof there brought down, the same might still remain in this his realm, yet that notwithstanding, by reason of the pretense of their necessity and scarceness of gold in those parts, no remedy at their hands can be had or obtained;

For these causes the King our sovereign lord, tendering above all things the wealth and enriching of this his realm and people, and willing to provide remedy herein and that gold and coin may remain and be plenteously brought into the same and not carried out into outward parts, as of long season to the great detriment and impoverishing of his said realm the same hath been; for the remedying whereof there can be none other means and ways studied and devised but that all gold now current within this realm should be of like price and valuation as the same is valued, esteemed, and current in other outward parts, realms, and countries:

The King therefore straightly chargeth and commandeth all and singular his subjects of what estate, degree, or condition soever they be, in all payments hereafter to be made, to receive and take the crown of gold of the sun having his due weight and fineness, or any other crown of the same weight and fineness, for 4*s*. 6*d*. sterling. And forasmuch as for the foresaid purpose the said crowns be valued as afore according to the price and valuation that the same be of in outward parts, the King's highness, with the deliberate advice of his council, considering that the said crown of the sun is a strange gold, have thought convenient that semblably there should be a piece of gold of his own coin of like fineness, poise, and goodness as the said crown of the sun is, to be also current within this his realm, the same to be called the crown of the rose.

Wherefore his highness, for the considerations afore specified, chargeth and commandeth that in all payments hereafter the said crown of the rose shall be likewise current and taken at 4*s*. 6*d*. sterling, as the said crown of the sun is; and the single ducat large of fine gold and due weight, at 4*s*. 8*d*. sterling; and the double ducat of due fineness and weight, for 9*s*. 4*d*. sterling.

And furthermore, whosoever shall bring unto the King's mint any gold, coined or uncoined, of the fineness of the sovereign, royal, noble, or half-noble, shall have paid unto him in crowns after the valuation aforesaid or other money current within this realm, after the value of 44*s*. the ounce. That is to say, for every piece of such gold weighing half an ounce, as a sovereign of weight, 22*s*.; for every piece of gold weighing the fourth part of an ounce, as a royal of weight, 11*s*.; for every piece of gold weighing the sixth part of an ounce, as a noble of weight, 7*s*. 4*d*.; for every piece of gold weighing the twelfth part of an ounce, as a forty pence of weight, 3*s*. 8*d*. And the same in likewise to be current and taken in all manner payments and receipts after the rates and valuation aforesaid.

By means whereof, not only all manner of such coins of gold as be now current within this realm shall be contained and kept within the same without carrying thereof into any outward parts, but also such the King's coins of gold as hath been conveyed into outward parts shall be brought in again from time to time to the enriching of this realm and abundance of all manner of coins within the same.

And moreover the King's highness straightly chargeth and commandeth that from henceforth all manner groats, half-groats, and pence of his coin, and all other groats and half-groats not being of his coin, having course and being current within this his said realm, not clipped nor fully broken albeit they shall be much cracked, to be taken, received, and paid throughout his said realm without any manner refusal or denial.

Wherefore his highness straightly chargeth and expressly commandeth all mayors, justices of peace, sheriffs, bailiffs, constables, and other his faithful officers and subjects, that if any person or persons of what estate, degree, or condition he or they be, refuse or deny to take and receive the said moneys of gold and silver in manner and form aforesaid, be it for merchandises, victuals, change or rechange, or other cause whatsoever, forthwith to take and arrest the same person or persons so making refusal or denial, and to put him or them in ward and prison, there to remain and further to be punished at the King's pleasure.

112. Revaluing Coins, Announcing New Coinage

[Westminster, 5 November 1526, 18 Henry VIII]

BM MS Harl 442, 47: date as above; writ to sheriff of Kent; schedule as below. *L&P 4* (2), 2609: writ to sheriffs of London and Middlesex, cited from PR. Hall 154: proclaimed in London on 5 November. Steele 105. Text (MS): Harl

THE KING our sovereign lord, of his gracious disposition having always tender zeal and mind to the preservation and increase of the common weal of this his realm, the furtherance and enriching of his loving subjects of the same; perceiving how of late years the price and valuation of the coins of his said realm hath been as well in the Emperor's Low Countries as in other outward parts raised, heightened, and enhanced to the intent that by mean thereof the same might be craftily and for particular lucre secretly (as it hath been) conveyed out of this said realm to the great impoverishment of the same and the enriching of the said outward parts; considering also that after sundry requisitions made by his highness for reformation of such heightenings and enhancements no remedy can be had, but that the same rather daily increaseth than otherwise, whereby in process (notwithstanding the good laws and ordinances made to the contrary) the coin and money of this realm by little and little should be so much stolen and conveyed out of the same that the King's said loving subjects and people should be clearly disgarnished thereof if speedy remedy be not provided: hath by deliberate advice of his council, upon great and mature consultation, devised, determined, and ordered that, as well for conservation of his said coins within this realm and to encourage folks to bring into the same from outward parts coin and bullion of gold and silver as also for the enriching of his said loving subjects, not only the coins of gold of this realm, which heretofore have been made, stricken, and coined within the same, and certain other hereafter mentioned, shall be in their valuation and price raised and enhanced, but also other coins of gold and silver shall be newly made, stricken, and coined from henceforth, so rated and proportioned in their fineness, price, and value as shall be both to the great profit, commodity, ease, and equal computation of the King's subjects in their receipts and payments thereof, and also a mean to enrich this realm and to replenish the same with great quantity of gold and silver hereafter.

That is to say: the sovereign of due weight and fineness shall be current in all manner receipts and payments, for 22*s.* 6*d.* sterling; the royal of due weight and fineness, for 11*s.* 3*d.*; and so the half-royal and quarter of the royal of due weight and fineness, after the same rate; the angel noble of due weight and fineness, for 7*s.* 6*d.*; and the half-angel of due weight and fineness, for 3*s.* 9*d.* And besides these golds which be coins of this realm, the crown of the sun having his due weight and fineness, and all other crowns being of like weight and fineness with the crown of the sun, not notably broken, shall be still current as it now is in all receipts and payments for 4*s.* 6*d.*

And to the intent that there may also be coins to run in receipts and payments after such computation, for the more ease and commodity of the people as hath been heretofore used, it is ordained, devised, and established that over and besides the angel noble, which shall have course and be enhanced to 7*s.* 6*d.*, as is aforesaid, there shall be another noble newly made, which shall be called the George noble and shall be of as fine gold as the angel noble is, lacking in the weight the value of 10*d.* sterling; so as the said George noble shall be current and have course in all receipts and payments for the sum of 6*s.* 8*d.* sterling, as the angel noble was accustomed. And likewise there shall be of the same fineness an half-George noble, which shall be current for 3*s.* 4*d.* sterling. And forasmuch as the crown of the sun and other of the like weight and fineness which have course for 4*s.* 6*d.*, as is aforesaid, be not of so easy a computation for the King's subjects and other not expert in reckoning, as crowns should be proportioned after an even rate to the pound sterling, it is therefore ordained, determined, and established by the King's highness, with the deliberate advice of his said council as is aforesaid, that there shall be a certain new coin of gold of the King's, made and devised, which shall be named a crown of the double rose, and shall be in weight after such rate above the crown of the sun that it may be current in all receipts and payments for 5*s.* sterling, so as four of them shall make in all computations 20*s.* sterling. And likewise there shall be another coin or piece of gold of like fineness with the said crown of the double rose of the half weight of the same, which shall be current for 2*s.* 6*d.* sterling.

And for like correspondence, equality, and evenness in the silver to the rate, proportion, and valuation of the said coins of gold, it is also devised and determined that to make the silver to accord in his rate with the said course of the gold, all manner coins of silver now already current in this realm, as groats not clipped nor notably broken, pence of 2*d.,* half-pence, and farthings shall hereafter be current in receipts and payments after the same rate as they have hitherto been. And likewise as 20 of the said groats, and so half-groats, pence, half-pence, and farthings, after the rate, were current for an angel noble, so shall they now be in likewise current for the noble of the George, and 15 groats for the crown of the double rose.

And over and besides the said coins of silver now current, it is determined that new coins of silver shall be from henceforth stricken and made, as well into groats as into pence of 2*d.,* half-pence, and farthings, which new coins of silver shall be mere sterling as the other be and shall be made and sized to be correspondent in value according to all manner the King's coins of fine gold before mentioned, so that every ounce troy of groats, half-groats, pence, half-pence and farthings, or the ounce troy of bullion, shall make 11 groats and one penny, whereof the merchant shall pay for the coinage 1*d.,* and so he shall receive for an ounce sterling, either at the mint or at the exchange (after it shall be molten), clearly 3*s.* 8*d.* in money current. Howbeit if any person having white money of the former coins of this realm shall think that the same is of more value than after the rate of the said new money devised now to be stricken, it shall be lawful for him at his pleasure and liberty to bring it unto the King's mint or exchange, where he shall receive for every ounce of the same groats or other white money of this realm (after the same shall be molten) 11 groats over and above the odd penny deducted for the coinage thereof as is aforesaid. And semblably in all bullion of silver being of the fineness of sterling. And if any such bullion be better than the sterling he shall be answered therefor after the rate, goodness, and fineness thereof accordingly.

And whereas the carolus placks of the old coin of the Duke of Burgundy, commonly called double placks, lack in their fineness of the sterling 20*d.* in a pound weight troy, it is ordained and determined that they not being clipped nor notably broken shall also be current in receipts and payments for 4*d.* sterling the piece, as they now be. Howbeit if any person shall think to take more advantage by them in bringing the same to the mint or exchange, converting them into the coin of silver newly devised, it shall be lawful for him so to do, where he shall receive for the pound weight which is 12 ounces Troy, after it shall be molten, 43*s.* 4*d.,* deducting of the same for the coinage of every ounce Troy, 1*d.* sterling as is aforesaid.

And whereas heretofore the merchant or other person bringing bullion unto the King's mint to be coined, paid for the coinage of every pound Tower weight, which was 11¼ ounces, 2*s.* 6*d.,* in which Tower weight there was a difference from the Troy weight of three quarters of an ounce in a pound weight, it is now determined by the King's highness as afore that the said pound Tower shall be no more used nor occupied, but that all manner gold and silver shall be weighed by the pound Troy being of 12 ounces Troy, which is three quarters of an ounce more than Tower weight as is aforesaid. For which cause the merchant or other person bringing gold to the mint to be coined shall pay for coinage of every pound of weight Troy of fine gold, being 12 ounces, to be made into George nobles or half nobles, or any other the King's coins of fine gold, 2*s.* 9*d.*; and for the coinage of every pound weight of gold to be made into the crowns of the double rose or the half thereof, 3*s.* sterling.

And forasmuch as it is by diligent search and trial well proved and known that there be many ducats coined in the parts of beyond the sea whereof some having one print, coin, and mark, be far different and lacking in the fineness and weight of other being of the same coin and mark, and that also in divers countries there be ducats made of divers fineness and weights; by reason whereof, if the same were current in receipts and payments within this his realm by the way of ordinance or proclamation, the King's people then not being expert in knowledge of the fineness of the gold might take great loss and be deceived therein: it is therefore ordained and determined as afore that there shall be no certain valuation, rate, or course assigned for receipt and payment of any ducats, double or single, of what country soever they be, current within this realm, nor of any other coin of gold or silver other than is before mentioned. But as well ducats as other coins of gold of outward parts not before named shall now be received and taken by any person at such value as the payer and the receiver of them can agree, and as between them they shall be found to be worth in weight and fineness. Nevertheless if any person shall think that he may take profit by bringing of such ducats of fine or coarse gold or other coins of gold or bullion unto the King's mint, it shall be lawful for him so to do, there to have them coined or to receive other money for them after the same rates and proportions, paying for the coinage thereof after the form before expressed.

It is also ordained and determined that all other ordinances, provisions, and proclamations heretofore passed for the valuation or course of any coins of gold and silver within this realm, for as much part of the same proclamations as may be prejudicial or contrary to the effect of these present ordinances, shall be from henceforth void and of none effect. And that no person, under color of this raising or enhancing of the valuation of money, do presume to heighten or raise the price of any wares, merchandises, victuals, or other thing in buying, selling, or changing of the same, except only bullion of gold and silver to the rates aforesaid, upon the uttermost pain that by so doing may ensue, considering that no man can or shall take loss or detriment by enhancing of the coins, but that the same with all other coins newly to be made shall be as much in value to the receiver thereof for any ware, victual, merchandise, or other thing as the coin and money was accustomed to be heretofore.

And forasmuch as by reason of the enhancing of the said coins of gold there may some doubt or question arise in what form and rate money already due either unto the King's highness or to the lords spiritual or temporal or other his nobles, commons, and subjects of this his realm, and other his dominions, shall and ought to be paid and received: it is for declaration thereof by his highness ordained and determined that all sums of money growing of rent, farms, or other revenues of lands, tenements, or other hereditaments, yet remaining in the hands of the tenants and not paid to the bailiffs, collectors, rent gatherers, reeves, or other persons appointed for gathering or receipt of the same, shall be paid, received and taken after such rate as the moneys of gold and silver shall be current by virtue of this proclamation and none otherwise. Nevertheless, if the same be paid by the tenants, farmers, or other occupiers of the premises, unto the hands of any of the said bailiffs, collectors, rent gatherers, reeves, or other persons appointed for gathering thereof, before the day of the date hereof, the same bailiffs, collectors, rent gatherers, reeves, or other persons appointed for that purpose shall make payment thereof in such money and after such price and valuation as they have received the same, according to reason, wherein they shall and may be tried as well by their oaths as by any other examination that may be made by any person having interest in the same.

It is also ordained that all other sums of money which upon any obligation, covenant, bargain, promise, bill, grant of parliament, or otherwise, was payable to the King's highness or any other person at any time between the date of the last proclamation made of coins, which was the 22nd day of August last past, and the day of the date of this present proclamation, shall be paid, received, and taken after such rate as the moneys and coins of gold and silver by virtue of the said last proclamation was valued and current. And semblably all such other sums of money which upon like respects or otherwise shall be payable to the King's highness or to any other person from the day of the date of this present proclamation forwards, shall be paid, received, and taken after such rate as the moneys and coins of gold and silver by this said proclamation be valued current and limited; and furthermore that all such sums of money as for like respects were payable and the day of payment come, passed, and expired before the date of the said last proclamation, that is to say, the 22nd day of August last past, shall be paid, received, and taken forasmuch as was the very debt and duty, not mentioning any penalty after such rate as the moneys and coins of gold and silver were current and going before the same last proclamation, like as to good reason, justice, and conscience it appertaineth.

Nevertheless forasmuch as both general and particular receivers, customers, collectors, bailiffs, and reeves, as also divers other officers, ministers, and accountants both unto the King's highness and to the lords spiritual and temporal and other noble men, subjects, and commons of this realm, have since and before the said last proclamation received divers sums of money as well of customs and subsidies for merchandises and of the subsidies and other sums granted to the King's highness in his last parliament, as also for rents, farms, and otherwise, in such money and after such rate as the same was current at the time of the receipt thereof; which said general and particular receivers and other officers and ministers aforesaid have not made immediate payment thereof before the times of the new proclamations, but have the same remaining in their hands till the time of their accounts and reckonings, intending percase under color of this ordinance to make their payments after these new rates, as money not payable till the yielding of the said accounts, and so detain in their hands the gain thereof without any ground of reason: it is therefore ordained that the said receivers, general and particular, customers, collectors, bailiffs, rent gatherers, reeves, and other officers and ministers aforesaid, which so by virtue of their offices have received any money of any farms, tenants, or other persons after the old or former rates of the same shall make payment thereof in such money and after such valuation as they received, gathered, and levied the same, without detaining any lucre or gain thereof in their hands, wherein they shall and may be tried as well by their oaths as by any other examination that may be made on the behalf of any person having interest in the same as is aforesaid.

Wherefore his highness straightly chargeth and commandeth all mayors, justices of peace, sheriffs, bailiffs, constables, and all other his faithful subjects and officers of what estate, degree, or condition soever he or they be, that if any person or persons do refuse or deny to obey and follow the effect of this his ordinance and proclamation, or any part thereof in form above specified, forthwith to take and arrest the same person or persons so refusing or denying, and to commit him or them to ward and prison, there to remain without bail or mainprize unto such time as the King's determinate pleasure be further known in that behalf.

113. Ordering Appearances for Enclosures

[Westminster, 21 November 1526, 18 Henry VIII]

Antiq 1, 41: date proclaimed in Chancery as above; schedule as below. Steele 106. Text (MS): Antiq

THE KING our sovereign lord straightly chargeth and commandeth all and singular persons summoned by his writ of subpoena or by his commissioners, or otherwise warned to appear in the King's Chancery for enclosures, that they and every of them appear in his said Chancery on Friday next coming or else writs of attachment shall be awarded against them and every of them without further delay.

114. Ordering Recognizances for Enclosures

[Westminster, 28 November 1526, 18 Henry VIII]

BM MS Harl 442, 52*v:* date proclaimed in Chancery as above; schedule as below. Steele 107. Text (MS): Harl

THE KING our sovereign lord straightly chargeth and commandeth all and singular persons called into this his Court of Chancery, by writs or other process or by commandment for enclosures, and as yet have not entered into the recognizance made and devised for reformation of the same, that they and every of them so not bound by recognizance appear before the commissioners appointed in that behalf from day to day, and by the same commissioners to be ordered and not to depart, upon pain of 500 marks.

115. Establishing Calais as a Market Town

[Calais, 13 July 1527, 19 Henry VIII]

BM MS Harl 442, 54: date as above; writ to mayor of Calais; schedule as below. Steele 108. Text (MS): Harl

THE KING our sovereign lord, minding and intending the wealth and increase and enriching of his realm of England and of this his town of Calais and the marches of the same; and that not only his own subjects but also other strangers, of what origin soever they be, might have the more desire and courage to repair to this his said town and marches; and for other great resorts and considerations: with the advice of his council, by these his letters patent of proclamation, freely giveth and granteth full liberty and license, and also ordaineth and determineth, that as well all and singular his subjects merchant and occupiers of all manner wares and merchandises, and also all other merchants stranger of what nation or country soever they be, that they and every of them from henceforth shall issue, resort, and repair from time to time with their goods, wares, and merchandises unto this his town of Calais and marches of the same, and there to buy and sell, change and rechange, with as large and ample freedoms and liberties and immunities as they have had and enjoyed at or in any mart or marts holden and kept at Antwerp, Bruges, or Bergen-op-Zoom, or within any other city, borough, or town within the Emperor's Low Countries of Flanders or Holland, Zeeland or Brabant, or any of them. Provided always and foreseen (inasmuch as the same town of Calais is a town of war) that no stranger enter the same town with any armor or weapons nor do nor attempt anything contrary to the statutes and ordinances made and established for the sure keeping thereof.

And further the King's highness willeth and giveth liberty as is aforesaid to all manner merchants, as well his subjects as other merchants stranger, resorting and repairing unto his said town of Calais and marches thereof, during their abode there to do and abide under his gracious protection, defense, surety, and safeguard in their bodies, goods, and merchandises; and thither to resort, come and go, pass and repass merchantly at all times at their liberties by land, sea, and fresh waters, and on horse or on foot, by chariot, wagon, cart, or with any manner of other carriage, with their factors, attorneys, familiars, or servants; and in the same town of Calais and marches to be conversant, remain, sojourn, and abide, there to occupy and exercise the feat of merchandise in buying, selling, bartering, changing, rechanging, or distributing their goods and merchandises at all times at their free wills and liberties without let, disturbance, arrest, vexation, impediment, or contradiction of the captains, deputy, lieutenant, the treasurer, marshal, and comptroller of the same town of Calais, or of the mayor there for the time being, or any customer, comptroller, voucher, bailiff, water bailiff, toller, warden of the passage, or of any other officer or officers whatsoever they be for the time being, or of the lieutenant or keeper of the castle of Calais, or of the keeper or constable of the tower of Rysbank, or of the keeper of Devononbridge for the time being, or of any other person or persons for them or for any of them, and without paying any head money, half-passage money, traverse money, sandgeld, wharfgeld, the Flemish toll, otherwise named brokage of the haven, or any other toll whatsoever they be, except only such customs and tolls as the King's merchants and subjects have paid and be accustomed to pay at the foresaid marts holden at Antwerp and elsewhere within the Emperor's said Low Countries; and that it be lawful also to the King's merchants adventurer, as also to all other merchants stranger, to ship their goods and merchandises from the said town and port of Calais in all ship or ships of what nation soever they be, at their choice and liberty without paying thenceforth any half-passage or any other exaction to be taken of them for their ships, goods, or merchandises. Upon pain to every person and persons offending in this behalf, to be forthwith put in ward and prison, there to remain without bail or mainprize and furthermore to pay and make fine at the King's pleasure. And that all the King's subjects merchant may peaceably and quietly resort, repair, and come into the same town of Calais and marches from time to time with their goods and merchandises, and from thence to pass and go at their liberties, and not to be vexed, troubled, grieved, or arrested in person or goods for any manner debt or duty, growing or rising upon or for any manner contract or bargain made out of the said town and marches (if the party grieved will require this freedom), except only for contracts and bargains made within the same town of Calais and marches there. And that all merchants stranger be as free in bodies and goods within the said town's port and marches of Calais as the King's subjects merchant be, or owe, or pretend to be, within the Emperor's Low Countries during the freedom of any mart holden or kept there, the provision before specified and made for guarding and surety of the town of Calais foresaid always saved.

And albeit that the merchants stranger exercising the feats of merchandise at the said marts heretofore holden in the said Emperor's Low Countries have been accustomed to pay divers and many more toll charges, customs, and impositions, and more larger, for their goods and merchandises thither brought than the King's subjects merchant repairing to the same mart: yet the King's highness, of his grace especial and bounteousness willing the merchants stranger which hereafter shall resort for cause of merchandises unto his said town and marches of Calais favorably and lovingly to be entertained and used within the same, so that by means thereof they may be encouraged to repair to the same towns and marches from time to time hereafter, hath therefore of his singular good grace and favor ordained and determined that all and every such merchant and merchants stranger pay for their goods and merchandises within the said town, port, and marches of Calais, coming and going to and from the same town, port, and marches of Calais for the said cause of merchandises, none other tolls, *gabels,* exactions, impositions, or customs than the King's subjects merchant have paid or owe to pay within the Emperor's said Low Countries at the marts holden there; and in likewise all merchants the King's subjects to pay for their goods and merchandises to be by them brought unto the said town, port, and marches of Calais, such customs, *gabels,* and tolls as the same merchants, the King's subjects, have paid, owe to pay, or have been accustomed to pay for the same in the said Emperor's Low Countries, and none other nor in none otherwise. And that no merchants stranger repairing to the said town and marches of Calais, or from thence going, be constrained within the said town, port, or marches to pay any other toll, custom, *gabel,* or exaction for their goods or merchandises, or any of them, than be rated and extended upon the King's subjects merchant in the privileges of Duke Philip of Burgundy, confirmed by the towns of Antwerp and Bergen-op-Zoom, according to certain tables thereupon to be made, whereof one table to be set in the open market place of Calais, the second in the customs house there, and the third in the King's exchequer of Calais. And if any officer of the said town, port, or marches, exact or levy any tolls or customs above the rate expressed in the said tables, and thereof found culpable, every such officer to be punished by imprisonment and fines at the King's pleasure, as is above expressed. And in case the said merchants stranger or any of them by covert concealing or not entering their goods and merchandises in the customer's books there to be appointed, bring in or convey out of the said town of Calais or marches in defrauding the King's highness of his said customs, then they to be mulcted and punished with like pains and forfeitures as the King's subjects, for like offense and concealment, have and owe to sustain and bear within the Emperor's said Low Countries.

And as touching the King's subjects, if they or any of them, by concealing or not entering their goods and merchandises in the customer's books there to be appointed, bring in or convey out of the said town or port of Calais or marches of the same, in defrauding the King's highness of his said customs, then they and every of them from time to time and as often as they shall so offend to pay unto the King's highness the said toll, and for their punishment of concealment 10 times so much over and besides the said toll. And also that the governor or governors of the said merchants adventurer, or such a person as they shall choose to be their ruler for the time being, may have and use like authority, power, and jurisdiction in the rule and government of the said merchants at the time of their abode at Calais and marches aforesaid, as the governor or governors of the same merchants have had, used, or ought to have in the said Emperor's Low Countries. And that all actions of debt, trespass, or other variance, to be moved or attained within the said town and marches by any merchant or merchants adventurer against any of the said merchants adventurer, stapler or others, for any cause or matter concerning the feat of merchants adventurer, or by any person or persons against any of the said merchants adventurer for causes concerning their said feat, be commenced afore the governor or governors and fellowships of the same merchants, there examined, pursued, and finally determined by sentence definitive without any further appeals, according and in like manner as the grants be made unto them in the said Emperor's Low Countries. And in likewise all actions of debt, trespass, or other variance to be moved or attained within the said town and marches by any merchant or merchants of the Staple against any of the merchants, fellowship, or servants of the said Staple, merchants adventurer or others, for any cause or matter concerning the feats of merchants of the Staple, or by any other person or persons against any of the said merchants of the Staple for cause or matter concerning their said feat, be commenced before the mayor of the said Staple, there examined, pursued, and finally determined by sentence definitive without any further appeal. The statute and ordinances of the said town of Calais provided for punishment of malefactors and trespassers in criminal causes, violators and breakers of the King's peace, or any of the ordinances within the same always standing in their full strength, vigor, and effect.

And that also all and every merchant of the Staple using and exercising the said feat of merchants adventurer, buying or bartering any of the merchandises belonging to the same feat, not only observe and keep the statute and ordinances made or to be made and ordained from time to time by the said merchants adventurer, but also be contributories unto them for the same, like as other merchants adventurer do or hereafter owe to do; and also that every merchant adventurer using or exercising the said feat of merchants of the Staple, buying or bartering any of the merchandises belonging to the same feat of the Staple, not only observe and keep the statutes and ordinances made or to be made and ordained from time to time by the said merchants of the Staple, but also be contributories unto them for the same like as other merchants of the Staple do or hereafter owe to do. And if any officer or officers within the said town, marches, or port of Calais constrain or compel the King's merchants adventurer or stranger, to pay any toll, custom, *gabel* or exaction for their goods and merchandises at the said town, marches, or port of Calais, inward or outward, or compel any merchants stranger to pay any toll, custom, or exactions other than by the effect of the said articles and the said tables shall be rated and extended, that then the King's treasurer and comptroller of the town for the time being and the said governor or governors and ruler jointly, or two of them at the least, whereof the governor to be one, have power and authority to examine the causes and complaints of the merchants grieved in this part and to levy of the officer or officers so offending six times the value of such exaction or exactions, besides imprisonment and other punishment of his body at the King's pleasure, whereof half to be paid to the King and the other half to be paid to the party grieved. Also that the said merchants adventurer may be corporate within the said town and marches as they be in the said Emperor's Low Countries, and that they may keep their courts and assemblies and make ordinances and statutes for their politic rule and government and ordain and levy fines, forfeitures, and impositions, and establish weights and measures and also admit meters, measurers, ployers, and packers, and order and extend peisage, cranage, carters, and rollwains in like manner and form as the said merchants have made, ordained, established, and used in the Emperor's said Low Countries, and this without interruption, let, impediment, or challenge of the mayor, water bailiff, or any other officer or officers within the said town, port, or marches, upon pain of imprisonment and fine to be cessed by the King's treasurer, comptroller, and governor of the said merchants or his deputy as is aforesaid rehearsed, half to be applied to the King and the other half to the party grieved. Also all persons having showhouses or packhouses within the said town or marches shall let to farm the same houses to the merchants adventurer for reasonable prices; and if the owners of such houses be unreasonable in that part, that then the ruler or governors of the said fellowships and the King's deputy and treasurer there have power to choose four merchants adventurer and four persons indifferent, inhabitants of the said town of Calais, the same persons or the more part of them to rate, cess, and extend the farm of every such showhouse or packhouse after a reasonable price so as the merchants and also the owner may both have reasonable cause to be contented.

And also it is ordained and established by the King's highness that merchants of the Hanse, France, Spain, Portugal, and all other merchants comprised in league and amity made by their princes and heads with the King's grace, and also Florentines, Genoese, Venetians, Luccans, Bolognese, Milanese, Italians, with all other merchants which be in the town or marches of Calais or hereafter shall be under the King's safe-conduct, shall not convey nor do to be conveyed, by themselves nor by any other for them, by fraud, color, or *mal engine* into the parts or any place within the said Emperor's Low Countries, any woolen cloths or other of the King's commodities, upon pain of forfeiture of all such goods and merchandises or the value of the same goods and merchandises; two parts of the said forfeiture to belong to the King's highness and the third part to the finder. Nevertheless if the said merchants of the Hanse, Italians, or other, intend to convey cloths or other merchandises of the commodities of the King's realm of England into their own countries through the said Emperor's Low Countries and dominions, the King's highness is contented that they so do and bring the commodities of their own countries through the said Emperor's Low Countries and dominions into his said realm of England, or to his said town and marches of Calais: provided always that before they ship the said commodities of his said realm of England to be conveyed into their own countries as above, they make sufficient sureties and bonds before the King's comptroller and customers of such town and port where the said goods and merchandises shall be shipped, in the custom house there, that they shall not break no bulk, open no pack for making sale, bartering, commutation, or dressing of any part of the said merchandises within the obeisance of the said Emperor's Low Countries and dominions, but only to be dried if necessity so require; also in likewise that none of the same merchants of the Hanse, or any other for them, bring or do to be brought into his said realm of England or into any other place under his obeisance, any goods, wares, or merchandises, unless they buy the same at the said town of Calais or the marches of the same. And furthermore and in like manner his highness giveth and granteth full liberty and license to all manner persons, victualers and other folks bringing victuals from any part on this side the sea, that they shall move in likewise at all times at their liberties and without let, interruption, or impediment of any person or persons, bring victuals of all manner kinds unto his said town and port of Calais and marches of the same for vitualing thereof; and there to abide, sojourn, pass, and repass with their ships, boats, horses, carriages, and other baggages; and as favorably to be used and entertained as any victualers be within the dominions of any other prince or princes whatsoever they be, without paying any manner imposition, toll, exaction, or other demand for the same as is abovesaid, either within this his said town and port of Calais or within any port of the marches of the same.

And all and singular the premises the King's highness commandeth duly and effectually from this day forward to be executed, upon the avoiding of his high indignation and displeasure; and over and besides that, the offender or offenders in the premises to be committed to ward, there to remain without bail or mainprize as is above specified.

And therefore his highness straightly chargeth and commandeth his deputy with all and singular his councilors and captains of the said town and marches of Calais and also the mayor and burgesses, bailiffs and constables of his said town and all other his faithful officers, servants, and subjects, that they and every of them be aiding, helping, counseling, furthering, and assisting the due, plain, and effectual execution of this the King's high pleasure and commandment, as they will answer unto his grace at their uttermost perils. And to the intent that all merchants, as well strangers as other, may have perfect knowledge and notice of every point and article comprised in this proclamation, the King our sovereign lord therefore hath ordained that the same shall with all diligence and speed be put in print so that therein no man shall or may pretend any ignorance.

116. Providing Victual for London

[Richmond, 25 September 1527, 19 Henry VIII]

LL O, 57: date as above; writ, under signet, to all mayors, sheriffs, bailiffs, constables, officers, ministers, and subjects; schedule as below. Not in Steele. Text (MS): LL

THE KING our sovereign lord, for many great and divers considerations his grace specially moving, willing his city and chamber of London to be substantially furnished and provided of wheat, malt, rye, and all other grains, as well for the benefit and commodity of the noblemen of this his realm and all other repairing to the same city, as of the citizens and inhabitants of the same, giveth full power, license, and authority to all and every person and persons within this his realm, as well within liberties as without, that will repair to the said city with any wheat, malt, rye, or other grain for the victualing of the same, may [*sic*] at all times from henceforth at their liberties freely, quietly, and peaceably without any let or interruption of any person or persons, lade, carry, and convey the same to the said city, as well by land as by water.

And further, his highness willeth and giveth straightly in commandment to all justices of peace, sheriffs, mayors, bailiffs, constables, customers, comptrollers, searchers and their deputies, and all other ministers and officers, as well within liberties as without, to whom it shall appertain, within this his realm, that they and every of them permit and suffer all and every such person and persons freely and quietly and also peaceably, without let or interruption of them or any of them, to lade, carry, and convey all such wheat, malt, rye, and all other grain to the said city for the victualing of the same, as they will avoid the King's high displeasure, and any act, proclamation, restraint, commandment, or provision heretofore had, made, or granted, to the contrary, under his Great Seal or otherwise, notwithstanding.

Foreseen and provided that the customers, comptrollers, searchers, or one of them, of every port, haven, or creek where any such wheat, malt, rye, or other grain or victual shall be laden to be conveyed to the said city, shall take sufficient bonds of the owners or conveyers of the said wheat, malt, rye, and other grain, that they and every of them shall truly convey the same to the said city of London, to and for the victualing of the same, and to none other place;

Provided also, that the effect of this power, authority, and license contained in this proclamation shall endure no longer but the space of three weeks after the publication of the same proclamation;

Provided also, furthermore, that the said proclamation be made in all such places, as the citizens of the said city trust to be relieved of within eight days of the date hereof at the furthest, not failing hereof as they will avoid the King's high displeasure.

117. Ordering Repairs in Calais

[Westminster, 12 October 1527, 19 Henry VIII]

BM MS Harl 442, 61: date as above; writ to mayor of Calais; schedule as below. Steele 109. Text (MS): Harl

THE KING our sovereign lord, calling to his remembrance, and by experience perfectly knowing, the great deformities and many other inconveniences evidently appearing and daily ensuing within his town of Calais by means of the decays of houses and mansions and habitations, to sundry lords and others appertaining within the said town, suffering the same by their negligence for lack of repairs to fall in extreme ruin, decay, and desolation: therefore straightly chargeth and commandeth that all and singular the same lords and others having such lands, houses, mansions, or habitations in ruins, desolation, or decay within the space of —— at the furthest after the day of this present proclamation, sufficiently to repair, build, and re-edify the same, so that by means thereof not only the deformities of the same town may be holpen and amended but also the habitation of the same continued, advanced, and increased; not failing so to do upon pain of such forfeitures and other dangers as be contained as well in the acts and statutes[1] made and ordained in that case by authority of parliament as also by other provisions and ordinances politicly devised and provided and made for the reformation of ruins and decays and the maintenance of the King's said town, which the King's grace purposeth to put in effectual execution without any further delays, respite, or favor. Charging also and straightly commanding all and singular his said officers of this his said town not only to register this the King's proclamation in the book of acts and ordinances, but also to be put in due and effectual execution and accomplishment thereof according to the tenor of the said statute and ordinances and the purport of this the King's proclamation, as they and every of them will answer to the King at their perils.

118. Prohibiting Grain Engrossing; Enforcing Statutes against Vagabonds, Unlawful Games

[Westminster, 12 November 1527, 19 Henry VIII]

BM MS Harl 442, 62: date as above; writ to sheriff of Kent; schedule as below. Steele 110. Text (MS): Harl

WHERE by diligent and due examination of sundry discreet, wise, and honest personages it is come to the knowledge of the King our sovereign lord that in all shires and countries within this his realm of England, by divers and many regraters, forestallers, and engrossers of wheat and other grain, which detain the same corn and grain, not bringing it to the open markets to be sold to the King's subjects; by means and occasion whereof there is pretended to be more scarcity of wheat and other grain within this realm than (God be thanked) there is indeed, whereby the prices of the same be unreasonably raised and enhanced to the great detriment of the King's loving subjects unless speedy remedy for the same be had and provided:

The King's highness therefore of his most gracious and virtuous disposition, having tender zeal and love to the common weal of this his realm and subjects, minding and intending the speedy redress of the premises, straightly chargeth and commandeth that no manner of person or persons, spiritual or temporal, of what estate, pre-eminence, or degree soever he or they be, do from henceforth in any manner of wise regrate, forestall, or engross any wheat or any other manner of grain; and that as well the said regraters, forestallers, and engrossers, as all and every other person and persons having plenty and store of wheat and other grain, do bring or cause to be brought weekly to some market or markets being within the county of their inhabitation or nigh thereunto, a convenient and reasonable portion of wheat and

1. 21 Richard II, c. 18, 1397, *SR* 2, 108; 10 Henry VI, c. 5, 1432, *SR* 2, 274.

other grain to be sold from time to time at a reasonable price, as they tender the King's high pleasure and will avoid his indignation and such other punishments as be provided by his laws and statutes in that behalf made.

And to the intent that no person or persons shall be found hereafter remiss or negligent in performing this the King's ordinance and high commandment but that every part thereof be duly observed, his highness, by deliberate advice of his most honorable council, hath appointed in every shire within this his realm certain wise, discreet, and substantial personages to be his commissioners; authorizing them by his commission to visit and search the barns, garners, ricks, and stacks of all and every such person and persons which is or be supposed to have more corn than shall be thought convenient by their discretions for the use of their households and seed; and to compel the owners thereof to bring the same unto the markets, there to be sold to the King's subjects at a reasonable and convenient price according to his said laws and statutes; causing the offenders and disobeyers of this his grace's commandment for the transgressing and breaking thereof not only to be punished according to his said laws but also to certify the names of them and only of them to the King and his most honorable council in the Star Chamber at Westminster in the octaves of St. Hilary next coming, there to be further ordered as shall stand with equity and the commonweal of this his realm.

But forasmuch as the city of London is a populous city, as well of the inhabitants and dwellers in the same as also of noblemen, strangers, and divers others, which daily do repair and resort unto the same city by reason of the laws there being ministered, merchandises, and other occasions and business; is in great indigence and scarcity of wheat and other grain: in consideration thereof, and to the intent the said city may in such necessity be the better served and relieved, the King's pleasure is that notwithstanding any words or restraint mentioned in this proclamation, his justices of the peace, commissioners, ministers, and subjects shall permit and suffer the purveyors of the said city, being authorized by the writing and the common seal of the same, to buy in every shire within this realm (where convenient plenty of grain is known to be) as much wheat and other grain as shall be needful and sufficient for the relieving of the said city, by the discretion, views, and estimation of the said commissioners without let or disturbance made to them by any person or persons. And also his like will and pleasure is that all meal-men and malt-men using to bring and carry meal and malt to serve the said city shall be suffered in likewise from henceforth to bring and carry meal and malt to the same as they have done in times past. Foreseen always that no shire or shires be thereby dispurveyed or unfurnished but that there be left within the same shire or shires sufficient wheat and other grain for the relief and sustentation of the same shire or shires and the inhabitants of the same.

Moreover our said sovereign lord, considering that by the remiss and negligent oversight of his justices of the peace, mayors, sheriffs, bailiffs, constables, petty constables, tithing men, and other his ministers of the law, the good and profitable statutes and ordinances made and ordained as well by his highness as other his noble progenitors concerning beggars, vagabonds, unlawful games, suspect inns and alehouses, and divers other good acts and ordinances, have not of long time been put in due and effectual execution; by reason whereof as well vagabonds and valiant beggars be increased to an infinite number and multitude, as also by long suffering of idleness and vice unpunished, divers and sundry thefts, burglaries, robberies, murders, and divers other heinous offenses against the King's laws be daily committed to the great inquietation of the King's true subjects and to the no little grief and displeasure of our said most dread sovereign lord.

His highness therefore, most graciously intending the due and speedy reformation of the premises, willing this his said realm to be in quietness and good order, straightly chargeth and commandeth all and every his said justices of the peace, mayors, sheriffs, bailiffs, constables, petty constables, headboroughs, and tithing men, and all other his ministers that they, laying apart all feigned and vain pity, affection, and dread and all other excuses and delays, from henceforth execute as to them appertaineth and as often as cause shall require the Statute of Winchester,[1] and all and every other statute and statutes concerning vagabonds, beggars, unlawful games, suspect inns, taverns, and alehouses, according to the true meaning and purport of the said acts and statutes in that case provided; with such circumspection and diligence as the King's highness shall not eftsoons have cause or need to send or give to them any further commandment in that behalf, as they will avoid his indignation and displeasure with condign punishment for their negligent demeanor, to the fearful example of other his subjects which shall happen hereafter to be in like authority and office.

119. Ordering Information Given on Enclosed Lands

[Westminster, 15 May 1528, 20 Henry VIII]

BM MS Harl 442, 65: date proclaimed in Chancery as above; schedule as below. Steele 111. Text (MS): Harl

THE KING our sovereign lord straightly chargeth and commandeth all and singular his subjects being relaters and furtherers of the commonwealth of this his realm, that they, by writing and bills, secretly disclose unto the Lord Legate, his Chancellor of England, the names of all such person and persons

1. 13 Edward I, c. 4 (Winchester), 1285, *SR 1*, 97.

of what estate, degree, or condition he or they be, who hath and keepeth in his hands and possession within any part of this the King's realm any more farms than one; and moreover by the same bills to disclose to the same Lord Chancellor the names of such persons as do enclose any grounds or pastures, to the hurt of the commonwealth of this the King's realm. And the same Lord Chancellor shall keep secret the same bills, so as no person shall fall into any indignation or displeasure of any man for his said disclosing. And for the receiving of the said bills from time to time, the said Lord Chancellor hath deputed Mr. Throgmorton and Mr. Clayburgh, Masters of the King's Chancery.

120. Announcing Truce with France and Empire

[Westminster, 17 June 1528, 20 Henry VIII]

STC 7770 (UM 5,25,296), BM C.18.3.2, 81: printed by R. Pynson (London, 1528); fragments of schedule below. *CSPSpanish* 3(2), 322: date, Vienna, 30 May; Emperor asks English ambassador to inform him of reported alliance with France. LJ 13, 53*v:* date as above; writ to mayor and sheriffs of London; schedule as below. Hall 176*v:* proclaimed in London on 19 June. Steele 112: date, 27 June. Text (MS): LJ

The King our sovereign doth give you knowledge that to the honor and praise of Almighty God, and to come unto universal peace to the weal of all Christendom, there is passed, accorded, and concluded between his highness for this his realm of England and all other his countries, isles, seigniories, and dominions, whatsoever they be on this side the sea or beyond, and the French King for the realm of France, his countries and seigniories on this side the mountains, and also the Emperor for his duchies, earldoms, countries, and seigniories of Brabant, Limburg, Faulquemont, Dalheim, Luxembourg, Flanders, Artois, Hainaut, Holland, Zeeland, Frisia, Onnreyselle, and Namur, and also Tournay, Tourneysies, and all other whereof the Lady Margaret, Archduchess of Austria, Duchess and Countess of Burgundy, and the Dowager of Savoy, hath the regime and governance, their heirs and successors, a good, true, sincere, and [firm] truce, abstinence of war, and deposition of armor by land, sea, and fresh waters, for the space and term of eight months next ensuing, to begin the 15th day of this present month of June, and to endure over and above the said eight months, till such time as one of the said princes shall have signified and given knowledge to the other that he will no longer hold and keep it; and also two months after any such signification, to the intent that the merchants and subjects of the one part and the other may in those two months bring home their persons, merchandises, and goods in surety.

By the which truce, abstinence of war, and putting off armor, it is covenanted, accorded, and concluded that during the same there shall cease between the said princes, their vassals, subjects, men of war, soldiers, and other whatsoever they be, being at their commandment, all force of arms, hostility, invasions, wastes, [in]roads, pilleries, burnings, and taking of people and of goods and all manner of exploits of war, as well by sea as by land and fresh water; so that all the said vassals, merchants, and other subjects of the said princes demurring and dwelling respectively in their said realms and countries may do their business and affairs in the same realms and countries; to sojourn, do their merchandises, traffic, sail, and return into their countries or elsewhere as they shall think good, be it by land, sea, or fresh water, paying only the customs, tolls, and other duties, rights, and impositions such as they paid in the time of peace, without any disturbance, let, or impeachment to be done unto them in their persons, merchandises, or other goods whatsoever they be. Provided always that if any person haunting, dwelling, or sojourning in the countries one of the other, by virtue of this present truce, conspire against the weal of the country or prince of the same, he shall not enjoy the benefit of the said truce but shall be punished as a breaker and infractor thereof; and nevertheless the truce shall remain and stand for all other in his force and strength. The subjects also and inhabitants of the countries, realms, lands, and seigniories aforesaid freely, and without disturbance or let, may fish for herrings and other fish in the seas where the said truce shall have place and where any fishing of herring may be, as they might have done before the war and as they might and were accustomed to do in time of peace.

It is also covenanted and accorded that the intercourse of merchandises between England and the Emperor's said countries, their vassals, merchants, and subjects whatsoever they be of, the same shall have wholly and entirely place and course not only for the said eight months as afore, but also for as long time after as the truce shall endure, in such form and manner as it was a year before the intimation of war made by the King's highness to the said Emperor; without paying any other customs, tolls, *gabels,* duties, or other exactions but such as they paid and were used to pay in the time aforesaid, that is to say, a year before the said intimation of war.

And the said truce shall not have place in the realms of Spain nor in any other countries and seigniories which the said Emperor hath and pretendeth to have as well beyond the mountain Pyrennees as also in Italy. Yet nevertheless it is covenanted, concluded, and accorded and expressly declared by the same truce that as long as the same shall last and endure, there shall cease between the said princes, as well in the sea which is called the Narrow Sea as in the rest of the sea, ocean, and marine sea for against England, Wales, Ireland, Scotland, France, Normandy, Gascony, Guines, Brittany, Flanders, Germany, and all other parts and regions of the Low Countries subject to the said Emperor, and also in all other seas on this side the confines and havens of Spain, howsoever they be called or named, all hostility, invasion, and exploits or feats of war for and between them, their vassals and subjects; so that all and every merchants, subjects, and vassals of the said princes shall move with their ships and other vessels, whatsoever they be, sail, go, tarry, sojourn, return, pass, and repass with their ships and of equippage of the same their merchandises, and goods whatsoever they be, by all and every the said seas safely and peaceably without any manner damage, grief, let, trouble, or disturbance to be done unto them in their persons, ships, merchandises, or goods whatsoever they be, by the subjects, vassals, or men of war of the said princes or other being at their commandment by any color or occasion whatsoever it be.

Wherefore the King our sovereign lord willeth and commandeth all his captains and men of war, his admiral, vice-admiral, the wardens of all and singular his marches and ports, keepers and rulers of his towns and castles, all mayors, sheriffs, bailiffs, constables, and all other his justices, officers, servants, ministers, and subjects, whatsoever they be, and to every of them to whom it shall appertain, that they keep and observe and do to be kept and observed the said truce and all and every the points, articles, and chapters before said, without doing or attempting anything directly or indirectly against the same in any form or manner whatsoever it be, upon pain to run into the indignation of his highness and to be punished and corrected at the King's pleasure as an infractor and breaker of the same.

121. Enforcing Statutes on Archery, Handguns, Unlawful Games; Reforming High Grain Prices

[Westminster, 4 December 1528, 20 Henry VIII]

STC 7771 (UM 1,6,297), BM C.18.e.2, 77: printed by R. Pynson (London, 1528); schedule as below. BM MS Harl 442, 69: date as above; writ to sheriffs of London; schedule as below. Steele 113. Text (*STC*): BM

THE KING our sovereign lord, of his high prudence and wisdom, considering how that in the times of his noble progenitors, Kings of this his realm of England, as also in the time of his most noble reign, by the exercising and using of his and their subjects in shooting in longbows, there did insurge, increase, and grow within the same realm great number and multitude of franc-archers which not only thereby defended this his said realm and subjects thereof against the danger and malice of their enemies, but also with a mean and small number and puissance, in regard and comparison to their enemies, have done many notable exploits and acts of war to the discomfiture of their said enemies; by reason whereof as well our said sovereign lord the King as also his noble progenitors have had and obtained great and triumphant victories against their enemies to the great honor, fame, renown, and surety of his and their noble persons, and of this his said realm of England and subjects of the same, as also to the terrible fear and dread of all outward and strange nations attempting anything by the way of hostility to the hurt or danger of this his said realm;

In consideration whereof and for the better maintenance and good continuation of the said archery and shooting in longbows, divers good and politic statutes [1] have been made, established, and devised as well in the time of our sovereign lord the King that now is as also in the days of his noble progenitors, Kings of this realm. Yet that notwithstanding, for lack of good and effectual execution of the laws and statutes, the said archery and shooting in longbows is sore and marvelously decayed and in manner utterly extinct; and specially by the newfangles and wanton pleasure that men now have in using of crossbows and handguns, whereby also great number of people be given to felonies and to the unlawful destruction of deer and other beasts and fowls within warrens, forests, chases, and parks, to the great loss and detriment as well of the King our sovereign lord and also of his noblemen and subjects. And it is thought by the King's highness and his most honorable council that the archery and shooting in longbows is like for evermore to be decayed and destroyed by the using hereof; and of divers and many other unlawful games as playing at tennis, bowls, closh, tables, dice, cards, and other unlawful games, contrary to the King's laws and honorable statutes [2] made in that behalf.

For the remedying and eschewing whereof, and for setting up again of longbows and advancing and increasing of the said archery, the King our sovereign lord straightly chargeth and commandeth that no manner of person or persons from henceforth, after the present proclamation and publication thereof, have, shoot in, or use any crossbow or handgun nor have, bear, or keep any crossbow or handgun in their houses or any other places contrary and against the said statute. And furthermore our said sovereign lord willeth, chargeth, and straightly commandeth that all and every person and persons of what degree or condition he or they be that shall see, perceive, or know any person or persons shooting in any crossbow or handgun, or have or bear any crossbow or handgun contrary to the said statutes as is before said, that then it shall be lawful for such person or

1. 13 Edward I, c. 6 (Winchester), 1285, *SR 1*, 97; 2 Edward III, c. 6, 1328, *SR 1*, 259; 22 Edward IV, c. 4, 1482, *SR 2*, 472; 19 Henry VII, c. 4, 1503, *SR 2*, 649; 3 Henry VIII, c. 3, 1511, *SR 3*, 25; 3 Henry VIII, c. 14, 1511, *SR 3*, 33; 6 Henry VIII, c. 13, 1513, *SR 3*, 132; 14 & 15 Henry VIII, c. 7, 1523, *SR 3*, 215.

2. 12 Richard II, c. 6, 1388, *SR 2*, 57; 11 Henry IV, c. 4, 1409, *SR 2*, 163; 17 Edward IV, c. 3, 1477, *SR 2*, 462.

persons to take and seize or cause to be taken and seized the said crossbow or handgun, crossbows or handguns, from the said person or persons shooting, using, bearing, having, or keeping the same. And the same so taken and seized to break in pieces in the next market town or other town in the presence of the owner or owners of the same, or in their absence in the presence of their deputy or deputies there. And in case the said person or persons do refuse to deliver the said crossbows or handguns to such person or persons as shall attempt to seize or demand the said crossbows or handguns, then and in that case the King's pleasure and commandment is that his good and loving subjects being near thereunto (being also required and desired) shall assist from time to time the same person or persons so intending to seize and take the said crossbows and handguns in the taking, seizing, and breaking of the same. And furthermore our said sovereign lord the King chargeth and straightly commandeth that if any person or persons shall know or probably suppose any crossbow or handgun to be kept in the house of any person or persons contrary to the tenor, form, and effect of the said statutes, that then it shall be lawful to the said person or persons, knowing or probably supposing the same to be true, to enter into the said house or houses where any such crossbows, handgun, or handguns shall be kept; commanding the same householder, or other person or persons there then being in the absence of the said householder, in the King's name, that he or they without any contradiction, denial, or refusal, incontinently and without delay deliver the said crossbow or handgun, crossbows or handguns being in the said house, to the person or persons so commanding the same. And if the said householder, or such persons as in his absence shall then be there, deny and refuse so to do, then and in that case the same person so demanding the same crossbow or handgun, crossbows or handguns, shall resort to the King's true and loving subjects near thereunto dwelling or being, charging them in the King's name to go with him to the same house for his better aid and assistance in executing this the King's high commandment, for the great and urgent causes moving his highness and council concerning the surety of his most royal person and realm; and to charge and command the said householder, or such as in his absence shall be then in the same, to make delivery of the said crossbow or crossbows, handgun or handguns, under pain of death; suffering the same to be broken in parts according as is above rehearsed.

And over this our said sovereign lord the King chargeth and commandeth that no manner of person, of what degree or condition he be, from henceforth after this present proclamation and publication thereof had and made, shall make any crossbow within this realm of England except it be to and for such person or persons as may lawfully therein shoot and use the same. And also in case any person or persons shall hereafter make the said crossbows, the King's pleasure is that the same makers of crossbows shall be first bound by his or their obligations, to the King's use, by the governor or ruler of such places where they shall then dwell, in such sums as shall be thought by the same rulers and governors convenient, upon condition that they shall not make any crossbow or crossbows but for such persons as may lawfully use the same.

And furthermore our sovereign lord the King chargeth and commandeth that no manner of person or persons shall bring into this his realm any crossbows or handguns but only for and to the use of our said sovereign lord and such other as may lawfully use the same, upon pain of the King's high indignation and imprisonment, there to remain without bail or mainprize till his gracious pleasure be further known in that behalf. And also his highness chargeth and commandeth that no person or persons (not lawfully authorized to have and use crossbows) presume to buy the same of any stranger, denizen, or Englishman being within this his realm, upon like pain as is afore rehearsed.

Furthermore our said sovereign lord the King chargeth and commandeth that no manner of person or persons use, exercise, or haunt any playing at the tennis, dice, bowls, cards, tables, or any other unlawful games contrary to such laws, ordinances, and good statutes as be provided and made in that behalf. And that every person and persons keeping any hostelry, inn, or alehouse within this his realm of England, immediately after this proclamation and publication of this the King's pleasure had and made, shall not only eschew all manner unlawful games to be used in their houses, but also shall without contradiction suffer such persons as be and shall be authorized by the King for that purpose to take and burn the said tables, dice, cards, bowls, closhes, tennis balls, and all other things pertaining to the said unlawful games. For the King's express determination and pleasure is, for great respects and causes, that the said unlawful games shall not from henceforth in any wise in the foresaid places and houses be exercised, haunted, or used, under the pain of the King's indignation and imprisonment as is before rehearsed.

Furthermore our said sovereign lord, considering that there is great abundance and plenty of all manner of grains within this his realm of England (our Lord God be thanked), yet nevertheless by the inordinate iniquity and covetousness of certain evil disposed persons, more regarding their own particular enriching than the due order of charity and commonwealth of this his realm, [who] do sell the same grains at great and excessive prices throughout this his realm, to the great hurt and impoverishing of his subjects of the same.

Wherefore the King our said sovereign lord, by the advice of his said council, chargeth and commandeth that every person and persons within the counties and places where their abiding shall be, do show and detect unto one or some of the justices of peace within the said counties and places aforesaid, as near as they can imagine or conjecture what should be the occasion or cause why that grains should be at so great and excessive prices; and whether the same do insurge and arise by forestalling, regrating and engrossing of grains (as it is thought to his highness and his honorable council that it should be), which is contrary to his laws; and to detect and show (all favor and dread put apart) the name and names of such persons as they shall think to be regraters, forestallers or engrossers of grains; or whether there be used any undue means by reason whereof the price of grains should be so excessively enhanced.

And furthermore the King's pleasure is that all and singular justices of peace through this his realm of England do diligently inquire and search for reformation of the premises and punish the malefactors and offenders in that case offending, not failing this to do as they will answer unto the King's highness at their uttermost peril; commanding and straightly charging all and singular mayors, sheriffs, justices of peace, bailiffs, constables, headboroughs, and other his officers and ministers of justice as well within liberties and places privileged as without, that from henceforth and from time to time they shall see this the King's proclamation, commandment, and pleasure to be put in due and effectual execution (all favor, dread, malice, and meed utterly set apart) as they will deserve his grace's special thanks, and by doing the contrary to be in his high indignation and displeasure.

122. Enforcing Statutes against Heresy; Prohibiting Unlicensed Preaching, Heretical Books

[London, before 6 March 1529, 20 Henry VIII]

AC (HM Ellesmere 436): date, Star Chamber, 25 February 1531; John Borstick committed to the Tower for keeping books contrary to proclamation. *STC* 7772 (UM 5,25,298), Antiq 1, 54: printed by R. Pynson (London, 1529); schedule as below, incomplete. *L&P 5*, 311: date, 6 March; warrant for payment to R. Pynson for printing. Foxe *4*, 676: date, 1530. Wilkins *3*, 738: schedule as below. Steele 114: date as above. Text (*STC*): Antiq, first sheet only; completed after asterisk from Wilkins.

The King our sovereign lord of his most virtuous and gracious disposition, considering that this his noble realm of England hath of long time continued in the true Catholic faith of Christ's religion, and that his most noble progenitors, kings of this his said realm, hath before this time made and enacted many devout laws, statutes,[1] and ordinances for the maintenance and defense of the said faith against the malicious and wicked sects of

1. 5 Richard II, st. 2, c. 5, 1382, *SR 2*, 25; 2 Henry IV, c. 15, 1400, *SR 2*, 125; 2 Henry V, st. 1, c. 7, 1414 *SR 2*, 181.

heretics and Lollards who by perversion of Holy Scripture do induce erroneous opinions, soweth sedition among Christian people, and finally do disturb the peace and tranquillity of Christian realms, as late happened in some parts of Germany, where by procurement and sedition of Martin Luther and other heretics were slain an infinite number of Christian people; considering also that as well by the corruption and malice of indiscreet preachers, fautours of the said erroneous sects, as by certain heretical and blasphemous books lately made and privately sent into this realm by the disciples, fautours, and adherents of the said Martin Luther and other heretics, whereby the King's subjects be likely to be corrupted, unless his highness (as defender of the faith) do put to his most gracious help and authority royal to the due and speedy reformation thereof:

His highness therefore, like a most gracious prince, of his most blessed and virtuous disposition for the incomparable zeal which he hath to Christ's religion and faith, and for the singular love and affection that he beareth to all his good subjects of this his realm, and specially to the salvation of their souls, according to his office and duty in that behalf, willeth and intendeth to provide with all convenient expedition that this his noble realm may be preserved from the said pestiferous, cursed, and seditious errors.

And forasmuch as his highness is credibly informed that some of the said errors be already sown and spread within this his realm, partly by the corruption of indiscreet preachers, partly by erroneous books copied, printed, and written as well in the English tongue as in Latin and other languages, replete with most venomous heresies, blasphemies, and slanders intolerable to the clean ears of any good Christian man: his highness therefore, like a most gracious and Christian prince, only intending the safeguard of this his realm, the preservation of his subjects, and salvation of their souls, willeth to put now in execution with all diligence possible all good laws, statutes, and ordinances concerning the premises before this time provided, made, and ordained by his most noble progenitors, kings of England, for that purpose and intent; which laws and statutes by our said sovereign lord and his most honorable council by long and deliberate advice for the extirpation, suppressing, and withstanding of the said heresies, have been seen and examined, and by them in every part thought good and necessary to be put in execution.

Wherefore his highness chargeth and straightly commandeth all and every his lords spiritual and temporal, judges, justices of the peace, sheriffs, mayors, bailiffs, constables, and all other his officers, ministers, and all his true and loving subjects, that all favor, affection, and partiality laid aside, they effectually with all diligence and study endeavor themselves substantially to the executing of all and every the articles hereafter ensuing without dissimulation, intermission, or excuse, as they will avoid his high indignation and displeasure.

First, that no man within the King's realm or other his dominions, subject to his highness, hereafter presume to preach, teach, or inform anything openly or privily, or compile and write any book, or hold, exercise, or keep any assemblies or schools in any manner of wise contrary to the Catholic faith or diminution of Holy Church, nor that any person within this his said realm and dominions do presume to preach openly or secretly without they have first obtained license of the bishop of the diocese where they intend to preach; curates in their parishes, persons privileged, and other by the law of the Church only except.

Also that no man wittingly hereafter favor, support, or maintain any person which preacheth in form aforesaid, or that maketh any such or like conventicles and assemblies, holdeth or exerciseth any schools, maketh, writeth, or publisheth any such book, teacheth, informeth, or stirreth the people, or any of them in any manner of form to the said errors. Moreover that all and every person and persons having any books or writings of any such erroneous doctrine and opinion do deliver or cause to be delivered effectually and actually all and every such books and writings to the bishop of the diocese or to the ordinary of the place within 15 days after this proclamation [be] pronounced.

And in case any person or persons, of what estate, condition, or degree soever they be, do or * attempt anything contrary to this act and proclamation, or do not deliver or cause to be delivered such books within the time aforesaid, that every bishop in his diocese, or ordinary, shall cause that person or persons and every of them in that behalf defamed, or evidently suspected, to be arrested; and detain and keep them under safe custody in their prisons until such time that the said persons and every of them either have purged themselves of the said errors or else do abjure the said erroneous sects, preachings, doctrine, or opinions, as the law of Holy Church doth require.

Furthermore if any person by the law of Holy Church be convicted before the bishop of the diocese or his commissary in any case above expressed, that the said bishop may keep in prison the said person or persons so convicted, as it shall seem best to his discretion, after the grievousness or quality of the crime; and further may set a fine to be paid to the behoof of the King by the person or persons convicted, as it shall be thought convenient to the said bishop, having respect to the grievousness of the offense of the said person or persons, the said fine to be certified by the bishop into the King's Exchequer, there to be levied to the King's use: except in such cases in which by the laws of Holy Church the said persons convict of heresies ought totally to be left to the secular jurisdiction.

Also if any person within this his realm of England or other his dominions be by sentence judicial convicted of the said preachings and doctrines prohibited, erroneous opinions, schools, and informations, or any of them, and before the bishop or his commissary do abjure according to the form of the laws of Holy Church, the aforesaid erroneous sects, doctrines, schools, or informations; or else be pronounced by the bishops or their commissaries after their abjurations by them before made, to be relapsed, so that after the laws of Holy Church they ought to be relinquished to the jurisdiction secular (wherein faith is to be given to the bishop or his commissary in that behalf): then the sheriff of the county, mayor, sheriffs, or mayor and bailiffs of the same city, town, or borough next unto the said bishop or commissaries shall be personally present at the sentence given by the said bishop or commissaries thereunto required, and after the said sentence given, shall receive the said persons and every of them, and put them to further execution, according to the laws of this realm.

Also the chancellor, treasurer of England, the justice of the one bench and the other, justices of peace, sheriffs, mayors, and bailiffs of cities and towns, and other officers having governance of the people, which now be or for the time hereafter shall be, shall make oath in taking their charge and ministration to give their whole power and diligence to put away and to make utterly to cease, and destroy all manner of heresies and errors, commonly called Lollardies, within the precincts of their offices and administrations, from time to time, with all their power.

Also they shall assist the bishops and their commissaries, and them shall favor and maintain, as oftentimes as that to do they or any of them shall be required by the said bishops or their commissaries, so that the bishops or their commissaries shall bear and pay the reasonable costs of the said officers and ministers, when or as often as they shall travel or ride to arrest heretics and Lollards, or to assist the said bishops or commissaries by virtue of the King's laws and statutes.

Moreover, the justices of the King's bench, justices of peace, and justices of assize shall inquire at their sessions and sittings of all those that hold any errors or heresies: and who be their maintainers, recepters, favorers, and supporters; common writers of books, as also of their sermons, schools, conventicles, congregations, and confederacies.

Furthermore if any person be indicted of any of the points aforesaid, the justices of the peace have power to award against them a *capias,* and the sheriffs be bound to arrest such persons so indicted as soon as they may be found, by themselves or by their officers. And forasmuch as cognizance of heresies, errors, and Lollardies appertaineth to the judge of Holy Church and not to the judge secular, the persons so indicted to be delivered to the bishop of the places or their commissaries, by indenture between them to be made, within 10 days after their arrest, or sooner if it can be done: thereof to be acquit or convict by the laws of Holy Church, in case that those persons be not indicted of other things whereof the knowledge appertains to the judges and officers secular; in which case, after they be acquit and delivered afore the justices secular of those things pertaining to the judge secular, that they be conveyed in safeguard to ordinaries or their commissaries, and to them to be delivered by indentures as is abovesaid, after the laws of Holy Church. Provided that the indictments be not taken in evidence, but for an information afore the judges spiritual against such indicted, but that the ordinaries commence their process against those indicted in the same manner as if no indictment had been, having no regard to such indictments.

Moreover that no manner of person or persons, of what estate, degree, or condition he or they be, do from henceforth presume to bring into this realm, or do sell, receive, take, or detain any book or work printed or written, which is made or hereafter shall be made against the faith Catholic, or against the holy decrees, laws, and ordinances of Holy Church, or in reproach, rebuke, or slander of the King, his honorable council, or his lords spiritual or temporal. And in case they have any such book or work, they shall incontinent upon the having of them bring the said book or work to the bishop of the diocese without concealment or fraud. Or if they know any person having one of the said books, they shall detect them to the said bishop, all favor or affection laid apart; and that they fail not thus to do as they will avoid the King's high indignation.

Books prohibited

A Disputation Between The Father and Son.[2]
A Book of The Old God and New.[3]
Godly Prayers.[4]
The Christian State of Matrimony.[5]
The Burying of The Mass.[6]
The Sum of The Scripture.[7]
Matins and Evening Songs, vii Psalms and Other Heavenly Psalms, with The Combination, in English.[8]
An Exposition of The Seventh Chapter of The First Epistle to The Corinthians.[9]
The Chapters of Moses, Called Genesis.[10]
The Chapters of Moses, Called Deuteronomy.[10]

2. Attributed to William Roy. See *A Brief Dialogue between A Christian Father and His Stubborn Son* (1530), ed. Adolph Wolf, Vienna, 1874.

3. Herbert 483: printed by John Byddle, 15 June, 1533.

4. See *STC* 20,197.

5. By Heinrich Bullinger, translated by Miles Coverdale, *STC* 4045.

6. By William Roy, *STC* 21,427.

7. Translated by Simon Fish, *STC* 3036. See Foxe *4*, 658.

8. See *STC* 15,989.

9. Printed in Marburg, 1529. See J. F. Mozley, *William Tyndale* (London, 1937), p. 345. More 342. Wilkins *3*, 733.

10. Both by William Tyndale, *STC* 2351.

The Matrimony of Tyndale.[11]
The Practice of Prelates.[12]
Hortulus Animae, in English.[13]
A.B.C. Against The Clergy.[14]
The Examination of William Thorp, etc.[15]

123. Ordering Destruction of Enclosures

[Westminster, 15 February 1529, 20 Henry VIII]

BM MS Harl 442, 73; date as above; writ to sheriff of Kent, ordering certification at once to Chancery after making proclamation; schedule as below. Steele 115. Text (MS): Harl

THE KING our sovereign lord straightly chargeth and commandeth all and singular those his subjects of what estate, degree, or condition soever he or they be, that have in right use or possession to his own profit any lands, tenements, pastures, or commons, ditched or enclosed, contrary to the statutes [1] and laws of this his realm and contrary to the commonwealth of the same, by reason whereof insurgeth the decaying of husbandry and tillage within the said realm, that they and every of them, at this side the 15th of Easter next coming, without any further delay or contradiction, clearly break and cast down all and singular the said hedges, ditches, and enclosures so made or enclosed, as is aforesaid; upon pain to them and every of them not following this the King's commandment to run into his high indignation and displeasure, and also upon such pains as be expressed in the King's laws and statutes made and provided in that behalf; declaring furthermore expressly that in case they do not execute this the King's said commandment and pleasure by the day before limited, that then and in that case they shall not only run into the forfeiture of the said penalties, but also direction is therein further taken that the same shall be hereafter executed and done by the King's sheriffs and other his commissioners to be appointed and authorized in that behalf.

For the King's highness is determinably resolved that the same enclosures shall no longer continue, forasmuch as the same be to the express hindrance of the commonweal of this his realm, and to the extreme impoverishing of his true and loving subjects of the same.

11. Another title for 9: see Mozley, *Tyndale.*
12. By William Tyndale, *STC* 24,465.
13. Unidentified.
14. See More 343.
15. *STC* 24,045.
1. 4 Henry VII, c. 19, 1488, *SR 2,* 542; 6 Henry VIII, c. 5, 1514, *SR 3,* 127; 7 Henry VIII, c. 1, 1515, *SR 3,* 176.

124. Continuing Truce with France

[Richmond, 18 March 1529, 20 Henry VIII]

LL O, 151*v:* date as above; writ to mayor and sheriffs of London; proclaimed in London on 20 March; schedule as below. BM MS Harl 442, 74: writ to sheriff of York. Steele 116. Text (MS): LL

THE KING our sovereign lord doth you to understand that whereas truce and abstinence of war [1] by land, sea, and fresh water was accorded between his highness for his realms of England, countries, dominions, isles, and seigniories wheresoever they be on this side and beyond the sea; the right excellent, right high, and mighty prince the elect Emperor for his countries, dominions, lands and seigniories on this side the mountains; and the right excellent, right high, and mighty prince the French King for his realms, countries, lands and seigniories; in the which is comprised as well the Narrow Sea as also all the rest of the sea ocean for against England, Wales, Ireland, Scotland, France, Normandy, Gascony, Guines, Brittainy, Germany, Flanders, and other parts of the said Emperor's Low Countries, and all other seas on this side the confines and parts of Spain whatsoever they be or howsoever they be named: during the time and space of eight months then following, beginning the 15th day of June last past and to endure not only for the said eight months but also shall and continually afterward without any end limited or prefixed, till such time as any of the said princes shall certify to the residue that he will keep it no longer.

And yet whensoever any of the said princes would make such certification to the residue, the truce shall nevertheless endure in all the countries, seas, and parts aforesaid two months after such certification, to the intent that the merchants and other subjects haunting or being in the realms and countries, the one of the other, may during these two months after such certification withdraw their persons and goods in surety like as more at length heretofore was cried, proclaimed, and published, and as the treaty of truce more largely containeth, inasmuch as divers merchants and subjects of the one part and the other, not knowing the drawing of the truce after the manner and form beforesaid may go, adventure, be in dread, and doubt to adventure themselves, their goods and merchandises, supposing the said truce to be expired if never proclamation and publication be not made.

It hath therefore been ordered by all the said three princes that every of them in his countries and dominions should of now make such publication, which is already done in the French King's countries, and also the Emperor for this cause, and to the intent that it may well appear and be known to all manner of subjects of the said princes that they may truly, safely and

1. See 120.

without doubt or fear haunt, pass, go, come, abide, sojourn, remain, and resort into or from any of the said countries, seas, waters, or places in feat of merchandise and other their business as they shall think good. The King's highness also for his part doth publish and give knowledge to you all that the said truce and abstinence of war doth and shall continue, endure, and have place till such time as one of the said three princes shall have signified to the residue that he will keep no longer for his part, and two months after; which signification whensoever any such shall fortune, shall be openly proclaimed and published through all the principal parts and frontiers of the King's realm and obeisance, to the intent that (if any such significance or declaration shall chance to be) the merchants and subjects of the said princes on every part may within two months after any such signification and proclamation withdraw themselves and their goods as is aforesaid.

Wherefore the King's highness straightly chargeth and commandeth all and singular his subjects of what estate, degree, or condition soever they be, truly to observe and keep the said truce and abstinence of war as well by all the seas and fresh waters as by land, in all the parts and places before specified, and nothing to do or attempt against the same but to see it in every part obeyed and kept, at their uttermost perils, accordingly.

125. Prohibiting Grain Regrating

[More, 19 August 1529, 21 Henry VIII]

BM MS Harl 442, 76: date as above; writ to sheriffs of Bedford and Bucks; schedule as below. Steele 117. Text (MS): Harl

THE KING our sovereign lord, considering how the great scarcity of corn and grain and the high prices of the same hath of late risen within this his realm of England, by means of such evil-disposed persons as do regrate the same corn and grain and do combine and confederate together in fairs and markets to set unreasonable prices upon the said corn and grains, to the great damage of his loving subjects and contrary to divers acts and statutes in that case provided; of his gracious disposition willing speedy remedy to be had against such offenders in this behalf, straightly chargeth and commandeth that no person, of what degree or estate soever he be, do regrate or combine himself with other to make or set such unreasonable prices; nor that any person, being no victualer, buy or take into his hands in market or other place any more corn or grain than shall be needful for his household and seed corn for his land, upon pain of the King's high displeasure and forfeiture of the same corn and grain.

126. Announcing Peace with Emperor

[More, 27 August 1529, 21 Henry VIII]

BM MS Harl 442, 77: date as above; writ to sheriff of Kent; schedule as below. Calais 41: proclaimed in Calais on 30 August. Steele 118. Text (MS): Harl

THE KING our sovereign lord doth you to understand that to the laud and praise of Almighty God, the exaltation and increase of Christ's faith and religion, and the repose and tranquillity of all Christendom, there is passed, accorded, and concluded between his highness of the one party; and the right high, right excellent, and mighty prince, his dearest brother and nephew, Charles, Emperor-elect of the other party, for them, their heirs and successors, realms, countries, dominions, seigniories, lands, vassals, and subjects whatsoever they be, present and to come, as well spiritual as temporal, of whatsoever estate, degree, or condition they be, good, sincere, true, whole, perfect, and firm amity, league, intercourse, peace,[1] and union, by land, sea, and fresh water, as well on this side the mountains as beyond and in every place under their dominions and obeisances, perpetually to endure. So that it shall be lawful to the merchants and subjects of either of the said parties whatsoever they be, to pass out and to come from, henceforth surely, freely, and liberally at their pleasures, to pass and enter into any of their realms, countries, dominions, and lands, cities, towns fortified and not fortified, ports, and straits, by land, sea, or fresh water; and in the same as long as they will to abide, sojourn, demur and remain there, to buy, sell, exercise traffic and course of merchandise, or do their other lawful business; and from the same, as often as it shall please them, into any other place to depart their goods, merchandises, armor, ships, baggages and other things as they might in their own countries, and as the proper subjects of any of the same princes may do, without any manner license or safe-conduct to be had or obtained in that behalf, with all other special and general mutual intercourses of merchandises and liberties and privilege for the same, both in this realm of England and all other places of the King's obeisance; and also in Flanders, Holland, Zeeland, Brabant and all other the Emperor's Low Countries on their side the mountain; and in Spain, Italy, and all other places beyond the mountains and wheresoever under the said Emperor's obeisance and dominion for as large form as, and ample manner as, they did or might have done at any time heretofore if never war had been had, made, moved, or denounced between the King's highness and the said Emperor. Wherefore the King's grace straightly chargeth and commandeth

1. See 120, 124.

all and singular his officers, ministers, and subjects duly and inviolably to observe and keep the said peace accordingly.

127. Prohibiting Grain Forestalling and Regrating

[Westminster, 8 October 1529, 21 Henry VIII]

BM MS Harl 442, 78: date as above; writ to sheriff of Suffolk; schedule as below. Steele 119. Text (MS): Harl

THE KING our sovereign lord, considering how the great scarcity of corn and grain and the high prices of the same hath of late risen within this his realm of England, by means of such evil-disposed persons as do forestall and regrate the same corn and grain, and do combine and confederate together in fairs and markets to set an unreasonable price upon the said corn and grain, to the great damage of his loving subjects, and contrary to divers acts and statutes in that case provided: of his gracious disposition willing speedy remedy to be had against such forestallers, regraters, and other offenders in this behalf, straightly chargeth and commandeth that no person, of what degree or estate soever he be, do forestall, regrate, or combine himself with other to make or set such unreasonable prices; nor that any person, being no victualer or purveyor for any towns, cities, shires, or householders, buy or take into his hands, in market or other place, any more corn or other grain than shall be needful for his household and seed corn for his land, and the reasonable provision whereunto he is assigned or appointed without making any sale of the same provision or other; that any husbandman or other person, whatsoever he be, having corn sufficient of his own (as is aforesaid) shall buy any seed corn or other corn at the market or elsewhere, unless he from time to time bring to the market as much of his own corn, there to be sold and put to sale as the same corn amounteth unto which he buyeth at the said market or other place; upon pain to run into the King's high displeasure and to forfeit the same corn and grain used, bought, and sold contrary to this his proclamation; and the body of the person offending to be committed to ward without bail or mainprize, there to remain the King's determinate pleasure in that behalf.

And in case any person or persons have made any bargain or bargains for any manner of corn or grain contrary to the effect and purport of this the King's proclamation, that then the same bargain and bargains to be frustrate, void, and of none effect. And if any money in this case be paid by force and virtue of any such bargain, the King's pleasure and commandment is that the same money be repaid and restored as reason appertaineth.

Furthermore the King's highness straightly chargeth and commandeth that all such person and persons, as have more corn than shall suffice for the expenses of their household and their seed corn, shall from time to time send or bring to the markets, there to be sold, part of the same corn remaining above the expenses of his said household and seed corn, so that the market may be sufficiently furnished at all times. Provided always that this present proclamation extend not to any person or persons being common malters and buyers of barley or oats to the same purpose of malting. And furthermore his highness straightly chargeth and commandeth all and singular mayors, sheriffs, justices of peace, bailiffs, and other his faithful officers to whom it appertaineth in this behalf, that they and every of them within any shire, city, borough, town, and other place and market within this his said realm, so cause and procure in that they may [see] that this proclamation be put in effectual and due execution; and also to aid, assist and help the executors of the same proclamation, as they will answer to his grace at their extreme perils.

128. Ordering Punishment of Vagabonds and Beggars

[Westminster, June 1530, 22 Henry VIII]

STC 7774 (UM 2,10,318), Antiq 1, 55: printed by T. Berthelet (London, 1530); date as above; schedule as below. *L&P 5,* 322: date October 1530: payment to T. Berthelet for printing. Steele 121: date as above. Text (*STC*): Antiq

THE KING our most dreaded sovereign lord, having always in his most blessed remembrance as well the cure and charge of his dignity royal, as also the present estate of this his realm and his subjects of the same, considereth that in all places throughout this his realm of England vagabonds and beggars have of long time increased and daily do increase in great and excessive numbers, by the occasion of idleness, mother and root of all vices; whereby have insurged and sprung, and daily insurge and spring, continual thefts, murders, and other sundry heinous offenses and great enormities, to the high displeasure of God, the inquietation and damage of his true and faithful subjects, and to the disturbance of the whole commonweal of this his said realm; and whereas many and sundry good laws, statutes,[1] and ordinances have been before this time devised and made, as well by his highness

1. 13 Edward I, c. 4 (Winchester), 1285, *SR 1,* 97; 13 Edward I (London), 1285, *SR 1,* 102; 5 Edward III, c. 14, 1331, *SR 1,* 268; 23 Edward III, c. 7, 1349, *SR 1,* 308; 34 Edward III, c. 10, 11, 1360, *SR 1,* 367; 7 Richard II, c. 5, 1383, *SR 2,* 32; 12 Richard II, c. 7–9, 1388, *SR 2,* 58; 11 Henry VII, c. 2, 1495, *SR 2,* 569; 19 Henry VII, c. 12, 1503, *SR 2,* 656; 22 Henry VIII, c. 12, 1530, *SR 3,* 328.

as also by divers his most noble progenitors, kings of England, for the most necessary and due reformation of the premises; yet that notwithstanding, the said numbers of vagabonds and beggars be not seen in any part to be minished, but daily to be augmented and increased into great routs and companies: which his grace evidently perceiveth to happen, forasmuch as his said laws, statutes, and ordinances be not from time to time put in effectual execution, according to his gracious expectation, pleasure, and commandment.

His highness therefore, willing to declare to all his subjects his most godly and virtuous purpose, and perseverance in the persecution, correction, and reformation of that most damnable vice of idleness, chief subverter and confounder of commonweals, eftsoons willeth and straightly commandeth all justices of the peace, mayors, sheriffs, constables, burseholders, tithing men, and other his ministers, as they will avoid his high indignation and displeasure, that if they or any of them shall, after two days next ensuing after this proclamation [be] published, happen to find any vagabond or mighty beggar (be it man or woman) out of the hundred where he or she was born, or out of the town or place where he or she last dwelled in and continued by the space of three years next before; and that upon knowledge of the said proclamation he or she hath not demanded a billet to convey themself to the said hundred or dwelling place, and to be in their journey thitherward within the said two days: that then the said justices and ministers and every of them shall cause the said vagabonds and beggars and every of them to be stripped naked, from the privy parts of their bodies upward (men and women of great age or sick, and women with child only except) and being so naked, to be bound and sharply beaten and scourged. And after that they be so beaten in form aforesaid, that there be delivered to them and every of them so whipped or scourged a schedule or billet, the form whereof appeareth in the end of this present proclamation; and that the said schedule or billet be signed with the hand of the justice of peace, mayor, sheriff, constable, burseholder, tithing man, or other minister, by whose commandment the said vagabond or beggar was whipped or scourged. And in case that any of them cannot write, then the same billet to be signed by one of the best and most substantial inhabitants next adjoining. And if it happen the person beaten in form aforesaid, to be eftsoons found in the said place, as a vagabond or beggar, that than he or she to be taken and eftsoons beaten and scourged as is aforesaid; and so from time to time, and as often as they shall happen to be taken out of the place to them limited for their abode, by the statute.[2]

Moreover, if any of the said vagabonds or mighty beggars, whipped in form aforesaid, do after the said whipping make their abode in any place longer than a dinner time, or the space of one night, until they be come to the said place of their habitation appointed (being not verily sick or hurt), that than

2. 13 Edward I, c. 1–6 (Winchester), 1285, *SR 1*, 96–98.

they shall be eftsoons whipped, and ordered as is before written. Semblably if any vagabond or mighty beggar, being taken, will affirm that he was late whipped, and cannot show forth a schedule or billet signed, as before is mentioned, he shall notwithstanding his said affirmation be stripped naked and seen by the justice or some of the ministers before named. And if it may evidently appear unto them by the tokens on his body that he hath been already scourged or beaten, they shall then suffer him to depart without other harm, with a billet signed by them, mentioning where and at what time he was beaten. And if they find no tokens or signs of scourging or beating on his body, then they to see him to be whipped or scourged, and further ordered as is before written.

And moreover, the King's highness commandeth all justices of the peace, mayors, sheriffs, constables, burseholders, tithing men, and other his said ministers that, all vain pity and other excuses laid apart, they endeavor themselves with all their power, study, and diligence to put this his said ordinance in effectual execution, without any delay. And also that they endeavor themselves to keep their watches and searches, according to the laws and statutes of this realm, and according to the instructions before this time made and devised by his highness and his honorable council, and by his grace to them sent to be put in due execution: as they will answer to his highness at their uttermost perils.

The form and tenor of the schedule or billet above mentioned.

> A. B. taken at C. in the county of D. as a vagabond, without a schedule or token of scourging, and therefore whipped at C. aforesaid, the ——— day of the month of ——— the ——— year of the reign of our sovereign lord King Henry VIII, in the presence of T. E., constable, and other of the inhabitants of the same town.

129. Prohibiting Erroneous Books and Bible Translations

[London, 22 June 1530, 22 Henry VIII]

AC (HM Elesmere 436, 1): date, Star Chamber, 14 October 1531; John Croker cited for keeping a New Testament contrary to the King's proclamation. *STC* 7775; (UM 2,7,319), Antiq 1, 56: printed by T. Berthelet (London, 1530); schedule as below. Another edition, *STC* 7776; Steele 123. Foxe *5*, 258. Hall 182*v:* Tyndale's Testament prohibited in Star Chamber on 25 May. Wilkins *3*, 740. Steele 122: date as above. Text (*STC*): Antiq

THE KING our most dread sovereign lord, studying and providing daily for the weal, benefit, and honor of this his most noble realm, well and evidently perceiveth that partly through the malicious suggestion of our ghostly enemy, partly by the evil and perverse inclination of seditious disposition of sundry persons, divers heresies and erroneous opinions have been late sown and spread among his subjects of this his said realm, by blasphemous and pestiferous English books, printed in other regions and sent into this realm, to the intent as well to pervert and withdraw the people from the Catholic and true faith of Christ, as also to stir and incense them to sedition and disobedience against their princes, sovereigns, and heads, as also to cause them to contemn and neglect all good laws, customs, and virtuous manners, to the final subversion and desolation of this noble realm, if they might have prevailed (which God forbid) in their most cursed persuasions and malicious purposes.

Whereupon the King's highness, by his incomparable wisdom, foreseeing and most prudently considering, hath invited and called to him the Primates of this his grace's realm, and also a sufficient number of discreet, virtuous, and well-learned personages in divinity, as well of either of the universities, Oxford and Cambridge, as also hath chosen and taken out of other parts of his realm; giving unto them liberty to speak and declare plainly their advices, judgments and determinations concerning as well the approbation or rejecting of such books as be in any part suspected, as also the admission and divulgation of the Old and New Testament, translated into English.[1] Whereupon his highness, in his own royal person, calling to him the said Primates and divines, hath seriously and deeply, with great leisure and long deliberation, consulted, debated, insearched, and discussed the premises; and finally, by all their free assents, consents, and agreements, concluded, resolved, and determined that these books ensuing, that is to say, the book entitled *The Wicked Mammon,*[2] the book named *The Obedience of a Christian Man,*[3] the *Supplication of Beggars,*[4] and the book called *The Revelation of Antichrist,*[5] *The Summary of Scripture,*[6] and divers other books made in the English tongue, and imprinted beyond the sea, do contain in them pestiferous errors and blasphemies: and for that cause shall from henceforth be reputed and taken of all men for books of heresy, and worthy to be damned and put in perpetual oblivion.

The King's said highness therefore straightly chargeth and commandeth all and every his subjects of what estate or condition soever he or they be, as they will avoid his high indignation and most grievous displeasure, that they from henceforth do not buy, receive, or have any of the books before

1. By William Tyndale, *STC* 2350 and 2824.
2. Tyndale, *STC* 24,454.
3. Tyndale, *STC* 24,446.
4. By Simon Fish, *STC* 10,883.
5. By John Frith, *STC* 11,394.
6. Translated by Simon Fish, *STC* 10,883.

named, or any other book being in the English tongue and printed beyond the sea, of what matter soever it be, or any copy written, drawn out of the same, or the same books in the French or Dutch tongue. And to the intent that his highness will be ascertained what number of the said erroneous books shall be found from time to time within this his realm, his highness therefore chargeth and commandeth that all and every person or persons which hath or hereafter shall have any book or books in the English tongue printed beyond the sea, as is afore written, or any of the said erroneous books in the French or Dutch tongue, that he or they, within fifteen days next after the publishing of this present proclamation, do actually deliver or send the same books and every of them to the bishop of the diocese wherein he or they dwelleth, or to his commissary; or else before good testimony to their curate or parish priest, to be presented by the same curate or parish priest to the said bishop or his commissary. And so doing, his highness freely pardoneth and acquitteth them, and every of them, of all penalties, forfeitures, and pains wherein they have incurred or fallen by reason of any statute, act, ordinance, or proclamation before this time made concerning any offense or transgression by them committed or done by or for the keeping or holding of the said books. Foreseen and provided always that they from henceforth truly do observe, keep, and obey this his present gracious proclamation and commandment.

Also his highness commandeth all mayors, sheriffs, bailiffs, constables, burseholders, and other officers and ministers within this his realm, that if they shall happen by any means or ways to know that any person or persons do hereafter buy, receive, have, or detain any of the said erroneous books, printed or written anywhere, or any other books in English tongue printed beyond the sea, or the said erroneous books printed or written in the French or Dutch tongue, contrary to this present proclamation, that they being thereof well assured do immediately attach the said person or persons, and bring him or them to the King's highness and his most honorable council, where they shall be corrected and punished for their contempt and disobedience, to the terrible example of other like transgressors.

Moreover his highness commandeth that no manner of person or persons take upon him or them to print any book or books in English tongue concerning Holy Scripture, not before this time printed within this his realm, until such time as the same book or books be examined and approved by the ordinary of the diocese where the said books shall be printed; and that the printer thereof, upon every of the said books being so examined, do set the name of the examiner or examiners, with also his own name upon the said books, as he will answer to the King's highness at his uttermost peril.

And furthermore, forasmuch as it is come to the hearing of our said sovereign lord the King, that report is made by divers and many of his subjects that it were to all men not only expedient but also necessary to have in the English tongue both the New Testament and the Old, and that his highness, his noblemen, and prelates were bounden to suffer them so to have it, his highness hath therefore semblably thereupon consulted with the said Primates and virtuous, discreet, and well-learned personages in divinity foresaid: and by them all it is thought that it is not necessary the said Scripture to be in the English tongue and in the hands of the common people, but that the distribution of the said Scripture, and the permitting or denying thereof, dependeth only upon the discretion of the superiors, as they shall think it convenient. And that having respect to the malignity of this present time, with the inclination of people to erroneous opinions, the translation of the New Testament and the Old into the vulgar tongue of English should rather be the occasion of continuance or increase of errors among the said people than any benefit or commodity toward the weal of their souls, and that it shall now be more convenient that the same people have the Holy Scripture expounded to them by preachers in their sermons, according as it hath been of old time accustomed before this time. Albeit if it shall hereafter appear to the King's highness that his said people do utterly abandon and forsake all perverse, erroneous, and seditious opinions, with the New Testament and the Old corruptly translated into the English tongue now being in print, and that the same books and all other books of heresy, as well in the French tongue as in the Dutch tongue, be clearly exterminate and exiled out of this realm of England forever: his highness intendeth to provide that the Holy Scripture shall by great, learned, and Catholic persons translated into the English tongue, if it shall then seem to his grace convenient so to be.

Wherefore his highness at this time, by the whole advice and full determination of all the said Primates and other discreet and substantial learned personages, of both universities, and other before expressed, and by the assent of his nobles and others of his most honorable council, willeth and straightly commandeth that all and every person and persons of what estate, degree, or condition soever he or they be, which hath the New Testament or the Old translated into English, or any other book of Holy Scripture so translated, being in print, or copied out of the books now being in print, that he or they do immediately bring the same book or books, or cause the same to be brought, to the bishop of the diocese where he dwelleth, or to the hands of other the said persons, at the day afore limited, in form afore expressed and mentioned, as he will avoid the King's high indignation and displeasure. And that no person or persons from henceforth do buy, receive, keep, or have the New Testament or the Old in the English tongue, or in the French or Dutch tongue, except such persons as be appointed by the King's highness and the bishops of this his realm for the correction or amending of the said translation, as they will answer to the

King's highness at their uttermost perils, and will avoid such punishment, as they, doing contrary to the purport of this proclamation, shall suffer, to the dreadful example of all other like offenders.

And his highness further commandeth that all such statutes, acts, and ordinances as before this time have been made and enacted, as well in the time of his most gracious reign as also in the time of his noble progenitors, concerning heresies, and having and detaining erroneous books contrary and against the faith Catholic, shall immediately be put in effectual and due execution over and beside this present proclamation.

130. Prohibiting Bulls from Rome

[Westminster, 12 September 1530, 22 Henry VIII]

CW (C82/668): date, 24 Henry VIII; sign manual; schedule as below. LL O, 199*v:* date as above; writ to mayor and sheriffs of London; schedule as below. Foxe 5, 55: excerpts. Hall 193*v:* proclaimed in London on 19 September. *CSPSpanish 4(1)*, 433: published before 20 September, to a great flourish of trumpets. Steele 124. Text (MS): CW

Forasmuch as the King our sovereign lord, perceiving how much the people and subjects of this his realm have been vexed, inquieted, and troubled by authorities and jurisdictions legatine in times of the reigns of his noble progenitors, and something touched in his time, to the great diminution and prejudice of the jurisdiction and prerogative royal of this his grace's realms; and also where his highness hath by authority of his parliament lately holden at Westminster ordained and established divers and sundry acts [1] for the good order and reformation of divers abuses by the clergy maintained to the noyance of his said subjects; to interrupt and let the due execution thereof, his grace feareth that ways and means be sought from the court of Rome; for these considerations, and for that his grace, by the advice of his council and authority of his said parliament, intendeth to take such order and direction for the remedying of the premises as shall be agreeable with God's laws, reason, and conscience, for the wealth, benefit, commodity, and quietness of his said subjects, with the preservation of the liberties, immunities, privileges, and prerogatives of his grace's said realm:

His highness therefore straightly chargeth and commandeth that no manner of person of what estate, degree, or condition soever they be of, do pursue or attempt to purchase from the court of Rome or elsewhere, nor use, put in execution, divulge, or publish anything heretofore within this year passed, purchased or to be purchased hereafter, containing matter prejudicial to the high authority, jurisdiction, and prerogative royal of this his said

1. 21 Henry VIII, c. 13, 1529, *SR 3*, 292.

realm, or the let, hindrance, or impeachment of his grace's noble and virtuous intended purposes in the premises, upon pain of incurring the King's high indignation and imprisonment of their bodies for their so doing, and further punishment at his grace's pleasure to the dreadful example of others.

131. Enforcing Statutes against Beggars and Vagabonds

[Westminster, 16 June 1531, 23 Henry VIII]

L&P 5, 332: warrant to pay T. Berthelet for printing. LL O,228*v:* date as above; writ to mayor and sheriffs of London; proclaimed in London on 18 June; schedule as below. Steele 125. Text (MS): LJ

THE KING our sovereign lord straightly chargeth and commandeth that all beggars and vagabonds being within the city of London and the suburbs of the same, or within any liberties, franchises, or places privileged of the same city of London, that they and every of them, this side the Feast of St. John Baptist next coming, do depart from the same city into their countries where they were born, or else where they last dwelled by the space of three years: upon pain of such imprisonment as is contained in an act[1] made in this present parliament the 31st day of March last past, prorogued unto the 14th day of October next coming.

And moreover his highness straightly chargeth and commandeth all and singular his justices of peace, mayors, sheriffs, bailiffs, constables, petty constables, and all other his officers to whom it shall appertain, that they and every of them with all effectual diligence execute and cause to be put in due and effectual execution the said act accordingly, as they tender his high pleasure and commandment and will avoid the contrary.

132. Enforcing Statutes against Beggars and Vagabonds

[Westminster, 16 June 1531, 23 Henry VIII]

BM MS Harl 442, 81*v:* date as above; writ to sheriffs of London; schedule as below. Steele 126. Text (MS): Antiq

WHERE at this our instant parliament holden at Westminster the 31st day of March last past and prorogued unto the 14th day of October next coming,

1. 22 Henry VIII, c. 12, 1530, *SR 3*, 328.

amongst other things it was enacted[1] that all beggars and vagabonds shall, before the Feast of the Nativity of St. John Baptist next coming, depart into their countries where they were born, or else where they last dwelt by the space of three years, and further to do and abide such directions upon certain pains as in the said act more plainly appeareth:

We therefore will and command you that immediately upon the sight hereof in all wards, parishes, and suburbs thereof within the said city, you make solemn and public proclamation that all beggars and vagabonds, according to the said act, do depart and avoid the same city before the said Feast of St. John Baptist, upon the pain in the said act contained.

And moreover we will and command all and singular our justices of peace, mayors, sheriffs, bailiffs, constables, and all other our officers to whom it shall or may appertain, that they and every of them do substantially and effectually see this act put in due and effectual execution accordingly, as they will answer unto us at their uttermost perils.

133. Prohibiting Export of Gold and Silver

[Westminster, 18 July 1531, 23 Henry VIII]

PR (C66/659/32*d*): date as above; writ to sheriffs of Bedford, Bucks; similar writs to sheriffs throughout England; schedule as below. Hall 200: proclaimed during Midsummer term. Steele 127. Text (MS): PR

THE KING our sovereign lord by the advice of his honorable council, considering that in the time of his noble progenitor King Richard II, in the fifth year of his reign, it was ordained and enacted[1] by authority of his parliament, and the same King Richard defended and forbade, that no manner persons, merchants, clerks, nor other as well strangers or denizens of what estate or condition that they be, upon pain of forfeiture of as much as they can forfeit, privily or openly should send or carry or cause to be sent or carried out of the realm any gold or silver or money, bullion, plate, vessels, neither by exchanges to be done nor in any other whatsoever manner, except the wages of Calais and of other the King's fortresses beyond the sea; and specially excepted those prelates, lords and other of the realm, which of necessity must at some time make payments beyond the sea, which payments only they may make exchanges in England by good and sufficient merchants to pay beyond the sea, and thereof to have such the King's special leave and license as well for the exchanges as for the persons that oweth the payment containing expressly the same, which had been so exchanged; and that the merchants which so should make the said exchanges shall be diligently

1. 22 Henry VIII, c. 12, 1530, *SR 3*, 328.

1. 5 Richard II, st. 1, c. 2, 1381, *SR 2*, 17.

examined and sworn in their proper persons as often as they shall have the said license, that they shall not convey to beyond the sea any manner of gold and silver under color of that exchange; and that if after proclamation of the said ordinance any person be duly attainted that he have conveyed or brought to beyond the sea any gold or silver against the said ordinance, he shall forfeit unto the King the same sum so being sent or conveyed. And the royal majesty of the King's said noble progenitor, by the said authority, utterly forbade the passage to all manner of people, as well clerks as others, in any port and other town and place upon the seacoast, upon pain of forfeiture of all their goods, except alonely to the lords and other great persons of the realm and true and notable merchants and the King's soldiers, and every other person other than before be not excepted, and after the proclamation of the said ordinance made, to pass out of the said realm without the King's special license; which license the said King willed and commanded not to be made from henceforth but only in one of the ports underwritten in the said statute, upon pain of forfeiture to the King all that he hath in goods as is aforesaid. And nevertheless the master or mariner of the ship or of other vessel wherein he hath brought to beyond the sea, without the King's license, any person, except only those which above be excepted, and thereof be duly convicted, shall forfeit to the King the said vessel. And furthermore the said King Richard II by the said statute commanded to all keepers and searchers of the ports and passages throughout England, that they should use from thenceforth diligently their offices, and make good and straight searches; and that if any searcher or keeper of the ports and passages throughout the said realm by negligence or otherwise do or suffer to be done wittingly to any point the contrary of the said two articles touching the money of gold and silver and the said passages of people, and thereof be duly convicted, [he] shall forfeit to the King his said office and therewith all his goods, and that his body should be committed to prison, there to abide by an whole year without redemption. And thereupon, whatsoever person that should espy and duly prove that anything be done against the intent of the said two last articles, whereby the said forfeiture should fall upon any person, shall have the one half of the same forfeiture for his travail of the King's gift, as by the said statute evidently appeareth.

Our said sovereign lord the King, considering that notwithstanding the said good and beneficial statute and all other good laws, ordinances, and statutes heretofore made for the preservation and keeping of the treasure of this realm within the same for the commonwealth of all his subjects, yet many persons having intercourse between this realm and other foreign countries, some by occasions and feats of merchandise and some by other occasions, saving such inordinant affection to themself that for the furtherance of their own private lucre they little or nothing regard what harm, loss, or detriment they do to the commonwealth of the realm, have used commonly at many times heretofore to convey, send, and carry out of this realm by many secret means the coins of this realm and of other realms, plate, bullion, jewels, and other mass of gold and silver, whereby the treasure of this realm hath at sundry times been greatly diminished, and were also now like within short time to be much more diminished to the great impoverishment of this realm, if remedy be not therefore speedily provided.

Our said sovereign lord the King therefore, by the advice of his most honorable council, straightly chargeth and commandeth that no manner of person, Englishman, stranger, nor denizen, of what estate or degree soever he be, from henceforth in any wise so convey, send, or carry, or cause to be sent, carried, or conveyed out of this realm by any craft, means, or conveyance, any manner of coin of gold or silver of this realm or of any other realm, country, region, or dominion, or any manner of plate, vessel, bullion, jewels, or mass of gold or silver, under pain of forfeitures specified in the said statute.

And furthermore our said sovereign lord the King notifieth and declareth that whatsoever person hereafter by any manner of means espy, perceive, find, or know any person or persons conveying, sending, or bearing, or which shall cause to be conveyed or sent, any gold or silver, plate, bullion, vessels, jewels, or mass of gold or silver out of this realm, contrary to this proclamation, and thereof make seizure or give information to the lords of his most honorable council or before the Treasurer and Barons of his Exchequer, whereupon due proof may be made of the same, whether the same coin, plate, bullion, jewels, or mass of gold or silver be seized in the carrying or conveying out of this realm, and thereby still remain within the same, or else happen to be conveyed or carried out of this realm before any seizure or knowledge had of the same, shall have the one half of the said gold or silver, and of both; and that the party so offending shall, besides the said forfeiture, stand in the King's extreme indignation and be reputed forever after as an enemy to the realm, and one that hath a mind, for his part, to confound the commonwealth of the same.

134. Prohibiting Export of Victual

[Chelsea, 7 September 1531, 23 Henry VIII]

PR (C66/659/12*d*): date as above; writ to sheriffs of Bedford, Bucks; similar writs to sheriffs throughout England; schedule as below. LJ 13, 284*v*: date, Waltham, 17 October; schedule as below. Steele 128. Text (MS): PR

THE KING our sovereign lord, tendering the commonwealth and commodity of his loving subjects and people, and considering what annoyance and danger might ensue by scarcity and excessive dearth of corn and other victual; forasmuch as his grace by his high wisdom foreseeth and in experience knoweth divers persons so to regard their own private lucre and advantage as without respect of the violation and breaking of his highness' commandment heretofore given to the contrary, or consideration which damage and hurt they do therein to the residue of his grace's people and consequently to themselves, they only intending to apply all their policies daily how to convey out of this his grace's realm into other countries the said victuals in great quantities; by reason whereof this present year not being so fruitful as was trusted and in many parts of this his grace's realm by unseasonable weather failing, this his grace's realm should be shortly brought into extreme necessity and penury of victuals requisite for the sustenance of man's body, unless by dreadful penalties the covetous affection of such persons were therein in time restrained:

For these causes and considerations his highness, and by the advice of his council, for the avoiding of this unnecessary mischief in his commonwealth, hath for remedy thereof, and to notify the same unto his people, causeth this proclamation to be made in all countries and parts within this his grace's realm, straightly charging and commanding that no manner of person born under his grace's obeisance, or stranger, of what estate, degree, or condition soever he be, do convey or cause to be conveyed out of England or Wales into any other country, by sea or land, any manner corn, butter, cheese, tallow, beer, beeves, muttons, or other victuals, unless it be for the necessary victual of their ship, crayer, or boat, under pain of the King's high indignation, and forfeiture of the said corn, butter, cheese, tallow, beer, beeves, muttons, and other victuals so conveyed, the same to be levied of their lands, goods, and chattels to the King's use.

And for eschewing of such color and craft as hath been practiced heretofore for conveyance of such victuals, the King's highness signifieth to all and singular his subjects and other, that whensoever any corn, butter, cheese, tallow, beer, beeves, muttons, or other victuals above the value of 40*s*. be found or afterward known to have been laden in any ship, crayer, or boat for any pretense or cause, be it for victuals or else, to be carried into any other place of this realm in any haven, port, creek, or such river as passeth to the sea, without knowledge given thereof before the customers or other the King's officers there appointed for that purpose, then the owner of that corn, butter, cheese, tallow, beer, beeves, muttons, or other victuals above the value of 40*s*. so laden, to forfeit unto our said sovereign lord the value of the said corn, butter, cheese, tallow, beer, beeves, muttons, or other victuals, as though it had been conveyed contrary to the effect of this proclamation. Wherein no excuse nor allegation of ignorance shall be heard or admitted.

Wherefore the King's highness chargeth and commandeth not only all and singular his subjects to observe and keep the effect of this proclamation, as they will avoid the penalties of the same; but also all customers, comptrollers, searchers, and other officers in the ports and creeks of this his grace's realm, so diligently to attend to the due execution of the premises as no default or blame may be aretted unto them in that behalf: whose duty shall be not only to seize such corn, butter, beer, tallow, beeves, muttons, and other victuals as shall be conveyed or laden contrary to the effect of this proclamation, and signify unto the Exchequer the names of such persons as they shall know to offend in the same, but also by themselves or their deputies to give such attendance as his grace's subjects intending to victual their ships, crayers, or boats, may commodiously give knowledge thereof, without their great hindrance, according to the purport of this proclamation. And to the intent the said customers, searchers, and other officers shall the more fear and dread to offend in the execution of their charges, and others also be encouraged to deprehend and disclose their default in the permises, the King's said highness doth further order in this his proclamation, that whosoever can make due information of any customer, comptroller, searcher, or other officer to have suffered by covin any ship, crayer, or other vessel laden with corn, butter, cheese, tallow, beer, beeves, muttons, or other victuals, contrary to the purport hereof, the same person proving that information before the Lord Treasurer and other of the King's council shall recover of that customer, comptroller, searcher, or other officer so offending, half the just value of such corn, butter, cheese, tallow, beer, beeves, muttons, and other victuals so conveyed or laden contrary to this proclamation, with his costs and charges sustained in that behalf.

The King's highness nevertheless, for mutual relief between his loving subjects of this his realm of England and of Wales, hath ordered that it shall be lawful to any person or persons to convey from one country to another within his said realm of Wales any of the victuals aforesaid, so that before the lading and conveying thereof, the same person or persons make and deliver an obligation to the King's use, in the double value of the same victuals, to the customers and comptrollers or their deputies where the same victuals shall fortune to be shipped, that within the space of three months after, they shall bring a true certificate from the customers, comptrollers, mayors, sheriffs, bailiffs, or head officers of the place, whereunto he shall divert and assize of the employing of the same to the use of the King's subjects there, in which case and none other the same persons shall move lawfully from time to time, lade the said victuals or any kind thereof as aforesaid, without any manner danger, forfeiture, let, or molestation.

135. Proroguing Parliament

[Westminster, 4 October 1531, 23 Henry VIII]

LL O, 234: date as above; further prorogation, on 21 October to 15 January 1532; schedule as below. Not in Steele. Text (MS): LL

THE KING our sovereign lord, considering the great plague and sickness now remaining in the borough of Westminster where his high court of parliament is holden, and for other considerations moving his highness, giveth understanding and knowledge to all his subjects which be bounden to give their attendance at the same court of parliament the 16th day of this present month of October, shall not repair and come to the said parliament till the 6th day of November next coming; at which said day of November, his pleasure is that all such persons as be bound to come to the same give their attendance thereunto.

136. Appointing Council of State during King's Absence

[London, before 11 October 1532, 24 Henry VIII]

STC 7778 (UM 5,25,316), Antiq 1, 61: printed by T. Berthelet (London, 1532): schedule as below. Stow 945: Henry lands at Calais on 11 October. Steele 130: date, London. Text (*STC*): Antiq

THE KING our sovereign lord, being his grace resolved and determined upon such causes and grounds as tendeth to the wealth of this his realm and the benefit of Christendom to accomplish such appointment as between his highness and his good brother and perpetual ally, the French King, concerning their meeting beyond the seas, hath been concluded and taken: the tender zeal and princely affection which his majesty beareth to his most dear and well-beloved subjects hath steered and provoked his high wisdom to consider the due and perfect establishment of good order, rest, and quiet among his people to be preserved and maintained by due administration of justice in his grace's absence, and to make convenient provision for the same.

Wherefore his highness doth you to understand that for the causes before specified, his grace hath, by the advice of his council, named and appointed certain personages of nobility, wisdom, great experience, and knowledge, whom his highness hath authorized by sufficient commission to order and direct such matters as shall chance in his grace's absence, needing and requiring reformation: and therefore willeth all and every of his subjects, as they shall find themself grieved, to repair unto them, and also straightly chargeth and commandeth his said subjects, of what estate, degree, or condition soever they be, to obey such orders and directions as shall be made by the said council, with no less regard and respect than if the same proceeded and passed directly from his grace's own person.

This council is established at Westminster.

137. Ordering Muster against Scottish Invasion

[Westminster, 26 October 1532, 24 Henry VIII]

BM MS Harl 442, 82: date as above; writ to sheriff of York; schedule as below. Steele 131. Text (MS): Harl

FORASMUCH as the King's highness, by his letters of commission under his Great Seal, of late hath assigned, committed, and deputed his dear well-beloved cousin and councilor, the Earl of Shrewsbury, steward of his Majesty's honorable household and Knight of the honorable Order of the Garter, in this the absence of his grace, his Lieutenant-General of an army to be levied for defense and resistance of the Scots, in case they should attempt to invade any part of this his realm in his absence; and also hath given to the same Earl full power and authority to levy and assemble all and singular his subjects able for war inhabited in any of the shires of Nottingham, Derby, Stafford, Salop, Lancaster, Chester, York, Northumberland, Cumberland, and Westmorland, if case so require or necessity happen in that behalf, as in the same commissions more at large is contained:

His highness therefore straightly chargeth and commandeth all and singular his subjects of what estate, degree, or condition soever he or they be, within this his said shire, being within the ages of 60 and 16, able and meet for the wars, that they and every of them after their estate, behavior, and degree, upon the warning and commandment of the said Earl, to be ready, defensibly arrayed for the wars, to serve his grace in the leading and conducting of his said cousin and councilor in resistance and defense of the said Scots; and that every of his subjects with all diligence provide for harness, arms and other habiliments of war, as doth appertain to their duties and behaviors in that behalf: and not to fail thus to do, as they will answer unto his highness at their uttermost perils and avoid his high indignation and displeasure.

138. Ordering Local Officers to Enforce Statutes

[London, after 1532, 24 Henry VIII]

Rev.STC 7779.5 (BM Microfilm A.607,2) Chapin: printed by T. Berthelet (London, ?1533): schedule as below. LL P, 147: proclaimed in London on 6 March, 29 Henry VIII. Steele 132: date as above. Text (*STC*): Chapin

WHERE DIVERS and many good wholesome statutes and laws have been made and established as well in the time of the most gracious reign of our most dread sovereign lord as in the time of sundry of his noble progenitors, for the weal, profit, and utility of this realm, and for conservation of the King's loving subjects in good peace, concord, and unity, according to the estates and degrees that every of them is called to;

And in especial among other, the statutes made against such as craftily imagine, invent, make, and publish new-fangled news, tidings, and false tales to provoke and stir sedition, murmur, grudge, and division among the people; [1] the statutes provided for idle beggars and vagabonds; [2] the statutes for unlawful games and play; [3] and for maintenance and using of artillery and archery; [4] the statute made for reformation of excess in apparel; [5] and the statute made for sewers; [6]

For lack of due execution of which good statutes, the offenders for whom they were made daily increase and be encouraged, and the offenses for which the said statutes were provided be not reformed, punished, nor repressed, to the great hurt of the commonwealth of this realm; the very default whereof resteth in the King's justices of the peace, mayors, sheriffs, bailiffs, chief constables, constables, tithing men, and other ministers of justice in every shire, city, borough, and place of this realm, which for the most part so negligently, dulcetly, favorably, and unwillingly use their offices that justice is decayed, no punishment is done for common and open offenses;

By reason whereof, the offenders, being shameless, stand without dread of the laws, and so daily increase in multitude and numbers, and take courage

1. 3 Edward I, c. 34 (Westminster I), 1275, *SR 1*, 35; 2 Richard II, st. 1, c. 5, 1378, *SR 2*, 9.

2. 22 Henry VIII, c. 12, 1530, *SR 3*, 328. See 128, n. 1.

3. 19 Henry VII, c. 12, 1503, *SR 2*, 656. See 108, n. 1.

4. 6 Henry VIII, c. 2, 1514, *SR 3*, 123. See 108, n. 2.

5. 11 Edward III, c. 2, 1337, *SR 1*, 280; 11 Edward III, c. 4, 1337, *SR 1*, 280; 3 Edward IV, c. 5, 1463, *SR 2*, 399; 22 Edward IV, c. 1, 1432, *SR 2*, 468; 1 Henry VIII, c. 14, 1509, *SR 3*, 8; 6 Henry VIII, c. 1, 1513, *SR 3*, 121; 7 Henry VIII, c. 6, 1515, *SR 3*, 179; 24 Henry VIII, c. 13, 1532, *SR 3*, 430.

6. 23 Henry VIII, c. 5, 1531, *SR 3*, 368.

and boldness without shame or dread to commit daily offenses contrary to the form of the said good laws and statutes of this realm, to the high displeasure of Almighty God, and to impeachment, hindrance, damage, and the whole subversion of the commonwealth of this realm, if speedy remedy be not otherwise provided in this behalf;

The King's most royal majesty, who nothing more earnestly desireth than the advancement of the commonwealth of this realm, the due execution and equal administration of justice, and the good peace, rest, and quietness of his loving subjects, much lamenteth that his justices, officers, and ministers, to whom his highness hath committed the cure of administration of justice and the due execution of such statutes, do so negligently and unwillingly use the things committed to their charge, within the limits of their authorities, contrary to the good expectation and trust that his majesty hath in them.

His highness therefore, most prudently considering the premises, and minding first most graciously to admonish them of their negligences and defaults in the same, doth straightly charge and command all and singular his justices, commissioners, mayors, sheriffs, bailiffs, constables, underconstables, tithing men, burseholders, and all other his ministers of justice, of what authority, degree, or estate soever they be, that they endeavor to do and exercise the offices, cures, and authorities committed to their charges, without dread, corruption, affection, or partiality; and that especially they shall put into execution the laws and statutes above mentioned, having also most vigilant and earnest eye and regard to the apprehension and committing to sure prison all such persons as shall set forth any new rumors, tales, or reports, that shall in any wise sound to the slander or damage of his majesty or of any of his council, or to the provocation of sedition or murmur among his subjects, or to the violation of any good law or custom of this his realm.

And in their good doings and proceedings, his majesty will earnestly from time to time assist them and, for the same, love them, favor them, and in all their reasonable suits most graciously hear them; and over that, requite their good services and diligences in his commonwealth in such wise that they shall think their travails and pains right well employed and bestowed in that behalf.

And in case that after this his most gracious admonition no amendment be had, nor respect to their duties, his highness then signifieth to such as do and will obstinately continue and persist in their negligences, follies, and defaults, that they and every of them shall run into his most high indignation and displeasure.

And over that, his grace will pursue them as very enemies of his commonwealth, and punish them in their bodies, lands, and goods, after their demerits, that it shall be to their confusions and undoings, to the most terrible example of such offenders.

And furthermore, his majesty straightly chargeth and commandeth all and singular persons within this his realm and dominions, of what estate, degree, or condition soever they be, that they and every of them, for their parts do from henceforth observe and keep the said good laws and statutes, upon the pains and penalties contained in the same; which his highness intendeth to take and levy without pardon or remission, in case they do obstinately persist in the breaking of the said statutes and laws, after this his grace's proclamation.[7]

139. Enforcing Statute on Sale of Meat by Weight

[Westminster, 3 July 1533, 25 Henry VIII]

LJ 13, 376*v:* date as above; writ to mayor and sheriffs of London; schedule as below. LL P, 11: schedule includes a mayoral addition for London. Steele 133. Text (MS): LJ

WHERE by an act[1] made in the parliament begun the third day of November, *anno* 21 Henry VIII, and yet prorogued and continued, it is ordained amongst other things that butchers, and all other persons putting flesh to sale, shall sell the same by weight by retail, to all and every of the King's subjects after such rates as by the same act is expressed and specified; which act, the King's pleasure and high commandment is, shall be duly put in execution for the weal and benefit of all his loving subjects of this his realm according to the true meaning and tenor of the same. And therefore [he] chargeth and commandeth all and every his subjects exercising the craft or mystery of butchers, and all other putting flesh to sale, that they shall use and order themselves according to the tenor of the said act, upon the pains limited and contained in the said act.

And forasmuch as the butchers and such other victualers as shall put flesh to sale by retail will peradventure refuse or grudge to obey and use themselves in retail of flesh by weight, according to the tenor of the same act, objecting for their excuses that they cannot buy of the graziers, and such other farmers as shall sell cattle in gross by the poll, at such reasonable prices as they, having any living, may utter the same by retail by weight, according to the tenor of the said act: the King's highness therefore, by his excellent wisdom considering that like as the said act obligeth the butchers and other victualers to sell by retail by weight at reasonable prices limited by the same act, so likewise it is and ought to be understood, interpreted, and intended by good reason and equity, that the graziers, and other putting cattle to sale

7. See 17.

1. 24 Henry VIII, c. 3, 1532, *SR 3,* 420.

in gross by the poll, should and ought to sell the same cattle by poll to the butchers and other victualers in gross, after such reasonable prices as the butchers may reasonably accomplish and perform the effects of the said act.

In consideration whereof, the King our sovereign lord straightly chargeth and commandeth all and every graziers, farmers, and all other his subjects intending to put any manner cattle to sale by the poll in gross of the said butchers, or to any other persons intending to retail the same by weight according to the same act, shall utter and sell the said cattle in gross, of what kind soever it be, at such reasonable prices as the butchers and other buyers thereof, intending to retail the same by weight to the King's subjects, reasonably leaving to themselves a competent gain for their living, utter and sell the said cattle to the King's subjects by weight by retail, according to the tenor of the said act. And in case the said graziers, farmers, or any other the King's subjects refuse this to do by reason of their greedy covetousness and willfulness, whereby the said good act shall be letted to take good effect according to the tenor of the same, then the King our sovereign lord is not only determined to punish the offenders in that behalf, but also to put such redress therein as shall stand with equity and justice for the weal of all his subjects of this realm, and every the offenders to incur into his indignation and displeasure, and to suffer punishment for the same at his will.

140. Depriving Catherine of Royal Style; Warning of Praemunire

[London, 5 July 1533, 25 Henry VIII]

STC 7779 (UM 2,7,317) BM C.18.e.2, 56: printed by T. Berthelet (London, 1533); date missing; schedule as below. *CSPSpanish* 4(2), 1058: date, 10 April; report from Chapuis to Emperor that Henry is about to prohibit speaking in favor of the Queen under pain of death. Stow 959: Catherine proclaimed Arthur's widow on July 5. Steele 134. Text (*STC*): BM

FORASMUCH as the unlawful matrimony between the King's highness and the Lady Catherine, Princess Dowager, late wife to Prince Arthur, by just ways and means is lawfully dissolved, and a divorce and separation had and done between his said highness and the said Lady Catherine, by the most reverend father in God the Archbishop of Canterbury, Legate and Primate of all England, and Metropolitan of the same; and thereupon the King's majesty hath lawfully married and taken to his wife, after the laws of the church, the right high and excellent Princess Lady Anne, now Queen of England, and she solemnly crowned and anointed as appertaineth, to the laud, praise, and honor of Almighty God, the surety of the King's succession and posterity, and to the great joy, comfort, and contentation of all the subjects of this realm; all which premises have grandly proceeded and taken their effects, as well by the common assent of the lords spiritual and temporal, and the commons of this realm, by authority of parliament, as also by the assent and determinations of the whole clergy in their several convocations holden and kept in both provinces of this realm.

And for perfect and sure establishment thereof, it is enacted among other things that whatsoever person or persons of what estate, degree, or condition they be of, do attempt or procure any manner process, or do or move any act or acts to the let or derogation of any such proceedings, sentences, and determinations, as is and have been done and had as well in and about the said divorce, as in the solemnation of the lawful matrimony had and concluded between the King's highness and the said Queen Anne, shall incur and run in the pains and penalties comprised in the Statute of Provisers and Praemunire[1] made in the 16th year of the late King Richard II, which is no less pain than the offenders to be out of the King's protection, and their goods and lands to be forfeited, and their bodies imprisoned at the King's will, as by the said act more at large is expressed; by reason whereof and forasmuch as the said divorce and separation is now had and done, and the King's highness lawfully married, as is before rehearsed.

It is therefore evident and manifest that the said Lady Catherine should not from henceforth have or use the name, style, title, or dignity of Queen of this realm, nor be in any wise reputed, taken, accepted, or written by the name of Queen of this realm; but by the name, style, title, and dignity of Princess Dowager, which name she ought to have because she was lawfully and perfectly married and accoupled with the said Prince Arthur. And whatsoever officers, ministers, bailiffs, receivers, farmers, servants, keepers of parks or chases of the said Princess Dowager, or any other person or persons of what estate, degree, or condition they be of, contrary to the premises, do name, repute, accept, and write, or in any wise obey the said Lady Catherine by virtue of any manner of warrant or writing to them directed by the name of Queen, or attempt, do, or move any other act or acts, thing or things, to the let or derogation of such doings and proceedings as is determined and accomplished as well for the dissolution of the said unlawful marriage, as for the solemnization and confirmation of the said lawful matrimony justly finished and concluded, as is above rehearsed, shall and doth plainly and manifestly incur and run in the said great dangers and pains comprised and specified in the said act.

In consideration whereof, albeit that the King our most dread sovereign lord nothing mistrusteth his loving subjects for any attempt, act, or acts, or anything to be done, moved, or spoken by them contrary to the true meaning of the said act, and the due execution and proceedings in the

1. 16 Richard II, c. 5, 1392, *SR* 2, 84.

premises, yet nevertheless to the intent that his said humble and loving subjects shall have plain, open, and manifest notice of the great perils, dangers, and penalties comprised and specified in the said act, whereby they may eschew the dangers thereof: his majesty therefore of his most gracious and benign goodness, more coveting and desiring the good obediences and conformities of his said subjects than to be advanced and enriched by their offenses or contempts, by the advice of his said council, hath caused this proclamation to be made for a plain overture and publication of the premises, whereby as well all and every his loving subjects, as others, may (if they will) avoid and eschew the said great pains, dangers, and penalties above specified. Whereunto his grace's pleasure and high commandment is that every person from henceforth take good heed and respect, at their perils.

And yet nevertheless the King's most gracious pleasure is that the said Lady Catherine shall be well used, obeyed, and entreated according to her honor and noble parentage, by the name, title, state, and style of Princess Dowager, as well by all her officers, servants, and ministers as also by others his humble and loving subjects, in all her lawful businesses and affairs, so it extend not in any wise contrary to this proclamation.

141. Ordering Vagabonds to Leave Court

[ca. 1533, 25 Henry VIII]

ETR (E36/231/188): schedule as below. Steele 135: date as above. Text (MS): ETR

THE KING'S royal majesty straightly chargeth and commandeth that all vagabonds, masterless folk, rascals and other idle persons which have used to hang on, haunt, and follow the court, do depart from thence within 24 hours of this proclamation made, upon such pains as in his laws therefor is appointed.

And furthermore the King's high commandment is that no manner of person or persons, of what estate or degree soever he or they be of, do from thenceforth keep any more number of persons or servants retaining unto them within the court than doth appertain unto them, nor that any of them shall keep any pages of boys to be attendant upon any of them within the said court contrary unto the King's ordinance in that behalf made, as they and every of them will avoid the King's grievous displeasure; and that no officer of the household nor any other person lodged within the King's house do suffer any vagabonds, masterless folk, rascals, or other idle persons to resort unto their office or chamber at any time, upon pain of imprisonment, and utterly forever to be excluded the King's service; nor that any of the said officers do keep any servants within the King's said house, nor suffer or support them with meat and drink within the King's house, but such as by the King's ordinance be appointed to have servants, upon like pain and loss of their service.

And also the King's gracious pleasure and commandment is that no manner of person, of what estate or degree he or they be of, shall suffer any of his or their servants to enter the King's gate but such as shall be like men to rest in good order, excluding from them in any wise all boys and rascals, upon pain of the King's grievous displeasure. And also his highness most straightly chargeth and commandeth that no persons, upon pain of his majesty's most high indignation, shall move or make any assault or fray, or in any wise attempt or break the peace, either within the great court or within any other place within the verge of the same; and that neither officer nor chamber keeper suffer, or in their offices or rooms, support any follower of the court, be they craftsmen, other rascals or [*illegible*], or cause any meat or drink to be carried out of the gates for them; and also that no officer nor chamber keeper, upon pain of loss of their service and imprisonment, lodge any person in their office or his majesty's chambers, other than be appointed by the King's highness' ordinary and statutes of his household.

142. Enforcing Statutes on Sale of Meat

[Westminster, 29 January 1534, 25 Henry VIII]

LJ 13, 393*v:* date as above; writ to mayor and sheriffs of London; proclaimed in London on 3 February; schedule as below. Steele 137. Text (MS): LJ

Forasmuch as it is come to the knowledge of our most dread sovereign lord the King, to his no little displeasure, as well by relation of many his noblemen and the complaint of others his subjects of good parts resorting to his high court of parliament, as also upon the piteous and lamentable exclamation of others his poor subjects that, notwithstanding the good and laudable statute [1] of late made to the relief of the commonwealth of this his realm for the prices of beef, mutton, veal, and pork to be sold by weight, yet nevertheless the butchers of London and other resortants to this city of London with the same victuals, not regarding any law nor fearing the forfeitures and penalties contained in the same, refusing and contemning the execution thereof, will in no wise sell the same victuals according to the purport and prices expressed in the same statute:

The King's highness therefore straightly chargeth and commandeth all

1. 24 Henry VIII, c. 3, 1532, *SR 3,* 420.

and every the said butchers and victualers and all other resorting to the same city and other places adjoinant, as well within the liberties and places privileged as without, in every part of this his realm, that they and every of them sell the said victuals of beef, mutton, veal, and pork according to the purport of the same statute, upon pain not only to forfeit the penalties contained and expressed in the said statute, but also to pay for their disobedience and contempt such other exactions, penalties, fines, and sums of money as by the King's grace and his council shall be set upon them for their offenses in this behalf, and also to make further answer at their uttermost perils.

And moreover the King's highness straightly chargeth and commandeth all mayors, sheriffs, bailiffs, constables, and others his officers and faithful subjects to whom it appertaineth, that they with all diligence see the same act put in effectual and perfect execution, as they will answer thereto, and also avoid the King's highness' displeasure and indignation; and to see the offenders so continuing their obstinacy to be put in ward and prison, there to remain without bail or mainprize until the King's pleasure be further known in that behalf.

143. Enforcing Statute of Apparel

[February 1534, 25 Henry VIII]

BM MS Harl 442, 86: heading date as above; schedule as below. Steele 138. Text (MS): Harl

WHEREAS in the act of reformation of excess of apparel[1] passed in this present parliament it is provided that all such officers and servants waiting and attending upon the King and the Queen and the Princess Elizabeth yearly or quarterly in their households, or being in their exchequer rolls, as shall be admitted or assigned and licensed by his grace to use or wear any manner of apparel on their bodies, horses, mules, or other beasts, otherwise than is in the said statute expressed, shall now lawfully do the same according to the license which shall be given unto them in that behalf; the same license to be declared in writing by the King's highness or the Lord Steward of his most honorable household or the Lord Chamberlain knowing the King's most gracious pleasure in the same.

You shall understand that the King's pleasure is that all officers and servants waiting or attending upon his guard, the Queen, or the Princess Elizabeth, yearly or quarterly in their household, or being in their exchequer rolls, may wear all manner such apparel as they now have unto the Feast of Palm Sunday next coming; and that none other persons, their servants so-

1. 24 Henry VIII, c. 13, 1532, *SR 3*, 430.

ever, nor any other person or persons of what degree soever he or they be, wear in their apparel of their bodies, horses, or mules, more than is limited and to them appointed by the said act, upon pain to forfeit the penalties in the same statute limited, and the King's further displeasure for doing of the same.

144. Suspending Statute on Sale of Meat until 24 June

[Westminster, 14 March 1534, 25 Henry VIII]

Antiq 1, 68: writ to mayor and sheriffs of London, sheriff of Middlesex: schedule as below. BM MS Harl 442, 87: date as above; writ to mayor and sheriffs of London; MS note, printed by T. Berthelet; schedule as below. Schanz 2, 650. Steele 139. Text (MS): Harl

Forasmuch as the King's majesty is credibly advertised and informed that beeves, muttons, and veals are likely to be more scarce and dear now at this holy time of Easter than in other seasons of the year by reason of the charges of keeping of such cattle with hay and other stover; by occasion whereof the butchers and other than shall sell such beeves, muttons, and veals by retail by weight, can not buy them of the breeders, broggers, farmers, drovers, owners, and feeders of such cattle at such reasonable prices in gross as they may sell the same again by weight by retail at such prices as are limited in the act[1] made for selling of flesh by weight, unless it should be to their utter loss and undoing:

His highness therefore, willing the same butchers to be so conveniently provided for in the premises as they should not have any cause reasonable to forbear their provisions for such victual to be sold by retail, against this holy time of Easter, for relief and succor of his subjects, in as ample manner as heretofore hath been accustomed, is contented and pleased that from henceforth unto the 24th day of June next coming, butchers and all other that shall sell flesh of the kinds aforesaid by weight by retail, shall and may sell unto the said 24th day of June next coming every pound of beef good and wholesome for man's body for ⅝*d.* and no more; and every pound of mutton for ¾*d.* only and no more; and every pound of veal for ⅝*d.* and no more. The said act of provision heretofore had or made for selling flesh by weight by retail to the contrary hereof notwithstanding.

And over this, it shall be lawful to all such butchers and others selling flesh by retail as is aforesaid from henceforth unto the first day of January next coming to kill and sell calves at their free liberty and pleasure at the

1. 24 Henry VIII, c. 7, 1532, *SR 3*, 423.

prices afore rehearsed. The act[2] late made for killing calves to endure for two whole years to the contrary thereof made notwithstanding.

The King's highness straightly charging and commanding all and every the said breeders, broggers, drovers, farmers, feeders, and owners of such cattle, that they and every of them furnish the fairs and markets with such fat cattle as they have to sell, in as large and ample manner as hath been accustomed; and to sell their said cattle at such reasonable prices as the said butchers, and such other as shall retail the same again by weight, may utter and sell the same to his loving subjects at such prices as are above limited, as they will avoid his grace's high displeasure and answer to the same at their uttermost perils. And that after the said 24th day of June, the said butchers and other selling flesh by retail shall from thenceforth sell by weight by retail according to the said act made and provided for the same, and at such prices as are limited in the said act: upon the pains and penalties contained in the said act, till such hour and time as the King's highness shall otherwise limit by his proclamation for the same.

Wherefore the King's highness straightly chargeth and commandeth all and singular mayors, justices of peace, sheriffs, bailiffs, constables, and other his officers and faithful subjects, to whom it shall or in any manner of wise may appertain, that they and every of them cause this his proclamation to be put in due and effectual execution, as they will answer to his highness at their uttermost perils.

145. Ordering Londoners to Pay Tithes Set by Commission

[Westminster, 2 April 1534, 25 Henry VIII]

BM MS Harl 442, 89: date as above; letters patent to mayor, aldermen, and sheriffs of London; schedule as below. Steele 140. Text (MS): Harl

To OUR TRUSTY and well beloved the mayor, aldermen, and sheriffs of London and to every of them, greeting.

Where variance between the parsons and curates of our city of London on the one part, and our loving subjects inhabitants of the same our city of the other part, for and concerning tithes and other duties, hath long depended undiscussed, and being lately compromised by both of the said parties to the arbitrament of the most reverend father in God, Thomas, Archbishop of Canterbury, Primate and Metropolitan of England; and to our right trusty and entirely beloved councilor, Sir Thomas Audley, knight, our

2. 25 Henry VIII, c. 1, 1533, *SR 3*, 436.

Chancellor of England; and to our trusty and well beloved councilor, the Bishop of Winchester; Thomas Cromwell, esquire, master of our jewels; and our two Chief Justices of either bench; who travailing therein have taken this order to be kept at this holy time of Easter: that is to say, that every our subjects shall pay to the parson or curate where he inhabiteth after the rate of *2s. 9d.* the pound, and 16½*d.* the half-pound, and so always ascending from half-pound to half-pound; and also that men's wives, their servants, children, and apprentices, taking and receiving the holy sacrament, shall give, every of them for their four offering days, *2d.* And this is to be done freely and charitably without grudge or murmur at the holy time of Easter, till such time as our said councilors shall finally and definitively end and determine the variance for this and all other causes depending between the said parties as to right, equity, and good conscience shall appertain.

We therefore will and command you and every of you to signify to all our loving subjects in every parish in our said city that our pleasure is that they and every of them shall obey, observe, and fulfill at this holy time of Easter the order of the said councilors in form above rehearsed without any contradiction thereof in any behalf: declaring to them that they so doing it shall not turn nor be alleged to their prejudice, hurt, or damage in and upon the final conclusion and determination of all their said variances to the definitive arbitrament whereof our said councilors intend, God willing, to proceed with all speed and diligence after the said Feast of Easter. And if any contemn the order of our said councilors in this behalf, we will then, if he after honest monition refuse so to do, he be committed to ward, safely to be kept till our further pleasure be known in this behalf: not failing this to do as you intend the advancement of justice and quietness of our people.

146. Enforcing Statute of Apparel

[Richmond, 27 May 1534, 26 Henry VIII]

LL L, 415: schedule as below. BM MS Harl 442, 90: date as above; schedule as below. Steele 141. Text (MS): LL

WHEREAS in the act of reformation of excess of array [1] passed in the parliament one proviso mentioning these words following is contained, "Provided always that all such officers and servants waiting or attending upon the King, the Queen, the Princess Elizabeth, yearly or quarterly in their household or being in their exchequer roll, as shall be admitted, assigned, or licensed by his grace to use or wear such manner apparel on their bodies,

1. 24 Henry VIII, c. 13, 1532, *SR 3*, 430.

horses, mules, or other beasts otherwise than is afore expressed, shall now lawfully do the same according to the license which shall be given unto them in that behalf, the same license to be declared in writing by the King's highness, or the lord steward of his most honorable household, or the lord chamberlain knowing the King's most gracious pleasure in the same":

We by this writing signed with our hand do declare that all manner of person and persons specified in the same proviso may wear all manner of such apparel as they now have unto the Feast of All Saints next coming: declaring our further pleasure to be that none other person nor persons use to wear none other sorts of apparel than is limited unto them by the said act, as they will avoid the danger that may ensue to them by virtue of the said act.

147. Announcing Peace Treaty with Scotland

[Westminster, 29 August 1534, 26 Henry VIII]

LJ 13, 420*v*: partial schedule. BM MS Harl 442, 91: date as above; writ to mayor and sheriffs of London; schedule as below. Steele 142. Text (MS): Harl

THE KING our sovereign lord doth you to understand that to the laud and praise of Almighty God and the repose and tranquillity of this his realm of England and his subjects of the same, there is passed, accorded, and concluded between his highness of the one part, and the right excellent prince his dearest brother, cousin, and nephew, James, King of Scots, on the other part; for them, their heirs and successors, realms, countries, dominions, lands, vassals, and subjects whatsoever they be, present and to come, as well spiritual as temporal, of whatsoever estate, degree, or condition they be: a good, sincere, true, whole, perfect, and firm amity, league, confederation, peace, and union, as well by land, sea, and fresh water, as in every place under their dominions and obeisances perpetually to endure during both their lives, and by one year next after the decease of such of them as shall first happen to depart this present life.

So that it shall be lawful to the merchants and subjects of either of the said princes whatsoever they be, present and to come, from henceforth surely, freely, and liberally at their pleasure to pass and enter into any of their realms, countries, dominions, and lands, cities, towns, ports, and straits, by land, sea, or fresh water, and in the same as long as they will to abide, sojourn, demur and remain; there to buy, sell, exercise traffic and course of merchandise, or do their other lawful business, and from the same as often as it shall please them into any other place to depart with their goods and merchandises, ships, baggages, and other things, as they might in their own countries, and as the proper subjects of any of the same princes may do; with all other special and general mutual intercourses of merchandise and liberties and privileges for the same, both in the realm of England and also in the realm of Scotland, in as large, frank, and ample manner as they did or might have done in any time heretofore if never war had been had, made, moved, or denounced between the King's highness and the said King of Scots.

Wherefore the King's highness chargeth and commandeth all and singular his officers, ministers, and subjects that they and every of them do duly and inviolably observe and keep the said peace accordingly, as they will avoid his highness' displeasure and indignation, and answer to him if they attempt the contrary, at their uttermost perils.

148. Suspending Statute on Sale of Meat until 24 June

[Westminster, 23 October 1534, 26 Henry VIII]

STC 7781 (UM 2,10,324), Antiq 1, 72: printed by T. Berthelet (London, 1534); date as above; writ to mayor and sheriffs of London; schedule as below. LJ 13, 428: proclaimed in London on 24 October; schedule as below. Steele 143. Text (*STC*): Antiq

WHERE at this present parliament begun at London the third day of November in the 21st year of the reign of our most dread sovereign lord the King, and from thence adjourned to Westminster, and there holden and prorogued by divers and sundry prorogations, and yet continued, it is ordered and provided[1] among other things that butchers should sell, by weight, beef and pork for ½*d.* the pound, and mutton and veal for ⅝*d.* the pound, as by the same act more at large is contained: forasmuch as the butchers of the said city of London and of the suburbs of the same can not so conveniently utter and sell their victuals at such prices as butchers inhabited in other parts of the realm may do, by reason that the said butchers of London and of the suburbs of the same, as well for maintenance of their houses and servants, and bearing lots and scots by the orders and customs of the said city, as for hiring of grounds lying nigh the same city, for the preservation of their cattle till they be killed, at such high farms and rents, be daily put to much more higher, greater, and excessive charges, costs, and expenses than butchers inhabited in other parts of this realm be.

The King our most dread sovereign lord therefore, being advertised of

1. 25 Henry VIII, c. 1, 1533, *SR 3*, 436.

the premises, considering also that in the same season of winter cattle are much more dearer than they be in the summertime, when they are nourished and fed with plenty fullness of grass; and willing that the butchers of his said city and suburbs of the same, being his loving subjects, should have and take such reasonable gains, by exercise of their mysteries, as they might honestly live withal according to their behaviors; and to give them courage that his said city, as well at the assembly of this his present parliament now to be holden as at all other times, should be plentifully furnished with good victuals: is pleased and contented, by the advice of his council, that the butchers of his said city of London and suburbs of the same, from the date of this his grace's proclamation unto the Feast of the Nativity of St. John Baptist next coming, shall and may sell beef and pork for ⅝*d.* the pound, and mutton and veal for ⅝*d.* the pound. And that this his most gracious letter of proclamation shall be to every of the same butchers of his said city and suburbs sufficient warrant and discharge against his highness and all other, for selling of flesh at the prices afore limited in the same: anything contained in the same act to the contrary thereof notwithstanding.

Provided always that the said butchers see his said city well and plentifully provided and furnished with good and wholesome victuals.

And furthermore his highness straightly chargeth and commandeth the mayor and sheriffs of his said city, that now is and hereafter shall be, that they from time to time survey and see the same to be effectually done, as they will answer to his majesty at their uttermost perils in that behalf.

And over this, the King's highness straightly chargeth and commandeth that as well all butchers inhabited in other parts of his realm, as also all graziers, farmers, broggers, and breeders of cattle, shall utter and sell their cattle at reasonable and convenient prices, and in such manner and form as by the said statute and by divers other statutes heretofore made is ordained and provided, as they will answer at their uttermost perils for the same.

149. Pricing Wines

[Westminster, 7 November 1534, 26 Henry VIII]

LJ 13, 429*v:* date as above; writ to mayor and sheriffs of London; proclaimed in London on 12 November; schedule as below. Steele 144. Text (MS): LJ

FORASMUCH as the King our sovereign lord, his most dear and trusty councilors, Sir Thomas Audley, knight, Lord Chancellor of England; Thomas, Duke of Norfolk, Lord President of his council; Thomas, Earl of Wiltshire, Keeper of his Privy Seal; Sir John Fitz-James, knight, Lord Chief Justice of his pleas before him to be holden; and Sir Robert Norwich, knight, Chief Justice of his common bench, in the due execution of an act[1] made and established in this his parliament, yet considering for the commonwealth of this his realm and subjects of the same, have limited, assigned, and appointed the prices of Gascon and French wines to be sold within this his realm; that is to say, every tun of the best Gascon wine or French wine to be sold after the price and rate of £4 sterling the tun and not above, and every pipe, hogshead, puncheon, tierce, and other vessel of the same wine to be sold for their quantities after and according to the same rate and not above; and for small and thin wines to be sold under the same rate as the buyers and sellers thereof can agree:

The King's highness, our said sovereign lord, therefore straightly chargeth and commandeth all manner his subjects and others putting any manner Gascon or French wines to sale within this his realm, that they nor any of them in any manner of wise sell any manner of Gascon or French wines above the said price and rate of £4 the tun; and every pipe, hogshead, puncheon, tierce, and other vessel of the said wines to be sold for their quantities after and according to the same rate; and to sell the said small and thin wines under the said value in manner and form specified and not above, upon pain to forfeit and pay such penalties as is contained in the said act.

And moreover his high pleasure and commandment also is that all and singular mayors, sheriffs, bailiffs, constables, and other officers to whom it appertaineth, that they and every of them with all diligence cause and see that this his proclamation be put in due execution after the tenor of the same, and also according to another act of parliament[2] in that case provided, as they will answer thereto at their uttermost perils.

150. Ordering Courtesies to French Ambassador

[Westminster, 7 November 1534, 26 Henry VIII]

LJ 13, 430*v*: date as above; writ to mayor, aldermen, and sheriffs of London and Middlesex; proclaimed in London on 12 November; schedule as below. Steele 145. Text (MS): LJ

Forasmuch as the King's most dear brother and perpetual ally, Francis the French King, sendeth now shortly to the King's majesty his dear and honest councilor, the Grand Admiral of France, ambassador, accompanied with many noblemen and gentlemen, for great and urgent causes concerning as well the honor and wealth of his realm as also the wealth of the realm of

1. 23 Henry VIII, c. 7, 1531, *SR 3*, 374.
2. 24 Henry VIII, c. 6, 1532, *SR 3*, 422.

France: wherefore it is thought to the King our said most dread sovereign lord, and to his council, to be very honorable and convenient that the said ambassador and also all his company and train should quietly, peaceably, and most lovingly be used, entreated, and entertained at all times, by day and by night, during their abode within this realm, and do all their business and affairs without any quarrels, occasions of quarrels, or other inquietations to be made or attempted unto any of them:

The King's majesty therefore straightly chargeth and commandeth the mayor, aldermen, and sheriffs of the city of London, and all other faithful subjects, of what degree, estate, or condition soever they be, that they nor any of them in any wise do use, offer, or suffer to be done or attempted to the said ambassador, or to any of his said company and train, within any place of the said city or suburbs of the same, both within the liberties there or without, any occasions, quarrels, displeasures or unkindness by any manner of color or means, by day or by night, upon pain to incur the King's most high displeasure and indignation, and as they will answer to the same at their uttermost perils.

And furthermore the King's highness straightly chargeth and commandeth all and singular his subjects, of what estate, degree, or condition soever he or they be, that they and every of them be aiding, helping, counseling, and assisting to all such as shall execute this the King's pleasure, as they will answer to the King's majesty for the same.

151. Ordering Punishment of Grain Hoarders

[Westminster, 11 November 1534, 26 Henry VIII]

STC 7782 (UM 5,25,325), Antiq 2, 121: printed by T. Berthelet (London, 1534); schedule as below. *L&P* 7, 1415: date 11 November; Cromwell requests a true copy to be printed this night. Steele 146: date, Westminster. Text (*STC*): Antiq

Forasmuch as corn of all grains, and especially wheat and rye, is suddenly enhanced at unreasonable prices, and one special cause is by occasion that it is used for a common merchandise, and most commonly bought by such persons as have plenty of their own growth, to the intent to make a dearth thereof; and divers husbandmen and farmers do color such buyings for feed, where they have no such necessity so to do;

For reformation whereof, the King's most royal majesty, willing that his loving subjects should be provided of corn at reasonable prices; considering that (thanks be to God) there is no just ground or cause why such grain should be so high enhanced in price as it is, but that the enhancement thereof groweth by the occasion aforesaid, and by the subtle invention and craft of divers covetous persons having convenient plenty of the same: doth therefore straightly charge and command, that no person nor persons, after this present proclamation, till his grace's pleasure be further known, shall buy or bargain any wheat or rye to sell again, except it be to be conveyed by water or land for provision of the city of London or other cities or towns having necessity therefor, or to bake in bread to be sold to his subjects, or else for provision of Iceland Fleet. And such as shall buy for any such causes, shall find sureties to one of the commissioners assigned for search of corn, to employ it accordingly. And that no person having wheat or rye of his own tilth and growth, or by provision of his buying, sufficient to find his family and household and for his seed, shall buy any such grain, upon pain that every offender contrary to the premises or any part thereof shall not only incur into his grace's most high displeasure and indignation, but also suffer imprisonment, and make fine at his pleasure. And also that no person occupying tillage and husbandry shall buy any wheat or rye for seed, unless it be first examined and proved before one or two of the commissioners assigned for search of corn, that such person hath necessity to buy such seed; or else that such person, so buying any wheat or rye for seed, within eight days after the buying thereof, do bring as much of his own wheat or rye, not being able for seed, into the market and there sell the same to the King's subjects having need thereof for keeping of their houses, and bring a certificate to one of the said commissioners from the bailiff or other chief officer of the market where he shall so sell his corn, that he hath sold the same: upon pain that every offender to the contrary hereof, to incur the danger, pains, imprisonment and fine above remembered.

And also his majesty straightly chargeth and commandeth that no person or persons shall regrate or engross any manner of corn, upon pain of imprisonment and forfeiture of all their goods and chattels. And that every of his subjects having corn of their own tilth, or by provision of their buying, more than will suffice for their families, households, and seed, shall furnish the markets with the overplus from time to time, by the order of the commissioners assigned for the same, and there sell at reasonable prices; and observe and obey the said commissioners in all such orders as they shall take for the due execution of their commission, upon pain of imprisonment and fine making at his grace's will.

And over this, the King's highness straightly chargeth and commandeth all and singular his justices of peace, mayors, sheriffs, bailiffs, constables, and all other his loving subjects, that they and every of them shall put their true diligence and effectual endeavors for the due execution of this his gracious proclamation, and to make relation of the offenders thereof to the said commissioners assigned for search of corn or to the Lord Chancellor of England and other his most honorable council from time to time as shall appertain, as they will answer to his highness at their uttermost perils.

152. Regulating Wool Cloth Manufacture

[Westminster, 23 November 1534, 26 Henry VIII]

LL P, 53: date as above; writ to sheriffs of London and Middlesex; schedule as below. Steele 147. Text (MS): LL

THE KING'S HIGHNESS our most loving and dread sovereign lord, for certain great and weighty causes and considerations specially moving his highness, for conservation of the ancient honor of this his realm concerning the true making of all sorts of woolen cloths, whereby a great multitude of his true and loving subjects daily be set in work and preserved from idleness, straightly chargeth and commandeth all and every his said subjects, cloth makers and others, that they and every of them, from the Feast of Easter next ensuing this present proclamation, do make and cause to be made all and every the same woolen cloths (being sale ware) of what kind, country, city, borough, town, village, or hamlet soever they be, well, sufficiently, truly, and without any craft or deceit, according unto such assize, length, breadth, order, and limitation as is ordained and appointed by the tenor of sundry statutes and acts [1] heretofore made for that purpose, and according to the true meaning of every of the same acts and statutes made for that intent as well by the King's said highness, as by divers others his most noble progenitors at sundry times, upon pain of forfeiture of all and every cloth, cloths, penalties, and fines of money contained in any of the same acts and statutes, in whose hands soever they may be found, as well within liberties as without.

And over this, the King's said highness straightly chargeth and commandeth all and every his alnager and alnagers and their deputies, that they and every of them be diligent and circumspect from the said Feast of Easter, as well in doing and executing of their said office according to the true meaning of every of the said acts and statutes, as in making of their informations before the Barons of his Exchequer, and in seizing of all and every woolen cloth and cloths made contrary to the purport, form, and effect of any of the said acts and statutes, upon pain of forfeiture of their said offices, and also of all such sums of money and penalties as be contained in any of the said acts and statutes for non-doing or not putting in due and plain execution of the same their office.

And besides this, our said sovereign lord straightly chargeth and com-

1. 27 Edward III, st. 1, c. 4, 1353, *SR 1*, 330; 27 Edward III, st. 2, c. 4, 1353, *SR 1*, 334; 27 Edward III, st. 2, c. 23, 1353, *SR 1*, 341; 47 Edward III, c. 1, 1373, *SR 1*, 395; 3 Richard II, c. 2, 1379, *SR 2*, 13; 11 Henry IV, c. 6, 1409, *SR 2*, 163; 11 Henry VI, c. 9, 1433, *SR 2*, 284; 4 Edward IV, c. 1, 1464, *SR 2*, 403; 3 Henry VII, c. 11, 1487, *SR 2*, 520; 3 Henry VIII, c. 6, 1511, *SR 3*, 28; 5 Henry VIII, c. 4, 1513, *SR 3*, 94; 6 Henry VIII, c. 9, 1514, *SR 3*, 130.

mandeth all mayors, sheriffs, bailiffs, constables, and all other his officers, servants, true liegemen, and subjects whatsoever they be, that unto the said alnagers and unto any of them and unto their deputy or deputies for the time being, they be from time to time helping, aiding, furthering, and assisting for the due executing of the premises, as often as they or any of them thereunto shall be required by and of the same alnagers or any of their deputies, upon pain to incur the high displeasure of the King's said highness, and as they and every of them will answer unto his highness at their uttermost perils.

153. Penalizing Failure to Pay Tithes

[Westminster, February 1535, 26 Henry VIII]

STC 7783 (UM 2,10,329), Antiq 1, 76: printed by T. Berthelet (London, 1535); date, MS note, February; schedule as below. Steele 148: date, Westminster. Text (*STC*): Antiq

THE KING's most royal majesty, having perfect knowledge and understanding that as well his loving subjects citizens of his city of London of the one part, as the parsons, curates of the churches of his said city of the other part, by their mutual assents compromitted themself to stand, abide, and perform the order, decree, and arbitrament of his right trusty and right entirely beloved councilors, the most reverend father in God, Thomas, Archbishop of Canterbury, Metropolitan and Primate of England; Thomas Audley, knight, Lord Chancellor of England; the reverend father in God, Stephen, Bishop of Winchester; Thomas Cromwell, esquire, Chief Secretary to the King's highness, and Master of the Rolls; John Fitz James, knight, Chief Justice of pleas to be holden before the King's highness; and Robert Norwich, knight, Chief Justice of the King's common bench, in and upon the debate and variance that has moved between the said parties for the rate and certainty of tithes, offerings, and other duties claimed by the said parsons and curates to be paid by the King's said subjects, the citizens of his said city: whereupon the said councilors of our said sovereign lord by great advice and deliberation, by one accord and assent, among other things have ordained and decreed that every the King's said subjects, citizens and inhabitants of his said city should from the time of their award and decree pay for their tithes after the rate of 16½*d.* for every 10*s.* of their house rent, and for every 20*s.* to pay 2*s.* 9*d.*; and so accounting and ascending always by 10*s.*, should pay for every 10*s.* after the rate of 16½*d.* and not above. And yet nevertheless the King's highness is informed that divers and sundry persons inhabited within his said city not only refuse to pay their said tithes, according as is limited by his said councilors, but also that many of the said citizens, and of other the King's subjects inhabited in sundry parts of this realm, grudged and murmured to pay their tithes, offerings, and other lawful duties to the parsons, vicars, and other having the cure of their souls, like as heretofore by the laudable customs of this realm they have done and been accustomed to do, and obstinately and willfully withdraw and detain their said duties, against justice, equity, reason, and good conscience, to the great peril of their souls.

For reformation whereof, the King's said royal majesty, being the supreme head in earth under God of the Church of England, minding and intending to maintain and sustain the honor of God and the godly observance and rightful duties customably and by laudable customs due to the ecclesiastical ministers of the Church of England, in as large and ample manner as heretofore hath been laudably and honorably used and accustomed within this his realm, doth therefore by this his present proclamation straightly charge and command all and every his said subjects of his said city to satisfy, pay, and content to their parsons, vicars, and other having cure of their souls, in the name and lieu of their tithes, after the rate above expressed limited by the King's said councilors. And that all such of his said city as pay less of yearly farm than 10*s.*, and all and every other person and persons, men, women, and children, inhabited within the said city, being of age to receive the blessed and holy sacrament of the altar, the very body of our Lord Jesus Christ, shall pay yearly for their four offering days 2*d.*; the householders inhabited within the said city, paying above the yearly rent of 10*s.*, only for their own persons, excepted and to be discharged of the 2*d*. for the said four offering days.

And over this, his highness straightly chargeth and commandeth that all and every his other subjects, in all other parts of this his realm, shall pay and content to the parsons, vicars, and other the ministers of the church, and having cure, such tithes as well predial as personal offerings and other duties, which by the laudable customs of this realm they heretofore have been obliged, accustomed, and bounden to pay, without detaining any part thereof and without further denial, contradiction, molestation, or trouble in any behalf, upon pain that every person offending this his gracious proclamation to have imprisonment, and to make fine at his grace's will and pleasure, and over that the offenders shall run into his highness' displeasure and indignation.

And his majesty also chargeth and commandeth as well all and singular archbishops, bishops, and other having ecclesiastical jurisdiction, as all and singular mayors, sheriffs, bailiffs, aldermen, and all other his ministers, true liegemen, and subjects, as well of his city of London as elsewhere within his realm, that they and every of them put their effectual endeavor for the due execution of this his proclamation from time to time as to them shall appertain, upon the pains above rehearsed.

154. Suspending Statute on Sale of Meat until 24 June

[London, 25 March 1535, 26 Henry VIII]

STC 7784, Antiq 1, 77: printed by T. Berthelet (London, 1535); schedule as below. LJ 13, 441: date as above; schedule as below. Steele 149. Text (*STC*): Antiq

FORASMUCH as the King's majesty is credibly advertised and informed that beeves, muttons, and veals are likely to be more scarce and dear now against this holy time of Easter than in other seasons of the year, by reason of the charges of keeping of such cattle with hay and other stover in the winter; by occasion whereof the butchers and other that shall sell such beeves, muttons, and veals by retail by weight cannot buy them of the breeders, broggers, farmers, drivers, owners, and feeders of such cattle at such reasonable prices in gross as they may sell the same again by weight by retail at such prices as are limited in the act[1] made for selling of flesh by weight, unless it should be to their utter loss and undoing:

His highness therefore, willing that the same butchers, and other selling flesh by retail, for the time hereafter limited in this proclamation, should be so conveniently provided for in the premises as they should not have any cause reasonable to forbear their provisions for such victual to be sold by retail against this holy time of Easter, for relief and succor of his subjects, in as ample manner as heretofore hath been accustomed, is therefore contented and pleased that from henceforth unto the 24th day of June next coming, butchers and all other that shall sell flesh of the kinds aforesaid by weight by retail, shall and may sell from time to time, unto the said 24th day of June next coming, every pound of beef good and wholesome for man's body, for ⅝*d.* and no more; and every pound of mutton for ¾*d.* only and no more; and every pound of veal for ⅝*d.* and no more; the said act of provision heretofore had and made for selling flesh by weight by retail, or anything therein contained, to the contrary hereof notwithstanding.

Provided always that no butchers or other shall kill any calves to sell by retail for the term of two years ensuing, from the first day of January last, upon the pains limited in the act[2] made for killing of calves, this proclamation notwithstanding. And his highness hath ordained that if any butcher or other selling by retail do sell any of the kinds of victuals aforesaid otherwise than by weight, or at any other prices than is afore limited, or refuse to sell according to this proclamation: then every butcher or other so offend-

1. 24 Henry VIII, c. 3, 1532, *SR 3*, 420.
2. 21 Henry VIII, c. 8, 1529, *SR 3*, 289.

ing shall suffer loss and forfeit all such pains and penalties, and also be ordered in all things as is contained and limited in the act made for the premises, this proclamation in any wise not letting.

And furthermore the King's highness straightly chargeth and commandeth all and every the said breeders, broggers, drovers, farmers, feeders, and owners of such cattle, that they and every of them furnish the fairs and markets with such fat cattle as they have to sell from time to time, in as large and ample manner as hath been accustomed; and to sell their said cattle at such reasonable prices as the said butchers or such other as shall retail the same again by weight may utter and sell the same to his loving subjects at such prices as are above limited, as they will avoid his grace's high displeasure and answer to the same at their uttermost perils.

And that after the said 24th day of June, the said butchers and other selling flesh by retail shall from thenceforth sell by weight by retail according to the prices limited in the said act made and provided for the same, upon the pains and penalties contained in the said act, without any abstinence or redress to be had thereof after the said 24th day.

Wherefore the King's highness straightly chargeth and commandeth all and singular mayors, justices of peace, sheriffs, bailiffs, constables, and other his officers and faithful subjects to whom it shall or in any manner of wise may appertain, that they and every of them cause this his proclamation to be put in due and effectual execution according to the tenor thereof, as they will answer to his highness at their uttermost perils.

155. Ordering Anabaptists to Depart the Realm

[London, March 1535, 26 Henry VIII]

STC 7785 (UM 5,25,330), Antiq 2, 120: printed by T. Berthelet (London, 1535); schedule as below. Stow 965: date, 25 May; twenty-four Anabaptists examined at St. Paul's. Wilkins *3*, 779: date, 1534. Steele 150: date, March. Text (*STC*): Antiq

For because that of late many strangers, born out of the King's obedience, are arrived and come into this realm, which, albeit that they were baptized in their infancy and childhood according to the ordinance of the universal Church of Christ; yet that notwithstanding, in contempt of the holy sacrament of baptism so given and received, they have of their own presumption and authority lately rebaptized themselves; and over and beside that, they deny the most blessed and holy sacrament of the altar to be really the very body of our Lord Jesus Christ; and yet further, they keep, hold, and teach other divers and sundry pestilent heresies against God and his Holy Scriptures, to the great unquietness of Christendom, and perdition of innumerable

Christian souls: wherefore a great number of them been judicially and lawfully convicted of their detestable heresies, and have and shall for the same suffer pains of death, as reason and justice requireth in that behalf.

The King's most royal majesty, being supreme head in earth under God of the Church of England, always intending to defend and maintain the faith of Christ and sacraments of Holy Church; and daily studying and minding above all things to save his loving subjects (members of the said church) from falling into any erroneous opinions and damnable heresies, into which they might happen to fall, and be infected by the communion and conversation of such corrupt, seditious, and erroneous persons: ordaineth and straightly chargeth and commandeth that all and singular strangers now being in this his realm, as well such as have recanted and revoked their said heresies as all other that have or do hold or teach those or any other erroneous opinions or heresies against God and his Holy Scriptures, shall within twelve days next after this present proclamation depart out of this his realm and of all other his dominions, on pain to suffer death if they, contrary to this proclamation, do abide and be apprehended or taken. And that no person hereafter being of the same sects and holding such erroneous opinions and heresies, upon like pain repair into this his realm or into any part or place of his dominions.

And over this his highness straightly chargeth and commandeth that none of his own loving and natural subjects be so hardy to hold, keep, or teach any errors or heresies contrary to God and his Holy Scriptures, upon like pains above remembered; willing and commanding as well all prelates of Holy Church as all nobles, justices, mayors, sheriffs, bailiffs, constables, and all other his ministers and loving subjects, that they and every of them shall put their good and effectual endeavor for the apprehending of such as they shall hear or know to keep, hold, or teach any such heresies, to the intent the offenders may receive due punishment and pains of death, from time to time as the case shall require, according to their merits, not failing so to do as they will avoid and eschew the King's most high indignation and displeasure and answer to his majesty for the same, at their uttermost perils.

156. Ordering Members of Parliament to Their Homes for Defense and Subsidy

[? May 1535, 27 Henry VIII]

BM MS Add. 9835, 22*v:* schedule as below. Steele 151: date as above. Text (MS): Add.

THE KING'S MOST ROYAL MAJESTY, considering most graciously how meet and necessary it is that all such noblemen, gentlemen, and others as repaired hither to this parliament, not being specially appointed to attend upon his most royal person or the Queen's highness or commanded by the council to attend here or elsewhere for any other purposes, should repair into their countries, as well for the putting of themselves in order for their defense and annoyance of our enemies, as occasion shall serve and as his majesty shall hereafter appoint and determine, as for service to be done to his majesty touching the subsidy and other his affairs in the parts where they do inhabit, doth straightly charge and command that all noblemen, gentlemen, and others, except only as such as before excepted, shall immediately depart home unto their countries upon pain of his majesty's displeasure, and to be further punished as to his highness or his most honorable council shall be thought convenient.

157. Limiting Access to Court

[ca. 1535, 27 Henry VIII]

BM MS Add. 9835, 11: schedule as below. Steele 152: date as above. Text (MS): Add.

THE KING'S MAJESTY straightly chargeth and commandeth that no manner of person or persons of what estate or degree soever they be of, inhabiting within the city of London or having his or their abode there, do presume to enter the gates of any of the houses wherein his majesty's or the Queen's grace shall be present, upon pain of his highness' most grievous displeasure; nor that none of the King's servants nor [the] Queen's, other than such as shall be appointed, nor no other man's servants of what estate or degree soever they be of, shall depart from the court to the city of London and from thence to resort to the court again, as they and every of them will avoid the King's majesty his like grievous displeasure and further punishment at his highness' pleasure.

158. Enforcing Statutes Abolishing Papal Authority in England

[Westminster, 9 June 1535, 27 Henry VIII]

STC 7786 (UM 2,10,331), Antiq 1, 78: printed by T. Berthelet (London, 1535); date, under signet, as above; letters patent to the sheriffs; schedule as below. Wilkins *3*, 772. Steele 153. Text (*STC*): Antiq

AND WHEREAS not only upon good, just, and virtuous grounds and respects, edified upon the laws of God and Holy Scripture, by due consultation, deliberate advisement, and consent as well of all other our nobles and commons temporal assembled in our high court of parliament, and by authority of the same, we have by good and wholesome laws and statutes [1] made for the purpose, extirped, abolished, separated, and secluded out of this our realm, the abuses of the Bishop of Rome, his authority and jurisdiction of long time usurped as well upon us and our realm as upon all other kings and princes and their realms, like as they themselves have confessed and affirmed; but also forasmuch as our said nobles and commons both spiritual and temporal, assembled in our said court of parliament, have upon like good, lawful, and virtuous grounds and for the public weal of this our realm, by one whole assent granted, annexed, knit, and united to the crown imperial of the same the title, dignity, and style of supreme head in earth immediately under God of the Church of England, as we be and undoubtedly have hitherto been:

Which title and style both the bishops and clergy of this our realm have not only, in convocation assembled, consented, recognized, and approved lawfully and justly to appertain unto us, but also by word, oath, profession, and writing under their signs and seals, have confessed, ratified, corroborated, and confirmed the same, utterly renouncing all other oaths and obedience to any foreign potentate and all foreign jurisdictions and powers as well as of the said Bishop of Rome as of all other whatsoever they be, as by their said profession and writings corroborated with the subscription of their names and appension of their seals more plainly appeareth.

We let you wite that, calling unto our remembrance the power, charge, and commission given unto us of Almighty God; and upon a vehement love and affection towards our loving and faithful subjects, perceiving right well what great rest, quietness, and tranquillity of conscience and manifold other commodities might insurge and arise unto them, if that the said bishops and other of the clergy of this our realm should set forth, declare, and preach unto them the true and sincere word of God, and (without all manner color, dissimulation, and hypocrisy) manifest and publish the great and innumerable enormities and abuses which the said Bishop of Rome, as well in the title and style as also in authority and jurisdiction, of long time unlawfully and unjustly hath usurped upon us and our progenitors and all other Christian princes:

[We] have therefore addressed our letters unto the bishop of the diocese, straightly charging and commanding him in the same that not only he in his own proper person shall declare, teach, and preach unto the people forthwith, upon the receipt of our said letters unto him directed, every Sunday and other high feast through the year, the true, mere, and sincere word of God; and that the said same title, style, and jurisdiction of supreme head

1. 23 Henry VIII, c. 20, 1531, *SR 3*, 385; 25 Henry VIII, c. 20, 1533, *SR 3*, 462; 26 Henry VIII, c. 1, 1534, *SR 3*, 492.

appertaineth only unto our crown and dignity royal, likewise as the said bishop and all other the bishops of our realm have by oath affirmed and confirmed by subscription of their names and setting to their seals; but also give warning, monition, and charge to all manner abbots, priors, deans, archdeacons, provosts, parsons, vicars, curates, and all other ecclesiastical persons who in his said diocese as well to preach, teach, publish, and declare in all manner churches our foresaid just title, style, and jurisdiction every Sunday and high feast through the year; and furthermore to monish and give commandment to all manner schoolmasters within his said diocese to instruct and teach the same unto the children committed unto them; as also to cause all manner prayers, orisons, rubrics, canons in mass books, and all other books used in the churches, wherein the said Bishop of Rome is named or his presumptuous and proud pomp and authority preferred, utterly to be abolished, eradicated, and erased out, and his name and memory to be nevermore (except to his contumely and reproach) remembered, but perpetually suppressed and obscured; and finally, to desist and leave out all such articles as be in the general sentence which is usually accustomed to be read four times in the year, and do tend to the glory and advancement of the said Bishop of Rome, his name, title, or jurisdiction.

Whereupon we, esteeming and reputing you to be of such singular and vehement zeal and affection towards the glory of Almighty God, and of so faithful, loving, and obedient heart towards us, as you will not only do and accomplish with all your wisdom, diligence, and labor, whatsoever should or might be to the preferment and setting forward of God's word, but also practice, study, and endeavor yourself with all your policy, wit, power, and good will to amplify, defend, and maintain all such interest, right, title, style, jurisdiction, and authority as is in any wise appertaining unto us, our dignity, prerogative, and crown imperial of this our realm, have thought good and expedient not only to signify unto you by these our letters the particularities of the charge, monition, and commandment given by us unto the said bishop, as before is specified, but also to inquire and straightly charge and command you upon pain of your allegiance and as you will avoid our high indignation and displeasure at your uttermost peril, laying apart all vain affections, respects, or other carnal considerations, and setting only before your eyes the mirror of truth, the glory of God, the dignity of your sovereign lord and King, and the great concord and unity and inestimable profit and commodity that shall by the due execution of the premises ensue to yourself and all other faithful and loving subjects, you make or cause to be made diligent search, wait, and espial, in every place of your sheriffwick, whether the said bishop do truly, sincerely, and without all manner cloak, color, or dissimulation, execute and accomplish our will and commandment as is aforesaid.

And in case you shall hear, perceive, and approvably understand and know that the said bishop or any other ecclesiastical person within his diocese, doth omit and leave undone any part or parcel of the premises, or else in the execution and setting forth of the same do coldly and unfeignedly use any manner sinister addition, wrong interpretation, or painted colors: then we straightly charge and command you that forthwith upon any such default, negligence, or dissimulation by the said bishop or any other ecclesiastical person of his diocese committed, contrary to the true tenor, meaning, and effect of the said charge by us to him appointed aforesaid, you do make indelayedly, and with all speed and diligence, declaration, and advertisement to us and our council of the said default, and of the behavior, manner, and fashion of the same.

And forasmuch as we, upon singular trust and assured confidence which we have in you, and for the special love and zeal which we suppose and think you bear toward us and the public and common weal, unity, and tranquillity of this our realm, have especially elected and chosen you among so many for this purpose, and have reputed you such men as unto whose wisdom, discretion, truth, and fidelity we might commit a matter of such great weight, moment, and importance, as whereupon the unity, rest, and tranquillity of our realm doth consist and is stabilized: if you should, contrary to our expectation and trust which we have in you, and against your duty and allegiance toward us, neglect, be slack, or omit to do with all your diligence, dexterity, and wisdom whatsoever shall be in your power for the due and true performance and execution of our mind and pleasure to you before declared in this behalf, or halt, stumble, or wink at any part or specialty of the same, be you assured that we like a prince of justice will so extremely correct and punish you for the same that all the world besides shall take by you example and beware, contrary to their duty, oath, and allegiance to frustrate, deceive, and to disobey the just and lawful commandment of their sovereign lord and prince in such things as the true, hearty, and faithful execution. Whereby you shall not only prefer and advance the honor and glory of Almighty God, and set forth the majesty and imperial dignity of your sovereign lord, but also import and bring an inestimable weal, profit, commodity, unity, and tranquillity to all the public and common state of this our realm, whereunto both by the laws of God, nature, and man you be utterly obliged and bound.

159. Suspending Statute on Sale of Meat until 2 February

[Westminster, 12 July 1535, 27 Henry VIII]

BM MS Harl 442, 96: date as above; writ to mayor and sheriffs of London; schedule as below. See 154. Steele 154. Text (MS): Harl

FORASMUCH as the King's majesty is credibly advertised and informed that the butchers resident or repairing within the said city have been and daily be at far higher charges, as in house rent, lease rent, servants' wages, and otherwise, than any foreign butchers dwelling within the said city be at; by reason whereof the said butchers citizen cannot have a living if they should continually be constrained to sell beeves, muttons, veals, and porks by weight by retail, within the said city, at such prices as be limited in the act [1] made for the selling of flesh by weight, unless it should be to their utter loss and undoing:

His highness therefore, willing all the same butchers citizen to have a reasonable living for the defense of their manifold charges, is contented and pleased that from henceforth unto the second day of February next ensuing the said butchers citizen shall sell flesh of the kinds aforesaid by weight by retail unto the said second day of February in manner and form following: that is to say, every pound of beef good and wholesome for man's body for ⅝*d.* and no more, and every pound of mutton for ¾*d.* only and no more, and every pound of veal for ¾*d.* and no more, and every pound of pork for ⅝*d.* and no more, the act of provision heretofore had or made for selling of flesh by weight by retail to the contrary hereof notwithstanding.

The King's highness straightly charging and commanding all and every the breeders, broggers, drayers, farmers, feeders, and owners of such cattle, that they and every of them furnish the fairs and markets with such fat cattle as they have to sell, in as large and ample manner as hath been accustomed, and to sell their said cattle at such reasonable prices as the said butchers citizen which shall retail again the same by weight may utter and sell the same to his loving subjects at such prices as are above limited, as they will avoid his dread highness' displeasure and answer to the same at their uttermost perils. And that after the said second day of February next coming, the said butchers citizen selling flesh by retail shall from henceforth sell by weight by retail according to the said act [2] made and provided for the same, and at such prices as is limited in the said act, upon the pains and

1. 21 Henry VIII, c. 8, 1529, *SR 3*, 289.
2. 24 Henry VIII, c. 3, 1532, *SR 3*, 420.

penalties contained in the said act, unto such day and time as the King's highness shall otherwise limit by his proclamation for the same.

Wherefore the King's highness straightly chargeth and commandeth all and singular mayors, justices of peace, sheriffs, bailiffs, constables, and other his officers and faithful subjects to whom it shall or in any manner of wise may appertain, that they and every of them cause this his proclamation to be put in due and effectual execution, as they will answer to his highness at their uttermost perils.

160. Prohibiting Access to Windsor Castle

[Westminster, 25 October 1535, 27 Henry VIII]

LL P, 74: date as above; writ to mayor and sheriffs of London; schedule as below. Not in Steele. Text (MS): LL

THE KING our most dread sovereign lord, calling to his remembrance how the contagious plague called the Great Sickness hath reigned a long season in this his grace's city of London and the vicine parts to the same adjoining; and like a most gracious prince tendering the safeguard and preservation of his people, the members of his politic body, whereof his grace is the only head under God; and the avoiding of all occasions which in any wise might nourish, continue, or increase the said plague, hath now of late as well prorogued his high court of parliament, as for a time adjourned his term, for eschewing of such dangers as by the confluence of fresh people might thereby have ensued unto them; and being (his highness) minded now, in the end of his most prosperous progress, wherein his grace hath much travailed for the advancement of his politic weal, to lie and repose himself for a season at his castle of Windsor; forasmuch as it is thought that all men might have their free access and recourse thither for their pursuits and other affairs or business, albeit the greater number, being personages of honor, do undoubtedly so remember their duties to their prince and sovereign lord, who employeth his labor, study, and travail for their defense, preservation, and advancement, as they will in no wise molest, annoy, or displease his highness by their repair to his court from any place where the said infection hath reigned; yet some other lewd and indiscreet persons, on the other side, more regarding and coveting the accomplishment and fulfilling of their fantastical desires than remembering their bounden duties, might, percase, resort thither, which other have been diseased of the said sickness themself, or have been or continued in this city, or else where the said sickness hath reigned, whereby might ensue to his highness and his train which have continually waited upon his grace this summer in clean and incorrupt air, great danger of infection to the annoyance of his grace and the discomfort of all his loving, faithful, and obedient subjects:

His highness therefore, minding as well to have these occasions of inconvenience removed, as in such sort to open, publish, and manifest his pleasure concerning the same, as no man shall now excuse himself therein by negligence or ignorance, straightly chargeth and commandeth that no person, of what estate, degree, or condition soever he be, which during this time of the plague hath continued here in London, or in any other place where the infection thereof hath been or reigned, shall in any wise presume to repair or resort to his grace's said town of Windsor, or to any other place where his majesty shall chance to be or lie, between this and the Feast of Christmas next ensuing; upon pain of his grace's high indignation and displeasure, and further to be punished by imprisonment and otherwise, at his highness' will and pleasure, for the example of all other with their extreme perils.

161. Ordering Surrender of Bishop Fisher's Sermon, Books

[London, 1 January 1536, 27 Henry VIII]

STC 7787 (UM 2,10,333), Antiq 1, 79: printed by T. Berthelet (London, 1536); schedule as below. *L&P 8,* 55: date, 16 January; answering proclamation, Bishop of London asks for more time in which to send books to chancellor. Herbert 426: date, 8 July. Steele 155: date as above. Text (*STC*): Antiq

Whereas the King's highness is informed that divers and sundry writings and books, as well imprinted as other, especially one book imprinted comprising a sermon made by John Fisher, late bishop of Rochester, who according to the laws of this realm was justly attainted and convicted of divers and sundry manifest and detestable high treasons by him committed against the King's highness, his crown, and dignity royal, are dispersed abroad in this realm and been come to the hands of divers of the King's subjects; in which writings and books many open and manifest errors and slanders are contained, not only in derogation and diminution of the dignity and authority royal of the King's majesty and of his imperial crown, but also directly and expressly against the good and laudable statutes of this realm; by reason whereof the King's said subjects having such erroneous writings and books might happen by the keeping or reading of them to incur into great perils, dangers, and losses of their lives, lands, and goods.

In consideration wherof, the King's most royal majesty, who of his most noble and gentle heart more desireth the reformation of his loving subjects by gentle warnings and monitions than by rigor and extremity of his laws, trusting that every humble, loving, and honest subject, being admonished of their offenses whereby they can pretend no ignorance, will take more regard and respect of their duties of allegiance that they owe to bear to their sovereign lord, or else they may well think that his highness, taking just occasion by their obstinacy, will proceed to their reformation and punishment according to his laws after their merits and deserts without any ministration of his mercy in that behalf: doth therefore straightly charge and command that all and every person and persons which have or hereafter shall happen to have any of the said books containing the said sermon of the said late traitor, or any other writing or book wherein shall be contained any error or slander to the King's majesty, or to the derogation or diminution of his imperial crown or of any authority knit to the same, or repugnant to his statutes of this realm made for the surety of his grace's succession, or for the abolition of the usurped power of the Bishop of Rome, shall within 40 days next after this his grace's proclamation bring and deliver the said books and writings to the Lord Chancellor of England or to Thomas Cromwell, esquire, the King's Chief Secretary and Master of his Rolls, as they will avoid his most high indignation and displeasure and the perils and dangers of his laws and statutes provided for the same, which his highness intendeth to execute against the offenders of this his grace's proclamation, according to their offenses, without any pity or mercy to them to be given by his majesty in any behalf.

And furthermore the King's highness straightly chargeth and commandeth all and singular justices of peace, mayors, sheriffs, bailiffs, constables, and all other his loving subjects, that every of them shall put their good and effectual endeavors for the finding, espying, and bringing in of the said books and writings according to this his grace's proclamation, as they will avoid his most high displeasure and indignation and answer for their doing contrary hereof at their uttermost perils.

And over this, where his majesty is also informed that divers and sundry light persons, called pardoners, go daily abroad in this his realm, declaring and publishing to his people, as well in parish churches as elsewhere, divers indulgences and pardons corruptly and deceitfully obtained of the Bishop of Rome, and by color thereof exact and gather of his subjects great and innumerable sums of money; and the most part of the said pardoners, being confederate with the great errant thieves of this realm, by going about espy where the richest and most substantial men inhabit and dwell, to whose houses many times they give and bring the said thieves their confederates, to rob and spoil; and also the money, unlawfully by them exacted of the poor innocent people by color of their indulgences, they spend in ribaldry and carnal vices, carrying about with them drabs, whores, and cut-purses, to the great slander of the realm and to the damage, deceit, and impoverishing of the King's good loving subjects:

For repressing whereof, the King's most royal majesty, who daily studieth to extinct vice and exalt and increase virtue in this his realm, to the glory and honor of God and quietness of his people, considering that by occasion of such corrupt and deceitful indulgences many of his loving subjects have been more encouraged to commit sin and to withdraw their faith, hope, and devotion from God, and have been the more negligent to fulfill his precepts and commandments, which all Christian people are bound to observe, doth therefore straightly charge and command that no person or persons from henceforth take upon him or them to send or go about in this his realm to publish any such pardon or indulgence, nor declare, publish, use, or practice any such pardon or indulgence in any monasteries, churches, or places, nor by color thereof exact, give, or receive any sums of money, upon the pains comprised in his laws in that case provided, and as they will answer for doing contrary hereof to his majesty at their uttermost perils. And if any person or persons go vagrant in any part of his realm, as pardoners, taking upon them anywhere to publish such indulgences and pardons, or by color thereof exact any sums of money, that then his highness straightly chargeth and commandeth all and singular justices of peace, mayors, sheriffs, bailiffs, constables and all other his loving subjects, that they shall apprehend from time to time such offenders, and cause them to be ordered and whipped, according to the act [1] provided for valiant beggars and vagabonds, not failing thus to do, as they will avoid the King's most high displeasure and indignation and also the perils of the pains contained in the said act.

162. Suspending Statute on Sale of Meat until Pentecost

[Westminster, 8 February 1536, 27 Henry VIII]

LL P, 82: date as above; writ to sheriffs of London; schedule as below. Not in Steele. Text (MS): LL

FORASMUCH as by occasion of murrain of sheep and other great beasts there is not plenty, nor such reasonable prices of such cattles to be sold in gross as the butchers and victualers killing such beasts and selling the same by retail can well sell the same by weight in such form and at such prices as is limited to them by the act [1] in that case provided, and specially now from

1. 22 Henry VIII, c. 12, 1530, *SR 3*, 328.

1. 24 Henry VIII, c. 3, 1532, *SR 3*, 420.

the first day of February unto the Feast of Pentecost next coming, by reason of the said murrain; and also for that such cattles during the same time be commonly sold at greater and higher prices than in other seasons of the year because of the costly keeping of them in the winter season;

In consideration whereof, the King's most royal majesty, who hath full and plenary power and authority, upon reasonable grounds, as well to abrogate and suspend the said act in that case provided, at his own pleasure and will, as also to revive the same from time to time, as plenty, scarcity, or other causes of necessity shall require in that behalf:

Of his most excellent goodness is now pleased and contented, by the advice of his council, for sundry respects that his highness hath to this present time and season of the year, that all manner of butchers (and other killing any such kind of cattles as they may kill, between the 12th day of February and the said Feast of Pentecost next ensuing, to sell by retail) shall and may lawfully, during the said time, utter and sell the same by retail, by pieces and parcels, without any weighing thereof, at convenient and reasonable prices, as they did and might do before the making of the said act;

Willing and commanding nevertheless to all graziers, breeders, farmers, and other owners of all kinds of cattles to sell their said cattles from time to time, at such reasonable and convenient prices as the said butchers, and other victualers killing flesh to sell by retail, may sell the same by pieces and parcels, for relief and comfort of his loving subjects, at reasonable and convenient prices;

And the said butchers and other victualers selling by retail in like manner [to] use their prices by retail as they will avoid the King's most high indignation and displeasure, and answer to his highness at their uttermost perils, for the same;

Commanding also all justices of peace, mayors, sheriffs, bailiffs, constables, and all other his ministers, to survey and see from time to time the due execution of his grace's proclamation, as well for excessive prices in selling of such victuals, as for the goodness and wholesomeness thereof, as they tender his most gracious pleasure and will answer to his highness if they be remiss or negligent in that behalf;

Signifying also to all and singular his loving subjects that his pleasure is that, after the said Feast of Pentecost, the said butchers and victualers shall sell by retail according to the said act, anything mentioned in his grace's proclamation notwithstanding.[2]

2. See 154, 159.

163. Enforcing Statutes on Archery, Unlawful Games

[London, February 1536, 27 Henry VIII]

STC 7788 (UM 5,25,334), Antiq 2, 113: printed by T. Berthelet (London, 1536); schedule as below. Steele 156: date as above. Text (*STC*): Antiq

WHERE amongst many good and wholesome laws and statutes of this realm there is made and ordained one statute [1] for maintenance of archery; and sundry statutes [2] for repress and reformation of playing at dice, cards, tennis, bowling, and other unlawful games; a statute [3] made for reformation of apparel and raiment; and another statute [4] made for punishment and ordering of sturdy beggars; all which statutes, as well by obstinacy and willfulness of the subjects of this realm, as also by negligence and affection of the King's justices of peace and other ministers that have power to put them in due execution, have not been observed and kept, but neglected and contemned, to the great discontentation and displeasure of the King's highness, and to the great hurt of the commonweal of this his realm:

The King's majesty therefore, by the advice of his lords spiritual and temporal and the commons in this present parliament assembled, deeply pondering and considering that the said statutes greatly tend to the advancement of the commonweal and surety of this his realm and to the great commodity of his loving subjects of the same, doth straightly charge and command all and singular his subjects, of what estate, degree, or condition soever he or they be, that they and every of them from the Feast of the Annunciation of Our Lady next coming do keep and observe the Statute of Apparel in such manner, form, and condition as in the same statute particularly is contained and expressed; and shall also from henceforth keep and observe all the other statutes made for or concerning maintenance of archery, punishment of beggars, and reformation and abuse of unlawful games, and put all and every of the same statutes abovesaid in due and perfect execution according to their tenors, purports, and effects: upon the pains and losses of the forfeitures limited in every of the said statutes, which pains and forfeitures the King's highness will not hereafter at any time remit, pardon, nor forgive to any of the offenders in any of the said statutes, but intendeth to

1. 6 Henry VIII, c. 2, 1514, *SR 3*, 123.
2. 12 Richard II, c. 6, 1388, *SR 2*, 57; 11 Henry IV, c. 4, 1409, *SR 2*, 163; 17 Edward IV, c. 3, 1477, *SR 2*, 462; 11 Henry VII, c. 2, 1495, *SR 2*, 569.
3. 22 Henry VIII, c. 12, 1530, *SR 3*, 328.
4. 24 Henry VIII, c. 13, 1532, *SR 3*, 430.

take the same pains and forfeitures according to his laws from time to time as the case shall require in that behalf.

And over this, his highness straightly chargeth and commandeth as well his lords spiritual and temporal as also all justices of peace, mayors, sheriffs, bailiffs, and all other ministers and officers whatsoever they be, that they and every of them within their authorities, as well within liberties as without, without favor, affection, or corruption, shall put their effectual endeavor and diligences for the due observation and execution of the said statutes and every of them; and especially every of the said lords, and all other householders, amongst their own families and household servants, as they and every of them and all other his loving subjects will have his most gracious favor and thanks, and avoid the penalties limited by the said statutes and his most dreadful indignation and displeasure, and will answer to his majesty for contemning his laws and this his grace's proclamation at their uttermost perils.

164. Suspending Statute on Sale of Meat until 24 April 1540

[Westminster, 14 April 1536, 27 Henry VIII]

BM MS Harl 442, 97: date as above; writ to mayor and sheriffs of London; schedule as below. Steele 157. Text (MS): Harl

WHERE in the parliament begun at London the third day of November in the 21st year of our reign and there adjourned to Westminster and there by divers prorogations continued in one session there holden the 24th year of our said reign, amongst divers beneficial statutes there made, it was enacted [1] that every person which did sell after the first day of August in the said 24th year any beef, pork, mutton, or veal, or any part or parcel thereof, should sell the same by lawful weight called *avoirdupois* and none otherwise, after the price in the same act contained and specified, as in the same act more plainly is contained;

And where afterwards forsomuch as sufficient authority was not given by the said act to the justices of the peace, mayors, bailiffs, sheriffs, and other officers rehearsed in the said former act, to punish the offenders and such other as would not sell by weight according to the force of the said act, at another session holden in the 25th year of our said reign, it was then by another statute [2] enacted that from the 20th day of February in the year of our

1. 24 Henry VIII, c. 3, 1532, *SR 3*, 420.
2. 25 Henry VIII, c. 1, 1533, *SR 3*, 436.

Lord God 1533 it should be lawful to all and every mayors, sheriffs, constables, bailiffs, and other governors of cities, boroughs, and market towns, as well within liberties as without, to whom any complaint should be made upon any butcher, his wife, servants, or other his ministers, refusing to sell the said victuals by true and lawful weight according to the tenor of the said former act, not only to commit every such butcher or other such offender to ward, there to remain without bail or mainprize unto such time as they and every of them shall have paid all forfeitures and penalties comprised in the same former act, but also every of the said mayors and other head officers and their deputies should sell or cause to be sold all such victuals by true weights and for ready money as in the said act made in the said 25th year more at large is expressed:

We therefore, well considering the great dearth of all manner of victuals which be now, and since the making of the said statutes hath fallen and happened within this our realm, as well by murrain of death of such cattle as by great waters and unseasonable weather, whereby the breed and increase of the same is much impaired and minished, in such wise that if the said former statutes were put in execution the butchers and sellers of such victuals were not able to live, nor that our commons should be well served thereof: we therefore, the premises considered, are contented, with the assent of our lords spiritual and temporal and of the commons of the same parliament assembled, and by authority of the same, that it be ordained, established, and enacted that from the 12th day of April in the year of our Lord God 1536 unto the 24th day of April, the which shall be in the year of our Lord God 1540, all butchers and others selling flesh by retail may lawfully kill and sell all manner beefs, pork, mutton, and veal, being good and wholesome for man's body, at their pleasures and liberties as freely and liberally as they or any of them did or might have done at any time before the making of the said statutes made in the 24th and 25th years of our said reign, without any loss, pain, imprisonment, forfeiture or penalty to be to them or any of them or the successors of them, or any of them, had lost, borne, or sustained in that behalf (during the time before limited), the same statutes made in the said 24th and 25th years or either of them, or any clause, sentence, forfeiture, pain, loss, or any other thing in them or any of them, to the contrary in any wise notwithstanding; and that the same statutes and either of them and every clause, sentence, and article in them, and either of them contained, shall be in suspense and not put in execution during the said time.

165. Announcing Neutrality with Both France and Empire

[Berechurch, 19 August 1536, 28 Henry VIII]

LL P, 103: date as above; writ to mayor and sheriffs of London; schedule as below. Steele 158. Text (MS): LL

THE KING'S MOST ROYAL MAJESTY, most prudently considering the great wars and hostility both by land and sea commenced and like to continue between the Emperor and the French King; and calling to his most gracious remembrance that his highness is knit in league and amity with either of the said princes, not intending without honest and just occasions to violate the same, but so to order and direct himself and his subjects in all his proceedings that no manner of suspicion of the leaning more to the one part than to the other shall appear at any time in his grace, but that always he may declare himself in this point of neutrality upright and indifferent, as to a prince of honor, truth, and virtue appertaineth; and forasmuch as it is credibly reported unto his highness that divers his subjects, not regarding the amity and league between his highness and the said princes, do daily cloak and color in their names the goods and merchandises as well of Frenchmen as of Flemings, whereby both parties suffer loss and detriment in their prices, contrary to his grace's mind and pleasure:

His grace therefore, willing to redress and reform the same, straightly chargeth and commandeth all and singular his most loving subjects that from henceforth none of the same do enterprise or attempt to cloak or color by any means directly or indirectly any manner goods or merchandises of any of the subjects either of the Emperor or the French King's, upon pain of the King's high displeasure and indignation and forfeiture of all their goods, and also imprisonment of their bodies at the King's will and pleasure.

166. Regulating Wool Cloth Manufacture

[Westminster, 5 October 1536, 28 Henry VIII]

BM MS Harl 442, 100: date as above; writ to mayor and bailiffs of Chichester; schedule as below. Steele 159. Text (MS): Harl

FORASMUCH as by divers statutes lately made it is ordained and enacted that woolen cloths made within this the King's realm should contain certain lengths and breadths according to the purport and tenor of the same statutes, as in the same acts and statutes it is more plainly expressed and specified, nevertheless the King's majesty, prudently considering that his said statutes cannot be suddenly put in execution unless it should be to the great grief, loss, and damage of his true and loving subjects, the weavers, tuckers, fullers, and other workers and makers of woolen cloths, not having as yet their looms, stays, and other instruments convenient for making of the same cloth, to keep the assize of length and breadth, neither any time limited for preparation of the same according to the said statutes:

Wherefore and in consideration of the premises, the King's highness, by the advice of his council, willeth and commandeth all his faithful and loving subjects, workers and makers of woolen cloths, that they, before and against the Feast of St. Michael the Archangel next coming, do endeavor themselves to make looms, stays, and other instruments and engines convenient and necessary for making of woolen cloths according to the forms of the said statutes; and that all workers and makers of woolen cloths betwixt this and the said Feast of St. Michael shall and may use to make and work woolen cloths of such lengths and breadths as they were wont to do before the making of the said statute, without incurring or running into any penalty or forfeiture for the same.

Provided always that the same workers and makers of woolen cloths, after the said Feast of St. Michael, shall observe and keep the effects of the said statute [1] concerning the size of the length and breadth of woolen cloths, and not to trust after that time to sue any dispensation or remission for the same.

167. Providing Victual for Army in North

[Westminster, 27 October 1536, 28 Henry VIII]

BM MS Harl 442, 103: letters patent to all subjects; schedule as below. Steele 160: date as above. Text (MS): Harl

FORASMUCH as the King's most royal majesty intendeth, God willing, to advance in his most noble person with an army royal towards the north parts of this his realm, for full repress of the traitorous rebellion in those parts lately most heinously attempted and begun; minding that all such his loving subjects, as well of his nobility as other which shall repair to his grace, giving their attendance in his most royal voyage and foray, should be most and plenteously victualed at reasonable prices in all places and nigh thereunto where they shall come, advance and resort:

The King's most noble majesty therefore straightly chargeth and com-

1. 27 Henry VIII, c. 12, 1535, *SR 3*, 544.

mandeth all and singular his subjects, as well victualers as all other intermeddling with buying and selling of any kind of victual by retail or in gross, that every of them with all diligence cause and put to their effectual endeavors and helping hands to cause large, ample, and plenteous provisions of all kinds of victuals to be had for the same army at reasonable prices from time to time and from place to place where the said army shall be come, and not to fail hereof as they will answer to the King's highness at their uttermost perils.

And furthermore his highness straightly chargeth and commandeth all and singular captains and soldiers of every degree that they and every of them satisfy and pay for their said victuals as justly and reasonably as shall appertain and not to ravin nor spoil, upon pain of their lives.

168. Ordering Punishment for Seditious Rumors; Martial Law for Unlawful Assemblies

[Westminster, ?29 October 1536, 28 Henry VIII]

Antiq 1, 84: date, October; schedule as below. BM MS Harl 442, 101: letters patent to all subjects; schedule as below. Holinshed *3*, 941: Lincolnshire men submit on 19 May. Stow 968: date, Windsor, 9 October; a priest and butcher executed by martial law for supporting Lincolnshire rebellion. Steele 161: date, as above. Text (MS): Antiq

FORASMUCH as it is come to our knowledge that divers devilish and slanderous persons have sown, bruited, and spread abroad that we should pretend to have all the gold in the hands of our subjects to be brought to our tower to be touched, and all their chattels being unmarked, and the chalices, goods, and ornaments of parish churches, and fines for christening, wedding, and burying; and for license to eat wheat, bread, pig, goose, or capon, with many other slanderous, false, and detestable rumors, tales, and lies, not only to alienate the true and loyal heart of our people from that their natural love and affection which they ought to bear unto us, their sovereign lord and King, but also to procure and stir up division, strife, commotion, contention, and sedition among our people; whereby divers of the same in sundry parts of the realm, and especially in our county of Lincoln, have lately most traitorously conspired and assembled themselves together in open and manifest rebellion toward God and us their natural sovereign lord: for repress whereof we were constrained to advance towards them part of our royal power and force, and for dread thereof they, lamenting their miserable mischiefs and traitorous offenses, be retired, dispersed, and put down, and have submitted themselves to our mercy and grace to do with them our pleasure.

We, considering that there is nothing more odious to God nor more pernicious and hurtful to the commonwealth than the contempt and inobedience of people against their sovereign lord, willing our true and faithful subjects to be admonished to take heed and beware to give light credence to any false forged tales and lies and to seek thereby any occasion to enterprise or attempt any rebellion against the duty of their allegiance; whereby they shall not only bring upon themselves the vengeance and indignation of God, to the peril and damnation of their souls, but also give us just cause to proceed against such rebels with our most royal power and force, to the utter destruction of them, their wives, and children: do therefore, by this our present proclamation, charge and command all and singular our true and faithful subjects of what estate, degree, or condition soever they be, that they, by all good means and policies they can, shall put their effectual endeavors to take and apprehend all and every such person and persons that they can prove to have bruited or set forth any forged false rumors, tales, and lies whereby any commotion, sedition, or encouragement of unlawful assemblies hath, or might be, among our people to the disturbance of our peace; and commit such offenders to ward, there to remain in safe and sure keeping till our pleasure shall be further known therein. And we shall so acquit such our good subjects as shall apprehend or report any of them that they shall think their travail well bestowed in that behalf.

And furthermore we charge and command all and singular our said subjects that they nor any of them, by color of such lies or otherwise, take or seize any occasion to stir, move, or attempt any routs, riots, or unlawful assemblies, or enterprise any gatherings of our people together without our special license and commandment thereunto had. And if any routs or assemblies be now presently had in any part of our realm by any our people, that every of them do forthwith retire and return to their houses, [and] there employ themselves about their lawful business without further enterprise or attempt. And if they after this our proclamation refuse thus to do, we plainly declare unto them that we will withdraw our eye of mercy and clemency from such as will contemn this our proclamation, and proceed against them with all our royal power, force, and minions of war which we now have in a readiness, and destroy them, their wives, and children, with fire and sword, to the most terrible example of such rebels and offenders.

169. Pardoning Pilgrimage of Grace

[Richmond, 9 December 1536, 28 Henry VIII]

PRO (SP 1/112/194*v*): date as above; letters patent to the rebels; schedule as below. *L&P 11*, 1276: proclaimed at Doncaster on 12 December. Steele 163 (for 2 November date, see Steele 162). Text (MS): SP

ALBEIT that you the King's highness' subjects and commons dwelling and inhabiting in the shires of York, Cumberland, Westmorland, Northumberland, the bishopric of Durham, the city of York and the shire of the same, the town of Kingston-upon-Hull and the shire of the same, the town of Newcastle-upon-Tyne and the shire of the same, and in other shires, towns, valleys, places privileged, franchises, and liberties within the limits of the said shires, cities, towns, or in any of them, or being reputed or taken for any part, parcel, or member of any of them, and such other the King's said subjects inhabited in the town of Lancaster and elsewhere by north in the shire of Lancaster, have now of late attempted and committed manifest and open rebellion against his most royal majesty; whereby was like to have ensued the utter ruin and destruction of these whole countries to the great comfort and advancement of your ancient enemies the Scots, which, as his highness is credibly informed, do in a great readiness watch upon the same; and to the high displeasure of God, who straightly commandeth you to obey your sovereign lord and King in all things and not with wickedness to resist his will or commandment for any cause whatsoever it be. Nevertheless, the King's royal majesty, perceiving as well by the articles of your petitions freely sent to his highness as also truly informed by credible reports that your said offenses proceeded of ignorance and by cause of sundry false tales never minded or intended by his highness or any of his council, but most craftily, untruly, and most spitefully set abroad amongst you by certain malicious and seditious persons: and thereupon his highness, inclined to extend his most gracious pity and mercy towards you, having the chief charge of you under God, both of your souls and bodies, and desiring rather the preservation of the same and your reconciliation by his merciful means than by the order and rigor of justice to punish you according to your demerits, of his inestimable goodness and singular mercy and pity, and at the most humble petitions and submissions made unto his gracious highness, is contented and pleased to give and grant, and by this present proclamation doth give and grant, unto you all and to all and every your confederates, wheresoever they dwell, of what estate, degree, or condition soever you or they be, or in what name or names soever they or you be or may be called, his general and free pardon for all manner treasons, rebellions, insurrections, misprisions of treasons, murders, robberies, felonies, and of all accessories of the same and of every of them, unlawful assemblies, unlawful conventicles, unlawful speaking of words, confederations, conspiracies, riots, routs, and all other trespasses, offenses, and contempts done and committed by you or any of you against the King's majesty, his crown, or dignity royal upon and from the time of the beginning of the said rebellion, whensoever it was until now this present day of proclaiming of this proclamation; and of all pains, imprisonments, and executions of death, and all other penalties, fines, and forfeitures of lands, tenements, hereditaments, [and] chattels by any of you incurred by reason of the premises or any of them: which fines, forfeitures, lands, tenements, hereditaments, goods, and chattels the King's said highness, of his special grace and mercy minding, by these presents giveth to such of you as have or should have forfeited or lost the same by occasion of the premises or any of them. And also his highness is pleased and contented that you and every of you from time to time shall and may have, upon your suit to be made hereafter in the King's chancery, his said most gracious and free pardon under his great seal thereof, and that you may sue without any further bill or warrant to be obtained for the same, and without paying anything for the Great Seal thereof. And that you and every of you from time to time may freely and liberally sue for his said pardon when and as often as it shall like you, without any trouble, vexation, or impediment for the processes or any of them, by his highness or by any of his officers, ministers, or subjects, by any manner of means or in any manner of wise. Provided always that you and every of you, in token of a present declaration and knowledge that you do heartily lament and be sorry for your said offenses, shall make your humble submission unto his highness in the presence of his right trusty and right entirely beloved cousins and councilors, the Duke of Norfolk and the Earl of Shrewsbury, his Lieutenants General, or of any of them, or to the deputy or deputies of them or of any of them, or to such other person or persons as the King's highness shall appoint for the same.

Furthermore the King's most royal majesty straightly chargeth and commandeth that you and every of you shall from henceforth like true and faithful subjects use yourselves in godly peace and his, according to your duties and allegiance; and that you shall in no wise hereafter attempt to make or presume any such rebellions, unlawful assemblies, routs, riots, and conspiracies; nor at the commandment nor by the authority of any person of what estate or degree or for what cause soever it be, shall arise in any forcible manner, way, and array, unless it be at the special commandment of the King's highness or his lieutenant sufficiently authorized for the same.

170. Pricing Wines

[Westminster, 12 January 1537, 28 Henry VIII]

LJ 14, 27: date as above; writ to mayor and sheriffs of London; schedule as below. BM MS Harl 442, 114: date 1 December; writ to bailiff of Colchester; schedule as below. Steele 169. Text (MS): LJ

FORASMUCH as the King our sovereign lord's most dear and trusty councilors, Sir Thomas Audley, knight, Lord Chancellor of England; Thomas, Duke of Norfolk, Treasurer of England; Charles, Duke of Suffolk, Lord President of his council; Thomas, Lord Cromwell, Keeper of his Privy Seal; Sir John Fitz James, knight, Chief Justice of his pleas before him to be holden, and Sir John Baldwyn, knight, Chief Justice of his common bench; in the due execution of an act [1] made and established in his parliament begun and holden at Westminster the third day of November in the 21st year of his reign, and continued by divers prorogations unto the 15th day of January in the 23rd year of the same his grace's reign, and there holden and continued for the commonwealth of this realm and his subjects of the same, have limited, assigned, and appointed the prices of Gascon and French wines to be sold within his said realm; that is to say, every tun of the best Gascon wine or French wine to be sold after the price and rate of seven marks sterling the tun and not above; and every pipe, hogshead, puncheon, tierce, and other vessel of the same wine, to be sold for their quantities after and according to the same rate and not above; and for small and thin wines to be sold after the same rate as the buyers and sellers thereof agree:

The King's highness, our said most dread sovereign lord, therefore straightly chargeth and commandeth all manner his subjects and others putting any manner Gascon or French wines to sale within this his realm, that they nor any of them in any manner of wise sell any manner Gascon or French wine above the said price and rate of seven marks sterling the tun, and every pipe, hogshead, puncheon, tierce, and other vessel of the same wine to be sold for their quantities after and according to the same rate, and not above; and to sell the same small and thin wines under the said rate in manner and form above specified and not above: upon pain to forfeit and pay such penalties as be contained and expressed in the said act.

And moreover his high pleasure and commandment also is that all and singular mayors, sheriffs, bailiffs, constables, and other officers to whom it appertaineth, that they and every of them with all diligence cause and see that this his proclamation be put in due execution after the tenor of the same

1. 23 Henry VIII, c. 7, 1531, *SR 3*, 374.

and also according to another act of parliament in that case provided: as they will answer thereto at their uttermost perils.

171. Prohibiting Use of Handguns and Crossbows

[Westminster, 24 January 1537, 28 Henry VIII]

BM MS Harl 442, 104: date as above; writ to mayor and sheriffs of London; schedule as below. Steele 164. Text (MS): Harl

FORASMUCH as in the parliament begun and holden the third day of November in the 21st year of our most dread sovereign lord the King's reign and continued by prorogations unto the 25th year of his said grace's reign, it was then amongst divers other good, laudable, and wholesome laws and statutes,[1] enacted, established, and provided that no manner of person or persons, of what estate or degree he or they be, except he or they in their own right or in the right of his or their wives to his or their own uses or any other to the use of any such person or persons, have lands, tenements, fees, annuities, or offices to the yearly value of £100, should shoot in any handgun or crossbow, or use or keep in his or their houses or elsewhere any crossbow or handgun, upon pain to forfeit for every time that he or they so offended contrary to this act, £10; and that it should be lawful to every person which be not prohibited by the said act to use and keep any crossbow or handgun to seize and take any such crossbow and handgun, or any of them, from the keeping or possession of every offender of the said act, and the same to keep or retain to his or their own use; and that no lords or owners of any leets should bear or maintain any of their tenants or servants, within the precinct or jurisdiction of their leets, to do or offend contrary to the said act, upon pain to forfeit for every time so offending £10, the one moiety of which forfeiture to be to the King our sovereign lord, and the other to the party that will pursue for the same, as in the same act amongst other things it is more at large expressed and mentioned:

The King's most royal majesty, considering that the said act is profitable for the commonwealth of his realm, doth therefore straightly charge and command as well all and singular his subjects, as other of, what estate, degree, or condition he or they be, that they nor any of them in any manner of wise shall from henceforth shoot in any handgun or crossbow, or use or keep any of them, contrary to the form, purport, and effect of the said statute and the provisions in the same, upon the pains in the said statute limited and expressed.

And over this, the King's majesty straightly chargeth and commandeth

1. 25 Henry VIII, c. 17, 1533, *SR 3*, 457.

that all such persons which be not restrained nor prohibited by the said act to shoot in any crossbow or handgun, and such as have or hereafter shall have his grace's placard for the same, that they nor any of them shall from henceforth use or bear abroad any manner of handgun, unless it be of the length with the stock two foot and a half of the standard at the least, upon pain of imprisonment and fine making at the King's will and pleasure.

And furthermore the King's highness straightly chargeth and commandeth all mayors, sheriffs, justices of peace, bailiffs, and all other his ministers and lords and owners of leets, that they, without favor, dread, affection, or corruption, shall put their effectual endeavors for the due execution of the said statute and this proclamation and for the punishment of the offenders thereof, as they will answer to his grace for the same at their uttermost perils, and will avoid the King's most high displeasure and indignation.

172. Redistricting Western Shires

[Westminster, 20 February 1537, 28 Henry VIII]

BM MS Harl 442, 106: date as above; writ to Bishop of Coventry and Lichfield, President of the Council of Wales; schedule as below. Steele 165. Text (MS): Harl

WHERE in the parliament begun and holden the third day of November in the 25th year of the reign of our sovereign lord, King Henry VIII, and from thence adjourned unto Westminster and there after divers prorogations and continuances holden the third day of February in the 27th year of his most gracious reign, the King's majesty, by the assent of the lords spiritual and temporal and the commons in the said parliament assembled, and by the authority of the same, made, provided, and ordained divers sundry good laws, ordinances, and statutes for the commonwealth of his realm of England; amongst the which his highness by the assent abovesaid constituted, ordained, and made many good, notable, and wholesome laws, ordinances, and statutes [1] for and concerning the preservation and wealth of the principality, dominion, and country of Wales and confines of the same, and of his most loving and obedient subjects inhabiting and dwelling within the said country of Wales, whom his majesty right entirely and most tenderly loveth, trusteth, and favoreth; the terms of which laws, statutes, and ordinances more plainly and at large appeareth in a certain act expressed in a schedule imprinted and onto this his highness' present proclamation annexed; amongst the which his royal majesty willeth it to be notified, published, declared, and known unto his said loving and obedient subjects of his said dominion, principality, and country of Wales, that his full mind,

1. 27 Henry VIII, c. 26, 1535, *SR 3*, 563.

will, and pleasure is that the laws, provisions, and ordinances contained in the said act hereafter specified, rehearsed, and declared by this his present proclamation to be observed and kept, shall be firmly holden, observed, performed, and executed in all and every thing and things without violation or infringing of them or any of them.

That is to say, that the lordships, towns, parishes, commotes, hundreds, and cantreds of Oswestry, Whittington, Masbroke, Knoking, Ellesmere, Downe, and Churbury hundred in the marches of Wales aforesaid, and every of them; and all and singular honors, lordships, castles, manors, towns, hamlets, lands, tenements, and hereditaments lying and being within the compass or precinct of the said lordships, towns, parishes, commotes, hundreds, and cantreds, or any of them, in whose possession soever they be or shall be, and every part thereof: shall stand and be forever from and after the Feast of All Saints last past, gildable, and shall be united, annexed, and joined to and with the county of Salop as a member, part and parcel of the same; and that the said lordships of Oswestry, Whittington, Masbroke and Knoking, with their members, shall be taken, named and known by the name of the hundreds of Oswestry in the county of Salop; and the inhabitants thereof shall be attendant and do every thing and things at every sessions, assize, and jail delivery to be holden within the county of Salop as the inhabitants of all other hundreds do within the said county of Salop according to the laws of this realm of England. And that the lordships of Ellesmere, with the members of the same, shall be united and knit to the hundred of Pymhill in the county of Salop, and shall be taken, named, and known to be parcel of the same hundred; and the inhabitants thereof shall be attendant and do every thing and things which the inhabitants of the same hundred now do and use according to the laws of this realm of England: and that the lordship of Downe, with the members, shall be united, joined, and knit to the hundred of Churbury in the county of Salop; and that the inhabitants of the said hundred of Churbury and lordship of Downe shall be attendant and do every thing and things at every sessions, assize, and jail delivery to be holden within the said county of Salop as the inhabitants of all other hundreds do within the said county of Salop, according to the laws of the realm of England. And that the said hundred of Churbury, from the said Feast of All Saints now last past, nor the said hundreds of Oswestry, nor yet the lordships of Ellesmere, shall be in no wise otherwise privileged nor have no other liberty nor privilege but as hundreds united, annexed, and knit to the said county of Salop as other hundreds be within the said county. And that the lordships, towns, parishes, commotes, hundreds, and cantreds of Ewyas Lacy, Ewyas Harold, Clifford, Wynforton, Yerdsley, Huntingdon, Whitney, Wygmore, Logharneys, and Stapleton, in the said marches of Wales, and every of them, and all and singular honors, lordships, castles, manors and lands, tenements and hereditaments lying and being within the compass or precinct of the said lordships, towns, parishes, commotes, hundreds, and cantreds, or any of them, whose possession soever they be or shall be, and every part thereof, shall stand and be forever from and after the said Feast of All Saints, gildable, and shall be united, annexed and joined to and with the county of Hereford as a member, part or parcel of the same county of Hereford. And that the lordships of Wygmore and Logharneys, with their members, shall be taken, named and known by the name of the hundred of Wygmore in the county of Hereford aforesaid; and that the inhabitants thereof shall be attendant and do every thing and things at every sessions, assize, and jail delivery to be holden within the said county of Hereford as the inhabitants of all other hundreds do within the said county of Hereford according to the laws of the realm of England, and the whole lordship of Ewyas Lacy, with the members, shall be taken, named, and known by the name of the hundred of Ewyas Lacy within the said county of Hereford; and the inhabitants thereof shall be attendant and do every thing and things at every sessions, assize, and jail delivery to be holden within the said county of Hereford as the inhabitants of all other hundreds do within the said county of Hereford, according to the laws of this realm of England. And that the lordship of Eways Harold, with the members, shall be united, joined, and knit to the hundred of Webtre in the said county of Hereford, and shall be taken, named, and known to be parcel of the said hundred of Webtre; and the inhabitants thereof shall be attendant and do every thing and things with the inhabitants of the same hundred of Webtre as the inhabitants of the same hundred now do, according to the laws of this realm of England, and that the lordships of Clifford, Wynforton, Yerdsley, Whitney, and Huntingdon, with their members, shall be taken, named, and known by the name of the hundred of Huntingdon within the county of Hereford aforesaid; and that the inhabitants thereof shall be attendant and do every thing and things at every sessions, assize, and jail delivery to be holden within the said county of Hereford as the inhabitants of all other hundreds do within the said county of Hereford, according to the laws of this realm of England. And that the said hundred of Wygmore, with the members, and the said hundred of Ewyas Lacy, and the said hundred of Huntingdon, and the lordship of Ewyas Harold annexed unto the hundred of Webtre, from the said Feast of All Saints now last past, shall be in no wise otherwise privileged nor have no other privileges, franchises, nor liberty, but as hundreds united and annexed to the said county of Hereford, and as other hundreds be within the said county of Hereford. And that the lordship, towns, and parishes of Willaston, Tydnam, and Bechcley in the said marches of Wales, and all honors, lordships, castles, manors, lands, tenements, and hereditaments lying or being between Chepstowe bridge in the said marches of Wales and Gloucestershire, in whose possession soever they be or shall be, and every part thereof, shall stand and be gildable from and after the said Feast of All Saints, and shall be united, annexed, and joined to and with the said county or shire of Gloucester as a member, part and parcel of the same. And that the said lordships, towns and parishes of Willaston, Tydnam, and Bechcley, and all honors, lordships, castles, manors, lands, tenements, and hereditaments lying or being between Chepstowe bridge and the shire of Gloucester as is aforesaid, shall be united, joined, and knit to the hundred of Westbury within the said shire of Gloucester, and shall be taken, named, and known to be part and parcel of the same hundred; and the inhabitants thereof shall be attendant and do every thing and things which the inhabitants of the same hundred of Westbury now do, according to the laws of this realm of England. And that the said lordship of Willaston, Tydnam, and Bechcley, from the said Feast of All Saints now last past shall be in no wise privileged nor have no other liberties, franchises nor privileges but as parcel of the said hundred of Westbury in the said county of Gloucester.

And it was further enacted by the authority aforesaid that all and every temporal and lay person now being lords marcher, or having any lordship marcher or lordship royal, shall from and after the said Feast of All Saints, have all such mises and profits of their towns as they have had or used to have at the first entry into their lands in times past; and also shall have, hold, and keep within the precinct of their lordship's courts, baron courts, leets, and law days, and all and every thing to the same courts belonging; and also shall have within the precinct of their said lordship or law day, waif, stray, infangthef, utfangthef, treasure troves, deodands, goods and chattels of felons and of persons condemned or outlawed of felony or murder, or put in exigent for felony or murder, and also *wreck de mer,* wharfage, and customs of strangers, as they have had in times past, and as though such privileges were granted unto them by his highness by point of eyre, anything in the said act to the contrary notwithstanding.

And where also it is provided, contained, and expressed in the said act and schedule that his highness, notwithstanding the said act or anything therein contained, shall have full power and authority for the term of three years then next after the end and dissolution of that said parliament to suspend, for such time as shall please his grace, or utterly to repeal, revoke, and abrogate the same whole act or any part thereof from time to time as should stand with his most gracious pleasure; so that every such suspending, repeal, and revocation from time to time, as often as any such case shall happen, shall be made in writing under the Great Seal of England and be annexed to the roll of the said parliament, wherein the said act shall be enrolled, and proclamation thereupon to be made in every shire within the said country and dominion of Wales; and that every such suspending, repeal, and revocation so to be had and made by the King's highness shall be as good and effectual to all intents and purposes as if the same had been done by authority of the said parliament, any act or thing therein contained to the contrary thereof notwithstanding.

His most royal majesty, for the tender zeal, love, and favor which he hath and beareth and at all times heretofore hath had and borne unto his said most loving and obedient subjects, willing and minding his said subjects to stand and live in and under such good laws, ordinances, and statutes as might be to and for their most commodity, wealth, weal, comfort, ease, and quietness, for divers and sundry considerations his highness specially moving, willeth it to be known, published, declared, and notified unto his loving subjects of his said dominion, principality, and country of Wales, and by this his present proclamation notifieth, publisheth, and declareth unto his said subjects and to every of them: that all and singular the articles, laws, provisions, and ordinances made, ordained, provided, and comprised in the said schedule unto this present proclamation annexed, concerning the said principality, dominion and country of Wales, except such ordinances and provisions had and made in the said act for and concerning the uniting and annexing of the said lordships, towns, parishes, commotes, hundreds, and cantreds severally assigned, united, annexed, and appointed by the said act onto the said counties of Salop, Hereford, and Gloucester, before published and proclaimed, to be kept and observed; and the laws of the same shall from the Feast of All Saints last past be respected and put in suspense unto the Feast of All Saints next coming, and not to be put in execution according to the said act, anything contained in the said act notwithstanding.

Nevertheless his highness, by this his present proclamation, willeth, notifieth, ordaineth, establisheth, and declareth that the laws and usages heretofore had, used, and exercised concerning or in any wise touching only the making of presents of any truck or trucks, of any manner beasts or cattles, within the said lordships, towns, parishes, commotes, hundreds, and cantreds, or within any of them, and all fines and payments of money for the same, commonly called truck silver, shall from and after the said Feast of All Saints last past be maintained and put in exercise and due execution within the said lordships, towns, parishes, commotes, hundreds, and cantreds, united and annexed unto the said counties of Salop, Hereford, and Gloucester, and in every of them, in such like and ample manner and form as heretofore hath been there used, done, paid, and exercised; and that no manner bargains or sales made or hereafter to be made in any fair or market holden or hereafter to be holden or kept within any of the said lordships, towns, parishes, commotes, hundreds, and cantreds, severally united and annexed unto the said counties of Salop, Hereford, and Gloucester, as is aforesaid, shall by any such bargains or sales, alter or change the property of the thing or things so bargained, bought, or sold, anything contained in the said act or in this present proclamation to the contrary notwithstanding.

Therewith his said highness' pleasure concerning the suspending of the articles contained in the said act according to this his said proclamation, his majesty by his letters patent under his Great Seal hath lawfully put in suspense, and the same letters patent hath caused to be annexed unto the said parliament roll according to the tenor of the said act, and forasmuch as at the said session in the said parliament it was by one other act,[2] not contained in the said schedule imprinted to this proclamation annexed, further enacted, established, ordained, and provided that no person or persons, of what estate or degree soever he or they be of, from the first day of July which was in the year of our Lord God 1536, should have power or authority to pardon and remit any treasons, murders, manslaughters, or any kind of felonies whatsoever they be, nor any accessories to any treasons, murders, manslaughters, or felonies or any outlawries for any such offenses aforesaid committed, perpetrated, done, or divulged by or against any person or persons in any parts of the realm of England, Wales, or the marches of the same; but that the King's highness, his heirs and successors, Kings of the said realms, should have the whole and sole power and authority thereof united and knit to the imperial orders of the realm of England, as of good right and equity appertaineth, any grants, usages, prescription, act or acts of parliament, or any other thing to the contrary thereof notwithstanding, as by the same act more plainly appeareth.

Wherefore the King's highness straightly chargeth and commandeth that the said act last and next before remembered be observed and kept in all things, and that no manner of person or persons, officer, minister, or other, of what degree, condition, or estate soever he or they be, at any time or times hereafter take upon him or them to remit, release, or pardon any person or persons of or for any offense or offenses contained in the said act last before rehearsed and declared, nor take any fine or fines for the same.

173. Regulating Exchange and Rechange

[Westminster, 9 July 1537, 29 Henry VIII]

LJ 14, 39: date as above; writ to mayor and sheriffs of London; schedule as below. Not in Steele. Text (MS): LJ

WHERE in a statute[1] made in the third year of the reign of the most noble prince of famous memory King Henry VII, father to our sovereign lord the King that now is, it is rehearsed that forasmuch as there hath grown and daily groweth, to the great displeasure of God and great hurt to the King our sovereign lord and to his realm, by and for the inordinante changes and rechanges that have been of long time used and yet continued in that said realm without authority given of the King's good grace for such changing and rechanging; for remedy whereof one especial statute was made in the 25th year of King Edward III,[2] another special statute made the fifth

2. 27 Henry VIII, c. 24, 1535, *SR 3*, 555.

1. 3 Henry VII, c. 6, 1387, *SR 2*, 515.

2. 25 Edward III, st. 5, c. 12, 1351, *SR 1*, 322.

year of King Richard II,[3] with other divers statutes made for the same remedy in the time of King Henry IV,[4] King Henry V,[5] and King Henry VI; [6]

Wherefore it was ordained by the said late King that all such statutes should be put in due execution from thenceforth, and that no man make any exchange without the King's license, nor make any exchange nor rechange of money to be paid within this land but only such as the King shall depute thereunto to keep, make, and answer such exchanges and rechanges, upon the pain in the same statutes of King Richard contained:

The King our sovereign lord, willing as well the said statute made in the time of his most noble father, as all other statutes and ordinances made in that behalf to be inviolably kept and observed, straightly chargeth and commandeth that no manner of person or persons, of what estate, degree or condition soever they be, do presume to make any exchange into any outward parts, or rechange of money to be paid within this his realm, without the King's special license or the license of such persons to whom it hath pleased the King's highness to appoint and depute thereunto by his most gracious letters patent; upon pain contained in the said several statutes, and also to incur into the displeasure and indignation of the King's said highness.

And furthermore his highness straightly chargeth and commandeth that all and singular such persons as heretofore have made any exchange or rechange contrary to the form of any the said statutes without his special license or the license of such whom his majesty by his letters patent hath deputed for the same, shall compound and reasonably agree with such as his highness hath deputed by his letters patent in that behalf, in which composition and agreement they shall be reasonably entreated and ordered as to reason and equity shall appertain; and such as shall refuse thus to do, then they to the peril and danger of his said laws and statutes.

174. Pardoning Bigod's Rebellion

[East Hampstead, 24 July 1537, 29 Henry VIII]

CW (C82/728): date of delivery as above; sign manual; schedule partially legible. ETR (E36/118/109): schedule, corrected by Cromwell, as below. *L&P 12*(2), 329: date, Terling; thirty true copies sent from Chancellor, under Great Seal, to Cromwell. Steele 166: date, Westminster. Text (MS): ETR

Albeit divers and many of you, the King's highness' subjects and commons, dwelling and inhabiting in the counties of York, Northumberland, Cumber-

3. 5 Richard II, st. 1, c. 2, 1381, *SR 2*, 17.
4. 2 Henry IV, c. 5, 6, 1400, *SR 2*, 122.
5. 4 Henry V, c. 6, 1415, *SR 2*, 195.
6. 2 Henry VI, c. 9, 1423, *SR 2*, 221.

land, and Westmorland, and the bishopric of Durham, and for the cities of York, Kingston-upon-Hull, Durham, and Carlisle, and the shires of the same, and in all other towns and places, liberties and franchises and dales within the limits of the same counties, cities, bishoprics, and dales, or in any of them; notwithstanding his highness' most generous benignity, clemency, and mercy lately extended unto you [1] upon your late most heinous and most detestable rebellion and most ingrate insurrection attempted against his majesty, to the great danger of his most royal person and of the utter ruin and subversion of the whole state of this noble realm; and have eftsoons been seduced and deceived and so, by the false, subtle, and crafty means of the traitor Bigod and his complices, been trained into such a manner rebellion as like as your most notable unkindness therein showed against his majesty and this your own natural country, had been able to have moved his grace's courage to have taken such punishment upon the offenders therein for the same as might have been terrible for all men to have thought on, that should hereafter have only heard the name of sedition and rebellion, had not his most merciful and benign nature, with the fervent zeal he hath to the preservation of his subjects, surmounted his princely courage in that behalf; so the same second conspiracy and rebellion might have grown to no less inconvenience than is before mentioned in the dangers in the first insurrection, that is to the destruction of the King's most noble person and to the turning up-so-down of the whole state of this realm.

Yet the King's most royal majesty, of his most tender pity and great desire that he hath rather to preserve you from the stroke of justice imminent upon your deserts than to put you to the extremity of the same, trusting and supposing that the punishment of a few offenders, in respect of the multitude which have suffered, only for an example to others to avoid like attempts will be sufficient forever to make all you and your posterities eschew semblable offenses, of his inestimable goodness, benignity, mercy, and pity, is contented and pleased to give and grant, and by this present proclamation doth give and grant, unto you all and every of you, of what state, degree, or condition soever they be or may be called, his general and free pardon for all manner treasons, rebellions, insurrections, misprisions of treasons, murders, robberies, felonies and of all accessories of the same and every of them, unlawful assemblies, unlawful conventicles, unlawful speaking of words, confederacies, conspiracies, riots, routs, and all other trespasses, contempts, and offenses done and committed by you or any of you against the King's majesty, his crown, or dignity royal upon and from the time of the beginning of the first rebellion, whatsoever it was, until the day of the date of this present proclamation; and of all pains, judgments, and executions of death and all other penalties, fines, and forfeitures of lands, tenements, hereditaments, goods, or chattels by any of you incurred by reason of the premises or any of them, which fines, forfeitures, lands, tenements,

1. See 169.

hereditaments, goods, and chattels the King's said highness, of his especial grace, by this present proclamation giveth to such of you as have or shall have forfeited or lost the same by occasion of the premises or any of them.

And also his highness is pleased and contented that you and every of you from time to time shall and may have, upon your suit to be made hereafter in the King's Chancery, his said most generous and fair pardon under his Great Seal covering the premises, without any further bill or warrant to be obtained for the same, and without paying anything for the Great Seal thereof; and that you and every of you from time to time may freely and liberally sue his said pardon, when and as often as it shall like you, without any trouble, vexation, or impediment for the premises or any of them, by his highness or by any his officers, ministers, or subjects, by any manner of means or in any manner of wise.

Furthermore the King's most royal majesty straightly chargeth and commandeth that you and every of you shall from henceforth like true and faithful subjects use yourselves in godly peace and his, according to your duties of allegiance, and that you shall in no wise hereafter attempt to make or presume any such rebellion, unlawful assemblies, riots, routs, and conspiracies, nor at the commandment nor by the authority of any person of what state, dignity, or degree, or for what cause soever it be, shall arise in any forcible manner and array, unless it be at the special commandment of the King's highness or his lieutenant sufficiently authorized for the same.

175. Suspending Statute on Wool Cloth Manufacture

[Terling, 28 September 1537, 29 Henry VIII]

LL P, 125*v:* date as above; writ to mayor and sheriffs of London; schedule as below. BM MS Harl 442, 112: date, Westminster, 9 October; writ to bailiffs of Colchester; schedule as below. Steele 167: date, Westminster. Text (MS): LL

WHERE at the humble suit of the King's loving subjects, the clothmakers, it pleased the King's most royal majesty by his grace's proclamation this last year, made for divers and sundry respects, to suspend the execution of the act [1] late made for lengths and breadths of woolen cloths unto the Feast of St. Michael the Archangel next following after the same proclamation, willing and straightly charging his said subjects by the same proclamation that they and every of them in the meantime should so provide that from the said feast they should make woolen cloths according to the said act, as

1. 27 Henry VIII, c. 12, 1535, *SR 3,* 544.

by the said proclamation more largely appeareth; and, that notwithstanding, it is now complained by divers and many of the clothmakers inhabited in sundry places of the realm that the weavers have not provided, nor many of them be yet able to provide, their looms, stays, and other necessaries for the making of woolen cloths in lengths and breadths according to the provision of the said act, alleging also that they can by no means possible observe the just breadths of woolen cloths in such form as is limited by the said act.

The King's most royal majesty, not a little marveling at the negligences and defaults of the said subjects in this behalf, considering that they have had long time as well for provision for due execution of the said act as to prove the impossibility of observation of the same (if any such be) as they have alleged; and yet nevertheless, minding that the complaints and suggestions of his said subjects shall be duly and indifferently examined before the proceeding to the straight execution of the said act to their trouble and molestation, is therefore at the most humble suit of his said subjects eftsoons pleased and contented of his most gracious and excellent goodness to suspend the execution of the said act late made (like as it was by his other proclamation) from the Feast of St. Michael the Archangel in the year of our Lord God 1537 unto the Feast of St. Michael then next following; that is to say, for one whole year, during which time his grace's pleasure is that his said subjects shall in no wise be molested by authority of the said act, intending within the said year upon deliberate examination of the contents of the said act by the advice of his council finally to determine and resolve his grace's pleasure for the due execution and observation of the same act, accordingly as for the advancement of the commonwealth of his realm shall be thought expedient.

176. Limiting Attendance at Baptism of Prince Edward

[Westminster, 12 October 1537, 29 Henry VIII]

LJ 14, 47*v:* writ to mayor and sheriffs of London; schedule incomplete. BM MS Harl 442, 113: date as above; writ as LJ; schedule as below. Steele 168. Text (MS): Harl

FORASMUCH as it hath pleased Almighty God of his infinite goodness to send unto the King our most dread sovereign lord a noble prince to the great comfort and wealth of this realm, and that his majesty intendeth by the grace of God the same noble prince to be christened upon Monday next coming:

His highness, being credibly informed that there is and hath been great infection of the plague within the city of London and the suburbs of the same, doubting that a great multitude of his loving subjects being joyous (as they have cause) of the birth of the said noble prince would make their access to his grace's court, whereby peril might ensue, doth therefore straightly charge and command all and singular his subjects, of what estate, degree, or condition soever he or they be, that they nor any of them shall repair or resort unto his said grace's court upon Monday next but only such as be appointed by his special letters from his highness or some of his council; and furthermore that no duke repairing thither shall bring in his company and family above the number of six persons, no marquis above five persons, no earl above four persons, no baron above three persons, no knight or squire above two persons, and that no bishop or abbot repairing or resorting thither shall bring in their company and family above the number of four persons nor any of the King's or Queen's graces' chaplains above the number of two persons: upon pain of the offenders of this his grace's proclamation to incur into his majesty's most high indignation and displeasure.

177. Dispensing with Lenten Fast from White Meats

[Westminster, 11 March 1538, 29 Henry VIII]

LJ 14, 69: date, MS note, 11 March; schedule as below, omitting Continental place-names. BM MS Harl 442, 115: schedule as below. See 209. Steele 170: date, Westminster. Text (MS): Harl

Forasmuch as by divers and sundry occasions, as well herring, lings, saltfish, salmon, [and] stockfish as other kinds of fish been this year scant, and and also enhanced in prices above the old rate and common estimation of their value, so that if the King's loving subjects should be enforced only to buy and provide herring and other salt store of fish for the necessary and sufficient sustentation and maintenance of their households and families all this holy time of Lent, according as they have been wont in times past to do, and should not be by some other convenient means relieved therein, the same might and should undoubtedly redound to their importable charge and detriment; and forasmuch as his highness considereth how this kind and manner of fasting, that is to say, to abstain from milk, butter, eggs, cheese, and all other white meats, is but a mere positive law of the church, and used by a custom within this realm, and of none other sort or necessity, but the same may be upon good considerations and grounds altered and dispensed with from time to time by the public authority of kings and princes whensoever they shall perceive the same to tend to the hurt and damage of their people:

The King's highness therefore, most graciously considering and tendering the wealth and commodity of his people, hath thought good, for the considerations above rehearsed, to release and dispense with the said law and custom of abstaining from white meats this holy time of Lent, and of his especial grace and mere motion giveth and granteth unto all and singular his subjects within this his realm of England, Wales, Calais, Guines, Hamme, and in all other his grace's dominions, free liberty, faculty, and license to eat all manner of white meats, as milk, eggs, butter, cheese, and such like, during the time of this Lent, without any scruple or grudge of conscience: any law, constitution, use, or custom to the contrary notwithstanding.

Wherein nevertheless his highness exhorteth, and in the name of God requireth, all such his faithful subjects as may, will, or shall enjoy this his said grant or faculty, that they be in no wise scruple or doubtful thereof, nor abuse or turn the same into a fleshly or carnal liberty, but rather endeavor themselves to their possible powers, with this liberty of eating of white meats, to observe also that fast which God most specially requireth of them; that is to say, to renounce the world and the devil, with all their pomps and works, and also to subdue and repress their carnal affections, and the corrupt works of their flesh, according to their vow and profession made at the font-stone. For in these points specially consisteth the very true and perfect abstinence and fasting of a Christian man.

This to endure and continue from year to year, till the King's highness' pleasure shall be by his majesty's proclamation published to the contrary.

178. Revaluing Coinage

[27 March 1538, 29 Henry VIII]

LJ 14, 136*v:* schedule as below. Steele 179a: date, 27 March 1539; "Not found." Text (MS): LJ

THE KING our sovereign lord, for divers great and urgent considerations and respects, by the advice of his council, straightly chargeth that from henceforth these moneys of gold and silver, here expressed, shall be current and have course within all places throughout this his realm of England, Ireland, Wales, Calais, and the marches of the same, to be taken, paid, repaid, by change, rechange and all other payments, as well betwixt his subjects as betwixt his subjects and all other, whatsoever they be, at the rate and value hereafter following, that is to say:

Every double ducat large of gold and weight, at 10*s.* sterling; every single ducat large of gold and weight, at 5*s.;* every crown called crown of the sun, porpentine, and dolphin, being gold and weight as the crown of the sun is, at 4*s.* 8*d.* (that is to say, weighing the crown weight accustomed, with two grains abated); and every half crown of the sun, porpentine, and dolphin, being gold and weight, at 2*s.* 4*d.;* and every crown of gold and weight, not *soleil,* at 4*s.* sterling;

And all manner of gold of the coin of this realm to go and be current after their value and rates as they were used and accustomed before this present proclamation; and all other groats and half groats, not being of the King's coin, having course and being current within this his said realm, not clipped nor fully broken, albeit they shall be much cracked, to be taken, received, and paid throughout his said realm without any manner refusal or denial.

And moreover, the King's highness straightly chargeth and expressly commandeth all mayors, sheriffs, bailiffs, constables and other his faithful officers and subjects, that if any person or persons, of what estate, degree or condition he be, refuse or deny to take the said moneys of gold and silver in manner and form aforesaid, be it for merchandise, victuals, change or rechange, or other cause whatsoever, forthwith to take and arrest the same person or persons making refusal or denial, and put him in ward and prison, there to remain, and further to be punished, at the King's pleasure.

179. Making Assault of Officers Punishable by Death

[Westminster, 18 April 1538, 29 Henry VIII]

LJ 14, 70: date as above; writ to mayor and sheriffs of London; schedule as below. Steele 171. Text (MS): LJ

WHERE divers and sundry officers having authority under the King's majesty for due execution of justice to attach and arrest by their bodies as well the King's subjects as other within the limits of their authorities, by virtue of writs, warrants, precepts, and other lawful commandments granted, taken, and affirmed by the due course of the laws of this realm, have divers and sundry times been hurt, maimed, slain, and murdered in and for the ministration and execution of their office, to the high displeasure of Almighty God and in contempt of the laws, power, and jurisdiction royal of the King our sovereign lord, ordained and given to his majesty by God; and after such offenses done, the offenders have taken and have privilege of sanctuary, and also of their clergy, and by such means have divers times escaped without punishment to the great boldness of such offenders and to the subversion of all good civil orders; the King's most royal majesty, considering like as his highness is ordained the minister of God and by his kingly office obliged and bounden by God's law to administer equal justice to all such, as well poor as rich, which be under his rule, cure, charge, governance, and dominion, so like manner of wise his subjects and other living within his realm, countries, and dominions, are straightly bounden and obliged by the laws of God semblably to obey his majesty's laws, precepts, and commandments, and all and singular his officers and substitutes ministering and executing the same:

And therefore his highness, earnestly minding to maintain his authority and jurisdiction royal given to him by God, and to reduce and constrain as well his subjects as other abiding in this his dominions to their duties of obedience as appertaineth to God's honor, and to the wealth, unity, and tranquillity of his realm, does straightly charge and command as well all and singular his loving subjects as other abiding within any his dominions, of what estate, degree, or condition soever they be of, that they and every of them from henceforth do obey and yield themselves to the arrests and attachments of all mayors, sheriffs, bailiffs, sergeants, and other his ministers without refusal, rescue, or resistance; and if any person or persons of what estate, degree, or condition soever they be, do hurt or maim any of the said officers or ministers in and for execution and doing of their offices in arresting or attaching any of them by their bodies, that then the offenders in cases and their aiders, maintainers, and procurers shall lose and forfeit all their lands, goods, and chattels, and their bodies to be committed to perpetual prison; and if any person or persons slay and murder any of the said officers or ministers in and for executing and doing of their offices in attaching or arresting any of them by their bodies, that then in every such case the offenders, aiders, maintainers, and procurers shall suffer death, without remission or pardon; and that they nor any of them shall have or enjoy the privilege of any sanctuary nor their clergy.

And furthermore his majesty, being credibly informed that divers and sundry his subjects have lately been murdered and slain in sundry frays happening by chance by reason of sudden foins with swords and other weapons, minding to take away the occasion of such sudden slaying and murdering, doth straightly charge and command that no person or persons in any fray or fight that shall happen or chance between them shall use in his fight any foin or foins with his sword or other his weapon; and if any person or persons from henceforth slay or murder any by occasion of such foin or foins, that then the offender contrary to this proclamation shall suffer death without remission or pardon, and shall also lose his clergy and privilege of sanctuary.

180. Revaluing Coinage

[Westminster, 27 July 1538, 30 Henry VIII]

LL P, 186: date as above; schedule as below. Not in Steele. Text (MS): LL

THE KING our sovereign lord, for divers great and urgent considerations and respects, by the advice of his council, straightly chargeth:

From henceforth these moneys of gold and silver here expressed shall be current and have course within all places throughout this his realm of England, Ireland, Wales, Calais and the marches of the same, to be taken, paid, repaid, by change, rechange, and all other payments, as well betwixt his subjects as betwixt his subjects and all other, whatsoever they be, at the rate and value hereafter following. That is to say:

Every double ducat, large, of gold and weight, at 10*s.* sterling.

Every single ducat, large, of gold and weight, at 5*s.*

Every crown, called crown of the sun, porpentine, and dolphin, being gold and weight as the crown of the sun is, at 4*s.* 8*d.;* that is to say, weighing the crown weight accustomed, with two grains abated.

And every half crown of the sun, porpentine, and dolphin, being gold and weight, at 2*s.* 4*d.*

And every crown of gold and weight, not *soleil,* at 4*s.* sterling.

And all manner of gold of the coin of this realm to go and be current after their value and rates, as they were used and accustomed, before this proclamation.

And all manner groats, half-groats, and pence of the King's coin, and all other groats and half-groats not being of the King's coin, having course and being current within this his said realm, not clipped nor fully broken, albeit they shall be much cracked, to be taken, received, and paid throughout this his said realm without any manner refusal or denial.

And moreover the King's highness straightly chargeth and commandeth all mayors, sheriffs, bailiffs, constables and other his faithful officers and subjects that if any person or persons, of what estate, degree or condition soever he be, refuse or deny to take the said moneys of gold and silver, in manner and form aforesaid, be it for merchandise, victual, change or rechange or otherwise, forthwith to take and arrest the same person or persons making refusal or denial, and so to put him in ward and prison, there to remain, and further to be punished at the King's pleasure.

181. Permitting Exchange and Rechange

[Sudbury, 30 July 1538, 30 Henry VIII]

BM MS Harl 442, 119: date as above; writ unspecified; schedule as below. Schanz 2, 634. Steele 172. Text (MS): Harl

ALBEIT the King's most royal majesty might justly and rightfully proceed and take great advantage and profit by reason of exchanges and rechanges made as well by his own subjects as by strangers merchant of this realm, by the express terms and words contained in divers and sundry statutes heretofore made, yet nevertheless his highness, being informed by the said merchants that if they should not have free liberty to exchange and rechange without anything paying therefor, that then the interruption thereof should not only be to their undoing but also to the let of traffic of merchandise, whereby great damage might grow to the commonwealth of this his realm; and also for that the said statutes have not been commonly put in use for exchanges and rechanges made on this side the mountains: is therefore pleased and contented of his own excellent goodness, by the advice of his council, that the said merchants, as well his own loving subjects as strangers, shall and may frankly, freely, and liberally, between the date of this his present proclamation and the Feast of All Saints next coming, make their exchanges and rechanges in as large and ample manner and condition as they have done heretofore in times past, without any exaction, loss, damage, or penalty for the same, any act or statute to the contrary notwithstanding.

And furthermore the King's most royal majesty, more considering the commonwealth of this his realm than the singular profit and advantage which his grace might lawfully take by the occasion of the said statutes, is fully minded and determined of his own most gracious goodness, at the humble suit of the said merchants, on this side the Feast of All Saints to put such final order and determination concerning the said exchanges and rechanges, by the advice of his council, as shall stand with equity, right, and good conscience.

182. Permitting Exchange and Rechange

[Terling, 6 August 1538, 30 Henry VIII]

LJ 14, 99: date as above; writ to sheriffs of London; schedule as below. Harl 442, 118: date, Westminster. Steele 173. Text (MS): LJ

ALBEIT the King's most royal majesty might justly and rightfully prove and take great advantage and profit by reason of exchanges and rechanges made as well by his own subjects as by strangers merchant of this realm by the express terms and words contained in divers and sundry statutes heretofore made, yet nevertheless his highness, being informed by the said merchants that the said statutes have not been commonly put in use for changes and rechanges on this side the mountains, and also for divers other considerations at this present time moving:

His majesty is pleased and contented of his own excellent goodness, by the advice of his council, that the said merchants, as well his own loving subjects as strangers, shall and may frankly, freely, and liberally make their exchanges and rechanges in as large and ample manner and condition as they have done heretofore in times past, without any exaction, loss, damage, or penalty for the same, any act or statute to the contrary thereof notwithstanding, and that this present proclamation shall be sufficient warrant and discharge to them and every of them against his highness in this behalf.

183. Enforcing Statutes against Unlawful Games

[London, 13 September 1538, 30 Henry VIII]

STC 7789 (UM 2,7,338), BM K.T.C.115.a.4, 2: printed by T. Berthelet (London, 1538); schedule as below. *L&P 13* (2), 4,3,2: proclaimed at Cheapside, 13 September. Steele 174. Text (*STC*): BM

WHEREAS in the statute [1] made at Canterbury the 12th year of the reign of King Richard [II] amongst other things it was accorded and assented that the servants and laborers of husbandry and laborers and servants of artificers and of victualers should have bows and arrows, and use the same the Sundays and other festival days, and utterly leave playing at the balls, as well handball as football, and other games called quoits, dice, bowling, and kailes and other such unthrifty games, and that the sheriffs, mayors, bailiffs, and constables should have power to arrest all that doth contrary, as in the said

1. 12 Richard II, c. 6, 1388, *SR 2*, 57.

statute is more fully contained: it is ordained the 11th year of King Henry IV[2] that the said statute be firmly holden and kept, joining to the same that every such laborer or servant that doth contrary to the same statute shall have imprisonment by six days. And the mayors and sheriffs, or the mayors and bailiffs of cities and boroughs, and the constables in other towns, shall have power to put this statute in execution from time to time; and if they do not thereof execution, the same mayors and sheriffs, or mayors and bailiffs aforesaid, shall pay to the King for every default 20*s.;* and the constables or constable of every town that doth not like execution of this statute shall pay for every their or his default 6*s.* 4*d.;* and that the justices of assizes shall have power to inquire in this case in their sessions from time to time of them that do contrary to this statute and thereof to certify in the chancery.

Item, it is ordained the 17th year of King Edward IV[3] that after the Feast of Easter next coming, no person, governor, nor occupier of any house, tenement, garden, or other place within this realm shall willingly suffer any person to occupy or play any of the said games called closh, kailes, halfbowl, hand-in and hand-out or quickboard and any of them within any of their said houses, tenements, gardens, or any other place, upon pain to have the imprisonment of three years and to forfeit and lose for every offense £20; the one half thereof to our sovereign lord the King to be applied to the use of his house in all such places where such forfeiture shall happen to fall, other than where any person ought to have the forfeiture of the goods of felons and fugitives by any lawful grant, authority of parliament or otherwise. And it is ordained by the said authority that all such persons, their heirs and successors, which ought to have any such forfeitures in such places, shall have all such half as shall be hereafter forfeit by any of the premises; and the other half thereof to him or them that in this behalf will pursue by action of debt at the common law. In which action, like process, trial, judgment, costs, damages, and execution shall be had as is used in other actions there pursued. And that no person from the said Feast of Easter shall use any of the said games called closh, halfbowl, kailes, hand-in and hand-out or quickboard, upon pain of two years' imprisonment and to forfeit for every default £10., the one half thereof to our sovereign lord the King, to be applied to the use of his house in all such places where such forfeiture shall happen to fall, other than where any person ought to have the forfeiture of the goods of felons and fugitives by any lawful grant, authority of parliament, or otherwise. And it is ordained by the said authority that all such persons, their heirs and successors, which ought to have any such forfeitures in such places shall have all such half that shall be hereafter forfeit by any of the premises, and the other half thereof to him or them that in this behalf

2. 11 Henry IV, c. 4, 1409, *SR* 2, 163.
3. 17 Edward IV, c. 3, 1477, *SR* 2, 462.

will sue by action of debt in like manner and form as be had, tried, ruled, and ordered as is aforesaid.

Item, it is ordained and enacted the 11th year of the reign of the most noble King of famous memory, Henry VII,[4] that none apprentice nor servant of husbandry, laborer, nor servant artificer play at the tables from the 10th day of January next coming but only for meat and drink, nor at the tennis, closh, dice, cards, bowls, nor any other unlawful game in no wise out of Christmas; and in Christmas to play only in the dwelling house of his master, or where the master of any of the said servants is present, upon pain of imprisonment by the space of a day in the stocks openly. And that the householder where dicing, carding, tennis playing, bowls, closh or any other unlawful game afore rehearsed shall be used otherwise than is afore rehearsed, and that lawfully be presented before the justices of peace, the mayor, sheriff in his tourn, or steward in his leet, or by examination had afore the said justices of peace that process be made upon the same as upon indictment of trespass against the King's peace: and that the said misdoer be admitted to no fine under the sum of 6*s*. 8*d*.

Item, it is ordained and enacted the 19th year of the said most noble King Henry VII[5] that none apprentice, nor servant at husbandry, laborer, nor servant artificer, play at the tables from the Feast of Easter next coming, nor at tennis, closh, dice, cards, bowls, nor any other unlawful games in no wise out of the twelve days at Christmas, and then to play only in dwelling houses of his master or where the master of any of the said servants is present, upon pain of imprisonment by the space of a day in the stocks openly. And that the householder where dicing, carding, tennis playing, bowls, closh, or any other unlawful game afore rehearsed shall be used otherwise than is afore rehearsed, and that lawfully be presented before justices of the peace, mayor, sheriff in his tourn, or steward in his leet, or by examination had before the said justice of peace, that process be made upon the same as upon indictment of trespass against the King's peace, and that the said misdoer be admitted to no fine under the sum of 6*s*. 8*d*.

184. Prohibiting Export of Leather, Hides, Tallow

[Westminster, 14 October 1538, 30 Henry VIII]

BM MS Harl 442, 120: date as above; letters patent to all customers, comptrollers, and searchers within port of London; schedule as below. Schanz 2, 668. Steele 175. Text (MS): Harl

FORASMUCH as the King's most royal majesty is perfectly and credibly informed that leather, hides, and tallow is suddenly enhanced and risen in

4. 11 Henry VII, c. 2, 1495, *SR* 2, 569.
5. 19 Henry VII, c. 12, 1503, *SR* 2, 656.

prices and much scantness thereof is uttered and employed for the necessaries, utility, and commodity of his loving subjects within this his realm, to their great lack thereof, loss, and detriment; the occasion whereof groweth and cometh by reason that sundry greedy persons, studying their own singularities, buy and engross these commodities, and carry the same into the parts of beyond the seas:

The King's highness therefore of his most gracious goodness and disposition, minding the reformation of the premises and the advancement and relief of his own natural subjects in all their necessities, straightly chargeth and commandeth that no person or persons, of what estate, degree, or condition soever they be, shall from henceforth carry or convey any leather, hides, or tallow into any of the parts of beyond the seas, upon pain of forfeiture of the double value thereof, and over that imprisonment and fine making at the King's will; which forfeiture all searchers and finders thereof shall have for their labor a reasonable portion according to their merits, provided always that this proclamation shall not be extended to the let of conveyance of any such commodities to the King's town of Calais or the marches thereof, for the relief and necessity of the same, nor to any master or mariner of ships, but that they and every of them may have in their ships passing beyond the seas, hides, leather, or tallow necessary for defense and safeguard of their said ships, according as by the said statutes of this realm is limited in that behalf.

185. Confirming Annual Collection for Exeter Cathedral

[Westminster, 9 November 1538, 30 Henry VIII]

Rev.STC 7789.7, Exeter Cathedral Library 3498/94: printed by T. Petyt (London, 1538); date as above; schedule as below. Not in Steele. Text (*rev.STC*): Exeter Cathedral Library

HENRY VIII, by the grace of God King of England and of France, defender of the faith, lord of Ireland, and in earth supreme head of the Church of England, to all and singular persons of both sexes being wheresoever within the city and diocese of Exeter, greeting.

It agreeth with reason and is consonant to equity that those things which by a long godly custom have been reasonably brought forth to preserve and keep cathedral churches in their prosperous and honest estate should be most strongly and undoubtedly so confirmed.

Whereupon, insomuch as we by credible testimony are informed that in the city and diocese of Exeter aforesaid, such custom, time out of mind, hath been observed and used, that all and singular persons, men and women being housekeepers or abiders within the aforesaid city or diocese are bounden to yield and pay every year to and for the use of the fabric or building of the Cathedral Church of St. Peter, in Exeter, one farthing of our English money:

We, reputing such custom to be godly and commendable, upon our proper motion and certain knowledge, confirm and allow, by these presents, the said custom perpetually and forever. So that it shall be lawful for the messengers or proctors of the said Cathedral Church to repair and come to you and to your parochial churches, to and for gathering of the said farthings, according to the old ancient custom, and the same to ask, require, and levy for the use aforesaid; without let of us, our heirs, or of any other, whatsoever they be.

186. Prohibiting Unlicensed Printing of Scripture, Exiling Anabaptists, Depriving Married Clergy, Removing St. Thomas à Becket from Calendar

[Westminster, 16 November 1538, 30 Henry VIII]

STC 7790 (UM 2,10,339), Antiq 2, 96: printed by T. Berthelet (London, 1538); date as above; schedule as below. BM MS Cleo. E.5, 431: incomplete draft, with correction in King's handwriting. Wilkins *3*, 776. Steele 176. Text (*STC*): Antiq

THE KING'S MOST ROYAL MAJESTY, being informed that sundry contentions and sinister opinions have, by wrong teaching and naughty printed books, increased and grown within this his realm of England and other his dominions among his loving subjects of the same, contrary to the true faith, reverence, and due observation of such sacraments, sacramentals, laudable rites, and ceremonies as heretofore have been used and accustomed within the Church of England, whereof his highness is justly and lawfully sovereign, chief, and supreme head in earth immediately under Christ; esteeming also that by occasion of sundry printed books in the English tongue that be brought from outward parts, and by such like books as have been printed within this his realm, set forth with privilege, containing annotations and additions in the margins, prologues, and calendars, imagined and invented as well by the makers, devisers, and printers of the same books, as by sundry strange persons called Anabaptists and Sacramentaries, which be lately come into this realm, where some of them do remain privily unknown, and by some his highness' subjects, using some superstitious speeches and rash words of erroneous matters, and fanatical opinions, both in their preachings and familiar communications, whereby divers and many of his loving simple subjects have been induced and encouraged, arrogantly and superstitiously, to argue and dispute in open places, taverns, and alehouses, not only upon the Holy Sacrament of baptism, but also upon the most Blessed Sacrament of the altar, and further to break, contemn, and despise of their own private wills and appetites, other Holy Sacraments, laudable rites, and ceremonies heretofore used and accustomed in his grace's realm and Church of England, not only to the great slander of sundry the King's true, simple, and unlearned subjects and other, but also to the reproach and vituperation of this said whole realm and church, to his grace's high discontentation and displeasure, with danger of increase of the said enormities and abuses, unless his highness should speedily reform and redress the same:

Whereupon his majesty, most prudently pondering and considering the great cure and charge which it hath pleased Almighty God of his infinite goodness to commit to his majesty over all the congregation of the said Church of England, and above all things earnestly willing and desiring to advance and set forth the holy word of God, to his divine honor and glory, and to conserve his said realm and church, committed to his charge, in peace, unity, rest, and tranquillity, clear and void from all wicked errors, erroneous opinions, and dissension, doth therefore straightly charge and command by this his present proclamation, as well all and singular his subjects, of what degree or quality soever they be, as all other residents or inhabitants within this his realm, or within any his grace's dominions, that from henceforth they and every of them for his part shall obey, keep, and observe all and singular such articles as hereafter follow, upon the pains and penalties contained and specified in the same.

First, for expelling and avoiding the occasion of the said errors and seditious opinions by reason of books imprinted in the English tongue, brought and transported from outward parts, the King's most royal majesty straightly chargeth and commandeth that no person or persons, of what estate, degree, or condition soever he be, shall from henceforth (without his majesty's special license) transport or bring from outward parts into this his realm of England, or any other his grace's dominions, any manner books printed in the English tongue, nor sell, give, utter, or publish any such books from henceforth to be brought into this realm, or into any his highness' dominions, upon the pains that the offenders in that article shall not only incur and run into his grace's most high displeasure and indignation but also shall lose and forfeit unto his majesty all his or their goods and chattels and have imprisonment at his grace's will.

Item, that no person or persons in this realm shall from henceforth print any book in the English tongue, unless upon examination made by some of his grace's Privy Council, or other such as his highness shall appoint, they shall have license so to do; and yet so having, not to put these words *cum privilegio regali,* without adding *ad imprimendum solum,* and that the whole copy, or else at the least the effect of his license and privilege be therewith printed, and plainly declared and expressed in the English tongue underneath them; nor from henceforth shall print or bring into this his realm any books of divine Scripture in the English tongue with any annotations in the margin, or any prologue or additions in the calendar or table, except the same be first viewed, examined, and allowed by the King's highness or such of his majesty's council, or other, as it shall please his grace to assign thereto, but only the plain sentence and text, with a table or repertory instructing the reader to find readily the chapters contained in the said book, and the effects thereof; nor shall henceforth print any book of translations in the English tongue unless the plain name of the translator thereof be contained in the said book; or else that the printer will answer for the same as for his own privy deed and act, and otherwise to make the translator, the printer, and the setter forth of the same, to suffer punishment, and make fine at the King's will and pleasure.

Item, that no person or persons using the occupation of printing of books in this realm shall print, utter, sell, or cause to be published any books of Scripture in the English tongue until such time as the same books be first viewed, examined, and admitted by the King's highness, or one of his Privy Council, or one bishop of this realm, whose name also his grace willeth shall be therein expressed, upon pain not only to incur and run into the King's most high displeasure and indignation but also to lose and forfeit all their goods and chattels and suffer imprisonment at his grace's will and pleasure.

Item, forasmuch as divers and sundry strangers of the sect and false opinion of the Anabaptists and Sacramentaries been lately come into this realm, where they lurk secretly in divers corners and places, minding craftily and subtly to provoke and stir the King's loving subjects to their errors and opinions, whereof part of them by the great travail and diligence of the King's highness and his council be apprehended and taken: the King's most royal majesty declareth and notifieth to all his loving subjects that his highness, like a godly and a Catholic prince, abhorreth and detesteth the same sects and their wicked and abominable errors and opinions, and intendeth to proceed against such of them as be already apprehended, according to their merits and the laws of his realm, to the intent his subjects shall take example by their punishments not to adhere to their false and detestable opinions, but utterly forsake and relinquish the same, which his highness straightly commandeth them to do, upon pain of like punishment; and also wheresoever any such be known, they shall be detected, and with as convenient diligence as may be, disclosed unto his majesty, or some of his council, to the intent they may be punished according to their deserts;

and the maintainers, abettors, printers, sellers, keepers, or utterers of any books, out of the which any such lewd opinions, either against the most Blessed Sacrament of the altar, or setting forth any erroneous opinion of the said Anabaptists, may be gathered, his highness also intendeth in like case to punish, as is aforesaid, without any favor or mercy to be showed to any of them offending in any of the premises.

And over this his majesty straightly chargeth and commandeth all other strangers of the same Anabaptists' and Sacramentaries' erroneous sects, not being apprehended or known, that they within eight or ten days after this present proclamation, with all celerity shall depart out of this realm and all other his dominions, upon pain of loss of their lives and forfeiture of all their goods, without any favor, remission, or indulgence to be administered to any of the offenders against the tenor of this present article.

Item, forasmuch as the most Blessed and Holy Sacrament of the altar is the very body and blood of our Lord Jesus Christ, our only Savior and Redeemer, and so hath and ought to be taken and believed by the whole congregation of Christian men, upon the peril of damnation, truly and without any sinister arguments or sophistical opinions grounded without faith upon fantastical reasons, his highness therefore, minding earnestly to conserve his people in the true and just faith of the said Holy and Blessed Sacrament, and that they shall not be seduced or beguiled by fantastical reasons and arguments, straightly chargeth and commandeth all and singular his loving subjects, and other residents within this his realm and all other his dominions, that they nor any of them from henceforth shall reason, dispute, or argue upon the said Holy and Blessed Sacrament nor of the mysteries thereof, upon pain of loss of their lives and forfeiture of their goods, without any favor or pardon to be shown by his majesty to any offending in this behalf; except and reserved to learned men in Holy Scripture, instructed and taught in the universities, their liberty and privilege in their schools and places accustomed concerning the same, and otherwise in communication without slander of any man, for the only confirmation and declaration of the truth thereof.

Item, forasmuch as divers and sundry persons have presumed and do arrogantly attempt of their own sensual appetites and froward rash wills to contemn, break, and violate divers and many laudable ceremonies and rites heretofore used and accustomed in the Church of England, and yet not abrogated by the King's highness' authority; whereby daily riseth much difference, strife, and contention among divers and sundry his loving subjects, as for and concerning the ceremonies of holy bread, holy water, procession, kneeling and creeping on Good Friday to the Cross, and Easter day, setting up of lights before the Corpus Christi, bearing of candles upon the day of the Purification of Our Lady, ceremonies used at the purification of women delivered of child, and offering of their chrisoms, keeping of the four offering days, payment of tithes according to the old customs of the realm, and all other such like laudable ceremonies heretofore used in the Church of England, which as yet be not abolished nor taken away by the King's highness: his majesty, for avoiding such contentions and the occasions of the same among his loving subjects, doth straightly charge and command all and singular his subjects, and other residents within this his realm, that they and every of them shall observe and keep all and singular the ceremonies before specified, and all other such like ceremonies heretofore used and accustomed in this realm, and not abrogated nor abolished by his highness, nor by his laws or authority royal, so as they shall use the same without superstition, and esteem them for good and laudable ceremonies, tokens, and signs to put us in remembrance of things of higher perfection, and none otherwise, and not to repose any trust of salvation in them, but take them for good instructions until such time as his majesty doth change or abrogate any of them, as his highness upon reasonable considerations and respects, if it shall hereafter seem to his most excellent wisdom so to be convenient and expedient, for the quietness of his people and the advancement of his commonwealth, both may and intendeth to do.

Finally his majesty, understanding that a few in number of this his realm being priests, as well religious as other, have taken wives and married themselves, contrary to the wholesome monitions of St. Paul *ad Timotheum, ad Titum,* and *ad Corintheos,* both in the First and Second, and contrary also to the opinions of many of the old Fathers and expositors of Scripture, not esteeming also the avow and promise of chastity which they made at the receiving of their holy orders: his highness, in no wise minding that the generality of the clergy of this his realm should with the example of such a few number of light persons proceed to marriage without a common consent of his highness and his realm, doth therefore straightly charge and command as well all and singular of the said priests as have attempted marriages that be openly known, as all such as will hereafter presumptuously proceed in the same, that they nor any of them shall minister any sacrament or other ministry mystical, nor have any office, dignity, cure, privilege, profit or commodity heretofore accustomed and belonging to the clergy of this realm, but shall utterly, after such marriages, be expelled and deprived from the same, and be had and reputed as lay persons to all purposes and intents; and that such as shall after this proclamation, contrary to this commandment, of their presumptuous mind take wives and be married, shall run in his grace's indignation and suffer further punishment and imprisonment at his grace's will and pleasure.

And whereas his most royal majesty heretofore, most prudently considering as well the great and manifold superstitions and abuses which have crept into the hearts and stomachs of many his true, simple, and unlearned loving subjects for lack of the sincere and true explication, and the declaring of the true meaning and understanding of Holy Scripture, sacramentals, rites and ceremonies, as also the sundry strifes and contentions which have and may grow among many of his said loving subjects for lack of the very perfect knowledge of the true intent and meaning of the same, hath divers times most straightly commanded all and singular his archbishops, bishops, and other ministers of the clergy of this his most noble realm, in their sermons and preachings, plainly, purely, sincerely, and with all their possible diligence, to set forth first the glory of God and truth of his most blessed word, and after, the true meaning and end of the said sacramentals and ceremonies, to the intent that, all superstitious abuses and idolatries being avoided, the same sacramentals, rites, and ceremonies might be quietly used for such only intent and consideration as they were first instituted and meant:

His majesty, having knowledge that this his most godly and most virtuous commandment hath not been executed according to his trust and expectation, therefore straightly eftsoons chargeth and commandeth all his said archbishops and bishops of this his realm not only in their own persons with more diligence to preach, teach, open, and set forth to his people and loving subjects within their cures, committed to them by his highness for that purpose, as often as they conveniently may, the word of God, sincerely and purely declaring such difference between things commanded by God, and the rites and ceremonies aforesaid, and the use of them, in such wise as his people, being under their cures, by his highness to them committed, may be brought to the true knowledge of their lively faith to God, and obedience to his highness, with their love and charity also to their neighbors; but also his highness straightly chargeth and commandeth all archdeacons, deans, provosts, parsons, vicars, curates, and other ministers, and every of them, in their own persons, within their cures, truly and diligently to do the same, and further in all their said sermons and collations to stir and exhort the people to charity, love, and obedience, and also to read and hear with simplicity and without any arrogancy the very Gospel and Holy Scripture, and to conform by earnest deeds their minds and wills unto the same, avoiding all manner of contention, strife, and occasions thereof: upon pain not only to incur his majesty's indignation, but also for their slackness and negligence in the executing of their cures and charges, committed unto them by his highness, to be imprisoned and punished at his majesty's pleasure.

Item, forasmuch as it appeareth now clearly that Thomas Becket, sometime Archbishop of Canterbury, stubbornly to withstand the wholesome laws established against the enormities of the clergy by the King's highness' most noble progenitor, King Henry II, for the commonwealth, rest, and tranquillity of this realm, of his froward mind fled the realm into France and to the Bishop of Rome, maintainer of those enormities, to procure the abrogation of the said laws, whereby arose much trouble in this said realm;

and that his death, which they untruly called martyrdom, happened upon a rescue by him made; and that, as it is written, he gave opprobrious words to the gentlemen, which then counseled him to leave his stubbornness and to avoid the commotion of the people risen up for that rescue; and he not only called the one of them bawd, but also took Tracy by the bosom and violently shook and plucked him in such manner that he had almost overthrown him to the pavement of the church, so that upon this fray one of their company perceiving the same, struck him, and so in the throng Becket was slain; and further that his canonization was made only by the Bishop of Rome because he had been a champion to maintain his usurped authority and a bearer of the iniquities of the clergy: for these and for other great and urgent causes, long to recite, the King's majesty, by the advice of his council, hath thought expedient to declare to his loving subjects that, notwithstanding the said canonization, there appeareth nothing in his life and exterior conversation whereby he should be called a saint, but rather esteemed to have been a rebel and traitor to his prince.

Therefore his grace straightly chargeth and commandeth that from henceforth the said Thomas Becket shall not be esteemed, named, reputed, nor called a saint, but Bishop Becket, and that his images and pictures through the whole realm shall be put down and avoided out of all churches, chapels, and other places, and that from henceforth the days used to be festival in his name shall not be observed, nor the service, office, antiphons, collects, and prayers in his name read, but erased and put out of all the books; and that all other festival days, already abrogate, shall be in no wise solemnized, but his grace's ordinance and injunctions thereupon observed, to the intent his grace's loving subjects shall be no longer blindly led and abused to commit idolatry as they have done in times past, upon pain of his majesty's indignation and imprisonment at his grace's pleasure.

Finally his majesty willeth and chargeth all his said true, loving, and obedient subjects, that they and every of them for his part shall keep and observe all and singular the injunctions made by his majesty, upon the pain therein contained, and further to be punished at his grace's pleasure.

187. Pricing Wines

[Westminster, 20 November 1538, 30 Henry VIII]

LJ 14, 119*v:* date as above; writ to mayor and sheriffs of London; proclaimed in London on 21 November; schedule as below. Not in Steele. Text (MS): LJ

WHEREAS it is ordained and provided by statute[1] that the prices of Gascon and French wines should be limited and declared by the Lord Chancellor of England, Lord Treasurer of England, Lord President of the King's most honorable council, Lord Privy Seal, and other the councilors of our said sovereign lord specified and named in the said statute, as by the same statute made and established in the parliament begun and holden at Westminster the third day of November in the 21st year of the King's most gracious reign and continued by divers prorogations, more plainly appeareth;

Forasmuch as the said lords and councilors in execution of the said act have by their deliberate advices taxed, limited, assigned, and appointed the prices of Gascon and French wines to be sold within this his realm, that is to say, every tun of the best Gascon wine or of French wine to be sold after the price and rate of £5 sterling the tun and not above, and every pipe, hogshead, puncheon, tierce, and other vessel of the same wine to be sold after and according for their quantities to the same rate, as the buyers and sellers thereof can agree:

The King's most royal majesty therefore straightly chargeth and commandeth all manner his subjects and others putting any manner Gascon or French wines to sale within this his realm, that they nor any of them in any manner of wise, by any craft, covin, or private agreement shall sell any manner Gascon or French wine above the said price and rate of £5 sterling the tun, and every pipe, hogshead, puncheon, tierce, and other vessel of the same wine to be sold for their quantities after and according to the same rate and not above, and to sell the said small and thin wines, under the said rate in manner and form above specified and not above:

Upon pain to forfeit and pay such penalties as be contained and expressed in the same act.

And moreover his highness' pleasure and commandment also is that all and singular mayors, sheriffs, bailiffs, constables, and other officers to whom it appertaineth, that they and every of them with all diligence cause and see that this his proclamation be put in due execution after the tenor of the same, and also according to another act[2] of parliament established in

1. 23 Henry VIII, c. 7, 1531, *SR 3,* 374.
2. 24 Henry VIII, c. 6, 1532, *SR 3,* 422.

the parliament above rehearsed, against such as will refuse to sell their wines at prices as is aforesaid; as they will answer thereto at their uttermost perils.

188. Prescribing Rites and Ceremonies, Pardoning Anabaptists

[Westminster, 26 February 1539, 30 Henry VIII]

CW (C82/749): date as above; sign manual; schedule as below. *STC* 7791, Antiq 2, 97: printed by T. Berthelet (London, 1539); date as above; schedule as below. Wilkins *3*, 842. Steele 177. Text (*STC*): Antiq

THE KING'S MOST ROYAL MAJESTY, having by the late proclamation made in the month of November last past [1] commanded and straightly charged all and singular his loving subjects, and all other residents within this his grace's realm, to observe and keep the ceremonies of holy bread, holy water, procession, kneeling, and creeping on Good Friday to the Cross, and on Easter day setting up of lights before the Corpus Christi, bearing of candles upon the day of the Purification of Our Lady, ceremonies used at the purification of women delivered of child, and offering of their chrisoms, keeping of the four offering days, payment of tithes according to the old custom of the realm, and all other like laudable ceremonies heretofore used in the Church of England, which as yet be not abolished nor taken away by his highness, so as they shall use without superstition:

His majesty, for the tender zeal which his highness hath borne to the good instruction of his people in truth, and being desirous that the said ceremonies should be observed and used in their right use (all ignorance and superstition clearly taken away) straightly chargeth and commandeth, that in such places, and all such days as the said ceremonies shall be chiefly celebrated, the bishop, dean, curate, or parish priest, for that time the minister, shall truly and plainly instruct the people, the good and right use and effects of such ceremony as is used that day, by which knowledge the people so using and observing the same ceremony may be fruitfully edified in renewing and stirring up spiritual cogitations and godly thoughts of such things as those ceremonies, well understood, were ordained to preach unto us.

Wherefore every Sunday it shall be declared how holy water is sprinkled, to put us in remembrance of our baptism, and of the blood of Christ sprinkled for our redemption upon the Cross; and that giving of holy bread is to put us in remembrance of unity, that all Christian men be one mystical

1. See 186.

body of Christ, as the bread is made of many grains, and to put us also in remembrance of the housel, which in the beginning of Christ's church men did oftener receive than they use now to do.

On Candlemas day it shall be declared that the bearing of candles is done in the memory of Christ, the spiritual light, of whom Simon did prophesy, as it is read in the church that day.

On Ash Wednesday it shall be declared that these ashes be given to put every Christian man in remembrance of penance at the beginning of Lent, and that he is but earth and ashes.

On Palm Sunday it shall be declared that bearing of palms reneweth the memory of the receiving of Christ in like manner into Jerusalem before his death.

On Good Friday it shall be declared how creeping of the Cross signifieth an humbling of ourself to Christ before the Cross, and the kissing of it a memory of our redemption made upon the Cross. And at four times in the year at the least to declare the signification of the other ceremonies.

And so it shall be well understood and known that neither holy bread nor holy water, candles, bows, nor ashes hallowed, or creeping and kissing the cross be the workers or works of our salvation, but only be as outward signs and tokens whereby we remember Christ and his doctrine, his works and his passion, from whence all good Christian men receive salvation, which is the undoubted truth and the sincere understanding of the catholic doctrine. And as the word doth no good to him that abuseth it, nor unworthily receiveth it, so is not the ceremony fruitful to him that would superstitiously abuse it, or by his own malice withstand the good use of it: wherein every man's fault shall work his own detriment. And to the whole body it shall be greatly profitable, each one to see other, and all together to see the whole congregation under the King's majesty's governance, so to profess and outwardly to declare a loving and charitable obedience, as all instructed by one true doctrine set forth by his majesty, and in their hearts consenting to the same do likewise in their several acts and manners, in their preachings and teachings, their words and writings; and jointly together with their devout behavior in rites and ceremonies laudable, and by the King's majesty approved, make evident demonstration of a concord and agreement in one God, one Redeemer, one Spirit, one teaching, with an humble and meek heart to be obedient to one governor and ruler, the King's most excellent majesty, supreme head of the Church of England: always submitting their judgments and showing themselves ready and gladly to obey that which for the time shall be by his highness commanded.

And therefore his majesty, having thus, as above is declared, taken order how to have his people taught the right use and understanding of rites and ceremonies; like as his grace did, in the foresaid proclamation made in November last past, straightly charge and command his people to observe the rites and ceremonies aforesaid: so now eftsoons his highness chargeth and commandeth all and singular his loving subjects, and all other residents within this his grace's realm, to observe and keep all and singular the rites and ceremonies afore mentioned and all such other like as have been laudably accustomed in the Church of England not yet abolished; so long and unto such time as the same rites and ceremonies, or any of them, shall by his highness be taken away or altered; and that in the mean season none of his highness' subjects, nor other resident within this his highness' realm, do neither by deed, word, nor behavior despise these ceremonies afore mentioned, nor superstitiously abuse them, nor any of them, as they will avoid his majesty's most grievous indignation and displeasure.

And where of late certain Anabaptists and Sacramentaries, coming out of outward parts into this realm, have by divers and many perverse and crafty means seduced many simple persons of the King's subjects, which as his highness trusteth now be sorry for their offenses and minding fully to return again to the Catholic church and the doctrine of the same, and never hereafter to adhere nor stick to those damnable opinions, but clearly to forsake and abandon them forever: the King's highness, like a most loving parent much moved with pity, tendering the winning of them again to Christ's flock, and much lamenting also their simplicity, so by devilish crafts circumvented, and fearing also that great fear of extreme punishment might turn their simplicity to obstinacy, whereby they might perish and be lost out of Christ's flock forever, of his inestimable goodness, pity, and clemency is content to remit, pardon, and clearly forgive, and by this present proclamation remitteth, pardoneth, and forgiveth to all and singular persons, as well his grace's subjects as other, all such faults as they have committed by falling into such wrong and perverse opinions, by words or writings, whereof they be not yet convicted nor condemned afore any judge or ordinary of this realm. So that for any such fault done or committed before the 23rd day of February in the 30th year of his grace's reign not already judged against them, they shall not be further troubled or vexed, but clearly acquitted from all worldly punishment therefor, upon trust that they will better regard not to fall hereafter into like folly.

And if it should be so fortune, as God forbid, that either any of those persons by this proclamation so pardoned, or any other hereafter, shall fall to any such detestable and damnable opinions, the King's highness declareth expressly by this his proclamation to all his subjects that without further mercy his grace's laws shall be straightly executed against them that so shall offend, to the extreme punishment of them in example of all other like offenders hereafter.

189. Taxing Foreign Merchants at Same Rates as English

[Westminster, 26 February 1539, 30 Henry VIII]

CW (C82/749): date as above; sign manual; schedule as below. *STC* 7792, Antiq 2, 98: printed by T. Berthelet (London, 1539); date as above; schedule as below. Schanz 2, 607. Steele 178. Text (*STC*): Antiq

FORASMUCH as it is the office and duty of chief rulers and governors of all civil commonalties to study, devise, and practice by sundry ways and means to advance, set forth, and increase their commonwealths committed to their cures and charges, and to maintain and observe such ordinances and orders as by them should be devised for the same, if by the experience of them, such goodness, profit, commodity, and benefit succeed thereof in and among their civility as they intended; and if not, then to revoke, repeal, and reform their said ordinances and orders, and establish new from time to time as the necessity of their commonwealth should require:

The King's most royal majesty, Henry VIII, by the grace of God King of England and of France, defender of the faith, lord of Ireland and in earth supreme head of the Church of England, of his most excellent goodness, deeply pondering and considering his kingly office and charge, and that although in the time of his most gracious reign, a great multitude of laws, ordinances, and orders have been devised, made, and ordained by his most excellent wisdom and policy for advancement and increase of the commonwealth of his realm, and the great profit and commodity of his loving subjects of the same, yet his most gracious highness, like a most godly and worthy ruler, not minding to cease, but daily to travail and labor in devising and setting forth orders and ordinances from time to time, as his grace by his most excellent wisdom may perceive just occasion of necessity in his commonwealth; and now among other things calling to his most gracious remembrance, that albeit his highness is justly and lawfully entitled in the right of his imperial crown to take and perceive for custom and subsidy of merchants stranger conveying or transporting into this his realm or out of the same, their wares, goods, and merchandises, greater and larger sums of money than of his own loving and natural subjects; and being in good hope and confidence that although the moderation thereof should tend to his grace's own detriment and loss, that yet it shall be a great occasion to have more plentiful resort, traffic, and commutation within this his grace's realm, with and among his loving subjects of the same, for their enriching wealths and commodities:

Taking therefore more respect to the advancement of his grace's commonwealth than to his own singular profit, and like the most godly and most worthy chief ruler of this realm, minding to prove and assay, whether by the attemperance and moderation of the said custom and subsidy of strangers, goodness, profit, and commodity shall succeed, increase, and grow to the commonwealth of this his realm, according to his grace's hope and expectation in that behalf, is therefore, and for other considerations moving his highness, pleased and contented, for the experiment thereof, that from the sixth day of April in the 30th year of his grace's reign, during the full and whole term of seven years from thence next following, no person or persons being strangers or denizens, conveying or transporting any goods, wares, or merchandises into any port, creek, or other place of this realm, or out of the same, shall for and during the same time of seven years pay any other more or larger custom and subsidy than the King's own loving and natural subjects have used and been accustomed to do and pay at this present time (custom and subsidy for wools only excepted).

And his highness straightly chargeth and commandeth all and singular customers, comptrollers, and other his ministers having charge of receipt of his customs and subsidy, that they nor any of them by any manner of color or means during the said time of seven years shall exact, take, or receive of any stranger or denizen any other more or larger custom and subsidy than is above specified in this his grace's proclamation, upon pain of forfeiture of their offices and making fine at his grace's will, and over that upon pain to yield and render to the parties grieved 10 times so much as they shall exact and take contrary to this present proclamation.

And his highness also chargeth and commandeth as well the treasurer, chancellor, chamberlains, and barons of his exchequer, and every of them, as all other his auditors having charge to take accounts of his customs and subsidies, that they nor any of them, from the said sixth day of April, during the said time of seven years from thence next following, shall charge any the said customers, comptrollers, and ministers of any other, further or more custom and subsidy for strangers or denizens than above is expressed, as they will answer to his highness at their uttermost perils:

Signifying and declaring as well to the said treasurer, chancellor, chamberlains, barons, and auditors, and to every of them, as to all and singular the said customers, comptrollers, and ministers, that they following and ensuing this his grace's proclamation, the same shall be to them, and to every of them, their heirs and executors, and to the heirs and executors of every of them, a sufficient warrant and discharge against his majesty, his heirs and successors for the same, without any other bill, warrant, writ, or other commandment to be sued in this behalf.

Provided always, that this present proclamation, nor any thing therein contained, shall not extend to give license or liberty to any person or persons, strangers or other, to convey or transport into this realm or out of the same, any goods, wares, or merchandises contrary to the form and effect of the laws and statutes of this realm; but that it shall be understood, taken, and expounded alonely, that custom and subsidy of strangers and denizens shall be agreeable and equal with the custom and subsidy of the King's own natural subjects, and not above, during the time of seven years afore limited.

190. Making Unlicensed Shipping Punishable by Death

[Westminster, 28 February 1539, 30 Henry VIII]

BM MS Harl 442, 121: date as above; writ to sheriffs of London; schedule as below. *L&P 14,* 408: date, 1 March. Steele 179. Text (MS): Harl

THE KING'S MOST ROYAL MAJESTY, for divers respects and considerations moving his highness for the surety and defense of this realm, hath ordained and decreed by the advice of his council, and straightly chargeth and commandeth, that no manner of ship, hulk, hoy, or crayer, of what burden or portage soever they be, now being and remaining within any port, haven, creek, or other place within this his realm, or any other his dominions, whether they belong or appertain to his own natural subjects or to any other strangers, whatsoever they be, shall be taken or conveyed out of his highness' dominions, ports, or jurisdictions by any person or persons, upon pain of death and forfeiture of all the lands, goods, and chattels of the offenders in this behalf, without his grace's special license first obtained for the same.

And his majesty straightly chargeth and commandeth all mayors, sheriffs, bailiffs, customers, comptrollers, and all other his ministers, of what estate, degree, or condition soever they be, that they and every of them shall have a vigilant and earnest respect that no person or persons by fraud, covin, or any other indirect mean, shall offend or contemn this his grace's present proclamation, as they will avoid his majesty's most high indignation and displeasure, and answer to his highness at their uttermost perils.

191. Limiting Exposition and Reading of Scripture

[April 1539, 30 Henry VIII]

BM MS Cleo. E.5, 311: heading "Proclamation for uniformity in religion"; schedule, with corrections in King's hand, as below; endorsement "Minute of an act of parliament." Strype *1*(*2*), 434. Wilkins *3*, 810: date, 1536. Steele 180: date as above. Text (MS): Cleo

THE KING'S MOST ROYAL MAJESTY hath been informed that great murmur, malice, and malignity is risen and sprung amongst divers and sundry of his subjects by diversities of opinions; some of them minding craftily by their preaching and teaching to restore into this realm the old devotion to the usurped power of the Bishop of Rome, the hypocrite religion, superstitious pilgrimages, idolatry, and other evil and naughty ceremonies and dreams justly and lawfully abolished and taken away by authority of God's word, and to allure the people again to the same; and some other, taking and gathering divers Holy Scriptures to contrary senses and understanding, do wrest and interpret and so untruly allege the same to subvert and overturn as well the sacraments of Holy Church as the power and authority of princes and magistrates, and in effect generally all laws and common justice, and the good and laudable ordinances and ceremonies necessary and convenient to be used and continued in this realm, which were ordained for the increase and edifying of virtue and good Christian living; some of them also using the Scripture permitted to them by the King's goodness in the English tongue [*much contrary to his highness' expectation; for his majesty's intent and hope was that they that would read the Scripture, would with meekness and wish to accomplish the effect of, read it, and not to maintain erroneous opinions and preach, nor for to use the reading or preaching of it in sundry times and places and after*] such fashions and feats as it is not convenient to be suffered. And thus each of them dispute so earnestly [*arrogantly*] against the other of their opinions as well in churches, alehouses, taverns, and other places and congregations, that there is begun and sprung among themselves slander and railing each at other as well by word as writing, one part of them calling the other papist, the other part calling the other heretic; whereby is like to follow sedition [*dissension*] and tumult [*to their own confusions*] and destructions, [*not only to their own confusions that teach and use the same, but also to the disturbance and likelihood of destruction of all the rest of the King's true and well-beloved subjects*], by punishment of the King's laws according to their merits, if his majesty, like a godly and catholic prince, of his excellent goodness, by his princely power and authority given him by God, should not politicly in the beginning provide for the same.

For remedy whereof, his most royal majesty, by his most excellent wisdom, knowing and considering his kingly office and charge touching the premises, and daily painfully studying and devising with a most noble and earnest heart to reduce his people, committed by God to his cure, to unity of opinion, and to increase love and charity amongst themselves and constantly to conserve them in the same, intendeth (God willing), by advice of his prelates and clergy and other of his council, to proceed to a full power [*order*] and resolution to extinct all such diversities of opinions by terrible [*good and just*] laws to be made for the same by authority of his parliament; and yet nevertheless, now in the beginning of his parliament, of his most excellent and virtuous goodness, mindeth by this his [*a*] proclamation set forth by the advice [*his highness with the advice*] of his council, by authority of parliament [*according to an authority of parliament already to his highness, successors, and council granted*] [1] to extirpate and take away some occasions [*as hereafter followeth*] which have moved and bred division among sundry of his subjects: and therefore, by authority of this his present parliament, straightly chargeth and commandeth that no person or persons shall from henceforth slanderously and maliciously name or call any other papist nor heretic, unless the person or persons so using themselves can and do lawfully and justly prove the same to be true, upon pain of ———.

And over this, his majesty straightly chargeth and commandeth that no person, except such as be curates or graduates in any of the universities of Oxford or Cambridge, or such as be or shall be admitted to preach by the King's license or by his vice-regent or by any bishop of the realm, shall teach or preach the Bible or New Testament, nor expound the mysteries thereof to any other; nor that any person or persons shall openly read the Bible or New Testament in the English tongue in any churches or chapels [*or elsewhere*] with any loud or high voices, [*and specially*] during the time of divine service or of celebrating and saying of masses, but virtuously and devoutly to hear their divine services and masses, and use that time in reading or praying with peace and silence, as good Christian men ought to do [*for his own erudition*], upon the like pains as is afore rehearsed.

And also [*Notwithstanding*], his highness is pleased and contented that such as can [*and will*] read in the English tongue shall and may quietly and reverently read the Bible and New Testament [*quietly and with silence*] by themselves [*secretly*] at all times and places convenient for their own instruction and edification, to increase thereby godliness and virtuous living; and if they shall happen to stand in [*with this admonishment, nevertheless,*

1. This statutory reference is obscure. Henry's revising hand at this point seems to anticipate the authorities granted by parliament in the Statute of Proclamations (31 Henry VIII, c. 8, 1539). The Act of Supremacy (26 Henry VIII, c. 1, 1539, *SR 3*, 739), which empowers crown action in church reform, and to which the textual change might be an appeal, does not include mention of the King's council.

that if they shall happen to find] any doubt of any text or sentence in the reading thereof, to beware to take heed of their own presumptions and arrogant expositions of the letter, but [*to*] resort humbly to such as be learned in Holy Scripture for their instruction in that behalf.

Finally his highness signifieth to all and singular his loving and obedient subjects that his majesty was, nor is, compelled by God's word to set forth the Scripture in English to all [*his*] lay subjects, but of his own liberty [*liberality*] and goodness was and is pleased that his said loving subjects should have and read the same in convenient places and times, to the only intent to bring them from their old ignorance and blindness to virtuous living and godliness, to God's glory and honor, and not to make and take occasion of sedition or division [*dissension or tumult*] by reason of the same.

Wherefore his majesty chargeth and commandeth all his said subjects to use the Holy Scripture in English according to his godly purpose and gracious intent, as they would avoid his most high displeasure and indignation, beside the pains above remembered.

192. Appointing Cromwell to Approve New Translation of Bible

[14 November 1539, 31 Henry VIII]

PR (C66/689/15): date as above; letters patent as below. Not in Steele. Text (MS): PR

To ALL and singular printers and sellers of books within this our realm, and all other officers, ministers and subjects, these our letters hearing or seeing, greetings:

We let you wite that, being desirous to have our people at all times convenient give themselves to the attaining the knowledge of God's word, whereby they will the better honor him and observe and keep his commandments, and also do their duties the better to us, being their prince and sovereign lord;

And considering that as this our zeal and desire cannot by any mean take so good effect as by granting to them the free and liberal use of the Bible in our own maternal tongue, so unless it be foreseen that the same pass at the beginning by one translation to be perused and considered, the frailty of men is such that the diversity thereof may breed and bring forth manifold inconveniences, as when willful and heady folk shall confer upon the diversity of the said translations:

We have therefore appointed our right trusty and well-beloved councilor the Lord Cromwell, Keeper of our Privy Seal, to take for us and in our name special cure and charge that no manner of person or persons within this our realm shall enterprise, attempt or set in hand to print any Bible in the English tongue, of any manner of volume, during the space of five years next ensuing after the date hereof, but only such as shall be deputed and admitted by the said Lord Cromwell;

Willing and commanding all sheriffs, bailiffs, constables, and all other our officers, ministers, and subjects to be aiding to our said councilor in the execution of this our pleasure, and to be conformable in the accomplishment of the same, as shall appertain.

193. Suspending Statute on Sale of Meat until 1 November

[Westminster, 4 March 1540, 31 Henry VIII]

LJ 14, 198*v:* date as above; writ to mayor and sheriffs of London; proclaimed in London on 20 March; schedule as below. BM MS Harl 442, 122: date, 30 Henry VIII; schedule as below. Steele 182. Text (MS): LJ

WHERE in the parliament begun at London the third day of November in the 26th year of our reign and from thence adjourned to Westminster and there by divers prorogations continued unto the fourth day of February in the 27th year of our said reign, amongst divers good and wholesome statutes, it was enacted [1] that all butchers and others selling flesh by retail from the 12th day of April which shall be in the year of our Lord God 1540 might lawfully kill and sell all manner beef, mutton, pork, and veal being good and wholesome for man's body at their pleasures and liberties without weighing the same, as freely and liberally as they or any of them might have done before the making of a statute [2] ordained and established before that time for selling of flesh by weight; any thing contained in the said statute ordained for selling of flesh by weight to the contrary thereof notwithstanding; and where also by the same statute made in the session of the said 27th year of our reign it was ordained and enacted that the statute made for killing of calves should begin and take effect the first day of January in the year of our Lord God 1539, as by the articles of the said statute more plainly and particularly doth appear.

We, considering the multitude, number, increase, and multiplication of our people, and being in doubt of plenty of victuals of flesh for their sus-

1. 27 Henry VIII, c. 9, 1535, *SR 3,* 538.
2. 21 Henry VIII, c. 8, 1529, *SR 3,* 289.

tenance and relief now against this holy time of Easter and now this summer season, considering also the great confluence of our nobles and subjects to our city of London for attendance of our parliament there next to be holden, are contented and pleased by the advice of our council that all butchers and other victualers selling flesh within our said city of London and suburbs of the same, and elsewhere in any parts of our realm, at and from the Feast of Easter next coming unto the first day of November next after that following, shall and may lawfully kill and sell calves and also all manner of flesh, without weighing the same, being good and wholesome for man's body, at their pleasures and liberties, as freely and liberally as they or any of them did or might have done at any time before the making of any statute to the contrary thereof, without any loss, pain, forfeiture, imprisonment, or penalty to be to them or any of them for the same, any statute, act, or ordinance made to the contrary of this our present proclamation notwithstanding: commanding them and every of them to utter and sell the said victuals to our loving subjects at honest and reasonable prices, so that there be no complaint of their greedy and covetous appetites in that behalf; willing them also to take no boldness or courage of this our dispensation proceeding of our love and affection that we have for this time to our loving subjects, but that they persuade with themselves to observe and obediently keep the statutes made to the contrary of this proclamation from the said first day of November next coming, without disobeying or offending the same, at their perils.

194. Limiting Use of Handguns

[Westminster, 27 July 1540, 32 Henry VIII]

LJ 14, 215: date as above; writ to mayor and sheriffs of London; proclaimed in London on 28 July; schedule as below. Not in Steele. Text (MS): LJ

THE KING'S ROYAL MAJESTY, by divers grievous complaints of sundry his loving subjects, and also by divers other ways and means, hath been lately informed that, whereas by his majesty's grant and permission sundry persons have had and obtained license for their exercise to shoot with handguns (and sundry other, of their own mind, and against the statute[1] provided in that behalf, do take upon them to shoot with handguns), in cities, boroughs and towns, and other unmeet places, without having any regard or respect where their pellets do fall or light down after their shot; whereby sundry his grace's officers and subjects, being in the highway, in the open

1. 25 Henry VIII, c. 17, 1533, *SR 3*, 457.

street, or in their own houses, chambers, or gardens, have been put in great jeopardy of their lives:

Therefore his most excellent highness, by the advice of his most honorable council, by this his present proclamation straightly chargeth and commandeth that no manner of person or persons, of what quality, condition, degree, or estate soever he or they be, shall from henceforth shoot with any handgun or hack, unless it be at places of the marks, pricks, and butts appointed for the shooting and exercising of the said handguns or hacks;

Upon pain that every person offending to the contrary of this present proclamation shall suffer imprisonment, and make fine at the King's pleasure; any his grace's license, *congé,* permission or liberty, or anything or things heretofore granted, had, or used, to the contrary hereof in any wise notwithstanding.

195. Suspending Statute against Foreigners

[Walden, 1 September 1540, 32 Henry VIII]

AC (Nicolas 7, 21): date, Grafton, 30 August; Privy Seal informed on the King's behalf that a proclamation should be sent forth at once. Ibid., 7, 23: date, Grafton, 31 August; proclamation with writs sent to Chancellor. LJ 14, 122: proclaimed in London on 1 September; schedule as below. BM MS Harl 442,123: date, Walden, September; writ to mayor and sheriffs of London; schedule as below. Steele 183: date, 2 September. Text (MS): LJ

WHEREAS in the parliament holden at Westminster begun the 28th day of April in the 31st year of the reign of our most dread sovereign lord, Henry VIII, by the grace of God King of England and of France, defender of the faith, lord of Ireland, and in earth immediately under Christ supreme head of the Church of England, and from thence by divers prorogation prorogued unto the 25th day of May in the 32nd year of the reign of our said sovereign lord the King, it was amongst other things enacted,[1] ordained, and established by the most royal assent of the King's majesty, his lords spiritual and temporal, and the commons in the same parliament assembled, and by the authority of the same, that all manner of strangers born out of his grace's obeisance which then before have been made denizens, or that then after should be made denizens from and after the first day of September then next coming, should be bounden and obedient by and unto all the foresaid acts and statutes and to all the contents of the same, and to all other acts and statutes of this realm theretofore made then being in their force and not repealed; any letters patent or ordinances then before made or then after to be made to the contrary thereof in any wise notwithstanding.

1. 32 Henry VIII, c. 16, 1540, *SR 3,* 765.

And where it was further enacted by authority aforesaid that all leases of any dwelling house or shop within this realm or any the King's dominions then made to any stranger artificer or handicraftman born out of the King's obeisance, not being denizens from and after the Feast of St. Michael the Archangel then next coming, should be void and of none effect, and that no strangers artificer or handicraftman born out of the King's obeisance, not being denizen, should after the same Feast take any lease or any dwelling house or shop within this realm or in any other the King's dominions, upon pain to lose and forfeit for every time doing or offending contrary to that act, 100*s.* And that no person after the same Feast should grant or let to farm any dwelling house or shop to any such stranger artificer or handicraftman not being denizen, to the intent to dwell or inhabit in the same upon like pain of 100*s.*, the moiety of which pains and forfeitures to be to the King our sovereign lord and the other moiety to such as will sue for the same in manner and form as in the same act amongst other things and provisions is declared and specified.

Nevertheless the King's majesty, of his excellent goodness, much moved with pity considering that there be now at this present divers and many aliens and strangers, as well denizens as not denizens, being artificers or handicraftmen remaining, dwelling, and abiding within this his realm of England, which be bounden and chargeable to obey and perform all the articles, contents, and penalties contained and specified in the same and other statutes and ordinances before made concerning the same, and also that such a multitude within so brief a time may not conveniently prepare and furnish themselves to execute and accomplish the said act and every thing therein contained according to the tenor, purport, and effect of the true meaning of the same statute, of his most excellent clemency and benignity is contented and pleased to dispense concerning all strangers artificer or handicraftmen in manner and form hereafter ensuing.

That is to say: first, his majesty is contented and pleased that every stranger, being an artificer or handicraftman and born out of his grace's obeisance, and not being denizen, which at the 26th day of August in the 32nd year of his most gracious reign, were sworn servant or servants to his highness and to the excellent and most virtuous lady Queen Catherine, his most dear and entirely beloved wife, the most noble Prince Edward, the King's first begotten son, or any other of the King's children, or the noble Lady Anne of Cleve, or to any of them or within the yearly fee, wages, or livery of the King's majesty, the Queen, the Prince, the King's children, the Lady Anne of Cleve, or of any of them from and after the Feast of St. Michael the Archangel next coming, may at his or their free will, liberty, or pleasure, hold, keep, take, and procure any lease or any dwelling house or shop within this his realm of England for and during the time the same strangers artificer or handicraftmen shall be and remain in the said fee, wages, or livery of our said sovereign lord the King, the Queen, the Prince, the King's children, and the Lady Anne of Cleve, or of any of them; and furthermore that every of his grace's subjects may at their free will, liberty, and pleasure from and after the said Feast of St. Michael the Archangel let, set, and devise to every such strangers artificer or handicraftmen being in fee, wages, or livery in form before specified; also that the same strangers artificer may retain, receive, and keep any shop or dwelling house within this his realm of England for and during such time and space as the same strangers artificer or handicraftmen shall be in wages, fee, or livery as is aforesaid and no longer; any article, clause, matter, sentence, penalty, or forfeiture in the same act or in any other act or acts, laws or ordinances heretofore made, ordained, or devised concerning the same to the contrary in any wise notwithstanding.

And furthermore the King's highness of his most gracious benignity and liberality and for the considerations before specified, is contented and pleased that every other stranger artificer and handicraftman not being in fee, wages, or livery as is aforesaid, being born out of the King's obeisance for and to the Feast of Easter next coming, at their free will and pleasures may hold, keep, take, or receive any lease, demise, or grant of any of the King's subjects, made or to be made, of any shop or dwelling house being within this realm of England, and that every such stranger may dwell and inhabit in the same shop or dwelling house for and to the said Feast of Easter next coming without any danger, forfeiture, or penalty of them to be demanded or forfeited, any statute, law, ordinance, penalty, or forfeiture heretofore made concerning the premises to the contrary notwithstanding. Also the King's highness is further pleased and contented that all strangers artificer or handicraftmen not being denizens and born out of the King's obeisance, at their free will and pleasure until the said Feast of Easter, shall stand, remain, and be abiding and demurrant within the realm of England to all intents, purposes, and constructions in the same form, condition, quality, and degree as they were before the making of the same act made and ordained in the 32nd year of the reign of our said sovereign lord.

196. Suspending Statute on Sale of Meat until 1 November 1541

[Windsor, 27 October 1540, 32 Henry VIII]

LJ 14, 231: date as above; writ to mayor and sheriffs of London; proclaimed in London on 30 October; schedule as below. Steele 185. Text (MS): LJ

WHERE in the parliament begun at London the third day of November in the 26th year of the King's most gracious reign, and from thence adjourned to Westminster and there by divers prorogations continued unto the fourth day of February in the 27th year of his said gracious reign, amongst divers good and wholesome statutes it was enacted[1] that all butchers and others selling flesh by retail from the 12th day of April in the year of our Lord God 1536 unto the 24th day of April which should be in the year of our Lord God 1540 might lawfully kill and sell all manner beef, mutton, pork, and veal, being good and wholesome for man's body, at their pleasure and liberty without weighing the same, as freely and liberally as they or any of them might have done before the making of a statute ordained and established before that time in the said parliament for selling of flesh by weight; anything contained in the said statute ordained for selling of flesh by weight to the contrary thereof notwithstanding.

And where also by the same statute made in the session of the said 27th year of his said majesty's reign it was ordained and enacted that the statute[2] made for the killing of calves should begin and take effect the first day of February in the year of our Lord God 1539, as by the articles of the said statutes more plainly and particularly doth appear. And where also the King's most royal majesty of his most excellent goodness, for divers considerations concerning the wealth of his subjects, by his most gracious proclamation suspended the execution of the said statutes until the Feast of All Saints next coming; his majesty now being credibly informed by divers and sundry ways that if the said statutes should be put in execution forthwith after the Feast of All Saints next coming, that then it is to be dread that his loving subjects, most especially of the city of London and other thither resorting, as also other his subjects in sundry parts of this his realm, shall lack victuals of such flesh sufficient for their sustenance and relief, is therefore, and for other good considerations moving his highness, contented and pleased by the advice of his council that all the butchers and other victualers selling flesh within the said city of London and suburbs of the same and elsewhere in any parts of his realm, at and from the said Feast of All Saints next coming unto the Feast of All Saints from thence after that following, shall and may lawfully kill and sell calves and also all manner flesh without weighing the same, being good and wholesome for man's body, at their pleasure and liberty, as freely and liberally as they or any of them did or might have done at any time before the making of any statutes to the contrary thereof, without any loss, pain, forfeiture, imprisonment, or penalty to be to them or any of them for the same; any act, statute, or ordinance made to the contrary of this our present proclamation notwithstanding: commanding them and every of them to utter and sell the said victuals to our loving subjects at honest and reasonable prices so that there be no complaint of their greedy and covetous appetities in that behalf; willing them also to take no boldness or courage of this our dispensation, proceeding of

1. 27 Henry VIII, c. 9, 1535, *SR 3*, 538.
2. 21 Henry VIII, c. 8, 1529, *SR 3*, 289.

our love and affection that we bear for this time to our loving subjects, but that they persuade with themselves to observe and obediently keep the statutes made to the contrary of this proclamation from and after the expiration thereof without disobeying or offending the same at their perils.

197. Prohibiting Irish Currency

[Westminster, 16 November 1540, 32 Henry VIII]

AC (Nicolas 7, 77): date, Windsor, 5 November; letter informing council in Ireland that King has sent £2,000 in harp groats. LJ 14, 233: date as above; writ to mayor and sheriffs of London; proclaimed in London on 17 November; schedule as below. *L&P 16,* 281: copy to sheriff of Hants. BM MS Harl 442, 186: date, 19 September; schedule as below. Steele 186. Text (MS): LJ

WHERE the King's most royal majesty at his grace's great costs and expenses hath a long time sustained and yet keepeth a great army in his land of Ireland, as well for conservation and defense of the said land as also for the avoidance of such his highness' enemies as attempt daily great displeasures against the subjects of the same, and for the maintenance and relief of the said army and subjects by his most excellent wisdom hath ordained a coin of money as well of groats as pence of 2*d.*, to be current only within the said land of Ireland, bearing the print of the harp of the one side thereof; which coin divers and sundry persons have lately transported and brought out of the said land and uttered the same within this his realm of England, not only to the great detriment and hurt of his said grace's land of Ireland and of his said army and subjects of the same but also to the great deceit of his highness' loving subjects of this his realm of England:

For remedy whereof his majesty by this his proclamation straightly chargeth and commandeth that no person or persons of what estate, degree, or condition soever he or they be, shall from henceforth transport or bring out of his said highness' land of Ireland any of the said coin of groats or pence of 2*d.* ordained to be current for and within the said land, nor utter nor pay for any payment within this his realm of England, Wales, Berwick, Calais, or the marches of the same, any of the said coin upon pain of the forfeiture of the treble value of the said coin brought, transported, or uttered for payment contrary to this proclamation, and over that to suffer imprisonment and make fine at his grace's will and pleasure.

198. Suspending Statute on Kersey Manufacture until 24 June

[Westminster, 17 March 1541, 32 Henry VIII]

AC (Nicolas 7, 156): date, Westminster, 15 March; notice of King's pleasure to prorogue statute. LJ 14, 248: date as above; writ to mayor and sheriffs of London; proclaimed in London on 21 March; schedule as below. Steele 190. Text (MS): LJ

ALBEIT divers and sundry statutes heretofore hath been made for the lengths and breadths of woolen cloths called kersey, and that such cloths should be marked with the mark of the makers and also sealed with their seals of lead comprising the certainty of the length of such cloths at the water, as by the said statutes, and in especial by one statute [1] thereof made in the 27th year of the King's majesty's most royal reign amongst other things more plainly appeareth:

Yet nevertheless the King's most royal majesty, at the most humble petition of the makers of such cloths of kersies, for divers respects, causes, and considerations moving his highness and his council, is pleased and contented that the said makers of kersies, between this and the Feast of the Nativity of St. John Baptist next coming, shall and may freely and liberally make cloths called kersies after such form, fashion, length, and breadth, without marking or sealing of them with their own marks and seals, as they did and might have done before the making of any statute made to the contrary thereof. And that arrangers may lawfully seal such kersies so by them made without any pain, loss, or forfeiture of any thing or things by them or any of them to be had or taken for the same; any thing or things specified in any statute of this realm or in any proclamation to the contrary thereof notwithstanding.

Wherefore his majesty straightly chargeth and commandeth all and singular his subjects, and all other residents in any his dominions that they permit and suffer the makers of kersies to do and use themselves according to this his highness' proclamation, without any molestation or trouble.

And the King's majesty straightly chargeth and commandeth that no person or persons shall falsely or untruly make or stop any kersies with flocks to the deceit of the King's subjects as they will answer for the contrary thereof at their uttermost perils.

1. 27 Henry VIII, c. 12, 1535, *SR 3*, 544.

199. Ordering Alien Artisans to Register

[Westminster, 16 April 1541, 32 Henry VIII]

LJ 14, 253*v:* date as above; writ to mayor and sheriffs of London; proclaimed in London on 16 June; schedule as below. Schanz 2, 607. Steele 191. Text (MS): LJ

WHERE by an act made and established in the last parliament holden at Westminster in the 32nd year of the King's majesty's most royal reign it was ordained and enacted[1] among other things that all strangers artificer not being denizens should use and behave themselves as is limited in the said act, or else to depart and avoid the realm by the Feast of St. Michael the Archangel last past, with divers other articles and provisions contained and specified in the said act; and sithen the dissolution of the said parliament the King's most royal majesty for divers and sundry respects and considerations by his highness' proclamation under his grace's Great Seal ordained and determined that strangers, although they then were not denizens, might at their pleasure and wills demur, abide, and dwell within this his realm of England unto the Feast of Easter next after the said proclamation and liberally do and use their mysteries, occupations, and crafts of merchandise and enjoy all such commodities as they might do afore the making of the said act; anything in the said act contrary to the said proclamation notwithstanding, as by the said proclamation more plainly declared.

And now the King's majesty minding the due execution of the said act doth straightly charge and command by this his present proclamation that all strangers, except only such whose names be entered, or before the 24th day of April next coming, shall be entered before the Lord Chancellor of England to be made denizens, shall do, use, and behave themselves after the 24th day of April next coming according to such form, fashion, and condition as is limited and expressed in the said act, upon the pains, losses, and forfeitures therein contained without any further delay or remission for the same; and that such strangers whose names be entered, or before the said 24th day of April shall be entered, before the said Lord Chancellor of England to be made denizens as aforesaid shall procure and sue out their letters patent for the same in due form to be made under the King's highness' Great Seal before the Feast of Midsummer next coming after the date of this present proclamation, upon the pains, forfeitures, and penalties contained in the said act.

And his highness' pleasure and commandment is that such strangers whose names be entered, or before the said 24th day of April shall be entered, before the said Lord Chancellor of England to be made denizens as is

1. 32 Henry VIII, c. 16, 1540, *SR 3,* 765.

aforesaid, shall not be molested, troubled, or inquieted by reason of the said act nor that they nor any other for them shall lose any forfeitures or penalties therein contained, so that such strangers whose names be entered before the said Lord Chancellor as is aforesaid, do sue and procure out their letters patent of denizens under the King's highness' Great Seal before the Feast of Midsummer next coming in form as is to them afore limited for the same.

And also the King's royal majesty minding of his most excellent goodness that such strangers which be servants in fee or wages to his highness, or to his most dear and entirely beloved wife Queen Catherine, should be made denizens under his Great Seal if they would humbly sue for the same before the Feast of Midsummer next coming, is therefore pleased and contented that such strangers as be servants in fee, wages, or livery to his highness or to the Queen's grace may demur and abide within this his realm and use and behave themselves as they might do before the making of the said act unto the said Feast of Midsummer next coming, without any loss, foreitures, or penalties to them or any for them by reason of the said act: and therefore straightly chargeth and commandeth that no person or persons shall molest or trouble any such strangers so being servants to his majesty or to the Queen's grace, nor any other for them, by virtue and authority of the said act, unto the said Feast of Midsummer be past and expired.

And finally his highness' pleasure and commandment is that all such persons of what estate, degree, or condition soever they be, having authority by the said act to retain and keep any number of strangers in their service shall, within six months next after the date of this present proclamation, or after the time that they shall receive any strangers into their service by authority of the said act, cause the names of such strangers to be entered before the said Lord Chancellor of England, upon pain to forfeit, for every month after the time to them limited for every stranger being in their service not entered according to this proclamation, 20*s*. to the King's use.

200. Ordering Great Bible to Be Placed in Every Church

[Waltham, 6 May 1541, 33 Henry VIII]

AC (Nicolas 7, 186): date, Greenwich, 1 May; agreement that proclamation be made, in response to petition by A. Marler. *STC* 7793 (UM 2,10,362), Antiq 2, 106: printed by R. Grafton and E. Whitchurch (London, 1541); date 6 May; schedule as below. Foxe *5*, 828: date, Westminster, 7 May; writ to Bishop of London. Wilkins *3*, 856. Steele 192: date, Waltham. Text (*STC*): Antiq

WHERE, by injunctions heretofore set forth by the authority of the King's royal majesty, supreme head of the Church of this his realm of England, it was ordained and commanded amongst other things that in all and singular parish churches there should be provided by a certain day, now expired, at the costs of the curates and parishioners, Bibles containing the Old and New Testament in the English tongue, to be fixed and set up openly in every of the said parish churches. The which godly commandment and injunction was to the only intent that every of the King's majesty's loving subjects, minding to read therein, might by occasion thereof not only consider and perceive the great and ineffable omnipotent power, promise, justice, mercy, and goodness of Almighty God, but also to learn thereby to observe God's commandments, and to obey their sovereign lord and high powers, and to exercise godly charity and to use themselves according to their vocations, in a pure and sincere Christian life without murmur or grudgings. By the which injunctions the King's royal majesty intended that his loving subjects should have and use the commodity of the reading of the said Bibles for the purpose above rehearsed, humbly, meekly, reverently, and obediently; and not that any of them should read the said Bibles with loud and high voices in time of the celebration of the holy mass and other divine services used in the church, nor that any his lay subjects reading the same should presume to take upon them any common disputation, argument, or exposition of the mysteries therein contained, but that every such lay man should humbly, meekly, and reverently read the same for his own instruction, edification, and amendment of his life, according to God's holy word therein mentioned.

And notwithstanding the King's said most godly and gracious commandment and injunction in form as is aforesaid, his royal majesty is informed that divers and many towns and parishes within this his realm have negligently omitted their duties in the accomplishment thereof; whereof his highness marveleth not a little. And minding the execution of his said former most godly and gracious injunctions, doth straightly charge and command that the curates and parishioners of every town and parish within this his realm of England, not having already Bibles provided within their parish churches, shall on this side the Feast of All Saints next coming, buy and provide Bibles of the largest and greatest volume, and cause the same to be set and fixed in every of the said parish churches, there to be used as is aforesaid according to the said former injunctions; upon pain that the curate and inhabitants of the parishes and towns shall lose and forfeit to the King's majesty for every month that they shall lack and want the said Bibles, after the same Feast of All Saints, 40*s.*, the one half of the same forfeit to be to the King's majesty and the other half to him or them which shall first find and present the same to the King's majesty's council.

And finally, the King's royal majesty doth declare and signify to all and singular his loving subjects, that to the intent they may have the said Bibles of the greatest volume at equal and reasonable prices, his highness by the advice of his council, hath ordained and taxed that the sellers thereof shall not take for any of the said Bibles, unbound, above the price of 10*s.* And for every of the said Bibles well and sufficiently bound, trimmed, and clasped, not above 12*s.*, upon pain the seller to lose for every Bible sold contrary to this his highness' proclamation 40*s.*, the one moiety thereof to the King's majesty, and the other moiety to the finder and presenter of the default, as is aforesaid.

And his highness straightly chargeth and commandeth that all and singular ordinaries having ecclesiastical jurisdiction within this his Church and realm of England and the dominion of Wales, that they and every of them shall put their effectual endeavors that the curates and parishioners shall obey and accomplish this his majesty's proclamation and commandment as they tender the advancement of the King's most gracious and godly purpose in that behalf, and as they will answer to his highness for the same.

201. Providing Victual for Calais

[Westminster, 20 May 1541, 33 Henry VIII]

STC 7794 (UM 2,10,363), Antiq 2, 107: printed by T. Berthelet (London, 1541); date, 20 May; schedule as below. Steele 193: date, Westminster. Text (*STC*): Antiq

Albeit by a proclamation devised by the King's most royal majesty, with the assent and advice of his highness' council, according to the act [1] of parliament in that case provided, which proclamation beareth date the 16th day of February, in the 32nd year of his majesty's reign,[2] it is ordained and declared among other things, after what sort, form, fashion, and condition any person or persons may transport and convey to the King's majesty's town of Calais, victuals and other things expressed in the said proclamation, necessary for the victualing of the said town, and for the castles of Guines, and Hamme in the marches of the same:

Yet nevertheless the King's most royal majesty, minding more speedy remedy for the victualing of his said town of Calais and castles, and the marches thereof, than is ordained by his said proclamation, is therefore pleased and contented, and also ordaineth by this his highness' proclamation, made and devised by his majesty, by the advice and consent of his highness' council, by authority of the said act, that it shall be lawful to all and singular his subjects, to transport and convey to his highness' said town of Calais, or the marches of the same, all and singular such kinds of victuals and other things, as is specified in the said former proclamation, without any certificate to be made to his highness' council, from his grace's deputy of Calais and other his highness' captains, officers, and ministers of his said town of Calais

1. 32 Henry VIII, c. 14, 1540, *SR 3*, 760.
2. Not found. See Steele 189.

and marches of the same, and without his majesty's license under his grace's Great Seal to be obtained for the same, as is limited and ordained by his said former proclamation; anything in the said former proclamation to the contrary thereof notwithstanding. So that always such person or persons as shall carry or tansport to his highness' said town of Calais or marches of the same, any such victuals or things mentioned in the said former proclamation, before the shipping thereof, shall be bound with one sufficient surety with him, unto the customer and comptroller of the port or creek where such victuals or other things shall be shipped, or to their deputies, by an obligation sufficient in the law to the King's use in a certain sum of money, amounting to the double value of the victual or things that shall be so transported, that the said victuals and other things so shipped, shall be truly without fraud or covin transported and conveyed to the said town of Calais or the marches of the same for the victualing and relief thereof; and not to discharge the same in any other place out of the King's dominions. And that also the transporters and conveyors of such victuals or things aforesaid shall within such convenient time as shall be limited by the discretion of the customer and comptroller, or their deputies, taking such bond, bring a true and just certificate from the King's deputy of Calais, and lieutenants and captains of the castles of Calais, Guines and Hamme, and the treasurer, marshall, comptroller, porter, captain of Rysbank and under marshall of the said town and marches, or from three of them, under their seals and names, or under the seals and names of three of them at the least, that the said victuals and things so shipped were there discharged and delivered accordingly.

And the King's most royal majesty declareth and signifieth by this his highness' present proclamation, that if any person or persons that shall provide and take upon him to convey and transport such victuals or things to his highness' said town of Calais, as is aforesaid, do not the same accordingly, but falsely and untruly convey such victuals and things to other places out of his dominions, or if by fraud or covin of any of the said deputy captains and other ministers aforesaid of his said town and castles, or by any his subjects or inhabitants in the same, the said victuals or things thither transported, and there delivered for the relief thereof, shall be conveyed and carried from thence out of the King's dominions; that then the offenders in such and in all other cases, not repugnant or contrary to this present proclamation, nor dispensed with by the same, shall incur and run into the dangers, losses, pains, and penalties expressed and mentioned in the said former proclamation made the said 16th day of February in the 32nd year of the King's majesty's reign; any thing in this his highness' present proclamation to the contrary thereof notwithstanding.

202. Suspending Statute on Kersey Manufacture until 25 December

[Westminster, 1 June 1541, 33 Henry VIII]

BM MS Harl 442, 135: date as above; writ to mayor and sheriffs of London; schedule as below. Steele 194. Text (MS): Harl

ALBEIT divers and sundry statutes heretofore hath been made for the lengths and breadths of woolen cloths called kersies, and that such cloths should be marked with the mark of the makers and also sealed with their seals of lead comprising the certainty of the length of such cloths at the water, as by the said statutes and in special by one statute[1] made in the 27th year of the King's majesty's most royal reign amongst other things more plainly appeareth:

Yet nevertheless the King's most royal majesty, at the most humble petition of the makers of such cloths of kersies and for divers respects, causes, and considerations moving his highness and his council, is pleased and contented that the said makers of kersies between this and the Feast of the Nativity of Our Lord next coming shall and may freely and liberally make cloths called kersies after such form, fashion, length, and breadth, and without marking or sealing of them with their own marks and seals, as they did and might have done before the making of any statute made to the contrary thereof, and that the arrangers may lawfully seal such kersies so by them made without any pain, loss, or forfeiture of any thing or things by them or any of them to be had or taken for the same; any thing or things specified in any statute of this realm or in any proclamation to the contrary thereof notwithstanding.

Wherefore his majesty straightly chargeth and commandeth all and singular his subjects and all other residents in any his dominions that they permit and suffer the makers of kersies to do and use themselves according to this his highness' proclamation without any molestation or trouble.

And the King's majesty straightly chargeth and commandeth that no person or persons shall falsely or untruly make or stop any kersies with flocks to the deceit of the King's subjects, as they will answer for the contrary thereof at their uttermost perils.

1. 27 Henry VIII, c. 12, 1535, *SR 3*, 544.

203. Altering Feast Days and Fast Days

[Northampton, 22 July 1541, 33 Henry VIII]

STC 7795 (UM 2,10,364), Antiq 2, 109: printed by T. Berthelet (London, 1541); date 22 July; schedule as below. Wilkins *3*, 859. Steele 195: date, Northampton. Text (*STC*): Antiq

FORASMUCH as the Feasts of St. Luke and St. Mark, Evangelists, occurring within the terms holden at Westminster, and also the Feast of St. Mary Magdalen, falling within the time of harvest, were amongst other abrogated and commanded not to be observed as holy days; the King's highness considering that the same saints been often and many times mentioned in plain and manifest Scripture, willeth and commandeth that the said three feasts from henceforth shall be celebrated and kept holy days as in times past they have been used.

And furthermore, where as in divers parts of this realm St. Mark's day hath been used as a fasting day, and in some other places of this his realm the people have used customably to eat flesh, the King's most gracious majesty, willing an uniform manner and fashion therein to be observed throughout this his realm and dominions of the same, and for that the day of no saint hath been used to be fasted, but only the said day of St. Mark, willeth and commandeth that from henceforth throughout all this his realm the said day of St. Mark shall not be taken nor kept as a fasting day, but that it shall be lawful to all and every his grace's subjects to eat flesh or such other meat as to them shall be thought expedient, without grudge or scruple of conscience.

And where also as by the variable and uncertain falling of the Feast of Easter, the Feast of the Invention of the Cross, commonly called St. Elyn's day, for the most part chanceth within Easter term, holden at Westminster, and yet some year out of the said term, ambiguity and doubt hath risen amongst the King's subjects whether the said Feast should be celebrate and kept holy day or no. The King's most benign grace, of his infinite goodness willing one uniform order herein to be observed among all his faithful subjects, ordaineth and commandeth that, as the said Feast falling within the term is not kept holy day, so likewise at all times from henceforth it shall not be observed, accepted, nor taken as holy day, though it fall out of the term, but that it shall be lawful unto all the King's subjects to use and exercise all manner of labors and occupations as of any other working day. And likewise the Exaltation of the Cross, falling in harvest or out of harvest shall not be kept as holy day, but that all the King's subjects to use all manner labors as of any other work day.

Also whereas the day of St. Lawrence, falling within the time of harvest, was abrogated and commanded not to be observed as holy day, and yet that notwithstanding many of the King's subjects do observe and keep the fast upon the eve, thinking themself to be bound in conscience so to do, in as much as in the abrogation of the holy day there was no express mention made of the taking away of the fast upon the eve; some others (like as indeed it was meant at the making of the said ordinance) do omit as well the fasting of the said eve as the hallowing of the day: the King our sovereign lord, willing to remove and put away from amongst his liege people all occasion of variance, diversity, discord, dissension, or debate, and to establish them all in one conformable and uniform order in all such public observances, declareth and commandeth that from henceforth the said eve of St. Lawrence shall not be taken nor kept as a fasting day, but that it may be lawful to all and every his grace's loving subjects to eat flesh and all other kinds of meats without any grudge or scruple of conscience.

And whereas heretofore divers and many superstitious and childish observations have been used, and yet to this day are observed and kept in many and sundry parts of this realm, as upon St. Nicholas, St. Catherine, St. Clement, the Holy Innocents, and such like, children be strangely decked and appareled to counterfeit priests, bishops, and women, and so be led with songs and dances from house to house, blessing the people and gathering of money, and boys do sing mass and preach in the pulpit, with such other unfitting and inconvenient usages, rather to the derision than to any true glory of God, or honor of his saints: the King's majesty therefore, minding nothing so much as to advance the true glory of God without vain superstition, willeth and commandeth that from henceforth all such superstitious observations be left and clearly extinguished throughout all this his realm and dominions, for as much as the same do resemble rather the unlawful superstition of Gentility than the pure and sincere religion of Christ.

204. Ordering Vagabonds to Leave Court

[after October 1541, 33 Henry VIII]

ETR (E36/231/190): schedule as below. Steele 196: date as above. Text (MS): ETR

WHEREAS the King's highness, by the advice of his lords spiritual and temporal and the commons in his parliament assembled holden at Westminster the 16th day of January in the 33rd year of his most noble reign, considering the great and manifold inconveniences, as well thefts, murders, as other hurts and annoyances which did rise and grow by the great number and multitude of vagabonds, strong and mighty beggars, and other idle persons being vagrants, to go abroad in all places universal throughout this his realm, for the reformation thereof did establish, ordain, and enact[1] in

1. 33 Henry VIII, c. 17, 1541, *SR 3*, 853.

his said parliament that all such mighty vagabonds and idle persons such as might conveniently get their livings by the labor of their bodies should from the Feast of St. John Baptist last past, being taken within any place of this his realm going vagrant and being idle, be scourged or otherwise punished in the stocks or in prison by the justices of the peace, mayors, sheriffs, bailiffs, constables, or other the King's ministers assigned to the same, as by their discretion should be thought meet and convenient: the King's said highness minding and intending the due execution of the said act to be executed and followed within this his court, as in all other places within his realm, doth straightly charge and command that all vagabonds, mighty beggars, and other idle persons which do haunt and follow the court, do depart from thence within 24 hours after this proclamation, upon such pain of imprisonment as in the said statute is appointed.

And furthermore the King commandeth that no manner of person or persons of what degree or condition soever he or they be, do from henceforth keep any more number of persons or servants retained unto them within the said court than appertaineth unto them to do, or to have any vagabonds to resort unto their chambers or offices contrary unto the King's ordinances in that behalf heretofore made, but if they do avoid within 24 hours next and immediately after this proclamation made, upon pain of imprisonment in the Marshalsea at the King's pleasure.

And also the King commandeth that no manner of person of the court do keep any hound or greyhound, but such as please his grace to license so to do, and that none of them so licensed do presume to hunt with any of the said hounds or greyhounds in any place without they be lawfully licensed thereunto, as they will avoid the King's high displeasure. And furthermore the King commandeth that no person keep any ferrets.

205. Enlarging Hatfield Chase

[Westminster, 3 November 1541, 33 Henry VIII]

BM MS Harl 442, 137: date as above; schedule as below. TRS 2, 51: warrant to pay T. Berthelet, King's printer, 10*s*. for twenty copies on fine vellum delivered to Chancellor on 9 December. Steele 197. Text (MS): Harl

WHERE in the late parliament begun and holden at Westminster the 28th day of April in the 31st year of the King's most gracious reign, an act [1] was made and established by the authority of the said high court of parliament, that the King, with the advice of his most honorable council, or with the advice of the most part of them, may set forth at all times, by authority of the same act, his proclamation under such penalties and pains, and of such sort,

1. 31 Henry VIII, c. 8, 1539, *SR 3*, 726.

as to his highness and his most honorable council or the most part of them shall seem necessary and requisite, as in the said act, amongst other things, more plainly appeareth;

And where also the King's highness and his most noble progenitors have been lawfully seized of the lordship and manor of Hatfield, in the county of York, within this his realm of England, as in the right of his crown, within which said lordship and manor of Hatfield his highness and his most noble progenitors have ever had and used a chase of red deer for their pleasure and pastime, and now forasmuch as the said game of red deer is well replenished, meet and convenient for his grace's pleasure and pastime, intending also to enlarge the said chase of Hatfield:

Therefore his high pleasure and commandment is that his manor of Armethorpe with the appurtenances which were parcel of the possessions of the late monastery or priory of Routh, within the said county of York, and also the manor of Crowell with the appurtenances in the county of Lincoln, whichever parcel of the possessions of the late monastery and priory of Selby in the said county of York being very near adjoining unto the said chase of Hatfield, and meet and convenient for the defense, scope, and increase of the deer there, shall be from the Feast of Christmas next coming part and parcel of the said chase of Hatfield, and also shall be and go, deemed and taken as part, parcel, and member of the same chase to all purposes, constructions, and intents whatsoever it be, and shall have like liberties and privileges in them and every of them as the same chase of Hatfield hath had. His highness' pleasure and commandment is also that all and every person and persons, whatsoever he or they be, which shall at any time after the said Feast of the Nativity of our Lord God wrongfully attempt, hurt, chase, or kill any deer within the said manors of Armethorpe and Crowell, or in either of them or within the precincts of the said manors or any of them, that every such offender and offenders which shall be thereof convicted and attainted according to the laws of this his realm shall have and suffer such like punishment and incur such loss and forfeitures for the same as be ordained for such offenders in any other the King's forests, parks, or chases within this his realm of England. And that also the said manors of Armethorpe and Crowell shall remain and be from henceforth in the order, rule, and surety of the Court of the Augmentations, and that the issues and profits thereof and every parcel of the same shall be answered before the chancellor and other officers of the said court, to the King's use, his heirs and successors, in such manner and form as though this proclamation, act, or law or anything therein contained had never been had nor made. And further that the said manors and either of them shall be from the said Feast of the Nativity, within the rule and direction of the King's justices of his forests, parks, and chases, and that all offenders therein shall from time to time after the said Feast of the Nativity be called and punished by the same justices as if the same offense had been done and committed within any other park, forest, or chase within this his grace's realm; any law, article, custom, or prescription to the contrary notwithstanding. And further his majesty doth will and command that this his most gracious proclamation be to all intents and purposes observed and kept without any violation of the same, as they intend to avoid his grace's displeasure.

206. Pricing Wines

[Westminster, 7 December 1541, 33 Henry VIII]

STC 7796 (UM 2,10,417), ULC: printed by T. Berthelet (London, 1541); schedule as below. LJ 14, 288: date as above; writ to mayor and sheriffs of London; proclaimed in London on 17 December; schedule as below. Steele 198: "Only found in MS." Text (*STC*): ULC

WHERE it is ordained and provided by statute [1] that the prices of Gascon and French wines should be limited and declared by the Lord Chancellor of England, Lord Treasurer of England, Lord President of the King's most honorable council, Lord Privy Seal and other the councilors of our said sovereign lord specified and declared in the said statute, as by the same statute made and established in the parliament begun and holden at Westminster the third day of November in the 21st year of the King's most gracious reign and continued by divers prorogations more plainly appeareth.

Forasmuch as the said lords and councilors, in executing of the said act, have by their deliberate advices taxed, limited, assigned, and appointed the prices of Gascon and French wines to be sold within this his realm; that is to say, every tun of the best Gascon wine and French wine to be sold after the price and rate of £5 sterling the tun and not above; and every tun of the said wines of the second best to be sold after the rate of £4. 6*s*. 8*d*. sterling and not above. And every pipe, hogs-head, puncheon, tierce, and other vessel of the said several wines to be sold for their quantities after and according to the same rates and not above. And for small and thin wines to be sold under the same rates as the buyers and sellers thereof can agree.

The King's most royal majesty therefore straightly chargeth and commandeth all and singular his subjects and others putting any manner Gascon or French wines to sale within this his realm, that they nor any of them in any manner of wise by any craft or covin or other private agreement shall sell any Gascon or French wines otherwise than is above limited, upon pain to forfeit and pay such penalties as be contained and expressed in the same act.

And moreover his high pleasure and commandment also is that all and

1. 23 Henry VIII, c. 7, 1531, *SR 3*, 374.

singular mayors, sheriffs, bailiffs, constables, and other officers to whom it appertaineth, that they and every of them with diligence cause and see that this his proclamation be put in due execution after the tenor of the same, and also according to another act[2] of parliament established in the parliament above rehearsed against such as will refuse to sell their wines at prices taxed as is aforesaid, as they will answer thereunto at their uttermost perils.

207. Suspending Statute on Kersey Manufacture until 24 June

[Westminster, 7 December 1541, 33 Henry VIII]

BM MS Harl 442, 140: date as above; writ to mayor and sheriffs of London; schedule as below. Steele 199. Text (MS): Harl

ALBEIT divers and sundry statutes heretofore hath been made for the lengths and breadths of woolen cloths called kersies, and that such cloths should be marked with the mark of the makers and also sealed with their seals of lead comprising the certainty of the length of such cloths at the water as by the said statutes, and in especial by one statute[1] thereof made in the 27th year of the King's majesty's most royal reign amongst other things more plainly appeareth;

Yet nevertheless the King's most royal majesty, at the most humble petition of the makers of such cloths of kersies and for divers respects, causes, and considerations moving his highness and his council, is pleased and contented that the said makers of kersies between this and the Feast of the Nativity of St. John the Baptist next coming, shall and may freely and liberally make and put to sale cloths called kersies after such form, fashion, lengths, and breadths and without marking or sealing of them with their own marks and seals as they did and might have done before the making of any statute made to the contrary thereof. And that the arrangers may lawfully seal such kersies so by them made without any pain, loss, or forfeiture of any thing or things by them or any of them to be had or taken for the same; any thing or things specified in any statute of this realm or in any proclamation to the contrary thereof notwithstanding.

Wherefore his majesty straightly chargeth and commandeth all and singular his subjects and all other residents in any his dominions that they permit and suffer the makers of kersies to do and use themselves according to this his highness' proclamation without any molestation or trouble. And the

2. 24 Henry VIII, c. 6, 1532, *SR 3*, 422.
1. 27 Henry VIII, c. 12, 1535, *SR 3*, 544.

King's majesty straightly chargeth and commandeth that no person or persons shall falsely or untruly make or stop any kersies with flocks to the deceit of the King's subjects as they will answer for the contrary thereof at their uttermost perils. Provided always that such kersies as shall be made to be retailed within this realm shall bear such lengths and breadths and have such marks and seals by the makers as is limited and appointed by the statutes of the realm, any thing contained in this proclamation to the contrary thereof notwithstanding.

208. Adding "King of Ireland" to the Royal Style

[Westminster, 23 January 1542, 33 Henry VIII]

CW (C82/790): date, Westminster, 19 January; letters patent to Chancellor, ordering proclamation. *STC* 7797 (UM 2,10,374), Antiq 2, 114: printed by T. Berthelet (London, 1542); date as above; schedule as below. TRS *2,* 51: warrant to pay printer 50*s.* for 600 copies delivered to Chancellor on 25 January. LL Q, 300*v:* proclaimed in London on 6 February. Steele 219. Text (*STC*): Antiq

Where we be justly and rightfully King of our realm of Ireland, and ought [1] to have the title, style, and name thereof by right of inheritance, and the non-use thereof in our style hath caused much disobedience, rebellion, dissension and sedition in our said realm, to the great impoverishing and peril of destruction of the same, if we had not for the redress thereof put to our kingly hand, as we have done, in such wise, as by reason thereof our said realm (thanks be to God) is now brought and reduced to better order, peace, and civility than it hath been many years past;

And forasmuch as our loving subjects of our said realm, both the prelates, nobles, and commons, do think and determine, that the good estate, peace, and tranquillity, wherein our said realm now standeth, shall the better and longer continue, if we would as we ought of right, accept and take upon us the title and name of King of the same; which to do all our said subjects, of our said realm, by their mutual assents, by authority of parliament holden within the same, have agreed and assented unto, and most instantly desired us, that the said title and name of King of Ireland, together with our said whole realm, should be united and annexed to our imperial crown of our realm of England:

To which their desires and humble requests, for the better conservation of the good peace of our said realm, we have assented, and have caused for that purpose our style to be altered and reformed, as well in the Latin as in the English tongue, as hereafter followeth: *Henricus octavus dei gratia*

1. See 35 Henry VIII, c. 3, 1543, *SR 3,* 958.

Anglie, Franciae & Hibernie rex, fidei defensor, & in terra ecclesiae Anglicanae & Hibernicae supremum caput. Henry VIII, by the grace of God King of England, France, and Ireland, Defender of the Faith, and of the Church of England and also Ireland in Earth the Supreme Head.

And to the intent that our said subjects should not be ignorant of the alteration of our said style, in form as is aforesaid, we have caused this present proclamation to be made, and by the same will and command all and singular our officers, justices and ministers, and all other our subjects and residents within this our realm of England, and elsewhere within any our dominions, that they shall accept, take, and use our style, in form above written, in like form, as they used and accepted our old style before this alteration. Nevertheless, to the intent that no discord, variance, occasion, trouble, impeachment, or molestation should be had or made to any our justices, officers, ministers, and other our subjects or residents, before they may have convenient knowledge of the change and alteration of our late style; we are therefore pleased and contented, that none of our said justices, officers, ministers, subjects, or other residents within our realm of England, the dominion of Wales, Calais, and of the Isles of Jersey and Guernsey, for omitting of our said title and name of King of Ireland in writs, patents, process, or other writings, to be passed under any our seals, or for non-acceptation or mis-acceptation thereof, or for any offense touching the same, done or committed, or to be done or committed, before the last day of April next coming, shall be vexed, troubled, impeached, or by any wise molested or troubled, but that all writs, patents, process, or other writings that be passed or shall pass under any our seals, before the said last day of April, wherein shall happen our said title and name of King of Ireland to be omitted, shall be taken, construed, accepted, and admitted to be of the same force, strength, quality, and condition in all things, as they were before the said title and name of King of Ireland was annexed to our style. And that the non-acceptation or mis-acceptation of our said title and name of King of Ireland, or any acts or things done, or that shall chance to be done, before the said last day of April, by any our subjects or residents, touching or concerning our said title or name of King of Ireland, shall be construed and expounded any offense or occasion of trouble to any of our said subjects or residents; anything contained in this proclamation, or anything that shall be expressed in the same, or any other thing or things to the contrary thereof in any wise notwithstanding.

209. Dispensing Lenten Fast from White Meats

[Westminster, 3 February 1542, 33 Henry VIII]

STC 7798 (UM 2,10,375), BM 1851.b.3, 1: printed by T. Berthelet (London, 1542): date 3 February; schedule as in 177 above. TRS *2*, 52: warrant to pay printer 25*s*. for 600 copies delivered to Chancellor on 4 February. *L&P 17*, 85: proclaimed in London on 6 February. Dibdin *3*, 316: other editions, dated 6 and 9 February. Stow 985: proclaimed on 9 February. Steele 220: date, Westminster. Text: see 177.

210. Granting Anthony Marler Patent to Print Bible in English

[Westminster, 12 March 1542, 33 Henry VIII]

PR (C66/707/33): date as above; letters patent to all printers in realm, all officers, ministers, and subjects; schedule as below. Not in Steele. Text (MS): PR

We let you wite that we, for certain causes convenient to our grace especial, have given and granted to our well beloved subject Anthony Marler, citizen and haberdasher of our city of London, only to print the Bible in our English tongue authorized or hereafter to be authorized by us, by himself or his assignees.

And we command that no manner person within these our dominions shall print the said Bible, or any part thereof, within the space of four years next ensuing the printing of the said book by our said subject or his assignees.

And further, we will and command our true subjects and all strangers, that none presume to print the said work, or break this our commandment and privilege, as they intend to eschew our punishment and high displeasure.

211. Prohibiting Hawking

[Westminster, 16 April 1542, 33 Henry VIII]

AC (Nicolas 7, 329): date, Westminster, 22 March; inquiry into illegal hunting. BM MS Harl 442, 141: date as above; schedule as below. TRS *2*, 54: warrant to pay T. Berthelet, King's printer, 35*s*. for 400 copies delivered to Chancellor on 11 April; another warrant to pay the same 16*s*. 4*d*. for another 400 delivered to Chancellor on 16 April; a third warrant to pay the same 16*s*. 4*d*. for 400 of the same "new made." See 217. Steele 222. Text (MS): Harl

The King's most royal majesty having knowledge by credible information that divers and sundry evil-disposed persons have and do daily take, steal, convey, and otherwise by conceit obtain and come to the eggs or young birds of goshawks, tercels, lanners and lannerets, within this his realm and other his grace's dominions, and also do take, keep, sell, convey, and willfully destroy the foresaid kinds of hawks, to the great discommodity and detriment of the King's said majesty's disport, pastime, and pleasure, and the nobility of this his realm, and also like to be within short space the plenary destruction of great part of the said hawks if great remedy should not speedily be provided for the same:

His highness therefore, of his most excellent goodness, by the advice of his honorable council, by his royal power dilated and confirmed by act [1] of parliament, doth by this present proclamation straightly charge and command that no person or persons of what estate, degree, nation, or condition soever he or they be, from and after this present proclamation openly published and proclaimed, shall steal, nor without the King's majesty's license under his Great Seal, take, keep, or otherwise by conceit or covin, directly or indirectly convey any egg or eggs, bird or birds, of any goshawks, tercels, or lannerets within this realm or other the King's dominions, nor during the space of one whole year next after this present proclamation published and proclaimed as is aforesaid, keep or bring up, or cause to be kept or brought up, any sore hawk of any of the kinds of hawks above remembered, upon hand, in mew or otherwise within this realm or other the King's dominions upon pain to lose and forfeit for every such offense £100 sterling, whereof one tenth to the discoverers and takers, the rest to the King's highness, and to have and suffer such further punishment by imprisonment of his and their bodies as by the King's majesty and his most honorable councilors shall be thought meet and convenient.

And further his highness with his council, considering that this proclamation is set forth somewhat late, and that mayhap thereby some hawks or eggs of hawks before the same proclaimed to be already taken, that then the takers, conveyers, sellers, or stealers shall incur the foresaid danger and penalty except he or they bring or cause to be brought the same to the King's majesty or some of his council within 14 days after this proclamation made, and so then he or they to follow therein his or their commandments.

1. 32 Henry VIII, c. 11, 1540, *SR 3*, 755.

212. Declaring Town of Stafford a Sanctuary

[Westminster, 30 May 1542, 34 Henry VIII]

BM MS Harl 442, 142: date as above; writ to sheriff of Chester; schedule as below. Steele 223. Text (MS): Harl

WHERE at the parliament begun at Westminster the 28th day of April in the 31st year of our reign and there continued by divers prorogations unto the 30th day of May in the 32nd year of our said reign and holden unto the 24th day of July the said 32nd year, at which day the said parliament was by authority finished and ended; at which said parliament amongst many other things by us, with the assent of the lords spiritual and temporal and the commons in the said parliament then assembled, it was enacted[1] that the town of Manchester in the county of Lancaster amongst other towns and places from thenceforth should be admitted, allowed, and taken to be sanctuary and a place of privilege and tuition for term of life of all and singular offenders and malefactors of whatsoever quality, kind, or nature all and every their offenses were, for the which said offenses and crimes the pains and punishment of death should ensue by the statutes, laws, and customs of this realm, other than such as by and in the said act of parliament be expressed and foreprised. That notwithstanding at our parliament, begun at Westminster the 16th day of January the 33rd year of our said reign and unto the first day of April then next ensuing for divers causes prorogued upon divers great matters and considerations, then and there purposed and alleged it was by us, the lords spiritual and temporal and the commons in the said parliament then assembled, and by the authority of the same ordained, established, and enacted[2] that the said former act of parliament concerning the privilege, sanctuary, and tuition for the said offenders only within the said town of Manchester should and might be from the Feast of the Nativity of St. John Baptist next coming repealed, annihilate and made frustrate, and the same town of Manchester from the said Feast of the Nativity of St. John Baptist should be of like condition, estate, and quality discharged of the said sanctuary and privilege as the same town of Manchester was before the making of the said former act; anything, sentence, clause, or article in the said former act contained to the contrary notwithstanding. And by our said last parliament it was by us, and the lords spiritual and temporal and the commons then and there assembled, and by the authority of the same ordained, established, and enacted that the city of Manchester for divers causes and considerations in the said act recited and expressed among other

1. 32 Henry VIII, c. 12, 1540, *SR 3*, 756.
2. 33 Henry VIII, c. 15, 1541, *SR 3*, 850.

towns and places from thenceforth should be admitted, allowed, and taken to be a sanctuary and a place of privilege and tuition for term of life of all and singular offenders and malefactors of whatsoever quality, kind, or nature all and every their said offenses were, or should be for the which said offenses and crimes the pains and punishment of death should ensue by the statutes, laws, and customs of this realm, other than such as by and in the said act of parliament be expressed and foreprised, with a promise contained in the said last act of parliament that if hereafter upon any reasonable matter or cause it should appear to us by information or otherwise that the said city of Chester is not meet to be sanctuary nor a place of privilege and tuition for the said offenders and malefactors as been before remembered or for such like of their conditions, that then it should be lawful to us by our proclamation to extinct and determine the said sanctuary within the said city of Chester and clearly to discharge the same city thereof, and thereupon to appoint, ordain, and make another town or place to be sanctuary and a place of privilege and tuition for the said offenders and malefactors, anything in the said last act contained to the contrary notwithstanding.

And for that now it appeareth unto us by credible information that the said city of Westchester, which not only standeth near the borders of Wales by means whereof such offenders and malefactors might lightly for their safeguard and tuition pass and go from the said city unto the parts of Wales so that justice should not be had of the said offenders, but also that the said city is a port town near the sea and unto the same city great resort of merchants stranger from time to time, by means whereof such offenders and malefactors for their tuition and safeguard may by ship sail from the said city of Westchester unto the parts of Scotland, Ireland, and other outward parts, to the increase and comfort of such offenders and malefactors, and for other good causes and considerations as appearing concerning the same, we therefore clearly discharge and exonerate the said city of Westchester concerning the said sanctuary, privilege, and tuition there to be had and used as is expressed in the said last act, and will by these presents that the said city of Westchester shall be, upon proclamation, have of this our writing of like condition, estate, and quality forthwith, discharged of the said sanctuary and privilege as the said city was before the making of the said last statute; any thing, sentence, clause, or article in the said act contained to the contrary notwithstanding. And further will by these our letters, that from the said Feast of the Nativity of St. John Baptist next coming the town of Stafford within the county of Stafford among other towns and places shall be admitted, allowed, and taken to be a sanctuary and a place of privilege and tuition for term of life of all and singular offenders and malefactors of whatsoever quality, kind, or nature all and every the said offenses be, for the which said offenses and crimes the pains and punishment of death should ensue by the statutes, laws, and customs of this realm, other than such as by and in the said former act of parliament be expressed and foreprised.

And further by these presents will and ordain that the constables of the town of Manchester for the time being taking and associating with them 20 of the inhabitants of the same town by their discretions shall have the safe-conduction, leading, and bringing of all sanctuary men now or hereafter, before the said Feast of the Nativity of St. John Baptist next coming, being in the town of Manchester, to conduct, lead, and safe bring from the said town of Manchester to the said town of Stafford, there to remain as sanctuary men and to be delivered to the bailiffs or head officers of the said town of Stafford by indenture to be made between the foresaid constables and the said bailiffs or head officers of the said town of Stafford for the time being, in which indentures shall be comprised and specified the names of all such sanctuary persons as shall be so delivered and that the said sanctuary persons and every of them shall be in all places mean between Manchester and Stafford in the time of their said conduction, leading, and bringing from Manchester to Stafford, as they and every of them had been and remain sanctuary persons in Manchester aforesaid, and further we do by these presents clearly discharge the mayor, sheriffs, and commonalty of the said city of Westchester and their successors for the having and receiving of such sanctuary persons from Manchester after the said Feast of the Nativity of St. John Baptist now next coming.

213. Pricing Bows, Arrows, and Armor

[Westminster, 31 August 1542, 34 Henry VIII]

BM MS Harl 442, 146: date as above; writ to mayor and sheriffs of London; schedule as below. Steele 224. Text (MS): Harl

The King's most royal majesty, being informed that divers covetous persons having harness, artillery, and other habiliments for the war to sell, hold them at such unreasonable and excessive prices that his loving and obedient subjects cannot buy nor provide the same at reasonable and convenient prices to serve this majesty and the realm as the case shall require, and as by the laws, statutes, and customs of his highness' realm they are bounden to do; hath therefore made and ordained this his highness' present proclamation, by the advice and consent of his grace's council, and by the same hath taxed and set reasonable prices of bows, arrows, bills, harness, and other habiliments for the war as hereafter followeth: that is to say, first, every bow of the best sort at 3*s.* 4*d.* and not above; every bow of the second sort at 2*s.* 6*d.* and not above; every bow of the third sort at 2*s.* and not above; every shaft of livery arrows at 2*s.* and not above; every leather case at 6*d.* and not above; every girdle at 2*d.* and not above; every shaft of arrows of eight inch or nine inch the feather at 2*s.* 4*d.* and not above; every gross of bowstrings containing 12 dozen, at 3*s.* 4*d.* and not above; every demi-lance with curase, vambrace, polren, head-piece with a beaver at 45*s.* and not above; every demi-lance called a collincliff ready made and headed, at 2*s.* 8*d.* and not above; every arming sword for a horseman at 2*s.* 8*d.* and not above; every pair of gauntlets with joints at 2*s.* 8*d.* and not above; every almain rivet of the best sort at 7*s.* 6*d.* and not above; every almain rivet of the second sort at 6*s* 8*d.* and not above; every javelin of the best sort ungilt at 14*d.* and not above; every javelin of the second sort at 10*d.* and not above; every fighting bill ready helmed at 12*d.* and not above; every Flemish halberd of the best sort at 20*d.* and not above; every Flemish halberd of the second sort at 16*d.* and not above.

Wherefore his highness straightly chargeth and commandeth that every person and persons having any bows, arrows, harness, artillery, or other habiliments aforesaid, upon the reasonable request of any of his highness' loving subjects offering to buy the same, show it in their shops or other houses without concealing any part thereof by any fraud or covin, and for and at the reasonable prices aforesaid sell it to such as will buy the same, upon pain of imprisonment without bail or mainprize and to lose and forfeit £10 for every offense and default done or attempted by any person contrary to this present proclamation.

And also his majesty straightly chargeth and commandeth all and singular mayors, sheriffs, justices of peace, bailiffs, and other head ministers of cities, boroughs, and towns, that they upon every complaint or information given to them by any of his subjects minding to provide or buy any bows, arrows, bills, harness, artillery, or other habiliments aforesaid, that any person having the same or any part thereof to sell, will not show, utter, and sell the same at the prices aforesaid, shall not only attach such persons offending contrary to this present proclamation and commit them to ward, there to remain as is aforesaid, but also search their shops and houses where any such harness, artillery, or munition shall be, and view and sell the same to such of his highness' subjects as will buy it at the prices aforesaid, saving and keeping the money to the use and behoof of the owners thereof, not failing thus to do from time to time as the case shall require, upon pain of the King's majesty's most high displeasure, all which forfeitures to be levied of the lands, goods, and chattels of the offenders as often as the case shall require.

214. Dispensing with Lenten Fast from White Meats

[Westminster, 9 February 1543, 34 Henry VIII]

STC 7800 (UM 5,25,382), Antiq 2, 122: printed by T. Berthelet (London, 1543); schedule as in 177 above. TRS *2*, 57: warrant to pay printer 25*s*. for 600 copies delivered to Chancellor on 9 December. LJ 15, 14: date as above. Wilkins *3*, 867. Steele 226. Text: see 177

215. Regulating Thames Fishing

[ca. 15 March 1543, 34 Henry VIII]

LJ 15, 18*v:* date, based on neighboring entries, as above; schedule as below. Not in Steele. Text (MS): LJ

FORASMUCH as now of late all kinds of fish, as well salt as fresh, brought and conveyed unto our city of London to be sold, by reason of the greedy and covetous mind and appetite of the fishmongers and other of our subjects using and occupying the trade and course of buying and selling of the same, have been brought and enhanced to very great, high, and excessive prices, to the great grief and hindrance of all our loving subjects, as well the citizens and inhabitants within our said city as of our nobles and other repairing and resorting unto the same:

We therefore straightly charge and command that no person or persons using the said trade and course of buying and selling of fish be so hardy or so bold at any time hereafter, until our further pleasure shall be known therein to the contrary, to utter or sell any part or portion of the several kinds of fish hereafter specially mentioned and rehearsed at any higher or greater price or prices that they at this present by the mayor and aldermen of our said city, with the consent and advice of our council, are rated and assessed at;

And further that they and every of them truly and obediently at all and every time and times hereafter do observe, keep, and obey all and every price and prices by the said mayor and his successors, upon all and every other kind and sort of fish hereafter to be rated and set, upon pain of imprisonment and our high indignation and displeasure;

And further that they and every of them, upon pain of incurring of our like indignation and displeasure, do not only faithfully and truly bring forth and put to sale within our said city, in the open markets and places and at the days and times heretofore commonly accustomed for the same, all such kinds of salt fish and other fish as they or any of them now have in their hands and possession to the uttered and sold as is aforesaid, but also that they and every of them earnestly, studiously, and diligently apply and endeavor themselves from time to time to buy and provide all such sorts and kinds of fish, and as great plenty, store, and quantity thereof as they or any of them heretofore have used at any season [or] been accustomed to buy and meddle withal; so that we, our nobles, and loving subjects aforesaid may from henceforth be the more readily and at more easy and indifferent prices there served, provided, and sped of the same.

And further, where the mayor of our said city for the time being and his predecessors, as well by reason of divers and sundry grants of our right noble progenitor unto them made and by us confirmed as by virtue of divers and sundry acts[1] of parliament in that behalf heretofore established and made, have of long time had and enjoyed the conservancy of our river of Thames and of the fish, broad and fry, of the same river without interruption, contradiction, or impediment of us or of any of our true and faithful subjects, and also the punishment and just correction of all the fishermen within and upon the same river, and of all their unlawful and defective nets and other engines, until now of late that divers obstinate, forward, and evil-disposed persons, fishermen upon the said river, commonly using and occupying upon the same river very unlawful nets and other engines to the great destruction and consumption of the small fish and fry of the said river, have obstinately, stubbornly, and contemptuously neglected, refused, and utterly denied to obey or give place unto the said mayor and his predecessors and his and their deputies and ministers in their just and lawful administration and execution of the good, ancient, politic, and reasonable laws, acts, and ordinances heretofore made, devised, and provided for the conservancy, safeguard, maintenance, and increase of the said river, and of the fish and fry of the same, which is and will be to the most utter destruction, spoil, and decay of the small fish and fry of the said river, if good reformation be not shortly had in this behalf.

We therefore semblably straightly charge and command that from henceforth no manner of person or persons, of whatsoever condition, estate, or degree he or they be of, presume or be so bold either to use or occupy any such unlawful net or nets or other engines whatsoever upon the said river, or to impugn, deny, resist, or disobey the said mayor or his successors or his or their deputies or ministers at any time or times in making of their due search, stenting, and investigation for the said offenders and their said unlawful nets and other engines, and in doing and executing due punishment and correction upon the same, or in any other their doing and executing of their said office for and concerning the conservation of the said river and of the fish and fry of the same, according to the said grants and statutes, or in any manner of wise, or by any manner of color or means, at any time here-

1. 13 Edward I, c. 47 (Westminster II), 1285, *SR 1*, 94; 13 Richard II, st. 1, c. 19, 1389, *SR 2*, 67; 17 Richard II, c. 9, 1393, *SR 2*, 89; 2 Henry VI, c. 12, 1423, *SR 2*, 222.

after intermit or meddle with the execution or administration of any of the points or articles aforesaid, in derogation, let, or hindrance of the power, jurisdiction, and lawful authority of the said mayor and his successors, or of any his or their deputies or ministers, upon pain above remembered, and as they will further answer unto us at their uttermost perils;

And that this our proclamation shall be proclaimed not only in our said city of London, but also in as many other cities, towns, and places nigh unto the said river of Thames, as the said mayor and his successors shall think convenient in his or their discretions.

216. Establishing One Authorized Grammar

[London, before 25 March 1543, 34 Henry VIII]

STC 15,605, BM C.21.b.4, 2: printed by T. Berthelet (London, 1543); letters patent to all schoolmasters and grammar teachers; schedule as below. Reprinted in *The Vulgaria of John Stanbridge and the Vulgaria of Robert Whittinton* (ed. Beatrice White, Early English Text Society Publications, o.s. 187, London, Kegan Paul, 1932), xxxviii. Not in Steele. Text (*STC*): BM

HENRY VIII, by the grace of God King of England, France, and Ireland, defender of the faith, and of the Church of England and also of Ireland in earth the supreme head, to all schoolmasters and teachers of grammar within this his realm, greeting:

Among the manifold business and most weighty affairs appertaining to our regal authority and office, we forget not the tender babes and the youth of our realm, whose good education and godly bringing up is a great furniture to the same, and cause of much goodness.

And to the intent that hereafter they may the more readily and easily attain the rudiments of the Latin tongue without the great hindrance which heretofore hath been, through the diversity of grammars and teachings:

We will and command, and straightly charge, all you schoolmasters within this our realm and other our dominions, as ye intend to avoid our displeasure and have our favor, to teach and learn your scholars this *English Introduction* [1] here ensuing and the *Latin Grammar* [2] annexed to the same, and no other; which we have caused, for your ease and your scholars' speedy preferment, briefly and plainly to be compiled and set forth.

Fail not to apply your scholars in learning and godly education.

1. By William Lily, *STC* 15,605.
2. Ibid., *STC* 15,604.

217. Prohibiting Hawking

[St. James, 4 April 1543, 34 Henry VIII]

Antiq 2, 123: date, 4 April; schedule as in 211. Steele 227: date, St. James. Text: see 211

218. Pricing Sugar

[Westminster, 2 May 1543, 35 Henry VIII]

Antiq 2, 124: date, from marginal note, 2 May; schedule as below. TRS 2, 57: warrant to pay T. Berthelet, King's printer, 16*s.* 8*d.* for 200 copies delivered to Chancellor on 4 May. Steele 228: date, Westminster. Text (MS): Antiq

WHERE in the parliament holden at Westminster the 28th day of April in the 31st year of the most victorious reign of the King's royal majesty, and there continued unto the 28th day of June in the said year, one act[1] for proclamations to be made in this realm was ordained and established that the King's highness, with the advice of his honorable council named and expressed in the same act, or the most part of them, might set forth at all times his highness' proclamation under such penalties and pains and of such sort as to his majesty and his said most honorable council or the most part of them should seem necessary and requisite, and that such proclamations should be obeyed, observed, and kept as though they had been made by act of parliament for the time in them limited unless the King's majesty dispensed with them or any of them under his Great Seal, as by the said act amongst other things therein contained more plainly is mentioned and expressed.

The King's most royal majesty is credibly informed that albeit a great plenty and quantity of sugar is lately come to his port of his city of London to be sold, and also is remaining already in the hands of divers of the said city to sell, yet nevertheless by the greedy appetites and affections of such as have the same sugar, and by crafty conspiracies between them and other for their singular avail and lucre, the price thereof is enhanced far exceeding that which hath been accustomed in times past; for where within few years it hath been at 2*d.*, 3*d.*, and 4*d.* the pound, it is now brought to 9*d.* and 10*d.* the pound against all reason and equity, and to the great detriment of his highness' loving and obedient subjects having necessity to occupy the same for the maintenance of their hospitalities and families. And also sundry persons after they have bought such sugar at the first hand do new-cast again the same in mounds, mixing therewith other things perilous and unwholesome for man's body.

1. 31 Henry VIII, c. 8, 1539, *SR 3*, 726.

His majesty therefore, minding the reformation of the premises and to impedite and let such greedy appetites and affections as daily increase, to the hurt of his commonweal not only in this case but in all kinds of victuals, hath ordained and devised this his highness' proclamation, by authority of the said act, by the advice of the most part of his council named in the same, in manner and form following; that is to say, his highness straightly chargeth and commandeth by this present proclamation that no person or persons, being his natural subjects or strangers denizen, after three days next following the proclamation and publication of these presents according to the act above said, shall sell the best sugar above the price of 7*d.* the pound upon pain to lose and forfeit for every pound of sugar sold contrary to this present proclamation 3*s.* 4*d.*, and for every half pound 20*d.*, and so after the rate, and also to suffer imprisonment by the space of one month, the one moiety of which forfeiture to be to his majesty and the other moiety to such as will sue for the same by original writ, bill, plaint, or information in any of the King's courts, in which action or suit no wager of law shall be admitted nor any essoin or protection allowed.

And his majesty hath further ordained by these presents, by the advice aforesaid, that no person or persons shall (at any time after proclamation hereof made, as is aforesaid) alter and new-cast again any sugar into loaves or masses to be sold: upon pain to lose and forfeit all his goods and chattels and also suffer imprisonment at the King's will, the two parts of which forfeiture to be to the King's majesty's use and the third part thereof to be to such as will sue for the same as is aforesaid, in which action or suit no wager of law shall be admitted nor any essoin or protection allowed.

And his majesty signifieth to all and singular persons that his highness' intent is not that sugar should or ought always continue at the great price limited by this proclamation, but that as occasion shall serve so his majesty will raise and decrease and default the price of the same as shall stand with reason and equity and for the commonwealth of his realm.

219. Prohibiting Londoners from Approaching Court

[Hampton Court, 15 July 1543, 35 Henry VIII]

AC (Dasent *1*, 156): date, Oatlands, 18 July; order for proclamations against Londoners coming to court. ETR (E36/231/186): date as above; schedule as below. Steele 242. Text (MS): ETR

THE KING'S MAJESTY straightly chargeth and commandeth that no manner of person or persons, of what estate or degree they be of, inhabiting within the city of London or having their abode there, do presume to enter the gates of any of the houses wherein his majesty or the Queen's grace shall be present, upon pain of his highness' most grievous displeasure, nor that none of the King' servants, or Queen's, other than such as shall be appointed, nor no other man's servant, of what estate or degree soever they be of, shall depart from the court to the city of London, and from thence to resort to the court again, as they and every of them will avoid the King's majesty's like displeasure and further punishment at his highness' pleasure.

The King's highness, considering that peril oftentimes ensueth by occasion of infections and assemblies of much people, doth therefore straightly charge and command that no manner of person or persons inhabiting within the city of London or the suburbs of the same, not being household servants to his grace nor necessary persons for provision of his household, do presume to resort or come unto the court wheresoever his said highness shall please to be or be, until such time as his pleasure shall be to them further known for any manner of suit or other cause, whatsoever it be, upon pain of imprisonment and as they and every of them will avoid his displeasure.

220. Declaring War against France

[Terling, 2 August 1543, 35 Henry VIII]

STC 7801 (UM 5,25,383), Antiq 2, 125: printed by T. Berthelet (London, 1543); date as above; writ to mayor and sheriffs of London; schedule as below. LJ 15, 46*v:* schedule as below. Wriothesley *1,* 143: proclaimed in London on 3 August. Steele 243. Text (*STC*): Antiq

Forasmuch as by credible means it hath been declared to the King's majesty that the French King, omitting the duty and office of a good Christian prince (which is much to be lamented), hath not only by a long time and season aided the great Turk, common enemy to Christendom, and also by sundry ways and means encouraged, procured, and incited, and daily procureth the said Turk, to arraise and assemble great armies and forces of war to enter and invade the same, which daily the said Turk attempteth and putteth in execution, to the great trouble, perturbation, and molestation of all good Christian princes and their subjects, and to the peril and danger of the state of Christian religion and imminent destruction of the universal weal and quiet of all Christendom, if good and godly kings and princes, with the aid and assistance of all Christian people, should not speedily provide for the defense and relief of the same: but also the said French King, forgetting the great kindness, gratuitous and manyfold benefits exhibited and ministered to him by the King's most royal majesty, our sovereign lord, by sundry ways and means in his great and extreme necessity, hath by a long season unkindly withholden and withdrawn from the King's highness his yearly pension, contrary to his liege oath and promise made for the same. The arrest whereof, besides the perpetual payment, amounteth to great sums of money. And although the King's most royal majesty hath been by a long time in good hope and trust that the said French King with gentle and friendly admonitions (which hath not lacked) would not only have desisted from intelligence with the said Turk, but also paid and satisfied the said pension. Yet nevertheless his highness now perceiving that the said French King will not be induced by any gentle means to honesty and reason, but still persist and be obstinate against his liege fidelity, oath, and honor, most specially concerning the common cause of Christendom; and next weighing his majesty's just title to the crown of France and other dukedoms and dominions unjustly withholden by the said French King, for recompense whereof the said pension was granted: hath therefore entered into a most Christian and straight league and amity with his good brother and perpetual ally the Emperor's majesty, who, joined together as well for the causes aforesaid as for other good grounds and occasions touching their private affairs, have intimate war to the same French King, he first refusing to receive their heralds which were sent to him to offer honorable and reasonable conditions of peace, which conditions have also been declared to the French King's ambassador here resident, and no convenient nor reasonable answer made to the same; by reason whereof the Emperor's and King's majesties, being assuredly knit and constantly joined together, intend jointly to proceed in the wars against the said French King, and never to cease the same until he shall be enforced, not only to desist from the Turk and all his factions but also yield and render to either of them all such rights, things, and recompenses as to honor, reason, honesty, and equity shall appertain.

Wherefore like as the King's majesty our sovereign lord hath thought meet to notify the premises unto all and singular his most loving and obedient subjects, so his highness by virtue of this his majesty's proclamation doth declare the said French King to be his highness' enemy, giving license and authority to every his said subjects to use the said French King, and all those which depend upon him, to their most advantage and commodity, as his majesty's enemies, as hath in such like cases heretofore been used and accustomed.

221. Exempting Mariners from Military Service

[Terling, 25 August 1543, 35 Henry VIII]

AC (Dasent *1*, 23): date, Hampton Court, 25 August; order to Chancellor to proclaim. LJ 14, 342: date, 25 August; writ to mayor and sheriffs of London; proclaimed on 28 August; schedule as below. BM MS Harl 442, 148: date, Terling; writ to sheriff of Essex; schedule as below. Steele 244. Text (MS): LJ

We will and command you that you nor any of you which have received or hereafter shall receive any our letters to retain or press any person to serve us in our affairs of war, shall not in any wise retain or press any shipman or mariner, but suffer them to remain without molestations or trouble to serve us when war shall otherwise dispose them at our pleasure as the case shall require; not failing thus to do as you will answer to the contrary at your uttermost perils; anything contained in our letters to you directed, or hereafter to be directed, to the contrary hereof notwithstanding.

222. Prohibiting Hawking or Hunting

[Woodstock, September 1543, 35 Henry VIII]

ETR (E36/231/187): date, Woodstock; schedule as below. Steele 245: date, September. Text (MS): ETR

The King's royal majesty straightly chargeth and commandeth that no manner of person or persons of what estate or degree soever he or they be of, do from henceforth hawk neither pheasant nor partridge, nor hunt the hare within the space of four miles foragainst of any of the King's castles, lands, and manors, his majesty being present or absent in any of the same, during the time of his majesty's progress, upon pain of his high and grievous displeasure.

223. Adjourning Michaelmas Term

[Walden, 28 October 1543, 35 Henry VIII]

BM MS Harl 442, 152: date as above; writ to sheriff of Herts; schedule as below. Steele 246. Text (MS): Harl

Forasmuch as the city of London, where the term hath been of long time accustomed to be kept, is sore infected with the pestilence, by occasion whereof the King's majesty, trusting the same would have ceased, did therefore in avoiding of the peril of his subjects that would have resorted thither, adjourn this term of St. Michael from the *utas* thereof unto *crastino,* being in good hope that the said plague by that time should have ceased; and now being credibly informed that the same still continueth; and if great confluence of people should resort thither it might be occasion the rather to increase than diminish; therefore, minding the preservation of his loving subjects from the peril and danger of infection, is resolved and determined to adjourn the said term of St. Michael from the city of Westminster unto the town of St. Albans, there to begin *crastino* St. Martin next coming, which his majesty notifieth to all and singular his loving subjects by this his highness' proclamation, willing and commanding them to observe and keep their assemblies and appearances in his highness' courts there to be holden in like manner, form, and condition as they would, should, or ought to have done if the said term and courts had been holden and kept at Westminster, as they will answer at their perils.

224. Prohibiting Unlicensed Imports from France

[Westminster, 18 December 1543, 35 Henry VIII]

STC 7802 (UM 26,152,384), Antiq 2, 128: printed by T. Berthelet (London, 1543): date, 18 December; schedule as below. Steele 247: date, Westminster. Text (*STC*): Antiq

THE KING'S MOST ROYAL MAJESTY being informed that notwithstanding there is open war proclaimed and manifestly known between his highness and the French King, upon sundry occasions only ministered on the part of the same French King, yet nevertheless divers of his majesty's subjects and others do daily transport, convey, and bring into this his highness' realm of England and other his majesty's dominions, out of the realm of France and other the French King's countries, divers and sundry kinds of wares and merchandises to sell, exchange, barter, and utter, whereby the said French King and his subjects and adherents, being the King's majesty's enemies, have taken and daily take great commodities, benefits, profits, and advantages, and be thereby enriched and encouraged to maintain their wrongful and unjust wars, annoyances, attempts, and malicious purposes moved by them and their occasion against oath, honor, truth, and all honesty.

For reformation whereof the King's said majesty straightly chargeth and commandeth all and singular his loving subjects and all other persons as well denizens as strangers, of whatsoever estate, degree, or condition soever they be, that they nor any of them shall not at any time after 14 days now next ensuing after this present proclamation proclaimed, by any manner of means convey, transport, or bring into this realm or in any other his highness' dominions, to be sold, exchanged, bartered, given or by any other ways or means uttered, any manner of wares, merchandise, or other commodities, of what name, nature, kind, or quality soever they be of, being made, growing, or increased within the said realm of France or any other the French King's dominions, without special license under his Great Seal to be obtained of the King's highness for the same, upon pain that every such person, bringing into this realm any such wares, merchandises, or commodities contrary to the form of this his majesty's proclamation as is aforesaid, to forfeit and lose the same wares, merchandises, and commodities or the value of them, and to suffer punishment by imprisonment or otherwise at his highness' pleasure.

225. Providing Penalties for Export of Grain

[Walden, 7 January 1544, 35 Henry VIII]

AC (HM Ellesmere 4361): date, Star Chamber, 15 June; Edward Baker bound for maintenance in a case of shipping corn against the King's proclamation, and the said corn and hay forfeited. BM MS Harl 442, 153: date as above; writ unspecified; schedule as below. Steele 248. Text (MS): Harl

Forasmuch as [in] the necessary affairs of this realm there must be presently made furniture of beer, wheat, malt, oats, beans, butter, and cheese, the want and lack whereof may be great hindrance, loss, and detriment to such exploits and enterprises as for defense of the King's majesty's subjects and annoyance of his grace's ancient enemies be thought requisite:

The King's majesty therefore straightly chargeth and commandeth that all other provisions of beer, wheat, malt, oats, beans, butter, and cheese made or to be made by virtue of special licenses or otherwise to be conveyed beyond the seas into outward parts be stayed, and that from henceforth none shall carry or transport or be suffered to pass with any of the said grains or victuals until such time as the necessary furniture aforesaid be sufficiently made and satisfied as appertaineth;

Upon pain that every person offending this present proclamation shall lose and forfeit the corn and victuals transported or carried contrary to the form hereof, and also suffer imprisonment and make fine at the King's pleasure, and that every customer, comptroller, and searcher or their deputies suffering the same shall lose and forfeit £100 and also have imprisonment at the King's majesty's pleasure.

226. Suspending Statute on Fuel

[Westminster, 11 February 1544, 35 Henry VIII]

Antiq 2, 130: date, 11 February; writ, crossed through, to mayor and sheriffs of London; schedule as below. Steele 250: date, Westminster. Text (MS): Antiq

WHERE in the session of this present parliament holden upon prorogation at Westminster the 22nd day of January in the 34th year of the King's majesty's reign one act[1] was made and established in the said session that no person from the Feast of the Purification of Our Lady last past should bargain, sell, bring, or convey, to be uttered or sold in the city of London or elsewhere within this realm, nor to Calais, nor to the marches of the same, any coals, fagots, billets, or talwood but of the measures, quantities, lengths, and assizes mentioned in the said act, upon certain pains and forfeitures specified in the same as by the same act amongst other things more at large appeareth.

Forasmuch as the King's most royal majesty is credibly informed that divers and sundry persons which have been accustomed to bring to his highness' said city of London, coals, fagots, billets, and talwood have already made and provided great quantity of the said coals, fagots, billets, and talwood long before the Feast of Christmas last past and intended to have brought and sold the same in the said city for relief thereof before the said Feast of the Purification of Our Lady last past, as they might have done without danger of the said act, but that they were interrupted to transport and convey the same to the said city by water by occasion of such great continual frosts and ice as hath happened before the said Feast of Our Lady, and there is not at this present already coals, fagots, billets, and talwood made and provided of the assize limited in the said act for relief of the said city, so that in case they should not be permitted by the King's excellent goodness to sell the said coals, fagots, billets, and talwood in the said city which is already provided for that purpose, that then the King's loving subjects, the citizens and other inhabitants of the said city, should lack wood for their necessary relief.

In consideration whereof, the King's highness of his most excellent goodness, for the comfort and relief of the said city, is pleased and contented and by this his present proclamation giveth free liberty and license to all and singular his loving subjects to sell, bargain, transport, and convey to his said city of London, between the 11th day of February in the 35th year of his highness' reign, being the day of this his highness' proclamation, and the first day of March next coming, all such coals, fagots, billets, and talwood

1. 34 & 35 Henry VIII, c. 3, 1542, *SR 3*, 899.

which hath been made before the said Feast of the Purification of Our Lady last past; albeit the same or any part thereof be not of the quantity, length, and assize mentioned and comprised in the said act, without any loss, penalty, or danger, anything in the same act to the contrary of this present proclamation notwithstanding; signifying to all and singular his loving subjects that from and after the said first day of March the said act shall be duly and inviolably performed, kept and obeyed upon the pains specified in the same without any further or other dispensation or permission to the contrary thereof in any behalf.

227. Ordering Alien French to Leave Realm

[Westminster, 16 May 1544, 36 Henry VIII]

STC 7804 (UM 2,10,388), Antiq 2, 131: printed by T. Berthelet (London, 1544); date, 16 May; schedule as below. Steele 251: date, Westminster. Text (*STC*): Antiq

THE KING'S MOST ROYAL MAJESTY being informed that where by a statute [1] made in the parliament holden at Westminster in the 32nd year of his most noble reign it was ordained and enacted, amongst other things, that such of his subjects as be rehearsed in the same may retain and keep in their service certain number of strangers; which statute extendeth only to strangers born in such realms, dominions, and countries as be in league and amity with his highness.

Divers of his grace's said subjects, notwithstanding his proclamations heretofore made touching the wars and hostility at this time moved between his majesty and the French King,[2] by reason whereof all Frenchmen not being denizens [3] may and ought to be reputed and taken for his grace's enemies, the retaining and nourishing of whom in this case welleth no less then to the nourishing and maintenance of his majesty's enemies, do still keep and entertain great multitudes of Frenchmen not being denizens which for many respects and considerations were meet to be expelled and avoided out of this realm.

His majesty therefore, by the advice of his most honorable council, straightly chargeth and commandeth that all manner of persons born under the French King's obeisance (not being denizens) shall depart and go out of this his highness' realm of England within 20 days next after this present proclamation made; except such as in the meantime shall

1. 32 Henry VIII, c. 16, 1540, *SR 3*, 765.
2. See 220.
3. See 195, 199.

upon special suit to his highness be made denizens upon pain that every one of them doing contrary to this proclamation shall be forthwith apprehended, and either sent to his grace's galleys, there to be ordered as shall appertain, or to be otherwise used as the case shall require.

Furthermore his highness, considering the danger of his laws, which his loving and obedient subjects may incur by entertaining of any Frenchman not being denizen during the time of the wars between his majesty and the French King, straightly chargeth and commandeth all and singular his subjects of this his realm of England, that they and every of them within 20 days next after this his majesty's proclamation shall be made and published, shall expel and put out from their service, families, and wages, all manner of Frenchmen not being denizens, and in no wise, or by any color, respect, or means, shall after the said 20 days next after this present proclamation, retain, succor, aid, comfort, or maintain within this his highness' said realm of England any of the said Frenchmen; upon pain that every one of them doing or attempting contrary to this present proclamation, or any part thereof, shall be accompted, taken, accepted, and reputed as an aider, fautour and succorer of the King's enemies, and shall have and suffer such punishment for the same as the laws of this realm do in such cases appoint and determine accordingly.

228. Revaluing Gold, Announcing New Coinage

[16 May 1544, 36 Henry VIII]

L&P 19, 513: date, 16 May. Antiq 2, 118: writ, unspecified; schedule as below. Grey Friars 47: proclaimed in London on 16 May. Schanz *2*, 636. Steele 252. Text (MS): Antiq

Forasmuch as now of late in outward parts beyond the sea, as well in Flanders as in France, the price of money and gold, not only coined in those countries but also gold of the King our sovereign lord's coin of this realm, is so enhanced in the valuation thereof that not only strange golds, as crowns and ducats, but also the gold of this realm, as nobles, half-nobles, and royals, by merchants as well strangers resorting hither as the King's subjects repairing into those parts, for the great gain and lucre that they find thereby, daily be transported and carried out of this realm to the no little impoverishing thereof, and finally to the total exhausting and drawing out of all the coins out of the same, unless speedy remedy be provided in that behalf;

And albeit the King our sovereign lord hath given straight charge and commandment to all and singular his customers, comptrollers, and guardians of his ports to put all such good acts and statutes in execution as heretofore have been made for conserving of the King's coin within this his realm, yet nevertheless for the great gain and advantage thereof rising by reason of this high price of money beyond the sea, the King's coin is daily by secret means (such as cannot be espied nor deprehended) still carried over:

For these causes the King our sovereign lord, tendering above all things the wealth and enriching of this his realm and people, and willing to provide remedy herein, and that gold and coin may remain and be plenteously brought into the same and not carried out into outward parts as of long season to the great detriment and impoverishing of his said realm, the same hath been for the remedying whereof there can be none other means and ways studied and devised, but only a convenient enhancement of the values of gold and silver in this realm whereby the same may countervalue the values and rates of the same in outward parts, hath therefore, by the advice of his council, resolved that the ounce of fine gold of 24 carats shall be from henceforth of the value of 48*s.* of lawful money of this realm, and the ounce of the finest sterling silver shall be of the value of 4*s.* of the said lawful money of this realm of England.

And to the intent money and coin may be the more plentiful in this realm, his majesty therefore hath caused a piece of gold to be newly made which his highness will shall be called the sovereign, and shall be current for 20*s.* of the lawful money of this realm. Item, an half-sovereign which his majesty will shall be current for 10*s.* Item, his majesty will that the royal of gold, being weight, shall from henceforth be of the value of 12*s.* Item, that the angel, being weight, shall be current for 8*s.*, the half-angel for 4*s.*, and the quarter-angel, being also newly made, for 2*s.* And his majesty hath likewise caused to be newly made certain pieces of silver which his pleasure is shall be current within this his grace's realm after the rates hereafter specified; that is to say a piece called a teston which shall be current for 12*d.* Item, a groat with a whole face which shall be current for 4*d.*, and half-groat of the same stamp which shall be current for 2*d.*

And his majesty is further pleased that whosoever will bring unto his mint in the Tower of London any gold coined or uncoined of the fineness aforesaid shall receive for the ounce of the same 48*s.*, and for the ounce of silver of the fineness aforesaid 4*s.*, and if the gold or silver so brought thither be not found of the just fineness aforesaid, the said bringers to allow for the lack thereof, like as they shall be allowed for the betterness thereof as the goodness of the same shall require.

And moreover the King's highness straightly chargeth and commandeth that from henceforth all manner groats, pence, half-pence and farthings of this coin having course and being current within this his said realm, not clipped nor fully broken, albeit they shall be much cracked, to be taken, received, and paid throughout his said realm without any manner refusal or denial.

Wherefore his highness straightly chargeth and expressly commandeth all mayors, justices of peace, sheriffs, bailiffs, constables, and other his faithful officers and subjects that if any person or persons of what estate, degree, or condition he or they be, refuse or deny to take or receive the said moneys of gold, being weight, or any of the moneys of silver before expressed or now current in this realm, be it for merchandises, victuals, change or rechange, or other cause whatsoever, forthwith to take and arrest the same person or persons so making refusal or denial and to put him or them in ward and prison, there to remain and further to be punished at the King's pleasure. Provided always that all such sums of money as were due to the King's majesty or to any other person before the first day of this present month of May shall be paid after *7s. 6d.* the angel, and so ratably; anything in this present proclamation to the contrary notwithstanding.

229. Suppressing Publication of Military Rumors

[Westminster, 18 May 1544, 36 Henry VIII]

Antiq 2, 132: date as above; writ to mayor and sheriffs of London; schedule as below. Steele 253. Text (MS): Antiq

THE KING'S MOST EXCELLENT MAJESTY, understanding that certain light persons, not regarding what they might report, write, or set forth, have caused to be imprinted and divulged certain news of the prosperous success of the King's majesty's army in Scotland; wherein although the effect of the victory be indeed true, yet the circumstances in divers points be in some part overslenderly, in some part untruly and amiss, reported: his highness therefore, not content to have any such matters of so great importance set forth to the slander of his captains and ministers, nor to be otherwise reported than the truth, straightly chargeth and commandeth all manner of persons into whose hands any of the said printed books be come, immediately after they shall hear of this proclamation, to bring the same books to the lord mayor of London or to the recorder or some of the aldermen of the same to the intent they may suppress and burn them, upon pain that every person keeping any of the said books 24 hours after the making of this proclamation shall suffer imprisonment of his body and be further punished at the King's majesty's will and pleasure.

230. Pricing Wines

[Westminster, 20 May 1544, 36 Henry VIII]

BM MS Harl 442, 156: date, 20 May; schedule as below. Steele 254: date, Westminster. Text (MS): Harl

WHEREAS it is ordained and provided by statute [1] that the prices of Gascon and French wines should be limited and declared by the Lord Chancellor of England, Lord Treasurer of England, Lord President of the King's most honorable council, Lord Privy Seal, and other the councilors of our said sovereign lord specified and declared in the said statute, as by the same statute made and established in the parliament begun and holden at Westminster the third day of November in the 21st year of the King's most gracious reign, and continued by divers prorogations, most plainly appeareth.

Forasmuch as the said lord and councilors, in execution of the said act, have by their deliberate advice taxed, limited, assigned, and appointed the prices of Gascon and French wines to be sold within this his realm; that is to say, every tun of the best Gascon wine to be sold after the price and rate of £8 sterling the tun and not above; and every tun of the best French wines to be sold after the rate of £6 sterling the tun and not above; and every pipe, hogshead, puncheon, tierce, and other vessel of the same several wines to be sold for their quantities after and according to the same rates and not above; and for small and thin wines to be sold under the said rates as the buyers and sellers thereof can agree.

The King's most royal majesty therefore straightly chargeth and commandeth all and singular his subjects and others putting any manner Gascon or French wines to sale within this his realm, that they nor any of them in any manner of wise by any craft, covin, or private agreement shall sell any Gascon or French wines otherwise than is above limited upon pain to forfeit and pay such penalties as be contained and expressed in the same act.

And moreover his high pleasure and commandment also is that all and singular mayors, sheriffs, bailiffs, constables, and other officers to whom it appertaineth, that they and every of them with diligence cause and see that this his proclamation be put in due execution after the tenor of the same, and also according to another act [2] of parliament established in the parliament above rehearsed against such as will refuse to sell their wines at prices taxed as is aforesaid as they will answer at their uttermost perils.

1. 23 Henry VIII, c. 7, 1531, *SR 3*, 374.
2. 24 Henry VIII, c. 6, 1532, *SR 3*, 422.

231. Pricing Meats

[Westminster, 21 May 1544, 36 Henry VIII]

STC 7805 (UM 2,10,389), Antiq 2, 134: printed by T. Berthelet (London, 1544); date, 21 May; schedule as below. See 232. Steele 255: date, Westminster. Text (*STC*): Antiq

Forasmuch as it is come to the knowledge of our sovereign lord the King that butchers and other victualers, having more respect to their own private lucre and advantage than the commonwealth of this his highness' realm, have raised the prices of flesh, as of beeves, muttons, veals, and other kind of poultry and victuals, to such excessive and high prices that his loving subjects cannot gain with their labors and salary sufficient to pay for their convenient victuals and sustenance unless that speedy remedy be provided in that behalf.

His highness therefore, by the advice of his most honorable council, and by the authority of the act [1] of parliament made in the 31st year of his majesty's reign, straightly chargeth and commandeth that all and every the said butchers and victualers, selling flesh by retail as well within the city of London and the suburbs of the same as in all other places within this his realm of England, as well within franchises and liberties as without, shall from and after 14 days next ensuing this present proclamation published and proclaimed, according to the said statute, sell the flesh of beef, mutton, veal, pork, and lamb, being good and wholesome for man's body, by retail by weight, not above the prices and rates hereafter ensuing; that is to say, between the 15th day of June and the feast of the birth of our Lord God yearly, every pound of beef to be sold not above the price of ⅝*d.* the pound; every pound of mutton not above the price of 1*d.* the pound; and every pound of veal not above the price of 1*d.* the pound. And that the flesh of beeves, muttons, and veals to be sold between the said feast of the birth of our Lord God and the said 15th day of June not above the prices and rates hereafter following: that is to say, the pound of beef to be sold not above ¾*d.* the pound; the pound of mutton not above 1*d.* the pound; and every pound of veal not above ⅞*d.* the pound. And furthermore that the flesh of lamb and pork shall be sold at all times in the year not above the prices and rates hereafter following: that is to say, the best lamb to be sold not above the price of 2*s.*; the second lamb not above the price of 20*d.*; and the meanest lamb not above the price of 16*d.*; and the half and quarters of every such lambs to be sold not above the rates of the said prices of lambs. And also the flesh of pork to be sold by retail or otherwise not above the price of ¾*d.* the pound.

1. 31 Henry VIII, c. 8, 1539, *SR 3*, 726.

And furthermore his highness, by the same authority, straightly chargeth and commandeth all and singular his subjects, inhabiting within the cities of London and Westminster, and in the suburbs of the same, and in the borough of Southwark, being free men of the said cities and borough, or of any of them, to sell all manner of wild fowl and poultry wares not above the rates and prices hereafter ensuing: that is to say, the best swan not above the price of 5*s.;* the best crane, bustard, or stork not above the price of 4*s.;* hernshaws, shovelers, and bitterns of the best not above the price of 18*d.* the piece; peacock old, the best, not above the price of 20*d.;* peachickens the best, not above the price of 14*d.* the piece; the capon of Greece of the best, not above the price of 20*d.;* capon of Kent, otherwise called boiling capon, of the best, not above the price of 8*d.;* capon good, not above the price of 14*d.;* hen of Greece the best, not above the price of 7*d.;* brew and egret of the best, not above the price of 12*d.* the piece; bitterns of the best, not above the price of 12*d.* the piece; gulls of the best, not above the price of 12*d.* the piece; green geese fat, sold between Easter and Midsummer, not above the price of 7*d.* the piece; geese great, sold between Midsummer and Shrovetide, of the best, not above the price of 8*d.* the piece; godwits fat, not above the price of 12*d.* the piece; a dozen dotterels of the best, not above the price of 3*s.* 4*d.* the dozen; quails of the best, the dozen, not above 4*s.;* sparrows the dozen, not above 3*d.* the dozen; pigeons of the best, not above 8*d.* the dozen; rabbits, suckers fat, not above 18*d.* the dozen; conies between Easter and Allhallowtide, the best, not above 2*s.* the dozen; winter conies between Allhallowtide and Shrovetide, not above 2*s.* 6*d.* the dozen; mallard, of the best, not above 4*d.* the mallard; teals of the best, not above 2*d.* the teal; widgeons fat, not above 3*s.* the dozen; woodcocks of the best, not above 4*d.* the piece; plovers green, of the best, not above 3*s.* the dozen; bastard plovers, fat, not above 2*s.* 6*d.* the dozen; martlets of the best, not above 18*d.* the dozen; hen snites of the best, not above 18*d.* the dozen; larks of the best, not above 6*d.* the dozen; buntings of the best, not above 4*d.* the dozen; great birds of the best, not above 6*d.* the dozen; eggs from Easter to Michaelmas, not above 16*d.* the hundred; eggs from Michaelmas till Easter, not above 20*d.* the hundred; butter, sweet, between Easter and the Feast of All Saints, not above 2*d.* the pound; butter, sweet, from the Feast of All Saints till Easter, not above 3*d.* the pound.

And furthermore his highness straightly chargeth and commandeth by the same authority that no foreign or foreigners sell or cause to be sold within the markets of Leaden Hall, Cheapside, and Newgate market, or any of them, or elsewhere within the said city of London and suburbs of the same, after the time of the open markets finished and ended, any of the poultry, wares, and victuals hereunder mentioned above such rates and prices as be hereafter set, rated, and assessed of and upon the same; that is to say, the mean swan 3*s.;* the best swan 4*s.;* the mean crane 2*s.* 4*d.;* the best crane 3*s.*; the mean bustard 2*s.*; the best bustard 2*s.* 8*d.*; the best hern, bittern, or shoveler 14*d.*; the mean curlew 6*d.*; the best curlew 8*d.*; the mean woodcock 2½*d.*; the best woodcock 3*d.*; the best teal, green plover, or grey 2*d.*; the lapwing 1½*d.*; the best wild mallard 4*d.*; the best wild duck 3*d.*; the best dozen larks 5*d.*; the mean dozen larks 3*d.*; the best dozen snites 16*d.*; the mean dozen snites 12*d.*; the mean dozen great birds 4*d.*; the best dozen great birds 6*d.*; the mean cony 2*d.*; the cony, the kidney half covered with fat 2½*d.*; the best cony 3*d.*; the mean dozen chickens 14*d.*; the best dozen chickens 18*d.*; the dozen lean quails 2*s.*; the dozen best quails 4*s.*; the mean goose 5*d.*; the best goose 7*d.*; the mean dozen pigeons 6*d.*; the best dozen pigeons 8*d.*; the boiling capon 6*d.*; the mean roasting capon 10*d.*; the best roasting capon of Greece 16*d.*; the best pig 6*d.*; the mean hen 3*d.*; and the best hen 5*d.*

And furthermore the King's most royal majesty, by the advice of his said council, ordaineth and establisheth by the authority aforesaid, that every person, of what estate, degree, or condition soever he be, the which at any time after the end of 14 days next ensuing the publishing of this present proclamation, shall sell any part or parcel of the flesh or fowl aforesaid above the rates and prices above rated and expressed, contrary to the tenor of this present proclamation, shall lose and forfeit for every time so doing and offending £10 sterling, the one moiety whereof shall be to the King's majesty, and the other moiety to the party that will sue for the same by information, bill, plaint, action of debt, or otherwise in any of the King's Courts of his Exchequer, King's Bench, or Common Pleas or else before such of the King's most honorable council, as be appointed to hear and determine the same by authority of the said act; in which suits none essoin or protection shall be allowed nor wager of law received or admitted for the defendant.

And also the King's most royal majesty straightly chargeth and commandeth all mayors, sheriffs, justices of peace, bailiffs, constables, and all other his officers and faithful subjects, that they and every of them, without favor, dread, affection, or corruption, shall put their effectual endeavors for the due execution of this his highness' proclamation, and for the punishment of the offenders thereof, as they will answer to his grace for the same at their uttermost perils, and will avoid the King's most high displeasure and indignation.

Provided always that where the said flesh of beeves, muttons, veals, porks, and lambs, within any parts or counties of this realm, be uttered and sold, by retail or otherwise, better cheap or after less prices than in this present proclamation is limited and expressed, that they shall sell the same at such like prices and after such rate as they do and have used to do before the making of this proclamation; any thing or things in this proclamation had or made to the contrary notwithstanding.

232. Pricing Meats

[Westminster, 22 May 1544, 36 Henry VIII]

BM MS Harl 442, 157: date, 22 May; schedule as in 230 (omitting section on fowl). Steele 256: date, Westminster. Text (MS): Harl

FORASMUCH as it is come to the knowledge of our sovereign lord the King that butchers and other victualers, having more respect to their own private lucre and advantage than the commonwealth of this his highness' realm, have raised the prices of flesh as of beeves, muttons, veals, and porks to such excessive and high prices that his loving subjects cannot gain with their labors and salary sufficient to pay for their convenient victuals and sustenance, unless that speedy remedy be provided in that behalf.

His highness therefore, by the advice of his most honorable council, and by the authority of the act[1] of parliament made in the 31st year of his majesty's reign, straightly chargeth and commandeth that all and every the said butchers and victualers selling flesh by retail, as well within the city of London and the suburbs of the same as in all other places within this his realm of England, as well within the franchises and liberties as without, shall from and after 14 days next ensuing this present proclamation published and proclaimed, according to the said statute, sell the flesh of beef, mutton, veal, and pork, being good and wholesome for man's body, by retail by weight, not above the prices and rates hereafter ensuing; that is to say, between the 15th day of June and the feast of the birth of our Lord God yearly, every pound of beef to be sold not above the price of ¾*d.* the pound; every pound of mutton not above the price of 1*d.* the pound; and every pound of veal not above the price of 1*d.* the pound. And that the flesh of beeves, muttons, and veals to be sold between the said feast of the birth of our Lord God and the said 15th day of June not above the prices and rates hereafter following; that is to say, the pound of beef to be sold not above ¾*d.* the pound; the pound of mutton not above 1*d.* the pound; and every pound of veal not above ⅞*d.* the pound; and also the flesh of pork to be sold by retail or otherwise not above the price of ¾*d.* the pound.

And furthermore the King's most royal majesty, by the advice of his said council, ordaineth and establisheth by the authority aforesaid, that every person of what estate, degree, or condition soever he be, the which at any time after the end of 14 days next ensuing the publishing of this present proclamation, shall sell any part or parcel of the flesh aforesaid above the rates and prices above rated and expressed contrary to the tenor of this present proclamation, shall lose and forfeit for every time so doing

1. 31 Henry VIII, c. 8, 1539, *SR 3*, 726.

and offending £10 sterling, the one moiety whereof shall be to the King's majesty and the other moiety to the party that will sue for the same by information, bill, plaint, action of debt, or otherwise in any of the King's Courts of Exchequer, King's Bench, or Common Pleas, or else before such of the King's most honorable council as be appointed to hear and determine the same by authority of the said act, in which suits none essoin or protection shall be allowed nor wager of law received or admitted for the defendant.

And also the King's most royal majesty straightly chargeth and commandeth all mayors, sheriffs, justices of peace, bailiffs, constables, and all other his officers and faithful subjects, that they and every of them without favor, dread, affection, or corruption shall put their effectual endeavors for the due execution of this his highness' proclamation and for the punishment of the offenders thereof as they will answer to his grace for the same at their uttermost perils, and will avoid the King's most high displeasure and indignation. Provided always that where the said flesh of beeves, muttons, veals, and porks within any parts or counties of this realm, be uttered and sold, by retail or otherwise, better cheap or after less prices than in this present proclamation is limited and expressed, that they shall sell the same at such like prices and after such rate as they do and have used to do before the making of this proclamation; anything or things in this proclamation had or made to the contrary notwithstanding.

233. Ordering Alien French to Register

[Westminster, 2 June 1544, 36 Henry VIII]

BM MS Harl 442, 160: date as above; writ to mayor and sheriffs of London; schedule as below. Schanz 2, 609. Steele 257. Text (MS): Harl

WHERE the King's most royal majesty hath of late published and declared by his proclamation [1] that all Frenchmen not being denizens should within 20 days next after the said proclamation proclaimed avoid this his highness' realm of England, upon pain that every one of them doing contrary to the said proclamation should be forthwith apprehended and either sent to his highness' galleys or otherwise punished; and further that all and singular his subjects having or keeping any of the said Frenchmen, not being denizens, in their families or services, should within the said 20 days next after the said proclamation [be] published and made, expel and put out the said Frenchmen from their families and not retain, succor, or maintain them or any of them, upon pains that every one of them doing or attempting the contrary should be arrested, taken, and reputed as an aider, favorer, and

1. See 227.

succorer of his highness' enemies; except such as in the meantime should upon special suit made to his grace be made denizen, as by the same proclamation more plainly appeareth:

Forasmuch as divers and many of the said Frenchmen since the time of the said proclamation made and published have made humble suit to his majesty to be denizens, and have by his highness' commandment entered their names for that purpose before the Lord Chancellor of England, his majesty therefore is contented and pleased that, as well all the said Frenchmen which have so already entered their names as all others of that nation which shall enter their names within six days next after the publishing of this proclamation, shall remain and abide within this his highness' realm without any punishment, danger, or forfeiture, till his majesty shall determine his pleasure how many it shall please him to enfranchise and make denizens, and how many shall avoid according to the said former proclamation made and published in that behalf.

And his highness is further pleased and granteth that none of his subjects keeping or retaining any of the said strangers in their families or services which be or shall be entered in form aforesaid shall incur any penalty, danger, or forfeiture for the same till his majesty's said pleasure shall be eftsoons expressed, declared, and published in manner and form before expressed; willing and commanding nevertheless all other Frenchmen not entered or to be entered, as is above specified, to avoid the realm according to the former proclamation, as they and their keepers, aiders, and succorers will avoid the pains mentioned in the same.

234. Ordering All French to Become Denizens or Leave the Realm

[Westminster, 19 July 1544, 36 Henry VIII]

BM MS Harl 442, 161: by the Queen Regent; date as above; writ to mayor and sheriffs of London; schedule as below. Schanz 2, 610. Steele 258. Text (MS): Harl

WHERE the King's most royal majesty hath of late published and declared by his proclamation[1] that all Frenchmen not being denizens which hath entered their names before the Lord Chancellor of England to the intent to be made denizens should remain, dwell, and abide within this his highness' realm without any punishment, danger, or forfeiture to them or any of them, or to any man keeping them in his house or company, unto such time as his grace's determinate pleasure were further known and declared

1. See 227, 233.

in that behalf; forasmuch as at this present his majesty hath now determined his pleasure how many of the said Frenchmen so entered shall be made denizens and signed a roll with his most gracious hand containing the names of the same:

His highness therefore straightly chargeth and commandeth by this his present proclamation that all Frenchmen and others whose names be entered before the said Lord Chancellor of England to be made denizens as is aforesaid, eftsoons repair to the house of the said Lord Chancellor, there to know whether they be in the said roll or no, and that all such as his highness is pleased shall be denizens and be in the said roll signed as aforesaid shall procure and sue out their letters patent for the same in due form to be made under his majesty's Great Seal before the first day of September next coming. And all those Frenchmen and others that be not in the roll aforesaid signed with his majesty's hand for this purpose, and all such as being in the same as shall not procure or sue out their letters patent of denizen as before specified before the said first day of September next coming, shall forthwith avoid this his highness' realm according to his highness' former proclamation upon the pains and penalties contained and expressed in the same.

235. Pricing Armor

[Hampton Court, 18 August 1544, 36 Henry VIII]

BM MS Harl 442, 162: by the Queen Regent; date as above; writ to mayor and sheriffs of London; schedule as below. Steele 259. Text (MS): Harl

FORASMUCH as the King's most royal majesty hath of late sent forth his several commissions of justices into all parts of this his realm of England for mustering and levying of his loving, faithful, and obedient subjects, a great number whereof be charged by virtue of the same to provide them harness for the defense of themselves and of the realm at days by the commissioners for that purpose appointed; his highness understanding that harness hath of late days been sold at unreasonable and excessive prices, and minding to have now such a certain price set upon the same as shall be reasonable for all his good subjects, as well the buyers as the sellers of the same, hath therefore ordained and determined by this his highness' present proclamation, made by the advice and consent of his grace's most honorable council, that no manner of person or persons, having any almain rivets to sell, shall sell any pair of the same of the best sort with all the furniture thereof above the price of 9*s.* 6*d.* of the lawful money of England upon pain of imprisonment without bail or mainprize and to lose and forfeit £5 sterling for every pair sold contrary to this his highness' proclamation. And his highness further straightly chargeth and commandeth that every person and persons having any such almain rivets to sell shall make some show of the same outward in their shops and outward houses, that such of his said subjects as will buy the same may thereby know where to be served thereof for the price aforesaid, upon the pains and penalties above expressed. And also his highness straightly chargeth and commandeth all and singular mayors, sheriffs, justices of peace, bailiffs, constables, and other his officers and ministers, that they and every of them from time to time as often as the case shall require see this his present proclamation to be put in due execution as they will avoid his most high displeasure and indignation and will answer to the contrary at their uttermost perils.

236. Ordering Arrest and Trial of Deserters

[Westminster, 10 September 1544, 36 Henry VIII]

Antiq 2, 139: by the Queen Regent; date as above; writ to mayor and sheriffs of London; schedule as below. Steele 260. Text (MS): Antiq

FORASMUCH as it is come to the perfect knowledge and understanding of the King's most royal majesty that divers and sundry persons, being retained to serve his highness in his wars beyond the seas, be returned into England in great numbers and companies without any manner of safeconduct, passport, or license from his majesty or any of his grace's lieutenants or of any of the captains of his highness' army, leaving his majesty (being there in his most royal person) unfurnished of his prescribed and determined force and company, to the great peril and danger of the same, and of all his nobility and the rest of his good subjects attending upon him:

His highness therefore, by the advice of his most honorable council, straightly chargeth and commandeth all and singular his justices of peace, mayors, sheriffs, bailiffs, constables, and all other his officers and ministers to whom it shall appertain, to examine all such persons as shall come from the army, and if they shall not be able to show sufficient passport and license for their return, signed with his majesty's hand or with the hand of some of his highness' lieutenants or at the least with the hand of the captain or head officer under whom they were pressed and appointed to do service in the said army, they shall forthwith attach the bodies of the same persons and that him or them commit to prison there to remain and abide without bail or mainprize unto such time as they shall be tried according to his laws provided in that behalf.

237. Limiting Access to Court

[Woking, 18 September 1544, 36 Henry VIII]

BM MS Harl 442, 164: by the Queen Regent; date as above; writ to mayor and sheriffs of London; schedule as below. Steele 261. Text (MS): Harl

FORASMUCH as the Queen's highness, general regent of the realm in the King's majesty's court, hath been credibly informed that the infection of the plague reigneth in sundry parts within these the cities of London and Westminster, whereby great danger might ensue to her grace's person, the Prince's grace, and other the King's majesty's children, in case any of the inhabitants of the said cities who have had the infection in their houses, or have resorted to any infected persons or dwell near any place where the infection is or lately hath been, should repair to the court or permit any of those which attend in the court to enter their houses: her highness straightly chargeth and commandeth that no manner of person or persons in whose houses the plague is or hath been, or have resorted to any other infected persons, or dwell near any place where the infection is or lately hath been, do from henceforth repair to the court or do suffer any of the attendants of the said court to enter their houses where the infection hath been, upon pain of her grace's indignation and further punishment at her highness' pleasure.

238. Permitting French to Remain

[Eltham, 30 September 1544, 36 Henry VIII]

BM MS Harl 442,165: by the Queen Regent; date as above; writ to mayor and sheriffs of London; schedule as below. Schanz 2, 611. Steele 262. Text (MS): Harl

WHERE the King's most royal majesty hath of late published and declared by his proclamation [1] that all Frenchmen and others whose names were entered before the Lord Chancellor of England should repair to the house of the said Lord Chancellor, there to know whether they were in the roll signed with his most gracious hand or not, and that all such as his highness was pleased should be made denizens should procure and sue out their letters patent for the same in due form to be made under his majesty's Great Seal before the first day of September now last past, and all those

1. See 227, 233, 234.

Frenchmen that were not in the roll aforesaid signed with his majesty's hand for that purpose should forthwith avoid this his highness' realm according to his highness' former proclamation in that behalf made, upon the pains and penalties contained and expressed in the same act by the same proclamation more plainly appeareth.

His majesty, upon a merciful disposition and for certain respects and considerations his highness thereunto moving, hath resolved, and is contented and pleased that all Frenchmen which be not yet denizens nor have not entered their names before the said Lord Chancellor of England shall by his gracious toleration remain, dwell, and abide within this his highness' realm without any punishment, danger, or forfeiture to them or any of them, or to any man keeping them in his house or company, unto such time as his grace by his proclamation shall determine his further pleasure in that behalf.

239. Providing Victual for Boulogne and Calais

[Otford, 6 October 1544, 36 Henry VIII]

LJ 15, 241: date, 6 October; writ to mayor and sheriffs of London; schedule as below. BM MS Harl 442,166: date, Otford, 5 October; writ to sheriff of Kent; schedule as below. For 5 October date, see 241. Steele 263. Text (MS): LJ

Forasmuch as the King's majesty, being (thanks be to Almighty God) in his most royal person safely returned into this his realm of England, is nevertheless desirous to have the noblemen and others yet remaining for the fortification and defense of his majesty's town of Boulogne and other piers of that side [of] the sea well and sufficiently furnished with wheat, malt, rye, oats, beans, peas, beeves, muttons, bacon, bread, beer, meal, and other kinds of victuals, wood, coals, hay, and straw, in such and so ample and large sort as they may have as good plenty thereof as need shall require. Considering also that the utterance of the premises may be to the great commodity of his loving subjects dwelling near the seacoasts, is of his great clemency and goodness pleased and contented that it shall be lawful to all and singular his highness' subjects, at their liberties and free wills, from time to time to embark, ship, and carry over the seas to be delivered at the ports of Calais and Boulogne and not elsewhere as much of the kinds aforesaid, that is to say, as much wheat, malt, rye, oats, beans, peas, beeves, muttons, bacon, bread, beer, meal, and all other kinds of victuals, wood, coals, hay, and straw as they or any of them will, until such time as his highness shall by his majesty's proclamation determine the contrary; any statute, law, proclamation, or restraint to the contrary notwithstanding.

Provided always that every person transporting any of the kinds aforesaid by force of this the King's majesty's license shall first enter the same in the customers' books and bind themselves to deliver the same at the said ports of Calais and Boulogne and not elsewhere, and to bring with them certificate in writing subscribed with the hands of two of the council of Calais or Boulogne for the delivery of the same, upon pain not only to forfeit the pains and forfeitures of their said several obligations but also the incurring all such other penalties as by the statutes and proclamations be provided in this behalf, and further to be punished by imprisonment of their bodies and otherwise, to the terrible example of all other.

240. Limiting Performance of Interludes and Plays

[October 1544, 36 Henry VIII]

LJ 15, 241*v:* date, based on neighboring entries, as above; schedule, incomplete, as below. Not in Steele. Text (MS): LJ

FORASMUCH as by reason and occasion of the manifold and sundry interludes and common plays that now of late days have been by divers and sundry persons more commonly and busily set forth and played, than heretofore hath been accustomed, in divers and many suspicious, dark, and inconvenient places of this our most dread and most benign sovereign lord the King's city and chamber of London, wherein no such plays ought to be played, and that namely and chiefly upon the Sunday and other holy days in the time of evensong and other divine service celebrated and said in the said city; to which places a great part of the youth of the same city, and many other light, idle, and evil-disposed persons daily and continually frequenting, haunting, and following the same plays, have not only been the rather moved and provoked thereby to all proneness, proclivity, and readiness of divers and sundry kinds of vice and sin, and the said youth by that occasion not only provoked to the unjust wasting and consuming of their master's goods, the neglecting and omission of their faithful service and due obedience to their said masters, but also to the no little loss and hindrance of God's honor and the divine service aforesaid, and to the augmenting of many other inconveniences more which daily spring and ensue thereof, to the high displeasure of Almighty God, the great nourishment and increase of much vice, sin, and idleness, and to the great decay and hurt of the commonwealth of the said city, as of archery and other lawful and laudable exercises, as our said most gracious and sovereign lord is credibly informed:

His highness therefore straightly chargeth and commandeth that no manner of person or persons from henceforth, of whatsoever estate, degree, or condition he or they be of, presume or take upon him or them at any time hereafter to play or set forth, or cause to be played, any manner of interlude or common play [1] within any manner of place or places of this his grace's said city; unless it be in the houses of noblemen or of the lord mayor, sheriffs, or aldermen of the same his highness' city for the time being; or else in the houses of gentlemen or of the substantial and sad commoners or head parishioners of the same city, or in the open streets of the said city, as in time past it hath been used and accustomed; or in the common halls of the companies, fellowships, or brotherhoods of the same city, and that at the request and desire of the same companies, fellowships, and brotherhoods, and in their common assemblies and presence, at times meet and convenient for the same, and in none other wise; and further, that no manner of person or persons, of what estate, degree, or condition soever he or they be of, presume at any time hereafter, or take upon him or them, to set up or affix.

241. Requiring Licenses for Export of Butter, Cheese

[Westminster, 6 November 1544, 36 Henry VIII]

BM MS Harl 442, 167: date as above; writ to mayor and sheriffs of London; schedule as below. Steele 264. Text (MS): Harl

WHERE the King's majesty, by his proclamation [1] bearing date at Otford the fifth day of October last past, did license to all and singular his subjects that they at their liberties from time to time (for the victualing of his towns of Boulogne and Calais) should embark, ship, and carry over the seas to be delivered at his ports of Boulogne and Calais and not elsewhere, as much wheat, malt, rye, oats, beans, peas, beeves, muttons, bacon, bread, meal, and all other kinds of victuals, wood, coals, hay, and straw as they or any of them would, unto such time as his highness by his proclamation should determine the contrary;

Forasmuch as divers and sundry of his said subjects have since made great provisions of butter and cheese, pretending the same to be for the victualing of the said towns of Calais and Boulogne, which in truth hath not been sent thither but conveyed otherwise to their own private lucres and com-

1. See 34 & 35 Henry VIII, c. 1, 1542, *SR 3*, 894.

1. See 239.

modities, whereby his highness' expectation is deceived and the said towns of Calais and Boulogne unfurnished:

His majesty therefore straightly chargeth and commandeth all and every his subjects of what estate, degree, or condition soever they or any of them be, that none of them, by themselves or any other for them, shall from henceforth transport or carry over the seas any butter or cheese without his highness' special license, had and obtained for the same, upon the pain not only to incur all such penalties as by the statute and proclamations be provided in that behalf, but also to be further punished by imprisonment of their bodies and otherwise, to the terrible example of all other.

242. Ordering Sale of Grain

[Westminster, 15 November 1544, 36 Henry VIII]

BM MS Harl 442, 168: date, crossed through, as above; schedule as below. Schanz 2, 669. Steele 265. Text (MS): Harl

FORASMUCH as it is come to the knowledge of our sovereign lord the King how that divers persons, as well his own subjects as other, having more respect to their own private lucre and advantage than to the commonwealth of this his highness' realm, have by divers and sundry means accumulated and gotten unto their hands and possession a great number and multitude of corns and grain far above the necessary finding of their household, sowing of their lands, paying their rent-corn, and performing of their lawful bargains of corn without fraud or covin; and the same, of their covetous minds, do willfully detain and keep in their possessions without bringing any part or parcel thereof into any market to be sold, intending thereby for to cause the prices of corns to arise so that they may sell their corns and grain at such unreasonable prices as they will themselves; by reason whereof the prices of corns and grains as wheat, rye, maslin, barley, malt, beans, peas, and oats, be raised to such excessive and high prices that his majesty's loving subjects cannot gain, with their great labors and pains, sufficient to pay for their convenient victuals and sustenance, and worse are like to be hereafter unless speedy remedy be provided in that behalf: his highness therefore by the advice of his said most honorable council, and by authority of the said act[1] of parliament made in the said 31st year of his majesty's reign, straightly chargeth and commandeth all justices of peace being, inhabiting, or abiding within any shire, city, borough, or place within this his realm of England, Wales, or any other his grace's dominions, within 20 days next ensuing the publishing of this proclamation, according

1. 31 Henry VIII, c. 8, 1539, *SR 3*, 726.

to the said act and oftener after that, by their discretions to assemble themselves together; that is to say every member of them within the limits of their commissions wherein they be named justices of peace and do inhabit or dwell, and at and upon such their assembly they shall divide and sever themselves, limiting and assigning always the number of two of them at the least, or more, into hundreds, wapentakes, rapes, commotes, or number of towns and villages, by their discretions, and that the said justices so divided, or two of them at the least, shall with all convenient speed search the houses, barns, and yards of such persons as have been accustomed or used to sell corns and grain, and have abundance of corns and grain more than shall be necessary for the sowing of their lands, paying their rent-corn, performing their said lawful bargains of corn, and finding of their houses until the Feast of All Saints next coming: and where they shall find any such abundance or surplusage, shall by their discretions straightly garner and command, in the name of our said sovereign lord the King, the owner or owners thereof to convey and bring or cause to be brought such part and portion of their said corns and grain unto the market and markets there near adjoining, or to such other market or markets where they aforetime have used or accustomed to sell their corn, there to be sold at and during such time as shall be thought meet by the said justices of the peace, or two of them at the least; the said justices delivering unto every of the said owner and owners a bill subscribed with their hands mentioning and declaring the days, places, number, and certainty of the bringing of the said corns and grain to the said market and markets to be sold as is aforesaid, according to their said commandments and appointments. And if any person or persons do willfully refuse to convey or bring or cause to be brought unto the said market or markets to be sold, such part or portion of any such corns and grain as by the said justices, or two of them at the least, shall be to him and them limited and appointed as is aforesaid, that then every such person and persons so offending shall lose and forfeit for every bushel, whereof eight bushels maketh the quarter, of the said kinds of corns and grain not brought into the market or markets, to be sold by and according to the appointment of the said justices or two of them as is aforesaid, 3*s.* and 4*d.*, the one moiety of all which said forfeitures shall be to the King's majesty, and the other moiety to the party and parties that will sue for the same by information, bill, plaint, action of debt, or otherwise in any of the King's Courts of his Exchequer, King's Bench or Common Pleas, or else before such of the King's most honorable council as be appointed to hear and determine the same by authority of the said act; in which suits none essoin or protection shall be allowed, nor wager of law received or admitted for the defendant. This proclamation to continue and endure until the Feast of All Saints next coming and no longer, provided always that this present proclamation or anything therein contained shall not in anywise extend to give authority to the said justices of peace or to any of them to appoint or compel any person or persons to bring any of the said corns or grain to any market or markets to be sold, which now be or before the said Feast of All Saints next coming shall be provided, or brought for the city of London and the inhabitants of the same, anything in this proclamation or in the said act contained to the contrary notwithstanding.

243. Granting Letters of Marque against Scots and French

[Westminster, 20 December 1544, 36 Henry VIII]

Antiq 2, 145: date, 20 December; letters patent to all subjects; schedule as below. Steele 266: date, Westminster. Text (MS): Antiq

The King's most royal majesty, being credibly informed that divers and many of his most loving, faithful, and obedient subjects, inhabiting upon the seacoasts, using traffic by sea, and divers others, be very desirous to prepare and equip sundry ships and vessels, at their own costs and charges, to the sea for the annoyance of his majesty's enemies, the Frenchmen and the Scots, so as they might obtain his most gracious license in that behalf, hath of his clemency, tender love, and zeal which he beareth to his subjects, by the advice of his most honorable council, resolved and determined as hereafter followeth: first his majesty is pleased, and by the authority hereof giveth full power and license to all and singular his subjects of all sorts, degrees, and conditions, that they and every of them may at their liberties without incurring any loss, danger, forfeiture, or penalty, and without putting in of any bonds or recognizance before the council or in the Court of the Admiralty, and without suing forth of any other license, *videndum,* or other writing from any council, court, or place within this realm or any other his majesty's realms and dominions, prepare and equip to the seas such and so many ships and vessels furnished for the war, to be used and employed against his grace's said enemies the Scots and Frenchmen, as they shall be able to think convenient for their advantage and the annoyance of his majesty's said enemies.

And his majesty is further pleased, and by these presents granteth to every of his said subjects, that they and every of them shall enjoy to his and their own proper use, profit, and commodity all and singular such ships, vessels, munitions, merchandises, wares, victuals, and goods of what nature and quality soever it be which they shall take of any of his majesty's said enemies, without making account in any court or place of this realm or any other the King's realms or dominions for the same, and without paying any part or share to the Lord Admiral of England, the Lord Warden of the Cinque Ports, or to any other officer or minister of the King's majesty, any use, custom, protection, or order to the contrary hereof used heretofore in any wise notwithstanding.

And his majesty is further pleased that all and every his said subjects which upon the publication of this proclamation will sue for a duplicate of the same under his Great Seal of England shall have the same, paying only the petty fees to the officers for writing the same. And seeing now that it hath pleased the King's majesty of his most gracious goodness to grant unto all his subjects this great liberty, his highness desireth all mayors, sheriffs, bailiffs, aldermen, and all other his grace's faithful officers, ministers, and subjects of his realm, and other his highness' realms and dominions, and specially those which do inhabit in port towns and other places near the seaside, to show themselves worthy of such liberty, and one to bear with another and to help another in such sort as their doings hereupon may be substantial and bring forth that effect that shall redound to his majesty's honor, their own sureties, and the annoyance of the enemies.

Provided always that no man which shall go to the sea by virtue hereof presume to take anything from any his majesty's subjects or from any of his majesty's friends; that is to say, of their own goods nor from any man having his grace's safe-conduct, upon the pains by his majesty's laws provided for the same. And his grace is further pleased that no manner officer or other person shall take any mariner's munition or tackle from any man thus equipping himself to the sea, but by his own consent, unless his majesty for the furniture of his own ships do send for any of them by special commissions. And where need shall require his majesty will also grant commission to such as will sue for the same for their better furnitures in this behalf.

244. Providing Death Penalty for Deserters from Ships

[Westminster, 24 January 1545, 36 Henry VIII]

BM MS Harl 442, 172: date as above; writ to all sheriffs, mayors, bailiffs, constables, officers, and ministers; schedule as below. Steele 267. Text (MS): Harl

FORASMUCH as the mariners and soldiers serving in the King's majesty's ships have in times past, and yet continually do, use not only unlawfully to depart from their ships unto the towns near where they have and do arrive without any license or leave of their admiral or captain, and tarrying a-land most ungodly and unlawfully using themselves contrary to the King's highness' laws, spending his majesty's money and victuals in vain, by means whereof his majesty's enemies have done divers exploits, enormities, and hurts to divers his majesty's loving and true subjects within this his realm (in defense whereof his majesty to his great charge hath set forth his said ships), but also contrary to the most just laws of his grace's realm the said mariners and soldiers do run and steal away from the said ships, taking the King's wages, prests, and conduct money to their most extreme perils; by which means, contrary to the King's majesty's expectation and trust, his said ships are constrained for want of men to lie still in the harbors and docks, neither being able to do any enterprise themselves nor yet to defend the King's majesty's people traveling in the seas, without speedy redress whereof great danger is like to ensue.

His majesty's pleasure and straight commandment is that no mariner nor soldier nor any other able person, unless he be sick or hurt, serving or pressed to serve in any of his majesty's ships, do after this present proclamation proclaimed, depart or go from their ships without testimonial signed with their captain's hands, to any place of the land, neither for victuals, water, or any other necessaries, nor for any other lawful or unlawful occasion, upon pain of death. And that no manner of person or persons shall retain into their houses, hide, or succor the said mariners, soldiers, or any other person or persons pertaining or belonging to any of the King's majesty's ships, upon pain of the King's highness' most grievous displeasure, loss of their goods, and imprisonment of their bodies. And that all mayors, bailiffs, and constables of all towns, ports, and boroughs do see this proclamation thoroughly executed and used as they will answer to the contrary at their most extreme perils. And that no mariner or soldier so by his captain licensed to come to the land do bring with him any manner of weapon upon pain of three days imprisonment.

245. Raising Wages of Mariners

[Westminster, 24 January 1545, 36 Henry VIII]

BM MS Harl 442, 173: date as above; writ to all sheriffs, mayors, bailiffs, constables, officers, and ministers; schedule as below. Steele 268. Text (MS): Harl

THE KING'S MOST ROYAL MAJESTY, graciously considering that whereas the mariners within this his grace's realm hath heretofore taken pains in the serving of his majesty, not only at his late sundry voyages into Scotland and France, having for their wages but only 5*s*. for every month as in times past hath been accustomed, his highness therefore, remembering their true, faithful service to him done in the same, considering also the dearth and excessive prices of all things at this present, of his most bountiful goodness, hath given and granted unto every of the said mariners from henceforth that shall be diligent and attendant in and about to serve his highness in his ships, for every month *6s. 8d.,* willing and commanding all such as will and be meet to serve for the said wages immediately after the publishing of this present proclamation to resort and repair unto Deptford, Strand, Portsmouth, Dover, Calais, and to such other places where his ships be, whereas they shall be retained accordingly.

246. Recruiting Volunteers for Ships of Marque

[Westminster, 11 April 1545, 36 Henry VIII]

LJ 15, 239*v:* date as above; writ to mayor and sheriffs of London; schedule as below. Steele 269. Text (MS): LJ

Forasmuch as it hath pleased the King's majesty to be presently served, amongst other his grace's men of war in the parts of beyond the seas, with a certain number of adventurers, like as in all the wars heretofore hath been accustomed, his highness upon the knowledge of the experience of his well-beloved servant, John of Calais, hath appointed him to be captain of all such adventurers as shall serve his majesty in this war, and doth for that purpose authorize the said John of Calais by this his grace's proclamation to levy, take, or retain in all places as well on this side the seas as on the other, such and as many of his highness' subjects as shall offer themselves to serve at their own adventure, as at like times hath been used; willing and commanding all such as will presently enter themselves with the said captain here in England to repair to the Sign of the Gun at Billingsgate before the Feast of St. George next coming, where order shall be taken with them for the time of their passage.

Provided that under color hereof no prentice, nor no servant to any man, nor soldier already retained, be so hardy to depart from his master or captain without his special license, nor that any of them presume to interrupt, disquiet or peril any of his majesty's subjects, or in any wise being once entered, to disobey the said captain or to depart from him without his license signed with his hand as they and every of them will avoid his grace's indignation and abide such further punishment, as for the contrary is ordained by the laws of this realm and also by the laws martial accordingly.

247. Prohibiting Deer Hunting in Combe Park

[Westminster, 13 April 1545, 36 Henry VIII]

BM MS Harl 442, 174*v:* date as above; writ to sheriff of Surrey; schedule as below. Steele 270. Text (MS): Harl

WHERE our most dread sovereign lord the King's majesty is credibly informed that a good number of his red deer, bred in his chase of Hampton Court, and also certain fallow deer of his parts thereabouts, be strayed abroad and lie at this present in his grace's woods and bushes between London and Cobham, and specially at and about a place called Combe Park, between London and Kingston-upon-Thames, his majesty much desiring to have the same deer preserved and kept for his own disport and pastime, doth straightly charge and command all and singular his subjects of what estate or degree soever they be, that they nor any of them do in any wise chase, hunt, or kill any deer lying abroad in any place between London and Cobham aforesaid, but suffer the same deer either to remain for his grace's own pastime or to return to his said chases and parts again at their liberties, upon pain of imprisonment of their bodies and further to be punished at his grace's will and pleasure.

248. Authorizing English Primer

[Westminster, 6 May 1545, 37 Henry VIII]

STC 16,034 (UM 19,112,2037), BM C.35.c.15: printed by R. Grafton (London, 1545); date, 29 May: letters patent (date, 6 May) to all subjects; schedule as below. Wilkins *3,* 875. Steele 271: date as above. Text (*STC*): BM

AMONG the manifold business and most weighty affairs appertaining to our regal authority and office, we, much tendering the youth of our realms (whose good education and virtuous bringing up redoundeth most highly to the honor and praise of Almighty God), for divers good considerations, and especially for that the youth by divers persons are taught the Pater Noster, the Ave Maria, Creed, and Ten Commandments all in Latin, and not in English, by means whereof the same are not brought up in the knowledge of their faith, duty, and obedience, wherein no Christian person ought to be ignorant; and for that our people and subjects which have no understanding in the Latin tongue and yet have the knowledge of reading, may pray in their vulgar tongue, which is to them best known, that by the mean thereof they should be the more provoked to true devotion and the better set their hearts upon those things that they pray for; and finally for the avoiding of the diversity of primer books that are now abroad, whereof are almost innumerable sorts, which minister occasion of contentions and vain disputations rather than to edify, and to have one uniform order of all such books throughout all our dominion, both to be taught unto children and also to be used for ordinary prayers of all our people not learned in the Latin tongue: have set forth this Primer,[1] or book of prayers in English, to be frequented and used in and throughout all places of our said realms and dominions, as well of the elder people as also of the youth for their common and ordinary prayers; willing, commanding, and straightly charging that for the better bringing up of youth in the knowledge of their duty toward God, their prince, and all other in their degree, every schoolmaster and bringer up of young beginners in learning, next after their A.B.C., now by us also set forth, do teach this Primer or book of ordinary prayers unto them in English, and that the youth customably and ordinarily use the same until they be of competent understanding and knowledge to perceive it in Latin, at what time they may at their liberty either use the Primer in English or this which is by our authority likewise made in Latin and English, the Latin being in all points correspondent to the English.

And furthermore we straightly charge and command as well all and singular our subjects and sellers of books, as also all schoolmasters and teachers of young children within this our realm and other our dominions, as they intend to have our favor and avoid our displeasure by the contrary, that immediately after this our said Primer is published and imprinted, that they nor any of them buy, sell, occupy, use, nor teach, privily or apertly any other primer either in English or Latin than this now by us published, which with no small study, travail and labor we purposely made to the high honor and glory of Almighty God and to the commodity of our loving subjects and edifying of the same in godly contemplation and virtuous exercise of prayer.

249. Adjourning Trinity Term

[Westminster, 13 May 1545, 37 Henry VIII]

LJ 15, 239*v:* date as above; writ to mayor and sheriffs of London; schedule as below. Antiq 2, 150: date, 11 May; schedule as below (final paragraph omitted). Steele 272. Text (MS): LJ

THE KING our most dread sovereign lord, singularly tendering the commonwealth and safe preservation of this his realm and other his majesty's

1. *The Primer, Set Foorth by the Kynges Maiestie and His Clergie* (London, R. Grafton, 29 May 1545), *STC* 16,034. See 34 & 35 Henry VIII, c. 1, 1542, *SR 3,* 894.

dominions, and of his subjects of the same, for certain great and urgent causes his highness moving, and chiefly for that his most royal majesty hath appointed sundry armies royal with a main army for the sea, to be levied for the defense and annoyance of his majesty's ancient enemies, the Scots and Frenchmen, which intend as much as in them is to do annoyance and displeasure to his said subjects, which his highness, by God's might and power, intendeth to defend as well by sea as by land, and to put all his majesty's forces in such order as he may be as able and ready to annoy the enemies at home in their own countries as they shall be to damage any of his majesty's subjects in any of his dominions;

Hath most graciously considered that his good and loving subjects inhabiting in divers parts of this his realm of England cannot conveniently attend these matters of the war and follow also their suits and causes in his sundry courts holden at Westminster, and that it shall be therefore expedient that the next term commonly called Trinity term shall be adjourned from the first day thereof unto the *utas* of St. Michael next ensuing and to spare the execution of part of his laws for that little time to the intent that his said subjects should be the more ready this present summertime at their habitations and dwelling places or elsewhere the King's majesty shall appoint to and for the same defense and annoyance of his grace's enemies, and for the execution of all such his most dread commandments, proclamations, and commissions as between this and Michaelmas next, shall be addressed unto them.

Wherefore his majesty, by the advice and assent of his most honorable council, doth by this present proclamation publish and declare that the said next term, usually called Trinity term, from and at the first day of the said term shall be wholly and fully adjourned unto the *utas* of St. Michael next ensuing in all his majesty's courts at Westminster,[1] except the Court of the Exchequer and the Court of the Tenths and First Fruits, which shall be kept open to all intents and purposes as though the said Trinity term were not in any wise adjourned. And his majesty's pleasure is that all such of his said subjects as should or ought to appear in any of his said highness' courts in the said Trinity term shall keep their day at the said *utas* (except before excepted).

And his highness further chargeth and commandeth that all justices of the peace, sheriffs, mayors, bailiffs, and other his ministers, subjects, which heretofore by virtue of any commission have travailed or meddled for or touching the benevolence or subsidy, fifteenth, or any other debt or duties due unto the King's highness, or do know any receiver, collector, bailiff, or other person whatsoever which hath any money in his hands now due to his highness, or that shall be due at any time between this and Michaelmas aforesaid, and doth retain and keep the same in their hands, to cause them

1. 26 Henry VIII, c. 3, 1534, *SR 3*, 493.

to bring it up with diligence to be paid to the officers assigned for the receipt thereof, who shall give continual attendance for that purpose. And if they shall know any person or persons that upon their monition will refuse or do delay so to do, then to certify his majesty's council thereof, that such order may be taken for them as shall appertain.

250. Ordering Vagabonds to the Galleys

[Westminster, 26 May 1545, 37 Henry VIII]

Antiq 2, 151: date as above; writ to mayor and sheriffs of London; schedule as below. Steele 273. Text (MS): Antiq

THE KING'S MOST ROYAL MAJESTY, seeing daily before his most noble eyes that notwithstanding the sundry good and wholesome laws and statutes made by his highness and his most noble progenitors for the good and virtuous occupation of his people, the persuasion of the same from idleness, the mother and root of all mischiefs, and the punishment of vagabonds, ruffians, and idle persons, there do remain yet in this realm of England, specially about the city of London, a great number of ruffians and vagabonds, to whom albeit God hath given personage and strength apt and able to labor, work and do service for their living, yet be they so wasted in mischief and idleness that they give themselves to no labor or honest kind of living, but entertain themselves with theft [and] falsehood in play, whereby many simple young men be polled and some utterly undone, and with other detestable vices and fashions commonly used at the bank and such like naughty places where they much haunt and in manner lie nightly for the accomplishment and satisfying of their vile, wretched, and filthy purposes.

For reformation whereof, like as his most royal majesty hath thought convenient and doth determine to use and employ all such ruffians, vagabonds, masterless men, common players, and evil-disposed persons to serve his majesty and his realm in these his wars in certain galleys, and other like vessels which his majesty's highness intendeth to arm forth against his enemies before the first of June next coming:

Even so his majesty straightly chargeth and commandeth that no person of what estate, degree, or condition soever he be, do in any wise hereafter name or avow any man to be his servant unless he be his household servant or his bailiff or keeper or such other as he may keep and retain by the laws and statutes of this realm, or be retained by the King's majesty's license, upon pain of the incurring of extreme danger of his grace's laws and imprisonment of his body, and as he will further answer for his contempt in that behalf at his highness' pleasure.

251. Granting Grafton and Whitchurch Patent to Print Primer

[Greenwich, 28 May 1545, 37 Henry VIII]

STC 16,034 (UM 19,112,2039), BM C.35.c.15, *Epilogue:* printed by R. Grafton (London, 1545); date as above; letters patent to all other ministers and subjects; schedule as below. Not in Steele. Text (*STC*): BM

HENRY VIII, by the grace of God of England, France, and Ireland, King, defender of the faith, and of the Church of England and Ireland in earth the supreme head, to all printers and booksellers, and to all other our officers, ministers, and subjects:

We do you to understand that of our grace especial we have granted and given privilege and license to our well-beloved subject, Richard Grafton, printer and servant to our most dearest son Prince Edward, and Edward Whitchurch, citizen of London, to print or cause to be printed our Primer,[1] now by us and our clergy set forth, both in English and in Latin; and none other person nor persons of what estate, degree, or condition soever they be of, to print or cause the same Primer to be printed, or any part thereof, but only the said Richard and Edward, and either of them, or the assignees of any of them; neither to sell nor buy of any other impressions than such as shall be printed by the said Richard or Edward, or the assignees of any of them.

Wherefore we will and straightly command and charge all and singular our subjects, as well printers as booksellers, and all other persons within our dominions, that they nor any of them presume to print or sell, or cause to be printed or sold, the said book or any part thereof, contrary to the meaning of this our present license and privilege; upon pain of our high displeasure.

1. See 248, n. 1.

252. Ordering Northern Gentry to War against Scots

[Westminster, May 1545, 37 Henry VIII]

Antiq 2, 152: date, Westminster; writ to mayor and sheriffs of London; schedule as below. Steele 274: date, May 1545. Text (MS): Antiq

THE KING'S MOST ROYAL MAJESTY, having appointed an army royal to be levied beyond the river Trent for the defense and annoyance of his most ancient enemies, the Scots and the Frenchmen, intending as much as in them is to do displeasure to his good subjects inhabiting in those parts, doth straightly charge and command all and singular such gentlemen and others as be inhabiting beyond Trent aforesaid, all other business or excuse set apart, immediately to depart hence and repair to their houses and dwelling places, there to do as by his majesty's lieutenant in those parts shall appoint unto them, except only such as by special commandment be appointed to give their personal attendance here, without failing, as they will answer for the contrary at their extreme peril.

253. Ordering Penalties for Deceitful Winding and Packing of Wool

[Westminster, 17 June 1545, 37 Henry VIII]

Antiq 2, 153: date as above; writ to sheriff of Lincoln; schedule as below. Steele 276: date, 27 June. Text (MS): Antiq

WHERE in the parliament holden in the 27th year of the reign of our most noble progenitor, King Edward III, it was enacted[1] and ordained among other things that all wool packers and winders of wools should be sworn and take a corporal oath before the mayor and constables of the Staple of Westminster (for the time being) truly and justly to wind and pack all the wools within this realm; by force of which statute and by the good ordinances made in the said Staple, the fellowship of wool winders, otherwise called woolmen, have ever since justly and truly wound and packed all such wools as they have meddled with throughout this realm, unto now of late that divers and many persons contrary to the said statute, taking upon them

1. 27 Edward III, st. 2, c. 23, 1353, *SR 1*, 341.

to be wool winders in many places of this realm, neither being sworn nor expert in winding and folding of wools, of the which some of them be tailors, weavers, cordwainers, barbers, husbandmen, and other artificers, have gone and do daily go about throughout this realm in many places. And in winding and folding of the said wools by the procurement and means of the owners and breeders of the said wools, do wind up and deceitfully put into the said fleeces of wool, sand, stone, dust, pitch, tar, clay, iron, lead, double marks, shearlocks, dung, lamb's-wool and other deceivable things, not only to the great slander of this realm but also to the slander of the merchants of the said Staple. And also as well to the great hindrance and deceit of the merchants of the Staple buying the same, as also to the great loss and prejudice of the King's subjects using the mystery and craft of cloth-making within this his realm.

For reformation and redress whereof the King's most royal majesty, by the advice of his most honorable council, straightly chargeth and commandeth that no manner of person or persons whatsoever he be, at any time hereafter go about or take upon him or them to wind or fold any manner of wools within the county of Lincoln before he or they have taken a corporal oath before two justices of the peace within the same county, whereof one of the said justices to be of the quorum, or else before the mayor of the Staple of Westminster for the time being, that he or they shall truly and justly, without fraud or deceit, wind and fold all and singular such wools as he or they shall take upon him or them to wind and fold, without leaving or putting within any fleece or fleeces any manner of clockettes, locks, hindershanks, tails, passellys, washlocks, stones, sand, dust, or any wool of worse nature or growing than the same fleece is, or any other filth to be left upon the breech of any fleece whereby any such fleece may be impaired or made the weightier or minished, or take away any part or portion of the goodness of any of the same fleeces to the intent to deceive the buyers, upon pain of imprisonment by the space of ten days, and then to be set upon the pillory in the next market town with a fleece of wool hanging about his neck.

And his majesty further straightly chargeth and commandeth that no grower, breeder, brogger, or gatherer of any wool within the said county, shall at any time hereafter set on work any wool folder or wool winder to fold or wind his or their wools unless the said wool folder or wool winder bring with him or them a testimonial or certificate either under the seal of the mayor of the Staple of Westminster for the time being or else a certificate sealed by the said justices of the peace, as is afore mentioned within the said county, or either of them, certifying him or them to be sworn and admitted as wool folders or wool winders, upon the pains as is above expressed.

254. Prohibiting Hunting and Hawking at Westminster

[Westminster, 7 July 1545, 37 Henry VIII]

AC (Dasent *1*, 201): date, Dartford, 21 June; order to Chancellor to make proclamation. LJ 15, 240*v:* date as above; writ to mayor and sheriffs of London; schedule as below. Steele 277. Text (MS): LJ

FORASMUCH as the King's most royal majesty is much desirous to have the game of hare, partridge, pheasant, and heron perserved in and about his honor at his palace of Westminster for his own disport and pastime; that is to say, from his said palace of Westminster to St. Giles-in-the-Fields, and from thence to Islington to Our Lady of the Oak, to Highgate to Hornesey Park, to Hamsted Heath, and from thence to Shotehop Hill, to Willesdon, to Acton in Chesweke, to Cheese Heath, and from then to his said palace of Westminster, to be preserved and kept for his own disport, pleasure, and recreation:

His highness therefore straightly chargeth and commandeth all and singular his subjects of what estate, degree, or condition soever they be that they nor any of them do presume or attempt to hunt or to hawk or in any manner of means to take or kill any of the said game within the premises aforesaid, as they tender his favor and will eschew the imprisonment of their bodies and further punishment at his majesty's will and pleasure.

255. Providing Victual for Army in France

[Westminster, 2 September 1545, 37 Henry VIII]

Antiq 2, 155: date as above; writ to mayor and sheriffs of London; schedule as below. Steele 278. Text (MS): Antiq

WHERE the King's most royal majesty intendeth (by the grace of God) to prepare and furnish with all diligence an army royal both of Englishmen and strangers, and with the same (if it shall so please God) not only to levy the siege before Boulogne, but also to do such other exploits upon his grace's enemies as shall be thought convenient: forasmuch as it is most expedient and necessary that such provision and preparation of victuals be made for furniture of the same as appertaineth, like as his highness for his part at his own great charge doth make all the preparation he can possibly. So minding to have the said army nourished with abundance of all things necessary, and considering that the free recourse of victuals thither by his grace's good subjects may not only help much to the furtherance of his highness' most godly purpose herein, but shall be also to their great benefit, gain, and commodities, being the seas and passages also now cleared by his highness, is of his great clemency and goodness pleased and contented that it shall be lawful to all and singular his highness' subjects at their liberties and free wills from time to time to embark, ship, and carry over the seas, at his or their own adventure, to be delivered at his port of Calais and not elsewhere, as much wheat, malt, rye, oats, beans, peas, beeves, muttons, bacon, bread, beer, butter, cheese, and all other kinds of victuals, wood, coal, hay, and straw, as they or any of them will, until such time as his highness shall by his majesty's proclamation determine the contrary; any statute, law, proclamation, or restraint to the contrary notwithstanding.

Provided always that every person transporting any of the kinds aforesaid, by force of this his majesty's license, shall first enter the same in the customer's books and bind themselves to deliver the same at the said port of Calais and not elsewhere and to bring with them certificate in writing subscribed with the hands of two of the council of Calais for the delivery of the same, upon pain not only to incur the pains and forfeitures of their said several obligations but also all such other penalties as by the statutes and proclamations be provided in this behalf, and further to be punished by imprisonment of their bodies or otherwise, to the terrible example of all other at the King's majesty's pleasure.

256. Adjourning Michaelmas Term

[Westminster, 22 September 1545, 37 Henry VIII]

Antiq 2, 156: date as above; writ to mayor and sheriffs of London; schedule as below. Steele 279. Text (MS): Antiq

WHEREAS the term commonly called Michaelmas term, appointed for ministration of justice, hath been accustomed to begin and holden at Westminster in the *utas* of St. Michael the Archangel next coming, and so continue to the *quindene* of St. Martin then next following, and forasmuch as the King's majesty intendeth for sundry great affairs of the realm to hold his high court of parliament at his majesty's town of Windsor, the same to begin the 23rd day of November next coming, by reason whereof the said term cannot continue so long as hath been observed and accustomed, but for furniture of the said parliament the same must take sooner end.

His highness therefore signifieth to all his loving subjects who shall have any cause to repair to the said term, that the same shall end the 18th day of November, which is the *utas* of St. Martin next coming, and that day be adjourned to the *utas* of St. Hilary then next following.

257. Continuing Michaelmas Term

[Westminster, 6 October 1545, 37 Henry VIII]

Antiq 2, 157: date as above; writ to mayor and sheriffs of London; schedule as below. Steele 280. Text (MS): Antiq

WHEREAS the King's most royal majesty by his former proclamation [1] did appoint this present term, commonly called Michaelmas term, to begin at Westminster in the *utas* of St. Michael the Archangel last past, and so continue to the 18th day of November next coming which shall be the *utas* of St. Martin, and that day to be adjourned to the *utas* of St. Hilary then next following, as by the same proclamation more plainly appeareth; and forasmuch as his majesty intended for sundry great affairs of this realm to hold his high court of parliament at his town of name Westminster, for the same to begin the 23rd day of November now next coming, by reason whereof the said term should not have continued so long as hath been accustomed:

His highness therefore, by the advice of his most honorable council, signifieth to all his loving subjects that his said high court of parliament shall begin and be holden at his city of Westminster the said 23rd day of November, and that this present term shall hold and continue unto the *quindene* of St. Martin next coming, as hath been in times past accustomed, and that day to be adjourned to the *utas* of St. Hilary aforesaid, the former proclamation notwithstanding.

258. Prohibiting Export of Victual

[Westminster, 4 December 1545, 37 Henry VIII]

Antiq 2, 158: date as above; writ to sheriff of Essex; schedule as below. Steele 281. Text (MS): Antiq

FORASMUCH as for the necessary furniture of Calais, Boulogne, and other the King's majesty's piers beyond the seas, there must be presently made a great provision of cheese and bacon within the county of Essex, the want and

1. See 256.

lack whereof might be great detriment and danger to the same, and likewise breed a great lack to such the King's majesty's subjects as reside there: for the defense of them and the annoyance of his grace's enemies, the King's majesty therefore, by the advice of his most honorable council, straightly chargeth and commandeth that all provisions of cheese and bacon made or to be made by any manner of person or persons within the said county of Essex be stayed unto the Feast of the Purification of our Blessed Lady next coming (the King's majesty's provisions only excepted), upon the pain that every person offending this present proclamation shall lose and forfeit the said cheese and bacon and also shall suffer imprisonment and make fine at the King's will and pleasure.

259. Limiting Export of Victual from Norfolk and Suffolk

[Westminster, 5 December 1545, 37 Henry VIII]

Antiq 2, 159: date as above; writ to sheriffs of Norfolk and Suffolk; schedule as below. Steele 282. Text (MS): Antiq

FORASMUCH as for the necessary furniture of Calais, Boulogne, and other the King's majesty's piers beyond the seas, there must be presently made a great provision of butter, cheese, and all kinds of grains within the counties of Norfolk and Suffolk, the want and lack thereof might be great detriment and danger to the same, and likewise breed a great lack to such the King's majesty's subjects as reside there: for the defense of them and the annoyance of his grace's enemies, the King's majesty therefore, by the advice of his most honorable council, straightly chargeth and commandeth that all provisions of butter, cheese, and of all kinds of grain made or to be made by any manner of person or persons within the said counties of Norfolk and Suffolk, be stayed unto the Feast of the Purification of our Blessed Lady next coming; the King's majesty's provisions and the provisions of such quantity of grain as is appointed and agreed upon to be made within the said counties for the city of London, and such as any person or persons shall ship, to be at his or their adventure, conveyed to Calais or Boulogne, only excepted, upon pain that every person offending this present proclamation shall lose and forfeit the said grain and victuals and also shall suffer imprisonment and make fine at the King's will and pleasure.

And to the intent the King's majesty may be advertised by his commissioners what quantity of grain hath been provided and bought by any person within the said counties, his highness straightly chargeth and commandeth all and singular his subjects inhabiting within the said counties that they and every of them do declare and certify to his commissioners appointed for the provision of grain by minding how much grain every of them have bought since Easter last past, and of whom and in what towns or villages, and how much thereof they have received from the sellers, and where the same grain doth now remain, in such form and sort as by the said commissioners shall be devised and commanded.

And moreover his highness straightly chargeth and commandeth all and singular his subjects selling any manner of grain, or making or malting any malt within the said counties, that they and every of them do well and truly make their malt good and ample without any long tails, and also cleanse and dight all the said grains, and also deliver to the buyers of the said grains good measure according to the custom of those counties; that is to say 21 for 20 and not 5 for 4 of malt in the corns or fluid.

And furthermore the King's majesty's pleasure is that all such persons as shall carry and transport any kind of grains either to Boulogne or to Calais at his or their own adventure do first indent for the same with his trusty and well-beloved, Sir John Jernyngham, knight; Osberte Moundeford, esquire; and Thomas Townesend, gentleman; or other deputy or deputies for that purpose. Which deputies, authorized by writing, shall remain at every port and creek where any shipping is used in those parts.

Provided always that every person or persons that shall carry and transport to his highness' said towns of Calais or Boulogne or the marches of the same, any such grain or victuals as is mentioned in the said proclamation before the shipping thereof, shall not only enter the same also with the customer but shall likewise be bound with one sufficient surety with him unto the customer and comptroller of the port or creek where such grain and victuals shall be shipped, or to their deputies, by obligation to the King's majesty's use, in a certain sum of money amounting to the double value of the said grain and victuals that shall be so transported and conveyed to the said towns of Calais and Boulogne for the victualing and relief thereof, and not to discharge the same in any other place out of the King's dominions. And also the transporters and conveyors of such grain and victuals aforesaid shall be bound to bring a true and just certificate within four months next after from the King's deputy of Calais or his lieutenant of Boulogne and two other of the council there at the least, that the said grain and victuals so shipped were there discharged and delivered accordingly.

260. Pricing Wines

[Westminster, 5 December 1545, 37 Henry VIII]

Antiq 2, 160: date as above; writ to mayor and sheriffs of London; schedule as below. Steele 283. Text (MS): Antiq

WHERE it is ordained and provided by statute[1] that the prices of Gascon and French wines should be limited and declared by the Lord Chancellor of England, Lord Treasurer of England, Lord President of the King's most honorable council, Lord Privy Seal and other the councilors of our said sovereign lord specified and declared in the said statute, as by the same statute made and established in the parliament begun and holden at Westminster the third day of November in the 21st year of the King's most gracious reign, and continued by divers prorogations, more plainly appeareth;

Forasmuch as the said lords and councilors in the execution of the said act have by their deliberate advices taxed, limited, assigned, and appointed the prices of Gascon and French wines to be sold within this his realm; that is to say, every tun of the best Gascon wine to be sold after the price and rate of £6. 13*s*. 4*d*. sterling the tun and not above. And every tun of the best French wines to be sold after the rate of £5. 6*s*. 8*d*. sterling the tun and not above. And every pipe, hogshead, puncheon, tierce, and other vessel of the same several wines to be sold after their quantities after and according to the same rates and not above. And for small and thin wines to be sold under the same rate as the buyers and sellers thereof can agree:

The King's most royal majesty therefore straightly chargeth and commandeth all and singular his subjects and others putting any manner of Gascon or French wines to sale within this his realm that they nor any of them in any manner wise by any craft, covin, or private agreement shall sell any Gascon or French wines otherwise than is above limited, upon pain to forfeit and pay such penalties as be contained and expressed in the same act.

And moreover his high pleasure and commandment also is that all and singular mayors, sheriffs, bailiffs, constables, and other officers to whom it appertaineth, that they and every of them with diligence cause and see that this his proclamation be put in due execution after the tenor of the same, and also according to another act[2] of parliament established in the parliament above rehearsed, against such as will refuse to sell their wines at prices taxed as is aforesaid, as they will answer thereto at their uttermost perils.

1. 23 Henry VIII, c. 7, 1531, *SR 3*, 374.
2. 24 Henry VIII, c. 6, 1532, *SR 3*, 422.

261. Ordering Nobles and Gentry to Their Homes for Military Service

[Westminster, 23 December 1545, 37 Henry VIII]

Antiq 2, 160*a:* date as above; writ to mayor and sheriffs of London; schedule as below. Steele 284. Text (MS): Antiq

THE KING'S MOST ROYAL MAJESTY, considering most graciously how meet and necessary it is that all such noblemen, gentlemen, and others as repair hither to this parliament, not being specially appointed to attend upon his most royal person, or the Queen's highness, or commanded by the council to attend here or elsewhere for any other purpose, should repair into their countries as well for the putting themselves in order for their defense and annoyance of our enemies as occasion shall serve and as his majesty shall hereafter appoint and determine, as for service to be done to his majesty, touching his subsidy and other his affairs in the parts where they do inhabit, doth straightly charge and command that all noblemen, gentlemen, and others, except only such as be before excepted, shall immediately depart home into their countries upon pain of his majesty's displeasure and to be further punished as to his highness or his most honorable council shall be thought convenient.

262. Prohibiting Export of Grain

[Westminster, 2 January 1546, 37 Henry VIII]

Antiq 2, 161: date as above; writ to sheriff of Wilts; schedule as below. Steele 285. Text (MS): Antiq

FORASMUCH as there must be presently made a great provision of all kinds of grain within the county of Wilts for the furniture of our army upon the sea, the want and lack thereof might be a great detriment and danger to the same, and likewise breed a great lack and danger to our subjects for lack thereof: we therefore, by the advice of our council, straightly do charge and command that all provisions of all kinds of grain made or to be made by any manner of person or persons within the said county of Wilts for the said furniture be stayed until the Feast of Easter next coming (our other provisions only excepted), upon pain that any person offending this present proclamation shall lose and forfeit the said grain and also shall suffer imprisonment and make fine at our will and pleasure.

263. Requiring Licenses for Food Export

[Westminster, 18 January 1546, 37 Henry VIII]

Antiq 2, 162: date as above; writ to sheriffs of Norfolk and Suffolk; schedule as below. Steele 286. Text (MS): Antiq

WHERE the King's most royal majesty, by his proclamation[1] bearing date at Westminster the fifth day of December last past (for the necessary furniture of the towns of Calais and Boulogne and other his highness' parts beyond the seas, there must be presently made a great provision of butter, cheese, and all kinds of grain within the said counties of Norfolk and Suffolk), by the advice of his most honorable council, did straightly charge and command that all provisions of butter, cheese, and of all kinds of grain then made or to be made by any manner of person or persons within the said counties, should be stayed unto the Feast of the Purification of our Blessed Lady next coming, his highness' provisions and such provisions as any person or persons should ship, to be, at his or their own adventure, transported and conveyed to his said towns of Calais and Boulogne only excepted, as by the said proclamation more plainly appeareth;

Forasmuch as divers and sundry persons have since made great provision of butter, cheese, and of all kinds of grain, pretending the same to be for the victualing of his said towns of Calais and Boulogne, which nevertheless have not been sent thither but conveyed otherwise to their own private lucres and commodities, whereby his highness' expectation is deceived and the said towns of Calais and Boulogne unfurnished:

His highness therefore straightly chargeth and commandeth all and every his subjects of what estate, degree, or condition soever they be, that they nor any of them shall from henceforth transport or carry over the seas unto his said towns of Calais or Boulogne or to any other place, any butter, cheese, or any kind of grain without special license to be had and obtained for the same either of his highness or of such of his highness' council as be appointed to the special charge of the provision of victual, upon pain not only to incur all such penalties as by the statutes and proclamations be provided in that behalf, but also to be further punished by imprisonment of their bodies and otherwise, to the terrible example of all other.

1. See 259.

264. Enforcing Staple's Control of Wool Export

[Westminster, 4 March 1546, 37 Henry VIII]

Antiq 2, 163: date as above; writ to sheriff of Staffordshire; schedule as below. See 278. Steele 287. Text (MS): Antiq

WHERE in the session of this present parliament holden upon prorogation at Westminster the 23rd day of November last past, among other things it was ordained and enacted[1] by authority of the said parliament, that no manner of person from and after the first day of March last past, other than merchants of the Staple and their servants and factors for the only provision of the said Staple, and for to be shipped only to the said Staple, and other than such as should convert the same into yarn or cloth within this realm by himself or by any other, should buy or bargain or take promise of bargain of any wools being now unshorn, of the growing of the shires of Kent, Surrey, Sussex, Southampton, Wilts, Dorset, Somerset, Gloucester, Worcester, Hereford, Salop, Warwick, Leicester, Nottingham, Derby, York, Lincoln, Rutland, Northampton, Norfolk, Suffolk, Essex, Cambridge, Huntingdon, Buckingham, Bedford, and Hertford or any of them before the Feast of the Purification of Our Lady next after the shearing or clipping of the same wools, or buy or bargain any wools or take promise of bargain of any wools that should grow in any of the said shires in any year or years to come after the said Feast of the Purification of Our Lady that shall be next after the shearing or clipping of the said wool, but only such persons, their servants and factors that of the said wools should make or do to be made yarn, hats, girdles, or cloths within this realm, and not to sell the same wool again, or the Stapler or his servants or factors, to be shipped only to the said Staple, upon pain of forfeiture of the double value of all the said wools bought or for to be bargained or taken by promise of bargain contrary to the said act, as by the said act amongst other things more plainly appeareth;

And forasmuch as the shires of Middlesex, Stafford, Oxford, and Berks be omitted and left out in the said act, the King's most royal majesty, with the advice of his most honorable council, straightly chargeth and commandeth that no manner of person or persons whatsoever he or they be, from and after the said first day of March, other than merchants of the said Staple and their servants and factors for the only provision of the said Staple, and for to be shipped only to the said Staple, and other than such as shall convert the same into yarn or cloths within this realm by himself or by any other, buy or bargain or take promise of bargain of any wools being now

1. 37 Henry VIII, c. 15, 1545, *SR 3*, 1004.

unshorn of the growing of the said shires of Middlesex, Stafford, Oxford, and Berks, or any of them before the same Feast of the Purification of Our Lady next after the shearing or clipping of the said wool, or buy or bargain or take promise of bargain of any wools that shall grow in any of the said shires of Middlesex, Stafford, Oxford, and Berks in any year or years to come after the said Feast of the Purification of Our Lady that shall be next after the shearing or clipping of the said wool, but only such persons, their servants, and factors that of the said wools shall make or do to be made yarn, hats, girdles, or cloth within this realm, and not to sell the same wool again, or the Stapler or his servants or factors, to be shipped only to the said Staple upon the pain expressed in the said act.

265. Ordering London Brothels Closed

[Westminster, 13 April 1546, 37 Henry VIII]

Antiq 2, 164: date as above; writ to mayor and sheriffs of London; schedule as below. Steele 288. Text (MS): Antiq

THE KING'S MOST EXCELLENT MAJESTY, considering how by toleration of such dissolute and miserable persons as, putting away the fear of Almighty God and shame of the world, have been suffered to dwell besides London and elsewhere in common, open places called the stews, and there without punishment or correction exercise their abominable and detestable sin, there hath of late increased and grown such enormities as not only provoke instantly the anger and wrath of Almighty God, but also engender such corruption among the people as tendeth to the intolerable annoyance of the commonwealth, and where not only the youth is provoked, enticed, and allowed to execute the fleshly lusts, but also, by such assemblies of evil-disposed persons haunted and accustomed, is daily devised and conspired how to spoil and rob the true laboring and well-disposed men, for these considerations hath by advice of his council thought requisite utterly to extinct such abominable license and clearly to take away all occasion of the same: wherefore his majesty straightly chargeth and commandeth that all such persons as have accustomed most abominably to abuse their bodies contrary to God's law and honesty, in any such common place called the stews now about the city of London, do, before the Feast of Easter next coming, depart from those common places and resort incontinently to their natural countries with their bags and baggages, upon pain of imprisonment and further to be punished at the King's majesty's will and pleasure.

Furthermore his majesty straightly chargeth and commandeth that all such householders as under the name of bawds have kept the notable and marked houses and known hostelries for the said evil-disposed persons; that is to say, such householders as do inhabit the houses whited and painted with signs on the front for a token of the said houses, shall avoid with bag and baggage before the Feast of Easter next coming upon pain of like punishment at the King's majesty's will and pleasure.

Furthermore the King's majesty straightly chargeth and commandeth that all such as dwell upon the banks called the stews near London, and have at any time before this proclamation sold any manner victuals to such as have resorted to their houses, do before the said Feast of Easter cease and leave off their victualing and forbear to retain any guest or stranger into their house either to eat and drink or lodge, after the Feast of Easter next coming, until they have presented themselves before the King's majesty's council and there bound themselves with surety in recognizance not to suffer any such misorder in their house, or lodge any serving man, prentice, or woman unmarried, other than their hired servants, upon the pain before specified.

The King's most excellent majesty also chargeth and commandeth that no owner or mean tenant of any such whited house or houses, where the said lewd persons have had resort and used their most detestable life, do from the said Feast of Easter presume to let any of the houses, heretofore abused with said mischiefs in the streets called the stews aforesaid, to any person or persons before the same owner or mean tenant intending to make lease as afore do present the name or names of such as should hire the same to the King's majesty's council, and that before them the lessee hath put in bond and surety not to suffer any of the said houses to be abused as hath been in times past with the said abomination, upon like pain as before is mentioned.

Finally, to the intent all resort should be eschewed to the said place, the King's majesty straightly chargeth and commandeth that from the Feast of Easter next ensuing there shall no bear-baiting be used in that row or in any place on that side the bridge called London Bridge, whereby the accustomed assemblies may be in that place thoroughly abolished and extinct, upon like pain as well to them that keep the bears and dogs which have been used in that purpose as to all such as will resort to see the same.

266. Providing Victual for Boulogne and Newhaven

[Westminster, 19 April 1546, 37 Henry VIII]

AC (Dasent *1*, 390): date, Greenwich, 18 April; order to Chancellor for proclamation to be made. Antiq 2, 165: date as above; writ to mayor and sheriffs of London; similar writs to sheriffs of Southampton, Somerset, Dorset, Sussex, Kent, Essex, Norfolk, Suffolk, Lincoln, and Cinque Ports; schedule as below. Steele 289. Text (MS): Antiq

FORASMUCH as at this present it is by the King's most excellent majesty thought most expedient and necessary that provision and preparation of all manner of victuals be forthwith made for the furniture of his grace's town at the Newhaven in Boulogne, minding to have his said town nourished with abundance of all things necessary: his highness therefore, by the advice of his most honorable council, of his great clemency and goodness is pleased and contented that it shall be lawful to all and singular his highness' subjects at their liberties and free wills from time to time to embark, ship, and carry over the seas, at his or their own adventure, to be delivered at the said Newhaven and not elsewhere, as much wheat, malt, rye, oats, beans, peas, beeves, muttons, bacon, bread, beer, butter, cheese, and all other kinds of victuals, wood, coals, hay, and straw as they or any of them will, until such time as his highness shall by his proclamation determine the contrary; any statute, law, proclamation, or restraint to the contrary notwithstanding.

Provided always that every person transporting any of the kinds aforesaid shall first enter the same in the customer's books and bind themselves in the double value of the said victuals to deliver the same at the said Newhaven and not elsewhere, and to bring with them certificate in writing subscribed with the hands of the King's majesty's lieutenant or two of his grace's council there for the delivery of the same, upon pain not only to incur the pains and forfeitures of their said several obligations but also all such other penalties as by the statutes and proclamations be provided in this behalf, and further to be punished by imprisonment of their bodies or otherwise, to the terrible example of all other at the King's majesty's will and pleasure.

267. Pricing Wines

[Westminster, 11 June 1546, 38 Henry VIII]

Antiq 2, 166: date as above; writ to mayor and sheriffs of London; schedule as below. Steele 290. Text (MS): Antiq

WHEREAS it is ordained and provided by statute [1] that the prices of Gascon and French wines should be limited and declared by the Lord Chancellor of England, Lord Treasurer of England, Lord President of the King's most honorable council, Lord Privy Seal, and other of the councilors of our said sovereign lord specified and declared in the said statute, as by the same statute made and established in the parliament begun and holden at Westminster the third day of November in the 21st year of the King's most gracious reign and continued by divers prorogations, more plainly appeareth.

Forasmuch as the said lords and councilors in execution of the said act hath by their deliberate advices taxed, limited, assigned, and appointed the prices of Gascon and French wines to be sold by retail within our city of London and suburbs of the same; that is to say, every gallon of the best Gascon or French wines shall be retailed and sold for 12*d.* the gallon. Item, every gallon of the best Sack or Rumney shall be retailed and sold for 10*d.* the gallon, and also that every gallon of the best Rhenish wine and Malmesey shall be retailed for 12*d.* the gallon, and also that every pottle, quart, and pint shall be retailed after and according to the same rates.

The King's most royal majesty therefore straightly chargeth and commandeth all and singular his subjects and others that shall sell any manner Gascon or French wines or any of the wines above named by retail within the city of London and suburbs of the same, that they nor any of them in any manner wise shall sell any of the said wines otherwise than is above limited, upon pain to forfeit and pay such penalties as be contained and expressed in the same.

And moreover his highness' pleasure and commandment also is that all and singular mayors, sheriffs, bailiffs, constables, and all other officers to whom it appertaineth that they and every of them with diligence cause and see that this proclamation be put in due execution after the tenor of the same, as they will answer thereto at their uttermost perils.

1. 23 Henry VIII, c. 7, 1531, *SR 3*, 374.

268. Announcing Peace Treaty with France

[Westminster, 11 June 1546, 38 Henry VIII]

STC 7806 (UM 2,10,392), Antiq 2, 167; printed by T. Berthelet (London, 1546); date, MS note as above; MS writ to mayor and sheriffs of London; schedule as below. Hall 252*v:* proclaimed in London on Whitsunday. Wriothesley *1*, 163: proclaimed in London on 13 June. Steele 291. Text (*STC*): Antiq

THE KING our sovereign lord, having always before his most gracious eyes the manifold benefits and commodities of peace, and considering how necessary it is at this time not only for his grace's own realms and dominions, but also for the whole state of Christendom, that Christian princes should agree and join in perfect love, concord and amity together, whereby they shall first please God, and be the more able to maintain their estates, and also procure great wealth and quietness to their subjects, being the wars of late years entered between his majesty and the right high and mighty prince the French King, hath upon deliberate advice and consideration removed all kind of enmity, displeasure, and unkindness, that hath been between them, and hath upon most godly and honorable conditions passed, concluded, and agreed a good, perfect, sincere, firm, assured and perpetual amity, peace, intelligence, confederation, union, and amity, to remain and continue forever between his most excellent majesty and his heirs and successors on the one part, and the said right high and mighty prince the French King on the other part, their realms, countries, cities, towns, lands, dominions, territories and seigniories, places, castles, vassals, and subjects by sea, land, fresh water, and elsewhere; by the which peace it is provided and ordained, that from henceforth all hostility and war shall cease on either part. And the said princes, their heirs, and successors with all their vassals and subjects to live together in peace, amity, intelligence, concord, love, unity, and friendship. And that it shall be lawful to all and singular the subjects of either of them, of what estate, degree, or condition soever they be, freely, quietly, peaceably, and at liberty, and without any safe-conduct or license to enter into the others' realms, there to remain, demur, haunt, frequent, be conversant, dwell, sojourn, abide, or through the same to pass at their pleasure. And all feats of merchandise, intercourse, exchange, buying, selling, or other business whatsoever it be, not prohibited or defended by the laws of the realms, to use, occupy, do and exercise; and from the same to pass and repass with their goods, merchandises, ships, carts, carriages, horses, armors, and other things whatsoever they be, not prohibited, without arrest, stop, molestation, contradiction, or impediment; and generally all other things to do, use, and exercise as freely, quietly, and liberally as they have done in time of peace taken between the realms of England and France heretofore accordingly. In which peace also is comprehended the most high and mighty prince Charles by the grace of God Emperor, and etc., with all his realms, dominions, lands, countries and subjects, and no manner of thing touching the friendship and perpetual amity with him, nor any intercourse of merchandises or other thing is by this present peace in any wise violated, broken, impaired, diminished, or hindered, but all remaining in full and perfect strength and virtue as firmly, wholly, entirely as they were before.

269. Prohibiting Unlicensed Export of Grain

[Westminster, 27 June 1546, 38 Henry VIII]

STC 7807 (Um 2,10,393), Antiq 2, 168: printed by T. Berthelet (London, 1546); date, MS note, as above; writ unspecified; schedule as below. Steele 292. Text (*STC*): Antiq

WHERE the King's most royal majesty, by his grace's proclamation [1] bearing date at Westminster the 19th day of April last past, did give license to all and singular his subjects, that they at their liberties and free wills from time to time should embark, ship, and carry over the seas, at their own adventure, for the furniture of his grace's camp at the Newhaven, wheat, malt, rye, and all such other kinds of grain and victuals as they or any of them would unto such time as his highness by his proclamation should determine the contrary;

Forasmuch as at this present (thanks be to Almighty God) there is passed, concluded, and agreed a good, perfect, sincere, firm, assured and perpetual amity and peace, to remain and continue forever between his most excellent majesty, and the right high and mighty prince the French King; by reason whereof it shall not be needful that so great quantities of grain and other victuals be conveyed over the seas, as in the time of the war were necessary; his highness therefore minding to provide that his pieces on that side the sea may from henceforth be furnished in such order as the same breed no lack or scarcity in this realm, doth, by the advice of his most honorable council, straightly charge and command all and singular his subjects, of what estate, degree, or condition soever they be, that they nor any of them shall, after the publishing of this his highness' proclamation, transport or carry over the seas, to the said Newhaven, or elsewhere, any manner, kind of grain or other victuals, without his highness' special license to be had and obtained for the same, under his Great Seal of England, upon pain not only to incur all such penalties as by the statutes and proclamations be provided

1. See 266.

in that behalf, but also to be further punished by imprisonment of their bodies, and otherwise by fine and ransom at his majesty's will and pleasure, to the terrible example of all other. Willing and commanding all and singular his justices of peace, mayors, sheriffs, bailiffs, constables, customers, comptrollers, and searchers, and all other his grace's officers, ministers, and subjects, to whom in this case it shall appertain, to see that this proclamation be duly and without respect observed, as they will answer at their extreme perils.

And to the intent the same may be the better and more certainly kept, according to the true meaning thereof, his majesty straightly chargeth and commandeth all and singular his customers, comptrollers, and searchers of this realm, that they permit no kind of grain or other victuals to be shipped and transported from one port, country, or shire to another within the same realm, but that the party which shall so ship and convey the same, do first bind himself by obligation in the treble value of the said corn or other victuals, that he shall only carry the same to that place which he shall name and appoint in the condition of his obligation, and from thence bring a certificate under the hands of the mayor, the customer, and comptroller of the town and port, where he shall unship it, or of two of them at the least, within four months after that he hath delivered the same there, to be there, and in those parts of the realm employed, and not elsewhere, without failing, as they will answer for that which shall pass contrary to this order upon like pain as is before rehearsed.

270. Requiring Certification of Barristers in Crown Courts

[Westminster, 28 June 1546, 38 Henry VIII]

BM MS Harl 442, 176: proclaimed on above date; schedule as below. Steele 293. Text (MS): Harl

FORASMUCH as it is ordered and agreed by the commandment of our most dread sovereign lord the King's highness, with the advice of the Lord Chancellor of England and all the justices of both benches, that no person except that he hath read in court shall be admitted nor suffered to be a pleader in any of his highness' honorable courts at Westminster; that is to say, in the Courts of Chancery, King's Bench, Common Pleas, Exchequer, Star Chamber, Duchy Chamber, Augmentations, Sewers, Tenths and First Fruits, and Wards and Liveries, unless he be thereunto admitted and appointed by the said Lord Chancellor and the two Chief Justices with the advice of two of the benchers and ancients of either of the four houses of court.

His majesty's express pleasure and most dread commandment is that no person presume to break this order, upon pain to be committed by the officers and ministers of every of the said courts to ward and to make fine at his highness' will and pleasure.

And it is further ordered at his majesty's pleasure that, before his justices of assize and *nisi prius* in their assizes and sessions, if there be no learned men present that hath been readers, that then his justices in their circuits may and shall appoint such other learned men to be of counsel with the parties as shall be thought meet by the justices for that time. This proclamation to begin and take effect the first day of Michaelmas term next coming.

271. Enforcing Statute on Handguns

[London, 8 July 1546, 38 Henry VIII]

STC 7808 (UM 2,10,39), Antiq 2, 169: printed by T. Berthelet (London, 1546); date, MS note, 28 June or 8 July; schedule as below. Herbert 450: date, 8 July. Steele 294: date, 28 June. Text (*STC*): Antiq

WHERE the King our most dread sovereign lord, considering how expedient it was to have his loving subjects practiced and exercised in the feat of shooting of handguns and hackbuts, as well for the defense of this his highness' realm and other his realms and dominions, as for the annoyance of his majesty's enemies in time of war and hostility, did, by his highness' proclamation set forth, by the advice of his majesty's council, according to the act and statute [1] made at Westminster the 28th day of April, in the 31st year of his most gracious reign, give license and liberty to all his majesty's subjects, born within his grace's dominions, being of the age of 16 years and upwards, that they and every of them, from and after the said proclamation made, might lawfully shoot in handguns and hackbuts without incurring any forfeiture, loss, or danger for the same; any statute thereof made before to the contrary notwithstanding, as by the same proclamation more at large doth and may appear;

Forasmuch as it hath pleased God to remove from us the plague of war and to send unto us a right honorable and profitable peace, which (by God's grace) shall continue to His glory, and to the honor and surety of his majesty and his succession, and to the quiet and benefit of this realm:

His most royal majesty therefore, by this his highness' present proclamation, set forth by the advice of his majesty's council, according to the act above mentioned, doth not only make void the said former proclamation, but

1. 31 Henry VIII, c. 8, 1539, *SR 3*, 726.

also straightly chargeth and commandeth all and singular his majesty's subjects, that they or any of them, from the last day of August next coming, shall not shoot in any handguns, hackbuts, or other guns, nor use or have the same contrary to the tenor, form, and effect of his gracious law and statute [2] made in the parliament begun at Westminster the 16th day of January, and continued until the first day of April, in the 33rd year of his most gracious reign; except any of his said loving subjects have his grace's license under his Great Seal for the same, or otherwise licensed or authorized by the same statute made the first day of April, in the said 33rd year of his said most gracious reign, upon the pain of the forfeiture mentioned in the same statute.

Willing and commanding all and singular justices of the peace, mayors, sheriffs, bailiffs, constables, and all other his majesty's officers, ministers, and subjects to have special regard to the due execution of this proclamation as they tender his majesty's pleasure and will answer for the contrary at their perils.

272. Prohibiting Heretical Books; Requiring Printer to Identify Himself, Author of Book, and Date of Publication

[Westminster, 8 July 1546, 38 Henry VIII]

STC 7809 (UM 2,10,395), Antiq 2, 171: printed by T. Berthelet (London, 1546); date, 8 July; schedule as below. Foxe *5*, 565. Wilkins *4*, 1. Wriothesley *1*, 168: proclaimed in London on 7 July. Steele 295: date Westminster. Text (*STC*): Antiq

THE KING'S MOST EXCELLENT MAJESTY, understanding how under pretense of expounding and declaring the truth of God's Scripture, divers lewd and evil-disposed persons have taken occasion to utter and sow abroad, by books imprinted in the English tongue, sundry pernicious and detestable errors and heresies, not only contrary to the laws of this realm, but also repugnant to the true sense of God's law and his word; by reason whereof certain men of late, to the destruction of their own body and soul, and to the evil example of others, have attempted arrogantly and maliciously to impugn the truth, and therewith trouble the sober, quiet, and godly religion united and established under the King's majesty in this his realm:

His highness, minding to foresee the dangers that might ensue thereof, and tendering therewith (like a most Christian prince) the conservation of

2. 33 Henry VIII, c. 6, 1541, *SR 3*, 832.

the true religion in his majesty's dominions from such corrupt and pestilent teaching as hath of late secretly crept in by such printed books, hath thought it necessarily requisite to devise, by his proclamation and authority of the same, how to avoid and eschew the said dangers and inconvenience, and to purge his commonwealth of such pernicious doctrine, as by books in the English tongue hath been of late divulged abroad in this his grace's realm. For which consideration, having the devil so tempered the setting abroad of his falsehood, as he many times annexed truths thereunto, whereby to induce and deceive the simple people. So as now the purging of that which is noisome and hurtful cannot, without taking away some part of that being tolerable, be put in execution, being the books increased to an infinite number, and unknown diversities of titles and names, whereby specially to revoke, annul or condemn the same, the King's majesty is enforced to use his general prohibition, commandment, and proclamation as followeth:

First, that from henceforth no man, woman, or other person, of what estate, condition, or degree soever he or they be, shall after the last day of August next ensuing, receive, take, have, or keep in his or their possession, the text of the New Testament of Tyndale's [1] or Coverdale's [2] translation in English, nor any other than is permitted by the act of parliament made in the session of the parliament holden at Westminster in the 34th and 35th year of his majesty's most noble reign; nor after the said day shall receive, have, take, or keep in his or their possession any manner of book printed or written in the English tongue which be or shall be set forth in the names of Frith, Tyndale, Wycliff, Joy, Roy, Basille, Bale, Barnes, Coverdale, Turner, Tracy, or by any of them, or any other book or books containing matter contrary to the King's majesty's book called *A Necessary Doctrine and Erudition for any Christian Man,*[3] or any thing therein contained, or any other book or books prohibited or forbidden to be had or kept by the act [4] of parliament holden at Westminster in the 34th and 35th year of the King's majesty's most victorious reign abovesaid.

And furthermore the King's majesty straightly chargeth and commandeth that whosoever, of what estate, degree, or condition soever they or he be, hath now in his or their custody any such book printed or written in English as doth contain matter contrary to the said doctrine set forth by the King's majesty, or be set forth in the name of Frith, Tyndale, Wycliff, Joy, Roy, Basille, Bale, Barnes, Coverdale, Turner, Tracy, or else the same book or books in English be the New Testament of Tyndale's or Coverdale's translation, or any other prohibited by the said act made *anno* 34th and 35th, shall before the last day of August next coming deliver the same Eng-

1. *STC* 2824.
2. *STC* 2842.
3. *STC* 5168.
4. 34 & 35 Henry VIII, c. 1, 1542, *SR 3*, 894.

lish book or books to his master in that household, if he be a servant, or dwell under any other; and the master or ruler of the house, and such others as dwell at large, shall deliver all such books of the sorts aforesaid as they have, or shall come to their hands, deliver as afore or otherwise, to the mayor, bailiff, or chief constable of the town where they dwell, to be by them delivered over openly within 40 days next following after the said delivery to the sheriff of the shire or to the bishop, chancellor, or commissary of the same diocese, to the intent the said bishop, chancellor, commissary, and sheriff, and every of them, shall cause them incontinently to be openly burned, which the King's majesty's pleasure is, that every of them shall see executed in most effectual sort, and of their doings therein make certificate to the King's majesty's most honorable council before the first of October next coming.

And to the intent that no man shall mistrust any danger of such penal statutes as be passed in this behalf for keeping of the said books, the King's majesty is most graciously contented by this proclamation to pardon that offense to the said time appointed by this proclamation for the delivery of the said books; and commandeth that no bishop, chancellor, commissary, mayor, bailiff, sheriff, or constable shall be curious to mark who bringeth forth such books, but only order and burn them openly as is in this proclamation ordered.

And if any man, after the last day of August next coming, shall have any of the said books in his keeping, or be proved convicted by sufficient witness before four of the King's most honorable council, to have hidden them or used them, or any copy of any of them, or any part of them, whereby should appear that he willingly hath offended the true meaning of this proclamation, the same shall not only suffer imprisonment and punishment of his body at the King's majesty's will and pleasure, but also shall make such fine and ransom to his highness for the same, as by his majesty or four of his grace's said council shall be determined.

Moreover the King's majesty straightly chargeth and commandeth, upon the pain aforesaid, that from henceforth no printer do print any manner of English book, ballad, or play, but he put in his name to the same, with the name of the author and day of the print, and shall present the first copy to the mayor of the town where he dwelleth, and not to suffer any of the copies to go out of his hands within two days next following.

Finally his majesty straightly chargeth and commandeth that no person or persons, of what estate, degree, or condition soever he or they be, from the day of this proclamation presume to bring any manner of English book concerning any matter of Christian religion printed in the parts of beyond the seas, into this realm, or sell, give, or distribute any English book, printed in outward parts, or the copy of any such book, or any part thereof, to any person dwelling within this his grace's realm or any other his majesty's dominions, unless the same shall be specially licensed so to do by his highness' express grant, to be obtained in writing for the same upon the pains before limited, and therewithal to incur his majesty's extreme indignation.

273. Encouraging English to Colonize French Territory

[Westminster, 7 August 1546, 38 Henry VIII]

BM MS Harl 442, 177: date as above; writ to sheriff of Kent; schedule as below. Steele 296. Text (MS): Harl

WHEREAS our most dread sovereign lord the King's majesty doth hold and enjoy the town of Boulogne in the parts of beyond the seas, with sundry other honors, castles, towns, fortresses, territories, and grounds within the marches of Boulogne and Newhaven, which his majesty did most victoriously win and conquer in his last wars against France, in such sort as by the treaty passed between his majesty and his good brother, cousin, and ally the French King doth appear;

For the better furniture of which towns and marches and the increase of the inhabitants within the same, and also for the increase of all kinds of grain and other necessaries for husbandry to be now newly set up upon the grounds there, of late by reason of the wars wasted and consumed, his majesty hath assigned by his commission under his Great Seal certain of his council and other of his commissioners to survey the said town of Boulogne and all other his highness' honors, castles, manors, lands and tenements, and hath given full power and authority to the said commissioners upon due survey thereof to let and set the same and any parcel thereof to any such persons the King's said sovereign lord's subjects for farm of year or years or otherwise at such reasonable prices or yearly rents as shall be to the great commodity of the occupiers of the same:

Wherefore his majesty doth signify unto all his loving subjects of this his realm of England that they and every of them between this and the fifth day of November next coming shall have free liberty to pass the seas towards his said town of Boulogne to commune or conclude with the said commissioners for the taking and occupying of the said houses, castles, manors, lands, and tenements or other grounds within the said territories, and upon such covenants and conclusion made shall have like liberty to convey from out of this realm into those parts all manner of such cattle, stuff, and other necessaries as shall be meet for the manuring of the said grounds so taken, without any customs or other thing to be answered unto his highness for the same.

274. Enforcing Statutes of Sewers, Vagabonds

[1546, 38 Henry VIII]

BM MS Harl 442, 181: writ to sheriff of Kent; schedule as below. Steele 297: date as above. Text (MS): Harl

The King our sovereign lord, considering that albeit many good and profitable statutes and ordinances hath been made for the commonweal of his realm and in especial for sewers,[1] and repress and punishment of vagabonds and sturdy beggars,[2] yet nevertheless his justices of peace and other his ministers in every shire, city, borough, and town, which by their oaths and duties be bound to see execution of the same laws and statutes, be and of long time hath been remiss and negligent in that behalf, whereby evil-doers much encouraged and boldened to contemn the same laws and statutes for lack of due execution thereof, much to the King's displeasure and discontentation, the whole default whereof his majesty imputeth to his justices of peace and other ministers being authorized and having charge of the same.

His highness therefore straightly chargeth and commandeth all and singular justices of peace, constables and all other his ministers and subjects to whom the charge of due execution of such good laws and statutes appertaineth that they, putting apart all favor, affection, and corruption shall endeavor themselves with all diligence and dexterity of the uttermost of their powers to the due and effectual execution of the said laws and statutes, and in especial the statutes made for sewers and vagabonds, as they will answer to the King's highness at their uttermost perils and will avoid the King's most high displeasure and indignation. And if it may appear to his highness that the said justices of peace, ministers and subjects shall hereafter neglect this to do, his majesty intendeth to proceed against the offenders as enemies of his commonwealth, to the terrible example of all other.

1. 6 Henry VIII, c. 10, 1533, *SR 3*, 131.

2. 13 Edward I, c. 4 (Winchester), 1285, *SR 1*, 97; 5 Edward III, c. 14, 1331, *SR 1*, 268; 23 Edward III, c. 7, 1349, *SR 1*, 308; 34 Edward III, c. 1, 1360, *SR 1*, 364; 34 Edward III, c. 10, 11, 1360, *SR 1*, 367; 7 Richard II, c. 5, 1383, *SR 2*, 32; 12 Richard II, c. 7–9, 1388, *SR 2*, 58; 11 Henry VII, c. 2, 1495, *SR 2*, 569; 19 Henry VII, c. 12, 1503, *SR 2*, 656; 22 Henry VIII, c. 12, 1530, *SR 3*, 328; 27 Henry VIII, c. 25, 1535, *SR 3*, 558; 28 Henry VIII, c. 6, 1536, *SR 3*, 655; 33 Henry VIII, c. 10, 1541, *SR 3*, 841; 37 Henry VIII, c. 23, 1545, *SR 3*, 1014.

The Proclamations of Edward vi

1547-53

275. Proclaiming Accession of Edward VI

[Westminster, 31 January 1547, 1 Edward VI]

CW (C82/865): date as above; sign manual; letters patent to all subjects; schedule as below; order for proclamation to be made in London and all shires in England and Wales. PR (C66/804/12*d*): date as above; schedule as below; order for proclamation as in CW. LJ 15, 303*v:* date, 31 January; order for mayor and aldermen on 31 January to return from Westminster at once and, in scarlet gowns, accompany the heralds proclaiming Edward VI. Rymer *15,* 123. Wriothesley *1,* 178: proclaimed in Westminster Hall on 31 January. Steele 300. Text (MS): PR

EDWARD VI, by the grace of God King of England, France, and Ireland, defender of the faith and of the Church of England and also of Ireland in earth the supreme head, to all our most loving, faithful, and obedient subjects, and to every of them, greeting.

Where it hath pleased Almighty God, on Friday last past in the morning to call unto his infinite mercy the most excellent high and mighty prince, King Henry VIII of most noble and famous memory, our most dear and entirely beloved father, whose soul God pardon; forasmuch as we, being his only son and undoubted heir, be now invested and established in the crown imperial of this realm, and other his realms, dominions, and countries, with all regalities, pre-eminences, styles, names, titles, and dignities to the same belonging or in any wise appertaining:

We do by these presents signify unto all our said most loving, faithful, and obedient subjects that like as we for our part shall, by God's grace, show ourself a most gracious and benign sovereign lord to all our good subjects in all their just and lawful suits and causes, so we mistrust not but they and every of them will again, for their parts, at all times and in all cases, show themselves unto us, their natural liege lord, most faithful, loving, and obedient subjects, according to their bounden duties and allegiances, whereby they shall please God and do the thing that shall tend to their own preservations and sureties; willing and commanding all men of all estates, degrees, and conditions to see our peace kept and to be obedient to our laws, as they tender our favor and will answer for the contrary at their extreme peril.

276. Proclaiming Accession of Edward VI

[Westminster, 1 February 1547, 1 Edward VI]

AC (Dasent *2*, 10): date, 2 February; order for proclamations of King's style to be sent to all sheriffs of shires. Antiq 3, 1: date as above; writ to sheriffs of Notts and Derby; schedule as below. Strype *2(1)*, 21. Steele 301. Text (MS): Antiq

THE KING our sovereign lord, Edward VI, by the grace of God King of England, France, and Ireland, defender of the faith and of the Church of England and also of Ireland in earth the supreme head, doth give to understand to all his most loving, faithful, and obedient subjects, and to every of them, that where it hath pleased Almighty God on Friday the 28th day of January last past in the morning to call unto his infinite mercy the most excellent high and mighty prince, King Henry VIII of most noble and famous memory, the King's majesty's most dear and entirely beloved father (whose soul God pardon); forasmuch as the King's majesty, now being his only son and undoubted heir, is now thereby invested and established in the crown imperial of this realm, and his majesty's realms, dominions, and countries, with all regalities, pre-eminences, styles, names, titles, and dignities to the same belonging or in any wise appertaining:

The same our sovereign lord doth signify unto all his said most loving, faithful, and obedient subjects, that like as his majesty for his part shall by God's grace show himself a most gracious and benign sovereign lord to all his good subjects in all their just and lawful suits and causes, so his majesty mistrusteth not but they and every of them will again for their parts at all times and in all cases show themselves unto his highness, their natural liege lord, most loving, faithful, and obedient subjects, according to their bounden duties and allegiance, whereby they shall please God and do the thing that shall tend to their own preservations and sureties. Willing and commanding all men of all estates, degrees, and conditions, to see his peace kept, and to be obedient to his laws as they tender his gracious favor and will answer for the contrary at their extreme perils.

277. Announcing Service Claims for Coronation

[Westminster, 4 February 1547, 1 Edward VI]

BM MS Harl 353, *1v*: date, February; letters patent to all subjects; schedule as below. Strype 2 (2), 24. Wriothesley *1*, 180: proclaimed on afternoon of 4 February. Steele 302: date, Westminster. Text (MS): Harl

WHEREAS by the laws and ancient customs of this realm of England the nobles, knights, and others the King's majesty's subjects, by sundry tenures of their lands and hereditaments, are bounden to attend upon his majesty's person royal, at the time and day of his grace's coronation; to do, exhibit, and minister to his highness their several services, duties, ministries, and offices; and thereupon to receive of his majesty such gifts, fees, and rewards as to their several services, offices, and duties of ancient time hath been accustomed and appertained:

His majesty royal, by his highness' proclamation, signifieth to all the said nobility, and other his subjects claiming to do service at his said coronation, that his majesty hath by his highness' commission appointed, assigned, and authorized his right well-beloved councilor, Sir Thomas Wriothesley, knight, of the noble Order of the Garter, Lord Wriothesley, Lord Chancellor of England; and his right trusty and right well-beloved cousins and councilors, Francis, Earl of Shrewsbury, William, Earl of Essex, and John Lord, Viscount Lisle, High Admiral of England; and his right trusty and well-beloved councilor Richard Listen, knight, Chief Justice of England, and Edward Montague, knight, Chief Justice of the Common Pleas; and five, four, or three of them, to be his commissioners for the receiving and allowance of the said claims; who shall begin his majesty's court for that purpose upon Monday, the seventh of this present month of February, within the White Hall of his majesty's palace of Westminster, then and there to receive, hear, determine, and allow the petitions and claims of the several services of his said nobles and other his faithful subjects, to be done by them and every of them by reason of their several tenures and services at the day of his majesty's coronation, which, God willing, shall be the 20th day of February next coming, according to their duties and his majesty's laws.

Wherefore his majesty's pleasure is that every man having any thing to do before the said commissioners shall give their attendance at the said day accordingly.

278. Enforcing Staple Control of Wool Export

[Westminster, 31 March 1547, 1 Edward VI]

BM MS Titus B.2, 4: date as above; schedule as below. See 264. Steele 303. Text (MS): Titus

WHERE in the session of parliament holden upon prorogation at Westminster the 23rd day of November in the 37th year of the reign of our most dearest father of famous memory, King Henry VIII (whose soul God pardon), amongst other things it was ordained and enacted [1] by authority of the said parliament that no manner of person from and after the first day of March then last past, other than merchants of the Staple and their servants and factors for the only provision of the said Staple and for to be shipped only to the said Staple, and other than such as should convert the same into yarn or cloth within this realm, by himself or by any other should buy or bargain or take promise of bargain of any wools being now unshorn of the growing of the shires of Kent, Surrey, Sussex, Southampton, Wilts, Dorset, Somerset, Gloucester, Worcester, Hereford, Salop, Warwick, Leicester, Nottingham, Derby, York, Lincoln, Rutland, Northampton, Norfolk, Suffolk, Essex, Cambridge, Huntingdon, Bucks, Bedford, and Hertford, or any of them, before the Feast of the Purification of Our Lady next after the shearing or clipping of the same wools; or buy or bargain any wools or take promise of bargain of any wools that should grow in any of the said shires in any year or years to come after the said Feast of the Purification of Our Lady that shall be next after the shearing or clipping of the same wools, but only such persons, their servants, and factors that of the said wools should make or do to be made yarn, hats, girdles, and cloth within this realm, and not to sell the same wool again, or the stapler or his servants or factors to be shipped only to the said Staple; upon pain of forfeiture of the double value of all the said wools bought or to be bargained or taken by promise of bargain contrary to the said act, as by the said act among other things more plainly appeareth:

And forasmuch as the shires of Middlesex, Stafford, Oxford, and Berks be omitted and left out in the said act, the King's most royal majesty, with the assent and consent of his most dear uncle Edward, Duke of Somerset, governor of his person, and of his realms and dominions protector, and of other of his councilors, straightly chargeth and commandeth that no manner of person or persons, whatsoever he or they be, from and after the first day of March, other than merchants of the said Staple, and their factors and servants, for the only provision of the said Staple and to be shipped only

1. 37 Henry VIII, c. 15, 1545, *SR 3*, 1004.

to the said Staple, and other than such as shall convert the same into yarn or cloth within the realm, by himself or by any other buy or bargain or take promise of bargain of any wools being now unshorn of the growing of the said shires of Middlesex, Stafford, Oxford and Berks, or any of them, before the said Feast of the Purification of Our Lady next after the shearing or clipping of the said wool, or buy or bargain or take promise of bargain of any wools, but only such persons, their servants and factors that of the said wools will make or do to be made yarn, hats, girdles, or cloth within this realm and not to sell the same wool again, or the stapler or his servants or factors to be shipped only to the said Staple: upon the pain expressed in the said act.

And furthermore his highness straightly chargeth and commandeth that no manner of person or persons, what estate or degree soever he or they be, shall pull, pluck, or slip the wool of any fell that is merchantable to the Staple of Calais, upon pain of forfeiture of the double value of the said fell and further to be punished at his majesty's will and pleasure.

279. Holding Subsidy Collectors Accountable

[Westminster, 14 May 1547, 1 Edward VI]

Antiq 3, 4: date as above; schedule as below. Steele 304. Text (MS): Antiq

THE KING our sovereign lord straightly chargeth and commandeth all and singular commissioners assigned to assess and have the second payment of the subsidy [1] granted to the late King of famous memory, King Henry VIII, father to our said sovereign lord, in the 37th year of the reign of the said late King, in all and singular shires, cities, boroughs, and towns corporate within this realm of England and Wales: that they and every of them return and certify into the Court of Exchequer, before the Treasurer and Barons of the same court, before the Feast of the Ascension of Our Lord next coming, their certificates and bonds of the said assessment of the same second part of the said subsidy; and that all knights of the shires in the same parliament and burgesses of cities, boroughs, and towns corporate, certify before the day to them appointed, the names and surnames of the collectors of the last payment of the 15th and 10th granted at the same parliament, and their bond concerning the same upon the pains and forfeitures limited in the act thereof made; and that all collectors of the same second payment of the said subsidy make undelayed payment into the receipt of the same Exchequer of all such sums of money as they be charged with for their said collections, before the Monday then next following the

1. 37 Henry VIII, c. 24, 1545, *SR 3*, 1016; 37 Henry VIII, c. 25, 1545, *SR 3*, 1019.

same Feast of the Ascension, upon the pains of forfeitures of the bonds therefore made, and upon pain of forfeitures of 4*s.* for every pound unpaid, according to the forms of the statutes in that behalf made.

280. Permitting Export of Grain

[Westminster, 16 May 1547, 1 Edward VI]

AC (Dasent 2, 492): date, 12 May; license to Sir William Peneston to export cattle and grain. Antiq 3, 5: date as above; writ to sheriff of Essex; schedule as below. Steele 305. Text (MS): Antiq

Whereas by a proclamation [1] bearing date at Westminster the 27th day of June in the 38th year of the reign of our late entirely beloved father of most famous memory, King Henry VIII (whose soul God pardon) did then by his proclamation straightly charge and command all and singular his subjects, of what estate, degree, or condition soever they were, that they nor any of them should after the publishing of the same his proclamation transport or carry over the seas into any outward parts any manner kind of grains or other victuals without his special license, to be had and obtained for the same under his Great Seal of England, upon pain not only to incur all such penalties as by the statutes and proclamations were provided in that behalf, but also to be further punished by imprisonment of their bodies and otherwise by fine and ransom at his will and pleasure, to the terrible example of all others, as by the same proclamation more plainly appeareth; and forasmuch (as thanks be unto Almighty God) there is at this present great plenty and abundance of wheat and other corn within this realm, whereby the farmers and others which use tilling and manuring of their lands may not sell their wheat and other grains but at very low prices to their utter undoing, unless that some remedy be provided in that behalf:

The King's most royal majesty, with the advice of his most dearest uncle Edward, Duke of Somerset, governor of his person and protector of all his realms, dominions, and subjects, and others of his most honorable council, of his special grace granteth and by this his present proclamation giveth free liberty and license to all and singular his loving subjects, of what estate or degree soever he or they be, to embark, ship, and carry over the seas at his and their liberties and free wills into all outward parts (being with his majesty in league and amity), all manner of wheat and all other kinds of grain (oats only excepted) so long as a quarter of wheat shall not exceed the prices of 6*s.* 8*d.* the quarter; barley, malt, and rye shall not exceed the price of 5*s.* the quarter; or unto such time as his highness by his other proc-

1. See 269.

lamation under his Great Seal of England shall determine the contrary; any act, law, statute, proclamation, or restraint to the contrary hereof in any wise notwithstanding. Provided always that of his customs, subsidies and other duties due unto his highness in this behalf, he be duly answered for the same as appertaineth.

Wherefore his majesty straightly chargeth and commandeth all and singular his customers, comptrollers, and searchers of all and singular his ports, that they and every of them shall permit and suffer all and sundry his subjects to transport and carry wheat and other grain, according to this his majesty's license of proclamation, as they and every of them will answer to his highness at their uttermost perils.

281. Enforcing Statutes on Seditious Rumors

[Somerset Place, 24 May 1547, 1 Edward VI]

Grafton *2v:* date, 24 May; schedule as below. Dibdin *3,* 457*n:* separate edition by Grafton. Steele 306: date, Somerset Place. Text: Grafton

FORASMUCH as the King's highness, the Lord Protector, and the residue of the King's majesty's council is informed that there hath been now of late divers lewd and light tales told, whispered, and secretly spread abroad by uncertain authors, in markets, fairs, and alehouses, in divers and sundry places of this realm, of innovations and changes in religion and ceremonies of the Church feigned to be done and appointed by the King's highness, the Lord Protector, and other of his highness' Privy Council, which by his grace or them was never begun nor attempted; and also of other things and facts sounding to the dishonor and slander of the King's most royal majesty, the Lord Protector's grace, and other the King's most honorable council, and no less to the disquietness and disturbance of the King's highness' loving subjects, contrary to divers wholesome laws [1] and ordinances, upon grave and weighty considerations heretofore made and ordained by the King's highness' most noble progenitors to reform, punish, and chastise all manner of lewd and vagrant persons telling and reporting false news and tales to the disquieting and disturbing of the King's highness, his nobles, and subjects of this realm:

The King's most royal majesty, by the most circumspect and laudable advice of his most dearly beloved uncle Edward, Duke of Somerset, Lord Protector of the King's majesty's realms, dominions and subjects, and governor of his most royal person, and other of his highness' Privy Council,

1. 3 Edward I, c. 34 (Westminster I), 1275, *SR 1,* 35; 2 Richard II, st. 1, c. 5, 1378, *SR 2,* 9; 12 Richard II, c. 11, 1388, *SR 2,* 59; 37 Henry VIII, c. 10, 1545, *SR 3,* 997.

considering and graciously pondering the great hurt, damage, loss, and disquietness amongst his grace's subjects which might ensue of such false and slanderous tales and news, and that nothing is more necessary than to provide and see that good and wholesome laws be put in ure and full execution, to the intent no manner of person may or shall have justly any occasion to surmise, invent, or disperse any kind of false tales or news to the discord or disturbance of the subjects of this realm, straightly chargeth and commandeth all manner of officers, ministers, and justices, that the said former laws and statutes be earnestly put in execution; that is to say, that no manner of person from henceforth be so hardy to find, say, or tell any false news, messages, or other such false things, whereof discord or occasion of discord or any slander might arise within this realm between the King, his people, or the nobles; and he that so doeth shall be kept in prison until he have brought in him which was his author of the tale.

And further his majesty, by his former gracious advice of the said Lord Protector and his said Privy Council, straightly chargeth and commandeth all manner of persons, of what estate, degree, or condition he or they be, hearing, reading, knowing or witting any such false tales or news to be by any manner of person, of and upon the King's highness, the Lord Protector or any of his said majesty's most honorable council, or other nobles of the realm, reported, told, written, or otherwise published and spread about within the King's highness' realms and dominions, immediately and without all delay, all other business set apart, either to repair and declare the same to his dearly beloved uncle, the Lord Protector, or some other of his majesty's Privy Council, if that do he may conveniently; or else at the least do declare and show the same to the justice of the peace next inhabiting. The which justice also, the King's majesty most straightly commandeth, after the hearing thereof immediately to apprehend the said person, and after he be apprehended to put the said person in jail or safe custody, so to remain unto such time he hath brought forth the author of the said tale or news who told the same to him; and so then to make further search from person to person, so much as lieth in them, to search forth and get out the first author and beginner of the said tales and news; and of their diligence done herein, and the knowledge by them gotten, to certify without delay, under their seals in writings, the King's highness' said dearly beloved uncle, upon pain of incurring, as well concerning the same party so hearing, reading, knowing, or witting, and not immediately declaring as is abovesaid, as concerning the justice of peace, so hearing and not immediately giving knowledge thereof, as is abovesaid, of extreme danger of his grace's laws and imprisonment of his or their bodies, and as he and they will further answer for the grievous attempts in that behalf at his grace's pleasure.

And whosoever shall reveal, bring to light, and utter the first inventor and author of such false news, untrue tales, and lies, which tend to the slander and reproach of the King's most royal person, the Lord Protector's grace, and other of the King's highness' honorable council, and other of his nobles, or else to the disturbance of the peace and quietness of these his grace's realms, dominions, or subjects, shall have not only his majesty's great and worthy thanks, but also convenient and good reward for faithfully doing his most bounden duty therein.

282. Announcing Payment of Henry viii's Debts

[Somerset Place, 29 May 1547, 1 Edward VI]

STC 7810 (UM 2,10,396), BM 1851.c.10, 89: printed by R. Grafton (London, 1547); schedule as below. Grafton 2: date, 29 May; schedule as below. Steele 307; date, Somerset Place. Text (*STC*): BM

WHEREAS the King's majesty hath been informed that sundry sums of money were and be due to divers his loving and faithful subjects, in the time of his most dear father of most worthy memory, for sundry things taken to the service of him and the realm; and that his dearest uncle the Duke of Somerset, protector of all his realms, dominions, and subjects, and governor of his most royal person, and others of his council, the executors of his majesty's said most noble father, have disbursed great sums of money to divers his highness' ministers in those affairs, for the payment of the said debts; desiring to know how much, and to whom any debt doth yet remain unsatisfied: willeth and requireth all and every his loving subjects to whom in this case it shall appertain to declare in writing unto ______________ before the Feast of St. John Baptist next coming what remaineth due unto them and wherefore; and the said ______________ to send the same declarations to the lord great master before the end of Trinity term to the intent that upon the knowledge of the certainty of the said debts the said Lord Protector, and the other executors to the said late King's majesty, may take an order for the full contentation of every debt, which they intend to do accordingly.

283. Holding Subsidy Collectors Accountable

[Westminster, June 1547, 1 Edward VI]

Antiq 3, 6: date, MS note, June; schedule as below. Steele 308: date, Westminster. Text (MS): Antiq

THE KING our sovereign lord straightly chargeth and commandeth all and singular collectors as well of payments of any subsidies as of all and singular

15ths and 10ths granted to the late King of famous memory, King Henry VIII, father to our said sovereign lord the King that now is, by act of parliament,[1] and accountable in the court of the King's majesty's Exchequer, that they and every of them do not only pay or cause to be paid all and every such sums of money as is in the charge of them, or any of them, by reason of their said collections being due and yet behind unpaid, but also fully account of the same their collections before the last day of this present month of June: upon pain of imprisonment and to make fine at the King's majesty's pleasure; and furthermore to incur such penalties and dangers as by the statute and laws of this realm in that behalf be ordained and provided.

284. Prohibiting Hunting of King's Deer

[Westminster, 9 July 1547, 1 Edward VI]

Antiq 3, 7: date as above; writ to Sir John Williams, chief steward of the honor of Grafton; schedule as below. Steele 309. Text (MS): Antiq

FORASMUCH as of late our deer within our honor of Grafton hath been by divers and sundry persons hunted and disquieted, as well in the night as in the day, not only with hounds and greyhounds, but also with crossbows, handguns, shewels by night, and divers other engines, without respect of their duties of allegiance which they ought to have borne towards us, and contrary to former orders and proclamations heretofore in that behalf made by our most dear father of famous memory, King Henry VIII:

We let you wite, therefore, our full mind, pleasure, and commandment is, by the advice of our dear uncle Edward, Duke of Somerset, protector of our realms, dominions, and subjects, and governor of our person, and the rest of our Privy Council, that from henceforth no manner of person or persons of what estate, degree, or condition soever he or they be, shall neither hunt, molest, disquiet, trouble, nor forestall any of our deer within our said honor of Grafton, nor yet use as purlieu any our woods, fields, pastures, and commons adjoining and being in any of our forests of Writted Cole or Sawsey, being parcel of our said honor of Grafton. And that all and every such person and persons which shall hereafter attempt to do the contrary, we, in consideration thereof, by the advice aforesaid, do fully authorize and appoint by virtue of this our proclamation that the high steward of our said honor, the master of our game, and his or their deputy or deputies, keepers of grounds next unto where any such unlawful act or acts shall be committed or done, to take away from such offenders and breakers of this our proclamation their hounds, greyhounds, crossbows,

1. 37 Henry VIII, c. 24, 1545, *SR 3*, 1016; 37 Henry VIII, c. 25, 1545, *SR 3*, 1019.

handguns, or other his or their engines, and the same incontinent to convey to our said uncle Edward, Duke of Somerset, with a bill as well of the names of such offenders as a declaration of their act or acts committed, so that there may be such punishment as shall seem meet by our said uncle ministered unto them in that behalf.

285. Prohibiting Export of Bell Metal, Food, Candles

[Westminster, 27 July 1547, 1 Edward VI]

Antiq 3, 8: date as above; letters patent to customers, comptrollers, searchers, and other officers and ministers of the port of London; schedule as below. Strype 2(*1*), 71. Steele 310. Text (MS): Antiq

To OUR CUSTOMERS, comptrollers, and searchers and other our officers and ministers within our port of London, and in all creeks and places to the said port belonging, and to every of them, greeting.

For certain causes and considerations, us and our most dearest uncle Edward, Duke of Somerset, governor of our person, and of our realms, dominions, and subjects protector, and other of our Privy Council, specially moving, we straightly charge and command you that you nor any of you permit or suffer to be carried or conveyed out of the said port or out of any creeks or places to the said port belonging, into any outward parts, any manner of bell metal, butter, cheese, tallow, or candles, unto such time as by our letters patent sealed under our Great Seal you shall specially have our further commandment for the same; the towns of Calais and Boulogne and the marches of the same always excepted and reserved.

Wherefore we will and command you and every of you that in execution of the premises you diligently do attend as you tender our pleasure, any act, statute, ordinance, or other restraint heretofore made to the contrary notwithstanding; and that upon pain of £200 to be levied of your lands, goods, and chattels to our use, you fail not hereof, as we specially trust you.

286. Prohibiting Hunting of King's Deer

[Westminster, 30 July 1547, 1 Edward VI]

Antiq 3, 9: date as above; writ to Sir Leonard Rede, chief steward of Barnwood Forest, Bucks; schedule as below. Steele 311. Text (MS): Antiq

FORASMUCH as of late our deer within our forest of Barnwood, within our county of Bucks, hath been by divers and sundry persons hunted and disquieted, as well in the night as in the day, not only with hounds and greyhounds but also with crossbows, handguns, shewels by night, and divers other engines, without respect of their duties of allegiance which they ought to have borne towards us, and contrary to former orders and proclamations heretofore in that behalf so made by our most dear father of famous memory, King Henry VIII:

We therefore let you wite that our full mind, pleasure, and commandment is, with the advice of our dearest uncle Edward, Duke of Somerset, governor of our person, and of our realms, dominions and subjects protector, and the rest of our Privy Council, that from henceforth no manner of person or persons of what estate, degree, or condition soever he or they be, shall neither hunt, molest, disquiet, trouble, nor forestall any our deer within our said forests, nor yet use as purlieu any our woods, fields, pastures and commons lately belonging and appertaining to the late dissolved monasteries of Notley and Studley adjoining and lying near to our said forest of Barnwood; and that all and every such person and persons as shall hereafter attempt to do the contrary, by the advice aforesaid do fully authorize and appoint by virtue of this our proclamation that the high steward of our said forest or his lieutenant, and his or their deputy or deputies, keepers of the grounds next unto such places where any such unlawful act or acts shall be committed and done, to take away from such offenders and breakers of this our proclamation their hounds, greyhounds, crossbows, handguns, or other his or their engines, and the same incontinent to convey to our said uncle Edward, Duke of Somerset, with a bill as well of the names of such offenders as a declaration of their act or acts committed, so that there may be such punishment as shall seem meet by our uncle ministered unto them in that case.

287. Injunctions for Religious Reform; Ordering Homilies to Be Read from the Pulpit

[London, 31 July 1547, 1 Edward VI]

AC (Dasent *2*, 517): date 12 September; Bishop of London protests Injunctions and Homilies. *STC* 10,088 (UM 2,10,399), BM, 697.f.1,1: printed by R. Grafton (London, 1549); date as above; letters patent to all subjects; schedule as below. Cardwell *1*, 2. Foxe *5*, 702. Wilkins *4*, 3. Not in Steele. Text (*STC*): BM

THE KING'S MOST ROYAL MAJESTY, by the advice of his most dear uncle, the Duke of Somerset, Lord Protector of all his realms, dominions, and subjects, and governor of his most royal person, and the residue of his most honorable council, intending the advancement of the true honor of Almighty God, the suppression of idolatry and superstition throughout all his realms and dominions, and to plant true religion, to the extirpation of all hypocrisy, enormities, and abuses, as to his duty appertaineth, doth minister unto his loving subjects these godly Injunctions hereafter following; whereof part were given unto them heretofore by the authority of his most dearly beloved father, King Henry VIII [1] of most famous memory, and part are now ministered and given by his majesty; all which Injunctions his highness willeth and commandeth his said loving subjects, by his supreme authority, obediently to receive and truly to observe and keep, every man in their offices, degrees, and states, as they will avoid his displeasure and the pains in the same Injunctions hereafter expressed.

The first is that all deans, archdeacons, parsons, vicars, and other ecclesiastical persons shall faithfully keep and observe, and as far as in them may lie, shall cause to be observed and kept of other, all and singular laws and statutes made as well for the abolishing and extirpation of the Bishop of Rome, his pretensed and usurped power and jurisdiction, as for the establishment and confirmation of the King's authority, jurisdiction, and supremacy of the Church of England and Ireland. And furthermore, all ecclesiastical persons having cure of soul shall to the uttermost of their wit, knowledge, and learning, purely, sincerely, and without any color or dissimulation, declare, manifest, and open, four times every year at the least, in their sermons and other collations, that the Bishop of Rome's usurped power and jurisdiction, having no establishment nor ground by the law of God, was of most just causes taken away and abolished, and that therefore no manner of obedience or subjection, within his realms and dominions, is due unto him; and that the King's power, within his realms and do-

1. *STC* 10,085 and 10,086. See 186, 303.

minions, is the highest power under God, to whom all men within the same realms and dominions, by God's laws, owe most loyalty and obedience, afore and above all other powers and potentates in earth.

Besides this, to the intent that all superstition and hypocrisy crept into divers men's hearts may vanish away, they shall not set forth or extoll any images, relics, or miracles, for any superstition or lucre, nor allure the people by any enticements to the pilgrimage of any saint or image; but reproving the same, they shall teach that all goodness, health, and grace ought to be both asked and looked for only of God, as of the very author and giver of the same, and of none other.

Item, that they, the persons above rehearsed, shall make or cause to be made, in their churches and every other cure they have, one sermon every quarter of the year at the least wherein they shall purely and sincerely declare the word of God, and in the same exhort their hearers to the works of faith, mercy, and charity specially prescribed and commanded in Scripture, and that works devised by man's phantasies, besides Scripture, as wandering to pilgrimages, offering of money, candles, or tapers to relics or images, or kissing and licking of the same, praying upon beads, or such like superstition, have not only no promise of reward in Scripture for doing of them, but contrarywise, great threats and maledictions of God, for that they be things tending to idolatry and superstition, which of all other offenses God Almighty doth most detest and abhor, for that the same diminish His honor and glory.

Item, that such images as they know in any of their cures to be, or have been, so abused with pilgrimage or offerings of anything made thereunto, or shall be hereafter censed unto, they (and none other private persons) shall, for the avoiding of that most detestable offense of idolatry, forthwith take down, or cause to be taken down, and destroy the same, and shall suffer from henceforth no torches nor candles, tapers, or images of wax, to be set afore any image or picture, but only two lights upon the high altar before the Sacrament; which for the signification that Christ is the very true light of the world they shall suffer to remain still, admonishing their parishioners that images serve for no other purpose but to be a remembrance whereby men may be admonished of the holy lives and conversation of them that the said images do represent; which images, if they do abuse for any other intent, they commit idolatry in the same, to the great danger of their souls.

Item, that every Holy Day throughout the year, when they have no sermon, they shall immediately after the Gospel openly and plainly recite to their parishioners, in the pulpit, the Pater Noster, the Credo, and the Ten Commandments, in English, to the intent the people may learn the same by heart; exhorting all parents and householders to teach their children and servants the same, as they are bound by the law of God, and in conscience to do.

Item, that they shall charge fathers and mothers, masters, and governors to bestow their children and servants, even from their childhood, either to learning or to some honest exercise, occupation, or husbandry; exhorting and counseling, and by all the ways and means they may, as well in their sermons and collations as other ways, persuading their said fathers and mothers, masters, and other governors diligently to provide and foresee that the youth be in no manner of wise brought up in idleness, lest at any time afterward, for lack of some craft, occupation, or other honest mean to live by, they be driven to fall to begging, stealing, or some other unthriftiness: forasmuch as we may daily see, through sloth and idleness, divers valiant men fall, some to begging and some to theft and murder, which, after [being] brought to calamity and misery, do blame their parents, friends, and governors which suffered them to be brought up so idly in their youth; where, if they had been well brought up in good learning, some occupation or craft, they should (being rulers of their own household) have profited as well themselves as divers other persons, to the great commodity and ornament of the commonwealth.

Also, that the said parsons, vicars, and other curates shall diligently provide that the sacraments be duly and reverently ministered in their parishes. And if at any time it happen them, in any of the cases expressed in the statutes of this realm or of special license given by the King's majesty, to be absent from their benefices, they shall leave their cure not to a rude and unlearned person, but to an honest, well-learned, and expert curate, that can by his ability teach the rude and unlearned of their cure wholesome doctrine, and reduce them to the right way that do err; and which will also execute these Injunctions and do their duty otherwise as they are bound to do in every behalf, and accordingly may and will profit their cure no less with good example of living than with the declaration of the word of God, or else their lack and default shall be imputed unto them (who shall straightly answer for the same if they do otherwise). And always let them see that neither they nor their curates do seek more their own profit, promotion, or advantage than the profit of the souls that they have under their cure, or the glory of God.

Also, that they shall provide within three months next after this visitation one book of the whole Bible, of the largest volume, in English; and within one twelve months next after the said visitation the *Paraphrases* of Erasmus, also in English, upon the Gospels; and the same set up in some convenient place within the said church that they have cure of, whereas their parishioners may most commodiously resort unto the same and read the same; the charges of which books shall be ratably borne between the parson or proprietary and the parishioners aforesaid; that is to say, the one half by the parson or proprietary and the other half by the parishioners. And they shall discourage no man (authorized and licensed thereto) from the reading of any part of the Bible, either in Latin or in English, but shall rather conform and exhort every person to read the same as the very lively word of God and the special food of man's soul that all Christian persons are bound to embrace, believe, and follow if they look to be saved; whereby they may the better know their duties to God, to their sovereign lord the King, and their neighbor; ever gently and charitably exhorting them, and in his majesty's name straightly charging and commanding them, that in the reading thereof no man to reason or contend, but quietly to hear the reader.

Also, the said ecclesiastical persons shall in no wise, at any unlawful time, nor for any other cause than for their honest necessity, haunt or resort to any taverns or alehouses. And after their dinner and supper they shall not give themself to drinking or riot, spending their time idly by day or by night at dice, cards, or tables-playing, or any other unlawful game, but at all times, as they shall have leisure, they shall hear or read somewhat of Holy Scripture, or shall occupy themselves with some other honest exercise; and that they always do the things which appertain to honesty, with endeavor to profit the commonweal; having always in mind that they ought to excel all other in purity of life, and should be example to the people to live well and Christianly.

Item, that they shall, in confessions every Lent, examine every person that cometh to confession to them whether they can recite the articles of their faith, the Pater Noster, and the Ten Commandments, in English, and hear them say the same particularly, wherein, if they be not perfect, they shall declare then that every Christian person ought to know the said things before they should receive the Blessed Sacrament of the altar, and admonish them to learn the said necessary things more perfectly, or else they ought not to presume to come to God's board, without perfect knowledge and will to observe the same; and if they do it is to the great peril of their souls and also to the worldly rebuke that they might incur hereafter by the same.

Also, that they shall admit no man to preach within any their cures but such as shall appear unto them to be sufficiently licensed thereunto by the King's majesty, the Lord Protector's grace, the Archbishop of Canterbury, the Archbishop of York in his province, or the bishop of the diocese. And such as shall be so licensed they shall gladly receive, to declare the word of God without any resistance or contradiction.

Also, if they have heretofore declared to their parishioners anything to the extolling or setting forth of pilgrimages, relics, or images, or lighting of candles, kissing, kneeling, decking of the same images, or any such superstition, they shall now openly, before the same, recant and reprove the same, showing them (as the truth is) that they did the same upon no ground of Scripture, but were led and seduced by a common error and abuse crept into the Church through the suffrance and avarice of such as felt profit by the same.

Also, if they do or shall know any man within their parish, or elsewhere, that is a letter of the word of God to be read in English, or sincerely preached, or of the execution of these the King's majesty's Injunctions, or a fautour of the Bishop of Rome's pretended power, now by the laws of this realm justly rejected, extirped, and taken away utterly, they shall detect and present the same to the King or his council, or to the justice of peace next adjoining.

Also, that the parson, vicar, or curate, and parishioners of every parish within this realm, shall in their churches and chapels keep one book or register, wherein they shall write the day and year of every wedding, christening, and burial made within their parish for their time, and so every man succeeding them likewise; and also therein shall write every person's name that shall be so wedded, christened, or buried. And for the safekeeping of the same book the parish shall be bound to provide, of their common charges, one sure coffer, with two locks and keys, whereof the one to remain with the parson, vicar, or curate, and the other with the wardens of every parish church or chapel wherein the said book shall be laid up. Which book they shall every Sunday take forth and, in the presence of the said wardens or one of them, write and record in the same all the weddings, christenings, and burials made the whole week before; and that done, to lay up the book in the said coffer as afore. And for every time that the same shall be omitted, the party that shall be in the fault thereof shall forfeit to the said church 3*s*. 4*d*. to be employed to the poor men's box of that parish.

Furthermore, because the goods of the Church are called the goods of the poor, and at these days nothing is less seen than the poor to be sustained with the same, all parsons, vicars, pensioners, prebendiaries, and other beneficed men within this deanery, not being resident upon their benefices, which may dispend yearly £20 or above either within this deanery or elsewhere, shall distribute hereafter among their poor parishioners or other inhabitants there, in the presence of the churchwardens or some other honest men of the parish, the fortieth part of the fruits and revenues of their said benefices, lest they be worthily noted of ingratitude which, reserving so many parts to themselves, cannot vouchsafe to impart the fortieth portion thereof among the poor people of that parish that is so fruitful and profitable unto them.

And to the intent that learned men may hereafter spring the more for the execution of the premises, every parson, vicar, clerk, or beneficed man within this deanery, having yearly to dispend in benefices and other promotions of the church £100, shall give competent exhibition to one scholar; and for as many hundred pounds more as he may dispend, to so many scholars more shall give like exhibition in the University of Oxford or

Cambridge, or some grammar school; which, after they have profited in good learning, may be partners of their patron's cure and charge, as well in preaching as otherwise in the execution of their offices; or may, when need shall be, otherwise profit the commonweal with their counsel and wisdom.

Also, that all proprietaries, parsons, vicars, and clerks having churches, chapels, or mansions within this deanery, shall bestow yearly hereafter, upon the same mansions or chancels of their churches, being in decay, the fifth part of that their benefices, till they be fully repaired; and the same, so repaired, shall always keep and maintain in good estate.

Also, that the said parsons, vicars, and clerks shall once every quarter of the year, read these Injunctions given unto them, openly and deliberately before all their parishioners, to the intent that both they may be the better admonished of their duty, and their said parishioners the more moved to follow the same for their part.

Also, forasmuch as by a law established every man is bound to pay his tithes, no man shall, by color of duty omitted by their curates, detain their tithes, and so redub and requite one wrong with another, or be his own judge, but shall truly pay the same as he hath been accustomed, to their parsons, vicars, and curates without any restraint or diminution; and such lack and default as they can justly find in their parsons and curates, to call for reformation thereof at their ordinaries' and other superiors' hands; who, upon complaint and due proof thereof, shall reform the same accordingly.

Also, that no person shall from henceforth alter or change the order and manner of any fasting day that is commanded, nor of common prayer or divine service, otherwise than is specified in these Injunctions, until such time as the same shall be otherwise ordered and transposed by the King's authority.

Also, that every parson, vicar, curate, chantry priest, and stipendiary, being under the degree of bachelor of divinity shall provide, and have of his own, within three months after this visitation, the New Testament, both in Latin and in English, with *Paraphrases* upon the same,[2] of Erasmus, and diligently study the same, conferring the one with the other. And the bishops and other ordinaries by themselves or their officers, in their synods and visitations, shall examine the said ecclesiastical persons how they have profited in the study of Holy Scripture.

Also, in the time of High Mass within every church, he that sayeth or singeth the same shall read, or cause to be read, the Epistle and Gospel of that Mass in English, and not in Latin, in the pulpit or in such convenient place as the people may hear the same. And also every Sunday and Holy Day they shall plainly and distinctly read, or cause to be read, one chapter of the New Testament in English in the said place, at Matins immediately

2. *STC* 2854.

after the lessons; and at Evensong, after Magnificat, one chapter of the Old Testament. And to the intent the premises may be more conveniently done, the King's majesty's pleasure is that when nine lessons should be read in the church, three of them shall be omitted and left out with their responses. And at Evensong time the responses with all the memories shall be left off for that purpose.

Also, because those persons which be sick and in peril of death be often times put in despair by the craft and subtlety of the devil, who is then most busy, and specially with them that lack the knowledge, sure persuasion, and steadfast belief that they may be made partakers of the great and infinite mercy which Almighty God of his most bountiful goodness and mere liberality, without our deserving, hath offered freely to all persons that putteth their full trust and confidence in Him; therefore, that this damnable vice of despair may be clearly taken away, and firm belief and steadfast hope surely conceived of all their parishioners being in any danger, they shall learn, and have always in readiness, such comfortable places and sentences of Scripture as do set forth the mercy, benefits, and goodness of Almighty God towards all penitent and believing persons, that they may at all times when necessity shall require, promptly comfort their flock with the lively word of God, which is the only stay of man's conscience.

Also, to avoid all contention and strife which heretofore hath risen among the King's majesty's subjects in sundry places of his realms and dominions by reason of fond courtesy and challenging of places in procession, and also that they may the more quietly hear that which is said or sung to their edifying, they shall not from henceforth in any parish church at any time use any procession about the church or churchyard or other place; but immediately before High Mass the priests with other of the choir shall kneel in the midst of the church, and sing or say plainly and distinctly the Litany which is set forth in English with all the suffrages following, and none other procession or Litany to be had or used but the said Litany in English, adding nothing thereto but as the King's grace shall hereafter appoint; and in cathedral or collegiate churches, the same shall be done in such places as our commissaries in our visitation shall appoint. And in the time of the Litany, of the High Mass, of the sermon, and when the priest readeth the Scripture to the parishioners, no manner of persons without a just and urgent cause shall depart out of the church; and all ringing and knelling of bells shall be utterly foreborne for that time, except one bell in convenient time to be rung or knelled before the sermon.

Also, like as the people be commonly occupied on the work day with bodily labor for their bodily sustenance, so was the Holy Day at the first beginning godly instituted and ordained that the people should that day give themselves wholly to God. And whereas in our time God is more offended than pleased, more dishonored than honored, upon the Holy Day because of idleness, pride, drunkenness, quarreling, and brawling, which are most used in such days; people nevertheless, persuading themselves sufficiently to honor God on that day if they hear Mass and service though they understand nothing to their edifying; therefore all the King's faithful and loving subjects shall from henceforth celebrate and keep their Holy Day according to God's holy will and pleasure. That is, in hearing the word of God read and taught; in private and public prayers; in acknowledging their offenses to God, and amendment of the same; in reconciling their selves charitably to their neighbors, where displeasure hath been; in oftentimes receiving the Communion of the very body and blood of Christ; in visiting of the poor and sick; in using all soberness and godly conversation. Yet notwithstanding, all parsons, vicars, and curates shall teach and declare unto their parishioners that they may with a safe and quiet conscience, in the time of harvest, labor upon the Holy and Festival Days and save that thing which God hath sent; and if for any scrupulosity or grudge of conscience men should superstitiously abstain from working upon those days, that then they should grievously offend and displease God.

Also, forasmuch as variance and contention is a thing which most displeaseth God, and is most contrary to the Blessed Communion of the body and blood of our savior Christ, curates shall in no wise admit to the receiving thereof any of their cure and flock who hath maliciously and openly contended with his neighbor, unless the same do first charitably and openly reconcile himself again, remitting all rancor and malice, whatsoever controversy hath been between them; and nevertheless, their just titles and rights they may charitably prosecute, before such as have authority to hear the same.

Also, that every dean, archdeacon, master of collegiate church, master of hospital, and prebendiary, being priest, shall preach by himself personally twice every year at the least, either in the place where he is entitled or in some church where he hath jurisdiction, or else which is to the said place appropriate or united.

Also, that they shall instruct and teach in their cures that no man ought obstinately and maliciously break and violate the laudable ceremonies of the Church, by the King commanded to be observed, and as yet not abrogated. And on the other side, that whosoever doth superstitiously abuse them doth the same to the great peril and danger of his soul's health: as in casting holy water upon his bed, upon images, and other dead things; or bearing about him holy bread, or Saint John's Gospel; or making crosses of wood upon Palm Sunday in time of reading of the Passion; or keeping of private Holy Days, as bakers, brewers, smiths, shoemakers, and such other do; or ringing of the holy bells, or blessing with the holy candle, to the intent thereby to be discharged of the burden of sin, or to drive away devils, or to put away dreams and phantasies; or in putting trust and confidence of health and salvation in the same ceremonies when they be only ordained, instituted, and made to put us in remembrance of the benefits which we have received by Christ. And if he use them for any other purpose he grievously offendeth God.

Also, that they shall take away, utterly extinct, and destroy all shrines, covering of shrines, all tables, candlesticks, trindles or rolls of wax, pictures, paintings, and all other monuments of feigned miracles, pilgrimages, idolatry, and superstition, so that there remain no memory of the same in walls, glasses, windows, or elsewhere within their churches or houses. And they shall exhort all their parishioners to do the like within their several houses. And that the churchwardens, at the common charge of the parishioners, in every church shall provide a comely and honest pulpit to be set in a convenient place within the same, for the preaching of God's word.

Also, they shall provide and have within three months after this visitation, a strong chest, with a hole in the upper part thereof, to be provided at the cost and charge of the parish, having three keys, whereof one shall remain in the custody of the parson, vicar, or curate, and the other two in the custody of the churchwardens or any other two honest men to be appointed by the parish from year to year. Which chest you shall set and fasten near unto the high altar, to the intent the parishioners should put into it their oblation and alms for their poor neighbors. And the parson, vicar, and curate shall diligently from time to time, and specially when men make their testaments, call upon, exhort, and move their neighbors to confer and give as they may well spare to the said chest; declaring unto them, whereas heretofore they have been diligent to bestow much substance, otherwise than God commanded, upon pardons, pilgrimages, trentals, decking of images, offering of candles, giving to friars, and upon other like blind devotions, they ought at this time to be much more ready to help the poor and needy; knowing that to relieve the poor is a true worshipping of God, required earnestly upon pain of everlasting damnation; and that also whatsoever is given for their comfort is given to Christ himself, and so is accepted of him that He will mercifully reward the same with everlasting life. The which alms and devotion of the people the keepers of the keys shall at times convenient take out of the chest, and distribute the same, in the presence of the whole parish or six of them, to be truly and faithfully delivered to their most needy neighbors; and if they be provided for, then to the reparation of highways next adjoining. And also the money which riseth of fraternities, guilds, and other stocks of the church (except by the King's majesty's authority it be otherwise appointed) shall be put into the said chest and converted to the said use, and also the rents of lands, the profit of cattle, and money given or bequeathed to the finding of torches, lights, tapers, and lamps, shall be converted to the said use, saving that it shall be lawful for them to bestow part of the said profits upon the reparation of the church if great need require, and whereas the parish is very poor and not able otherwise to repair the same.

And forasmuch as priests be public ministers of the Church, and upon the Holy Days ought to apply themselves to the common administration of the whole parish, they shall not be bound to go to women lying in child-bed, except in time of dangerous sickness, and not to fetch any corpse before it be brought to the churchyard; and if the woman be sick, or the corpse brought to the church, the priest shall do his duty accordingly in visiting the woman and burying the dead person.

Also, to avoid the detestable sin of simony, because buying and selling of benefices is execrable before God, therefore all such persons as buy any benefices, or come to them by fraud or deceit, shall be deprived of such benefices, and be made unable at any time after to receive any other spiritual promotion. And such as do sell them, or by any color do bestow them for their own gain and profit, shall lose their right and title of patronage and presentment for that time, and the gift thereof for that vacation shall appertain to the King's majesty.

Also, because through lack of preachers in many places of the King's realms and dominions the people continue in ignorance and blindness, all parsons, vicars, and curates shall read in their churches, every Sunday, one of the *Homilies*[3] which are and shall be set forth for the same purpose by the King's authority, in such sort as they shall be appointed to do in the preface of the same.

Also, whereas many indiscreet persons do at this day uncharitably contemn and abuse priests and ministers of the Church because some of them, (having small learning), have of long time favored phantasies rather than God's truth, yet forasmuch as their office and function is appointed of God: the King's majesty willeth and chargeth all his loving subjects, that from henceforth they shall use them charitably and reverently for their office and ministration's sake, and especially all such as labor in the setting forth of God's holy word.

Also, that all manner of persons which understand not the Latin tongue shall pray upon none other *Primer*[4] but upon that which was lately set forth in English by authority of King Henry VIII of most famous memory; and that no teacher of youth shall teach any other than the said *Primer*. And all those which have knowledge of the Latin tongue shall pray upon none other Latin *Primer* but upon that which is likewise set forth by the said authority. And that all graces to be said at dinner and supper shall be always said in the English tongue. And that none other grammar shall be taught in any school or other place within the King's realms and dominions but only that which is set forth by the said authority.

3. *STC* 13,639. See 248.

4. *STC* 16,034–16,039. See 248, n. 1.

Item, that all chantry priests shall exercise themselves in teaching youth to read and write, and bringing them up in good manners and other virtuous exercises.

Item, when any sermon or homily shall be had, the prime and hours shall be omitted.

The form of bidding the common prayers

You shall pray for the whole congregation of Christ's Church, and specially for this Church of England and Ireland, wherein first I commend to your devout prayers the King's most excellent majesty, supreme head immediately under God of the spirituality and temporality of the same church, and for Queen Catherine, dowager, and also for my Lady Mary and my Lady Elizabeth, the King's sisters.

Secondly you shall pray for my Lord Protector's grace, with all the rest of the King's majesty's council, for all the lords of this realm, and for the clergy and the commons of the same, beseeching Almighty God to give every of them, in his degree, grace to use themselves in such wise as may be to God's glory, the King's honor, and the weal of this realm.

Thirdly, you shall pray for all them that be departed out of this world in the faith of Christ, that they with us, and we with them, at the day of judgment may rest, both body and soul, with Abraham, Isaac, and Jacob in the kingdom of heaven.

All which and singular Injunctions the King's majesty ministereth unto his clergy and their successors, and to all other his loving subjects: straightly charging and commanding them to observe and keep the same, upon pain of deprivation, sequestration of fruits of benefices, suspension, excommunication, and such other coercion as to ordinaries or other having ecclesiastical jurisdiction, whom his majesty hath appointed for the due execution of the same, shall be seen convenient; charging and commanding them to see these Injunctions observed and kept of all persons being under their jurisdiction, as they will answer to his majesty for the contrary. And his majesty's pleasure is that every justice of peace (being required) shall assist the ordinaries, and every of them, for the due execution of the said Injunctions.

288. Making Assault of Officers Punishable by Death

[Westminster, 3 August 1547, 1 Edward VI]

LJ 15, 318: date as above; writ to mayor and sheriffs of London; schedule as in 178. Not in Steele. Text: see 178

289. Referring Religious Pensioners to Treasurer of the Court of Augmentations

[Hampton Court, 18 September 1547, 1 Edward VI]

AC (Dasent *2*, 97): date, 9 June; order for pensioners henceforth to be referred to Treasurer of Court of Augmentations. Grafton 5*v*: date, 18 September; schedule as below. Dibdin *3*, 457 n.: separate edition by Grafton. Steele 313: date, Hampton Court. Text: Grafton

ALL MEN shall understand that for divers causes and considerations it is lately ordered and decreed by the King's majesty, and his most honorable Privy Council, that all persons, as well religious as other, which have either pension, annuity, or corody granted to them by the King's majesty that dead is, or by any late abbot, prior, or other governor as abovesaid, heretofore paid by the receivers of the Court of Augmentations out of the issues, revenues, and profits of the same court, shall from henceforth receive the same pension, annuity, and corody yearly at the hands of the Treasurer of the said Court of Augmentations and Revenues or of his deputy or deputies, and not at the hands of the said particular receiver of the same Court as heretofore hath been accustomed; and the same to take effect at the next time of payment, at Michaelmas next coming.

Wherefore it is ordered for the ease and quietness of the pensioners and others as have either pension, annuity, or corody granted as before, of what house or houses soever they were of or had their grants, now dwelling within this shire, shall yearly receive the same within this said shire at the hands of the said Treasurer, his deputy, or deputies, at such time and places within this shire as shall be by the said Treasurer appointed. And for the better accomplishment whereof the King's majesty's pleasure, with the advice and consent of his grace's most honorable Privy Council, is that all persons within this shire having any of the said pensions, annuities, or corodies, and having knowledge of this proclamation and having no lawful impediment, shall appear at ________ the _____ day of ____________ next ensuing before the deputy of the said Treasurer being sent down with this proclamation, to take notice of their patents and grants, which they shall not fail but bring with them and exhibit to his said deputy, to the intent the said Treasurer may be the more better ascertained both of their state and states, and of the sum and sums of money which he shall appoint unto his said deputy for the contentation of their said pensions, annuities, and corodies which shall be due unto them at Michaelmas next coming; for the which apparency and exhibiting of the said patents, grants, and writings and taking of the said notice, no money shall be demanded nor required of any person or persons by the said deputy for the same; and that they shall now at this time repair to the place where the King's majesty's next audit shall be kept within this shire for the receipt of their said pensions, annuities, and corodies due unto them as before, and there to show themselves before the deputy of the said Treasurer, at whose hands they shall receive their said pensions, annuities, and corodies. And in case there be any which shall not so personally appear, that then they to send a certificate in writing under the hands of two justices of the peace, or of one justice of peace and one other gentleman of reputation of this shire, declaring that the same person or persons are living and in lawful state to receive his or their said pension, annuity, or corody, and thereupon the said Treasurer or his deputy to make payment accordingly.

290. Forbidding Nuisance in the Court

[Hampton Court, 21 September 1547, 1 Edward VI]

ETR (E36/231/196): date as above; schedule as above. Steele 314. Text (MS): ETR

THE KING'S MAJESTY, by the advice of his P[rivy] Council, straightly chargeth and commandeth that no persons, of what degree soever, shall make water or cast any annoyance within the precinct of the court, within the gates of the porter's lodge, whereby corruption may breed and tend to the prejudice of his royal person, as they regard his high displeasure.

291. Ordering Release of French Prisoners and Prizes

[Westminster, 26 October 1547, 1 Edward VI]

CSPForeign 1, 23: date, Westminster 4 March; commission formed to arrange defensive league with France. LJ 15, 318*v:* date as above; writ to the sheriffs of London; schedule as below. Steele 315. Text (MS): LJ

FORASMUCH as of late days it hath chanced that sundry prizes hath been taken upon the sea by our subjects upon the Frenchmen, and on the other side also the semblable hath been done against our subjects, to the prejudice of peace and contrary to the form and tenor of the treaty last made between the most noble prince of famous memory, our most dear father, and the late French King, by means of which prizes the poor subjects as well on the one side as the other which had interest in the same, have made divers complaints and supplications as well unto us and our dear uncle Edward, Duke of Somerset, governor of our person, and of our realms, dominions, and subjects protector, and other of our Privy Council, as also to our good brother the French King; whereupon for the weal, intercourse, the agreement and preservation of the said peace, and to the end that it might endure without that by such occasions it should be altered or troubled, it hath been by a common consentment accorded, prefixed, and determined that all such persons, ships, and merchandises which since the time of the said peace have been taken and arrested upon the sea shall be absolutely upon Sunday the 30th day of this present month, as well on the one side as the other, put in plain and entire deliverance and liberty:

We therefore, by the advice of our said dearest uncle and council, will and command expressly all and singular our subjects to whom in this case it shall appertain, that they fail not, the said 30th day within all our ports and their members, where they have to do, to see entirely released, delivered and set at full liberty all and every such prisoners, ships, goods, merchandises, and things whatsoever, which have been prized and taken upon the said Frenchmen by our said subjects since the said treaty of peace.

And further we straightly charge and command that none of our subjects from henceforth presume or be so hardy to make any prizes upon the said Frenchmen, nor to do any other thing in prejudice of the said treaty and peace, but that they shall have free gate amiably to converse, traffic, and do their trade of merchandise with our said subjects as with their good friends and allies, even as the semblable shall be done on the behalf of our good brother the French King's subjects, to the end that every of our said subjects may know that it is lawful and permitted to them quietly and freely to exercise their traffic of merchandise, or any other their trade by sea, as in time of peace they are accustomed.

292. Ordering Punishment for Assaults on Clergy and Scholars

[Somerset Place, 12 November 1547, 1 Edward VI]

AC (Dasent 2, 521): date, 12 November; schedule as below. BM MS Harl 352, 47*v*: date 12 November; schedule as below. Steele 316: date, Somerset Place. Text (MS): Harl

FORASMUCH as the misorders by the serving men and other young and light persons and apprentices of London towards priests, and those that go in scholars' gowns like priests, hath of late, both in Westminster Hall and in other places of the city of London, been so great that not only it hath offended many men, but also have given great occasion, if on the parts of the said priests more wisdom and discretion had not been showed than of the other, of sedition and murder or at the least of such other inconveniences as are not to be suffered in a commonwealth; as to the King's highness and his most entirely beloved uncle the Duke of Somerset, governor of his most royal person and protector of all his realms, dominions, and subjects, and the rest of his majesty's council, hath been credibly and certainly reported and showed:

For reformation whereof, the King's highness, by the advice of his said most dear uncle and other his majesty's honorable council, willeth and straightly commandeth that no serving man nor apprentice or any other person, whatsoever he or they be, shall use hereafter such insolence and evil demeanor towards priests, as reviling, tossing of them, taking violently their caps and tippets from them without just title or cause, nor otherwise to use them than as becometh the King's most loving subjects one to do toward another: upon pain that whosoever shall do the contrary and be upon the same taken with the manner, or if he shall appear upon complaint made by sufficient trial of witness or otherwise before the King's highness' council, or the mayor, sheriffs, or other sufficient judges to whom the complaint shall be made, the person thereof to be guilty; that then such offender or offenders, according to the quality of the fact for the time and place where it was committed, to suffer pain of imprisonment or other corporal pain, to the example of all others as to the discretion of the said Lord Protector, the King's majesty's council or of the judges before whom the same is proved, seem convenient; which shall be such that, by the punishment of a few, all other may be afraid to use such insolence, violence, and ill demeanor against any of the King's majesty's subjects.

293. Limiting Access to Court because of Plague

[Westminster, 18 November 1547, 1 Edward VI]

Antiq 3, 12: date as above; schedule as below. Steele 317. Text (MS): Antiq

FORASMUCH as the King's most royal majesty is credibly informed that the infection of the plague reigneth in sundry parts, as well within his city of Westminster as in other places near adjoining to the same, whereby great danger may not only ensue to his most royal person but also to his nobles and others his subjects repairing at this present to this his highness' court of parliament:

His highness therefore, with the advice of his most dear uncle Edward, Duke of Somerset, governor of his majesty's royal person and protector of all his realms, dominions, and subjects, and other of his most honorable council, straightly chargeth and commandeth all and singular person and persons inhabiting as well within the said city as in other places adjoining to the same, in whose houses the said infection of plague now reigneth or hereafter shall reign, that they and every of them do forthwith set forth a cross upon their street door, whereby the King's highness' said subjects may know that the said infection of plague is or hath been in their said houses.

And furthermore his highness, by the advice aforesaid, straightly chargeth and commandeth that no manner of person or persons in whose house the said infection of plague is or hath been, or have resorted to any other infected person by the space of three months last past, do from henceforth repair to the court or do suffer any of the attendants of the said court or other gentlemen's servants whose masters attend the said court, to enter their houses where the said infection of plague hath been, upon pain of his high indignation and displeasure and further to be punished at his majesty's will and pleasure.

294. Regulating Legal Pleading

[Westminster, 28 November 1547, 1 Edward VI]

Antiq 3, 13: date as above; schedule as below. Steele 318. Text (MS): Antiq

WHEREAS always heretofore the utter barristers and other students of the four houses of court for the time being have been from time to time admitted and allowed to be pleaders and setters forth of the causes and suits of the King's majesty's highness' subjects, in all and every his courts, the Court of the Common Pleas at Westminster only excepted, his most royal majesty therefore minding the due execution and ministration of justice, and the expedition of his said subject's causes in this behalf, is pleased and contented that all and every such person and persons, now being or that hereafter shall be student, utter barrister, or utter barristers in any of the said houses of court, and being fellow in any of the said houses by the space of eight years, shall and may from henceforth lawfully plead and be counselors and pleaders at or in any court of record within this his realm of England and the marches of the same, the said Court of the Common Pleas at Westminster only excepted; any proclamation, order, and decree heretofore had or made to the contrary in any wise notwithstanding.

And furthermore his highness straightly chargeth and commandeth that no manner of person or persons being no sergeant-at-law, reader, or utter barrister of any of the said four houses of court, nor any utter barrister not being a fellow of any of the said four houses of court by the space aforesaid, shall presume or enterprise to plead or be a pleader in any of his highness' said courts at Westminster, upon pain of imprisonment and further to make fine at his majesty's will and pleasure.

295. Limiting Grain Export

[Westminster, 7 December 1547, 1 Edward VI]

LJ 15, 335: date as above; writ to customers, searchers, comptrollers, and other ministers in port of London, and other ports and creeks adjacent thereto; schedule as below. Steele 319. Text (MS): LJ

Where the King's most royal majesty, by his proclamation[1] bearing date at Westminster the 16th day of May last past, did give free liberty and license to all and singular his loving subjects, of what estate or degree soever they were, to embark, ship, and carry over the seas at their liberties and free wills into all outward parts (being with his majesty in league and amity) all manner of wheat and all other kinds of grain, so long as a quarter of wheat should not exceed the price of 6*s.* 8*d.* the quarter, barley, malt, and rye 5*s.* the quarter, or unto such time as his highness by his other proclamation under his Great Seal of England should determine the contrary, as by the same proclamation more plainly appeareth;

And forasmuch as wheat, malt, and other grain before rehearsed doth exceed the prices abovesaid, his most royal majesty therefore, with the advice of his most honorable council, straightly chargeth and commandeth all and every his subjects of what estate, degree, or condition soever they be, that

1. See 280.

they nor any of them shall from henceforth transport or carry over the seas into any outward parts any manner of wheat or other grain without his special license under his Great Seal of England to be had and obtained for the same (his majesty's towns of Calais, Boulogne, and other his piers beyond the seas only excepted), upon pain not only to incur all such pains as by the statutes and proclamations are provided in this behalf, but also to be further punished by imprisonment of their bodies and otherwise, to the terrible example of all others.

Provided always that every person before the shipping or transporting of any manner of wheat or other kinds of grains aforesaid unto the said towns of Calais and Boulogne and other his piers beyond the seas shall not only enter the same into the customers' books but shall likewise with one sufficient surety with him be bound by obligation unto the King's majesty, to be taken by the customer and comptroller of the port or creek where the said wheat or other grain shall be shipped, or by their deputies, in the double value of the said wheat or other grain, to discharge the same at his said towns or other his piers and not elsewhere, and to bring a true and just certificate within two months next after from the King's deputies of the said towns of Calais and Boulogne and two others of his council there at the least, that the said wheat and other grain so shipped were there discharged and delivered accordingly. Provided also that of our customs, subsidies, and other duties due unto us for the same were duly answered as appertaineth.

296. Silencing Disputes on the Eucharist

[Hampton Court, 27 December 1547, 1 Edward VI]

STC 7812 (UM 2,10,398), Antiq 3, 15: printed by R. Grafton (London, 1547); date, 27 December; schedule as below. Cardwell *1*, 34. Strype 2(2), 340. Wilkins *4*, 18. See 287. Steele 320: date, Hampton Court. Text (*STC*): Antiq

WHEREAS the King's highness hath of late, with the assent and consent of the lords spiritual and temporal, and the commons in the parliament held the fourth day of November, in the first year of his most gracious reign, made a good and godly act[1] and statute against those who do contemn, despise, or with unseemly and ungodly words deprave and revile the Holy Sacrament of the body and blood of Our Lord, commonly called the Sacrament of the Altar; and in the same statute, hath most prudently declared by all the words and terms which Scripture speaketh of it, what is undoubtedly to be accepted, believed, taken, and spoken by and of the said Sacrament; yet this notwithstanding, his majesty is advertised that some of his

1. 1 Edward VI, c. 1, 1547, *SR 4(1)*, 2.

subjects, not contented with such words and terms as Scripture doth declare thereof, nor with that doctrine which the Holy Ghost by the Evangelists and Saint Paul hath taught us, do not cease to move contentions and superstitious questions of the said Holy Sacrament and Supper of the Lord, entering rashly into the discussing of the high mystery thereof, and go about in their sermons or talks arrogantly to define the manner, nature, fashion, ways, possibility, or impossibility of those matters, which neither make to edification, nor God hath not by His holy word opened; which persons (not contented reverently and with obedient faith to accept that in the said Sacrament, according to the saying of Saint Paul, the bread is the communion or partaking of the body of Our Lord, the wine likewise the partaking of the blood of Christ, by the words instituted and taught of Christ, and that the body and blood of Jesus Christ is there, which is our comfort, thanksgiving, love token of Christ's love towards us, and of ours as his members within ourself) searcheth and striveth unreverently whether the body and blood aforesaid is there really or figuratively, locally or circumscriptly, and having quantity and greatness or but substantially and by substance only, or else but in a figure and manner of speaking; whether his blessed body be there, head, legs, arms, toes, and nails, or any other way, shape, and manner, naked or clothed; whether He is broken and chewed, or He is always whole; whether the bread there remaineth as we see, or how it departeth; whether the flesh be there alone and the blood, or part, or each in other or in the one, both; in the other but only blood, and what blood, that only which did flow out of the side, or that which remained; with other such irreverent, superfluous and curious questions, which (how, and what, and by what means, and in what form) may bring into them, which of human and corrupt curiosity hath desire to search out such mysteries as lieth hid in the infinite and bottomless depth of the wisdom and glory of God, and to the which our human imbecility cannot attain, and therefore ofttimes turneth the same to their own and others' destruction, by contention and arrogant rashness; which simple and Christian affection, reverently receiving, and obediently believing, without further search, taketh and useth to most great comfort and profit:

For reformation whereof, and to the intent that further contention, tumult, and question might not rise among the King's subjects, the King's highness, by the advice of the Lord Protector and other his majesty's council, straightly willeth and commandeth that no manner person from henceforth do in any wise contentiously and openly argue, dispute, reason, preach, or teach, affirming any more terms of the said Blessed Sacrament than be expressly taught in the Holy Scripture, and mentioned in the foresaid act; nor deny none which be therein contained and mentioned, until such time as the King's majesty, by the advice of his highness' council and the clergy of this realm, shall define, declare, and set forth an open doctrine thereof, and what terms and words may justly be spoken thereby, other than be expressly in the Scripture contained and in the act before rehearsed.

In the meanwhile the King's highness' pleasure is, by the advice aforesaid, that every his loving subjects shall devoutly and reverently affirm and take that holy bread to be Christ's body, and that cup to be the cup of His holy blood, according to the purport and effect of the Holy Scripture contained in the act before expressed, and accommodate themself rather to take the same Sacrament worthily than rashly to enter into the discussing of the high mystery thereof.

Yet the King's highness mindeth not hereby to let or stop the ignorant and willing to learn, quietly, reverently, and privately to demand of those whom he thinketh knoweth more, the further instruction and teaching in the said Blessed Sacrament, so that the same be not done with contention nor in open audience, with a company gathered together about them, nor with tumult; nor doth prohibit any man hereby likewise so quietly, devoutly, and reverently to teach or instruct the weak and unlearned, according to the more talent and learning given to him of God; but only that all contention, strife and tumult and irreverence might be avoided, and in open audience or preaching nothing taught but which may have the Holy Scripture for warrant:

Upon pain that whosoever shall openly, with contention or tumult, and in a company gathered together, either in churches, alehouses, markets, or elsewhere, contrary to the form and effect of this proclamation, defend, and maintain, or irreverently and contentiously demand of any man, any of the questions before rehearsed, either on the one part or of the other, or any other such like, or do otherwise revile, contemn, despise the said Sacrament, by calling it idol or other such vile name, shall incur the King's high indignation and suffer imprisonment, or to be otherwise grievously punished at his majesty's will and pleasure; giving further in authority to all justices of peace, within the shires where they dwell, to apprehend and take all such as contentiously and tumultuously, with companies or routs assembled about them, do dispute, argue, or reason, or stiffly maintain, or openly preach and define the questions before rehearsed, or any of them, or suchlike, either on the one part or the other, and to commit the same to prison until such time as the King's majesty's pleasure herein be known, and that they immediately do certify the name or names of the party so offending, and of them who were there at the same time present, making the rout or assembly, to the King's highness' council; willing and commanding the said justices with all diligence to execute the premises according to the purport, effect, and true meaning of the same, and their most bounden duties, as they tender his highness' will and pleasure, and will answer to the contrary upon their peril.

297. Enforcing Lenten Fast and Abstinence

[Hampton Court, 16 January 1548, 1 Edward VI]

Grafton 10*v*: date, 16 January; schedule as below. Dibdin *3*, 463: separate edition by Grafton. Cardwell *1*, 38. Strype 2(2), 340. Wilkins *4*, 20. Steele 321: date, Hampton Court. Text: Grafton

THE KING'S HIGHNESS, by the advice of his most entirely beloved uncle Edward, Duke of Somerset, governor of his person and protector of all his realms, dominions, and subjects, and other of his Privy Council, considering that his highness hath not only cure and charge of the defense of his realms and dominions, as a King, but also as a Christian King and supreme head of the Church of England and Ireland, a desire, will, and charge to lead and instruct his people, to him committed of God, in such rights, ways, and customs as might be acceptable to God, and to the further increase of good living and virtue; and that his subjects, now having a more perfect and clear light of the gospel and true word of the Lord through the infinite clemency and mercy of Almighty God by the hands of his majesty and his most noble father of famous memory, promulgated, showed, declared and opened unto them, should and ought thereby in all good works and virtues increase, be more forward, diligent, and plentiful; as in fasting, prayer, and alms deeds, in love, charity, obedience, and other such good works commanded to us of God in His Holy Scripture; yet his highness is advertised and informed that divers of his subjects be not only to all these more slow and negligent, but rather contemners and despisers of such good and godly acts and deeds, to the which, if they were of their own minds bended and inclined, they need not by outward and princely power be appointed and commanded. But forsomuch as at this time now alate, more than at any other time, a great part of his subjects do break and contemn that abstinence which of long time hath been used in this his majesty's realm, upon the Fridays and Saturdays and the time commonly called Lent, and other accustomed times:

His highness is constrained to see a convenient order herein set and appointed,[1] not minding thereby that his subjects should think any difference to be in the days or meats, or that the one should be to God more holy, more pure, or more clean than the other; for all days and all meats be of one and equal purity, cleanness, and holiness, that we should in them, and by them, live to the glory of God, and at all times and for all meats give thanks unto Him, of the which none can defile us at any time or make us unclean, being Christian men to whom all things be holy and pure, so that they be not

1. See 2 & 3 Edward VI, c. 19, 1548, *SR 4(1)*, 65.

used in disobedience and vice. But his majesty hath allowed and approved the days and times before accustomed to be continued and still observed here in this Church of England, both that men should on those days abstain and forbear their pleasures, and the meats wherein they have more delight, to the intent to subdue their bodies unto the soul and spirit, unto the which, to exhort and move men, is the office of a good and godly head and ruler; and also for worldly and civil policy certain days in the year, to spare flesh and use fish for the benefit of the commonwealth and profit of this his majesty's realm, whereof many be fishers and men using that trade of living, unto the which this realm, on every part environed with the seas, and so plentiful of fresh waters, doth easily minister occasion, to the great sustenance of this his highness' people, so that hereby both the nourishment of the land might be increased by saving flesh, and specially at the spring time, when Lent doth commonly fall, and when the most common and plenteous breeding of flesh is; and also divers of his loving subjects have good livings and get great riches thereby in uttering and selling such meats as the sea and fresh water doth minister unto us; and this his majesty's realm hath more plenty of ships, boats, crayers, and other vessels by reason of those which by hope of lucre do follow that trade of living.

Wherefore his majesty, having consideration that where men of their own minds do not give themselves so oft as they should do to fasting, a common abstinence may and should be by the prince enjoined and commanded, and having an eye and mind to the profit and commodity of his realm and subjects, and to a common and civil policy, hath willed and commanded, and by these presents doth will and command, by the advice aforesaid, all manner of person and persons, of what estate, degree, or condition he or they be, other than such as already be or hereafter shall be excused by law or license, or authorized sufficiently to the contrary, to observe and keep from henceforth such fasting days, and the time commonly called Lent, in abstaining from all manner of flesh, as heretofore in this realm hath been most commonly used and accustomed; upon pain that whosoever shall, upon any day heretofore wont to be fasted from flesh, and not by the King's highness or his predecessors abrogate and taken away, eat flesh contrary to this proclamation, shall incur the King's high indignation, and shall suffer imprisonment and be otherwise grievously punished at his majesty's will and pleasure.

And further the King's highness, by the advice aforesaid, straightly chargeth and commandeth all mayors, bailiffs, and other head officers and rulers of cities and towns, and all justices of peace in the shires where they be in commission, to be attendant and diligent to the execution of this proclamation, in committing to prison the offenders contrary to this proclamation, upon sufficient proof thereof, by two sufficient witnesses before them had and made, there to remain during the King's pleasure according to the true purport, effect, and meaning of the same, as they tender the King's majesty's will and pleasure and will answer to the contrary at their peril.

And where the late King of most famous memory, father to his highness, hath given, divers years, license to his subjects in the time of Lent to eat butter, cheese, eggs, and other meats, commonly called white meats, the King's highness, by the advice aforesaid, considering the same to have been done not without great considerations, doth give likewise license and authority to all his loving subjects from henceforth freely forever in the time of Lent or other prohibited times by law or custom, to eat butter, eggs, cheese, and other white meats; any law, statute, act, or custom to the contrary notwithstanding.

298. Ordering Soldiers to Their Garrisons

[Westminster, January 1548, 1 Edward VI]

Antiq 3, 16: schedule as below. Steele 322: date as above. Text (MS): Antiq

THE KING'S HIGHNESS, by the advice of his most entirely beloved uncle, the Duke of Somerset, governor of his most royal person and protector of all his realms, dominions, and subjects, willeth and commandeth all captains and soldiers heretofore appointed to the keeping of any castle, fortress, or pier to his highness appertaining or belonging, and at this present in wages, do with such convenient haste as they may make their repair to the said castles, fortresses, or piers unto the which they are appointed so that they be there in person; all such as are appointed on the south parts of England or on the frontiers and parts of Picardy or France to be and remain at their charge before the Feast of the Purification next following; and all such as are appointed northwards to any castle, fortress, or pier in the north parts of England, or in any part of Scotland, to be and remain at their charges on the said north parts or in Scotland before the 10th day of February next following; upon pain that every captain or soldier which shall not be at the said place and charge, in or before the days heretofore severally limited, shall forfeit and lose all such part or portion of his wages as is heretofore unpaid and to him due, but that it shall be lawful to the high and chief captain of every such soldier so being absent at the time and days before limited for that cause to remove the same soldier or captain so absent from his room and to put and set another able man in the same, according to his or their discretion.

Giving further in commandment to all lieutenants, wardens, captains, and deputies of all such castles, forts, and piers, to be attendant and diligent to the execution of this proclamation according to the true intent, purport, and effect thereof, as they tender the King's highness' pleasure and will answer to the contrary at their perils.

299. Prohibiting Private Innovations in Ceremonies

[Hampton Court, 6 February 1548, 2 Edward VI]

STC 7813 (UM 2,10,410), Antiq 3, 17: printed by R. Grafton (London, 1548); date, 6 February; schedule as below. LJ 15, 352*v:* date, 6 February; schedule as below. Burnet *5,* 188. Cardwell *1,* 42. Wilkins *4,* 21. Steele 323: date, Hampton Court. Text (*STC*): Antiq

THE KING'S HIGHNESS, by the advice of his most entirely beloved uncle, the Duke of Somerset, governor of his most royal person, and protector of all his realms, dominions, and subjects, and others of his council, considering nothing so much to tend to the disquieting of his realm as diversity of opinions and variety of rites and ceremonies concerning religion and worshipping of Almighty God, and therefore studying all the ways and means which can be to direct this church and the cure committed to his highness in one and most true doctrine, rite, and usage; yet is advertised that certain private curates, preachers, and other laymen, contrary to their bounden duties of obedience, do rashly attempt of their own and singular wit and mind, in some parish churches and otherwise, not only to persuade the people from the old and accustomed rites and ceremonies but also themself bringeth in new and strange orders, every one in their church, according to their fantasies; the which as it is an evident token of pride and arrogancy, so it tendeth both to confusion and disorder, and also to the high displeasure of Almighty God who loveth nothing so much as order and obedience:

Wherefore his majesty straightly chargeth and commandeth that no manner person of what estate, order, or degree soever he be, of his private mind, will, or fantasy, do omit, leave down, change, alter, or innovate any order, rite, or ceremony commonly used and frequented in the Church of England, and not commanded to be left down at any time in the reign of our late sovereign lord, his highness' father, other than such as his highness, by the advice aforesaid, by his majesty's visitors, injunctions, statutes, or proclamations, hath already or hereafter shall command to be omitted, left, innovated, or changed; but that they be observed after that sort as before they were accustomed, or else now since prescribed, by the authority of his majesty, and by the means aforesaid; upon pain that whosoever shall offend contrary to this proclamation shall incur his highness' indignation and suffer imprisonment and other grievous punishments at his majesty's will and pleasure.[1]

1. At this point Burnet prints, from the MS register of Bishop Bonner, the following paragraph not in the printed schedule:

"Provided always, that for not bearing a candle upon Candlemas Day; not taking ashes on Ash Wednesday; not bearing palm upon Palm Sunday; not creeping [to] the cross; not taking

And to the intent that rash and seditious preachers should not abuse his highness' people, it is his majesty's pleasure that whosoever shall take upon him to preach openly in any parish church, chapel, or any other open place other than those which be licensed by the King's majesty, or his highness' visitors, the Archbishop of Canterbury or the bishop of the diocese where he doth preach (except it be the bishop, parson, vicar, dean, warden, or provost in his or their own cure) shall be forthwith upon such attempt and preaching contrary to this proclamation committed to prison, and there remain until such time as his majesty, by the advice aforesaid, hath taken order for the further punishment of the same.

And that the premises should be more speedily and diligently done and performed, his highness giveth straightly in commandment to all justices of peace, mayors, sheriffs, constables, headboroughs, church wardens, and all other his majesty's officers and ministers and rulers of towns, parishes, and hamlets, that they be diligent and attendant to the true and faithful execution of this proclamation, and every part thereof, according to the intent, purport, and effect of the same; and that they of their proceedings herein (or if any offender be) after they have committed the same to prison, do certify his highness, the Lord Protector, or his majesty's council, with all speed thereof accordingly, as they tender his majesty's pleasure, the wealth of the realm, and will answer to the contrary at their uttermost perils.

300. Proclaiming the Communion Order

[London, 8 March 1548, 2 Edward VI]

AC (Dasent *2*, 291): date 16 June 1549; order to Princess Mary to have the Service of Communion celebrated in her house. *STC* 16,457 (UM 55,*1450), DFo 16457: printed by R. Grafton (London, 1548); date as above: schedule as below. Wriothesley *2*, 2: date, March. Wilkins *4*, 11. Steele 324. Text (*STC*): DFo

FORASMUCH as in our high court of parliament lately holden at Westminster it was by us, with the lords spiritual and temporal, and commons there assembled, most godly and agreeably to Christ's holy institution, exacted[1] that the most Blessed Sacrament of the body and blood of our Savior Christ

---

holy bread or holy water; or for omitting such other rites and ceremonies concerning religion and the use of the Church, which the most reverend father in God the Archbishop of Canterbury, by his majesty's will and commandment, with the advice aforesaid known, hath declared or hereafter shall declare to the other bishops by his writing under seal, as heretofore hath been accustomed to be omitted or changed: no man hereafter be imprisoned nor otherwise punished; but all such things to be reputed for the observation and following of the same, as though they were commanded by his majesty's Injunctions." Gilbert Burnet, *The History of the Church of England*, ed. Nicholas Pocock, *5* (Oxford, 1865), 189.

See 186, 188, 287.

1. 1 Edward VI, c. 1, 1547, *SR 4(1)*, 2.

should from thenceforth be commonly delivered and ministered unto all persons within our realm of England and Ireland, and other our dominions, under both kinds, that is to say, of bread and wine (except necessity other ways require): lest every man fantasying and devising a sundry way by himself in the use of this most Blessed Sacrament of unity, there might thereby arise any unseemly and ungodly diversity:

Our pleasure is, by the advice of our most dearly beloved uncle the Duke of Somerset, governor of our person and protector of all our realms, dominions, and subjects, and other our Privy Council, that the said Blessed Sacrament be ministered unto our people only after such form and manner as hereafter, by our authority with the advice before mentioned, is set forth and declared: willing every man with due reverence and Christian behavior to come to this Holy Sacrament and most Blessed Communion, lest that by the unworthy receiving of so high mysteries they become guilty of the body and blood of the Lord, and so eat and drink their own damnation; but rather diligently trying themselves that they may so come to this holy table of Christ and so be partakers of this Holy Communion that they may dwell in Christ and have Christ dwelling in them; and also with such obedience and conformity to receive this our ordinance and most godly direction that we may be encouraged from time to time further to travail for the reformation and setting forth of such godly orders as may be most to God's glory, the edifying of our subjects, and for the advancement of true religion.

Which thing we (by the help of God) most earnestly intend to bring to effect, willing all our subjects in the meantime to stay and quiet themselves with this our direction, as men content to follow authority according to the bounden duty of subjects, and not enterprising to run afore and so by their rashness become the greatest hinderers of such things as they more arrogantly than godly would seem (by their own private authority) most hotly to set forward.

We would not have our subjects so much to mistake our judgment, so much to mistrust our zeal, as though we either could not discern what were to be done, or would not do all things in due time. God be praised, we know both what by His word is meet to be redressed, and have an earnest mind, by the advice of our most dear uncle and other of our Privy Council, with all diligence and convenient speed so to set forth the same as it may most stand with God's glory, and edifying and quietness of our people: which we doubt not but all our obedient and loving subjects will quietly and reverently tarry for.

301. Permitting Export of Grain

[Leigh, 30 March 1548, 2 Edward VI]

Antiq 3, 18: date as above; writ to customers, comptrollers, searchers, etc.; schedule as below. Strype 2(2), 140. Steele 325. Text (MS): Antiq

WHERE the King's most royal majesty, by his proclamation [1] bearing date at Westminster the seventh day of December last past, did then by his said proclamation straightly charge and command all and singular his subjects, of what estate or degree soever they were, that they nor any of them should, after the publishing of the same his proclamation, transport or carry over the seas into any outward parts any manner kind of grain without his grace's special license under his Great Seal of England should be had and obtained for the same, upon pain not only to incur all such pains as by the statutes and proclamations were provided in that behalf but also to be further punished by imprisonment of their bodies and otherwise to the terrible example of all other, as by the same proclamation more plainly appeareth; and forasmuch (as thanks be unto Almighty God) there is at this present great plenty and abundance of wheat and other corn within this realm, whereby the farmers and others which use tilling and manuring of their lands may not sell their wheat and other grains but at very low prices to their utter undoing unless that some remedy be provided in that behalf:

The King's most royal majesty, with the advice of his most dear uncle Edward, Duke of Somerset, governor of his majesty's person and protector of all his realms, dominions, and subjects, and other of his most honorable council, of his especial grace granteth and by this present proclamation giveth therefor free liberty and license to all and singular his loving subjects, of what estate or degree soever he or they be, to embark, ship, and carry overseas at his or their license and free wills into all outward parts (being with his majesty in league and amity) all and all manner of wheat and all other kinds of grain (oats only excepted), so long as a quarter of wheat shall be under the price of 6*s.* 8*d.* the quarter, barley, malt, and rye 5*s.* the quarter, peas and beans 4*s.* the quarter, at the time of the embarking and shipping of the same and in the pier, creek, or port where any of the same shall be so shipped or embarked, until such time as his highness by his other proclamation under his Great Seal of England shall determine the contrary; any act, statute, law, proclamation, or restraint to the contrary hereof in any wise notwithstanding. Provided always that of his majesty's customs, subsidies, and other duties due unto his highness in that behalf he be duly answered for the same as appertaineth.

1. See 295.

Wherefore his majesty straightly chargeth and commandeth all you his customers, comptrollers, and searchers of all and singular his ports, that you and every of you shall permit and suffer all and every his subjects to transport and carry the said wheat and other grains according to this his majesty's license of proclamation, as you and every of you will answer to his highness at your uttermost perils.

302. Calling in Testons because of Counterfeiting

[Greenwich, 10 April 1548, 2 Edward VI]

STC 7814 (UM 5,25,411), Antiq MS *116*, 112: printed by R. Grafton (London, 1548); date, 10 April; schedule as below; *rev.STC*, additional copies in Pembroke College, Lord Crawford Collection in ULC, and DFo. LJ 15, 359*v*: date, 10 April; schedule incomplete. Steele 326: date, Greenwich. Text (*STC*): Antiq

WHEREAS it is come to the knowledge of our sovereign lord the King's majesty what fraud and corruption hath of late time been used in the falsing of his highness' coin now current, specially of the pieces of 12*d*. commonly named testons, by reason that the same sort of coin, for the greatness and facility of counterfeiting, hath the rather given occasion to divers evil persons to stamp or cast pieces of the same form and bigness in great multitude, the practicers whereof (as is known) are not only men here dwelling, but also for the most part have been strangers dwelling in foreign parts who have found the means to convey privily and disperse the said counterfeit pieces abroad in his majesty's dominions, to the great deceit and detriment of his highness' most loving subjects which have received the same:

His majesty therefore, minding the due reformation hereof, and to prevent the like practice hereafter, by the advice and assent of his dearest uncle, the Lord Protector, and others of his council, doth will and command that from the last day of December next coming after the date hereof, the said coin or pieces of 12*d*. commonly named testons, shall no more be current within any his highness' realms or dominions, but be taken only for bullion. And further straightly chargeth and commandeth all and singular his highness' subjects and others whatsoever, being within any his majesty's said realms or dominions, that from the said last day of December, they or any of them shall not utter or receive in payment any of the said testons as his highness' coin current. And also, his highness by the advice aforesaid, willeth and commandeth that no manner of person or persons, after the said last day of December, shall buy or amass into his or their hands any of the said testons for a peculiar gain to be had thereof to him or their wards, upon pain of forfeiture.

Nevertheless, his highness' most gracious clemency, tendering his subjects' and other's interests, which by lawful means do possess the said testons as their proper goods, and for avoiding of the loss which otherwise they should sustain hereby, is pleased, and doth ordain by the advice aforesaid, that every person or persons so having and possessing the said testons, being of his highness' just standard, shall and may bring or send the same to the officers of any of his majesty's mints, where in exchange shall be delivered unto him or them the just value and recompense thereof, as they be now current, either in groats or other his highness' coins, accordingly.

303. Prohibiting Unlicensed Preaching, Specifically of Bigamy and Divorce

[Westminster, 24 April 1548, 2 Edward VI]

AC (Dasent 2, 164): date, 28 February; order to be taken after Lord Northampton's trial for bigamy. *STC* 7815 (UM 2,10,412), Antiq 3, 19: printed by R. Grafton (London, 1548); date, 24 April; schedule as below. Cardwell *1*, 59. Steele 327: date, Westminster. Text (*STC*): Antiq

WHEREAS the King's majesty our sovereign lord, by the singular gift and grace of Almighty God, with the advice of his most entirely beloved uncle, the Lord Protector, and other of his highness' council, hath made certain reformation [1] and orders according to the laws and commandment of God in this his majesty's Church of England, to the intent that one and a most godly conformity might be had throughout all this realm; and is advertised that divers unlearned and indiscreet preachers and other priests, of a devilish mind and intent, hath not only incited and moved his loving subjects, as well in confession as otherwise, to disobedience and stubbornness against his majesty's godly proceedings, but also that other light and perverse persons hath sown abroad false and traitorous rumors against his highness, their sovereign lord, telling that they hear say that his majesty will take and set upon them new and strange exactions, as of every one that is married, half a crown, likewise of every christening and of a burial, with other such lying and untrue surmises; whereby some lewd and light persons, and that of no small number, giving credit to such false tales, and other having confidence in those seditious preachers, hath been seduced and brought to much disorder of late, and in some parts, in manner to insurrection and rebellion, to his majesty's no little grief, and disquietness of his highness' other loving subjects:

For reformation whereof, and to the intent that by such light and seditious preachers and other such like false and vain tale-tellers his majesty's subjects should not hereafter be brought and induced to like disorder and inconvenience, his majesty by the advice aforesaid willeth and commandeth

1. See 299.

that no man tell forth, spread abroad or utter lies nor other such vain, lewd, and untrue tales of the King's majesty or his highness' proceedings and affairs, upon pain of his majesty's displeasure and grievous imprisonment of such offender's body.

And also, for to eschew the hurt that may come of seditious and contentious preaching, his highness straightly chargeth and commandeth, notwithstanding any former commandment or injunction, that no man hereafter be permitted or suffered to preach (not meaning yet hereby but that his highness' *Homilies* should be, according to his majesty's Injunctions,[2] read and declared) except the same be licensed thereto by his majesty, the Lord Protector, or the Archbishop of Canterbury, under his seal; and the same to be showed to the parson and curate, and two honest men of the parish beside, before his said preaching, upon pain of imprisonment both of the preacher so preaching without license and of the curate or parson which suffereth any such without license as before is expressed to preach in any of his or their churches or chapels or churchyards.

And for further execution of the premises, his majesty by the advice aforesaid willeth and commandeth all manner justices of peace to take diligent heed thereunto, and to commit, upon due examination, as well the said preacher so preaching, without license as aforesaid, as the curate or parson suffering any such preacher in his cure to preach, to prison, and thereupon certify immediately the Lord Protector, or the King's majesty's honorable council; and that they shall assist and aid all such as be licensed by his majesty, the Lord Protector or the Archbishop of Canterbury, as aforesaid, as they tender his highness' will and pleasure and will answer to the contrary at their peril.

And whereas other unlearned and evil-disposed persons have not sticked to instill and whisper into men's ears and to persuade abroad evil and perilous opinions against God's law and the good order of the realm, some teaching that a man may forsake his wife and marry another, his first wife yet living, and likewise that the wife may do to the husband; other, that a man may have two wives or more at once, and that these things be prohibited not by God's law, but by the Bishop of Rome's law; so that by such evil and fantastical opinions some hath not been afraid indeed to marry and keep two wives:

The which opinions, the King's majesty, as a most Christian prince, by the advice aforesaid, not allowing as godly and Christian or convenient to be spread abroad or maintained in the realm; straightly chargeth and commandeth all archbishops and bishops, and other which hath spiritual jurisdictions within the realm, to proceed against all such as hath or hereafter shall marry or keep two wives at once, (whereof the first is his lawful wife) or shall put away his wife and marry another, and to punish such offenders

2. See 287.

according to the ecclesiastical laws, with grave and severe punishment, to fear therewith others which else would fall to such insolent and unlawful acts; and that all his highness' officers and loving subjects who hath charge or zeal thereto shall detect all such offenders to the said archbishops and bishops and others that exerciseth spiritual jurisdiction, and aid the same to the punishing of such evil doers according to the order of the law in those cases; and if so be the said archbishops, bishops, or other who hath the exercise of spiritual jurisdictions, be slack and negligent in the execution of the said process and punishing of such evil doers as is before rehearsed, that then the justices of peace in every shire, or any others his majesty's loving subjects, shall declare and signify such offenders and misdoers to the King's highness' council by their letters, that his highness by the advice aforesaid might see a convenient redress made of such misorder, and look more straightly upon the archbishops and bishops which do not execute their duties in this behalf according to the trust committed unto them.

304. Prohibiting Export of Victual

[Westminster, 24 April 1548, 2 Edward VI]

Grafton *17v:* date, 24 April; schedule as below. Dibdin *3*, 463 n.: separate edition by Grafton. Steele 328: date, Westminster. Text: Grafton

FORASMUCH as at this present time, by reason that so many do daily carry over beyond the seas butter, cheese, bacon, and tallow to sell and retail the same into foreign parts, the said things being so necessary to be had, both for the King's majesty's provisions and also to the sustenance of his highness' subjects, be waxing very scarce and of great and excessive price: his highness, by the advice and council of his entirely beloved uncle, the Lord Protector, and the rest of his majesty's council, straightly chargeth and commandeth that no manner of merchant or other person, of what estate, condition, or degree soever they be (except such as be appointed to make provision for his highness' forts and piers, to be employed upon the same, and not otherwise) do from henceforth convey and lade into any ship, to carry the same over into the parts of beyond the seas, any butter, cheese, bacon, or tallow, to sell the same again there, upon pain of forfeiture of all such butter, cheese, bacon, or tallow as is so laden and shipped for that intent; any license or grant by his highness, or by the late King of famous memory, his majesty's father, made heretofore, notwithstanding.

And his highness straightly chargeth and commandeth all his mayors, bailiffs, sheriffs, portreeves, customers, comptrollers, and searchers and other his majesty's officers, that they be diligent and attendant in executing of the said proclamation, as they tender his highness' will and pleasure and will answer for the contrary.

305. Summoning Judges and Justices to Star Chamber

[Westminster, 30 April 1548, 2 Edward VI]

Antiq 3, 20: date as above; schedule as below. Steele 329. Text (MS): Antiq

THE KING our sovereign lord, upon certain urgent respects and great considerations, by the advice of his council straightly chargeth and commandeth all and singular his judges at Westminster and other justices of peace within any part or shire within this his realm of England, now being or that shall be within the cities of London and Westminster or the suburbs of the same, that they and every of them upon Friday next coming, by eight of the clock in the morning, personally appear before the Lord Chancellor of England and others his council in the Star Chamber, there to know further of his majesty's will and pleasure; and not to fail thereof upon pain of his highness' displeasure.

306. Prohibiting Export of Bell Metal

[Westminster, 5 May 1548, 2 Edward VI]

Antiq 3, 21: date as above; schedule as below. Steele 330. Text (MS): Antiq

WHEREAS it has been brought to the knowledge of the King's majesty, the Lord Protector's grace and council, that certain evil-disposed persons, preferring their singular wealth, gain, and commodity before all other respects, attempt daily to convey bell metal out of the realm into foreign parts, without regard of the penalty of the statute [1] made and provided in that behalf:

His majesty, by the advice of the Lord Protector's grace and council aforesaid, straightly willeth and commandeth all persons, of whatsoever condition they be, that they forbear to convey any of the said bell metal from henceforth, as they will avoid the King's majesty's displeasure besides the penalties expressed in the said statute; willing and commanding all and singular customers, comptrollers, and searchers and all other the officers of

1. 21 Henry VIII, c. 10, 1529, *SR 3*, 290.

his highness to whom it shall appertain, that they attend their duties herein without concealment, upon the pain before expressed.

307. Ordering Religious Pensioners to Return to Their Counties

[Westminster, 14 May 1548, 2 Edward VI]

Antiq 3, 22: date as above; schedule as below. Steele 331. Text (MS): Antiq

THE KING'S MAJESTY, of the tender zeal and love which he beareth to his loving subjects, understanding that divers chantry priests, poor men, and other men of the late dissolved colleges, chantries, free chapels, etc., which by the last act [1] of parliament be come to his highness' hands, daily repaireth hither to London, to his highness the Lord Protector's grace, the Chancellor of the Augmentations and to other courts for the assurance of their pensions, to their great costs and charges and no small travail, by the advice of his most entirely beloved uncle, the Lord Protector, governor of his person and protector of all his realms, dominions, and subjects, and the rest of his Privy Council, for avoiding of the same, hath taken order that commissioners shall repair down shortly into every shire, and there shall declare unto them the manner of the payment of their said pensions so by the said act due and to be appointed, and also for their said patents of their said pensions in such sort and manner and to that proportion as they shall therewith be right well contented.

Wherefore his highness, by the advice aforesaid, willeth and commandeth all manner of chantry priests, prebendaries, guild priests, or any other who hath repaired and be here for that purpose, to return immediately down into their counties, and to travail and expect not long here in this city for the same.

308. Pardoning Cornwall Rebels

[Westminster, 17 May 1548, 2 Edward VI]

CW (C82/884): date of delivery as above; sign manual; writ to sheriff of Cornwall; schedule as below. Steele 332. Text (MS): CW

ALBEIT that many of you, the King's highness' subjects and commons, dwelling and inhabiting in the shire of Cornwall, as well within liberties and

1. 1 Edward VI, c. 14, 1547, *SR 4(1)*, 24.

franchises as without, within the said shire or in any other place or isle being reputed or taken for any part, parcel, or member of the same shire, and such other the King's said subjects inhabiting in other places, have now of late attempted and committed manifest and open rebellion against his most royal majesty within the said shire or the limits of the same; whereby was like to have ensued the utter ruin and destruction of that whole shire, and to the high displeasure of Almighty God, who straightly commandeth you to obey your sovereign lord and King in all things, and not with violence to resist his will and commandment for any cause, whatsoever it be; nevertheless the King's most royal majesty, perceiving by credible report that your said offenses proceeded of ignorance and ill enticements and by occasion of sundry false tales never purposed, minded, nor intended by his highness nor any of his council, but most craftily contrived and most spitefully set abroad amongst you by certain malicious and seditious persons:

And thereupon his highness, inclined to extend his most gracious pity and mercy toward you, having the chief charge of you under God both of your souls and bodies, and desiring rather the preservation of the same and your reconciliation by his merciful means than by the order of rigor of justice to punish you according to your demerits, of his inestimable goodness, replenished with most godly pity and mercy, and at your most humble petitions and submissions made unto his highness, is contented and pleased to give and grant, and by this present proclamation doth give and grant, unto you all and to all and every your confederates, wheresoever they dwell, of what estate, degree, or condition soever you or they be, or by what name or names soever you or they be called, his general and free pardon for all manner of treasons, rebellions, insurrections, misprisions of treasons, murders, robberies, felonies, and of all manner of accessories of or to the same, and of and to every of them; and of and for all and all manner of unlawful assemblies, unlawful conventicles, unlawful speaking of words, confederacies, conspiracies, riots, routs, and all other offenses, trespasses, and contempts done and committed by you or any of you within and from the time of the beginning of the said rebellion, whensoever it was, until the first day of May last past; and of all pains, judgments, and executions of death, and all other penalties, fines, and forfeitures of lands, tenements, hereditaments, goods, and chattels by any of you incurred, by reason of the premises or any of them; which fines, forfeitures, lands, tenements, hereditaments, goods, and chattels, the King's said highness of his special grace and mere motion by these presents giveth to such of you as should have forfeited or lost the same by occasion of the premises or any of them.

And also his highness is pleased and contented that you and every of you from time to time shall and may have, upon your suits to be made hereafter in the King's Chancery, his said most gracious and free pardon under his Great Seal specially to be made for any of you concerning the premises, without any further bill or warrant to be obtained for the same and without paying anything for the Great Seal thereof; and that you and every of you from time to time may freely and liberally sue for his said pardon when and as often as it shall like you, without any trouble, vexation, or impeachment of the premises or any of them, by his highness or by any his officers, ministers, or subjects, by any manner of means or in any manner of wise.

Furthermore the King's most royal majesty straightly chargeth and commandeth that you and all and every of you shall from henceforth like true and faithful subjects use yourselves in God's peace and his, according to your duties of allegiance; and that you shall in no wise hereafter attempt to make or procure any such rebellions, unlawful assemblies, riots, routs, and conspiracies; nor at the commandment nor by the authority of any person of what estate or degree, or for what cause soever it be, shall arise, commit, or stir wars in any forcible manner and array, unless it be at the special commandment of the King's highness or such as his highness shall authorize for the same: provided always that this general and free pardon shall not extend, or in any wise be beneficial unto John Williams; William Kylter; John Kylter; John Kelyan; Richard Trewela; William Ames; John Chykose; Aleyn Raw; Lawrence Briton; Michael Dion Briton; Oliver Rise; John Tregena; Richard Raw; Pasco Trevian; Martin Rasse; James, Robert, Henry Tyrlever; John Trebo, the elder; Thomas Tyrland; Dion, Michael, John, Morice Triball; Sir Martin Geoffrey, priest; John Piers, mariner; William Thomas, *alias* Senys; Richard Hodge; Trebo, the younger; Edward Iryshe, and Hugh Maston, *alias* Wavers, *alias* Parker.

309. Announcing Enclosure Inquiry

[Westminster, 1 June 1548, 2 Edward VI]

CW (C82/885): date of delivery as above; sign manual; schedule. *STC* 7816 (UM 2,10,413), Antiq 3, 24: printed by R. Grafton (London, 1548); date, 1 June; schedule as below. Strype *2(1)*, 145. Steele 333: date, Westminster. Text (*STC*): Antiq

FORASMUCH as the King's majesty, the Lord Protector's grace, and the rest of his Privy Council, hath been advertised and put in remembrance, as well by divers supplications and pitiful complaints of his majesty's poor subjects as also by other wise and discreet men having care to the good order of the realm, that of late by the enclosing of lands and arable grounds in divers and sundry places of this realm many have been driven to extreme poverty and compelled to leave the places where they were born and to seek them livings in other countries, with great misery and poverty; insomuch that whereas in time past, 10, 20, yea, in some place 100 or 200 Christian people hath been inhabiting and kept household to the bringing forth and nourishing of youth and to the replenishing and fulfilling of his majesty's realms with faithful subjects who might serve both Almighty God and the King's majesty to the defense of this realm, now there is nothing kept but sheep or bullocks; all that land which heretofore was tilled and occupied with so many men, and did bring forth not only divers families in work and labor, but also capons, hens, chickens, pigs, and other such furniture of the markets, is now gotten, by insatiable greediness of mind, into one or two men's hands and scarcely dwelled upon with one poor shepherd, so that the realm thereby is brought to a marvelous desolation, houses decayed, parishes diminished, the force of the realm weakened, and Christian people, by the greedy covetousness of some men, eaten up and devoured of brute beasts and driven from their houses by sheep and bullocks; and that although of the same thing many and sundry complaints and lamentations hath been heretofore made, and by the most wise and discreet princes, his majesty's father and grandfather, the Kings of most famous memory, King Henry VII and King Henry VIII, with the consent and assent of the lords spiritual and temporal in divers parliaments assembled, divers and sundry laws and acts [1] of parliaments and most godly ordinances in their several times hath been made for the remedy thereof, yet the insatiable covetousness of men doth not cease daily to encroach hereupon and more and more to waste the realm, after this sort bringing arable grounds into pastures, and letting houses, whole families, and copyholds to fall down, decay, and be waste:

Wherefore his highness is greatly moved both with a pitiful and tender zeal to his most loving subjects, and specially to the poor which is minded to labor and travail for their living and not to live an idle and loitering life, and of a most necessary regard to the surety and defense of his realm, which must be defended against the enemy with force of men and the multitude of true subjects, not with flocks of sheep and droves of beasts; and further is advertised that by the ungodly and uncharitable means aforesaid the said sheep and oxen, being brought into a few men's hands, a great multitude of them being together and so made great droves and flocks, as well by natural reason as also as it may be justly thought by the due punishment of God for such uncharitableness, great rots and murrains, both of sheep and bullocks, hath lately been sent of God and seen in this realm (the which should not by all reason so soon fall if the same were dispersed into divers men's hands, and the said cattle also by all likelihood of truth should be more cheap, being in many men's hands, than as they be now in few, who may hold them dear and carry their advantage of the market); and therefore by the advice of his most entirely beloved uncle, the Duke of Somerset, governor of his person and protector of his realms, dominions and subjects, and the rest of

1. 4 Henry VII, c. 19, 1488, *SR 2,* 542; 6 Henry VIII, c. 5, 1514, *SR 3,* 127; 7 Henry VIII, c. 1, 1515, *SR 3,* 176; 25 Henry VIII, c. 13, 1533, *SR 3,* 451; 27 Henry VIII, c. 1, 1535, *SR 3,* 531.

his majesty's Privy Council, hath weighed most deeply all the said things, and upon the foresaid considerations, and of a princely desire and zeal to see that godly laws, made with great travail and approved by experience and by the wise heads in the time of the said most prudent princes, should not be made in vain but put in ure and execution, hath appointed, according to the said acts and proclamations, a view and inquiry to be made of all such as contrary to the said acts and godly ordinances hath made enclosures and pastures of that which was arable ground, or let any house, tenement, or mese decay and fall down, or otherwise committed or done anything to the contrary of the good and wholesome articles contained in the said acts; and therefore willeth and commandeth all his loving subjects who knoweth any such defaults and offenses, contrary to the wealth and profit of this realm of England and the said godly laws and acts of parliament, done and committed by any person, whosoever he or they be, to insinuate and give information of the offense to the King's majesty's commissioners, who be appointed to hear the same so truly and faithfully that neither for favor nor fear they omit to tell the truth of any, nor for displeasure name any man who is not guilty thereof, that a convenient and speedy reformation might be made herein to the honor of God and the King's majesty, and the wealth and benefit of the whole realm.

310. Prohibiting Export of Leather and Hides

[Westminster, 1 June 1548, 2 Edward VI]

Antiq 3, 25: date as above; writ unspecified; schedule as below. Steele 334. Text (MS): Antiq

Forasmuch it is given us credibly sundry ways to understand, that by the reason of so frequent exportation of leather out of this our realm there is great lack and scarcity thereof for the necessary use of our people, the prices also thereof being risen to great height and importable: our will and pleasure is, by the advice and consent of our dear uncle the Duke of Somerset, governor of our person and protector of our realms, dominions, and subjects, and the rest of our Privy Council, that no manner person or persons do carry or export out of this our realm any manner leather or salt hides unto any strange nation or foreign country, without express license and permission by us to be given for the same, mentioning the release of this our proclamation; upon pain of the incurring into our displeasure and indignation.

311. Prohibiting Encroachment in Waltham Forest

[Westminster, 17 June 1548, 2 Edward VI]

CW (C82/885): date of delivery as above; sign manual; schedule as below. PR (C66/810/34*d*): date as above; schedule as below. Steele 335. Text (MS): PR

WHERE we and our progenitors, Kings of England, by a very long continuance of time have been seized in our demesne as of fee, of and in the forest of Waltham in our county of Essex, and the same have used and enjoyed with all manner of franchises, privileges, pre-eminences, and liberties to the same forest appertaining and belonging; and although we do earnestly mind the preservation and continuance of the same forest accordingly, yet nevertheless, upon what occasion or ground we know not, it hath been much bruited and noised amongst divers of you our loving subjects, that our pleasure for certain considerations should be for to disforest, dissolve, and clearly to disprivilege our said forest of Waltham in our said county of Essex, and to destroy our deer and game there; which bruit and noise hath stirred and encouraged a number of you not well disposed not only to destroy our vert in the same our forest, but also to hinder and disquiet our said deer and game of their accustomed places of feeding within our said forest, semblably to murder and kill a number of the same deer, not a little to our displeasure; wherefore you have incurred the danger of our laws and deserved punishment provided for the same accordingly.

We, minding therefore to quench and pacify the said bruit from henceforth, and to signify our further pleasure herein by this our proclamation, do give notice unto you that neither our pleasure is to destroy the said game, vert, or venison, or otherwise to deface or in any part to diminish our said forest of Waltham, but that the same and every part thereof we are fully resolved and determined to support and maintain in as good state and condition, and with as great liberties and privilege, as our late father of famous memory, King Henry VIII, or any other our progenitors, have done heretofore, and that our deer, both red and fallow, shall and may have their feedings within the limits and bounds of our said forest in as ample manner as ever they had heretofore: willing and therefore commanding you and every of you our loving subjects, from henceforth to abstain and forbear to murder, kill, or destroy, chase or hunt, any of our said deer within our said forest of Waltham, or by any undue way or mean to let, impeach, or disturb the same from their accustomed feeding, contrary to the liberties and laws of our said forest; as you tender our favor and will avoid the contrary (except it be by virtue of our warrants or other licenses heretofore accustomed): which is, every offender being convicted of any such hunting, chasing, and killing of any our deer, they shall have and suffer imprisonment by the space of three years, and make fine at our will and pleasure if they have wherewith so to do, and shall find good surety to do no more hurt; and if they have not whereof so to do, that they shall abjure this our realm.

And where also we be credibly further informed that divers greedy persons, having in their hands sundry closes and pastures within our said forest, where many of our said deer have accustomably used to feed, under the color and pretense of sowing of some little parcel thereof with corn, have for their private gain and profit so enclosed the said closes and pastures with such unreasonable hedges and ditches as our said deer have been utterly defrauded and hindered of their feeding and liberties, contrary to our laws, and to the great famishing and destruction of our said deer:

Wherefore we will and straightly charge and command that none of you our said loving subjects do at any time from henceforth enclose with any such unreasonable hedges or ditches any of the said closes and pastures, unless the more part thereof be sown with corn, as you will avoid the extreme danger of our laws for the same; and also that you nor any of you do use at any time hereafter any such vain talk or communication of our doings or proceedings herein, contrary to this our will and meaning, as you tender our pleasure and will eschew the contrary at your uttermost perils.

312. Adjourning Michaelmas Term because of Plague

[Westminster, 6 September 1548, 2 Edward VI]

LJ 15, 381*v*: date as above; writ to mayor and sheriffs of London; schedule as below. Antiq 3, 27: date, Hatfield, 6 September; schedule as below. Steele 336. Text (MS): LJ

Forasmuch as the King's majesty is credibly informed that the infection of plague reigneth in sundry parts of this realm, and specially within the cities of London and Westminster and in other places near adjoining to the same; whereas by the continuance of the same through the greater repair and resort of his loving subjects, greater peril and danger might not only ensue unto his most royal person, but also unto his most loving subjects repairing thither for their suits and causes:

His majesty therefore, minding the preservation of his loving subjects from the peril and danger of the said infection, and being in good hope that the same will, by the help of Almighty God and through the coldness of the year, the rather cease by the adjournment of the next term of St. Michael from the *utas* of the same till the morrow after the Feast of All Saints next coming, of his especial favor and benignity is pleased and contented to adjourn the said term of St. Michael from the *utas* thereof unto *crastino animarum* next coming, which his majesty signifieth unto all and singular his loving subjects by this his majesty's proclamation; willing and commanding them to observe and keep their assemblies and appearances with all their returns and certificates, in his highness' court at Westminster, then to be holden in like manner, form, and condition as they should or ought to have been done if this present proclamation of adjournment had not been had, made, and proclaimed; as they and every of them will answer at their extreme peril.

313. Prohibiting Sermons; Ordering Homilies to Be Read

[Windsor, 23 September 1548, 2 Edward VI]

STC 7818 (UM 2,10,415), DFo 7818: printed by R. Grafton (London, 1548); date, 23 September; schedule as below; DFo copy noted in *rev.STC*. LJ 15, 382: date, 23 September; schedule imperfect. Cardwell *1*, 70. Dibdin *3*, 463 n.: edition dated 24 September. Wilkins *4*, 30. Wriothesley 2, 6: proclaimed on 28 September. Steele 337: date, Windsor. Text (*STC*): DFo

WHEREAS of late by reason of certain controversious and seditious preachers, the King's majesty, moved of tender zeal and love which he hath to the quiet of his subjects, by the advice of the Lord Protector and other his highness' council, hath by proclamation [1] inhibited and commanded that no manner of person except such as was licensed by his highness, the Lord Protector, or by the Archbishop of Canterbury, should take upon him to preach in any open audience, upon pain in the said proclamation contained; and that upon hope and experience that those being chosen and elect men, should preach and set forth only to the people such things as should be to God's honor and the benefit of the King's majesty's subjects: yet nevertheless his highness is advertised that certain of the said preachers so licensed, not regarding such good admonitions as hath been by the said Lord Protector and the rest of the council on his majesty's behalf by letters or otherwise given unto them, hath abused the said authority of preaching, and behaved themself irreverently and without good order in the said preachings, contrary to such good instructions and advertisements as was given unto them; whereby much contention and disorder might rise and ensue in this his majesty's realm.

Wherefore his highness, minding to see very shortly one uniform order

1. See 287.

throughout this his realm, and to put an end of all controversies in religion, so far as God shall give grace (for which cause at this time certain bishops and notable learned men, by his highness' commandment, are congregate), hath by the advice aforesaid thought good, although certain and many of the said preachers so before licensed have behaved themself very discreetly and wisely and to the honor of God and his highness' contentation: yet at this present and until such time that the said order shall be set forth generally throughout this his majesty's realm, to inhibit, and by these presents doth inhibit generally, as well the said preachers so before licensed, as all manner of persons, whosoever they be, to preach in open audience in the pulpit or otherwise, by any sought [sic] color or fraud, to the disobeying of this commandment, to the intent that the whole clergy in this mean space might apply themself to prayer to Almighty God for the better achieving of the same most godly intent and purpose; not doubting but that also his loving subjects in the meantime will occupy themself to God's honor, with due prayer in the church and patient hearing of the godly homilies heretofore set forth by his highness' injunctions unto them, and so endeavor themself that they may be the more ready with thankful obedience to receive a most quiet, godly, and uniform order to be had throughout all his said realms and dominions; and therefore hath willed all his loving officers and ministers, as well justices of peace as mayors, sheriffs, bailiffs, constables, or any other his officers, of what estate, degree, or condition soever they be, to be attendant upon this proclamation and commandment, and to see the infringers or breakers thereof to be imprisoned, and his highness or the Lord Protector's grace or his majesty's council to be certified thereof immediately, as they tender his majesty's pleasure and will answer to the contrary at their peril.

314. Ordering Arrest of Military Deserters

[Leigh, 30 September 1548, 2 Edward VI]

Antiq 3, 29: date as above; writ to sheriffs of Norfolk and Suffolk; schedule as below. Steele 338. Text (MS): Antiq

WHERE now of late it hath come to our knowledge and understanding as well by advertisement from our well beloved servant, Thomas Windeham, as others presently traveling upon the seas about our affairs committed unto their charge, that their mariners and soldiers, without any honest ground or cause, do privily steal and convey themselves from their ships and captains and from our service to them appointed in that behalf, leaving the same not furnished according to such expectation as we have appointed, by means whereof the charge committed unto our said servant and others for the executing our commandment is by the same occasion not executed in all points accordingly, whereby might also ensue not only loss of our ships and of such as serveth in the same but also dishonor to our realms and subjects and further loss to us, grief and trouble to the rest of our said subjects inhabiting within our said realms and dominions: we, minding as well the preservation of the same with the avoiding of further troubles which might ensue to our said loving subjects, as also the reformation of the misbehaviors of such contemptuous, disobedient, and ingrate persons as neither have respect for such godly orders as have been by us and our council devised and set forth, to such whom we have appointed to serve in that behalf for the preservation of our realms, dominions, and subjects against the power of foreign princes, nor unto the honor of us their natural liege lord, nor the defense of their own natural country, do straightly charge and command all and singular justices of peace, mayors, sheriffs, bailiffs, customers, comptrollers, searchers, constables, and all other officers, ministers, and subjects inhabiting nigh unto the seacoasts or elsewhere to whom in this case it shall appertain, that whensoever any such soldiers or mariners or other person before mentioned retained, waged, or hired to serve in our service aforesaid, shall depart from our said ships or their captains without the special license of the said Thomas Windeham or others having good authority thereunto, and shall arrive at any place within any port, creek, or haven within our counties of Norfolk and Suffolk, or in any of them, that then the said officers or other persons before mentioned shall forthwith apprehend the said soldiers or mariners or other person departing as is aforesaid, and him or them to commit to prison, there to remain without bail or mainprize, and thereupon to advertise our dearest uncle, the Duke of Somerset, protector of our realms, dominions, and subjects, and governor of our person, and the rest of our Privy Council attendant upon the same, immediately upon the apprehension of any such soldier, mariner, or other person as is beforesaid, with the name or names of him or them and the place or places of his or their arrival, with the name or names of his or their captains, and the cause why they departed from the same, to the intent that being by our said officers advertised such speedy order may be taken for the reformation of such offenders as by us and our said council shall be thought meet according to the laws and statutes of our realm, and to the terror and fear of others, lest they should attempt the like.

315. Prohibiting Export of Victual

[Leigh, 8 October 1548, 2 Edward VI]

LJ 15, 382*v:* date, 26 September; writ to customers, comptrollers, searchers, and other officers of the port of London, and other ports, creeks, and places adjacent; earlier draft of schedule below. Antiq 3, 30: date as above; writ as in LJ; schedule as below. Steele 339. Text (MS): Antiq

FORASMUCH as the King's most royal majesty, considering the prices of corn and other victuals lately increased, risen, and grown in divers and many places within his majesty's realms, dominions, and the marches and confines of the same, hath thought it meet, weighing most specially the wealth and commodity of his poor subjects, to have a restraint for a season of all manner of grain, tallow, and victuals in all places within this his realm of England:

His most excellent majesty therefore, with the advice and consent of his most dear uncle, the Duke of Somerset, protector of his realms, dominions, and subjects, and governor of his royal person, and the rest of his Privy Council, straightly chargeth and commandeth all manner of persons, as well denizens as strangers, that they nor any of them after the publishing of this proclamation shall transport or carry over the seas into any outward parts any manner of grains, butter, cheese, tallow, or any kind of victuals, without his special license under his Great Seal of England, after the date of this proclamation, to be had and obtained for the same (his majesty's towns of Berwick, Calais, Boulogne and other his ports beyond the seas, and all other his highness' towns, castles, forts, and piers in the realm of Scotland only excepted), upon pain not only to incur all such pains as by the statutes and proclamations are provided in this behalf, but also to forfeit the grains, tallow, and victuals so conveyed, and also to be further punished by imprisonment of their bodies or otherwise, to the terrible example of all other, as by the Lord Protector's grace and other of his highness' council shall be thought convenient and requisite.

Provided always that every person transporting any manner of grain, tallow, or other kind of victuals unto any of his majesty's said towns, castles, forts, or piers, shall not only enter the same in the customer's books but shall likewise with one sufficient surety with him be bounden by obligation unto the King's majesty, to be taken by the customer and comptroller of the port or creek where the said grain, tallow, or other kind of victuals shall be shipped, or by their deputies, in the double value of the said grain, tallow, and other victuals, to discharge the same at his said towns or other his castles, forts, or piers, and not elsewhere, and to bring a true and just certificate within four months next after, from his majesty's deputies of Calais, Boulogne, and four other of his council there, and in like manner from such other of his majesty's lieutenants, wardens, captains, and other officers in the north parts, and four of them at the least, if so many be there appointed to serve, that the said grain, tallow, or other victuals so shipped were there discharged and delivered accordingly. Provided also that of his customs, subsidies, and other duties due unto his majesty in this behalf, he be duly answered for the same as appertaineth. Provided also that this proclamation shall continue during the King's pleasure and no longer.

316. Referring Religious Pensioners to Court of Augmentation Local Officers

[Westminster, 31 October 1548, 2 Edward VI]

Grafton 23*v:* date, 31 October; schedule as below. Steele 340: date, Westminster. Text: Grafton

THE KING'S MOST EXCELLENT MAJESTY, by the advice of his most dear uncle Edward, Duke of Somerset, governor of his most royal person and protector of all his realms, dominions, and subjects, minding to provide for the late incumbents of colleges, chantries, stipendaries, fraternities, guilds, and such other within this shire of ———————, convenient and reasonable recompenses and pensions, according to the statute [1] in the first year of his highness' reign in that behalf ordained, hath commanded and appointed several letters patent to be made, under the Great Seal of the Court of the Augmentations and Revenues of his majesty's crown, for the pensions of the said late incumbents.

Which patents his majesty, by the advice aforesaid, doth all his faithful subjects to understand, are presently sent to the hands of his highness' auditor, receiver, and surveyor of this county, with straight commandment unto them to deliver the same patents immediately, and to make payment unto the parties whom they concern, now and hereafter yearly, frank and free, without fee, duty, or sum of money to be demanded or taken of the said pensioners, either to his majesty's use or to the use of any officer, minister, clerk, or other person.

Wherefore, his majesty willeth all those persons which have to do herein to resort to his highness' audit, now presently to be holden within the said county, or elsewhere the same officers shall be; and there they shall receive their pensions accordingly.

1. 1 Edward VI, c. 14, 1547, *SR* 4(*1*), 24.

317. Ordering Arrest of Irish Pirates

[Westminster, ca. January 1549, 2 Edward VI]

LJ 15, 401*v:* date, ca. January, based on neighboring entries; schedule as below. Antiq 3, 31: date, MS note, ?October 1548; schedule as below. Steele 341: date, Westminster, October 1548. Text (MS): LJ

WHERE sundry lewd and evil-disposed persons, forgetting their bounden duties towards God, the King's majesty, their sovereign lord and prince and their country, have of late not only committed divers notable and great piracies both upon his majesty's own merchants and other subjects, and the subjects also of other foreign princes, states, and potentates, being in league and amity with his highness; but also as his majesty is credibly informed, out of such ships as they have spoiled and robbed have taken prisoner divers men, mariners and others of honest sort and good disposition, both of his majesty's own subjects and of others, and the same do still detain with them and use them in their evil enterprises against their wills:

The King's majesty, being certainly informed hereof and considering the said honest mariners, soldiers, and others who have so perforce served under the said pirates, do perchance remain in some despair for fear of the rigor of the laws because they have been in company with the said pirates, minding to temper the extremity of his highness' laws in that behalf, have thought good to extend his majesty's clemency toward them, and with the advice of his highness' dearest uncle, the Lord Protector, and others of his majesty's council, is pleased to grant that as many of the said mariners, soldiers, and others, now serving or that heretofore hath served under the said pirates, as shall come in and render himself to his majesty's High Admiral of England or to his highness' Lord Deputy of Ireland betwixt this and the last day of March next ensuing, shall not only have his majesty's most gracious pardon but also as many of them as be willing to serve shall be received into wages and serve in his highness' ships.

And forasmuch as his majesty is forthwith advertised that John Thompson, Richard Cole, Thomas Freeman, David Poore, Morrice Kelly, Richard Eyre, Patrick King, Thomas Outlaw, and Michael James be the most notable pirates and the principal occasions and grounds of all their spoils, piracies, and robberies, his highness, minding the punishment of them for an example of others is pleased to grant that whosoever, either of the said mariners and soldiers, or any other whatsoever he be, shall bring unto the said Lord Admiral or Lord Deputy of Ireland on this side the last day of March, the bodies of the said John Thompson, Richard Cole, Thomas Freeman, David Poore, Morrice Kelly, Richard Eyre, Patrick King, Thomas Outlaw, and

Michael James, or of any of them, quick or dead, shall have not only his own pardon as aforesaid but also of his highness' further liberality and reward: for the bringing of John Thompson, 1000 crowns; for the bringing of Richard Cole, 600 crowns; for the bringing of Thomas Freeman, 400 crowns; and by the bringing of David Poore, Morrice Kelly, Richard Eyre, Patrick King, Thomas Outlaw, and Michael James, for every of them, 300 crowns the piece.

318. Ordering Captains and Soldiers to Garrisons in North

[Westminster, 3 January 1549, 2 Edward VI]

LJ 15, 397: date as above; schedule as below. Not in Steele. Text (MS): LJ

THE KING'S MOST EXCELLENT MAJESTY, upon certain important considerations, specially that those whom his highness hath presently in entertainment as captains or soldiers in the north parts against Scotland should be present upon their charges as the affair of war requireth, and not to commit that, through their absence elsewhere, inconveniences may happen in places where their present head and attendance were requisite, hath therefore determined, and (by the advice and assent of his dearest uncle Edward, Duke of Somerset, governor of his grace's royal person and protector of his realms, dominions, and subjects, and the rest of his highness' council) straightly chargeth and commandeth all and singular captains, petty captains, and other officers and soldiers whatsoever, having presently wages and entertainment for their service at any place upon the borders against Scotland, or kept to his majesty's behalf within Scotland, shall put themselves in undelayed order to repair unto their several charges and place of service:

So, all excuses and delays set apart, they find themselves there present within 15 days next after the date of this proclamation; as they and every of them neglecting to fulfill the effect hereof shall not only lose their rooms and wages, but will further make answer to his highness for their not doing hereof, at their extreme perils.

319. Prohibiting Export of Victual

[Westminster, 18 January 1549, 2 Edward VI]

LJ 15, 402: date as above; writ to mayor and sheriffs of London; schedule as below. Steele 342. Text (MS): LJ

FORASMUCH as the King's highness at this present shall occupy great provision, his highness by the advice of his most entirely beloved uncle, the Lord Protector, and the rest of his Privy Council, straightly chargeth and commandeth that no manner of person, whosoever he be, do ship or lade to the intent to carry out of this realm any wheat, malt, oats, barley, butter, cheese, bacon, beef, cask, or tallow, any license or grant by the King's majesty's letters patent under the Great Seal of England or any other license or grant heretofore made notwithstanding, until such time as his majesty's provisions be fully certified and stored; upon pain that whosoever shall after the 22nd day of January in this present year and before the 20th day of April transport or carry into the parts beyond the seas, or lade into any ship to that intent, any of the aforesaid things or provisions contrary to this present proclamation, the party so offending shall forfeit the said goods or provisions so transported or shipped and laden to that intent to be transported beyond the seas, or the value thereof: the one half unto the King's majesty, the other to the accuser or presenter demanding the same according to the laws of this realm; and the party so offending nevertheless to be imprisoned during the King's pleasure.

And his highness by the advice aforesaid straightly chargeth and commandeth all mayors, bailiffs, sheriffs, constables, and other head officers of all his highness' havens, ports, and creeks, and all customers, comptrollers, searchers, and other his loving subjects, to be vigilant herein and to stay all such ships or boats and the master or owners of them, as shall do or attempt anything contrary to this said proclamation, and certify the same accordingly, as they tender his highness' pleasure and will answer to the contrary. Provided that this present proclamation doth not extend to the necessary furnishing of such ships as goeth into Ireland for fishing, nor for such other provision as is made and sent in Boulogne or Calais or any other the King's majesty's fortresses or holds.

320. Prohibiting Arms near Court

[Westminster, ca. 23 January, 1549, 2 Edward VI]

LJ 15, 402*v:* date as above, based on neighboring entries; schedule as below. Not in Steele. Text (MS): LJ

FORASMUCH as divers evil disposed persons, as well lately resorting to the court from the garrisons in the north parts as others, do ordinarily go abroad in coats of mail and other armors, whereby they be rather enhardied to make frays and parties to the disturbance of the King's majesty's peace, and trouble and inquiet of his majesty's good subjects:

His highness, by the advice and consent of his dearest uncle the Lord Protector, and the rest of his majesty's Privy Council, straightly chargeth and commandeth that no manner of person, whatsoever he be, be so hardy to wear any kind of dags, short handguns, harness, or armor within the court or three miles round about the same, under pain of imprisonment during his majesty's will and pleasure.

321. Announcing New Coinage

[Westminster, 24 January 1549, 2 Edward VI]

LJ 14, 402*v:* date as above; writ to mayor and sheriffs of London; schedule as below. Steele 343. Text (MS): LJ

WHEREAS the King's majesty having of late upon just occasions called in the pieces of 12*d.* commonly called the testons,[1] and tendering the speedy help and relief of his loving subjects and others' interests, which either have brought in testons into his grace's mints or by lawful means do possess the same, and to the intent money and coin may be the more plentiful and richly hereafter made within this his grace's realms, his highness therefore by the advice and assent of his dearest uncle, the Lord Protector, and others of his council, hath caused certain new coins of gold and silver to be made according to their several valuations hereinafter ensuing:

That is to say, four several pieces of gold, whereof the first piece of gold shall be called the sovereign of gold, and shall be current for 20*s.* of the lawful moneys of England. Item, one other piece of gold which shall be called the half-sovereign, or Edward's royal, running for 10*s.* of the lawful moneys aforesaid. Item, one other piece of gold which shall be called the crown,

1. See 302.

running for 5*s*. of the aforesaid moneys. Item, one other piece of gold called the half-crown, running for 2*s*. 6*d*. of the said lawful moneys.

And his said majesty by the advice aforesaid hath likewise caused to be newly made certain pieces of coin of silver hereafter specified: that is to say, a piece of silver called a shilling, running for 12*d*. of the lawful moneys of England. Item, one other piece or coin of silver which shall be called the half-shilling, running for 6*d*. of the lawful moneys aforesaid.

All which several pieces or coins as well of gold or also of silver before specified, the King's majesty's pleasure and commandment is, shall be from henceforth current within his grace's realms and the dominions of the same, according to their several rates and valuations before expressed.

And moreover the King's highness straightly chargeth and commandeth that from henceforth all manner of groats, half-groats, pence, and half-pence of his coins, being not counterfeit, current within this said realm, not clipped nor fully broken, albeit they shall be much cracked, shall be taken, received, and paid throughout his said realm without any manner refusal or denial.

Wherefore his highness straightly chargeth and commandeth all mayors, justices of peace, sheriffs, bailiffs, constables, and other his faithful officers and subjects, that if any person or persons of what estate, degree, or condition he or they be, refuse or deny to take or receive the said moneys of gold, being weight, or any of the moneys of silver before expressed or now current within this realm, be it for merchandise, victuals, change, or rechange or other cause whatsoever: forthwith to take and arrest the same person or persons so making refusal or denial, and to put him or them in ward and prison, there to remain and further to be punished at the King's pleasure.

322. Extending Time for Calling in Testons until 1 May

[Westminster, 31 January 1549, 3 Edward VI]

STC 7819 (UM 5,25,433), Antiq 3, 34: printed by R. Grafton (London, 1549); schedule as below. LJ 15, 403: schedule as below. Grafton 24*v*: date, 31 January; schedule as below. Steele 344: date, Westminster. Text (*STC*): Antiq

WHEREAS the King's most excellent majesty, with the advice and assent of his dearest uncle Edward, Duke of Somerset, governor of his royal person, protector of his highness' realms, dominions, and subjects, and the rest of his grace's council, hath heretofore by proclamation [1] bearing date the 10th day

1. See 302.

of April in the second year of his reign given notice and commandment to all manner his loving subjects and others haunting his majesty's realms or dominions that from the last day of the month of December last past forwards, the pieces of 12*d*. commonly called testons should no longer be current nor pass in payment or receipt as his grace's coin, but be taken only for bullion; whereunto his majesty was moved upon such considerations as in the said former proclamation was more at large expressed.

Forasmuch as it hath since come to his highness' knowledge, that by reason of the great number of the same testons which at this present are dispersed abroad in so many men's hands; besides no less cautel and policy, used even hard upon the day, by divers making whole payments in the said coin, and especially for that those that have plenty of other money take unreasonable allowance of the poorer sort, which is most to be relieved for the exchange of those testons; much detriment and inconvenience should ensue to the possessors of the same, unless a remedy, by prolonging of the term then appointed for their calling in, were provided.

His majesty therefore, by the advice aforesaid, is most graciously pleased, willeth, and commandeth that the term of the calling in of the said pieces of 12*d*. commonly called testons, shall be yet further prolonged and extended to the first day of May next coming after the date hereof; and that during all the mean space, the said testons (being of his highness' standard) shall be current throughout his highness' realms and dominions after no less value and sort then if the said former proclamation for their calling in had not been made.

Provided always that after the said first day of May, the said testons shall no longer be current, but be used in such sort as that former proclamation doth specify, this present proclamation notwithstanding.

And further his majesty exhorteth all his said loving subjects, that like as his highness for their benefit was moved to revoke the said testons, and for their more commodity is pleased to prolong the day of their calling in, so they also in the meanwhile will have the better regard and heed that such testons as they take be of his majesty's standard and coin, seeing the number to be such of false and foreign testons as are now so dispersed abroad, to the deceit and loss of the takers; and that during this time of respite, they endeavor themselves, from day to day, by portions and smaller sums, to bring in such testons as they shall have into any his majesty's mints, as shall best serve for their purpose, there to receive the just exchange of the same; so as by lingering or deferring of the bringing in of such testons until the said first day of May limited by this peremptory admonition, their negligence be not cause that when the mints (if the whole mass come in at once) are pestered, their exchange shall not be so ready unto them as otherwise it should be.

Moreover, because his majesty, most graciously above other things tendering the relief of the poorer sort of his loving subjects, doth consider that their need or inability to forbear by a space (be it never so small) the exchange of their testons at his grace's mints might be an occasion that others of the richer sort, with whom they should perchance be driven to bargain for other money in lieu of their testons, should then exact or take of them unreasonably for the exchange (as it hath come to his highness' knowledge that some already have not been ashamed to demand and take so against all conscience and equity): his highness therefore, by the foresaid advice, doth straightly charge and command that no manner person or persons, whatsoever they be, do take by any means for the gain of the exchange of any testons above 2*d.* for every pound in testons (which is 20*s.*), and after that rate for smaller sums in testons, upon pain of loss and forfeiture of so much of the money or the value thereof as he or they for any higher rate of gain, in every pound or smaller sums, shall have delivered in exchange for testons to any person, the one moiety thereof to be applied to his highness, and the other to the party complaining.

And finally, his majesty's pleasure is that between this and the first day of May aforesaid no manner person be so hardy to refuse in payments great or small any such testons of his grace's standard, but shall accept them no less than other his highness' coin for the time, upon pain aforesaid.

In which behalf his majesty likewise chargeth all manner mayors, sheriffs, bailiffs, justices of peace, and others his grace's officers and ministers of justice, that they, or such of them as by information of the party complaining shall have due knowledge hereof, fail not to see the whole effect of this penalty executed upon the party complained on (if he be guilty), as otherwise they themselves shall be subject to the like danger upon further information against them given.

Provided also that such person or persons as already have collected together at other men's hands any testons for a gain, that is to say after a less rate and value than they were current, shall not by occasion of any thing or clause herein contained, otherwise utter, disperse, or put in ure any such testons so by them collected, but shall only bring them into the mints without failing; as every such offender, being upon like information found culpable, shall incur the like penalty in each behalf as is before expressed.

323. Providing Death Penalty for Aid to Pirates

[Westminster, 19 February 1549, 3 Edward VI]

Rev.STC 7819.3, NRO Brudenell (Deene) B.3, 1: printed by R. Grafton (London, 1549); date as above; schedule as below. LJ 15, 404: date as above; schedule as below. Steele 345. Text (*rev.STC*): NRO

THE MULTITUDE of piracies and robberies on the seas being of late greatly increased, to the King's majesty's high displeasure and no small slander of his highness' realm, by reason that such persons who had the chief care and charge thereof and should most especially have seen the same redressed and amended hath rather been concealers or maintainers of such piracies, as of late (by the grace of God) it hath been revealed and doth appear:

His majesty therefore, by the advice of the Lord Protector and the rest of his highness' council, most earnestly minding to proceed with all care and force against the said pirates and sea robbers, and to cause his laws[1] more severely to be executed, lest peradventure any of his loving subjects should either ignorantly fall into danger or willingly pretend ignorance of his laws, doth by this his majesty's proclamation straightly charge and command that no manner of person or persons do by any color or pretense from henceforth receive, aid, succor, relieve, defend, conceal, or abet any manner of pirate or pirates, whatsoever they be, either on the seas or in any port, haven, creek, or any other town of the King's majesty's, or in any other place within his majesty's realms and dominions, by sea or land,

Upon pain that whosoever shall offend contrary to this proclamation shall be taken for a pirate or fautor of them, and suffer such pains of death, loss of goods, and forfeitures, as the pirates themselves or their fautors by the laws of this realm should or ought to do. And whatsoever person or persons shall buy of any pirate, or by any other fraud or covin shall wittingly take any manner of goods or merchandise piratically taken, or conceal the same, the person so offending to be taken for a receiver of pirates and so judged and suffer according to the laws of this realm.

And whosoever hereafter shall buy or take by exchange or any other color any goods of any pirate or which were piratically taken, the King's highness by the advice aforesaid further willeth that the person so taking such goods as aforesaid shall not only be compelled to deliver the said goods and merchandises to the true owners of the said goods without any recompense therefor, if they require the same, but also be further punished by imprisonment or otherwise at his highness' pleasure.

1. 27 Henry VIII, c. 4, 1535, *SR 3*, 533; 28 Henry VIII, c. 15, 1536, *SR 3*, 671.

And for the better repressing of the like robberies and piracies hereafter, his majesty willeth and requireth all and every his majesty's loving subjects to endeavor themselves to the best of their powers to apprehend and take the said pirates by all ways and means they may; whereby they shall not only show themselves good subjects to his majesty, but also be well assured to be further rewarded and considered of his majesty in such sort as they shall have good cause to be well contented.

Wherefore his highness willeth and commandeth all justices of peace, all mayors, sheriffs, constables, headboroughs, portreeves, and all his officers and ministers, to see this proclamation executed and performed according to the true meaning thereof, without any partiality or favor, as they tender the King's majesty's pleasure and will avoid the contrary at their uttermost perils.

324. Announcing Payment of King's Debts

[Leigh, 1 April 1549, 3 Edward VI]

LJ 15, 414: date as above; schedule as below. Grafton 29*v*: date, 1 April; schedule as below. Herbert 529: separate edition by Grafton. Steele 346: date, Leigh. Text: Grafton

WHEREAS at the humble suit of our loving subjects in our late parliament we have condescended and agreed, by the advice of our dearest uncle, the Duke of Somerset, governor of our person and protector of our realms, dominions, and subjects, and the rest of our Privy Council, to forbear to make any provisions by any of our purveyors or takers but in such sort and for such times as in an act [1] made in our said parliament for that purpose doth more plainly appear:

Being now minded not only to put the said act in execution, according to the effect and true meaning of the same, but also to give order that such sums of money as is due to any our subjects for any things heretofore taken to our use by any our said purveyors and takers, we have though convenient to will and require all and every of our loving subjects within this, our county of ——————, to whom any money is justly due by us for things taken to our use as aforesaid, to bring in and deliver to the sheriff of the said county, before the Feast of St. Michael the Archangel now next coming, their bills, containing their own names, their dwelling place, and the debt and the things whereof the debt riseth, with the names and times, also by whom and when the same things were taken.

And furthermore our pleasure and commandment is that the sheriff of our said county for the year being shall receive all such bills of debts as

1. 2 & 3 Edward VI, c. 3, 1548, *SR 4(1)*, 41.

shall be before the said Feast of St. Michael brought unto him; and deliver safely within 20 days next ensuing the said Feast of St. Michael such of the said bills as concern the debt of our household to the hands of our cofferer; and such as concern our debts for any other our provisions to the hands of the Treasurer and Barons of our Exchequer, or their deputies for that purpose: without failing thereof, as they will answer to us for the contrary at their peril. Whereupon we mind shortly after, God willing, to give such order for the satisfaction of our good subjects as shall stand with good reason, equity and justice.

325. Ordering Reform of Military Discipline

[Leigh, 6 April 1549, 3 Edward VI]

Grafton 33*v:* date, 6 April; schedule as below. Dibdin *3,* 468 n.: separate edition by Grafton. Steele 347: date, Leigh. Text: Grafton

WHEREAS it is come to the knowledge of the King's most excellent majesty that, among other disorders of late time crept into the ancient discipline of war, heretofore observed most straightly by the subjects of this realm as the chiefest cause of so many victories which by means thereof have risen to the same, there is a notable and perilous sort of deceit and breach of that discipline, used as well by captains as soldiers entertained in his highness' wages; and specially such captains of lighthorsemen and those of their bands being of the counties of Northumberland, Cumberland, Westmorland, and other places of the borders, as for defense of the same are entertained still in wages to his majesty's no small charge and expense of treasure.

Which captains, having not so much before their eyes their duty toward their sovereign lord and country nor yet their own sureties as a vile mind and filthy respect to their own gain by deceiving of his highness and polling of the soldiers without shame or dread, do not only diminish their numbers appointed to serve under them (saving that for a color at the muster day they have some others to supply the void places) but also, by patisement with unmeet and unservicable men for a less wage than his highness alloweth, do in such sort disguise their numbers (contrary to his highness' expectation and trust reposed in them) as, in a manner, the third part of the numbers which his majesty appointeth and payeth for is not ready, able or sufficiently furnished to do that service which is looked for, to the great deceit of his majesty and no less danger of such other his highness' true subjects and soldiers as, upon confidence of the aid of such lighthorsemen to join with them at any encounter with the enemy, find themselves deceived and abandoned.

According to the which said most naughty and shameful behavior of such captains, the soldiers in like sort that are of their bands, taking thereat example and boldness, do neither provide themselves of horse or harness meet to serve withal nor yet, being commanded to set forth towards any place of service, do repair thither together but sometime more than the half part remaineth behind; or if they go, stick not to return home by small companies without leave, with several preys and booties more sought of them than service. And, that is worst of all, at any approach or affronture of the enemy, without order or respect of abiding by the standard, do use commonly upon every little moment, or causeless, to begin the flight, betraying their fellows, which through such their flying lose oftentimes that assured advantage of victory which with their tarrying they might both have been partakers of. And moreover, if so be they tarry, they do it not so much for discharge of their profession of service as only for desire of spoil and pillage, which pillage they seek not so much upon the enemies as rather upon his highness' own subjects or friends, namely the assured Scottishmen, whose goods and chattels divers of those lighthorsemen of Northumberland and others of the borders have of late most ravenously spoiled and robbed, as by sundry complaints of such assured men it hath been touched.

His majesty therefore, minding the reformation hereof, by the advice of his dearest uncle and councilor the Duke of Somerset, governor of his person and protector of his majesty's realms, dominions, and subjects, and the rest of his highness' Privy Council, hath determined, and straightly chargeth and commandeth, all and singular the captains of any bands or numbers of lighthorsemen, and specially captains of any bands or number of lighthorsemen being of the county of Northumberland or any other county or place upon any the borders against Scotland, that they, according to the numbers [to] them appointed and wages for the same allowed, fail not from henceforth to entertain and have in continual readiness the said whole and entire number, without diminishment in any part of the said number or defalcation of any part of the wages so allowed by his highness to every such lighthorseman of their band.

And furthermore, that the said captains fail not to have their said complete bands always in such readiness from time to time to serve, as upon one hour's warning to be given them by his highness' commissaries, wardens, or other chief officers there for the time being, they may be found ready to set forth to what place they shall be appointed.

And moreover, that none of the said captains or any lighthorsemen of their bands be so hardy at any inroad or other invasion of the enemy's ground, or defense of the borders, to depart from the standard, or otherwise forsake or scatter from the rest of the army or company, either with their whole bands or smaller parts, for spoil or other cause; nor yet be so hardy to forsake or depart from any fortress to the guard whereof they shall be appointed, unless they shall have express commandment or license of the chieftain of the enterprise or captain of the fort so to do.

And finally, that the said captains and lighthorsemen of the bands forbear and refrain from henceforth to commit any spoils or other pillages upon any of the assured Scottishmen, their goods, lands, or chattels, which have been received into his majesty's protection, unless the commissaries or chieftain for the time being, upon the not keeping of promise by those assured men, do give them commandment so to do.

And that in likewise, they forbear from the embezzling or pilfering either of horses, geldings, harness, weapons, or any other thing pertaining to any other soldier serving his majesty in the wars on that side, whereby the service of the party so robbed by any of the said lighthorsemen should be hindered and he endamaged. Also that no captain of lighthorsemen or soldier of his band be so hardy as to sell, give, exchange or otherwise, by any fraud, cautel, or train, directly or indirectly, procure or find, the means to set out of purpose any horse, mare, or gelding, to be taken or come into the possession of any Scottishman or other stranger being his majesty's enemy, upon pain that whatsoever captain or captains, soldier or soldiers of their bands aforesaid, which shall in any part neglect, disobey, or break any point of this his majesty's commandment and order of reformation in these several cases afore rehearsed, or else disobey or break the orders of reformation set forth by the last parliament, in the articles where pain of death is expressed, shall from henceforth upon due proof of the offense, incur the danger and loss of his or their lives by execution, at the direction of his majesty's lieutenant, warden, commissaries, or other general, captain, or governor, there by his highness for the time placed.

And semblably if any soldier or soldiers being placed in garrisons within any his majesty's places upon the borders or within Scotland, being by the captain of the said places assigned to any charge of watch or ward for the surety of the said place, do from henceforth be so hardy, before license or discharge of the captain to leave their watch or ward appointed, to the danger of loss of the place: his majesty by the foresaid advice doth will and order that the offender or offenders herein, upon due proof, shall incur the like danger and pain of death, at the direction aforesaid. And in case any assured Scottishman shall help to convey by any means of purpose any horse, mare, or gelding unto the enemy, his majesty willeth and is pleased that upon due proof thereof the party offending herein shall lose the benefit of his assurance and from thenceforth be used as if no such assurance had been made unto him; straightly charging and commanding all and singular his majesty's commissaries, wardens, and other generals upon the borders for the time being, and by whatsoever name of office it shall please his highness to name them, that they not only see the whole effect of this reformation to be put in ure and observed upon the publishing of this present proclamation, but also that they fail not to correct and punish the offenders hereagainst or any point hereof, in no less degree than is herein contained, as otherwise they will sustain his majesty's displeasure and indignation, and answer for the contrary at their uttermost perils.

326. Revaluing Coinage, Punishing Counterfeiters

[Westminster, 11 April 1549, 3 Edward VI]

Rev.STC 7819.5, BM MS Harl 5928: printed by R. Grafton (London, 1549); schedule imperfect. LJ 15, 415*v*: date, Westminster, 10 April; schedule as below. Grafton 30*v*: date, 11 April; schedule as below. See 10 and 173. Steele 348. Text: Grafton

FORSOMUCH as divers persons now of late time have found the means to convey the King's majesty's coin in gold, and especially the old coin of royals, angels, half-angels, crowns of the rose, and other of that or like standard, and also sovereigns, half-sovereigns, and other of his majesty's new coin of gold, to the great disfurnishing of the realm: his highness, by the advice of his most entirely beloved uncle, the Lord Protector, and the rest of the council, straightly chargeth and commandeth that no manner person, whatsoever he be, do from henceforth convey any of the said coins, broken or whole, into the parts beyond the seas; upon pain that every such offender or offenders shall incur the King's majesty's displeasure and suffer imprisonment of his or their bodies at his highness' will and pleasure, over and beside such pains and forfeiture as be in such case by the laws and statutes of the realm appointed and provided.

And further the King's majesty, by the advice aforesaid, straightly chargeth and commandeth that no manner person do buy or sell any of the said coins afore rehearsed for other price, than according as they be valued and appointed by this the King's majesty's proclamation: that is to say, the angel of gold at 9*s*. 8*d*.; the half-angel at 4*s*. 10*d*.; the old royal 14*s*. 6*d*.; the new sovereign at 20*s*.; the half-sovereign at 10*s*.; and the crown at 5*s*.; and so all other the King's majesty's coin accordingly as they be in this or others his majesty's proclamations cessed and valued; upon pain that if any man shall either buy or sell the said coins, or any of them, over and above the price aforesaid so in the proclamation cessed, valued, or limited, both the seller and buyer shall forfeit the said coins so bought or sold, and 10 times the value thereof, the one moiety to the King's majesty, the other to the presenter or demander in any of the King's majesty's courts, by bill, action of debt, or information, as in such cases heretofore hath been accustomed; and further to suffer imprisonment for every such offense at the King's majesty's will and pleasure.

And forasmuch as divers persons, within this realm, as well goldsmiths as merchants and men of other occupations, hath used now of late, contrary to the laws and statutes of this realm, to buy and sell the King's majesty's coin, of and for higher price than it is by his majesty's proclamation rated and valued, and so cull and try out the finest and heaviest and melt them down, or otherwise make gain upon them, leaving the lightest and least fine only to be current amongst the King's majesty's people, to the great impairing of his highness' coin, defrauding of his subjects and disfurnishing and slandering of the mints: it is his highness' will and pleasure, by the advice aforesaid, that the old and ancient laws, statutes and customs of this realm in this case be put in ure and execution; and that no manner person attempt from henceforth to sell or buy any manner of money or coin of this realm, whatsoever it be, or cull out the heaviest and finest of it, or melt any manner of coin of gold or silver current in this realm, by what name soever it be called; upon pain of forfeiture of the same money so exchanged, bought, sold, culled out, or melted, and of imprisonment of the body of the buyers, sellers, changers, cullers, or melters of the said money, without mainprize, at his highness' will and pleasure, the one moiety of the which forfeiture shall be to the King's highness, the other moiety to the informer or demander in any of the King's majesty's courts of record, by bill, action of debt, or complaint, where no essoin nor protection shall serve.

Provided that it shall be lawful to any person to sell the coins before rehearsed, or any other, into any of the King's majesty's mints upon such prices as his majesty there doth give, and the officers there may buy the same so to melt and coin them to the King's majesty's use, according to their indentures, anything in this present proclamation notwithstanding.

Furthermore, it is divers ways come to notice and knowledge that sundry persons, in the parts beyond the seas, have now of late attempted to counterfeit the testons, shillings, groats, and other the King's majesty's coins of silver, and in great multitude do privily bring them into this realm, to the prejudice of the King's majesty and his subjects. For redress whereof it is his highness' will and pleasure, by the advice aforesaid, that all mayors, sheriffs, bailiffs, constables, all customers, comptrollers, and searchers in their offices, all justices of peace in their sessions, and all other his highness' officers and ministers, do make the most diligent search and inquiry that they possibly may for such offenders; and that every such person who wittingly and willingly shall bring from beyond the seas into this realm, or in this realm utter or sell by exchange, or for other money or wares, any testons, shillings, half-shillings, groats, or any other moneys of gold or silver of the King's majesty's stamp, knowing the same to be coined in the parts beyond the seas, or in any other part or place out of the King's majesty's mints, shall suffer pains of death and loss of all lands, goods, and chattels, as by the laws of the realm counterfeiters of the King's majesty's coin, their adherents, fautors, abettors, or concealers hath been wont and accustomed.

And his highness, by the advice aforesaid, straightly chargeth and commandeth all mayors, sheriffs, bailiffs, constables, and headboroughs, all justices of peace, and all other his majesty's officers, ministers, and subjects, to be aiding and assisting to the executing of this present proclamation, as they tender the wealth of the realm, their own commodity and his majesty's will and pleasure, and will answer to the contrary at their uttermost perils.

327. Enforcing Statutes against Enclosures

[Westminster, 11 April 1549, 3 Edward VI]

LJ 15, 416*v:* date as above; schedule as below. Steele 352: date, 1 June 1548; mistaken for reissue of 309. Text (MS): LJ

WHERE in the fourth year[1] of the reign of the most noble prince King Henry VII, the King's majesty's grandfather, and in the seventh, the 25th and 26th years[2] of the reign of the most mighty prince King Henry VIII, the King's majesty's most worthy father, divers good and necessary statutes were made and enacted for the avoiding of destruction of towns, villages, hamlets, and houses of husbandry and tillage, against the unreasonable multitude of sheep, decay of farms and of houses of husbandry, by enclosing them into a few men's hands, and for maintenance of hospitality, upon the sites of monasteries and religious houses, dissolved by act of parliament, being of and under the yearly value of 300 marks, and for the tilling and sowing of the demesnes thereof; whereby there was a great hope conceived that the commonwealth of this realm should have been renewed and restored to the ancient force and wealth that it had in times past;

For execution of which statutes, being so godly and necessary for the commonwealth, it pleased the King's majesty, by the advice of his most entirely beloved uncle Edward, Duke of Somerset, governor of his most royal person and protector of all his realms, dominions, and subjects, and the rest of his grace's Privy Council, to send forth his proclamation, and to address his commissioners, into divers parts of this his realm, the last year. By reason whereof, it is come to his majesty's and his said councilors' knowledge that through the greediness of some persons, blind and ignorant in brotherly love and charity, that ought to be between Christian man and Christian man, and the natural love and amity of one Englishman to another, which ought to be as countrymen and supporters of one and the same realm, country, and language, the said laws and statutes, most tending

1. 4 Henry VII, c. 19, 1489, *SR 2,* 542.

2. 25 Henry VIII, c. 13, 1533, *SR 3,* 451; 27 Henry VIII, c. 1, 1535, *SR 3,* 531. See 3 & 4 Edward VI, c. 3, 1549, *SR 4(1)*, 102.

to that purpose, have not been observed; whereby that good and benefit that was both desired and also looked for hath not followed.

For some still, and willfully, have continued to pull down and destroy towns, villages, and houses of husbandry, and converted the lands from tilling to pasture for sheep, and into parks for deer; and others have neither kept hospitality on the same sites nor eared the demesnes, but either have pulled down the houses or suffered them to be uninhabited, and have converted the demesnes utterly from tillage to pasture. And some have retained and kept in their proper occupation many farms and men's livings; and others have and do keep great[er] number of sheep than the law permitteth.

And on the other part, some others have enclosed and taken their tenants' (and other poor men, their) commons, so that they be not able to breed, rear, or keep their cattle as they have done in time past, and have maintained and upholden the buildings, but have taken away all the lands from the houses, wherein honest husbandmen, their wives, children, and families have been sustained and maintained, and the number of people, to the great defense of the realm, increased; making thereof cottages for older and poor people, living for the most part only by alms, or dairy houses, keeping there only one or two women to milk kine, or sheep houses, wherein only a shepherd dwelleth.

And others have eared and sown part but not all the ground that they ought, and some have eared it but not sown it. Others also, selling and giving away the houses, sometimes with one acre of ground, and most times with nothing at all, have kept the lands in their hands, and converted the same into pasture. And others have destroyed cottages, albeit there were but little land thereto belonging, wherein laborers of husbandry, carters, plowmen, threshers, hedgers, and such like, and their wives have dwelt, to the intent that they and their cattle might have the larger scope and gate. And others have and do pay to the King's majesty the moiety of the yearly rent of the lands so increased, which, being rated after the old rent, is but a trifle in respect of the gains that they unlawfully take by decaying the houses and turning the lands from tilling to pasture; and used other divers and marvelous crafts to defeat the godly acts, and the minds and intents of the same, setting more by their privity and commodity than the augmentation of the nation, the strength and defense of the realm. Whereupon it was apparent that very many and heavy forfeitures were for such offenses due unto his grace.

Yet his highness, of his most princely and gentle mind, by the advice aforesaid, intending as well by clemency and kingly mercy to provoke his subjects to do well, and also pitying that those should be so fined and forfeiting, which did now begin to amend that that was past, was contented and pleased that all pains, losses, and forfeitures for every such act contrary to the said statute [3] that was passed before the last day of the last session of his highness' parliament should be pardoned by his majesty to his loving subjects; not that thereby they should be animated to do evil still, and to hurt the King's majesty's realm, people, and commonwealth; but that men so gently thereunto provoked should obediently again follow so noble, godly, and wholesome laws.

Or else if gentleness will not now provoke and cause that thing be amended which duty should do and laws may compel: his highness, of his most royal duty and love, which his majesty beareth to this his region and country and to the maintenance of the manred thereof, is fully minded from henceforth, by advice aforesaid, to put in ure all the said penal laws heretofore made for the repressing of such offenses, and straightly to see them executed against all such as shall be found culpable, without pardon or remission;

And therefore straightly chargeth and commandeth all his highness' officers and ministers, whosoever they be, to whom by statute or otherwise the redress or repressing of such offenses may appertain, to receive information given unto them, and to make diligent inquiry, and with all speed and earnest endeavor see to the redress and punishment of all such offenders as by the laws and statutes of the realm they may and ought to do, as they tender this his majesty's will and pleasure, and will answer to the contrary at their uttermost perils.

328. Ordering True Manufacture of Wool Cloth

[Westminster, 17 April 1549, 3 Edward VI]

LJ 15, 414*v*: date, Westminster, 7 April. Grafton 38: date, 17 April; schedule as below. Herbert 529: separate edition by Grafton. Steele 349: date, Greenwich. Text: Grafton

WHERE, by the making of untrue and false cloths within this realm now within few years practiced and used, not only great infamy and slander hath grown to the same realm, but also the King's majesty's faithful and true subjects have sustained great loss: the King's most excellent majesty, minding to put away all occasions of the said slanders and to set forth such an order in his commonwealth that truth may rule, and falsehood be utterly banished, hath thought it good, by the advice of his most dearly beloved uncle, the Duke of Somerset, governor of his royal person and protector of all his realms, dominions, and subjects, and the rest of his Privy Council, to set forth and publish to his subjects a perfect order of the making of cloths in all places of this his highness' realm, and other his majesty's

3. 1 Edward VI, c. 15, 1547, *SR* 4(*1*), 33.

dominions; which his highness willeth and straightly chargeth and commandeth all and singular his loving and obedient subjects that use to make and sell cloths to observe and keep, upon pain of his grace's displeasure and imprisonment of their bodies.

First, that every clothier, from and after the Feast of the Nativity of St. John Baptist next coming, shall set his seal of lead to the cloth, declaring thereby the just lengths thereof to be tried by water. And that no person, after the said Feast, keeping any tentor, or using to stretch cloths, shall strain or stretch any cloth above a yard in length and half a quarter of a yard in breadth. And that no person or persons shall from or after the said Feast put to sale any cloth which when it shall be wet shall shrink more than one yard in all the length and half a quarter of a yard in the breadth; and likewise narrows, straits, and kersies, after that rate; nor shall put to sale any cloth, narrow, strait, or kersey by retail, the pieces whereof, being wet, shall shrink more than after the same rate in the whole piece.

And further, that no person or persons occupying the feat of dyeing shall, from and after the said feast, dye or alter, or cause to be dyed or altered, any wool cloth or cloths, as brown, blues, pukes, tawnies, violets, hats, or caps, except the same woolen cloths, hats, and caps be perfectly boiled, grained, or maddered upon the woad and shot with good and sufficient cork or archil, after a due, substantial, and sufficient mean of workmanship, according to the ancient workmanship in time past used; nor that any person shall dye any wool to be converted into cloth called russets, mustards, marbles, greys, rays, and such like colors, unless the same wool be perfectly woaded, boiled, and maddered according to the true and ancient usage, nor shall dye with brazil or any other false color in cloth or wool; nor that any person shall occupy, in, to, or with any woolen cloth or cloths, hat or cap, or any other thing, in coloring of scarlet, than grain or powder.

And that no person or persons, shall put any flocks upon any cloth; nor upon any white cloth or kersey, any chalk, flour, or starch.

And that no person shall after the said feast occupy any iron cards or picards in rowing of any manner of woolen cloth, nor that any person shall sell any cloth by any other measure, more or less, than after the true content thereof, to be moten and measured by the yard, adding to every yard one inch of the rule, according to the statute [1] made in the sixth year of the reign of his highness' said father; and that after the Feast of Pentecost next coming, no person shall keep any press in his house to the intent to press any cloth therewith, or shall press any cloth.

And for the better execution of this proclamation, his majesty, by the advice aforesaid, willeth and commandeth all and singular justices of the peace, mayors, sheriffs, bailiffs, and others, governors of cities, boroughs, and towns where any cloth is made or sold, that they shall visit every clothiers, drapers,

1. 6 Henry VIII, c. 9, 1514, *SR 3*, 130.

clothworkers, and dyer's house, once every quarter of a year at the least, and view the cloths by him made and dyed or remaining to be sold, to know whether they be truly made and dyed according to this proclamation; and to cause them or as many of them as they shall think convenient, to be put in water and to be measured, to see whether they be drawn or strained otherwise then is before mentioned in the said proclamation. And that the aldermen of the Steelyard in London, for the time being, shall once every quarter enter into all and every the packhouses of the same Steelyard belonging, and shall prove in the water as many cloths or kersies as he [*sic*] shall suspect, whether they be drawn or strained otherwise than is mentioned in this proclamation. And that the wardens of the clothworkers in London shall once every quarter, at the least, search the house of every person occupying the mystery of clothworkers, or occupying pressing of cloths within the same city, or within three miles' compass thereof, for the said presses, iron cards, or picards.

And further, his majesty by the advice aforesaid straightly chargeth and commandeth all and singular persons to whom his highness hath committed the charge and trust to see this proclamation truly executed, as they tender his majesty's favor, to be diligent in the execution of the same proclamation; and that if they or any of them shall find any cloths to be falsely colored, or upon the wetting of them in the water to have been drawn or strained otherwise than before by this proclamation is prescribed, or any wool or cloth falsely dyed, or any flocks, brazil, chalk, flour, or starch to be put upon any cloth, or iron cards or picards, or any other misdemeanor by this proclamation prohibited, that they, upon pain of his grace's displeasure, shall present the names of all such offenders, with their misdemeanors, to the said Lord Protector and the rest of the Privy Council, that the same offenders may receive condign punishment for such their falsehood and deceit according to their demerits.

329. Providing Penalty for Rumors of Military Defeat

[Westminster, 29 April 1549, 3 Edward VI]

LJ 15, 418: date as above; schedule imperfect. Grafton 41: date, 29 April; schedule as below. Herbert 529: separate edition by Grafton. Steele 350. Text: Grafton

FORSOMUCH as some lewd persons now of late, notwithstanding divers laws, statutes, and proclamations heretofore made to the contrary, hath not ceased to spread abroad and tell vain and false tales, as well of the King's majesty's own person, the Lord Protector, and the rest of his highness' council, as of his highness' fortresses, captains, and soldiers in the north parts and beyond the seas, and of his majesty's other affairs; feigning falsely great overthrows, losses, and dangers, to the slander of the King's highness, impairing of his majesty's service and discouraging of the King's subjects; besides that thereby, they have given to strangers occasion to write into distant countries such tales for news, to the great dishonor of his highness, the same being most false and untrue.

Therefore his majesty, compelled by the manifold inconveniences which might ensue thereof if order, stay, and redress were not foreseen and provided for such malicious, vain, and seditious lie-tellers and sowers abroad of false and lying rumors, considering that all other punishment heretofore appointed will not suffice for the redress and amendment hereof, by the advice and consent of his most entirely beloved uncle, the Lord Protector, and the rest of his highness' council, willeth and straightly commandeth all justices of peace, all mayors, bailiffs, sheriffs, constables, headboroughs, and all other his highness' officers and ministers, whosoever they be, to do their best endeavor and put in effect by all possible means they can, to apprehend all such sowers and tellers abroad of vain and forged tales and lies of his highness, the Lord Protector, his majesty's council or affairs, and to commit them to ward until such time as they bring forth the author or first teller of such vain tale or lie; or if they can bring forth none, then to keep such teller, as the author or first maker of such lies, in straight prison, and certify thereof the Lord Protector and the King's majesty's council. And his majesty's pleasure, by the advice aforesaid, is that every such author or maker of such false tale or news shall be committed into the galley, there to row in chains as a slave or forcery during the King's majesty's pleasure, to the example and terror of all other.

And furthermore his highness' will and pleasure, by the advice aforesaid, is that this present proclamation be with all diligence and severity put in execution and ure, as his said highness' officers will answer to the contrary at their peril.

330. Ordering Captains and Soldiers to Leave London

[Greenwich, 29 April 1549, 3 Edward VI]

LJ 16, 13: date as above; schedule as below. Steele 351. Text (MS): LJ

THE KING'S MOST EXCELLENT MAJESTY, with the advice and assent of his dearest uncle, the Lord Protector, his majesty's Lieutenant General of all his armies, and the rest of his highness' council, straightly chargeth and commandeth all and singular captains, officers of bands and soldiers, English or strangers, of what nation soever they be, Italians, Spaniards, Albainns, Almains, and others having had and received his highness' wages or prests and thereupon assigned to repair to the parts of the north to serve his majesty there: that forthwith upon proclamation hereof, without further tarrying or delay, they and every of them not only to avoid and depart forth of the cities of London, Westminster and suburbs of both the same, but also that according to the several wages and payments to them advanced, they with all diligence and competent journeys repair to Berwick, where order is given for their further address; and also that no manner soldier, English or stranger, having once taken prest or wages, be so hardy to return back again or depart from his captain without a special license in writing of his captain or leader, upon pain of hanging of every such offender hereagainst, wheresoever the same be taken.

331. Regulating Wool Trade

[Greenwich, 18 May 1549, 3 Edward VI]

PRO (SP 10/7/55): MS draft, signed by Somerset. *Rev.STC* 7820.5, NRO Brudenell (Deene) B.3, 10: printed by R. Grafton (London, 1549); date as above; schedule as below. Steele 354. Text (*rev.STC*): NRO

Forasmuch as upon the pitful complaints made unto the King's majesty by his loving subjects the clothiers of this his realm, it appeareth that through the greediness of some persons, who, perceiving that wool is so necessary for the keeping of the multitude of his highness' subjects from idleness that it cannot be lacked, have colorably made and named themselves factors for clothiers or merchants of the Staple, and so have of late days used to buy and sell wools for their singular profit, whereby not only the price of the same wools is so advanced that within short time, if it be not foreseen, a great number of subjects shall be destitute of living and driven to such misery as is not tolerable in any good commonwealth; but also that the clothiers cannot make cloths of the just breadth, length, content, and goodness that is prescribed by the laws and statutes of this his realm; whereby great infamy hath in foreign nations grown to this realm, and the said cloths in some places have been burned to the great loss of the merchants, and in some places have been banished and forbidden to be brought thither:

His highness, considering the dangers that may thereby ensue to this his realm, and minding the prevention thereof, nothing doubting but such as be his loving, faithful, and obedient subjects will willingly do for the love of their country, that those that be evil must be forced to do for fear, by the advice of his entirely beloved uncle Edward, Duke of Somerset, governor of his royal person and protector of his realms, dominions, and subjects, and the rest of his majesty's Privy Council, straightly willeth, chargeth, and commandeth that, from and after the first day of June next coming, no person, upon pain of his majesty's displeasure and grievous imprisonment of his body, other than such persons and their household servants as shall convert the same only into yarn, cloth, hats, caps, girdles, worsteds, stamin, says, arras, tapestry, or any other kind of thing to be wrought within this realm, and merchants of the Staple and their household servants for the only provision of the said Staple and for to be shipped only to the said Staple, shall by him or herself, or by any other, buy or bargain or take promise of bargain of any wools being now unshorn of the growing of the shires or counties of Kent, Surrey, Sussex, Southampton, Wilts, Dorset, Somerset, Devon, Cornwall, Gloucester, Worcester, Hereford, Salop, Stafford, Cheshire, Warwick, Leicester, Lincoln, Nottingham, Derby, York, Rutland, Northampton, Essex, Cambridge, Huntingdon, Buckingham, Bedford, Hertford, Oxford, Berks, Middlesex, North Wales, South Wales and all the shires of Wales, or any of them; upon pain to incur his majesty's high displeasure, and to suffer imprisonment of his or her body at his grace's will and pleasure.

And further his highness by the advice aforesaid straightly chargeth and commandeth that no merchant of the Staple, from and after the said first day of June, shall by fraud, covin, or collusion, sell any wools within this realm, unless it be the refuse, coarse wools, shot and sorted by the shooter, such as be not meet for the said Staple, upon like pain of his highness' displeasure and imprisonment of his body. Also his highness, by the advice aforesaid, straightly chargeth and commandeth that no merchant of the Staple, from and after the said first day of June, shall buy or bargain for any yarn other than such [persons] or his or their household servants as shall convert the same into cloths, hats, caps, girdles, worsteds, says, stamin, arras, tapestry or other things to be wrought within this realm, upon like pain of his highness' displeasure and imprisonment of his body. And furthermore his highness straightly chargeth and commandeth that no manner of person or persons shall pluck or clip the wool of any fell that is merchantable to the Staple of Calais, upon like pain of his highness' displeasure and imprisonment of his body.

And for the better execution hereof, his highness by the advice aforesaid straightly chargeth and commandeth all and singular justices of peace, mayors, bailiffs, and sheriffs, not only to see this proclamation truly executed, but also if that any person be justly accused before him or them for contemning or breaking this proclamation or any part thereof, they shall commit such persons to ward, there to remain without bail or mainprize till the King's majesty's and his said council's pleasure shall be further known.

332. Extending Time for Calling in Testons until 31 July

[Greenwich, 22 May 1549, 3 Edward VI]

STC 7821 (UM 5,25,435), Antiq 3, 36: printed by R. Grafton (London, 1549); date as above; schedule as below. Steele 355. Text (*STC*): Antiq

WHEREAS the King's majesty, by the advice of his most dear uncle the Lord Protector, and the rest of his highness' council, for divers great and urgent considerations had commanded [1] that all manner of persons should bring all coin commonly called testons, coined with the face and stamp of his highness' most dear father, the late King Henry VIII, before the Feast of Christmas last past, into the Tower of London or other his majesty's mints, to the intent the same might be exchanged into shillings, groats, or other kind of moneys, it hath so chanced that by reason as well of the multitude of that coin heretofore made in the time of the said late King, his majesty's father, as also by the great quantity and foison of the same coin, counterfeited and brought into this realm, being current here, all the said testons hath not been changed. And thereupon his highness, by the advice aforesaid, was pleased that the said proclamation should be enlarged unto a longer day,[2] and so hath permitted and suffered the said coin of testons to be current among his subjects until the first of May last past, upon trust that in that space, upon the considerations in the said proclamation expressed, every man for his part helping that ways, all manner of the said testons of the stamp of the said late King of famous memory should have been brought into the mints and exchanged; in the which space yet many, abusing his highness' clemency, hath kept their testons still in their hands, or otherwise uttered them, and fewer since that time till now of late have been brought into his highness' mints; the which testons if they should now remain only mere bullion, should be great loss and hindrance to his majesty's subjects; and if the same stay or proclamation should in any wise be released, it should be [the] greatest loss and hindrance to the realm, and a present occasion of continual bringing in more counterfeit testons.

Therefore the King's majesty, by the advice of the Lord Protector and the rest of his highness' council, straightly chargeth and commandeth the said proclamation, of disannulling and crying down of the said testons, to be kept among all his loving subjects, so that the same be never hereafter taken for current or lawful money, but may lawfully be refused of any manner of per-

1. See 309.
2. See 322.

son. And yet nevertheless of his most princely clemency and liberality, his highness by the advice aforesaid is content that all such sums of money as shall be due to his majesty, as well for the relief granted in the last sessions of the parliament as for all other rents and debts, may be paid in good and lawful testons, of the stamp and coin of his majesty's father, at any time before the first of June next following, and so received of his highness' treasurers until the said first of June next following only, after the rate and value of 12*d.* every teston. After which time, his highness' pleasure is that in no wise the said testons be any more received of any his highness' officers of receipt, of or for that price.

Nevertheless for the space and time of two months after, that is to say, unto the end and last day of July next following, his highness is content that all good and lawful testons at his majesty's mints shall be received for bullion, after the rate of 12*d.* the piece, of any person who shall bring them thither; and further that it shall be lawful to any man to buy any good and lawful testons of the said coin and stamp of the late King, and made in any of the mints within this realm of England, to that intent to bring them to the mints, of any person not disposed to bring them himself, so that he do buy them for no less price than after 11½*d.* the piece and not under; upon pain that whosoever, for his own greediness and lucre, shall buy any such testons for less value than after 11½*d.* the piece, to the damage of the poor men who would sell the same, shall forfeit therefor the testons so bought, and 10 times the value of them, whereof one moiety to the King's majesty, the other to the demander of the said forfeit, by bill, action of debt, or information in any of the King's majesty's courts of record, where no essoin, protection, nor wager of law shall serve to be allowed.

And his highness further is content that all his officers and ministers may receive all such good and lawful testons, and to repay them again unto his highness, after the said price of 11½*d.* the piece, during only the said months of June and July. In the which time for that price of 11½*d.* the piece, they shall refuse no lawful and good testons of any his highness' subjects. After the which last day of the month of July next following, his highness' express will and pleasure, by the advice aforesaid, is that the coin called testons of his highness' father, King Henry VIII's stamp, shall neither be received of his highness' officers, nor of none others, nor yet at the mints or exchange, as coin or money of any valuation, but after such sort as plate or any other strange bullion is or then shall be, that is to say, according to the rate of the standard, and the quantity of fine silver in them contained, and none otherwise.

333. Ordering Punishment of Enclosure Rioters

[Greenwich, 23 May 1549, 3 Edward VI]

PRO (SP 10/7/55): MS draft, signed by Somerset. *STC* 7820 (UM 2,10,434), Lambeth 432: printed by R. Grafton (London, 1549); date 23 May; schedule as below. BM MS Harl 4943, 227: MS note, approved by council; schedule as below. Steele 353: date, Greenwich. Text (*STC*): Lambeth

WHEREAS upon credible information of sundry decays of houses and enclosures made by divers persons contrary to the King's majesty's laws and statutes of this realm, his highness, by the advice of his dearest uncle, the Lord Protector, and others of his majesty's Privy Council, minding a gentle reformation of the same, gave warning by proclamation [1] to the offenders to redress and amend their offenses in that behalf before a certain day, intending after the said warning to have executed his highness' said laws and statutes sharply against such as, notwithstanding the said warning, would have continued in their said offense; being informed that certain numbers of disobedient and seditious persons, assembling themselves together unlawfully in some parts of the realm, have most arrogantly and disloyally, under pretense of the said proclamation, taken upon them his majesty's authority, presumed to pluck his highness' sword out of his hand, and so gone about to chastise and correct whom they have thought good, in plucking down pales, hedges, and ditches at their will and pleasure, contrary to their duties of allegiance and to the danger of his majesty and all other his highness' good and loving subjects; like as his majesty, by the advice and counsel aforesaid, hath resolved to take such order for the one part as the said decays and enclosures shall, when his highness sees time convenient, be reformed according to his majesty's laws and statutes; [2] and on the other part, these outrageous attempts of the said seditious and lewd persons stayed, corrected, and punished according to justice for the more surety of his highness' good and loving subjects.

So hath his majesty thought good to will, charge, and command, like as by these presents his majesty doth straightly charge and command, all and singular his highness' good subjects, of what estate, degree, or condition soever they be, not only to beware how they presume at any time from henceforth to make any such riots or unlawful assemblies for any cause whatsoever, upon pain of his highness' utter indignation, and as they will avoid the extremity and uttermost peril that may ensue for the contrary; but also as soon as by any

1. See 309, 327.

2. See 4 Henry VII, c. 19, 1488, *SR 2*, 542; 6 Henry VIII, c. 5, 1514, *SR 3*, 127; 7 Henry VIII, c. 1, 1515, *SR 3*, 176; 25 Henry VIII, c. 13, 1533, *SR 3*, 451; 27 Henry VIII, c. 1, 1535, *SR 3*, 531; 27 Henry VIII, c. 22, 1535, *SR 3*, 553; 32 Henry VIII, c. 18, 1540, *SR 3*, 768; 32 Henry VIII, c. 19, 1540, *SR 3*, 769; 3 & 4 Edward VI, c. 3, 1549, *SR 4(1)*, 102.

means they shall have any certain knowledge, intelligence, or vehement suspicion of any secret or open conspiracy or unlawful assembly of any multitude, either for the breaking down of hedges, pales, ditches, or enclosures or for any other purpose whatsoever, that in every such case they and every of them, having any knowledge or vehement suspicion as is aforesaid, fail not with as much speed as he or they possibly may to give notice and information to the next justice of the peace for the more speedy stay and repression thereof.

And his highness' further pleasure is that if any person or persons (this the declaration of his majesty's pleasure notwithstanding) shall presume (as his majesty trusteth none will) to make any the like sedition, assemblies, routs, or riots, that the sheriff and justices of peace in every shire within this his highness' realm, and every of them, shall not only extend their forces with all their possible diligence for the stay thereof, as is aforesaid, but also that they and every of them fail not to prosecute by the sword, and with all force and extremity, all such offenders; and also when they shall be departed from their houses to any assembly for any such unlawful purpose, to spoil and rifle their houses and goods to their utter ruin and destruction, and the terrible example of others; straightly charging and commanding all mayors, bailiffs, headboroughs, constables, and all other his majesty's officers, ministers, true and faithful subjects, that they and every of them be aiding and assisting to the said sheriffs and justices and to every of them in and about the execution of the premises, as they will avoid his majesty's indignation and imprisonment during his highness' pleasure, without bail or mainprize, and make further answer at their uttermost peril.

And yet his majesty doth his highness' good and loving subjects to understand that if any of them do or shall suffer any wrong or injury in any of the said cases, or any like: upon their humble and quiet complaint, his majesty will command such order to be given for redress thereof as his majesty's laws, justice and equity requireth.

334. Pardoning Enclosure Rioters; Ordering Martial Law against Future Rioters

[Greenwich, 14 June 1549, 3 Edward VI]

STC 7822 (UM 5,25,436), Antiq 3, 37: printed by R. Grafton (London, 1549); date 14 June; schedule as below. LJ 16, 16: date, 14 June; writ, dated 16 June, to mayor and sheriffs of London; schedule as below. Herbert 529: separate edition, 12 June. Grafton 47: date 12 June; schedule as below. Steele 356: date, Greenwich. Text (*STC*): Antiq

WHEREAS of late the King's majesty, moved of a godly zeal and love to the commonwealth of the realm, by the advice of his dearest uncle Edward, Duke of Somerset, governor of his highness' person and protector of all his realms, dominions, and subjects, and the rest of his majesty's Privy Council, did by proclamation [1] will and command all manner of persons who had offended against the good and wholesome laws heretofore provided against the decay of houses and unlawful enclosures, to amend their such offenses and to redress all faults by them committed against the said acts and statutes [2] and against the benefit of the commonwealth, upon pain to incur the dangers and pains in the same acts and statutes provided; and for the better performance thereof, by the advice aforesaid, willed and commanded all his highness' officers and ministers to whom it did appertain to see the same redressed, to receive informations, make inquiry, and with all speed and earnest endeavor see to the redress and punishment of all such offenders as by the laws and statutes of the realm they might and ought to do:

Upon this most godly warning, admonishment, and proclamation, which was to keep order and laws, his highness is advertised that a great number of rude and ignorant people, in certain shires of England, hath taken occasion, or at the least pretended to take occasion, of doing great and most perilous and heinous disorder, and contrary to all good laws and statutes and the order of this realm, have riotously, with routs and companies, with force, strength, and violence, of their own head and authority, assembled themselves, plucked down men's hedges, disparked their parks and, being led by furious and light guides of uproar, taken upon them the direction of things, the King's royal power and sword, and committed thereby such enormity and offense as they have justly therefore deserved to lose life, lands, and goods, and to be made example to all other.

But forasmuch as they have humbly submitted themselves and demanded pardon, being sorry for their former offenses, the King's highness, of a most high clemency and tender love to his subjects, is content not to look upon his justice herein to be executed, but much more of natural mercy and clemency; and so for this time accepting that this outrage was done rather of folly and of mistaking the said proclamation, and at the instigation and motion of certain lewd and seditious persons, than of malice or any evil will that his said subjects did bear either to his highness or to the quiet of this realm, of his majesty's most abundant clemency and tender pity, by the advice of the said Lord Protector and the rest of his highness' Privy Council, is contented and pleased to remit and pardon all the said outrages, misbehaviors, riots, and conspiracies, to all and singular his said subjects, other than to such as be already apprehended and in prison as heads and stirrers of the said outrages and riots; and therefore willeth and commandeth all justices of peace, mayors, sheriffs, bailiffs, and all other his highness' officers and ministers, not to interrupt, vex, or trouble, for and in his majesty's behalf, any manner person, other than is specified before, of or for any offense,

1. See 333.
2. See 333, n. 2.

injury, contempt, or conspiracy done at the said stir or riots lately made about the breaking of enclosures, so that they do not attempt or go about any such thing hereafter. But if so be there be any just cause to complain for default of justice, or lack of redress in any such enclosure, or default made against the said acts and statutes before specified in this case provided, or other who find themself unjustly grieved or injured, may give information, make suit or complaint to the King's majesty, or other his highness' officers deputed to the redress of all such offenses, according to the laws of the realm and the good and lawful order of the same.

But if any man shall at any time hereafter attempt or go about to make any such riot or unlawful assembly for any such cause before rehearsed, his majesty's will and pleasure is, by the advice aforesaid, that all such offenders shall immediately be apprehended by the next justice or justices of peace, and lose the benefit of this most gracious pardon, and suffer such pains of death, loss of lands, goods, and chattels, as by the laws of the realm in such case is provided; anything in this present proclamation heretofore mentioned notwithstanding.

335. Pricing Book of Common Prayer

[London, June 1549, 3 Edward VI]

STC 16,275, ICN Case 8726.548, T6*v:* printed by R. Grafton (London, 1549); date as above; schedule as below. Not in Steele. Text (*STC*): ICN

THE KING'S MAJESTY, by the advice of his most dear uncle, the Lord Protector, and other his highness' council, straightly chargeth and commandeth that no manner person shall sell this present book [1] unbound above the price of 2*s.* 2*d.*, and bound in forel for 2*s.* 10*d.*, and not above; and the same bound in sheep's leather for 3*s.* 3*d.*, and not above; and the same bound in paste or in boards in calves' leather, not above the price of 4*s.* the piece.

336. Pricing Victual

[Richmond, 2 July 1549, 3 Edward VI]

STC 7823 (UM 5,25,437), Antiq 3, 38: printed by R. Grafton (London, 1549); date as above; schedule as below; *rev.STC*, another copy at Chatsworth. Steele 357. Text (*STC*): Antiq

THE KING'S MAJESTY, having the principal and continual charge of the commonwealth and tranquillity of this realm, for the which cause Almighty

1. *The Boke of the Common Prayer* (London, R. Grafton, June 1549), *STC* 16,275.

God hath given to his majesty power to rule and to all his people hath enjoined lowliness to obey, certainly understandeth, by the information and good advice of his most dear uncle Edward, Duke of Somerset, governor of his most royal person, and protector of his realms, dominions, and subjects, and others of his Privy Council, that of late time the prices of all manner of victual necessary for man's sustenance be so heightened and raised above the accustomed and reasonable values that thereby (except speedy remedy be provided) very great loss and damage must needs chance to his majesty's loving subjects; and therefore both of wisdom, wherewith his majesty useth to consider the state of his commonwealth, and of pity, which at all times his majesty conceiveth upon the lack and griefs of his people, hath by long and deliberate study of his said dear uncle the Lord Protector, and the rest of his Privy Council, concluded and finally resolved to provide remedy herein, the which (resting upon the former redress of sundry disorders in the whole commonwealth) although it cannot be so absolutely and speedily had as his majesty's most hearty desire is, yet it is thought by his majesty, for the present disorders a great relief to put in due execution divers good laws and statutes provided heretofore by the authority of parliament in the reigns of the King's majesty's most noble progenitors, and especially two politic good statutes [1] made at Westminster in the 25th year of the reign of his majesty's most dear father, late deceased, King Henry VIII, ordained, as by the same appeareth, very politicly for the redress of these like disorders of prices, which at any time thence after might happen.

The effect of which later statute is that the Lord Treasurer, the Lord Chancellor of England, the Lord President of the King's most honorable council, the Lord Privy Seal, the Lord Steward, the Lord Chamberlain, and all other lords of the King's council, the Treasurer and Comptroller of the King's most honorable house, the Chancellor of the Duchy of Lancaster, the Justices of either bench, the Chancellor, Chamberlain, Under-Treasurer, and the Barons of the King's Exchequer, or seven of them at the least, whereof the Lord Treasurer, the Lord Chancellor, the Lord President of the King's council, or the Lord Privy Seal to be one, should have power and authority from time to time (as the case should require) to set and tax reasonable prices of all kinds of victuals mentioned in the said act, how they should be sold in gross or by retail, for relief of the King's subjects; and that after such prices set and taxed in form aforesaid, proclamation should be made in the King's name, under the Great Seal, of the said prices in such parts of this realm as should be convenient for the same.

And it was further enacted by the said statute that all farmers, owners, broggers, and all other victualers whatsoever, having and keeping any of the kinds of victuals mentioned in the said act, to the intent to sell, should sell the same to such the King's subjects as would buy them at such prices as should be set and taxed by the said proclamation, upon the pains to be ex-

1. 25 Henry VIII, c. 1, 1533, *SR 3*, 436; 25 Henry VIII, c. 2, 1533, *SR 3*, 438.

pressed and limited in the said proclamation, to be lost, forfeited, and levied to the King's use, in such wise as by the said proclamation should be declared.

And it was further provided by the said act, that the same act or anything therein contained, should not be hurtful to mayors, sheriffs, bailiffs, and other officers of cities, boroughs, and towns corporate, nor to any person or persons or bodies politic having authority to set prices of such victuals, or of any of them, but that they and every of them might set prices thereof as if the same act had never been had nor made, as by the same act amongst other things more at large it doth and may appear.

And forasmuch as complaint hath been made of the enhancing of prices of the same victuals, without ground or cause reasonable in all parts of this realm.

In consideration whereof the Lord Treasurer, the Lord Chancellor of England, and all others requisite by the said statute, have by authority of the same act, set and taxed reasonable prices of all kind of victuals mentioned in the same act, to be sold in form following, to the intent the same should be proclaimed, according to the same act. That is to say, that from the day of this proclamation made, without delay, all and singular person and persons having or keeping any of the kinds of victuals mentioned in the said act within this realm, to the intent to sell, shall sell the same to such of the King's subjects as will buy them at the prices hereafter mentioned.

That is to say: from Midsummer to Hallowmas, every ox being primed or well stricken, of the largest bone, 38*s.*; of a meaner sort, 28*s.* An ox fat and of the largest bone, 45*s.*; of the meaner sort being fat, 38*s.* Steers and runts being primed or well stricken and large of bone, 20*s.*; of a meaner sort, 16*s.*; being fat and of the largest bone, 25*s.*; being fat of a meaner sort, 21*s.* Heifers and kine being primed or well stricken and large of bone, 16*s.*; of a meaner sort, 13*s.* 4*d.*; being fat and large of bone, 22*s.*; being fat and of a meaner sort, 18*s.*

And from Hallowmas to Christmas, every ox being fat and large of bone, 46*s.* 8*d.*; being fat of a meaner sort, 39*s.* 8*d.* Steers and runts, within the same time, being fat and large of bone, 26*s.* 8*d.*; being fat of a meaner sort, 22*s.* 8*d.* Heifers and kine, within the same time, being fat and large of bone, 23*s.*; of a meaner sort, 19*s.*

And from Christmas to Shrovetide every ox being fat and large of bone, 48*s.* 4*d.*; of a meaner sort, 41*s.* 4*d.* Steers and runts, within the same time, being fat and large of bone, 28*s.* 4*d.*; of a meaner sort, 24*s.* 4*d.*

And from shearing time to Michaelmas, every wether being a shear-sheep, being lean and large of bone, 3*s.*; of a meaner sort, 2*s.* 4*d.*; being fat and large of bone, 4*s.*; being fat of a meaner sort, 3*s.* Ewes, within the same time, being lean and large of bone, 2*s.*; being lean of a meaner sort, 20*d.*; being fat and large of bone, 2*s.* 8*d.*; being fat of a meaner sort, 2*s.*

And from Michaelmas to Shrovetide, every wether being a shear-sheep, being lean and large of bone, 3*s.*; being lean of a meaner sort, 2*s.* 4*d.*; being fat and large of bone, 4*s.* 4*d.*; being fat and of a meaner sort, 3*s.* 4*d.*

And from Midsummer to Michaelmas, the pound of sweet butter not to be sold above 1*d.* And from Michaelmas to the new year's crop, the pound not above 1½*d.* Barrelled butter of Essex, the pound not to be sold to any the King's subjects above ½*d.* farthing. And barrelled butter of any other parts, to be sold to the King's subjects not above ½ farthing. Cheese of Essex, to be sold to the king's subjects, from Midsummer to Michaelmas, the pound not above ½*d.* Cheese of other parts, not above ½*d.* farthing. And of Essex to the King's subjects, from Michaelmas to the new years crop, not above ½*d.* farthing. And of any other parts, not above ½ farthing.

Upon pain of forfeiture for every ox, steer, cow, heifer, and bullock that should be sold by virtue of the same act and this proclamation, and shall not so be sold, £5.; and for every sheep that should be sold by virtue of the same act and this proclamation, and shall not so be sold, 10*s.*; and for every pound of butter and cheese, 12*d.*; and that for all and every sum that shall be forfeited by virtue of the same act and this proclamation, the King our sovereign lord shall and may have his recovery and remedy, by information, bill, plaint, or action of debt, in any of his highness' courts of record.

Wherefore we, considering the premises to be for the wealth and commodity of this our realm, will and command you, our sheriff, of our county of ———, within two days next after the receipt of this said proclamation, that you with all speed shall proclaim the premises in all market towns within the said county of ———, and that all manner our subjects shall obey the same, not only upon the pains above said, but also to incur our indignation and displeasure.

And furthermore the King's majesty, of his authority and power royal, straightly chargeth and commandeth all manner his justices of peace, sheriffs, mayors, and bailiffs of any towns corporate, or any other ministers to be assigned or appointed by any two justices of peace of the said county, if any the market or markets within the same county shall lack wherewithal to furnish the markets for the relief of his loving subjects, that then they shall foresee and provide that the owners, graziers, drovers, farmers, broggers, or any other of any kind of estate or degree whatsoever, near adjoining, having such store of any kind of the aforesaid victual that he may spare part of his said store, be it lean or fat (over and besides the store necessary for the maintenance of his household, and allowance whereof must be made in respect of his accustomed expenses, and the time of another usual provision), toward the furniture of the market, shall, by the appointment and order of the said justices, and other officers above named, bring to the market and markets such number and quantity of the said victuals, at such time and times as they shall think the cause and necessity requireth, and the same shall sell there according to the prices by the said justices to be rated.

As for an example, where the markets cannot be served with sufficient quantity of mutton, so that in default thereof the people happen to have overmuch lack, then in that and like cases the King's majesty's will and commandment is that the said justices of every county, and officers above named, upon the certain knowledge of that lack, shall compel all and every such person and persons as shall have nigh to the said market towns the number of 500 shear-sheep, for every hundred of the same 500 and above to send to the market so lacking at the most 10 of the best and fattest sheep of that sort, to be sold from time to time, and at the prices to be rated by the said justices and other officers; and if less lack, then less in number, upon like pain aforesaid for every sheep not so brought to the market.

Furthermore because the prices of the beeves and muttons hereto adjoined be but the prices of beeves and muttons alive and sold in gross and not by retail as the butcher useth to do, his majesty, notwithstanding the tenor of this proclamation, licenseth the butcher, in such cases where he shall buy of those prices, so to sell above the said price as it shall be thought and ordered by the said justices and officers above named, according to the laws and statutes of the realm, meet for a convenient gain toward his living; and so in all cases the same to be observed, upon pains expressed in sundry statutes for the same.

Provided that nothwithstanding any article or clause above mentioned, every butcher being no grazier, having bought and in his possession any manner cattle above the prices herein contained, before the time of this proclamation, shall have license and full liberty to make sale of any such cattle so bought of those prices according to the rate and proportion of the price he paid or then became debtor for, without any covin, by the space of eight days after the proclamation shall be proclaimed, in the next market town to his dwelling place, or to the place where he shall that sell; and after those eight days then to remain subject to the whole tenor of the proclamation.

And herein the King's majesty (to whom only, under God, appertaineth avengement, punishment, and redress of his people's offenses, whatsoever the same be) most straightly chargeth, and upon the pain of his highness' extreme indignation commandeth all manner of people to seek the redress and amendment of any manner offense against the tenor of this proclamation, or any other statute or laws, only by order of his majesty's laws, without force, riot, menace, unlawful assemblies, or any other disturbance of peace.

And on the contrary, if any subject, of what degree or estate soever he be, shall contrariwise and unlawfully, that is to say, otherwise than by complaint or order of law, seek, begin, or enterprise to redress his own cause, or the cause of any other, be the same never so just: then his majesty ascertaineth and letteth the same to know, that without any manner favor or grace to be hoped upon, he and every of them, so offending, shall surely feel, by extreme punishment, the King's highness' utter indignation; and in such case no extremity to be spared, but to be taken and accepted, not only as unkind, unnatural, unloving, and disobedient subjects, but also as high traitors and rebels against the King's majesty's own royal person, his crown, state, and dignity.

337. Offering Reward for Arrest of Rumor Mongers

[Richmond, 8 July 1549, 3 Edward VI]

STC 7824 (UM 5,25,438), NRO Brudenell (Deene) B.3, 9: printed by R. Grafton (London, 1549); date as above; schedule as below; *Rev.STC,* other copies at Chatsworth and Northampton. LJ 16, 22: date as above; schedule as below. Steele 358. Text (*STC*): NRO

THE KING'S MOST EXCELLENT MAJESTY hath certain knowledge, given as well to his own majesty as to his most dear uncle Edward, Duke of Somerset, governor of his person and protector of all his realms, dominions, and subjects, and to the rest of his highness' council, that in divers his majesty's counties of this his realm there be dispersed and severed abroad sundry light, lewd, idle, seditious, busy, and disordered persons; whereof the most part have neither place to inhabit in, neither seeketh any stay to live by, but having been either condemned of felonies and prison-breakers run from the wars, and sea-rovers departed from the King's garrisons, and loiterers;

Whereby they become desperate persons, and now employ and labor themselves, running and posting from place to place, county to county, town to town, by day to day, to stir up rumors, raise up tales, imagine news, whereby they seek to stir, gather together, and assemble the King's true subjects, of simplicity and ignorance deceived; and by that pretense, such lewd ruffians, tale-tellers, and unruly vagabonds become ringleaders and masters of the King's people, seeking to spoil, rob, and ravin where and whom they list or may, and so to live, wax rich, and feed of other men's labors, money, and food; they themselves neither willing to serve where they might, neither abiding when they be well entertained;

And being thus in several places of this his realm, at the last not able long to continue together with their assemblies according to their mischievous purposes, the same assemblies being in substance of such the King's poor subjects as though by ignorance and enticements of those foresaid tale-tellers they offend, yet shortly by the goodness of God acknowledge their faults and return themselves to their duties, most sorrowfully repent, receiving for the same the King's majesty's great mercy by his pardon; and by the reason of the quiet order the falling, ceasing, and appeasing of such assemblies, the said renegades, tale-tellers, and seditious persons fail and lack their purposes and mischievous intents; so that they, accustoming their evil nature and escaping from the places of their first attempts, have and do daily resort to new places, and from place to place, shire to shire, never quieting themself but devising slanderous tales and divulging to the people such kind of news as they think may most readily move them to uproars and tumults, and for the further deceit also pretend to them they seek to redress the commonwealth:

Therefore his majesty, by the advice of his said dear uncle, the Lord Protector, and the rest of his majesty's Privy Council, to the avoiding of the great inconveniences which, of the sufferance hereof daily doth ensue, and to admonish his good subjects which hitherto have not felt the peril of these poisoned evil people, most straightly chargeth and commandeth all manner and every his justices, sheriffs, constables, bailiffs, headboroughs, and all other his majesty's ministers and officers, whatsoever they be, to be most diligent and from time to time to be in their charge attendant, and therein also to take some good special politic order for the apprehension and attaching of all manner of such persons, whatsoever they be, which either as vagabonds, wayfaring men, stragglers, or otherwise, in what manner soever he be, shall bring any tale to any place, or invent or tell any news, (or conceal and keep close, longer than he may convenient, the bringer, inventor, or teller) which tale or news so brought, invented, or told, shall, doth, or may cause any unlawful assembly of the people or any tumult and uproar, or shall sound slanderous to the King's majesty, his crown, the Lord Protector, and other of his council, or any otherwise shall move the people unlawfully to remedy or redress their own causes and griefs by force and without law; which office belongeth only to the King's majesty and to the magistrates under him; and therein daily his majesty's said dear uncle and council most studiously travaileth.

And the same lewd person or persons so apprehended, to be brought unto the King's majesty or his said uncle and council, or to any one of the said council. For every the which so brought, the King's majesty assureth his officer and minister, the bringer of him, not only his costs and charges fully to be paid, but also to have his majesty's most hearty and effectual thanks.

And if any other the King's majesty's loving subjects shall at any time know certainly any such tale-carrier or rumor-runner, news-spreader, or sedition-sower, and of him so inform and give knowledge to any of the King's majesty's officers or ministers, so that the same evil person either might [be] or is taken and apprehended by the same officer and by force of the said information, then likewise the same informer, knowledge giver, accuser, and utterer shall have of the King's majesty's reward, for every such malefactor by him disclosed and apprehended, in manner as is abovesaid, 20 crowns, besides like hearty thanks from his majesty.

338. Enforcing Statutes against Enclosures

[Richmond, 8 July 1549, 3 Edward VI]

STC 7825, Antiq 3, 42: printed by R. Grafton (London, 1549): date, July; schedule as below; *rev.STC* notes other copies at Chatsworth, BM. Strype 2(2), 359. Steele 359: date, Richmond, 8 July. Text (*STC*): Antiq

FIRST, you shall inquire what towns, villages, and hamlets have been decayed and laid down by enclosures within the shire contained within your commission, since the fourth year of the reign of King Henry VII.[1]

Item, what land was in tillage at the time of the said enclosures, and what was then in pasture.

Item, how many plows, by reason of the said enclosures, be decayed and laid down.

Item, how many meses, houses, cottages, and dwelling houses be fallen in decay, and the inhabitants of the same departed from their habitation there, by reason of enclosures taken away of the lands, or otherwise, and how much land belonged to the same.

Item, if any person have severed the lands from any house of husbandry, whereby it is made a cottage, a sheep house, a dairy house, or otherwise converted to any other use than for a dwelling place of an husbandman.

Item, by whom the said enclosures and decays were made, and how long ago, and if they were made within the same time, and of what yearly rents and profits they be.

Item, who hath now the state of inheritance and the profits of the same enclosure and houses decayed, and of whom the lands be holden.

Item, how many new parks be now made since the said time.

Item, what arable land at the time of the making of the said parks were imparked with the same.

Item, how many parks within the shire be enlarged since the said time, and how much of the same ground was then arable and put in tillage.

Item, how many plows, houses, inhabitations be decayed by reason of the said new imparking.

Item, if any person hath or doth keep above the number of 2,000 sheep, besides lambs of one year's age, either in his own right or in the name of his wife, child, kinsman, or any other person, and whether he hath kept the same upon his own lands or upon his farm lands, or otherwise, by covin or fraud, and how long he hath kept them.

Item, how many sheep you think have been necessary for the only expenses of such person's household for one year.

1. 4 Henry VII, c. 19, 1488, *SR* 2, 542. See 7 Henry VIII, c. 1, 1515, *SR* 3, 176.

Item, if any person hath let any lands to farm by copy of court roll reserving the sheep pasture of the same to himself, or if any person hath taken from any other their commons, whereby they be not able to breed and keep their cattle and maintain their husbandry as they were in times past.

Item, if any person hath had or occupied above the number of two houses or tenements of husbandry, living in any town, village, hamlet, or tithing, and how long they have occupied the same.

Item, whether such person hath taken the same in farm for term of life, years, at will, by indenture or copy of court roll or otherwise, since the Feast of the Nativity of our Lord God, 1545, and where such person dwelleth.

Item, if any person, or body politic or corporate, that hath by gift, grant, lease, or demise, the site or precinct and demesnes of any monastery, priory, or religious house dissolved by the act of parliament [2] made in the 27th year of the reign of the King that dead is, do keep an honest and continual house and household in the same site or precinct; and do occupy yearly as much of the same demesnes in plowing and tillage of husbandry as was commonly used to be kept by the governors, abbots or priors of the same houses, monasteries, or priories, or by their farmer or farmers occupying the same, within the time of 20 years next before the making of the same statute.

Item, that you our said commissioners, for your better instruction, take with you copies of all such offices as were found concerning the premises, in the 9th or 10th years of the reign of our most noble father, King Henry VIII.

Item, that you cause to appear before you, at all places where you shall sit, for the execution of this commission, six persons of every parish; that is to say, two freeholders, two farmers, two copyholders or tenants at will, if there be so many there dwelling, or else as many as be there dwelling, to make presentment by their oaths of all such things as be presentable before you by virtue of this commission.

Item, if any person hath or keepeth in his occupation in one town, parish, lordship, or hamlet any more tenements of husbandry than one, and by what title he so hath or keepeth them.

Item, if any commons or highways have been enclosed or imparked contrary to right and without due recompense, that then the same shall be reformed by the said commissioners.

2. 27 Henry VIII, c. 1, 1535, *SR 3*, 531

339. Declaring Forfeitures by Western Rebels

[Richmond, 11 July 1549, 3 Edward VI]

Grafton 59: date 11 July; schedule as below. Herbert 530: separate edition by Grafton. Steele 360: date, Richmond. Text: Grafton

WHEREAS divers evil-disposed persons are at this present rebelliously and traitorously assembled in sundry companies within these the King's majesty's counties of Devon and Cornwall, showing themselves not only to contemn and disobey his most royal majesty, his laws, ordinances, and most godly proceedings, but also to levy war against his highness, to the great displeasure of Almighty God:

His majesty, most graciously weighing and considering what appertaineth to the good order and quiet reformation of his good and loving subjects, by the advice of his most entirely beloved uncle the Lord Protector, and the rest of his Privy Council, is pleased and contented and, by this present proclamation, willeth it to be notified and known to all and singular his loving subjects, that all and every of his said subjects which at the time of the publishing of this present proclamation do continue in their unlawful and disobedient assemblies within the said counties, and within ———— days next after this proclamation shall not willingly and obediently submit and yield themselves unto the right honorable Lord Russell, his highness' lieutenant in those parts, shall be deemed, accepted, and taken for rebels and traitors against his highness' most royal person, his imperial crown and dignity. For more terror and example of whose punishment, and for the good encouraging and advancing of such his true, loving, and obedient subjects as shall withdraw themselves from the said rebellious traitors, and of such others as shall aid and assist his highness' said lieutenant to suppress and subdue the said rebels and traitors; forsomuch as the forfeiture of all manner of goods, chattels, offices, pensions, lands, tenements, farms, copyholds, and other hereditaments of all and every traitors and traitor within this his majesty's realm and dominions, only and most justly appertaineth and belongeth unto his majesty: the same is further pleased and contented that all and singular the forfeitures of all the goods, chattels, offices, pensions, manors, lands, tenements, farms, copyholds, and other hereditaments of the said rebels and traitors which shall persevere and continue in their rebellion and treason, shall grow, come, and be unto all and every such person and persons as shall first have, take, possess, and attain to the said goods and chattels, or shall first enter into the said manors, lands, tenements, and hereditaments; and the same shall have, hold, possess, and enjoy, to his and their own proper use, commodity, and behalf, in as large and ample sort as his highness, by means and right of the said forfeiture and confiscation, ought and may dispose of the same; and shall have thereof such assurance from his majesty by his letters patent, or otherwise, as they or any of them can or shall best imagine or devise.

340. Pardoning Unlawful Assemblers

[Richmond, 12 July 1549, 3 Edward VI]

STC 7826 (UM 5,25,440), Antiq 3, 40: printed by R. Grafton (London, 1549); date as above; schedule as below. Steele 361. Text (*STC*): Antiq

THE KING'S MAJESTY, by the advice of his entirely beloved uncle Edward, Duke of Somerset, governor of his person, and protector of all his majesty's realms, dominions, and subjects, and the rest of his Privy Council, considereth that as it is the fruit of his mercy to receive his humble, repentant, and sorrowful subjects acknowledging their offenses, to the benefit and grace of his mercy, so also is it the reputation of his majesty's mercy to defend and save, harmless, all such which submitteth themselves to his mercy, and to let them feel his protection with their quiet, as they have sought it with their devout repentance; and so to save his repentant people with mercy, as his majesty ought to punish his obstinate subjects with justice.

In consideration whereof, his majesty, by the advice aforesaid, willeth, admonisheth, and commandeth first, all manner of his subjects which of late by their humble submission and sorrowful repentance of their offenses committed in sundry unlawful and riotous assemblies, that they from henceforth be of such good behavior in the peace of God and the King's majesty, and in all their acts and deeds be so quiet, peaceable, and well ordered, that the King's majesty may think his grace and pardon bestowed upon them with effect.

And likewise his majesty willeth and straightly commandeth all manner his other subjects, of what degree soever he be, having suffered any manner of grief, damage, or loss, by the act of any of the abovesaid the King's subjects whilst they offended and before they received the pardon from his majesty, that they shall not by action, suit, violence, or compulsion, force, punish, avenge, or correct any manner of offense, trespass, or unlawful act committed by the same offenders, and pardoned by the same act; but shall suffer and permit them to enjoy and take the benefit of the King's majesty's pardon, with like intent and purpose as the same hath been meant and intended by the King's majesty.

341. Pardoning Enclosure Rioters; Ordering Martial Law against Future Rioters

[Richmond, 16 July 1549, 3 Edward VI]

STC 7827 (UM 5,25,441), Antiq 3, 41: printed by R. Grafton (London, 1549); date as above; schedule as below; *rev.STC*, another copy at Chatsworth. LJ 16, 27: date as above; schedule as below. Grey Friars 60: proclaimed in London on 18 July. Wriothesley 2, 15: proclaimed in London on 18 July. See 338. Steele 362. Text (*STC*): Antiq

FORASMUCH as the King's majesty hath of late, for the redress of unlawful enclosures and such like enormities, directed his several commissions with large instructions [1] for the same into every his counties, not only authorizing his commissioners to redress and reform all manner of things so far forth as the laws could any wise be construed or expounded, but also by special his majesty's letters missive hath charged the same commissioners upon great pain in the same letters contained to redress and amend their own proper faults; which commissions be now part in execution and part ready to be executed, and delayed only by the folly of the people seeking their own redress unlawfully; so that no subject can any more require of any prince, than by his majesty, his said uncle, and council, hath been devised, ordered, and commanded.

Yet nevertheless his majesty understandeth that divers of his subjects, neither considering how they be ordained by God to be subjects and obey, neither regarding their sovereign lord's most earnest good will and zeal which he beareth and daily declareth to his commonwealth, neither having in remembrance what destruction it is to themselves to trouble and disquiet the state of the commonwealth, thereby impoverishing themselves, weakening the realm and breeding sedition and continual contention betwixt one subject and another, do attempt and travail, from time to time and from place to place, to make assemblies, riots, conventions, stittes, and uproars; and by them so unlawfully made, presume to do and attempt that which ought only to be done by the authority of the King and his majesty's laws; yea, and in many points, according to the evil disposition of their assemblies, attempt with violence and fury such unlawful things as be extremely forbidden by all justice and law, and to be abhorred of any good Christian.

For the which causes his majesty, neither of good justice and honor, neither for the estate and safeguard of his highness' realm, will or may endure his subjects so to offend without present punishment and correction, but as a prince reigning by Almighty God's providence, most mighty, and in justice

1. See 338.

terrible, by the advice of his said dear uncle and Lord Protector and the rest of his majesty's Privy Council, straightly chargeth and with the threatening of his sword commandeth all manner his subjects, of what degree, condition, kind, or estate soever he or they be, to depart, return, and cease forthwith, upon this proclamation proclaimed, from all manner their unlawful assemblies, riots, and uproars, and quietly and in peace to take and receive his majesty's order and direction, the redress of their wrongs whatsoever they be; and that also no manner of subject, of what degree, condition, kind, or estate soever he or they be, shall from henceforth by drum, taboret, pipe, or any other instrument striking and sounding, bell or bells ringing, open crying, posting, riding, running, or by any news, rumors, and tales inventing, divulging, and spreading, or by any other means, device, or tokens, whatsoever the same shall happen to be, call, gather, assemble, congregate, and muster or attempt and practice to gather, assemble, congregate, and muster any number of people, whatsoever they be, either to pluck down any hedge, pale, fence, wall, or any manner of enclosure; or to hunt, waste, spoil, desolate, or deface any park, chase, warren, house, lodge, ponds, waters, or any other unlawful act, which is forbidden; or to redress any thing which shall and may be by the force of the King's majesty's commission reformed, redressed, and amended: upon pain of death presently to be suffered and executed by the authority and order of law martial, wherein no delay or differing of time shall be permitted or suffered, as in other cases being indeed of less importance it is accustomed.

And therefore his majesty most straightly chargeth and commandeth all manner his sheriffs, justices, ministers, and officers, upon the knowledge of any offender against the tenor of this proclamation, forthwith, with all expedition and with such power as thereto shall be requisite, to apprehend and attach the same offender, and him to commit to a safe jail, and thereupon undelayed to certify the Lord Protector and the rest of the council, or any of them, to the intent most speedy order may be given for the execution of the offender with such haste and expedition as is above mentioned.

342. Ordering Martial Law against Officers Raising Unlawful Assemblies

[Richmond, 22 July 1549, 3 Edward VI]

Grafton 64: date 22 July; schedule as below. Dibdin *3*, 468 n.: separate edition by Grafton. Steele 363: date, Richmond. Text: Grafton

Where amongst other ancient officers and ministers of old time established within this realm for the conservation of peace and good order, the office of a bailiff, constable, or headborough, within the limits of their charge and jurisdictions, was most politicly ordained, as well to be the stay in every city, town, or village, of quiet and peace according to the King's majesty's laws, as also to put in execution whatsoever by the said laws or by the higher ministers of the same should be appointed and limited; contrary to which the purpose of the execution of the said offices, his highness knoweth that in most places, where of late this unnatural stir and commotion hath been amongst his majesty's subjects the commons, either the bailiffs, constables, or headboroughs, whose bounden duty and office it had been to have most earnestly travailed and employed themselves for the pacifying and stay of their neighbors by showing them the dangers and perilous sequel of such heady and disobedient attempts, and apprehension of the sowers and spreaders of lewd tales and rumors, stirring them to riot, have nevertheless been the very ringleaders and procurers, by their example and exhortation, to the rest of their neighbors, to levy themselves, and have themselves levied then in his majesty's name, abusing the authority of the same, contrary to their duty of allegiance, to the great displeasure of God and his majesty, the destruction of themselves and the great damage and peril of the whole realm.

To the end therefore that this so notable an allurement and provocation to disorder may from henceforth by terror of punishment be redressed, the King's majesty, with the advice and assent of his dear and most entirely beloved uncle the Lord Protector, and the rest of his highness' Privy Council, chargeth and enjoineth to every bailiff, constable, and headborough now being, and that hereafter shall be, that they forbear and abstain from the raising or assembling of any of his highness' subjects for any act or purpose other than such as by the laws and statutes of this realm is limited for them to execute and do, as incident to their offices, and other than such as the sheriff of the county where they are bailiff, constable, or headborough, or the justices or justice of peace for the same county, or other his majesty's higher ministers having authority from his majesty, shall in his highness' name direct and address them unto; upon pain that whatsoever bailiff, constable, or headborough shall from henceforth offend against this proclamation, and shall by his example or inducement allure others to be his followers and accessories in any unlawful assembly for any seditious proceedings tending to tumult and rebellion, or shall procure any harness, weapons, or victuals for them, shall be deemed, accepted, and taken as traitor, and suffer loss of life, lands, and goods forever, with like penalties as to cases of treason is reserved.

343. Ordering Justices, Knights, and Gentlemen to Their Homes

[Richmond, July 1549, 3 Edward VI]

Antiq 3, 43: date, MS note, July; schedule as below. Steele 364: date, Richmond. Text (MS): Antiq

THE KING'S MOST EXCELLENT MAJESTY, by the advice of his most dearest uncle Edward, Duke of Somerset, governor of his most royal person and of his realms, dominions, and subjects protector, and the rest of his Privy Council, straightly chargeth and commandeth all and singular justices of peace, knights, and other gentlemen inhabiting and dwelling within any county of or place of this realm of England, that they and every of them with all convenient speed shall repair unto their dwelling houses, to put themselves in order and readiness to serve his highness, as they and every of them tender his majesty's pleasure and will answer to the contrary at their uttermost perils.

344. Prohibiting Plays and Interludes

[Westminster, 6 August 1549, 3 Edward VI]

Rev.STC 7827.3, NRO Brudenell (Deene) B.3, 5: printed by R. Grafton (London, 1549); date as above; schedule as below. LJ 16, 28: date as above; schedule as below. Steele 365. Text (*rev.STC*): NRO

FORASMUCH as a great number of those that be common players of interludes and plays, as well within the city of London as elsewhere within the realm, do for the most part play such interludes as contain matter tending to sedition, and contemning of sundry good orders and laws; whereupon are grown, and are daily like to grow and ensue much disquiet, division, tumults, and uproars in this realm:

The King's majesty, by the advice and consent of his dearest uncle Edward, Duke of Somerset, governor of his person and protector of his realms, dominions, and subjects, and the rest of his highness' Privy Council, straightly chargeth and commandeth all and every his majesty's subjects, of whatsoever state, order, or degree they be, that from the ninth day of this present month of August until the Feast of All Saints next coming, they nor any of them openly or secretly play in the English tongue any kind of interlude, play, dialogue, or other matter set forth in form of play, in any place, public or private, within this realm; upon pain that whosoever shall play in English any such play, interlude, dialogue, or other matter, shall suffer imprisonment and further punishment at the pleasure of his majesty.

For the better execution whereof, his majesty, by the said advice and consent, straightly chargeth and commandeth all and singular mayors, sheriffs, bailiffs, constables, headboroughs, tithing men, justices of peace, and all other his majesty's head officers, in all the parts throughout the realm, to give order and special heed that this proclamation be in all behalves well and truly kept and observed, as they and every of them tender his highness' pleasure and will avoid his indignation.

345. Prohibiting Unlicensed Export of Wool

[Westminster, 9 August 1549, 3 Edward VI]

Rev.STC 7827.7, NRO Brudenell (Deene) B.3, 4: printed by R. Grafton (London, 1549); date, 9 August; schedule as below. LJ 16, 29: date as above; schedule as below. Steele 366: date, Westminster. Text (*rev.STC*): NRO

FORASMUCH as divers men of late use to engross and gather into their hands divers great quantities of wools, to the intent to enhance and raise the prices, and so to convey the same into the parts beyond the seas; whereby not only wools and cloths but likewise divers other kinds of wares be grown to excessive prices, and other inconveniences thereof do follow: the King's majesty, by the advice and consent of his dearest uncle Edward, Duke of Somerset, governor of his person and protector of all his realms, dominions and subjects, and the rest of his Privy Council, straightly chargeth and commandeth all and every as well his majesty's subjects as any other strangers, denizens or not denizens, of what estate, order, or degree soever they be of, from and after the last day of August next coming, until such time as by like proclamation his majesty shall release this restraint, that they [in] no manner ways shall ship, load, or transport, carry, nor cause to be shipped, transported, or carried, any wools, of what kind or sort they be, out of any haven, port, or creek within this realm, into any parts beyond the seas, by virtue of any license heretofore granted, or any otherwise;

Upon pain to forfeit the double value of all and every such wools so loaded and shipped, to the intent to carry to the parts beyond the seas, by the owner or owners of the same wools, and to suffer imprisonment at the King's majesty's pleasure; and that no customer, comptroller, nor any other officer of any haven, port, or creek within this realm, suffer such wools to be loaded in any haven, port, or creek within their rules or offices, to be conveyed or carried to any the parts beyond the seas, upon pain of forfeiture of their office or offices and to suffer imprisonment and fine at the King's majesty's pleasure.

Provided always that notwithstanding anything in this proclamation contained, it shall be lawful for the merchants of the Staple to carry and transport such wools and Staple ware as they might lawfully have done before this proclamation proclaimed.

346. Providing Victual for Soldiers in London

[Westminster, 11 August 1549, 3 Edward VI]

LJ 16, 28*v:* date as above; schedule as below. Steele 367. Text (MS): LJ

WHEREAS divers bands, appertaining to the noblemen and gentlemen appointed to attend upon the King's majesty's most royal person, as well for the good and safety of the same as for other his majesty's service, be presently assembled here about London, which, being of so great number, for the more commodity and ease of lodging, be disposed and divided into sundry towns and villages within the county of Middlesex and other counties adjoining; wherefore that his majesty is duly informed the hosts that board them do utter their victuals and other provisions at prices so far unreasonable:

His highness, by advice of his dearest uncle Edward, Duke of Somerset, governor of his highness' person and protector of his majesty's realms, dominions, and subjects, and the rest of his highness' Privy Council, straightly chargeth and commandeth all and singular his highness' subjects [to] whom in this case it shall appertain, which do or shall lodge any of the said bands, to receive no more of them than 2½*d.* the meal for one man, upon pain of imprisonment and further punishment at his highness' will and pleasure.

For the good execution whereof, his majesty, by advice aforesaid, straightly and especially chargeth and commandeth all mayors, sheriffs, bailiffs, constables, and all other his highness' officers, ministers, and subjects to see this proclamation duly observed and kept as appertaineth.

347. Prohibiting Hunting at Westminster

[Westminster, 11 August 1549, 3 Edward VI]

LJ 16, 29*v:* date as above; schedule as below. Steele 368. Text (MS): LJ

FORASMUCH as sundry persons have lately attempted to hawk and hunt liberally near unto this the King's majesty's palace of Westminster, and so take away the disport of hawking and hunting his highness might have in case of repair abroad, his highness by the advice of his dearest uncle the Duke of Somerset, governor of his majesty's most royal person and protector of all his realms, dominions, and subjects, straightly chargeth and commandeth all manner of person or persons, of what estate soever they be, that they nor any of them, nor any other person or persons without special authority and warrant by his or their assent or commandment, attempt or presume to hunt, hawk, or by any other ways or means take or destroy any kind of deer, partridges, pheasants, or other fowl of warren within the precincts of his highness' honor and palace of Whitehall, or any other parks, chases, or warren grounds thereto adjoining, upon pain of imprisonment and to incur his majesty's displeasure and indignation.

348. Ordering Gentlemen to Military Service

[Westminster, 15 August 1549, 3 Edward VI]

LJ 16, 29*v*: date as above; schedule as below. Antiq 3, 46: date as above; schedule as below. Grey Friars 61: French ambassador declares war against England on 9 August. Strype 2(2), 274. Steele 369. Text (MS): LJ

THE KING'S MAJESTY, by the advice of his most entirely beloved uncle the Lord Protector, and the rest of his highness' council, straightly chargeth and commandeth all gentlemen, of what estate, degree, or condition soever they be, who hath their habitation and dwelling in Essex, to depart from the court and the city of London and other places near unto them into their several habitations in the said county of Essex with all convenient speed, there to remain till they shall know further of the King's majesty's pleasure; likewise all such gentlemen as hath their habitations and dwellings in Suffolk, to depart unto their said habitations in Suffolk and there to remain until such time as they shall have commandment from the King's majesty or from the Earl of Warwick; and further that all gentlemen inhabitants in Norfolk do repair to the said Earl of Warwick so that they be with the said Earl to attend upon him in the King's majesty's army in his conduct and leading, for his highness' better service, upon Saturday next following, or Sunday at the furthest. And this, his said majesty, by the advice aforesaid, most straightly chargeth all persons to whom it may appertain, to follow and execute with all convenient speed and diligence, upon pain of his highness' indignation and displeasure.

Provided always, and his highness nevertheless doth signify, that by this present proclamation it is not his majesty's mind that any such gentleman as be of the ordinaries of his highness' chamber or household should depart or go home, but that they shall give their attendance upon his highness here in the court as heretofore they were commanded, anything in this present proclamation notwithstanding.

349. Providing Victual for Calais

[Westminster, 23 August 1549, 3 Edward VI]

LJ 16, 30: date, Westminster, 27 August; schedule as below. Grafton 68: date, 23 August; schedule as below. Herbert 530: separate edition by Grafton. Steele 370. Text: Grafton

THE KING'S MAJESTY, by the advice and consent of his dearest uncle Edward, Duke of Somerset, governor of his person and protector of all his majesty's realms, dominions, and subjects, and the rest of his Privy Council, is pleased and contented, whatsoever restraint heretofore made notwithstanding, that all and singular his highness' subjects may at all times and by this proclamation have license and liberty to carry and transport out of any part of this his realm all manner of victuals, fuel, and other provision and furniture whatsoever to Calais, Boulogne, or Newhaven, for the relief of the same; those and every of them that shall transport the said victuals, fuel or provision, putting in good sufficient sureties to not transport the same victuals, fuel or provision to any other part than to the said Calais, Boulogne, or Newhaven, whereof to bring certificate within a time convenient to the customer of the port where he or they shall charge the said victual, fuel, or provision.

Whereupon his highness, by the said advice, is further pleased that all such as shall have discharged the said victual, fuel, and provision at Calais, Boulogne, or Newhaven, and bring certificate of the said discharge, subscribed with the hands of the Lord Cobham, deputy of Calais; the Lord Clinton, deputy of Boulogne; or of the Lord John Grey, deputy of Newhaven; or any other for the time so occupying the said places: shall immediately, upon the delivery of the said certificate to the customer of the port where the said victuals, fuel, or other provision were charged, be clearly acquitted of the custom for the same and have their bonds delivered to them accordingly.

350. Ordering Soldiers to Serve Where Sent

[Westminster, 30 September 1549, 3 Edward VI]

LJ 16, 32*v:* date, 30 September; schedule as below. Antiq 3, 47: proclaimed on 30 September. Steele 371: date, Westminster. Text (MS): LJ

THE KING'S MOST EXCELLENT MAJESTY, with the advice and assent of his dearest uncle the Lord Protector, his majesty's Lieutenant General of all his armies, and the rest of his highness' council, straightly chargeth and commandeth that all manner of soldiers, as well Englishmen as strangers, of what nation soever they be, having had and received his highness' wages, or prests, and thereupon assigned to repair to the parts of the north or elsewhere to serve his majesty, that forthwith, upon proclamation hereof, without further tarrying or delay, they and every of them not only avoid and depart forth of the city of London and the suburbs of the same but also that, according to the several wages and payments to them advanced, they with all diligence and competent journeys repair where they and every of them are appointed to serve the King's majesty; as they will answer the King's majesty at their most extreme perils to the contrary.

351. Mustering Forces to Protect Duke of Somerset

[Hampton Court, 1 October 1549, 3 Edward VI]

AC (Dasent 2, 330): date, Ely Place, 6 October; council learns of force raised by Somerset. PRO (SP 10/9/1): date as above; MS note, received (?in chancery) on 6 October; sign manual; schedule as below. Another draft; (SP 10/9/2): date, 5 October; letters patent to all justices of peace, mayors, sheriffs, bailiffs, headboroughs, and all other subjects; schedule as below. Steele 372. Text (MS): SP 10/9/1

THE KING'S MAJESTY straightly chargeth and commandeth all his loving subjects with all haste to repair to his highness at his majesty's manor of Hampton Court, in most defensible array, with harness and weapons, to defend his most royal person, and his most entirely beloved uncle the Lord Protector, against whom certain hath attempted a most dangerous conspiracy; and this to do in all possible haste.

352. Ordering Arrest of Persons Spreading Seditious Rumors

[Westminster, 30 October 1549, 3 Edward VI]

AC (Dasent 2, 385): date, Star Chamber, 6 February 1550; order to place William Whitered in pillory, and cut off one ear, because of seditious words. LJ 16, 39: date as above; schedule as below. Not in Steele. Text (MS): LJ

THE KING'S MOST ROYAL MAJESTY, being credibly informed that upon the apprehension and committing of the Duke of Somerset to ward (whose doings in his government enforced the same, for avoiding of extreme peril to his highness' most noble person and to his whole estate, as all men may see that list to look upon things indifferently) certain lewd and seditious persons (more favoring the said Duke than remembering their duties to his highness and natural country, to continue sedition and division among his majesty's subjects before begun, continued, and maintained by the said Duke) do spread abroad and (as they dare in conventicles and assemblies where they think they may speak their pleasure, without regard of his majesty, his council, or of the nobles of the realm) declare, publish, and put into men's heads that the good laws made for religion should be now altered and abolished, and the old Romish service, mass, and ceremonies eftsoons renewed and revived:

Hath thought good to let all his good subjects know that neither his majesty nor any of his most honorable council mindeth in any wise any such alteration, but will continue and maintain the good laws now made and established for religion, and further do in all things, as time and opportunity may serve, whatsoever may lend to the glory of God and the advancement of his most holy word.

Wherefore his most excellent majesty, for avoiding of the great and dangerous inconveniences that may ensue and grow of such seditious, lewd, and proud tongues, doth by the advice of his most honorable council, straightly charge and command all and singular his justices of peace, mayors, sheriffs, bailiffs, constables, headboroughs, and all other his majesty's officers and ministers, that they and every of them shall forthwith apprehend the bodies of every such person and persons as shall declare, bruit, or publish any such seditious tales and rumors, and them to commit to prison, there to remain without bail or mainprize until such time as upon their advertisement by the council, his majesty, by the advice of his council aforesaid, shall further signify unto them what they shall think convenient to be done for their punishment as their offense and doings shall require.

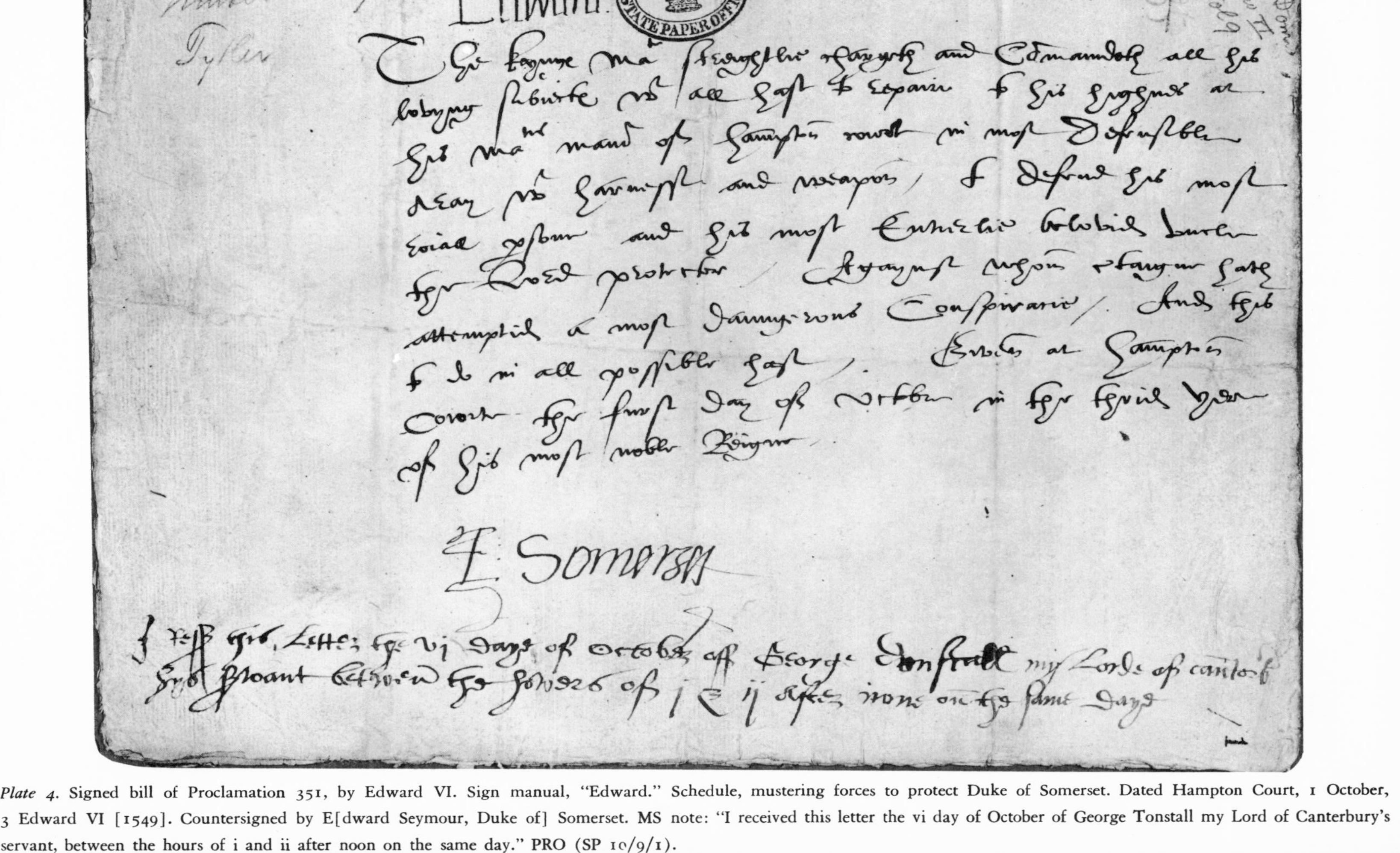

Edward

The kinges Matie streightlie chargeth and Commaundeth all his
lovyng subiectes wt all hast to repaire to his highnes at
his Mates manor of hampton court in most defensible
araye wt harnesse and weapons, to defend his most
roiall person and his most entirelie beloved uncle
the lord protector, agaynst whom certayn hath
attempted a most daungerous Conspiracie. And this
to do in all possible hast. Yeven at hampton
Courte the first day of October in the third yere
of his most noble Reigne.

E Somerset

I rec this letter the vj daye of october of George Tonstall my Lorde of cantorb
hys servant between the howres of i & ij after none on the same daye

Plate 4. Signed bill of Proclamation 351, by Edward VI. Sign manual, "Edward." Schedule, mustering forces to protect Duke of Somerset. Dated Hampton Court, 1 October, 3 Edward VI [1549]. Countersigned by E[dward Seymour, Duke of] Somerset. MS note: "I received this letter the vi day of October of George Tonstall my Lord of Canterbury's servant, between the hours of i and ii after noon on the same day." PRO (SP 10/9/1).

353. Ordering Bishops to Destroy Old Service Books

[Westminster, 25 December 1549, 3 Edward VI]

Cardwell *1*, 85: date as above; schedule as below. Wilkins *4*, 37. Not in Steele. Text: Cardwell

AND WHEREAS the book entitled the *Book of Common Prayers and Administration of the Sacraments and other Rites and Ceremonies of the Church After the Use of the Church of England* [1] was agreed and set forth by act of parliament,[2] and by the same act of parliament commanded to be used of all persons within this our realm; yet nevertheless we are informed that divers unquiet and evil disposed persons, since the apprehension of the Duke of Somerset, have noised and bruited abroad that they should have again their old Latin service, their conjured bread and water, with such like vain and superstitious ceremonies, as though the setting forth of the said book had been the only act of the aforenamed duke:

We therefore, by the advice of the body and state of our Privy Council, (not only considering the said *Book* to be our own act and the act of the whole state of our realm assembled together in parliament, but also the same to be grounded upon Holy Scripture agreeable to the order of the primitive church, and much to the edifying of our subjects, to put away all such vain expectation of having the public service, the administration of the sacraments, and other rites and ceremonies again in the Latin tongue, which were but a preferring of ignorance to knowledge and darkness to light, and a preparation to bring papistry and superstition again) have thought good by the advice aforesaid to require, and nevertheless straightly command and charge you, that you immediately upon the receipt hereof do command the dean and prebendaries of your cathedral church, the parson, vicar, and curate and churchwardens of every parish within your diocese, to bring and deliver to you or your deputy, every of them for their church and parish, at such convenient place as you shall appoint, all antiphonaries, missals, grails, processionals, manuals, legends, pyes, porcastes, tournals, and ordinals, after the use of Sarum, Lincoln, York, Bangor, Hereford,[3] or any other private use, and all other books of service, the keeping whereof should be a let to the using of the said *Book of Common Prayer;* and that you take the same books into your hands, or into the hands of your deputy, and them so deface and abolish, that they never hereafter may serve either to any such use as they were

1. *STC* 16,267.
2. 2 & 3 Edward VI, c. 1, 1548, *SR 4(1)*, 37.
3. See 3 & 4 Edward VI, c. 10, 1549, *SR 4(1)*, 110.

first provided for, or be at any time a let to that godly and uniform order which by a common consent is now set forth.

And if you shall find any person stubborn or disobedient in not bringing in the said book according to the tenor of these letters, that then you commit the same person to ward to such time as you have certified us of his misbehavior; and we will and command you that you also search or cause search to be made from time to time whether any books be withdrawn or hid contrary to the tenor of these our letters, and the same books to receive into your hands and to use as in these our letters we have appointed.

And furthermore, whereas it is come to our knowledge that divers froward and obstinate persons do refuse to pay toward the finding of bread and wine for the Holy Communion according to the order prescribed in the said *Book*, by reason whereof the Holy Communion is many times omitted upon the Sunday: these are to will and command you to convent such obstinate persons before you, and them to admonish and command to keep the order prescribed in the said *Book*, and if any shall refuse so to do, to punish them by suspension, excommunication, or other censure of the Church. Fail you not this to do as you will avoid our displeasure.

354. Announcing Peace Treaty with France

[Westminster, 28 March 1550, 4 Edward VI]

LJ 16, 52: date as above; writ to mayor and sheriffs of London; schedule as below. Grafton 69: date 28 March; schedule as below. Herbert 532: separate edition by Grafton. Stow 1020: proclaimed on 31 March. Wriothesley 2, 34: proclaimed in London on 29 March. Steele 375. Text: Grafton

THE KING our sovereign lord, having always before his eyes the manifold benefits and commodities of peace, and considering how necessary it is at this time, not only for his grace's own realms and dominions, but also for the whole state of Christendom, that Christian princes should agree and join in perfect love, concord, and amity together, whereby they shall first please God and be the more able to maintain their estates, and also procure great wealth and quietness to their subjects; the wars being of late entered between his majesty and the right high and mighty prince, the French King; hath upon deliberate advice and consideration removed all kind of enmity, displeasure, and unkindness that hath been between them, and hath upon most godly and honorable conditions, passed, concluded, and agreed a good, perfect, sincere, firm, assured, and perpetual amity, peace, intelligence, confederation, and union, to remain and continue forever between his most excellent majesty and his heirs and successors on the one part, and the said right high and mighty prince, the French King, on the other part, their realms, countries, cities, towns, lands, dominions, territories and seigniories, places, castles, vassals, and subjects, by sea, land, fresh waters, and elsewhere: by the which peace it is provided and ordained that from henceforth all hostility and war shall cease on either part. And the said princes, their heirs and successors, with all their vassals and subjects, to live together in peace, amity, intelligence, concord, love, unity, and friendship. And that it shall be lawful to all and singular the subjects of either of them, of what estate, degree, or condition soever they be, freely, quietly, peaceably, and at liberty and without any safe-conduct or license, to enter into the other's realms, there to remain, demur, haunt, frequent, be conversant, dwell, sojourn, abide, or through the same to pass at their pleasure. And all feats of merchandise, intercourse, exchange, buying, selling, or other business whatsoever it be, not prohibited nor defended by the laws of the realms, to use, occupy, do, and exercise, and from the same to pass and repass, with their goods, merchandises, ships, carts, carriages, horses, armors, and other things whatsoever they be, not prohibited, without arrest, stop, molestation, contradiction, or impediment; and generally all other things to do, use, and exercise as freely and liberally as they have done in time of peace taken between the realms of England and France heretofore accordingly.

In which peace is also comprehended the most high and mighty prince, Charles, by the grace of God, Emperor, etc., with all his realms, dominions, lands, countries, and subjects; and no manner of thing touching the friendship and perpetual amity with him, or any intercourse of merchandise or other thing is by this present peace in any wise violated, broken, impaired, diminished, or hindered, but all remain in full perfect strength and virtue, as firmly, wholly, and entirely as they were before. And moreover in the said peace is comprehended the right high and excellent Princess the Queen, and realm of Scotland, and subjects of the same.

355. Adjourning Trinity Term

[Westminster, 7 May 1550, 4 Edward VI]

LJ 16 60*v:* date as above; writ to mayor and sheriffs of London; schedule as below. Antiq 3, 50: date, 2 May; MS note, proclaimed in chancery on 22 April; schedule as below. Steele 376. Text (MS): LJ

THE KING our sovereign lord, for divers urgent causes and great considerations his majesty specially moving, and for the high commodity of his most loving subjects, by the advice of his most honorable council, is fully resolved and determined to adjourn part of the next term of Holy Trinity called

Trinity term, that is to say, the *utas* of the Holy Trinity, the 15th of the Holy Trinity, and *tres semaines* of the Holy Trinity, unto the *utas* of St. Michael next coming, being the first day of Michaelmas term. And therefore his majesty doth signify unto all and singular his loving subjects that they and every of them which hath cause or commandment to appear in any of his highness' courts at Westminster at the said *utas,* 15th, and *tres semaines* of the Holy Trinity, or at any of them or at any day mean between any of the said three returns, may tarry at their dwellings or where their business otherwise shall be, without resorting unto any of the said courts for that cause, and that without danger of forfeiture or penalty or contempt to incur towards his highness in that behalf.

And nevertheless his majesty's pleasure is that two of his justices; that is to say, of either of his benches one, shall the first day of this next Trinity term called *Crastino Trinitatis* according to the ancient order of his laws, keep the essoins of the said *Crastino Trinitatis,* and so keep and continue the said courts in his said two benches at Westminster unto the first day of the *utas* of the Holy Trinity next, to the intent that they may make an order for the continuing of process depending in the said courts, and also award writs and records of *nisi prius* and such other process as may be for the furtherance of the causes and suits depending before them. At which *utas* of the Holy Trinity writs of adjournment shall be directed unto the said justices giving them authority to adjourn the said *utas,* 15th, and *tres semaines* of the said Trinity term. And that the same adjournment shall be made in the first day of the said *utas* commonly called the Day of the Essoins. And whereas in the term of the Holy Trinity yearly it hath been used and accustomed that the days and places of the circuits of the King's justices for the jail deliveries, assizes, *nisi prius,* and oyer and terminer have been appointed and set up in open place, to the intent that every person having cause of suit before them might have knowledge of the said times and places for the better and readier expedition of their said suits, his majesty's pleasure is that the said order of appointment hath for the times, days, and places of the said jail deliveries, assizes, *nisi prius,* and oyer and terminer, shall now for this time be appointed and set up and notice made thereof this present term of Easter, for the better knowledge thereof to be had for them that shall have to do before them.

And his majesty's further pleasure is that all matters, causes, and suits depending in any of his other courts between party and party as in his highness' Courts of Chancery and Exchequer, Court of Wards and Liveries, the Court of the Augmentations of the Revenues of his Crown, and the Court of the First Fruits and Tenths, shall have continuance and the parties shall have day from the last day of this term unto the first day of Michaelmas term next coming. Provided always that all collectors, receivers, sheriffs, and all other accompters and all other persons that ought or should accompt or pay any money in any of the same Courts of the Exchequer, Court of the Wards and Liveries, the Court of the Augmentation, and First Fruits and Tenths, or in any of them, or to enter into any accompt in any of the same courts, shall be bounden to appear, pay, and do in every behalf as though no such proclamation or adjournment had been had, any thing mentioned in this present proclamation or in any writ of adjournment to the contrary in any wise notwithstanding. And the King's majesty straightly commandeth that no clerk nor officer of any of his said Courts of the King's Bench or Common Pleas shall make any process for the personal appearance of any person or persons in any of the same courts to be had in *Crastino* of the Holy Trinity next coming.

356. Ordering Vagabonds to Leave London

[Greenwich, 7 May 1550, 4 Edward VI]

AC (Dasent *3*, 27): date, 7 May; order for proclamation to remove vagabonds out of London, Southwark, and their liberties; *STC* 7830 (UM 5,25,444), Antiq 3, 51: printed by R. Grafton (London, 1550); date, May (MS note, 7 May); schedule as below. Grafton 70*v*: date, 4 May; schedule as below. Steele 377: date, Greenwich, 4 May. Text (*STC*): Antiq

THE KING our sovereign lord, by the advice and consent of his highness' most honorable Privy Council, straightly chargeth and commandeth that all and every person and persons of what estate, condition, or degree soever he or they be, being his grace's natural subjects born, which were not born within his majesty's city and chamber of London, the borough of Southwark, or the suburbs within the liberties of the same, nor be householders there, or have sufficient to live by, and good and reasonable cause there to remain, nor have continued and dwelled within the same by the space of three years together now last past, and now do continue, sojourn, and abide there within the said city, borough, or suburbs, not being retained in service with any person or applying themselves to any bodily labor or lawful occupation and taking stipend and wages for the same, do not only forthwith upon this proclamation, depart and avoid out of the said city, borough, and liberties thereof, but also with all convenient speed do return and get themselves home again either into their native countries where they were born, or else into the places within the realm where they last dwelt by the space of three years together according to the tenor, form, and effect of the statute [1] in that behalf, concerning the ordering of aged and impotent persons and the punishment of vagabonds, idle and loitering persons, and masterless men, lately made and provided, upon the pains in the same statute limited and expressed.

1. 1 Edward VI, c. 3, 1547, *SR 4(1)*, 5.

And that the said mayor, aldermen, and sheriffs and every of them and all and every other his majesty's officers and ministers within the said city, borough of Southwark, and liberties thereof (all excuses ceasing and set apart) endeavor themselves with all convenient diligence from henceforth from time to time to see, procure, and cause the said statute and every branch and article therein contained justly to be observed and put in due execution accordingly, as they and every of them tender his majesty's favor and will avoid his highness' indignation and displeasure.

357. Prohibiting Export of Victual

[Westminster, 7 May 1550, 4 Edward VI]

AC (Dasent *3*, 27): date, Star Chamber, 7 May; order for proclamation against transport of victual to any foreign dominion. Ibid., *3*, 135: date, Oatlands, 30 September; order for letters to certain justices of peace in every county to be diligent in setting forth the proclamation for victual. Ibid., *3*, 334: date, Hampton Court, 13 August 1551; order for letters of thanks to Sir Thomas Dennis and other Devonshire justices for their diligence in setting forth the proclamation. LJ 16, 61: date as above; writ to mayor and sheriffs of London; schedule as below. Grafton 72: date, 7 May; schedule as below. Herbert 532: separate edition by Grafton. Steele 378: date, Greenwich. Text: Grafton

The King our sovereign lord, having special regard and vigilant eye unto the wealth, commodity, and profit of this his realm of England, and of his most loving subjects of the same, considering the high prices of sundry kinds of victuals and other provisions which should seem to rise by reason of the scarcity thereof, to the great burden and charges of his said most loving subjects, is now earnestly minded to make special restraint for conveyance of such victuals and other provisions, in the parts of beyond the sea.

Wherefore his royal majesty, by the advice of his most honorable council, doth most straightly charge and command all and singular his said subjects and others, whatsoever they be, that neither they nor any of them, nor any other in their name or names, under the pain of imprisonment, and upon the pains of such forfeitures contained in the laws and statutes of this realm, shall from henceforth, until his majesty's pleasure be further known, carry or convey into the parts beyond the sea, any kind of beeves, muttons, veals, lamb, pork, butter, cheese, corn, grain, wood or woodcoal, ale, beer, tallow, hides, or generally any other kinds of victual, except only to the town of Calais and castles of Guines and Hamme, and that having sufficient license for the same. And also his majesty, by the advice of his said most honorable council, doth likewise most straightly charge and command all and singular his customers, comptrollers, searchers, and other officers and ministers within all and singular his highness' ports, havens, and creeks within this his realm of England and Wales and the marches of the same, that they shall make diligent search continually, for the further and better furtherance of this the King's majesty's high and dreadful commandment. And that they in no case do suffer any such victual or provision aforesaid to be shipped or conveyed out of any of the said ports, havens, or creeks or other places, except only unto the said town of Calais and castles aforesaid, having authority by special license to receive the same. And in that case the King's majesty's pleasure and commandment is that the said customers, comptrollers, searchers, or other officers, do take bond of the conveyers and enter into their books the time of the conveying, and the specialties of the things conveyed, and that the captains or other head officers of the said town and castles, upon the arrival of the conveyance of any such victuals or other provisions aforesaid unto those parts, shall make certificate thereof in writing under their hands and seals unto the King's Court of the Exchequer, within three weeks after the arrest thereof, and in case any thing by any person be hereafter attempted or done contrary to this present proclamation, the King's majesty, by the advice of his said most honorable council, doth signify and promise to any such person as shall show and reveal the offense so committed, shall have such portion thereof as is given by the statutes, and as the law shall permit.

This proclamation to continue to the Feast of All Saints next ensuing.

358. Offering Reward for Information of Sedition and Rebellion

[Greenwich, 17 May 1550, 4 Edward VI]

AC (Dasent *3*, 38): date Westminster, 28 May; order for proclamation granting £20 to informers on conspiracies. Grafton 73*v*: date, 17 May; schedule as below. Herbert 532: separate edition by Grafton; date, 17 May. Steele 379; date, Greenwich. Text: Grafton

THE KING our sovereign lord, upon the great and urgent causes concerning the quietness and tranquillity of this his realm and subjects, considering therewith how many and sundry ways divers evil-disposed persons have lately attempted and gone about in conventicles and secret places of this his majesty's realm, where they durst speak their pleasure without regard of his highness or his honorable council, determined and conspired divers and sundry evil facts and enterprises and disorders, tending to rebellion, murder, and unlawful assemblies, wherein Almighty God hath hitherto provided that their said determinations have come to his majesty's knowledge, to the subduing and present destruction of such persons, and as many as willingly take part with them in that behalf: his majesty foreseeing such dangers, and desiring the knowledge of such persons as shall hereafter go about or attempt the like matters, hath thought it meet to signify unto all and singular his loving subjects that if they or any of them shall know any manner of conspiracy or other privy intent of insurrection or rising to be made, moved, or attempted, by any person or persons within any shire, place, or places of this his said realm (and before open knowledge thereof had) do with all expedition make the same to be known, either to his highness or unto his Privy Council or unto his majesty's lieutenant of the county and shire where any such thing shall be intended, moved, or determined, and the same accusation, by any mean lawfully or duly proved, shall not only have of the King's majesty, for his pains and labor, for every such matter or privy intent so disclosed and proved (as is aforesaid), although he or they be one of the conspiracy, the sum of £20, but also his majesty's benign favor and pardon, with thanks for the same accordingly.

359. Regulating Wool Winding

[Westminster, 23 May 1550, 4 Edward VI]

PRO (SP 13/Eliz./Case H): Great Seal; writ to sheriff of Hants; schedule as below. *STC* 7831 (UM 5,25,445), Antiq 3, 52: printed by R. Grafton (London, 1550); date, May (MS note, 23 May); schedule as below. *L&P Addenda,* 404: date, Westminster, 21 May. Edward VI 267: 'proclamation made' on 11 May. Grafton 74*v:* date, 23 May; schedule as below. See 252. Steele 380: date, 21 May. Text (*STC*): Antiq

WHERE in the parliament holden in the 27th year of our most noble progenitor King Edward III, it was enacted[1] and ordained, among other things, that all wool packers and winders of wools should be sworn and take a corporal oath before the mayor and constables of the Staple of Westminster, for the time being, truly and justly to wind and pack all the wools within this realm, by force of which statute and by the good ordinances made in the said Staple, the fellowship of wool winders, otherwise called woolmen, have ever since justly and truly wound and packed all such wools as they have meddled with throughout this realm, unto now of late divers and many persons contrary to the said statute taking upon them to be wool winders in many places of this realm, neither being sworn nor expert in winding and folding of wools, of which some of them be tailors, weavers, cordwainers, barbers, husbandmen, and other artificers, have gone about and daily do go about throughout this realm, in many places, and practice themselves in winding and folding of the said wools by the procurement and means of the owners and breeders of the said wools, and do wind up and deceitfully put

1. 27 Edward III, st. 2, c. 23, 1353, *SR 1,* 341.

into the said fleeces of wool, sand, stones, dust, pitch, tar, clay, iron, lead, double marks, shearlocks, dung, lamb's-wool, and other deceivable things, not only to the great slander of this realm, but also to the slander of the merchants of the said Staple, and likewise also to the great hindrance and deceit of the said merchants, as also to the great loss and prejudice of the King's subjects using the feat or craft of clothmaking within this realm.

For reformation and redress whereof, the King's most royal majesty, by the advice of his most honorable council, straightly chargeth and commandeth that no manner of person or persons, whatsoever he or they be, at any time hereafter go about, or take upon him or them to wind or fold any manner of wools in any country where any endwools are accustomed to be wrought, had, or used for the merchant of the Staple or the clothier, before he or they shall be admitted and allowed by the masters and wardens of the company and fellowship of the woolmen of the city of London, or one of them for the time being, to the intent that he or they shall be expert and have knowledge in the said craft or mystery, for the true winding and folding of wools. And that every person or persons so allowed and admitted for an able and lawful workman or workmen by the said master and wardens or one of them for the time being, of the said company or fellowship of woolmen, that have a testimonial or certificate of his allowance and admittance under the seal of the mayor of the Staple of Westminster for the time being, and that none of the said persons so allowed and admitted, or that shall be so allowed and admitted, shall go about or take upon him or them to wind or fold any wools before he or they have taken a corporal oath before the said mayor for the time being, that he or they shall truly and justly, without deceit, wind or fold all and singular such wool or wools as he or they shall take upon him or them to wind or fold, without leaving or putting within any fleece or fleeces any manner clockettes, locks, hindershanks, tails, washlocks, stones, sand, dust, cummer or double marks, or any wool or wools of worse nature or growing than the same fleece is, or any other filth to be left upon the breech of any fleece or fleeces whereby any such fleece or fleeces may be impaired or made weightier, or minish or take away any part or portion of the goodness of any of the same fleeces to the intent to deceive the buyers, nor shall use any other deceit, craft, fraud, or guile therein, upon pain of imprisonment by the space of 10 days, and to be set upon the pillory in the next market town with a fleece of wool hanging about his neck.

And his majesty by the assent aforesaid, further straightly chargeth and commandeth that no grower, breeder, brogger, or gatherer of any wools within any of his grace's counties shall at any time hereafter set awork any wool folder or wool winder to fold or wind his or their wool or wools unless the said wool folder or wool winder bring with him or them a testimonial or certificate under the seal of the said mayor of the Staple of Westminster for the time being, testifying him or them to be sworn and admitted for an able workman to fold and wind wools, upon like pain and pains as are and be above expressed.

And forasmuch as it is perceived and certainly known, that divers covetous persons now of late of their greedy and insatiable minds, not being contented nor satisfied with such increase of wools of their sheep as God hath given them, but contrary to all godliness and honesty have abused the said gift of God, in letting their said sheep remain unshorn and unclipped by the space of three weeks or a month after their said washing and drying again of the same, before they will sheer or clip them, to the intent their said wools might be the weightier, partly by means of their sweating and partly also through other filth which doth increase by reason of their long deferring the shearing and clipping of the same, as well to the impairing of the same wools as also to the shameful deceit of the said merchants of the said Staple and the clothiers of this realm buying or working of the same. Whereupon, for the avoiding and eschewing as well of that craft and deceit as all other above named in time to come, the King's most royal majesty with the assent aforesaid, straightly chargeth and commandeth that from henceforth no grower or breeder of wools whatsoever he or they be shall permit or suffer his or their sheep being washed and dried again ready to be shorn to go above five or six days unshorn, or unclipped, upon pain of forfeiture for every 100 of the same sheep so remaining unclipped as is above specified, 40*s.*, or under or above 100 after the same rate, to be paid to our sovereign lord the King in his Exchequer at Westminster.

And further his majesty by the assent aforesaid straightly chargeth and commandeth all and every justice of peace, mayors, sheriffs, bailiffs, and all other officers and ministers, that they and every of them cause every such offender or offenders to be punished for such offense or offenses according as is afore expressed and declared, and that whatsoever justice of peace, mayor, sheriff, bailiff, or other officer, do refuse to punish any person or persons so to him or them presented according to this present ordinance, and his or their faults duly known and proved, shall forfeit to the King's majesty our sovereign lord £20. to be paid in his highness' Exchequer, and further to incur his grace's high displeasure.

360. Ordering Army Officers to Commands

[Greenwich, 11 June 1550, 4 Edward VI]

LJ 16, 64*v:* date as above; schedule as below. Edward VI 267: date, 9 May; proclamation made that soldiers should return to their mansions, and the mayor of London charged to look through all wards, to take them and send them to their counties. Steele 382. Text (MS): LJ

FORASMUCH as of late in divers parts of our dominions, through the departing of captains from their charges, the soldiers and laborers under their rule do not only neglect their duties but also break that good order that were convenient they should keep, our pleasure and commandment, by the advice of our Privy Council, is that all such captains as are retained in our wages for serving in any part of our dominions, being absent from their charges, shall immediately repair unto the same, upon pain not only to forfeit their said rooms, but also further to receive such punishment as by our Privy Council shall be in that case thought requisite, except they be such captains as by a special appointment of our said council are commanded to attend here on them.

361. Prohibiting Export of Victual

[Westminster, 3 July 1550, 4 Edward VI]

LJ 16, 66: date, 10 July; schedule as below. Grafton 79: date, 3 July; schedule as below. Herbert 532: separate edition by Grafton; date, 3 July. Steele 384: date, Westminster. Text: Grafton

THE KING'S MOST EXCELLENT MAJESTY, calling to his princely remembrance how, according to the regal power and state to him committed by Almighty God, over this realm of England, and other his highness' dominions, nothing can better declare the zeal and affection by his highness borne towards the commonweal, than when by all good means such orders proceed from his majesty as may best tend to the general plenty of things here needful for the commodious living of his highness' natural subjects; and namely such things as be brought forth and here given us by God, as the peculiar commodities of this realm may be perceived and enjoyed by the subjects of the same, to their utility and mutual benefit, among themselves in most plentiful sort and cheapness of price, before others, according as of ancient time hath been accustomed;

Forasmuch as of late years the said commodities have not only been reduced to a great scarcity, but thereby also, to an unwonted excessive price, the cause whereof to no one thing may sooner be credited, than that now commonly those commodities which ought specially to serve the turn and be employed to the use and sustentation of the subjects here inhabiting, are in overlarge manner conveyed into foreign regions, as well by color of licenses, unlawfully used, as also by stealth and covin, much to the defraudation and impoverishment of the commonweal, and to his highness' no less discontentment and displeasure:

Be it therefore published and known to all manner persons, that his majesty, by the advice of his highness' Privy Council, straightly chargeth and commandeth that no manner kind or sort of victuals, corn, beer, wools, fells, leather, hides, tallow, bell metal, wood, or coal, which have been usually bought or sold as merchandise, and are presently restrained from carrying forth of this realm by the laws and statutes of the same, shall from the day of the date hereof forwards be shipped, conveyed, or transported into any foreign parts out of this realm (the town of Calais only excepted) by any person or persons, English or strangers, by virtue or pretense of any license or licenses (heretofore made or granted) until hereafter upon further respects it shall please his majesty to enlarge the same, nor that by force of any other grant, allegation, color, pretense, or means any person or persons attempt or procure from henceforth to ship or transport into foreign parts any kind or sort of the aforesaid victuals, corn, beer, wools, fells, wood, coal, leather, hides, bell metal, or tallow, upon pain that whosoever shall do to the contrary hereof, shall not only therefore, besides the penalties expressed in the statutes restraining the transportation of the same, incur the loss and forfeiture of the said things, or any of them so shipped, contrary to this restraint, the one half to be immediately confiscated to his highness' coffers, and the other half to the presenter of the same into his grace's Court of the Exchequer, and likewise the ship or other vessel wherein any of the said things prohibited shall hereafter be shipped, to be forfeited to his highness, but also that the said principal offender, or offenders, and as many as shall be aiding and consenting to the shipping and conveyance of any of the aforesaid things prohibited, shall suffer imprisonment and fine at the King's majesty's pleasure. And that it shall be lawful to every of his highness' subjects, or others, to present and pursue the action against any such principal offender or offenders at any time within the space of three years next after the time of any such shipping or conveyance, as is before expressed, and to have pardon of his imprisonment, fine, or other penalty, in case he were before aiding or consenting to the said principal offenders' act.

Provided always that this present proclamation, nor any thing therein contained, shall not be prejudicial to the mayor and fellowship of the merchants Stapler at Calais, but that they may still continue their said trade according to their charters of privileges in as ample manner as before.

362. Barring Scottish Ships from English Ports

[Westminster, 15 July 1550, 4 Edward VI]

Grafton 81: date, 15 July; schedule as below. Herbert 532: separate edition by Grafton; date, 15 July. Steele 385: date, Westminster. Text: Grafton

THE KING'S MAJESTY, being sundry ways advertised, as well by the complaint of sundry his majesty's subjects trafficking the seas, as also by the like complaint of divers merchants stranger, subjects to his good brother and perpetual ally the Emperor, and others, of the great spoils, robberies, and injuries done unto them by certain Scottish ships haunting the seas upon the coasts of Cornwall, Ireland, Wales, Suffolk, and other parts of this realm, whereby not only the liberty of their traffic is much impeached, in such sort as they have presumed to commit some of the said spoils and robberies in the very entry and mouth of some of his majesty's havens and ports, and within his highness' streams and rivers.

Considering that the said Scots have no free traffic in this his majesty's realm, nor in any other his majesty's countries or dominions, his majesty, by the advice of his Privy Council, straightly chargeth and commandeth all mayors, sheriffs, bailiffs, constables, searchers, comptrollers, and all other his majesty's officers, ministers, and subjects, that they, nor any of them, from the publication of these presents, do not receive into any of his majesty's ports, havens, or creeks any of the said Scots, nor any other Scots (unless they have his majesty's safe-conduct) their vessels, ships, goods, factors, or servants, nor aid or succor with victuals, or any other necessaries, any of the said Scots so impeaching the traffic as is aforesaid; nor that they the said Scots, their factors, servants, or any other for them, or any of them, be permitted to sell, or do sell, any goods, merchandises, or wares whatsoever, so taken upon the seas of any of his majesty's subjects, or the subjects of any other prince being in amity or league with his said majesty, upon pain that whosoever shall or may be found to have transgressed any part of this his majesty's pleasure, shall suffer imprisonment without bail or mainprize, and also fine and ransom at his majesty's will and pleasure, over and besides the forfeiture of all such goods as shall be bought or received contrary to this proclamation.

Provided always that this proclamation shall not be prejudicial to any merchant or vessel of Scotland having the King's majesty's letters of safe-conduct, but that according to the tenor and effect of the same they may use their traffic of merchandise in this realm for the time limited in the said safe-conduct.

363. Ordering Disbanded Soldiers to Leave London

[Westminster, 20 July 1550, 4 Edward VI]

LJ 16, 66*v:* date as above; schedule as below. Grafton 78: date, 20 July; schedule as below. Herbert 532: separate edition by Grafton; date, 20 July. Steele 383: date, Greenwich, 20 June. Text: Grafton

THE KING'S MOST ROYAL MAJESTY, by the advice of his Privy Council, straightly chargeth and commandeth all manner captains, officers of bands, and soldiers, as well English as strangers of what nation soever they be, which are not presently entertained in his highness' wages and have been paid for their service by the treasurers thereunto appointed, according to their capitulations, until the day of their cassing and dismission, that they and every of them fail not to depart and avoid from this city of London, the suburbs and the members of the same, within three days after this present proclamation published, upon pain that if any of the aforesaid captains, officers of bands, or soldiers be found after that day to remain or lodge within the said city, suburbs, or members of the same, contrary to the tenor and effect hereof, he or they so offending shall suffer straight imprisonment, with further punishment at his majesty's pleasure.

Provided always that this proclamation, nor any thing therein contained, shall not extend to any ordinary pensioner, stranger, or to any other servant of the King's majesty, or servant to any other nobleman or gentleman, but that they may continue and remain here at their liberty as before, without danger or restraint hereof accordingly.

364. Raising Value of French Crowns to 7s.

[Windsor, 4 August 1550, 4 Edward VI]

AC (Dasent *3*, 94): date Windsor, 27 July; order for proclamation to be made that French crowns should be current at 7*s*. Ibid., *3*, 101: date, 10 August; minute that certain proclamations were sent forth, enhancing French crowns to 7*s*. Grafton 82*v:* date, 4 August; schedule as below. Herbert 532: separate edition by Grafton; date, 4 August. See 367. Steele 386. Text: Grafton

THE KING'S MAJESTY, by the advice and consent of his grace's Privy Council, is pleased and doth ordain, that from the day of the date and publication hereof forwards, all manner French crowns of the sun, being of the just standard, fineness, and weight, shall be deemed and accepted to be of the value of 7*s.* of current money of this realm, and that every such French crown of the sun, being of the just weight and fineness according to the standard of the same, shall commonly be paid and received throughout this his majesty's realm and other his grace's dominions in all payments and receipts for and after the rate and value of 7*s.* of the current money of this realm: straightly charging and commanding all and singular his majesty's subjects and others dwelling, conversing, or trafficking within the said his grace's realm and dominions, that they and every of them observe, fulfill, and execute the effect and tenor of this present proclamation, upon pain that whoso disobeyeth or refuseth so to do, being by due process thereof detected, shall suffer imprisonment and further punishment at his majesty's pleasure.

365. Prohibiting Export of Victual except to Calais

[Oatlands, 24 September 1550, 4 Edward VI]

AC (Dasent *3*, 125): date, Oatlands, 18 September; consideration of a French proclamation restraining victual from Calais. Ibid., *3*, 264: date, Greenwich, 20 April 1551; order dispensing Isle of Guernsey from proclamation. *STC* 7832 (UM 5,25,446), Antiq 3, 54: printed by R. Grafton (London, 1550); date, 24 September; schedule as below; *rev.STC,* another copy in Queen's, Oxford. Edward VI 293: proclamation set forth on 22 September. Steele 389: date, Oatlands. Text (*STC*): Antiq

WHEREAS heretofore by many good laws, statutes, and other good orders, it hath been upon divers pains straightly forbidden that no corn, cattle, or other things appertaining to the food and sustenation of the people of this realm, should in time of need be conveyed out of the same into foreign parts, or by covin and deceit so enhanced to unreasonable prices that thereby the native people of this realm, both lacking those sustenations which the natural soil of the realm yieldeth principally to them, and also burdened with the excessive prices of those things which remain, should thereupon sustain misery and danger of famine: yet nevertheless the insatiable and greedy desire of divers evil-natured people, neither minding due observation of good laws, neither any preservation of natural society within their own country, hath of late time, contrary to the provision of the said laws, both by frequent unlawful exportations of the said victuals out of the realm into foreign parts, and also by many detestable frauds and covins given and daily increased occasion of great scarcity and unreasonable prices of the said victuals and sustenations, which no longer may be endured.

Wherefore the King's majesty, by the advice of his highness' council, considering the great profit which may ensue of the execution of the said laws and proclamations and the necessity of the same at this present time, doth by proclamation as hereafter followeth provide and ordain, whereunto his majesty most straightly chargeth and commandeth all due and convenient regard to be given by all and every his majesty's subjects, as they will avoid both the pain therein expressed and also his majesty's high indignation.

First the King's majesty's pleasure is, by the advice of his council, that no person or persons of what estate, degree, or condition soever they be, shall after eight days immediately ensuing the publication of this proclamation, in the county where they or any of them dwelleth, transport, ship, or carry over the seas out of this his highness' realm of England, or any other his grace's dominions pertaining to the same, or into the realm of Scotland or elsewhere into any other foreign realms or countries, and there do make willingly port sale thereof, any wheat, malt, rye, barley, peas, beans, oats, or any other kind of grain, or the meals of any of the same; beeves, muttons, veals, cheese, butter, tallow, candle, beer, ale, bread, biscuit, leather, salt-hides, wood, wool, fells, or any other kind of victual, upon pain to forfeit as well all the goods and chattels that he or they have to their own use, their aiders, or consenters, at the time that they shall be found to offend this proclamation, as also the ship and ships wherein it shall fortune the premises or any of them to be transported, and also the thing or things itself so transported; any license, grant, or dispensation to the contrary heretofore granted in any wise notwithstanding, the one moiety of the said forfeiture to be to the use of him or them that shall find and present and approve the same, and the other moiety to the use of the King's majesty our sovereign lord, or to the lord or lords of the franchises who hath authority to have the same by his highness' grant or other lawful means. For the recovery whereof, the first presenter and party grieved shall have their remedy by bill or information, before the King's highness' Privy Council or any two of them, the Star Chamber, his grace's Courts of the Exchequer, King's Bench or Common Pleas, or before four justices of peace of the shire where the offense shall happen, and the premises or any part thereof so to be carried over or transported, so that one of the said justices of the shire be justice also of the quorum.

Provided always that the merchants of the Staple may lawfully carry over and transport their wools and fells to Calais, in such sort as they have been heretofore accustomed, this proclamation in any wise notwithstanding.

Provided also, that if at the time of the shipping or transporting of the premises or any of them, the best wheat be commonly sold in England for 6*s*. 8*d*. the quarter or under, and so after the rate, malt of the best sort for 5*s*. the quarter, beans or peas of the best sort for 4*s*. the quarter, oats of the best sort for 3*s*. 4*d*. the quarter, and rye of the best sort for 5*s*. the quarter or under, that then shall be lawful to all and every the King's majesty's subjects, being English or denizens, to carry over and transport every of the said kinds of grain at their will and pleasure, this proclamation notwithstanding.

Provided also that all and every of the King's highness' said subjects may carry over and transport any of the kinds of commodities aforesaid for the victualing and furnishing of Calais only, and the King's highness' other pieces for war thereunto adjoining, this proclamation notwithstanding, so that by color thereof the said kinds of commodities, nor any of them, be not in any other places bestowed or employed contrary to the intent and true meaning of this proclamation.

Provided also further that it shall be lawful for all manner of persons, as well merchants as other having good and lawful occasion to repair to the seas to furnish their ships and vessels with necessary provision of victual for the same and not otherwise, this proclamation or anything therein contained to the contrary notwithstanding.

Item, that no person of what estate, condition, or degree soever that he be, after the said eight days before expressed, shall buy or cause to be bought in open market or otherwise, to be sold again, any wheat, malt, barley, rye, peas, oats, beans, maslin, meal, or any kind of meals of any of the said grains, upon pain of forfeiture of the same grain or meal so bought to sell again, or the uttermost value of the same, and the moiety of his or their goods, chattels, leases, and farms, for term of life, lives, or years, or at will, which he or they have to their own use, the one moiety of the said forfeiture to be to the use of the party grieved that should first present and approve the same, and the other moiety to the use of the King's majesty or to such other as shall have good right to the same as is aforesaid, and the recovery thereof to be had in form aforesaid.

Provided always that all brewers and bakers may use all and every of the said kinds of grains and the meals of the same, so that they convert the same so by them bought, or to be bought, into bread and drink or one of them, and not to sell the premises or any of them in that kind or sort as they bought or shall buy the same or any part thereof.

Provided also, that all and every innkeeper and innkeepers may sell and utter in their inns or houses to be spent and consumed there, beans, peas, and oats, to such as be or shall be lodged with them or any of them; so that they sell the same at reasonable and convenient prices.

Provided also, that all broggers and common carriers of grain may buy and sell any of the said grains, so the same be sold to any bakers, brewers, innholders, or in open market, foreseeing always that the said broggers and common carriers nor any other to their use have at any one time of their own in their possession or in the possession of any other to their use above the number of 10 quarters of any one of the kinds of grain aforesaid.

Provided also that in case any person or persons meaning or pretending at the time of the buying of any of the said grains to expend the same only in his or their houses and afterward shall happen to be commanded to serve the King's majesty in his wars or otherwise, that then it shall be lawful to him or them that shall be so commanded by any his officer or servant to sell all the said kind of grains and every of them, in such sort and for like prices as the like grains shall then be commonly sold for in the market or under, anything in this proclamation notwithstanding.

Item, the King's majesty's pleasure by the advice aforesaid is that the justices of the peace in every shire, city, borough, or town corporate, shall divide themselves into hundreds, rapes, wards, and wapentakes, according as heretofore in other his highness' affairs they have done, and they or two of them at the least within the limits of their division shall with all diligence repair to all farms, barns, stacks, and garners within the precinct or limits of their said division, and there view, search, and try out as well by the verdict of honest men, as by all other good and lawful means and ways by their good discretions, what quantity and kinds of grain every person and persons have within the precinct of the same their division, and after the certainty thereof (as near as they can) known unto them, they shall allot, appoint, and allow to the owner of the said corn and grain so by them found in barns, stacks, or garners, sufficient and competent grain for the finding and maintenance of his or their houses, payment of their rent-corns, and performance of any bargain or bargains made or to be made for the King's majesty's house or to any nobleman, gentleman, or others for the only maintenance of his or their households and family until the 20th day of September now next coming, and also for necessary seed corn to be employed on his or their farm or farms to be sown before the 20th day of June now next coming.

And for the overplus of the said grain so found in barns, stacks, or garners, the said justices shall by virtue hereof have authority to charge and command in our name and behalf, upon pain by them to be limited, the said owner and owners to bring to the markets next adjoining such portion of the said overplus as the said justices shall think meet and requisite, and in such sort as by their good discretions shall be thought meet and convenient there to be sold.

And his highness' pleasure also is that the justices so viewing and seeing the premises as before shall, after the view taken, by their writing signify unto the chief officer or officers of the market or markets what quantity of grain is appointed to every man within their limits to bring to the said market or markets, and of what sorts and kinds of grains be appointed to be brought of every owner or farmer, willing and commanding the said officers of markets and every of them to note, and have continually good respect that their appointment be at all markets observed, wherein if any shall fail, the said officer or officers shall certify the justices of the names of him or them that shall be found faulty in this behalf.

Provided always that in case any of the said owners do sell such portion or part of the portion of the corn or grain as he or they shall so be appointed to bring to the market to any his neighbors being householders, or common laborers having not competent grain for his or their family, and for only sustenance and maintenance of himself, his house and family, that then the same owner and owners shall be discharged from the bringing of the said portion to the next market so to his neighbor sold in form aforesaid.

And in case any farmer or farmers, owner or owners, shall refuse, or do not bring to the markets his or their corn and grain according to the effect of this proclamation or as he or they shall be appointed by the said justices, that then every such offender shall forfeit for every such default £10 and suffer imprisonment by the space of three months, the one moiety of the said forfeiture to be to the use of the party that shall first present and approve the same, and the other moiety to the use of the King's majesty or to the use of such chief lord or lords of the franchises as by his grace's grant or otherwise shall have good right to the same, and the recovery thereof to be had and taken in form aforesaid.

Provided always, that if the said owner or owners shall not have so much grain as he or they shall be commanded to bring to the market, or if the same portion so appointed shall happen to be taken up afterwards to the King's majesty's use by any of his highness' takers or purveyors of grain, and the same duly proved before the said justices, that then the said owner and owners shall be clearly discharged of the said penalty and imprisonment and every part thereof, this proclamation or anything therein contained to the contrary notwithstanding.

And for the continual true and inviolable observation of this proclamation for bringing of all manner of grains to the markets, the King's majesty's pleasure is that the justices of peace of every shire, city, borough, or town corporate, shall, at their several divisions to be made as is aforesaid, take such order that some one justice of peace, at the least, be always from time to time personally present in every fair and market within their several limits, and there remain during all the time of the same fair or market, searching and examining with the assistance of the officers of the same place, whether every farmer and owner of corn do effectually, without all fraud and covin, bring to the market such proportions and quantities of every sort of grain as hath been appointed unto them, and such as shall be found faulty therein, his majesty's pleasure is that the said justices and every of them shall do the best that in them may be, to have every such offender forthwith punished according to the tenor of this proclamation, wherein his highness requireth and straightly chargeth the said justices to be diligent and upright, as they tender his majesty's pleasure and will answer for the contrary. This proclamation to endure during the King's highness' pleasure.

366. Pricing Victual, Prohibiting Export

[Westminster, 20 October 1550, 4 Edward VI]

AC (*CSPD 1,* 30): date, 17 November; council appoints special commissioners in each county to enforce proclamation for bringing victual to market. Ibid., *1,* 31: proclamation revoked on 6 December. *STC* 7833 (UM 5,25,447). Antiq 3, 55: printed by R. Grafton (London, 1550); date, 20 October; schedule as below. LJ 16, 97: date, 20 October; writ to mayor and sheriffs of London; schedule as below. Edward VI 295: proclamation dated 19 October. Ibid., 296, abolished on 29 November. Steele 390: date, Westminster. Text (*STC*): Antiq

WHEREAS at the parliament holden upon prorogation at Westminster the 15th day of January in the 25th year of the reign of our most dear father of famous memory, King Henry VIII, it was ordained and enacted [1] by authority of the same parliament, that the Lord Chancellor of England, the Lord Treasurer, the Lord President of the King's most honorable council, the Lord Privy Seal, the Lord Steward, the Lord Chamberlain, and all other lords of the King's council, the Treasurer and Comptroller of the King's most honorable house, the Chancellor of the Duchy of Lancaster, the King's Justices of either bench, the Chancellor, Chamberlains, Under-Treasurer, and Barons of the King's Exchequer, or seven of them at the least, whereof the Lord Chancellor, the Lord Treasurer, the Lord President of the King's council, or the Lord Privy Seal to be one, should have power and authority from time to time as the cause should require to set and tax reasonable prices of all kinds of cheese, butter, capons, hens, chickens, and other kinds of victuals necessary for men's sustenance mentioned in the said act; how they should be sold in gross or by retail for relief of the King's subjects; and that after such prices set and taxed in form aforesaid, proclamation should be made in the King's name under the Great Seal of the said prices in such parts of this realm as should be convenient for the same. And it was further enacted by the said statute that all farmers, owners, broggers, and all other victualers whatsoever, having or keeping any of the kinds of victuals mentioned in the said act, to the intent to sell, should sell the same to such the King's subjects as will buy them, at such prices as should be set and taxed by the said proclamation, upon the pains to be expressed and limited in the said proclamation, to be lost, forfeited, and levied to the King's use, in such wise as by the said proclamation should be declared. And further by the same act it was provided that the same act or any thing therein contained should not be hurtful to mayors, sheriffs, bailiffs, or other officers of cities, boroughs, or towns corporate, nor to any person or persons or bodies politic having authority to set prices of such victuals, or of any of them, but that they and every of them might set prices thereof as if that act had never

1. 25 Henry VIII, c. 2, 1533, *SR 3,* 438.

been had or made. And it was also enacted by the same act, that no person or persons unless it were by license under the King's Great Seal, from henceforth should carry or convey or cause to be carried or conveyed any corn, beeves, muttons, veals, porks, or any other of the victuals aforesaid to any the parts beyond the sea, except only for the victualing of the town of Calais, Guines, Hamme and the marches of the same, and except for victualing of masters, mariners, and merchants' ships passing the seas, and also except barreled butter and meal to be carried to the parts of Ireland as hath been accustomed, upon pain of forfeiting of the value of the thing conveyed and carried into the parts of beyond the sea contrary to the same act; the one half thereof to the use of our said sovereign lord the King, and the other half to the party that will sue for the same by bill, plaint, writ, or information in any of the King's courts of record. In which suits the defendant shall not wage his law, nor any protection or essoin for him shall be allowed, as by the same act more at large it may and doth appear.

And forasmuch as divers and sundry great complaints of enhancing of the prices of victuals necessary for man's sustenance, and in especial of corn, grain, butter, and cheese, be had and made not only to the King's most excellent majesty, but also to his most honorable councilors, by reason that divers his subjects and others upon their insatiable covetousness, minding and purposing of their perverse minds to make great dearth and scarcity, more than necessity requireth, of corn, grain, beeves, muttons, veals, porks, butter, cheese, and other victuals necessary for man's sustenance, not only by unlawful engrossing, forestalling and regrating of the same, but also by unlawful transporting and conveying the same victuals and other the premises into sundry parts beyond the seas, contrary to the said statute and contrary to the King's majesty's laws and proclamations [2] in that behalf had and made, and to the great hurt and peril of the commonwealth of this his realm: whereupon the King's most excellent majesty, having a vigilant and merciful eye and respect towards his loving subjects, and willing and straightly charging his said subjects and others from henceforth to enterprise no such offenses, contrary to his laws, statutes, or proclamations, upon the pains and forfeitures contained in the same, and upon his high indignation and displeasure, hath according to the tenor of the said act willed and required his honorable councilors named in the said act to set forth reasonable prices of all kind of corn, grain, butter, and cheese, according to the tenor of the said act. In consideration whereof, the Lord Chancellor of England, the Lord Treasurer of England, the Lord President of the King's most honorable council, the Lord Privy Seal, the Lord Chamberlain, and all other limited and appointed by the said act for taxing and setting the prices of all kind of victuals mentioned in the said act, have by authority of the said act set and taxed reasonable prices of all kind of grain mentioned in the said act

2. See 365.

to be sold in form following; that is to say, that from the Feast of All Saints next ensuing, without delay all and singular person and persons, having or keeping any of the kinds of grain, butter, or cheese within this realm to the intent to sell, shall sell the same to such of the King's subjects as will buy them at the prices hereafter mentioned, or under, and not above; that is to say, white wheat of the best sort, clean and sweet and not tailed, for 13*s*. 4*d*. the quarter and not above; and white wheat of the second sort, and red wheat of the best sort, clean, sweet and not tailed, for 11*s*. the quarter and not above; and grey wheat of the best sort, clean, sweet, and not tailed, for 10*s*. the quarter and not above. And all other wheat as well white, red, and grey, of the meanest sort, not clean or tailed, for 8*s*. the quarter and not above. And that malt, clean, sweet, and of the best sort, shall be sold for 10*s*. the quarter and not above; and malt of the second sort for 8*s*. the quarter, and not above. And rye of the best, cleanest, and sweetest sort, for 7*s*. the quarter and not above; and rye of the second sort for 6*s*. the quarter and not above. And barley of the best sort, clean and sweet, for 9*s*. the quarter and not above; and barley of the second sort for 7*s*. the quarter and not above. Beans or peas of the best sort, clean and sweet for 5*s*. the quarter and not above; and beans or peas of the second sort, for 3*s*. 8*d*. the quarter and not above. Oats of the best sort, clean and sweet, for 4*s*. the quarter and not above; accounting eight bushels to the quarter.

Provided always that in what place or county soever within this the King's realm of England or other his grace's dominions, the measure or raisure shall fortune to be more or less than is above expressed, that then the prices shall be likewise taxed, limited, and appointed according to eight gallons to every bushel of land measure and not otherwise.

And that from the said Feast of All Saints, the pound of sweet butter not to be sold above 1½*d*.; and barreled butter of Essex, the pound, not to be sold to any the King's subjects above ½*d*. farthing; and barreled butter of any other parts not to be sold to the King's subjects above ½ farthing. And cheese of Essex to be sold to the King's subjects from Hallowmas next till the new year's crop for ½*d*. farthing and not above; and cheese of other parts not above ½ farthing. And in case any person or persons, by himself or by any other, by his assent or procurement shall sell or attempt to sell any kind of grain, butter, or cheese above the prices aforesaid contrary to the said act and this proclamation, that then the offender or offenders in that behalf shall forfeit and lose to the King 13*s*. 4*d*. for every bushel of any kind of corn or grains before mentioned to be sold contrary to the tenor and effect of this proclamation, and upon pain of forfeiture of 2*s*. for every pound of butter or cheese to be sold contrary to the tenor and effect of this proclamation; the moiety of the which forfeitures, the King's majesty's pleasure is, that the first presenter or approver that will sue for the same shall have the same moiety of his highness' gift. And that for all and every such forfeiture the King our sovereign lord shall and may have his recovery and remedy by information, bill, plaint, or action of debt in any of his highness' courts of record, in which suit no essoin, protection, nor wager of law shall be allowed.

And to the intent this proclamation may be put in good execution, the King's majesty's pleasure, by the advice aforesaid, is, that the justices of the peace in every shire shall with all convenient speed after this proclamation made, divide themselves into hundreds, rapes, and wapentakes according as heretofore in other his highness' affairs they have done, and that three or two of them at the least within the limits of their division, shall with all diligence repair to all farms, barns, stacks, garners, cellars, sollers, lofts, wicks, dairies, granges, and other houses within the precinct or limits of their said division, and there shall, by all the ways and means they can, view, search, and try out by their good discretions what quantity of kinds of corn, grain, butter, and cheese every person and persons have within the precinct of the same their division, and after the certainty thereof (as near as it can) be known unto them, they shall allot, appoint, and allow to the owner of the said corn, grain, butter, and cheese, so by them found in barns, stacks, garners, granges, wicks, dairies, lofts, cellars, sollers, and other houses, sufficient and competent grain, butter, and cheese for the finding and maintenance of his or their houses and family until the 20th day of September now next coming, and also for necessary seed corn to be employed on his or their ground, farm, or farms, to be sown before the 20th day of June now next coming. And for the overplus of the said corn, grain, butter, and cheese found in barns, stacks, and other houses aforesaid, the said justices shall by virtue hereof have authority to charge and command in our name and behalf upon pain of imprisonment the said owner and owners, to bring to the markets next adjoining such portion of the same overplus as they the said justices shall think meet and requisite, and in such sort as by their discretions shall be thought meet and convenient, there to be sold according to the rate of prices before limited by this proclamation. And his highness' pleasure also is, that the justices, so viewing and seeing the premises as before, shall after the view taken by their writing, signify unto the chief officer or officers of the market or markets, fair or fairs, the just proportion of all such kind of grain as they shall so appoint to the same, and also what kind of grain it is, to the intent the same may be sold accordingly.

Provided always that in case any of the said owners do sell such portion or part of the portion of the corn, grain, butter, or cheese as he or they shall be so appointed to bring to the market, to any his neighbors being householders or common laborers, having not competent grain, butter, nor cheese, for his or their families and for the only sustenance and maintenance of himself, his house, and family, that then the same owner and owners shall be discharged from the bringing of the said portion to the next market so to his neighbor sold in form aforesaid.

And in case any farmer or farmers, owner or owners, shall refuse or do not bring to the markets his or their corn, grain, butter, or cheese according to the effect of this proclamation, or as he or they shall be appointed by the said justices; that then every such offender, shall for every such default, suffer imprisonment during the King's pleasure. And if it shall happen any variance or doubt to arise for the goodness or baseness of any of the kinds of grains aforesaid, then the same shall be tried and finally judged by any two justices of the peace within the same shire, or by the mayor, bailiff, or other head officer with the two constables, or one of them of the town, parish, village, fair, or market, where the said grain shall be put to sale or offered to be sold.

And furthermore the King's majesty, of his authority and power royal, straightly chargeth and commandeth all and singular his subjects, of what estate or degree soever he or they be, that they nor any of them from henceforth transport, ship, or carry over the seas, out of this his highness' realm of England or any other his grace's dominions pertaining to the same, or into the realm of Scotland, or elsewhere into any other foreign realms or countries, willing there to make port sale, of any wheat, malt, rye, barley, peas, beans, oats, mustard seed or any other kind of grain, or the meals of any of the same, or any beeves, muttons, veals, cheese, butter, tallow, candle, beer, ale, bread, biscuit, leather, salt-hides, wood, coal, wool, fells, or any other kind of victual, upon pain to forfeit the thing so transported or conveyed, and further to incur the danger, pains, and forfeitures of the King's laws and statutes in that behalf mentioned and provided, any license or dispensation to the contrary in any wise notwithstanding.

Provided also that all and every of the King's highness' said subjects, born within this realm, by virtue and authority of the King's letters patent, may carry over and transport any of the kinds of commodities aforesaid, for the necessary victualing and furnishing of Calais, Guines, Hamme, Rysbank, and the marches of the same, this proclamation notwithstanding, so that by color thereof, the said kinds of commodities nor any of them be not in other places bestowed or employed, contrary to the true intent and meaning of this proclamation.

Provided also that it shall be lawful for all manner of persons, as well merchants as other, having good and lawful occasion to repair to the seas, to furnish their ships and vessels with necessary provision of victual for the same, and not otherwise, this proclamation or any thing therein contained to the contrary notwithstanding.

Provided always that all brewers and bakers may buy all and every the said kinds of grains and the meals of the same, so that they convert the same so by them bought, or to be bought, into bread and drink, to be sold at reasonable prices according to the ancient statutes and laws of this realm, or one of them.

Provided also that all and every innkeepers may sell and utter in their inns or houses, beans, peas, and oats to such as be or shall be their guests and shall be lodged with them or any of them; so that they sell the same at reasonable and convenient prices, according to the laws and statutes of this realm.

Provided also that all baggers and common carriers of grain may buy and sell any of the said grains, so that the same be sold to any bakers, brewers, innholders, or in open market, according to the tenor and effect of this proclamation, foreseeing always that the said baggers and common carriers nor any other to their use have at any one time of their own in their possession or in the possession of any others to their use above the number of 20 quarters of any one of the kinds of grain aforesaid, over and above the grain and corn that he carrieth to the market to be sold from market day to market day, taking for the carriage of the same grain to the market such like gain and advantage as heretofore they have used for the same carriage.

And further the King's majesty most straightly chargeth and commandeth all and every his subjects of what degree soever he or they be, that in no wise any of them, upon his or their duty of allegiance, meddle or enterprise to put any article or clause of this proclamation in execution by color or pretense of the same, but only the justices of peace or such other as have especial authority by this present proclamation.

And we, considering the premises to be for the wealth and commodity of this our realm, will and command all sheriffs of our counties, mayors and bailiffs of every city and borough within this our realm, within six days next after the receipt of this our proclamation, that he or they with all speed shall proclaim the premises in all market towns within their limits, and that all manner our subjects shall obey the same, upon pain to incur our indignation and displeasure. And this proclamation to continue during our pleasure.

367. Lowering Value of French Crowns to 6s. 4d.

[Westminster, 1 December 1550, 4 Edward VI]

AC (Dasent *3*, 161): date, Westminster, 25 November; order for proclamation calling down French crowns. BD 13*v:* bill signed on 27 November. Ibid., 17: signed on parchment, 2 December. LJ 17, 103: date, 1 December; schedule as below. Grafton 99*v:* date, 1 December; schedule as below. Herbert 533: separate edition by Grafton; date, 1 December. Grey Friars 68: proclaimed on 5 December. Steele 391: date, Westminster. Text: Grafton

FORASMUCH as there cometh some hindrance and loss to the common traffic beyond the seas, and consequently hurtful increase of the exchange by the valuation of the French crowns as now they be valued, the King's majesty, being always ready and studying for the benefit in every part of his commonwealth, hath, by the advice of his highness' council, willed and commanded, and by this present proclamation straightly chargeth and commandeth all and every his said subjects and all other manner of persons having any traffic within these his realms, that they nor any of them from the last of December next ensuing shall utter or receive by any manner of means any of the crowns commonly called French crowns, above the value of 6*s*. 4*d*. of the current money of this realm, upon pain of forfeiture of the same, whereof the one half shall be to the King's majesty and the other to the accuser.

Nevertheless, for the avoiding of such present loss as hereby might be sustained by them, which by reason of the former valuation have any number of the said crowns, it is provided and ordained that whatsoever [*sic*] shall on this side or before the said last of December bring any of the said French crowns into any of the King's majesty's mints, he or they shall receive at the said mints for every such crown 7*s*. current money according to the valuation afore limited. And this the King's majesty will have duly observed.

368. Enforcing Statutes for Abstinence on Fridays, Saturdays, and during Lent

[Westminster, 9 March 1551, 5 Edward VI]

BD 55*v:* bill signed on 6 March. *STC* 7834, Antiq 3, 56: printed by R. Grafton (London, 1551); date, 9 March; schedule as below. LJ 16, 108: date, 9 March; schedule incomplete. Steele 392: date, Westminster. Text (*STC*): Antiq

THE KING our most dread sovereign lord, Edward VI, by the grace of God king of England, France and Ireland, defender of the faith, and in earth of the Church of England and also of Ireland the supreme head, calling to his remembrance the great scarcity of victuals and especially of flesh, that is presently grown within this his realm, and therewith remembering how great hurt and damage groweth and is like to grow daily to his most loving subjects by continual eating of flesh in the days and times accustomed to be abstained from flesh, and especially in the time of Lent, which for the most part is the greatest and chiefest time of breeding of all manner of flesh, and that by eating of fish and forbearing of flesh in the said times of usual abstinence from flesh, much flesh is bred and increased, to the continual and more plentiful sustenance of his loving subjects of this his realm; and likewise fishermen by taking of fish and utterance thereof, are the better able to live, and thereby the more exercised and made apt to serve his highness in his navy when need shall require for the defense of this his realm and subjects of the same. And further his highness, most godly remembering a profitable and necessary act of parliament made in the second year of his most gracious reign, whereby it is enacted,[1] that no person or persons of what estate, condition, or degree soever he or they be, should after the first day of May, in the year of our Lord God 1549, willingly and wittingly eat any manner of flesh, after what manner of kind or sort it should be ordered, dressed, or used, upon any Friday or Saturday or the Embering days, or in any day in the time commonly called Lent, nor in any other day that then was or should be at any time after commonly accepted or reputed as a fish day within this realm of England, wherein it hath been commonly used to eat fish and not flesh, upon pain that every person eating any manner of flesh upon any of the said days or times prohibited by the said act, to forfeit for the same first offense, 10*s.* and to suffer imprisonment for 10 days, and during the time of his or their imprisonment to eat no flesh, with other further pains concerning such eating of flesh as by the said act among other articles and provisions more plainly appeareth: which said act since the making thereof, hath been and daily is disobediently and stubbornly infringed, neglected, and broken, by divers and many willful, arrogant, and disobedient persons, in contempt of his highness and his laws.

For redress and due punishment whereof the King's majesty, our said most dread sovereign and liege lord, most straightly chargeth and commandeth that from and after the making of this his highness' present proclamation, and publishing of the same, no manner of person or persons dwelling, inhabiting, resident or abiding within this his realm of England, or any other his dominions or territories, having no license of his highness to eat flesh in the times prohibited by the said act, nor being provided, foreprised, or excepted by the said act, do willingly or wittingly eat any manner of flesh in the times of Lent or in or upon any other day prohibited by the said act, contrary to the effect, purport, and tenor of the said act, upon the pains and penalties contained in the said statute and as they will avoid his highness' indignation and displeasure.

And that no manner of person or persons keeping, or that shall keep any tavern, inn, hostelry, victualing house, common or usual table for any guests, or alehouses within his said realm or dominions, from and after the making of this his highness' proclamation, utter any flesh, in any kind of manner their houses or elsewhere in any the times prohibited by the said act or statute to be eaten by any person not licensed or provided for as is aforesaid, upon pain and penalties as shall be assessed and taxed by the lords of his highness' council, or by two justices of the peace within the county where the offense shall be committed, or by the mayors, aldermen, bailiffs, or other head officers of cities, towns, boroughs, within the said realm.

And that no butcher nor other person after the making of this present proclamation (except he shall be specially licensed by his highness under the Great Seal of England) shall kill or sell any flesh being dead within his said

1. 2 & 3 Edward VI, c. 19, 1548, *SR 4(1)*, 65.

realm or dominions, to be eaten in or upon any the days or times prohibited by the said act, and upon like pain and pains as is before last expressed and limited. And that as well the mayor of London for the time being, as all justices of peace, and all other mayors, sheriffs, bailiffs, constables, and head officers of all and every city, county, borough, town, and village within this his realm of England, and all other his highness' dominions and territories, as they will avoid his highness' displeasure and indignation, and will further answer at their peril, do from time to time, after the making of this his highness' proclamation, within their rules, jurisdictions, authorities, precincts, and circuits, truly and diligently with all speed inquire, search, and try out all and all manner the offenses, contempts, and inobediences aforesaid. And upon knowledge thereof, and due proof thereof made, that they and every of them forthwith commit all and every such offender and offenders to imprisonment, and there safe and surely to be kept and remain in prison according to the discretion of the same committers or any of them. And that all and every his loving and true subjects be from time to time aiding, helping, and assisting to all and every such mayor and mayors, justices, and other officers aforesaid in the doing and executing of the effect and purport of this his highness' proclamation, as they will answer to his majesty upon their uttermost guilt and as they will avoid his highness' grievous indignation and displeasure.

369. Adjourning Trinity Term

[Westminster, 22 April 1551, 5 Edward VI]

Antiq 3, 57: date, of proclamation in chancery, as above; schedule as below. Steele 393. Text (MS): Antiq

The King our sovereign lord, for divers urgent causes and great considerations his majesty specially moving, and for the high commodity of his most loving subjects, by the advice of his most honorable council, is fully resolved and determined to adjourn part of the next term of the Holy Trinity, called Trinity term; that is to say, the *utas* of the Holy Trinity, the 15th of the Holy Trinity and *tres semaines* of the Holy Trinity, unto the *utas* of St. Michael next coming, being the first day of Michaelmas term. And therefore his majesty doth signify unto all and singular his loving subjects that they and every of them which hath cause or commandment to appear in any of his highness' courts at Westminster at the said *utas,* 15th, and *tres semaines* of the Holy Trinity, or at any of them or of any day mean between any of the said three returns, may tarry at their dwellings or where their business otherwise shall lie without resorting into any of the said courts for that cause, and that without danger of forfeiture of penalties or contempt to incur towards his highness in that behalf.

And nevertheless his majesty's pleasure is that two of his justices; that is to say of either of his benches, one shall the first day of this next Trinity term, called *Crastino Trinitatis,* according to the ancient order of his laws keep the essoins of the said *Crastino Trinitatis,* and so keep and continue the said courts in his said two benches of Westminster unto the first day of the *utas* of the Holy Trinity next, to the intent that they may make an order for the continuing of process depending in the said courts and also award writs and records of *nisi prius* and such other process as may be for the furtherance of the causes and suits depending before them. At which *utas* of the Holy Trinity, writs of adjournment shall be directed unto the said justices giving them authority to adjourn the said *utas,* 15th, and *tres semaines* of the said Trinity term, and that the same adjournment shall be made in the first day of the said *utas* commonly called the Day of the Essoins. And whereas in the term of the Holy Trinity yearly it hath been used and accustomed that the days and places of the circuit of the King's justices for the jail delivery, assizes, *nisi prius,* and oyer and terminer have been appointed and set up in open place, to the intent that any person having cause of suit before them might have knowledge of the said times and places for the better and readier expedition of their said suits. His majesty's pleasure is that the said order of appointment both for the times, days, and places of the said jail deliveries, assizes, *nisi prius,* and oyer and terminer shall now for this time be appointed and set up, and notice made thereof this present term of Easter for the better knowledge thereof to be had for them that shall have to do before them.

And his majesty's further pleasure is that all matters, causes, and suits depending in any of his other courts between party and party, as in his highness' Courts of Chancery and Exchequer, Court of Wards and Liveries, the Court of the Augmentation of the Revenues of his Crown, and the Court of the First Fruits and Tenths, shall have continuance and the parties shall have day from the last day of this term unto the first day of Michaelmas term next coming. Provided always that all collectors, receivers, sheriffs, and all other accompters and all other persons that ought or should accompt or pay any money in any of the same Courts of the Exchequer, Court of the Wards and Liveries, the Court of the Augmentation, and First Fruits and Tenths, or in any of them or to enter into any accompt in any of the same courts, shall be bounden to appear, pay and do in every behalf as though no such proclamation or adjournment had been had, anything mentioned in this present proclamation or in any writ of adjournment to the contrary in any wise notwithstanding. And the King's majesty straightly commandeth that no clerk nor officer of any of his said Courts of the King's Bench or Common Pleas shall make any process for the personal appearance of any person or persons in any of the same courts to be had in *Crastino* of the Holy Trinity next coming.

370. Ordering Army Officers to Ireland

[Westminster, 27 April 1551, 5 Edward VI]

AC (Dasent *3,* 256): date, Greenwich, 11 April; order for letter inquiring into delay of captains now staying in Bristol. Ibid., *3,* 265: date, 26 April; warrant for £5,000 for King's affairs in Ireland. BD 84: bill signed on 24 April. Antiq 3, 58: date as above; writ to mayor and sheriffs of London; schedule as below. Steele 394. Text (MS): Antiq

THE KING'S MOST EXCELLENT MAJESTY, by the advice of his Privy Council, straightly chargeth and commandeth all manner of captains and soldiers that of late have received any prest or have been entertained to pass into Ireland since by the long seas or by Bristol, to depart forthwith or before the 28th of this month towards the same, according to the appointment signified unto them. And further also that no manner of person remain here after the said day within the city or anywhere nigh to the same under color or pretext of a soldier, or upon any such allegation that he is entertained or remaineth to be entertained upon pain of straight imprisonment and further punishment at his majesty's pleasure; for the execution whereof his majesty giveth straight charge and commandment to the mayor of London and the officers of the same city, and also to all justices of peace without the liberties in any of the counties adjoining to the same city, as they tender his pleasure and will avoid his indignation, to have diligent heed and regard and not to fail thoroughly to punish all and every the offenders of this proclamation.

371. Enforcing Statutes against Vagabonds, Rumor Mongers, Players, Unlicensed Printers, etc.

[Greenwich, 28 April 1551, 5 Edward VI]

AC (Dasent *3,* 260): date, Greenwich, 15 April; order for letters to justices in all shires commanding execution of statutes against vagabonds, watches, unlawful games, seditions, etc. Ibid., *3,* 262: date, 19 April; certain slanderous books and bills brought before council. *STC* 7835, Antiq 3, 59: printed by R. Grafton (London, 1551); date, 28 April; schedule as below. Steele 395: date, Greenwich. Text (*STC*): Antiq

THE KING'S MOST EXCELLENT MAJESTY, our natural sovereign lord, certainly knowing and understanding by the good advice and information of the lords and others of his Privy Council that by the setting forth of God's holy word and the establishment of a pure and sincere religion, conformable to God's institution and the usage of the holy Catholic church, with the administration of justice and the observation of the laws and statutes of this realm indifferently amongst all his subjects, he should not only discharge his duty to God, but also give an occasion of perfect quietness, humble obedience, charitable concord, great felicity and wealth to all his people, every man in his degree: and upon trust to see the effects and fruits of the same, having caused God's word to be truly and sincerely taught and preached, and a godly order for the administration of the sacraments, and other convenient and decent orders to be set forth in the Church, is most sorry and earnestly from the bottom of his heart doth lament, and so do all his councilors, to hear and see many of his subjects to abuse daily by their vicious livings and corrupt conversations that most precious jewel, the word of God, and by their licentious behavior, lewd and seditious talks, boldly and presumptuously without fear either of God's plague or the sword of their prince, to break continually the laws and statutes of the realm, to dispute of his majesty's affairs, to sow, spread abroad, and tell from man to man, false lies, tales, rumors, and seditious devices against his majesty, his councilors, magistrates, and justices; the seed and root whereof, as they first had beginning and sprang of the corrupt nature and ill disposition of naughty men (which therefore without short amendment must and shall be first scourged with the rod of the prince and afterward by most dreadful condemnation at God's hand). So the great fault for the continuance of the people in evil hath proceeded for want of execution of the good laws and statutes of the realm, and especially the statutes made against vagabonds, unlawful games, tellers of news, inventors of tales and rumors, unlawful assemblies, riots, routs, huntings, fishings, shooting in handguns and crossbows, keeping of alehouses, eating of flesh on fish days, regraters, forestallers, breakers of the order of religion, and sundry other like statutes, should undoubtedly not only have caused each man to have lived in quiet, and to have applied himself according to his vocation and degree; but also been causers of great wealth and felicity in this realm. No prince in the world is more loath to use the extremity of correction upon his subjects than is his majesty, nor no councilors more unwilling to advise his majesty thereunto than his highness' councilors be, but if the subjects do grow into such a contempt of their prince, of his laws and of his ministers, as they care not to use all such ways as may be dangerous to their sovereign lord and his estate, and desperately and obstinately in the end to cast themselves into utter ruin and destruction: in this case his majesty will severely and sharply look upon, correct, and punish the offenders, thereby to preserve his estate and to save the rest of the members of his politic body, which be his faithful, loving, and obedient subjects. And yet before his majesty proceed so far forth he will use a fatherly fashion and gently admonish and give warning ere his majesty fall to chastising.

Wherefore his highness on God's behalf, most heartily doth require, and nevertheless, by his royal power and princely authority, straightly chargeth and commandeth all and every his subjects, of what estate, degree, or condition soever he be, to dread and fear God and his plagues, to convert and amend their manners and to live according to the profession of Christian men, to love his majesty, and to fear his sword, to observe his highness' laws, statutes, and proclamations, to live every man within the compass of his degree, contented with his vocation, every man to apply himself to live obediently, quietly, without murmur, grudging, sowing of sedition, spreading of tales and rumors, and without doing or saying of any manner of thing (as near as God will give them grace) that may touch the dignity of his majesty, his council, his magistrates or ministers, or be hurtful to his neighbor, or in any wise contrary to his majesty's laws, statutes, or proclamations, whereby his majesty shall the rather be moved to study, devise, and put in use, by the good advice of his council, all good ways and means that may reduce again this realm unto that prosperity, estimation, and wealth which by sundry occasions in process of time hath and is decayed, a thing that his majesty and council do most desire, and doubt not with some convenient time to bring to pass if the naughtiness of some evil hearts give not cause of let and impeachment to the same; whereunto, if any shall be so unhappy as to give themselves, his majesty will, with the sharp sword of his princely power, so sharply chastise and correct them, as may be to the fearful example of all other.

And for the better avoiding of all such inconveniences, his majesty straightly chargeth and commandeth all justices, mayors, sheriffs, bailiffs, constables, headboroughs, tithing men, and all other officers and ministers of what estate, degree, or condition soever they be, from henceforth to look to their offices, and earnestly, truly and uprightly to execute and see executed all his majesty's laws, statutes and proclamations which be within the compass of their offices, and specially the statutes above rehearsed, and others of like kind and quality.

And for because that within the city of London there is at this present a great number of idle persons and masterless men, which seek rather by idleness and mischief to live by other men's labors and industries than to travail by any painstaking to live like good and obedient members of the commonwealth, his majesty straightly chargeth and commandeth all manner of vagabonds and masterless men, upon the pains not only all ready appointed by the laws and statutes made for such manner of men, but also upon such pains as his majesty may and will ordain to be inflicted upon them by his prerogative royal, to depart all such out of the city of London and the suburbs of the same, within four days after the making of this proclamation, home to the place either where they were born or where they have dwelt last three years within the realm, going at the least eight miles a day (if they have so far to go from London) and passing not above two or three or four at the most in a company, and not to abide above one night in a place, till they come home (except cause of sickness, the same cause to be allowed by a justice of the peace dwelling next to the place where he or they shall fortune to be sick). And that all vagabonds and masterless men in all other places within this realm, shall also within four days after the making of this proclamation, in the next market town where they shall fortune to be, depart likewise to the place where they were born, or last dwelled three years within the realm, without longer tarrying by the way or going more in company together, or fewer miles, in a day, than aforesaid; and upon like pains as is aforesaid for them which depart from London.

And furthermore his majesty straightly chargeth and commandeth that no man be so hardy either to devise any tale, rumor, or talk, touching his majesty, his council, magistrates, justices, officers, or ministers, nor hearing any such tale, rumor, or talk, to tell, report, or speak the same again to any other person or persons than to either one of his council or to a justice of peace, and there withal to show also of whom he had the same, to the intent that the same person from whom the tale or rumor cometh may be punished for the devising of it, if he devised it, or for the telling of it to any other person than by this proclamation is appointed.

And for because divers printers, booksellers, and players of interludes, without consideration or regard to the quiet of the realm, do print, sell, and play whatsoever any light and fantastical head listeth to invent and devise, whereby many inconveniences hath and daily do arise and follow among the King's majesty's loving and faithful subjects: his highness therefore straightly chargeth and commandeth that from henceforth no printer or other person do print nor sell within this realm or any other his majesty's dominions any matter in the English tongue, nor they nor any other person do sell or otherwise dispose abroad any matter printed in any foreign dominion in the English tongue, unless the same be first allowed by his majesty or his Privy Council in writing signed with his majesty's most gracious hand or the hands of six of his said Privy Council, upon pain of imprisonment without bail or mainprize and further fine at his majesty's pleasure. Nor that any common players or other persons upon like pains do play in the English tongue any manner interlude, play, or matter without they have special license to show for the same in writing under his majesty's sign, or signed by six of his highness' Privy Council; willing and straightly charging and commanding all justices, mayors, sheriffs, bailiffs, constables, and other officers and ministers, diligently to inquire for and search out all manner offenders within the limits and compass of their commissions, and specially all such as shall offend against any the points or branches expressly set forth in this proclamation, and to punish the same without remission: willing likewise, and also straightly charging and commanding all his good, true, loving, and faithful subjects to be aiding, helping, and assisting to all and every officer in the execution of their charges, as they tender the favor of his majesty and the preservation of the commonwealth, as they will answer to his majesty for the contrary at their uttermost peril.

372. Announcing Devaluation of Shillings and Groats on 31 August

[London, 30 April 1551, 5 Edward VI]

AC (Dasent *3*, 268): date as above; order for proclamation abasing shilling to 9*d*. and groats to 3*d*., to take effect on 31 August. BD 118: bill signed on 1 May. *STC* 7836, Antiq 3, 60: printed by R. Grafton (London, 1551); date, 30 April; schedule as below. Edward VI 317: proclaimed on 6 May. Steele 396. Text (*STC*): Antiq

WHEREAS the late King of most famous memory, King Henry VIII, father unto our most redoubted sovereign lord, the King's majesty that now is, considering at the beginning of his last wars that great and notable sums of money were requisite to be provided for the maintenance and supportation of the same, did therefore devise to abase and diminish the goodness of the coin, and thereupon cause to be coined and set forth [1] to be current among his subjects, certain pieces of money called testons valuing the same at 12*d*. sterling the piece, and likewise groats of the same baseness after the rate of 4*d*. sterling the piece; after which time our said sovereign lord that now is, perceiving that as well strangers in foreign parts as divers lewd persons within this realm did, by reason of the baseness of the said coin, counterfeit no small quantity of like money:

His majesty therefore, minding to remedy the same, devised and caused to be coined and set forth, to be current within this realm and other his dominions other pieces of money called shillings and groats, under another stamp, likewise valuing the said shillings at 12*d*. sterling the piece, and the groats at 4*d*. sterling the piece.

Forasmuch as this notwithstanding, it hath appeared since most certainly, unto our said sovereign lord and to his highness' council, that not only divers strangers of beyond the seas, but also sundry false and naughty persons within this realm, have in like manner from time to time counterfeited and falsely coined the said shillings and groats set forth by our said sovereign lord, and with the same counterfeit and false moneys in great and notable sums do traffic and buy all manner of victuals, wares, and other kind of merchandises, giving they care not what prices for the same; whereupon hath risen one great and special occasion of so great dearth of all manner of things as at this day doth appear among all men, to the great loss of his majesty and his sub-

1. See 112.

jects, and to the great slander of the whole realm, and to the impoverishment of every man in his degree that hath the same money, and would keep it in store.

His majesty therefore graciously considering, with the good advice of the lords, and others of the Privy Council, what great benefit, commodity, and reputation shall arise and follow very shortly after, to the whole body of the realm, if that the said coins were amended and brought to such a fineness, as may make the same certain, like as in times past it hath been. Albeit that the said first abasement of the coin was greatly beneficial unto his said majesty's father of famous memory, and also to the King our sovereign lord that now is, yet his majesty considering that this amendment of the coin shall be both great honor to this realm, and also a marvelous benefit unto the whole commonwealth, for the bringing down of the high prices of all things, hath like a most gracious prince determined to reform the same. And forasmuch as this cannot be brought to pass unless the said money called shillings, coined by his majesty, and groats coined both by his majesty and the King his father, might be rated at a value more near unto the goodness and fineness of the same, then now they be rated at, which thing taking place, his highness, with all the speed that may be, determineth to reform this present coin, and to bring it (with God's leave) to such perfect goodness and fineness as shall give all his loving subjects great cause to rejoice.

Therefore his majesty doth ordain and determine that from and after the last day of August now next ensuing, the said shillings coined and set forth by his majesty shall be current within this realm of England and the town of Calais and marches of the same for 9*d*. sterling, and not above; and the said groats at 3*d*. sterling and not above. And therefore straightly chargeth and commandeth all and every person and persons of what estate, degree, or condition soever the same be, to pay and receive after the said last day of August, the said coins of shillings for 9*d*. sterling and the said groats for 3*d*. sterling, and for no higher or lower price, within this his highness' realm, and the town of Calais and marches of the same, upon pain of forfeiture to his majesty of such sums of money as shall be paid or received otherwise than by this proclamation is set forth, and also upon pain of imprisonment with a further fine to be set upon the offenders at his majesty's pleasure.

373. Ordering Reform of Coinage, Engrossing, Enclosures

[Greenwich, 11 May 1551, 5 Edward VI]

AC (Dasent *3*, 272): date, Greenwich, 10 May; order to mayor, aldermen, and wardens of London to reform rise in prices. BD 95: bill signed on 11 May. *STC* 7837, Antiq 3, 61: printed by R. Grafton (London, 1551); date, 11 May; schedule as below; *rev.STC,* another copy in BM. Edward VI 318: proclaimed on 12 May. Steele 397: date, Greenwich. Text (*STC*): Antiq

THE KING'S MOST EXCELLENT MAJESTY, having of late season understanding and knowledge by divers and sundry consultations of the lords and others of his Privy Council, how necessary and beneficial it should be for the wealth of his whole realm to have his coin reduced to fineness which hath been made base from the beginning of the latter wars in the time of his majesty's father of most famous memory, and so remained by continuance of the like, hath had a great, godly, and earnest desire, daily increasing in his majesty's most noble and godly heart, to begin and attempt some towardness to so great a benefit, and so to proceed and achieve, with as much his own majesty's loss therein as possible were fit for him to sustain. Wherefore, of a most godly mind towards his people, and a most fervent desire to begin to do this notable great benefit, for the which all good subjects hath of late, as it were with groanings, longed, his majesty, with the advice of his council, who, with great reasons, were persuaded to advise his majesty thereto, caused his determination to be published by a proclamation [1] bearing date the last day of April last, that from the last day of August next following, the shilling coined and set forth by his majesty should be current for 9*d*. sterling and no more, and the groat for 3*d*. as further appeareth by the same proclamation, without the which means his majesty could never possibly attempt or come near to set forth and make the coin of fine silver according to his good desire, and as indeed ordinarily, his majesty from the beginning of the consultation hath meant and doth certainly mean.

Yet nevertheless such is the malice and naughty nature of a certain kind of people that live only for themselves, and as it seemeth by their doings, neither respect God, King, the surety of his majesty's crown, nor any other Christian creature, but going about to eat and devour, as well the estate of nobility as the lower sort, being serving men, artificers, handicrafters, poor husbandmen, laborers, and such like, and further maliciously overthwarting and hindering all good purposes of the King's majesty and his council, travailing to do to the commonwealth good and especially when they perceive any

1. See 372.

thing purposed to amend the unreasonable prices of victual and such necessary things for men's sustenance, that as it is come to his majesty's knowledge, and his council, by the information of divers credible persons from sundry parts of this his realm, since the aforesaid proclamation was published, which was the very ordinary and necessary beginning of a manifest amendment of the coin, the prices of victuals, wares, and such like things be purposely enhanced beyond all expectation, and the gracious meaning of the King's majesty and his council utterly perverted and sinisterly abused, the same most manifestly coming of the devilish malice and slight of the foresaid kind of naughty people injurious to the whole commonwealth: which things considered, his majesty, having the sword not in vain committed to him of God, and with the same as a minister of the Almighty, the very indignation and plagues from heaven to fall where his sword shall strike, cannot nor may not, without the offense of God, see and suffer such lewd persons as willfully be the causers hereof remain unpunished to their own damnations and the destruction of others.

Wherefore his majesty, meaning not in ire or passion to execute his indignation, but justly and with good ground, hath first by the advice of his council thought meet to admonish all kind of people in their degrees, and to let them clearly understand his pleasure and determination in this behalf, so as whosoever shall offend, the same shall not fail of sharp and due punishment for their offenses.

And therefore first of all, to all such as either willfully or ignorantly hath mistaken his majesty's good meaning upon the former proclamation, for the abasing of money, his majesty declareth his good and gracious meaning and determinate purpose, by the advice of his council, to be thereby to amend his coin and to reduce it to fineness of silver, although the same shall be most of all, without all comparison, to his majesty's loss and detriment, and yet to the benefit of his subjects and the honor of the realm. And next, to such farmers, graziers, and sheep masters which by unreasonable and fraudulent engrossing of farms, grain, victual, as well butter and cheese as other grosser things, as wool and such like, wood, coal, and other things pertaining to the daily sustenance of man, and enhancing the prices of the same, and by manifest decaying of towns and tillage, excessive increasing of sheep contrary to divers good laws and statutes of this realm provided for these cases, not unknown to the offenders therein; which kind of persons indeed his majesty and his council judgeth to be the principal occasions of these almost uncausable dearths: his majesty pronounceth and threateneth, that if they forthwith cease not their greedy, unlawful, and unnatural practices, colored with crafts and subtleties to avoid and deceive the meaning of the laws and all honesty, they shall suffer with his extreme indignation the justice of his laws to the uttermost, to the terror of all such as being thus often gently admonished have never amended.

Thus much doth his majesty in this behalf, partly of clemency of nature, admonish, that would have no cause to exercise extremity: partly (if the naughtiness of his subject shall give him cause) yet by this admonition the punishment shall be more just and necessary. And although his majesty considereth how convenient it is for his office, having indifferent charge and care over all manner his subjects, not only to reprehend the faults of offenders, but also to punish them severely, yet because, of late years, the lower sort of people, lacking indeed that part all manner of reason, and being like to those sick madmen that either will have no physic or else will be their own physicians, have presumptuously taken upon them the office of his majesty, both in reprehending of their superiors and attempting redress of things after their own fantasies, with force, and contrary to the due obedience of good subjects towards God and man.

Therefore also his majesty likewise pronounceth and declareth unto them, and every of them, that if they shall exceed their duties either in reprehending or attempting any manner of remedy or redress otherwise than shall stand with the laws and order of the realm, his majesty will not fail but minister unto them sharp terror of his sword and laws, which, as they be well provided of late for such offenders, so shall they not lack diligent and due execution.

374. Ordering Destruction of Seditious Bills against Privy Council

[Greenwich, 20 May 1551, 5 Edward VI]

BD 96*v:* bill signed on 17 May. *STC* 7838, Antiq 3, 62: printed by R. Grafton (London, 1551); date, 20 May; schedule as below. Steele 398: date, Greenwich. Text (*STC*); Antiq

Forasmuch as divers lewd and seditious persons, minding to sow contention in divers parts of this realm, have of their malicious and cankered affections forged and made many slanderous and wicked bills, as well against the King's majesty's most honorable council, as against other noble personages within this realm, and the same bills have spread and cast abroad in streets and in divers other places, and have fastened the same at such privy corners where they thought they might best publish their conceived malice: the authors whereof (because they have wrought their malice so covertly) cannot easily be found out to be punished according to the laws, statutes, and proclamations made in that behalf. And yet nevertheless their devilish device taketh place and effect for that the said bills have not been broken, defaced, and destroyed immediately, after they have been found, not only to the slander and infamy of many godly and well-disposed persons and defacing of their well-doings in the commonwealth, but also to the maintenance and encouraging of such malefactors to persevere and continue in their lewdness.

Therefore the King's majesty, with the advice of his most honorable council, straightly chargeth and commandeth all and singular his loving subjects to whose hands any such slanderous bills or writings shall come, or that shall find them cast abroad, or see them fastened to post, pillar, or other place, the same shall by the authority of this proclamation forthwith without further delay, break, burn, destroy, or deface without showing them to any other person or persons, that the effect and meaning of the said bill may not appear and be conserved thereby. And whosoever after his or their sight, reading, or knowledge thereof, shall suffer the same bills to stand still or remain not destroyed nor defaced as is beforesaid, or shall publish the same to any other by any manner of means, the same shall be taken and punished as the author, maker, and deviser of the same, and being brought before a justice of the peace lawfully convicted, shall suffer imprisonment and make fine at the King's majesty's pleasure.

375. Prohibiting Unlicensed Exchange and Rechange

[Leigh, 10 June 1551, 5 Edward VI]

BD 109*v:* signed on 9 June. CW (C82/934): date of delivery as above; sign manual; schedule as below. PR (C66/838/27): date, June; schedule as below. *STC* 7839, Antiq MS 116, 114: printed by R. Grafton (London, 1551); date, June; schedule as below. Edward VI 320; date, 7 June. Steele 399: Text (*STC*): Antiq

FORASMUCH as there hath grown, and daily groweth, great displeasure of God and inestimable damage and hurt to the King our sovereign lord and to his people of this his realm of England, by the inordinate exchanges and rechanges of money and carrying out of the realm gold or silver money, bullion, plate, or vessel, that hath been of long time used and yet continueth in this realm, without license and authority given by the King's majesty to such changing, rechanging and carrying out of the realm, to the great impoverishment of this his said realm: for remedy whereof divers and sundry notable and profitable statutes and ordinances have been made, provided, and ordained; amongst the which one very notable and profitable statute[1] was made, ordained, and enacted in the third year of the reign of the right noble and famous prince of worthy memory, King Henry VII, grandfather to our

1. 3 Henry VII, c. 6, 1487, *SR* 2, 515.

said sovereign lord, as well for the confirmation of divers and sundry profitable statutes before that time made and provided for that godly intent and purpose, as also for the due execution of the same. In the which statute of King Henry VII it is further contained that no man should make any exchange without the King's license, nor make any exchange or rechange of money to be paid within this land but only such as the King should depute thereunto to keep, make and answer such exchange and rechange, upon pain of forfeiture of such penalty as is contained in the statute[2] made in the time of King Richard II, which is that the offender shall forfeit as much as he may forfeit, as well for the privy and apert sending or bringing, or causing to be sent or brought out of the realm of any gold or silver in money, bullion, plate, or vessel, as also by exchange to be made; all which things be more at large contained in the said several statutes.

Our said sovereign lord, by the advice of his council, considering and right well perceiving the great enormities and prejudice which groweth unto his majesty and the commonwealth of this his said realm by occasion of the said carrying, changing, and rechanging, willeth, defendeth, and straightly by this his proclamation commandeth, that the said former statutes, and every of them, be observed and kept in all and every article and point, articles and points, and that due execution be thereof made as appertaineth upon such pains and penalties as in the said statutes been comprised. And that no manner of person or persons of what degree, estate, or condition soever he or they be, take upon him or them to carry out of the realm any gold or silver in coin or bullion, or make any exchange or rechange contrary to the form of the said statutes and this his highness' proclamation, without his majesty's license and authority to him or them to be given.

And his majesty willeth it to be understand and known unto all his subjects, his grace's full mind and pleasure is that they and every of them observe and keep his laws, ordinances, and statutes heretofore made concerning the premises as they will avoid his great indignation and displeasure, and further to incur the danger of his laws which his highness willeth duly to be put in execution, without respect or favor to be given unto any offender contrary to his said laws and this his highness' proclamation.

2. 5 Richard II, st. 1, c. 2, 1381, *SR* 2, 17.

376. Advancing Date for Devaluating Shillings and Groats

[Greenwich, 8 July 1551, 5 Edward VI]

AC (Dasent *3*, 315): date, Greenwich, 5 July; order for treasurers to forward certificates of King's money remaining in their hands. CW (C82/935): date as above; schedule as below. PR (C66/838/26): date as above; schedule as below. *STC* 7840, Antiq 3, 63: printed by R. Grafton (London, 1551); date, Greenwich, June; schedule as below. *CSPD 1*, 33: date, 1 July 1551; King's writ to sheriffs, ordering them to break seal of proclamation writ only on July 8. Edward VI 327: signed on 2 July, proclaimed on 9 July. Wriothesley *2*, 50: proclaimed in London on 9 July. Steele 400: date, June. Text (*STC*): Antiq

WHEREAS the King's majesty very lately by proclamation[1] did ordain upon divers great and profitable considerations that the piece of silver coin, called the shilling, should after the last day of August next, be current for 9*d*. and not above, and the piece of silver coin called the groat, should likewise after the same day be current for 3*d*. and not above: his majesty now understandeth, upon the advertisement of his Privy Council, that although his meaning was much favorable to his people in the setting so long a day, not minding that the so doing thereof should be over grievous; yet nevertheless the covetousness of certain kind of people is so insatiable that by the craft used in this behalf the goodness of his majesty towards his people is much abused by the excessive raising of the prices of victual and other things, in the hands of grafters, great farmers, merchants, and such like, that it appeareth now very needful to shorten the former day.

Wherefore his majesty, with the good advice of the lords and others of his Privy Council, doth ordain, determine, and publish his most royal pleasure to be that the said piece of silver coin named the shilling shall, at and immediately after this present proclamation published, be current, paid, and received but only for 9*d*. and not above. And likewise the piece of silver called the groat shall at and immediately after this proclamation published be current, paid, and received for 3*d*. and not above. Willing and straightly commanding all manner of persons so to receive and pay the same, neither for more nor less, upon like pains contained in the former proclamation; any thing in the said former proclamation notwithstanding.

1. See 373.

377. Enforcing Statutes against Regraters, Forestallers, and Engrossers

[Hampton Court, 24 July 1551, 5 Edward VI]

AC (Dasent *3*, 318): date, Hampton Court, 18 July; order to Chancellor to set forth proclamation. BD 119*v:* bill signed on 18 July. CW (C82/935): date, Westminster, 24 July; sign manual; schedule as below. PR (C66/838/12*d*): date, Leigh, 24 August [*sic*]; schedule as below. PRO (SP 10/12/14): date, Hampton Court, 20 July; sign manual; writ to sheriffs and justices; schedule as below. *STC* 7841, Antiq 3, 64: printed by R. Grafton (London, 1551); date, 17 July; schedule as below. Edward VI 333: proclamation made on 18 July. Steele 402: date 24/17 July. Text (*STC*): Antiq

THE KING'S MOST ROYAL MAJESTY, having perfect knowledge daily out and from all parts of this his realm that the great and excessive prices both of corn, cattle, butter, cheese, and other victuals necessary for men's sustenance, for the most part groweth by the greedy and insatiable covetous desires and appetites of the breeders, broggers, engrossers, graziers, victualers, and forestallers (minding only their own lucre without respect of the commonwealth, to the great damage, impoverishing, and disquieting of his majesty's subjects) cannot, in respect of the office committed unto his majesty of God for the preservation of his people, but forthwith provide speedy remedy for reformation thereof. And therefore his majesty letteth all manner his subjects to understand that by the advice of his council he purposeth most severely and straightly to execute all such laws[1] as have been heretofore most godly and wholesomely made the ordained against all such breeders, broggers, engrossers, graziers, victualers, regraters, and forestallers as well of victuals as of merchandises; and namely, one old statute made against forestallers, the tenor whereof hereafter followeth.

No forestaller shall be suffered to dwell in any town, the which for his lucre will make haste to mete any corn, fish, herring, and other things, to be sold sometime by water, sometime by land, the which so taken, doth imagine to sell it the more dear: also they that come to the merchants stranger offering them to the sale of their ware, and exhorting them to sell their ware more dear than they did purpose to sell it, and so by craft and engine beguileth both the towns and the country. The first time that he is thereof convict he shall be grievously amerced; the second time, he shall be put upon the pillory; the

1. 23 Edward III, c. 6, 1349, *SR 1*, 308; 25 Edward III, st. 3, c. 3, 1350, *SR 1*, 315; 27 Edward III, st. 1, c. 3, 1353, *SR 1*, 330; 27 Edward III, st. 1, c. 5, 1353, *SR 1*, 331; 27 Edward III, st. 2, c. 11, 1353, *SR 1*, 337; 28 Edward III, c. 13, 1354, *SR 1*, 348; 31 Edward III, st. 2, 1357, *SR 1*, 353; 35 Edward III, 1360, *SR 1*, 369; 37 Edward III, c. 16, 1363, *SR 1*, 382; 6 Richard II, st. 1, c. 11, 1382, *SR 2*, 28; 24 Henry VIII, c. 6, 1532, *SR 3*, 422.

third time, he shall be put in prison and make fine; the fourth time he shall be abjured and banished the town. And that shall be observed of all manner of forestallers and of them that give unto them council and aid. And it shall be inquired if any steward or bailiff, for any reward, did remit the judgment of the pillory or tumbrel, judged or of right to be judged.

And further, where there was in the 25th year of the reign of his majesty's most dear father, King Henry VIII, a good statute [2] made against regraters and forestallers of fish, his majesty commandeth that according to the form of the said statute, that the stewards of the fairs of Stourbridge, St. Ives, and Ely cause the said statute to be openly proclaimed and read within their limits, and that likewise the sheriffs of the counties of Essex, Suffolk, Norfolk, and Lincoln, and the mayors and bailiffs of cities and towns corporate within the same shires, shall before the last of July next coming publish and cause to be proclaimed the said statute at convenient places. And where there were in the last session of parliament holden at Westminster in the fourth year of his majesty's reign, good laws [3] made as well against them that should buy any manner of oxen, steers, runts, kine, heifers, or calves, otherwise than in open fairs or markets (except it be for his own provision of household, team, or dairy) or that should sell the same again alive in the said fair or market where the same cattle was bought; and against the butcher that should buy any fat cattle and sell the same again alive, as also against such which use to buy butter and cheese to sell again (except they sell the same by retail in open shop, fair, or market and not in gross) his majesty straightly chargeth and commandeth all manner of his subjects, to whom the same may appertain, that they shall duly observe and keep the good intent and meaning of all the said statutes and laws upon such pains and penalties as be contained in the same.

And further his majesty straightly chargeth and commandeth all and singular his majesty's justices of peace, mayors, sheriffs, and other head officers of every shire, city, borough, and town corporate within this his majesty's realm, that they and every of them within their limits to their uttermost power and ability shall endeavor themselves, with all diligence, from time to time to see and cause this his highness' proclamation and laws, to be executed and obeyed as they will enjoy his majesty's favor and avoid his indignation; that in case upon this admonition the greedy malice of covetous men shall by proof appear to be nothing amended, but to continue still in their corrupt intentions of disobeying the laws and impairing of the commonwealth; his majesty as head of the same, and of all his loving subjects, is resolved to provide in such wise for the redress and repression of such greedy disordinate enhancers of prices, as shall be much more sharp and penal than any former law or proclamation heretofore made or ordained hath been.

2. 25 Henry VIII, c. 4, 1533, *SR 3*, 440.

3. 3 & 4 Edward VI, c. 19, 1549, *SR 4(1)*, 119.

378. Ordering Punishment for Rumors of Further Coin Debasement

[Westminster, 24 July 1551, 5 Edward VI]

BD 119*v:* bill signed on 19 July. CW (C82/935): date of delivery as above; sign manual; schedule as below. PR (C66/838/12*d*): date, Leigh, 24 July; schedule as below. *STC* 7842, Antiq MS 116, 116: printed by R. Grafton (London, 1551); date, 18 July; schedule as below. Edward VI 332: proclamation made on 19 July. Steele 403: date, Hampton Court, 24/18 July. Text (*STC*): Antiq

WHEREAS the King's majesty, upon the publishing of the last proclamation [1] for the abasing of the shilling to 9*d.*, minded to have brought his coin unto a more perfection of fineness than it was, and so from time to time to have amended it, as in very deed he purposeth to do with all the speed that may be: now it is come to pass that by the spreading of false and untrue rumors the prices of all things are grown so excessively that it is intolerable for his loving subjects to endure it, by reason that certain lewd persons of their own light heads have imagined that because his highness hath already somewhat abated the value of his said coin therefore his majesty should yet more abase it, and of their imaginations have uttered this fond rumor in such sort as every man that hath corn, cattle, or other kind of victual meet to be brought to the markets rather will keep it than utter it, fearing their loss in the fall of the money; whereof followeth a scarcity in the market where no scarcity ought to be, and a marvelous dearth where plenty is of all manner of victuals. And, as this greedy restraining of them that hath plentifully breedeth the plague of God upon them, both for their light credit and for their insatiable covetousness, as in the death of a number of them it hath of late been seen; so the King's highness, having charge from God to see his commonwealth well governed, must have an earnest eye to the straight punishment of them that raise these slanders amongst his subjects.

Wherefore his majesty straightly prohibiteth and defendeth all and every of his subjects, of what estate, degree, or condition soever he or they be, that from the publishing of this present proclamation they invent not, speak, mutter, or devise any manner of tale, news, or report, either touching the abasing of the said coin or that in any manner of wise may sound either to the dishonor of his majesty's person or to the defacing of his highness' proceedings, or of his council, or to the disquieting of his loving subjects, upon pain of six months' imprisonment, and such fine to the King's majesty's use as shall be thought meet by the justices of the peace in the shire where the

1. See 376.

offense is committed, if the offender be able to pay it immediately before his delivery. And in case the offender be not able to pay it, then he to be put on the pillory and one of his ears cut off, or both, if the grievousness of his offense shall seem to the justices, mayor or other officer so to require. And whosoever shall hear any such tale, rumor, invention, or device and do not immediately reveal it unto some justice of the peace, mayor, bailiff, constable, or such other officer, he to incur no less pain than the first offender; the like whereof to be inflicted upon the justice, mayor, bailiff, constable, or other officer to whom the accusation shall be given in case that upon the trial thereof they do not put the effect hereof in execution upon the offenders; and the accuser of such officers to be rewarded at the King's majesty's hands for the uttering and declaration of the officer's fault in not executing his charge in such sort as they shall have good cause and other time to watch for the like.

379. Devaluing Shilling to 6d.

[Hampton Court, 16 August 1551, 5 Edward VI]

AC (Dasent *3*, 352): date, Windsor, 29 August; order admonishing mayor of London for not punishing rumors of a further fall of the groat to 4*d*. BD 118*v*: bill signed on 12 July for 17 August. CW (C82/935): sign manual; date of delivery, Westminster, 24 July; schedule as below. PR (C66/838/26): schedule as below. PRO (SP 10/13/34): date, 11 August; order for proclamation on 16 August; schedule as below. Edward VI 338: date, Hampton Court, 12 August; order prohibiting breaking of seal on writ of proclamation before 16 August. Wriothesley *2*, 54: proclaimed in Cheapside at 7 a.m. on 17 August by the common crier, "he first showing the proclamation to the audience under the King's seal, to witness that it was whole and not open." Steele 404: date, Hampton Court, 16 August. Text (MS): PR

WHERE the King's majesty, minding to reduce the coin of this his highness' realm to a more fineness, hath of late, for sundry weighty considerations partly mentioned in one proclamation [1] of the last of April last past, ordained and established that the piece of silver coin called the teston or shilling should be current for 9*d*. and not above, and the piece of silver coin called the groat should likewise be current for 3*d*. and not above; minding both at the time of the said proclamation and since also to have reduced the coin of this realm to a fineness by such degrees as should have been least burdensome to his majesty and most for the ease of his highness' most loving subjects; forasmuch as since that time his majesty is sundry ways informed that the excessive prices of victuals and other things, which of reason should have grown less (as the coin is amended), is rather by the malice and insatiable greediness of sundry men, especially such as make their gain by buying and selling, increased and waxen more excessive, to the great hindrance of the commonwealth and intolerable burden of his majesty's most loving subjects, especially

1. See 372.

of those of the poorer sort: for the remedy thereof nothing is thought more valuable than the speedy reducing of the said coin more near his just fineness.

His majesty therefore, by the advice of the lords and other his highness' Privy Council, more esteeming the honor and estimation of the realm and the wealth and commodity of his highness' most loving subjects than the great profit which by the baseness of the coin did and should continually have grown unto his majesty, hath and, by the advice aforesaid, doth ordain and determine that from the 17th day of the present month of August the piece of coin called the teston or shilling shall be current in the realm of England and the town and marches of Calais only for *6d.* sterling and not above; and the piece called the groat, for *2d.* sterling and not above; the piece of *2d.* shall be current for *1d.;* and the piece of ½*d.* for ¼*d.* and not above; and therefore straightly chargeth and commandeth all and every person and persons of what estate, degree, or condition soever he or they be, to pay and receive after the 17th day of this present month the said coins of shillings or testons for *6d.* sterling; and the said groats for *2d.;* and the piece of *2d.* for *1d.;* the piece of *1d.* for ½*d.;* and the piece of ½*d.* for ¼*d.* sterling; and for no higher nor lower values or prices within this his majesty's realm and the town and marches of Calais: upon pain of forfeiture to his majesty of all such money as shall be paid and received at other valors, or otherwise than by this proclamation is set forth, and also upon pain of fine and imprisonment during his majesty's pleasure.

380. Pricing Victual, Ordering Penalties for Violations

[Westminster, 11 September 1551, 5 Edward VI]

AC (Dasent *3,* 366): date, Hampton Court, 27 September; order for letter to all justices of peace and sheriffs in realm, commanding better diligence in executing the King's late proclamation on the price of cattle. Ibid., *3,* 394: date, Westminster, 22 October; citation of John Baker for selling twelve oxen at £5 per head. BD 129: bill signed on 4 September. *STC* 7843, Antiq 3, 65: printed by R. Grafton (London, 1551); schedule as below. Edward VI 342: proclamation set forth on 9 September. Steele 405: date, Westminster, 9 September. Text (*STC*): Antiq

WHERE by an act[1] of parliament holden at Westminster upon prorogation the 25th day of January in the 25th year of the reign of the most noble prince of worthy memory, King Henry VIII, it was enacted amongst other things, that upon complaints made of enhancing the prices of victuals necessary for

1. 25 Henry VIII, c. 2, 1533, *SR 3,* 438.

men's sustenance in any part of this realm, or in any other of the King's dominions, the Lord Chancellor of England, the Lord Treasurer, the Lord President of the King's council, the Lord Privy Seal, the Lord Steward, the Lord Chamberlain, and all other lords of the King's council, the Treasurer and Comptroller of the King's house, the Chancellor of the Duchy of Lancaster, the King's Justices of either bench, the Chancellor, Chamberlains, Under-Treasurer and the Barons of the King's Exchequer, or seven of them, whereof the Lord Chancellor, the Lord Treasurer, the Lord President of the King's council, or the Lord Privy Seal to be one, should have power and authority from time to time as the case should require, to set and tax reasonable prices of all kind of victuals necessary for man's sustenance, how they should be sold in gross or by retail; and that after such prices, set and taxed in form aforesaid, proclamation should be made in the King's name under the Great Seal, of the said prices; and that all farmers, owners, broggers, and other victualers, having or keeping any kind of victual to the intent to sell, shall sell the same to such the King's subjects as will buy them, at such prices as shall be set and taxed by the said proclamation, upon the pains to be expressed and limited in the said proclamation, to be lost, forfeited, and levied to the King's use in such wise as in the said proclamation should be declared, as in the said act more at large amongst other things appeareth.

Wherefore, upon divers good and pitiful complaints made of the great and excessive prices of victuals necessary for man's sustenance, the Lord Chancellor of England, the Lord Treasurer, the Lord Privy Seal, and other of the King's most honorable council, to the number expressed in the said act, by virtue and authority of the said act, assembled at Windsor together the 30th day of August last past, after deliberate consultation thereof, have set and taxed prices of certain victuals in form following.

First, that the greatest lean ox shall not be sold above the sum of 40*s*. Item, the lean ox of the second sort not to be sold above the sum of 33*s*. 4*d*. The lean ox of the third sort not to be sold above the sum of 26*s*. 8*d*. The best, greatest, and fattest ox shall not be sold above the sum of 53*s*. 4*d*. The fat ox of the second sort shall not be sold above the sum of 43*s*. 4*d*. The fat ox of the third sort shall not be sold above the sum of 33*s*. 4*d*. The lean sheep of the greatest sort not to be sold above the sum of 3*s*. 4*d*. The lean sheep of the second sort not to be sold above the sum of 2*s*. 8*d*. The lean sheep of the third sort not to be sold above the sum of 2*s*. The fat sheep of the greatest sort shall not be sold above the sum of 5*s*. The fat sheep of the second sort shall not be sold above the sum of 4*s*. The fat sheep of the third sort shall not be sold above the sum of 3*s*. And that no beef nor pork to be sold raw, by retail, above of the sum of 1*d*. ½ farthing the pound. Nor veal or mutton raw, by retail, above 1½*d*. the pound. And that no manner of person shall sell by retail any great thick Essex cheese above the rate of ½*d*. ½ farthing the pound, nor any other cheese by retail above ½*d*. farthing the pound.

The King's most excellent majesty, most graciously tendering the commonwealth of this his realm, besides divers remedies already provided as well in parliament as in other consultations, hath for remedy thereof of late to his own great loss, abated and decayed the valuation of his coin by his several proclamations, thinking thereby the excessive prices of all things, of good congruence should consequently fall and abate as by natural reason and equity necessarily it ought and should, (nevertheless, contrary to his grace's expectation, divers insatiable and greedy persons in whose hands a great part of the victual of this realm by regratings resteth, being void of all charitable regard and respect to the commonwealth of their natural country, for their own wealth and filthy lucre, do not only by their undue, subtle, and sinister practices continue their excessive prices of all manner of victuals, but also as much as in them lieth daily do invent and study for the increase of the same, to the great detriment and utter undoing of the greater part of his loving subjects, being forced to fetch their necessary victual at their hands, which his majesty will nor can in no wise suffer), and therefore, graciously assenting and agreeing to the said rates and prices and intending to proclaim and publish the same:

Most straightly chargeth and commandeth that no person or persons from henceforth do sell or cause to be sold the greatest lean ox above the sum of 40*s*. upon pain of forfeiture of £20. of current money of this realm for every lean ox so by him sold. Nor that any lean ox of the second sort be sold above the sum of 33*s*. 4*d*. upon pain of forfeiture of £10. of like money for every ox by him so sold. Nor any lean ox of the third sort above the sum of 26*s*. 8*d*. upon pain of forfeiture of £6. 13*s*. 4*d*. for every ox so sold by him. Nor the greatest, fattest, and best ox to be sold above the sum of 53*s*. 4*d*. upon pain of forfeiture of £20. for every ox so by him sold. Nor any fat ox of the second sort to be sold above the sum of 43*s*. 4*d*. upon pain of forfeiture of £10 for every ox so sold. Nor any fat ox of the third sort to be sold above the sum of 33*s*. 4*d*. upon pain of forfeiture for every such ox so sold, £6. 13*s*. 4*d*. Nor shall sell any lean sheep of the greatest sort above the sum of 3*s*. 4*d*. upon pain of forfeiture of £3. 6*s*. 8*d*. for every such sheep so sold. Nor any lean sheep of the second sort above the sum of 2*s*. 8*d*. upon pain of forfeiture of 53*s*. 4*d*. for every sheep so sold. Nor any sheep of the third sort above the sum of 2*s*. upon pain of forfeiture of 40*s*. for every sheep so sold. Nor shall sell any fat sheep of the greatest sort above the sum of 5*s*. upon pain of forfeiture of £3. 6*s*. 8*d*. for every sheep so sold. Nor any fat sheep of the second or meaner sort above the price of 4*s*. upon pain of forfeiture for every fat sheep so sold, 53*s*. 4*d*., nor any fat sheep of the third sort above the sum of 3*s*. upon pain of forfeiture of 40*s*. for every sheep so to be sold.

And that no butcher nor other person shall sell any raw beef or pork by retail above the rate and sum of 1*d*. ½ farthing the pound, upon pain of forfeiture of 6*s*. 8*d*. for every pound so sold, nor shall sell veal or mutton raw by retail above 1½*d.* the pound upon pain of forfeiture of 6*s.* 8*d.* for every pound so sold.

And that no manner of person shall sell by retail any great, thick Essex cheese above the rate of ½*d.* ½ farthing the pound upon pain of forfeiture of 2*s.* for every pound so sold, nor any other cheese by retail above ½*d.* farthing the pound upon pain of forfeiture of 2*s.* for every pound so to be sold. The same sums and forfeitures to be levied to the King's use in form following; that is to say, by bill, plaint, information, or action of debt to be taken before his justices of peace in their sessions in any county, city, or town corporate where any such offense shall be done, or in any of his courts of record, wherein no protection, essoin, or wager of law shall be allowed for the defendant; the one moiety of all such forfeit or forfeitures to be to the use of his majesty and the other moiety thereof to the use of him or them that shall first sue and pursue the same with effect. And that every person and persons that have reared or shall rear or keep, or have fatted or shall fat or keep any such cattle or sheep to the intent to sell the same, shall upon request made sell the same at the price aforesaid, upon pain of forfeiture for every such refusal £20., the same to be recovered and levied in form aforesaid, and to suffer imprisonment at the King's will and pleasure.

His highness also straightly chargeth and commandeth all and every his justices of peace, immediately after this proclamation published and proclaimed, to assemble themselves and to take order, by division or otherwise, for the good and perfect execution of this proclamation; and doth further signify to his said justices that as he will well consider and advance their diligence and well-doing in the premises, so will he severely and sharply punish their negligence in contrary doings.

And for the better effect, sequel, and success of this proclamation, his highness by the advice of his most honorable council hath determined to address his special commissioners for the hearing and examination of the defaults and negligent doings of his said justices in the premises, if any hap to be so, as his highness may proceed to the correction and punishment of such justices offenders as the importance of the case shall require.

His majesty also straightly chargeth and commandeth all and every his loving subjects, that they nor any of them from henceforth attempt to take from any owner any cattle or victual afore mentioned against the will of such owner, otherwise than is aforesaid, or by the delivery of the justices of the peace or some of them, upon pain of loss of all their goods and chattels and to suffer imprisonment during the King's pleasure.

381. Enforcing Statutes against Melting Silver Coin

[Farnham, 11 September 1551, 5 Edward VI]

BD 131: bill signed on 9 September. *STC* 7844, Antiq MS 116, 115: printed by R. Grafton (London, 1551): date, 11 September; schedule as below. Edward VI 343: proclamation set forth on 12 September. Steele 406: date, Farnham. Text (*STC*): Antiq

WHERE by divers and several acts of parliament holden in the ninth year of the reign of the noble prince, King Edward III,[1] and in the 17th year of King Richard II,[2] and in the fourth year of King Henry IV,[3] the King's majesty's noble progenitors, it was enacted, ordained, and established amongst other things that no groat, half-groat, halfpenny, nor farthing should be molten by any person or persons to make vessel or any other thing thereof, upon pain to forfeit and lose four times the value of the money so molten, and to suffer other grievous pains in the said statutes contained, as in the said several acts more at large amongst other things plainly appeareth. And where also the King's most excellent highness, graciously considering and tendering the commonwealth of this his realm and other his dominions, hath of late to his great loss abated and diminished the valuation of his coin by his several proclamations, in such order and form as in the said proclamations more amply and at large is contained and expressed, to the intent that his highness would reduce and bring his coin and mints to a certain better estate and estimation, for the honor of his majesty, the benefit of his subjects, and the commonwealth of this realm and other his grace's dominions. Which godly purpose and intent of his majesty as is aforesaid, and the said several statutes and forfeitures therein contained notwithstanding, his majesty is credibly informed, and also understandeth, that divers insatiable and greedy persons, as well goldsmiths as other, not regarding their duty of obedience towards his majesty, and being void of all charitable respect and regard to the commonwealth of this their country, have molten and daily do melt divers great sums of money, as well of groats as half-groats, halfpence, farthings, and other current money of his realm, to the great diminishing of his grace's coin and mints, to the great hurt and detriment of the commonwealth, contrary to his majesty's said godly intents and purposes, and against the tenor and effect of the said several statutes; to the great burdening and utter undoing of divers and many of the said offenders if his majesty should use and extend the rigor

1. 9 Edward III, st. 2, c. 3, 1335, *SR 1*, 273.
2. 17 Richard II, c. 1, 1393, *SR 2*, 87.
3. 4 Henry IV, c. 10, 1402, *SR 2*, 136.

and extremity of his laws against them for their offenses, which his highness intendeth to execute and do without favor if, by their unlawful doings, he be further moved and occasioned thereunto.

And therefore his majesty, being fully minded to have the said several statutes observed, and his coin not to be molten, doth straightly charge and command that no teston or shilling, groat, half-groat, penny, halfpenny, or farthing, or any other coin of silver being current within this realm, shall from henceforth in any wise be molten by any person or persons to make vessel, plate, or any other thing thereof, upon pain to forfeit and lose to his highness four times the value of the money so molten, and further to suffer imprisonment and other punishment at his majesty's will and pleasure.

382. Announcing New Coinage

[Westminster, 30 October 1551, 5 Edward VI]

AC (Dasent *3*, 387): date, Hampton Court, 13 October; order for Chancellor to print proclamation on new coin immediately, but to keep it from going abroad until the King's pleasure is signified. BD 141*v*: bill signed 12 October, schedule as below. Ibid., 164: date, 14 December; King and council sign a proclamation, not found, against seditious rumors concerning certain of the new coins. Edward VI 346: date, 1 October; commission for new coinage. Herbert 534: separate edition by Grafton; date, 30 October. Stow 1023: date, 30 September; summary of schedule. Strype 2(2), 211: schedule as below. Steele 408: date, 28 October. Text (MS): BD

THE KING'S MAJESTY hath ordered and established to be made within his mints these several coins, as well of silver in fineness of the standard sterling, as also of gold, as hereafter ensueth:

That is to say, one piece of silver money, which shall be current for 5*s*. of the lawful moneys aforesaid; another piece, which shall be called the piece of 2*s*. 6*d*. of the lawful moneys; the third piece, which shall be called the sterling shilling, current for 12*d*.; the fourth piece, which shall be half of the said sterling shilling, shall be current for 6*d*. of the lawful moneys aforesaid.

And also, the King's majesty has ordered to have three pieces of small moneys made likewise current: that is to say, the first piece shall be called a penny with a double rose, and shall be current for 1*d*. of the lawful moneys aforesaid; the second piece shall be called a halfpenny with a single rose; and the third piece, a farthing with a portcullis.

And of the coins of gold, as here ensueth: that is to say, the whole sovereign of fine gold, which shall be current for 30*s*. of lawful moneys of England; another piece of fine gold, called the angel, shall be current for 10*s*.; the third piece of gold, which shall be called the angelet, half of the angel, current for 5*s*. of lawful moneys aforesaid;

And further, a whole sovereign, of crown gold, shall be current for 20*s*.;

the second piece of crown gold, which shall be called the half-sovereign, shall be current for 10*s*.; and the third piece of crown gold, which shall be called a crown, current for 5*s*.; the fourth piece of crown gold, which shall be called the half-crown, which shall be current for 2*s*. 6*d*. of the lawful moneys aforesaid;

Straightly charg[ing] and command[ing] all manner of persons within his realms and dominions to receive and pay the said several pieces of moneys, as well of silver as of gold, at the several rates before rehearsed; under pain of the King's high displeasure, and to be further punished as his highness shall think convenient.

And his express commandment is that all such base moneys which his majesty did lately by his several proclamations [1] reduce to the value of a lower rate shall pass and go current in payment in like manner and sort as his highness' last proclamation did declare, until such time as his majesty's mints may with diligence convert the same into the said new coins, which his majesty mindeth to have done with all possible expedition.

And his majesty signifieth to all his loving subjects that, if they do bring in any quantity of moneys now current into his grace's mints within the Tower of London, they shall have the same received there by tale at the value as they be now current upon bills; and they shall, in as convenient time as may, be repaid for the said moneys now current by tale in other the King's majesty's new moneys afore declared.

383. Pricing Wines

[Westminster, 1 February 1552, 6 Edward VI]

BD 178*v*: bill signed on 20 January. LJ 16, 170: date, 1 February; proclaimed in London on 5 February; schedule as below. Steele 420: date, Westminster, February 1553; "Not found." Text (MS): LJ

Where it is ordained and provided by statute [1] that the prices of all manner of wines should be limited and declared by the Lord Chamberlain of England, Lord Treasurer of England, Lord President of the King's most honorable council, Lord Privy Seal, and other the councilors of our said sovereign lord, specified and declared in the same statute, as by the same statute made and established in the parliament begun and holden at Westminster the third day of November in the 21st year of the reign of the most noble prince of famous memory King Henry VIII, continued by divers prorogations, more plainly appeareth;

1. See 371, 372, 377, 378, 379.
1. 23 Henry VIII, c. 7, 1531, *SR* 3, 374.

Forasmuch as the said lords and councilors named and appointed for the execution of the said act have by their deliberate advice taxed, limited, assigned, and appointed, that all Gascon and French wines shall be sold within this realm, in sort following: that is to say, every tun of the best Gascon wine to be sold after the price and rate of £6 6*s*. 8*d*. the tun and not above; and every tun of the best French wine to be sold after the rate of £5 sterling the tun and not above; and every pipe, hogshead, puncheon, tierce, and other vessels, of the same several wines to be sold after their quantities after and according to the same rates, and not above:

The King's most royal majesty therefore straightly chargeth and commandeth all and singular his subjects and others putting any manner of Gascon or French wines to sale within this his realm, that they nor any of them in any manner wise, by craft, covin, or private agreement, shall sell any Gascon or French wines before mentioned otherwise than after the rates above limited; upon pain to forfeit and pay such penalties as be contained and expressed in the same act.

And moreover, his high pleasure and commandment is that all and singular mayors, sheriffs, bailiffs, headboroughs, constables, and other officers to whom it appertaineth, that they and every of them with diligence cause and see that this his proclamation be put in due execution, after the tenor of the same; and also according to another act of parliament[2] established in the parliament above rehearsed, against such as will refuse to sell their wines at prices taxed as is aforesaid: as they will answer thereunto at their uttermost perils.

384. Ordering Punishment for Irreverence in Churches

[Westminster, 20 February 1552, 6 Edward VI]

CR (C54/485/4): schedule as below. BD 181: bill signed on 20 February. Steele 412: date as above. Text (MS): CR

THE KING'S MAJESTY considering that churches, both cathedral and others, which at the beginning were godly instituted for common prayer, of the word of God, and the ministration of sacraments, be now of late times in many places, and especially within the city of London, irreverently used and by divers insolent, rash persons sundry ways much abused, so far forth that many quarrels, riots, frays, and blood-sheddings have been made in some of the said churches, besides shooting of handguns to doves, and the common bringing of horses and mules into and through the said churches, making the same,

2. 24 Henry VIII, c. 6, 1532, *SR 3*, 422.

which were properly appointed to God's service and common prayer, like a stable or common inn, or rather a den or sink of all unthriftiness, to the great dishonor of God, the offense of his majesty, and disquiet of all such as for the time be there assembled for common prayers and hearing of God's word.

Forasmuch as the insolence of great numbers using the said ill demeanors doth daily more and more increase, his highness, by the advice of the lords and others of the Privy Council, straightly chargeth and commandeth that no manner of person or persons, of what estate or condition soever he or they be, do from henceforth presume to quarrel, fray, or fight, shoot any handgun, bring any horse or mule into or through any cathedral or other church, or by any other ways or means irreverently use the said churches or any of them, upon pain of his highness' indignation and imprisonment of his or their bodies that so shall offend against the effect of this present proclamation at his majesty's pleasure.

And his highness further willeth and commandeth all justices of peace, mayors, sheriffs, constables, and other his majesty's officers, to see this his highness' proclamation duly executed accordingly without fail, as they will answer for the contrary at their uttermost perils.

385. Declaring True Meaning of Kneeling at Communion

[Westminster, 27 October 1552, 6 Edward VI]

AC (Dasent *4*, 154): date, Westminster, 27 October; order for Chancellor to cause declaration of the King's majesty touching the kneeling at receiving of the Communion to be joined to the *Book of Common Prayer*. BD 262: bill signed on 22 October. CR (C54/485/47): schedule as below. *STC* 16,282, BM G.12,099: printed by E. Whitchurch (London, 1552); schedule as below, in text. An earlier 1552 edition, *STC* 16,280, has the printed declaration inserted on a separate leaf, *sig*. N[8]–O[1]. Stow 1028: new *Book of Common Prayer* used first on 1 November in St. Paul's. Steele 417. Text (*STC* 16,282): BM

ALTHOUGH no order can be so perfectly devised but it may be of some, either for their ignorance and infirmity or else of malice and obstinacy, misconstrued, depraved, and interpreted in a wrong part, and yet because brotherly charity willeth that so much as conveniently may be, offenses should be taken away: therefore we willing to do the same, whereas it is ordained in the *Book of Common Prayer,*[1] in the administration of the Lord's Supper, that the communicants kneeling should receive the Holy Communion, which thing being well meant for a signification of the humble and grateful acknowledging of the benefits of Christ given unto the worthy receiving, and to avoid the

1. *STC* 16,279. See 5 & 6 Edward VI, c. 1, 1551, *SR 4(1)*, 130.

profanation and disorder which about the Holy Communion might else ensue; lest yet the same kneeling might be thought or taken otherwise, we do declare that it is not meant thereby that any adoration is done or ought to be done either unto the sacramental bread or wine there bodily received, or unto any real and essential presence there being of Christ's natural flesh and blood. For as concerning the sacramental bread and wine, they remain still in their very natural substances and therefore may not be adored, for that were idolatry to be abhorred of all faithful Christians. And as concerning the natural body and blood of our Savior Christ, they are in heaven and not here; for it is against the truth of Christ's true natural body to be in more places than in one at one time.

386. Enforcing Statutes for Abstinence on Fridays, Saturdays, and during Lent

[Westminster, 14 February 1553, 7 Edward VI]

AC (Dasent *4*, 217): date, Westminster, 12 February; letter to mayor of London, on adequacy of herring to provide city. BD 296*v:* bill signed on 15 February. *STC* 7845, Antiq 3, 66: printed by R. Grafton (London, 1553); date, 14 February; schedule as below. Steele 419; date, Westminster. Text (*STC*): Antiq

WHEREAS in the parliament holden at Westminster the second year of the King's majesty's reign, one act,[1] amongst divers others, was made, that no person or persons should after a certain time willingly and wittingly eat any kind of flesh upon any Friday, Saturday, any day within the time of Lent, nor at any such other day as was at that time, or should be at any time afterwards, commonly accepted and reputed as a fish day within this realm of England, under divers and great penalties as in the said act more largely doth appear. Forasmuch as the said act, founded upon sundry and wholesome considerations contained in the same, hath since been by divers and many fearless subjects, most disobediently and stubbornly infringed, broken, and neglected, to the great contempt of his majesty's laws, and the notable offense also of Almighty God, Who hath commanded princes' ordinances to be observed, not only for fear of their indignation, but also for conscience' sake.

His majesty, having due consideration of the great scarcity of victual, and specially of flesh that is grown within this realm, and that by the abstinence of eating of flesh in times prohibited, much flesh is bred and increased to the continual and more plentiful sustenance of his subjects, most straightly chargeth and commandeth that from and after the making of this his high-

1. 2 & 3 Edward VI, c. 19, 1548, *SR 4(1)*, 65.

ness' present proclamation and publishing of the same, no manner of person or persons dwelling, inhabiting, resident or abiding within this his realm of England, or any other his dominions or territories, having no license of his highness to eat flesh in the times prohibited by the said act, nor being provided, specified, or excepted by the said act, do willingly or wittingly eat any manner of flesh in the times of Lent, or in or upon any other days prohibited by the said act, contrary to the effect, purport, and tenor of the same, upon the pains and penalties contained in the said statute, and as they will, besides that, avoid his highness' indignation and displeasure.

And that no manner of person or persons keeping, or that shall keep, any tavern, inn, hostelry, alehouse, victualing house, common or usual table for any guests, within his said realm or dominions, from and after the making of this his highness' proclamation, utter any flesh in any kind of manner in their houses or elsewhere in any the times prohibited by the said act or statute, to be eaten by any person not licensed or provided for as is aforesaid, upon the selfsame penalties as against the eaters thereof in the said act is provided.

And that no butcher nor other person, after the making of this proclamation (except he shall be specially licensed by his highness under the Great Seal of England) shall sell any flesh, being dead, within his said realm or dominions, to be eaten in or upon any the days or times prohibited by the said act, upon like pain and pains as is before last expressed and limited.

And for the better example to be given by them which have any license, his majesty's pleasure is that no manner of person or persons having any license by his majesty's letters patent, or privilege by the said statute to eat flesh, do in any wise eat the same flesh upon any days prohibited in any open place of his or their house, or in any such assembly as they use on other days accustomed for eating of flesh, but that he and they having license use the same secretly and modestly.

And that as well the mayor of London for the time being, as all justices of peace, and all other mayors, sheriffs, bailiffs, constables, and head officers of all and every city, county, borough, town, and village within this his realm of England, and all other his highness' dominions and territories, as they will avoid his highness' displeasure and indignation and will further answer at their peril, do from time to time after the making of this his highness' proclamation, within their rules, jurisdictions, authorities, precincts, and circuits truly and diligently, with all speed from time to time, search and try out all manner the offenses, contempts, and inobediences aforesaid, and for the due execution of the aforesaid statute, and the tenor of this proclamation, do devise some weekly search so as by their diligence the law may have some fruit and profit, as it is very needful; and upon knowledge and due proof thereof made, that they and every of them forthwith commit all and every such offender and offenders to imprisonment, there safe and surely to be kept and remain, and further to be punished according unto the penalties by degrees contained in the foresaid act, and in case any be found upon the said punishments not amended, then such to be, as notable and incorrigible persons, certified to his majesty or his council that some grievous open punishment of such may be example to all others.

And that all and every his loving and true subjects be from time to time aiding, helping, and assisting to all and every such mayor and mayors, justices, and other officers aforesaid, in the doing and executing of the effect and purport of this his highness' proclamation, as they will answer to his majesty upon their uttermost peril, and as they will avoid his highness' grievous indignation and displeasure. For certainly such is the King's determinate purpose to have this thoroughly executed.

387. Permitting Merchants to Carry £4 out of Realm

[Westminster, 28 June 1553, 7 Edward VI]

CW (C82/968): date of delivery as above; sign manual; writ to mayor and sheriffs of London; schedule as below. LJ 16, 248*v:* date as above; writ to mayor and sheriffs of London; schedule as below. Steele 421. Text (MS): CW

WHERE in the parliament begun and holden at Westminster the first day of March in the seventh year of our reign and there continued till the last day of the same month of March, it is there recited by an act of parliament then and there made entitled, *An Act Reviving a Statute Made in the 17th Year of Our Most Noble Progenitor, King Edward IV,*[1] touching the carrying of gold and silver out of the realm as followeth:

> Where in the parliament begun and holden at Westminster the 16th day of January in the 17th year of our said most royal progenitor, King Edward IV, amongst other it was ordained and enacted[2] by authority of the same parliament, that no person should carry or make to be carried out of this realm or Wales from no part of the same any manner of money of the coin of this realm, nor money of the coin of other realms, lands, or lordships, nor plate, vessel, bullion, or jewel of gold garnished or ungarnished, or of silver, without the King's license, but such persons as be dispensed within the statute[3] made in the second year of the most noble progenitor, King Henry VI, and other divers statutes made upon pain of felony. The which

1. 7 Edward VI, c. 6, 1552, *SR 4(1)*, 170.
2. 17 Edward IV, c. 1, 1477, *SR 2*, 452.
3. 2 Henry VI, c. 6, 1423, *SR 2*, 219.

statute and ordinance so made in the time of our said most noble progenitor, King Edward IV, was made to endure from the feast of Easter in the 18th year of the said King Edward IV unto the end of seven years then next ensuing.

Which said statute and ordinance so before rehearsed, by authority of parliament holden in the fourth year of the late King of famous memory, King Henry VII,[4] was confirmed and established to be good and effectual from the Feast of the Purification of Our Lady in the year of our Lord God 1489, unto the end and term of 20 years then next ensuing, as by the same statute also more plainly appeareth. And where also at the said parliament holden at Westminster in the seventh year of our said reign it is enacted by authority of parliament that the said statute and ordinance before rehearsed, made in the 17th year of our most noble progenitor, King Edward IV, and every clause, article, sentence, or provision therein contained, is by authority thereof confirmed and enacted to be good and effectual from the first day of May then next ensuing and to endure unto the end of 20 years then next following, as by the said act made in the said seventh year of our said reign plainly appeareth.

Nevertheless, upon good and reasonable consideration us moving, we be pleased and contented that from and after the publication of this our proclamation, it shall be lawful unto all merchants and to all and every other person and persons, lawfully passing out of this our realm into any outward parts beyond the seas, to carry with them for their reasonable costs and expenses the sum of £4 of any money current within this realm or under and not above, or any rings or signets of gold or silver upon their fingers, without any loss of life, lands, or goods, or any other pain, forfeiture, imprisonment, or penalty to be to them or any of them for the same; the said statute or any other statute, ordinance, or law heretofore made to the contrary in any wise notwithstanding.

4. 4 Henry VII, c. 23, 1488, *SR 2*, 546.

Appendixes

Appendix 1. Acts

1.

An Act that Proclamations Made by
the King Shall Be Obeyed
[31 Henry VIII, c. 8, 1539, *SR 3*, 726]

FORASMUCH as the King's most royal majesty for divers considerations, by the advice of his council, hath heretofore set forth divers and sundry his grace's proclamations, as well for and concerning divers and sundry articles of Christ's religion, as for a unity and concord to be had amongst the loving and obedient subjects of this his realm and other his dominions, and also concerning the advancement of his commonwealth and good quiet of his people, which nevertheless divers and many froward, willful and obstinate persons have willfully contemned and broken, not considering what a King by his royal power may do, and for lack of a direct statute and law to cohort offenders to obey the said proclamations which being still suffered should not only encourage offenders to the disobedience of the precept and laws of Almighty God, but also sin too much to the great dishonor of the King's most royal majesty, who may full ill bear it, and also give to great hurt and boldness to all malefactors and offenders; considering also that sudden causes and occasions fortune many times which do require speedy remedies, and that by abiding for a parliament in the meantime might happen great prejudice to ensue to the realm; and weighing also that his majesty (which by the kingly and regal power given him by God may do many things in such cases) should not be driven to extend the liberty and supremacy of his regal power and dignity by willfulness of froward subject; it is therefore thought in manner more than necessary that the King's highness of this realm for the time being, with the advice of his honorable council, should make and set forth proclamations for the good and politic order and governance of this his realm of England, Wales, and other his dominions from time to time, for the defense of his regal dignity and the advancement of his commonwealth and good quiet of his people, as the cases of necessity shall require, and that an ordinary law should be provided by the assent of his majesty and parliament, for the due punishment, correction, and reformation of such offenses and disobediences.

Be it therefore enacted by the authority of this present parliament, with the King's majesty, the lords spiritual and temporal and the commons assent, that always the King for the time being, with the advice of his honorable council, whose names hereafter followeth, *or with the advice of the more part of them,*[1] may set forth at all times by *authority of this act his*[1] proclamations, under such penalties and pains and of such sort as to his highness and his said honorable council *or the more part of them*[1] shall seem necessary and requisite; and that those same shall be obeyed, observed, and kept as though they were made by act of parliament for the time in them limited, unless the King's highness dispense with them or any of them under his Great Seal.

Provided always that the words, meaning, and intent of this act be not understood, interpreted, construed, or extended, that by virtue of it any of the King's liege people, of what estate, degree, or condition soever he or they be, bodies politic or corporate, their heirs or successors, should have any of his or their inheritances, lawful possessions, offices, liberties, privileges, franchises, goods, or chattels taken from them or any of them, nor by virtue of the said act suffer any pains of death other than shall be hereafter in this act declared, nor that by any proclamation to be made by virtue of this act, any acts, common laws standing at this present time in strength and force, nor yet any lawful or laudable customs of this realm *or other his dominions*[1] nor any of them, shall be infringed, broken or subverted: and specially all those acts standing this hour in force which have been made in the King's highness' time; but that every such person and persons, bodies politic and corporate, their heirs and successors and the heirs and successors of every of them, their inheritance, lawful possessions, offices, liberties, privileges, franchises, goods, and chattels shall stand and be in the same state and condition, to every respect and purpose, as if this act or proviso had never been had or made; except such forfeitures, pains, and penalties as in this act and in every proclamation which *hereafter shall be set forth by authority of the same*[1] shall be declared and expressed; and except such persons which shall offend any proclamation to be made by the King's highness, his heirs or successors, for and concerning any kind of heresies against Christian religion.

Furthermore be it enacted by the authority of this present parliament, that to the intent the King's subjects should not be ignorant of his proclamations, every sheriff or other officer and minister to whom any such proclamation shall be directed by the King's writ under his Great Seal, shall proclaim or cause the same to be proclaimed within 14 days after the receipt thereof, in four several market towns if there be so many, or else in six other towns or villages within the limit of their authority; and they to cause the said proclamations to be fixed and set up openly upon places convenient in every such town, place or village, upon pain and penalty of such sum and sums of money or imprisonment of body as shall be contained in the said proclamation or proclamations.

1. Interlined in the original act. See *SR 3*, 726, n. 1.

And be it further enacted by the authority aforesaid, that if any person or persons, of what estate, degree, or condition soever he or they be, which at any time hereafter do willfully offend and break or obstinately not observe and keep any such proclamation or any article therein contained which shall proceed from the King's majesty, by the advice of his council as is aforesaid, that then all and every such offender or offenders, being thereof, within one half year next after their or his offense committed accused, and thereof within 18 months next after the same offense so [committed], convicted by confession or lawful witness and proofs before the Archbishop of Canterbury, Metropolitan, the Chancellor of England, the Lord Treasurer of England, the President of the King's most honorable council, the Lord Privy Seal, the Great Chamberlain of England, Lord Admiral, Lord Steward or Grand Master, Lord Chamberlain of the King's most honorable household, two other Bishops being of the King's council, such as his grace shall appoint for the same, the Secretary, the Treasurer and Controller of the King's most honorable household, the Master of the Horse, the two Chief Judges and the Master of the Rolls for the time being, the Chancellor of the Augmentations, the Chancellor of the Duchy, the Chief Baron of the Exchequer, the two General Surveyors, the Chancellor of the Exchequer, the Under-Treasurer of the same, the Treasurer of the King's Chamber for the time being, in the Star Chamber at Westminster or elsewhere, or at the least before the half of the number afore rehearsed, of which number the Lord Chancellor, the Lord Treasurer, the Lord President of the King's most honorable council, the Lord Privy Seal, the Chamberlain of England, the Lord Admiral, the two Chief Judges for the time being, or two of them shall be two, shall lose and pay such penalties, forfeitures of sums of money, to be levied of his or their lands, tenements, goods, and chattels to the King's use, and also suffer such imprisonment of his body as shall be expressed, mentioned, and declared in any such proclamation or proclamations which such offender or offenders shall offend and break or not observe and keep contrary to this act as is aforesaid; and that execution shall be had, done, and made against every such offender and offenders, with the addition of the names or surnames, towns or counties, mystery or occupation of the said offenders, by such order, process, ways and means, and after such manner, form, and condition as by the King's highness and the said council shall be devised and thought most convenient for example of such offenders: provided always that none offender which shall offend contrary to the form of any such proclamations shall incur the danger and penalty thereof, except such proclamation or proclamations be had, done or made in such shire or county where the offender hath or shall dwell or be most conversant within a year before.

And be it further enacted by the authority aforesaid, that the Lord Chancellor, the Lord Privy Seal and either of them, with the assent of six of the forenamed, shall have power and authority by their discretions, upon every information to be given to them or to either of them touching the premises, to cause process to be made against all and singular such offenders by writs under the King's Great Seal or under his grace's Privy Seal in form following; that is to say, first by proclamation under a pain or a penalty by the discretion of the aforesaid councilors appointed for the awarding of process, and if he appear not to the same without a lawful excuse, then the said councilors to award out another proclamation upon allegiance of the same offender, for the due examination, trial, and conviction of every such person and persons as shall offend contrary to this act, for the due execution to be had of and for the same in manner and form as is above remembered; except it be within the liberty of the County Palatine of the Duchy of Lancaster; and in case it so be, then to pass by the Chancellor of the King's Duchy of Lancaster under the seal of the said duchy, with the assent of six at least of the aforenamed councilors.

Be it also further enacted by the authority aforesaid that if any person or persons do commit any offense contrary to the form and effect of this act, and after the same offense done or committed do obstinately, willingly, or contemptuously avoid and depart out of this realm for and to the intent that he will not answer to such offense or offenses by him committed and done contrary to this act, that then every such willful and contemptuous person, avoiding or departing out of this realm, shall be adjudged a traitor, and his act high treason, and shall have and suffer such pains of death and also forfeit goods and chattels, lands and tenements, as in case of high treason: saving to all and singular person and persons, bodies politic and corporate, their heirs and successors, and to the heirs and successors of every of them, other than such person and persons, their heirs and successors, and the heirs and successors of every of them, that shall offend contrary to this act and thereupon obstinately, willingly or contemptuously avoid and depart out of this realm as is aforesaid, all such right, title, use, interest, rents, revisions, remainders, lease, leases, grants, annuities, offices, commons, profits, commodities, and other hereditaments whatsoever, in and to all and singular such honors, castles, manors, lands, tenements, and other hereditaments which any such offender or offenders shall have at the time of his or their offense or offenses of treason committed, or at any time after, in such like manner, form, and condition, to all intents, constructions, and purposes, as if this act had never been had or made; any thing contained in this act to the contrary in any wise notwithstanding.

And it is further enacted by authority aforesaid, that if any person or persons, offending contrary to this act, do willingly and contemptuously withdraw, absent, eloign, or secretly hide himself within any part of this realm or any of the King's dominions by the space of two months next after any writ or proclamation shall be made, directed and proclaimed against him or them as afore is rehearsed, and thereof by any convenient or reasonable mean may have knowledge, so that by eloigning of himself his offense cannot be examined, tried, and judged within the said time of 18 months, that then every such person and persons so offending shall stand and be as a person convicted of the offenses against him objected, and also lose and pay all and every such forfeiture, sums of money, and also suffer such imprisonment as to the same offense shall appertain.

And be it further enacted that if it happen our said sovereign lord the King to decease (whose life God long preserve) before such time as that person which shall be his next heir or successor to the imperial crown of this realm shall accomplish and come to the age of 18 years, that then all and singular proclamations which shall be in any wise made and set forth into any part of this realm or other the King's dominions by virtue of this act, within the foresaid years of the said next heir or successor, shall be set forth in the successor's name then being King, and shall import or bear underwritten the full names of such of the King's honorable council then being as shall be the devisers or setters forth of the same, which shall be in this case the whole number afore rehearsed, or at the least the more part of them, or else the proclamations to be void and of none effect.

Provided also that if any proclamation or proclamations hereafter shall be directed by virtue of this act to the justices of the peace of any shire or county, that then within 14 days after the receipt thereof the same justices shall and may by their discretions divide themselves in sundry parts and places within the limits of their commission for the due and speedy executions of the contents of the same proclamation or proclamations; and they and every of them doing or causing to be done with convenient speed in their limits as much as in them reasonably doth lie or rest to be done for the due and speedy execution of the same proclamation or proclamations, then every such of the same justices as so shall do his diligence or as much as in him reasonable resteth to be done, shall be discharged and exonerated against the King's highness, his heirs and successors, of and for every penalty or pain limited and appointed by the same proclamation to every of the same justices. Provided also that no justices of peace shall be charged hereafter by virtue of any such proclamations which or for any pain or penalty for not doing or executing of the same proclamations, but only in the shire or county where any such justices of peace shall or do inhabit, dwell, or be most conversant or abiding.

Provided also that the foresaid councilors appointed or to be appointed by virtue of this act or any part thereof, by the King's highness, his heirs or successors, to and for the hearing and determination of every offense committed contrary to any of his or their proclamation or proclamations, shall from time to time, knowing the King's determinate pleasure first therein, have full power and authority to diminish or mitigate the penalties of the sum or sums of money which shall be contained in any of the said proclamations hereafter to be made by the King's highness, his heirs or successors.

2.

An Act for the Due Execution of Proclamations
[34 & 35 Henry VIII, c. 23, 1542, *SR 3*, 923]

WHERE in the parliament holden at Westminster the 28th day of April in the 31st year of the King's most gracious reign that now is, and there continued till the 29th day of June then next ensuing, it was enacted amongst other things, by the King's majesty, with the assent of the lords spiritual and temporal and the commons in the said parliament assembled, and by the authority of the same parliament, that the King for the time being with the advice of his honorable council, whose names be mentioned in the same act, or with the advice of the more part [thereof], might set forth at all times, by the authority of the same act, his proclamations under such penalties and pains, and of such sort, as to his highness and his said honorable council, or the more part of them, should seem necessary and requisite, and that the same should be obeyed, observed, and kept, as though they were made by act of parliament, for the time in them limited, unless the King dispense with them or any of them under his Great Seal:

And it was then further enacted by the authority aforesaid, that if any person or persons of what estate, degree, or condition soever he or they be, which at any time from thenceforth did willfully offend and break, or obstinately not observe and keep, any such proclamation or any article therein contained which should proceed from the King's majesty by the advice of his council as is aforesaid, that [then] all and every such offender or offenders being thereof within one half year next after their or his offense committed, accused and thereof within 18 months next after the same convicted, by confession or lawful witness, [or] profess before the Archbishop of Canterbury, Metropolitan; the Chancellor of England; the Lord Treasurer of England; the President of the King's most honorable council; the Lord Privy Seal; and Great Chamberlain of England; the Lord Admiral; the Lord Steward, or Grand Master the Lord Chamberlain of the King's most honorable household; two other bishops being of the King's council, such as his grace shall appoint for the same; the Secretary, the Treasurer, and Comptroller of the King's most honorable household; the Master of the [horse]; the two Chief [Justices]; and the Master of the Rolls for the time being; the Chancellor of the Augmentations; the Chancellor of the Duchy; the Chief Baron of the Exchequer; the two General Surveyors; the Chancellor of the Exchequer; the Under-Treasurer of the same; the Treasurer of the King's Chamber for the time being; in the Star Chamber at Westminster, or elsewhere, or at the least before the half of the number afore rehearsed, of which number the Lord Chancellor; the Lord Treasurer; the Lord President of the King's most honorable council; the Lord Privy Seal; the Chamberlain of England; the Lord Admiral; the two Chief Judges for the time being; or two of them shall be two, shall lose and pay such penalties, forfeitures, or sums of money to be levied of his or their lands, tenements, goods, and chattels, to the King's use, and also suffer such imprisonment of his body as should be expressed, mentioned, and declared in any such proclamation or proclamations which such offender or offenders shall offend and break or not observe and keep contrary to the said act as is aforesaid, as by the same act more at large it may and doth appear:

Since the making of which said act the King's highness, with the advice of his said council, and according to the tenor and purport of the same act, hath, for the wealth, profit, and commodity of this his realm, caused divers good and [godly] proclamations to be made, which divers evil disposed persons have willfully and obstinately broken and not observed and kept, and thereupon divers and sundry informations have been given and had for the King against the same offenders before the said honorable council mentioned in the said act, according to the tenor and effect of the same act; and the same informations, after issue joined and witnesses published, have taken no effect, end, or perfect determination within the time limited by the same act, for and in default that there hath not been present so many of the King's said most honorable council as be limited and appointed by the same act; and so thereby offenders have been, and be like hereafter, to be unpunished, to the great encouraging of all such like offenders.

Wherefore be it [ordained and enacted] by the King our sovereign lord, with the assent of the lords spiritual and temporal and the commons in this present parliament assembled, and by the authority of the same, that all and every judgment, sentence, or decree hereafter to be had, taken, made, or given against any person or persons, in or upon any information, suit, or plaint concerning any offense or offenses done or committed, or hereafter to be done or committed, against the tenor, purport, or effect of any such proclamation, according to the true intent and meaning of the said former act, shall or may be given, had, and made by the said council, or any number of them, so there be then present the full number of nine persons of the said council, whereof the Lord Chancellor; the Lord Treasurer; the Lord President of the King's most honorable council; the Lord Privy Seal; the Chamberlain of England; the Lord Admiral; the two Chief Judges for the time being; or two of them at the least shall be two; and that the same judgment, sentence, or decree, so had, made, or given as is aforesaid, shall, by the authority aforesaid, be and stand good and available in the law, and of like force and effect in all and every thing and things contained or mentioned in the said former act, to all intents, constructions, and purposes, as if the same judgment or decree were given or made by the number of the said council appointed in the said former act, any clause, sentence, article, or matter in the same former act contained to the contrary hereof notwithstanding.

And this act to endure during the King's majesty's life, which Our Lord long preserve.

3.

An Act for the Repeal of Certain Statutes
Concerning Treasons, Felonies, etc.
[1 Edward VI, c. 12, 1547, *SR* 4(1), 19]

IV. AND be it also ordained and enacted by the authority aforesaid that one act made in the parliament holden at Westminster, in the 31st year of the reign of the said late King Henry the eighth, that proclamations made by the King's highness by the advice of his honorable council should be obeyed and kept as though they were made by authority of parliament, and also one other act made in the parliament holden in the 34th year of the reign of the said late King Henry the eighth, for the due execution of the said proclamations, and also all and every branch, article, and matter in the same statutes and in every of them mentioned or declared, shall from henceforth be repealed and utterly made void and of none effect.

Appendix ii. Proclamation 14a

Controlling Exchange Rates at Calais
[Westminster, before 20 August 1487, 3 Henry VII]

Campbell *2*, 195: date, 30 September; writs to lieutenant, deputy, and mayor of Calais; schedule as below. Pollard *2*, 275: omits textual reference to 20 August. Steele 8*a:* date, ca. July. Text: Campbell.

FORASMUCH as the King our sovereign lord Henry by the grace of God etc., considering how that in the time of his noble progenitor Edward IV, late King of England, for the public weal of the town and marches of Calais and the subjects and the inhabitants of the same, divers ordinances and establishments were ordained and made for and upon the course of all manner of coins of gold and silver, as well of the realm of England as of all other parts, and thereupon by the council of the said late King esteemed, rated, and valued, as more plainly appeareth in a table remaining in the Staple of the said town of Calais; and every coin in the said table specified, as well of gold as of silver, to have course within the said town and marches, for every 20*s.* sterling 30*s.* Flemish, and 30*s.* Flemish for every 20*s.*, and not above; and also how the aforesaid ordinances and establishments be now of late broken and discontinued, and all manner of coins have course within the said town and marches at over great and exceeding value and price, to the great damage of our said sovereign lord, and in especial of the subjects and inhabitants of the said town and marches:

For redress and reformation whereof, our said sovereign lord, by the advice of his council, straightly chargeth and commandeth that no manner of person or persons, of what estate, degree, or condition he or they be of, receive nor pay, privily nor apertly, within the said town and marches of Calais, for any manner of victual, merchandise to be bought or sold, house rent, or any other thing, whatsoever it shall be, any of the said coins in the aforesaid table specified, but after the rate of 30*s.* Flemish for the 20*s.* sterling, and the 20*s.* sterling for the 30*s.* Flemish, and not above, after the 20th day of August next coming; upon pain of forfeiture of all such coins to be paid or received, that one half of every such forfeiture to the King, and that other half to the finder of the same; and also that no man, upon pain of imprisonment of their bodies at the King's will, from henceforth receive nor utter any new devised coins brought or to be brought unto the said town and marches, for any victuals, merchandise, or other thing, as is above said, unto such time as by the advice of the King's council esteemed, rated and valued after the value of the coins specified in the foresaid table; and also that all victuals be priced and set after the rate and value of the said coins.

Glossary

[Proclamation text numbers are given for single special uses of a term]

Glossary

Abase reduce
Action of debt legal process to recover a debt
Adventure risk, 255, 259, 263, 266, 269
Adventurers mercenaries, 246
Advertise inform
Aids customary feudal payments and services rendered to a lord by his tenants
Albainns Scots
Alienation transfer of property title
Alleving aiding
Almain German
Almain rivet flexible German armor
Alnager collector of tax on woolen cloth
Amercement fine
Ancient demesne originally crown land
Ancients senior members of the Inns-of-Court
Angel noble English gold coin valued at 7*s.* 6*d.* in 1526, 112; 8*s.* in 1544, 228; 9*s.* 8*d.* in 1549, 326; 10*s.* in 1551, 382
Angelet English gold coin valued at 5*s.* in 1551, 382
Apatising extending peace in return for tribute
Apert open
Appearance attendance in court on the day prescribed, 60
Approof assay, 27
Archil violet dyestuff
Aretted imputed
As of fee with full dominion, 311
Assoil absolve
Attach arrest
Attaint declare in legal corruption
At the water testing the true length and breadth of woolen cloth by wetting and stretching it on a frame
Auncel weight weighing device made of wood

Baggers loaders of grain into bags
Banks a notorious section of London, 250
Baron court manorial court
Barretor disturber of the peace
Bastard plover lapwing
Bearing unlawful coercion
Bell metal copper-tin alloy
Benchers senior and governing members of the Inns-of-Court
Benches Courts of King's Bench and Common Pleas
Benevolences compulsory money contributions to the King
Best advantage highest ransom, 73
Bill hand-bill, 374; military weapon, 16, 213; written statement, 73
Billet safe-conduct, 73; small firewood, 226; written pass, 128
Black tin smelted tin, 27
Blessed bread unconsecrated ceremonial bread
Boiled submerged in hot dye solution to insure even and fast color
Brawn tough muscular cuts of flesh meat, 81
Brazil red dyestuff obtained from brazilwood
Break bulk open packed goods for purpose of sale
Breech flesh side of a sheepskin
Brew snipe
Brogger jobber
Brotherhoods guilds
Burseholder head market officer
By tale counted by a teller, 382

Cantred administrative unit containing 100 Welsh townships
Capias writ of arrest
Capitulations agreements, 362
Carolus Flemish gold coin valued at 6*s.* 10*d.*, in 1522, 95; in 1525, 102, 103
Carter cart loader
Cask ale and beer
Cassing discharging
Cast annoyance evacuate
Catherine, St., Feast of 30 April
Cautel and policy craftiness
Cessed priced, 115; rated, 73, 326
Chancery office of the King's chancellor
Chantry priest priest receiving a pension from an endowment fund
Chapman itinerant merchant
Chevisance unlawful evasion of laws against usury
Cinque Ports Dover, Sandwich, Romney, Hastings, and Hythe. Ordinarily the King's writ did not apply to these liberties
Clement, St., Feast of 23 November
Clockettes rough wool
Closes fenced areas
Closh game of bowls
Cofferer steward of the royal household
Cognizance device for recognition, 62; insignia, 73; knowledge, 122
Collations conferences
Colleges clerical institutions expropriated in 1547 by 1 Edward VI, c. 14
Collegiate church church having a chapter of canons
Collincliff light cavalry lance
Commissary bishop's agent
Commissions of array writs for mustering military forces
Commission of oyer and terminer writ authorizing a judge to hold court
Common players actors
Common Pleas one of the four superior courts at Westminster having exclusive jurisdiction in pleas between subject and subject
Commons manor land used in common for grazing purposes
Commote administrative unit comprising fifty Welsh villages
Commutation exchange
Compromitted pledged to mutual action
Conceit unlawful means
Conduct money travel allowance
Cony European rabbit
Congé permission
Contemn ignore, 168, 297
Convocation church council
Copyhold real estate title based on a court record
Cordwainers leather workers
Cork brownish hue, 328
Corodies pensions paid from sums of money due the crown by religious houses
Course circulation
Courser inspector, 331
Court of Augmentations court established by 27 Henry VIII, c. 27, having jurisdiction over the properties and incomes of suppressed religious houses
Court of Chancery the King's Chancellor's court, possessing the largest equitable powers and jurisdiction in England
Court of record any court whose acts were written into permanent public record
Court of Rome Holy See
Covert baron married woman
Covin deceit
Cranage fee for use of crane in unloading ships
Crastino day following
Crastino Animarum 3 November, the day following All Souls
Crastino Trinitatus Monday after Trinity Sunday
Crayer small trading ship
Cries proclamations and orders
Crown English gold coin, valued at 5*s.*, 321, 326, 382
Crown (*not* soleil) French gold coin, valued at 4*s.* in 1522–25, 88, 95, 102,

103; at 4*s*. 6*d*. in 1526, 111; at 4*s*. in 1537, 178; at 4*s*. in 1538, 180

Crown of the double rose English gold coin, valued at 5*s*. in 1526, 112

Crown of the rose English gold coin, valued at 4*s*. 6*d*. in 1526, 111

Crown of the sun (soleil) French gold coin, valued at 4*s*. 4*d*. in 1522, 88, 95; at 4*s*. 4*d*. in 1525, 102; at 4*s*. 6*d*. in 1526, 111, 112; at 7*s*. in 1550, 364; at 6*s*. 4*d*. in 1550, 367

Crown of the sun, dolphin French gold coin, valued at 4*s*. 8*d*. in 1537, 178; at 4*s*. 8*d*. in 1538, 180

Crown of the sun, porpentine French gold coin, valued at 4*s*. 4*d*. in 1525; at 4*s*. 8*d*. in 1537, 178; at 4*s*. 8*d*. in 1538, 180

Cry havoc shout order to pillage and destroy

Cummer waste

Cum privilego regali with royal permission

Curase body armor

Customer collector of duties

Customs of merchandise taxes on goods

Customs of strangers fees levied upon foreign merchants

Custos rotulorum keeper of public records

Cwt. hundredweight (112 lbs.)

Dag handgun

Damped rejected

Day of the essoins usually the first day of any of the four court terms

Decay diminution

Defended forbidden, 311

Deliberate reasoned, 268

Demeaned employed, 62

Demeaning conduct, 46

Demesne crown real property

Demilance light lance

Demise inheritance from will, 195; lease, 338

Demurrant dwelling temporarily

Denizen licensed alien resident

Denounced declared, 126

Deodand something "given to God," that is, forfeited to the crown for pious use

Deprehend detect and apprehend

Devoir duty

Devoured wasted, 58

Dight winnow

Disannuling voiding, 332

Discharge and recharge unload and load ships, 18

Disgarnished dispossessed, 112

Disme parliamentary subsidy theoretically equal to one tenth of the value of one's personal property

Dispurveyed left with insufficient food

Distraint legal constraint

Dolphin gold coin stamped with image of a dolphin

Dotterel European plover

Double ducat non-English gold coin valued at 9*s*. 4*d*. in 1526, 111; at 10*s*. in 1537, 178; 10*s*. in 1538, 180

Double mark metal marking piece

Double plack Burgundian coin valued at 4*d*. in 1526, 112

Dowager Catherine Parr, 287

Drayers cattle drivers and carters

Dressing altering, 56

Ducat non-English gold coin valued at 4*s*. 6*d*. in 1522, 88; 1525, 95, 102, 103; 4*s*. 8*d*. in 1526, 111; 5*s*. in 1537, 178; 5*s*. in 1538, 180

Duchy Chamber King's Chancellor's court to determine cases relating to land tenure in the Duchy of Lancaster

Eared cultivated

Easterling merchant engaged in the Baltic trade

Edward's royal English gold coin valued at 10*s*. in 1549, 321

Elyn (Helen), St., Feast of 3 May

Embattling preparing a castle for war

Embracery corruption of a jury, 60, 77

Endwools trimmings

Enforce criminally assault

Enfranchise grant privileges

Enhardied emboldened, 318
Entertainment service for wages, 319
Escheator official certifying estates forfeited to the crown
Essoin excuse for non-appearance
Exacted enacted, 300
Exaltation of the Holy Cross 14 September
Exigent writ of outlawry
Eyre by writ

Factor agent
Faith pledge, 73
Falsing counterfeiting, 302
Farm lands rented lands, 338
Fautor favorer
Feat act, 76, 133, 191; occupation, 115
Fell sheepskin
15th of Michaelmas the 15th day following the Feast of St. Michael; October 14
15th of the Holy Trinity the 15th day following Trinity Sunday
Find provide food and lodging, 73, 151
Finding supplying, 242
Flemish halberd battle-axe
Flemish toll Low Country tax on foreign goods
Flocks wool dust or shearings used to improve the appearance of finished cloth, 198, 328
Floren Holy Roman Empire import duty on wool
Florin, large English base gold coin, valued at 3*s.* 3*d.*, 1522–25, 95, 102, 103; *small,* 2*s.* 1*d.*, 1522–25, 95, 102, 103
Foin thrust
Foison abundance
Foist wooden cask
Font-stone baptismal font
Forcery forced laborer
Foreigns unincorporated areas within a sheriff's jurisdiction, 63
Forel parchment for binding books, 336
Foreprised excepted beforehand
Forestalling speculative purchase of goods en route to market
Four houses of court Inner Temple, Middle Temple, Lincoln's Inn, and Gray's Inn, 294
Franc-archers longbowmen
Franchises places legally exempt
Fraternities organizations incorporated for pious purposes, 316
Free gate liberty to enter and depart, 291
Freehold real estate title of uncertain duration
Fuller craftsman trained to make wool cloth thick and full
Furniture attendance by those elected, 256; fittings, 235; supply, 225, 243, 258

Gabel excise tax
Garner granary, 118; take possession of, 242
Gentility paganism
George noble English gold coin valued at 6*s.* 8*d.* in 1526, 112
George, St., Feast of 23 April
Gildable taxable
Godwit shore bird
Grafters those seeking illicit profits
Grail book of church services
Grain or powder scarlet dyestuff obtained from the dried bodies of the insect cochineal, 328
Grained dyed prior to weaving, 328
Grazier cattle feeder
Great bird bustard
Great Turk Suliman II, 220
Green geese young geese
Green plover small shore bird
Groat English silver coin valued at 4*d.*, 1504, 54; 1544, 228; debased to 3*d.* in 1551, 372; that of value of 3*d.* debased to 2*d.* in 1551, 379; that of value of 2*d.* to 1*d.*, that of 1*d.* to ½*d.*, that of ½*d.* debased to ¼*d.* in 1551, 379
Guild priest priest retained by artisans' and merchants' fellowships for religious services

Hack handgun
Half-angel noble English gold coin, valued

at 3*s.* 9*d.* in 1526, 112; at 4*s.* in 1544, 228; 4*s.* 10*d.* in 1549, 326

Half-crown English gold coin, valued at 2*s.* 6*d.*, 1549–51, 321, 382; of the double rose, 2*s.* 6*d.*, 1526, 112; of the sun (French, gold), 2*s.* 4*d.* in 1538, 178

Half-crown of the sun, porpentine and dolphin French gold coins, valued at 2*s.* 4*d.* in 1537, 178; 2*s.* 4*d.* in 1538, 180

Half-George noble English gold coin, valued at 3*s.* 4*d.* in 1526, 112

Half-groat English silver coin, valued at 2*d.* in 1544, 228

Half-passage money fee for entering port

Half-penny of the single rose English base metal coin, valued at ½*d.* in 1551, 382

Hallow tide first week of November

Hand-in and Hand-out game of hand-ball

Hanse association of German merchants

Harbinger official to provide lodging

Harborage lodging place

Hardy impure, 27

Harness armor

Havior estate or degree, 35, 73, 137

Headborough petty constable

Head money poll tax

Head-piece helmet

Hedger maker of hedge fence

Hen of Greece sterilized female chicken

Hernshaw heron

Hilary, St., Feast of 13 January

Hindershanks low grade wool

Holy Trinity eighth Sunday after Easter

Homilies Cf. *STC* 13,639, *Certayne Sermons or Homilies, appoynted by the Kinges Maiestie to be Declared and Read by All Parsons, Vicars, or Curates euery Sondaye in their Churches* (R. Grafton, London, 31 July 1547)

Honor estate held under the King

Horse meat fodder

Housel Eucharist

Hoy small passenger ship

Hulk heavy ship

Hundred originally, subdivision of 100 freeholders

Husbands tillers of the soil, 63

Iceland fleet English North Atlantic fishing fleet

Impedite obstruct, 218

Impetrate obtain on plea or entreaty

Importable intolerable, 24, 177, 310

Imposition import tax, 45

Inbarde attack

Incontinently immediately, 74, 121

Indenture formal contract, 46

Infangthef lord's right to try a suspected thief apprehended on his estate

Infold enroll

Insinuate report privately, 309

Interdict papal censure disallowing public religious services

Invention of the Cross, Feast of 3 May

Irish groat silver coin, minted for use in Ireland. Did not circulate legally in England. Valued at 2*d.* in 1540, 197

Irish pence (harp) coin, minted for use of the English armed forces in Ireland. Not circulated in England, 197

Jail delivery clearing of a jail by trying of the prisoners

John the Baptist, St., Feast of 24 June

Justice of assize and nisi prius circuit judge of the superior courts

Kailes game of bowls

King's Bench highest common law court of England

Kynkernell trading privilege from the Holy Roman Emperor

Laid down razed, 338

Law days days on which a local court was customarily held

Lawrence, St., Feast of 10 August

Leam navigable stream

Leet royally chartered lord's court

Legate de latere papal envoy

Legend book of saints' lives

Lents forty days, as in the period of penance preceding Easter, 84

Let allow, 115; hinder, 13, 17, 33, 35, 56, 66, 67, 70, 73, 77, 82, 86, 115, 116, 118,

120, 130, 134, 139, 140, 154, 181, 184, 185, 215, 218, 296, 311, 370; oppose, 93; rent, 56, 195, 265, 273

Letted not did not hesitate, 65

Letters missive written authorization

Letters patent open document issued by crown authority

Lewd evil, 333, 334, 337, 372, 374; ignorant, 160, 329

Lewd tales rumors and lies

Liberties convenience, 116

Lincoln, use (church rite) of. See *Use*

Ling codfish

Livery employment, 195, 199

Locks, shearlocks, 253

Lollards originally the followers of John Wycliffe; loosely applied to religious radicals in the 16th century

Long seas sea route from eastern England to Ireland

Lord legate Thomas Cardinal Wolsey, 119

Lordship royal domain held by grant of the King

Lots and scots local tax for poor relief

Luke, St., Feast of 8 October

Maddered upon the wood crimson (madder) added to the blue dye of woad

Mainprize surety bond similar to bail money

Maintenance interference in legal action involving others, 60; supporting and arming a retinue, 77

Mal engine evil contrivance

Manred leadership and government

Manual handbook of prayers

Manuring tilling

Marbles mixed colors

March wool of the northern borders

Marcher officer responsible for the defense of a border area

Mark, St., Feast of 7 October

Mark a money of account originally of the value of a mark of silver (13*s.* 4*d.*)

Marshalsea Southwark prison

Martin, St., Feast of 11 November

Mary Magdalen, St., Feast of 22 July

Maslin mixture of wheat and rye

Maugh in-law, or companion

Mean between, 212; standard, 328

Mean tenant sub-leaser

Meddled with worked upon, 253

Meed bribery

Merchants Adventurer members of a royally chartered international trade company

Merchants of the Staple merchants of a royally chartered central market

Merchants stranger foreign merchants

Mere pure, 158; solely, 64

Mese house and its appurtenances

Meter counter or gauger of merchandise and cargo, 115; measure, 56

Mew cage

Michael, St., the Archangel, Feast of 29 September

Michaelmas court term October 6 to November 25

Mighty beggars vagrants able to work

Mints the coins of a single minting, 382

Mise privilege purchased from the crown

Misuse noyous abuse of a right granted by the King

Misprision guilty knowledge

Moten judged

Mowe be able to

Muciana surety bond

Narrows cloth woven in ribbon width, 328

Narrow Sea English Channel

New fangles new and transient things, 121

Nicholas, St., Feast of 6 December

Noble English gold coin valued at 7*s.* 4*d.* in 1526, 111

Obeisance obedience

Obligation performance bond

Occupy use, 328; utilize, 218

Octave 21 January, 118

Offering of chrisoms offering to the church the equivalent to the value of the infant's baptismal garment

Old royal English gold coin, valued at 14*s.* 6*d.* in 1549, 326
Orators representatives, 21
Ordinal book of directives for daily church service
Ordinaries staff, 348
Ordinary prelate having ecclesiastical jurisdiction, 188
Orison collect, oration, prayer
Overthwarting opposing, 373

Packer baler of wool for sale by the Staple
Packhouse warehouse
Pales poles or posts, 110
Paraphrases of Erasmus *STC* 2854. Desiderius Erasmus, *First Tome of the Paraphrases Upon the New Testament* (E. Whitchurch, London, 31 January 1549)
Parcel area of command, 73
Pardoner itinerant preacher appointed to collect funds for a religious purpose through the offer of Indulgences
Parlement of Paris superior judicial court of France
Parliamentary Act of 31 Henry VIII Statute of Proclamations, 31 Henry VIII, c. 8
Park enclosed area
Passellys rejected wool
Patise to extend truce for tribute
Patisement covenanting, 325
Peachicken young of the pea-fowl
Peisage weighing fee
Pence, mullet, and spur English silver coins, debased to ½*d.*, 1499, 44; 1505, 57
Pence of the double rose English silver coin, issued by Edward VI in 1551, 382
Pence of 2d. English silver coins, 25, 112
Percase perchance
Personage physical capacity, 250
Picard toothed iron tool for raising the nap on cloth
Pieces territories, 269, 365
Pier port
Pilgrimage of Grace insurrection of 1536 centered in the northern counties
Pill rob
Pilleries pillages by soldiers, 120
Pioneers military scouts, 73
Pipe cask holding 126 wine gallons
Places of marks, pricks, and butts target ranges, 194
Plagues punishments, 371
Plain full, 17
Pocket bundle, 45
Poise weight
Poll by head, alive, 139
Polled despoiled, 250
Polling cheating, 325
Polren shoulder armor
Porcaste book of prayer
Porpentine gold coin stamped with the image of a porpoise
Porters of places gate-keepers, 73
Portreeve royal port official
Pottle half a wine gallon
Pound in 1543, one pound of silver, 10 ounces fine, was coined to 48*s.*; one pound of gold, 23 carats fine, to £28 16*s.* In 1544 the silver was weakened to six ounces fine and the gold to 22 carats; in 1545 the silver was 40 ounces fine and the gold 20 carats. One pound (£1) as money of account was equal to 20*s.*
Praemunire illegal appeal to ecclesiastical authority, 60
Predial landed, 153
Press device for smoothing of woolen cloth to impart a more finished appearance, 328; draft for military or marine service, 221
Pressed to serve paid for future service, 244
Prest forced loan, 55
Prests moneys paid for men drafted into military service, 20, 330
Primed and well-stricken of highest grade marbled with fat, 336
Promoters initiators of legal action, 59

Protections monopolies granted under royal writ, 91
Provision collection, 263, 266; supply, 264
Provost head of cathedral or collegiate chapter
Puncheon cask holding 84 wine gallons
Purification of the Blessed Virgin. Candlemas
Purlieu royal forest land used for other purposes
Purtenance animal organs used for food, 81
Purvey produce, 62; purchase for the King, 66
Purveyors of the ordnance procurers of military supplies, 73
Pye book of rules to ascertain the proper daily church service

Quarter-angel noble English gold coin, valued at 2*s.* in 1544, 228
Quarter Days 25 March, 24 June, 29 September, 25 December
Quickboard game of darts
Quindecim parliamentary subsidy to the King, theoretically equal to one-fifteenth of the value of the subject's personal property
Quindene fifteenth day following
Quint a fifth part
Quippage ship's gear, 120
Quorum select body of justices of peace

Raisure system of weights and measures
Rape subdivision intermediate between a hundred and a shire, 242, 365, 366
Ravin take by force, 167
Ravishment of ward marriage to an infant ward without the guardian's consent; also, expropriation of a ward's property or income, 60
Rays striped cloth, 328
Receptors patrons
Regrating speculative purchase of goods on the market
Rehearsed stated, 140, 227
Rent-corn annual payment of grain by the renter to the landlord
Reputed a bastard declared illegitimate for purposes of escheat, 45
Rollwain cart
Roman groat Imperial silver coin, valued at 2*d.* in 1498, 39
Roman pence. See *Roman groat*
Rooms areas of jurisdiction, 62
Rowing cloth raising the nap of newly finished cloth
Royal English gold coin, valued at 11*s.* in 1526, 111; at 11*s.* 3*d.* in 1526, 112; at 12*s.* in 1544, 228; 14*s.* 6*d.* in 1549, 326
Rumney sweet wine of Greece
Russet neutral brown or grey dye

Salt hides unfinished leather
Sandgeld beach rent
Sang royal royal family of France, 104
Sarum, use (church rite) of. See *Use*
Scry cry of panic, 13, 73
Scunage haven
Scutage payment in lieu of a knight's military service
Searcher customs officer appointed to search in suspect places for contraband
Seigniories domains
Serpler bale
Sewers court established pursuant to 6 Henry VIII, c. 10, with jurisdiction in matters pertaining to public health, 70; drains, 274
Shearlocks short wool, 253
Shewel scarecrow used in hunting deer
Shilling English silver coin, valued at 12*d.* in 1549, 321; debased to 9*d.* in 1551, 372; to 6*d.* in the same year, 379; minted by Edward VI in values of 12*d.* and 6*d.* in 1551, 382. Edward also minted silver coins valued at 5*s.* and 2*s.* in 1551, 382
Shoveler river duck
Showhouse place for displaying merchandise

Sign manual official royal signature
Single ducat non-English gold coin, valued at 5*s.* in 1538, 178, 180
Skepynbreef writ of delay from the Holy Roman Emperor
Slip skinning of a beast, 278
Small and thin wines of lower alcoholic content
Snite snipe
Soleil French gold coin, stamped with a sun
Soller garret (sollar)
Sore hawk yearling hawk
Sovereign English gold coin, valued at 22*s.* in 1526, 111; at 22*s.* 6*d.* in 1526, 112; at 20*s.* 1544–51, 228, 321, 326, 382; minted by Edward VI in 1551 at 30*s.*, 382
Sped fulfilled, 215
Spurs riding spurs engraved on coin, 44
Stall station
Stamin coarse woolen cloth
Staple royally chartered central market
Stapled rated and charged with duty, 27
Star Chamber ancient prerogative court remodeled by 3 Henry VII, c. 1, and 21 Henry VIII, c. 20
Statute of Provisors and Praemunire 16 Richard II, and 25 Edward III, st. 4
Statute of Winchester 13 Edward I
Staves crosspieces extending to the edge of coin, 57
Stay frame for stretching unfinished cloth, 166; stable force, 342
Steelyard establishment of the German Hanse merchants in London
Stipend priest (*stipendiary*) priest receiving a specific grant for specified religious services
Stittes unlawful assemblies and riots
Stockfish unsalted, dried fish
Stop fill, 198
Stover fodder
Strait cloth of single, unfolded width
Subsidy parliamentary grant to the King
Suckers sucklings
Sureties performance bonds, 151
Table of God communion rail or table
Tables game of backgammon
Tails beards on grain, 259
Taken in farm agreed to pay rent, 338
Takers or purveyors royal purchasing agents, 365
Talwood firewood cut to size
Tare administrative allowance, 65
Taxed rated, 368, 380; stipulated, 200
Tenements property rights
Tenths and First Fruits court established by 26 Henry VIII, c. 13
Teston English silver coin, valued at 12*d.* in 1544, 228; removed from circulation in 1548, 302, 321, 322. See also *shilling*
Thirds shares of ransom money, 73
Thomas (Becket) the Martyr, St., Feast of 29 December
Three Estates of France Estates General, 104
Tierce cask holding 42 wine gallons
Tithe customary payments to the parish church
Tithing men local peace officers
Toller collector of tolls
Toss jostle and wrestle, 292
Touched assayed and earmarked, 168
Tourn sheriff's circuit court
Tournal book of evening prayer
Tower weight system of weights for precious metals so-called because the standard pound, weighing 16 ounces, was kept in the Tower of London
Town of war garrison town, 56
Train attendants, 160; trickery, 325
Traverse money fee for passing through a country
Traverses actions to deny allegation or delay trial
Treasure trove treasure of unknown ownership
Tres semaines three weeks after
Trinity term court term of 22 May to 12 June
Truck barter for a right, 172
Truck silver bribe, 172

Tucker craftsman pleating and folding cloth
Tumbril chair used in punishment of misdemeanors
Tun cask holding 252 wine gallons
Tuition protection, 212
Tutelage guardianship, 89

Uncausable impossible, 373
Unfurnished bereft, 236; unsupplied, 241
Unmarked not registered, 168
Unneth scarcely
Upon hand in training for hunting, 211
Ure exercise, 59; operation, 281; use, 309, 322, 325, 326, 327, 329
Use engage in trade, 63; treat, 220; the form of Roman liturgy followed in certain areas, as Bangor (Wales), Sarum (south and central England), and York, 353
Utas octave or eighth day following
Utfangthef lord's right to try anyone with stolen goods in his possession regardless of the place of arrest
Utter absolute, 280, 333, 381; circulate, 272, 322, 326, 332, 367; distribute, 24, 139, 159, 162, 186, 213, 366, 378, 386; exchange, 25, 197, 302; issue, 57; proffer for sale, 196, 224, 226, 231, 232, 239, 297, 346, 365
Utter barrister outer (not yet admitted to privileged position within the bar)
Utterance offering for sale 368

Valiant able to work, 161; sturdy, 118
Valor of the marriage the value, in money, of the marriage of a ward, 60
Valors values, 379
Vambrace armor for the forearm
Verge privileged area around the royal court
Vert trees and greenery
Vicine neighboring
Videndum written document
Visitors official representatives of the King, 299
Voucher official responsible for certification of taxable merchandise entering port

Wager of law defense by oath-helpers
Wage his law base legal defense on character witnesses, 366
Waifs and strays unclaimed domestic animals or objects, 60
Wapentake administrative subdivision of the shires of Lincoln, Derby, Leicester, Nottingham, and parts of York
Ward custody, 16, 73, 88, 95, 101, 111, 112, 115, 127, 145, 164, 168, 180, 228, 321, 329, 331; guard, 73, 325; prison, 73, 213; subdivision of a city or town represented by an alderman, 132, 364; surveillance, 73
Wards and Liveries court established by 32 Henry VIII, c. 46
Wardens of fellowships head guild officers
Warden of the passage port official
Warrant proof, 296
Warren conservation area for wild game
Washlocks wool fiber gathered after washing sheep for shearing
Welleth amounts to, 227
Wharfgeld fee for space on a wharf, dock, or pier
White meats non-flesh foods derived from animals, as butter, milk, or eggs
White money silver coins
Wicks buildings for drying and storing grain
Winning loot and ransom, 73
Woolfells sheepskins
Wreck de mer right to wrecked ships and goods washed ashore
Writ of attachment court order to the sheriff to detain specified parties or attach their properties
Writ of nisi prius royal writ for assembly of a jury

Bibliography

Adair, Edward R., ed., *The Sources for the History of the Council in the Sixteenth and Seventeenth Centuries,* New York, Macmillan, 1924.

———, "The Statute of Proclamations," *English Historical Review, 32* (1917), 34–46.

Adams, George B., and Henry M. Stephens, eds., *Select Documents of English Constitutional History,* New York, Macmillan, 1901.

Allen, John W., *A History of Political Thought in the Sixteenth Century,* London, Methuen, 1928.

Anson, William R., *The Law and Custom of the Constitution,* 2 vols. Oxford, 1886–92.

Arber, Edward, ed., *A Transcript of the Registers of the Company of Stationers of London, 1554–1640 A.D.,* 5 vols. London and Birmingham, 1875–94.

Attenborough, F. L., ed. and trans., *Laws of the Earliest English Kings,* Cambridge, Cambridge University Press, 1922.

Bacon, Francis, *The History of the Reign of King Henry the Seventh* (1622), ed. J. R. Lumby, Cambridge, 1876.

Bagwell, Richard, *Ireland under the Tudors,* 3 vols. London, 1885–90.

Bainton, Roland H., *The Reformation of the Sixteenth Century,* Boston, Beacon Press, 1952.

Baldwin, James F., *The King's Council in England during the Middle Ages,* Oxford, Clarendon Press, 1913.

Barraclough, Geoffrey, "Law and Legislation in Medieval England," *Law Quarterly Review, 56* (1940), 75–92.

Baskerville, Geoffrey, *English Monks and the Suppression of the Monasteries,* New Haven, Yale University Press, 1937.

Baumer, Franklin L., *The Early Tudor Theory of Kingship,* New Haven, Yale University Press, 1940.

Bayne, Charles G. and William H. Dunham, Jr., eds., *Select Cases in the Council of Henry VII,* Selden Society Publications, 75, London, B. Quaritch, 1958.

Beard, Charles A., *The Office of Justice of the Peace in England in Its Origin and Development,* London, P. S. King, 1904.

Bibliotheca Lindesiana. See Crawford, James Ludovic Lindsay, Earl of; Steele, Robert.

Beveridge, William, *Prices and Wages in England from the Twelfth to the Nineteenth Century,* London, Longmans, Green, 1939.

Bills, Docquet-Book of Signed Bills Used as Warrants for the Great Seal, 1550–53, BM MS Royal 18.C.xxiv.

Bindoff, Stanley T., *Tudor England,* Harmondsworth, Middlesex, C. Nicholls, 1950.

———, *Ket's Rebellion,* London, G. Philip, 1949.

Blackstone, William, *Commentaries on the Laws of England,* 4 vols. Oxford, 1765–69.

The Boke of the Common Prayer, London, R. Grafton, June 1549, STC 16,275.

———, London, E. Whitchurch, 1552, *STC* 16,280.

———, London, E. Whitchurch, 1552, *STC* 16,282.

Brenner, Y. S., "The Inflations of Prices in Early Sixteenth Century England," *Economic History Review,* 2d series, *14* (1960–61), 225–39.

Brewer, John S., *The Reign of Henry VIII, from His Accession to the Death of Wolsey,* ed. James Gairdner, 2 vols. London, 1884.

———, et al., eds., *Letters and Papers, Foreign and Domestic, of the Reign of Henry VIII, 1509–47,* 21 vols, in 35 parts, London, H.M.S.O., 1862–1910; 2d ed. of Vol. 1, ed. Robert H. Brodie, 3 vols. London, H.M.S.O., 1920 (used in this edition for 1509–14); *Addenda,* 1 vol. in 2 parts, London, H.M.S.O., 1929, 1932.

British Museum Library, MS Additional 9835.

———, MS Arundel 26.

———, MS Cleopatra E. 5.

———, MSS Harleian 352, 442.

———, MSS Julius B. 1, B. 12.

———, MS Royal 18, C. xxiv.

———, MS Sloane 747.

———, MS Titus B. 2.

Brodie, Robert H. See Brewer, John S., et al.

Burnet, Gilbert, *The History of the Reformation of the Church of England,* ed. Nicholas Pocock, 7 vols. Oxford, 1865.

Calendar of Close Rolls: Henry VII, Vol. 1, 1485–1500, London, H.M.S.O., 1955.

Calendar of Patent Rolls: Edward VI, ed. Robert H. Brodie, 6 vols. London, H.M.S.O., 1914–29.

Calendar of Patent Rolls: Henry VII, 1485–94, eds. J. G. Black et al., 2 vols. London, H.M.S.O., 1914–16.

Calendar of State Papers Domestic: Edward VI, Vol. 1, ed. Robert Lemon, London, Longmans, Green, 1856.

Calendar of State Papers Foreign: Edward VI, ed. William B. Turnbull, London, 1861.

Calendar of State Papers . . . Rome, ed. J. M. Rigg, 2 vols. London, H.M.S.O., 1916–26.

Calendar of State Papers Spanish: Henry VII to Edward VI, eds. G. A. Bergenroth et al., 12 vols. London, H.M.S.O., 1866–1916.

Calendar of State Papers Venetian: Henry VII to Edward VI, Vols. 1–5, ed. Rawdon Brown, London, 1864–73.

Callendar, Geoffrey, "The Evolution of Sea-Power under the First Two Tudors," *History,* new series, 5 (1920–21), 141–58.

Campbell, John C., *The Lives of the Lord Chancellors and Keepers of the Great Seal of England, from the Earliest Times till the Reign of George IV,* 7 vols. London, 1845–47.

Campbell, William, ed., *Materials for a History of the Reign of Henry VII,* 2 vols. London, 1873–77.

Cardwell, Edward, ed., *Documentary Annals of the Reformed Church of England,* 1546–1716, 2 vols. Oxford, 1844.

———, *The Reformation of the Ecclesiastical Laws as Attempted in the Reigns of King Henry VIII, King Edward VI, and Queen Elizabeth,* Oxford, 1850.

Caspari, Fritz, *Humanism and the Social Order in Tudor England,* Chicago, University of Chicago Press, 1954.

Chapman, Hester W., *The Last Tudor King: A Study of Edward VI,* New York, Macmillan, 1959.

Cheyney, Edward P., ed., *Readings in English History Drawn from the Original Sources,* 2d ed. New York, Ginn, 1922.

Chrimes, Stanley B., *English Constitutional Ideas in the Fifteenth Century,* Cambridge, Cambridge University Press, 1936.

———, "Sir John Fortescue and His Theory of Dominion," *Transactions of the Royal Historical Society,* 4th series, *17* (1934), 117–47.

Constable, Robert, *Praerogativa Regis,* ed. Samuel E. Thorne, New Haven, Yale University Press, 1949.

Constant, Gustave, *The Reformation in England,* trans. R. E. Scantlebury, 2 vols. New York, 1934–42.

———, "Politique et dogme dans les confessions de foi de Henri VIII, roi d'Angleterre," *Revue Historique, 145* (1927), 1–38.

Cooper, J. P., "Henry VII's Last Years Reconsidered," *Historical Journal, 2* (1959), 103–29.

Coverdale, Miles, trans., *The Christen State of Matrimonye* by Heinrich Bullinger, 1541, *STC* 4045.

———, trans., *New Testament,* Antwerp, 1539, *STC* 2842.

Craig, John, *The Mint,* Cambridge, Cambridge University Press, 1953.

Crawford, James Ludovic Lindsay, Earl of, *Bibliotheca Lindesiana: Handlist of Proclamations,* 3 vols. and suppl. Aberdeen, Aberdeen University Press, 1893–1901. A revision of his *Bibliotheca Lindesiana: Handlist of a Collection of Broadside Proclamations Issued by Authority of the Kings and Queens of Great Britain and Ireland,* London, 1886. See also Steele, Robert.

Curtler, William H., *The Enclosure and Redistribution of Our Land,* Oxford, Clarendon Press, 1920.

Dasent, John R. et al., eds., *Acts of the Privy Council of England, 1452–1628,* 32 vols. London, H.M.S.O., 1890–1907.

Davies, Margaret G., *The Enforcement of English Apprenticeship,* Cambridge, Mass., Harvard University Press, 1956.

Dibdin, Thomas F., *Typographical Antiquities . . . Begun by the Late Joseph Ames . . . Augmented by William Herbert,* 4 vols. London, 1810–19. See also Herbert, William.

Dicey, Albert V., *The Privy Council,* Oxford, 1860.

Dickens, A. G., "The Edwardian Arrears in Augmentations Payments and the Problem of the Ex-Religious," *English Historical Review, 55* (1940), 384–418.

Dietz, Frederick C., *English Government Finance: 1485–1558,* Urbana, University of Illinois Press, 1921.

———, *The Finances of Edward VI and Mary,* Northampton, Mass., Smith College, 1918.

Dodd, Charles (pseud, for Hugh Tootell), *The Church History of England from 1500 to the Year 1688, Chiefly with Regard to Catholics,* 3 vols. [London], 1737–42; ed. M. A. Tierney, 5 vols. London, 1839–43.

Drake, Francis, *Eboracum: or the History and Antiquities of the City of York . . . Collected from Authentic Manuscripts,* 2 vols. London, 1736.

Drummond, Sir Jack Cecil, and A. Wilbrahmin, *The Englishman's Food: A History of Five Centuries of English Diet,* London, Jonathan Cape, 1957.

Dudley, Edmund, *The Tree of Commonwealth,* (1509), ed. D. M. Brodie, Cambridge, Cambridge University Press, 1948.

Duernberg, Ervin, *Henry VIII and Luther: An Account of Their Personal Relations,* Stanford, Stanford University Press, 1961.

Duncan, J. L., "Legal Theories in England in the Sixteenth and Seventeenth Century," *Juridical Review, 50* (1939), 257–81.

Dunham, William H., Jr., "The Ellesmere Extracts from the *Acta Concilia* of Henry VIII," *English Historical Review, 58* (1943), 301–18.

———, "Henry VIII's Whole Council and Its Parts," *Huntington Library Quarterly,* 7 (1943), 7–46.

———, and Stanley Pargellis, eds., *Complaint and Reform in England, 1436–1714,* New York, Oxford University Press, 1938.

Ellis, Henry, ed., *Original Letters Illustrative of English History,* ser. 1–3, 11 vols. London, 1824–46.

Elton, Geoffrey R., "An Early Tudor Poor Law," *Economic History Review,* 2d series, *6* (1952–53), 55–67.

———, *England under the Tudors,* London, Methuen, 1955.

———, "Henry VII: Rapacity and Remorse," *Historical Journal, 1* (1958), 21–39.

———, "Henry VIII's Act of Proclamations," *English Historical Review, 75* (1960), 208–22.

———, "Informing for Profit: A Sidelight on Tudor Methods of Law-enforcement," *Cambridge Historical Journal, 11* (1953–55), 149–67.

———, "State Planning in Early Tudor England," *Economic History Review,* 2d series, 13 (1956–60), 433–39.

———, *The Tudor Constitution: Documents and Commentary,* Cambridge, Cambridge University Press, 1960.

———, *The Tudor Revolution in Government: Administrative Changes in the Reign of Henry VIII,* Cambridge, Cambridge University Press, 1953.

Elyot, Sir Thomas, *The Book Named the Governor* (1531), ed. H. H. Croft, 2 vols. London, 1883.

The Examinacion of W. Thorpe, Preste, 1530, *STC* 24,045.

Exeter Cathedral Library, Broadside 3498/94.

Exposition on I Corinthians, VII, Marburg, June 1529.

Feaveryear, Albert E., *The Pound Sterling, A History of English Money,* Oxford, Clarendon Press, 1931.

Fish, Simon, *A Supplicacyon for the Beggars,* (ca. 1529), *STC* 10,883.

———, trans., *The Summe of the Holye Scripture,* Antwerp (ca. 1529), *STC* 3026.

Fisher, Frederick J., "Commercial Trends in Sixteenth Century England," *Economic History Review,* original series, *10* (1939–40), 95–117.

———, ed., *Essays in the Economic and Social History of Tudor and Stuart England,* Cambridge, Cambridge University Press, 1961.

Fisher, Herbert A., *The History of England from the Accession of Henry VII to the Death of Henry VIII,* New York, Longmans, Green, 1906.

Fitzherbert, Anthony, *The New Boke of Iustices of the Peas,* London, 1538, *STC* 10,969.

Fleetwood, William, *Chronicon preciosum: or, An Account of English Gold and Silver Money . . . ,* London, 1745.

Fortescue, John, *The Governance of England* (ca. 1471), ed. Charles Plummer, Oxford, 1885.

———, *De Laudibus Legum Angliae: A Treatise in Commendation of the Laws of England* (ca. 1469), ed. and trans. S. B. Chrimes, Cambridge, Cambridge University Press, 1942.

———, *De Natura Legis Naturae* (ca. 1469), ed. Thomas Fortescue, Lord Clermont, London, 1869.

Fox, Harold G. *Monopolies and Patents,* Toronto, Toronto University Press, 1947.

Foxe, John, *The Acts and Monuments of John Foxe,* ed. George Townshend, 8 vols. London, 1843–49.

Frith, John, *A Pistle to the Christen Reader: The Reuelation of Antichrist,* Antwerp, J. Luft, 12 July 1529, *STC* 11,394.

Froude, James A., *History of England from the Fall of Wolsey to the Defeat of the Spanish Armada,* 12 vols. London, 1856–70.

———, *The Reign of Henry the Eighth,* 3 vols. London, J. M. Dent, 1908.

Gairdner, James, *The English Church in the Sixteenth Century, from the Accession of Henry VIII to the Death of Mary,* London, Macmillan, 1902.

———, *Henry VII,* London, 1889.

———, ed., *Letters and Papers Illustrative of the Reigns of Richard III and Henry VII,* 2 vols. London, 1861–63.

Gasquet, Francis A., *Henry VIII and the English Monasteries,* 2 vols. London, 1888–89.

———, and Edmund Bishop, *Edward VI and the Book of Common Prayer,* London, 1890.

Gay, Edwin F., "Enclosures in England in the Sixteenth Century," *Quarterly Journal of Economics, 17* (1902–03), 576–97.

Gee, Henry, and William Hardy, eds., *Documents Illustrative of English Church History,* London, 1896.

Gerson, Armand J., et al., *Studies in the History of English Commerce in the Tudor Period,* Philadelphia, University of Pennsylvania Press, 1910.

Gierke, Otto von, *Natural Law and the Theory of Society, 1500–1800; with a Lecture on the Ideas of Natural Law and Humanity, by Ernst Troeltsch,* trans. Ernest Barker, 2 vols. Cambridge, Cambridge University Press, 1934.

Gilbert, Felix, "Sir John Fortescue's *'Dominium Regale et Politicum,'*" *Medievalia et Humanistica,* 2 (1944), 88–97.

Gilbert, Geoffrey, *The History and Practice of the High Court of Chancery,* London, 1758.

———, *A Treatise on the Court of Exchequer,* London, 1758.

A Goodly Prymer in Englyshe with Diuers Prayers, London, J. Byddel, ?1535, *STC* 15,989.

Grafton, Richard, ed., *All Suche Proclamacions as Haue Been Sette Furth by the Kynges Maiestie from the Last Day of January in the First Year of His Highnesses Reign unto the Last Day of Januarii Beeyng in the IIII Yere of His Reigne,* London, R. Grafton, 1550, *STC* 7758.

———, *A Chronicle at Large to the First Yere of Q. Elizabeth,* London, R. Grafton, 1569, *STC* 12,147.

Gras, Norman S., *The Early English Customs System,* Cambridge, Mass., Harvard University Press, 1918.

———, *Evolution of the English Corn Market from the Twelfth to the Eighteenth Century,* Cambridge, Mass., Harvard University Press, 1915.

Hales, John, *A Discourse of the Common Weal of This Realm of England* (ca. 1549), ed. E. Lamond, Cambridge, Cambridge University Press, 1929, *STC* 23,133.

Hall, Edward, *Henry VIII* (1532), ed. Charles Whibley, London, Jack, 1904.

———, *The Vnion of the Two Noble and Illustre Famelies of Lancaster and York,* (1532), *continued by Richard Grafton from 1532,* London, R. Grafton, 1550, *STC* 12,723.

Hallam, Henry, *Constitutional History of England from the Accession of Henry VII to the Death of George II,* 2 vols. London, 1827.

Halliwell-Phillipps, James O., *A Catalogue of Proclamations, Broadsides, Ballads, and Poems,* London, 1851.

Hamilton, E. J., "American Treasure and the Rise of Capitalism," *Economica, 27* (1929), 338–57.

Harmer, Florence E., ed., *Anglo-Saxon Writs,* Manchester, Manchester University Press, 1952.

Hatschek, Julius, *Englisches Staatsrecht,* 2 vols. Tübingen, J. B. Mohr, 1905–1906.

Henry VIII, *The Will of Henry VIII,* ed. Thomas Astle, London, 1844.

Herbert, William, *Typographical Antiquities . . . Begun by the Late Joseph Ames,* 3 vols. London, 1785–90.

Hewens, William A., "The Regulation of Wages by the Justices of the Peace," *Economic Journal, 8* (1898), 340–46.

Hinton, R. W., "English Constitutional Theories from Sir John Fortescue to John Elyot," *English Historical Review, 75* (1960), 410–25.

Holdsworth, William S., *History of English Law,* 9 vols. Boston, Little, Brown, 1922–27.

———, *"The Prerogative in the Sixteenth Century," Columbia Law Review, 21* (1921), 554–71.

———, "The Reception of Roman Law in the Sixteenth Century," *Law Quarterly Review, 27* (1911), 387–98; *28* (1912), 39–51, 131–47, 236–54.

———, *Sources and Literature of English Law,* Oxford, Clarendon Press, 1928.

Holinshed, Raphael, *The Chronicles of England, Scotlande, and Irelande,* 3 vols. London, 1587, *STC* 13,569.

Homilies, *Certayne Sermons or Homilies, appoynted by the Kinges Maiestie to be Declared and Read by All Parsons, Vicars, or Curates euery Sondaye in their Churches,* London, R. Grafton, 31 July 1547, *STC* 13,639.

Hooper, Wilfrid, "The Tudor Sumptuary Laws," *English Historical Review, 30* (1915), 433–49.

Hughes, Paul L., and Robert F. Fries, eds., *Crown and Parliament in Tudor-Stuart England: A Documentary Constitutional History, 1485–1714,* New York, Putnam, 1959.

Hughes, Philip, *The Reformation in England,* 3 vols. London, Hollis and Carter, 1954.

Huntington Library, MS Ellesmere 436.

———, MS Ellesmere 438.

———, MS Ellesmere 439.

———, MS Ellesmere 2654.

———, MS Ellesmere 2655.

———, MS Ellesmere 2758.

Hurstfield, J., "Corruption and Reform under Edward VI and Mary: The Example of Wardship," *English Historical Review, 68* (1953), 22–36.

Hutchins, B. L., "Notes towards the History of London Wages," *Economic Journal, 9* (1899), 599–605; 10 (1900), 103–04.

Iniunctions for the Clergy, London, T. Berthelet, 1538, *STC* 10,087.

Iniunctions gyuen by the Auctoritie of the Kynges Highnes to the Clergie, London, T. Berthelet, 1536, *STC* 10,085.

Innes, Arthur D., *Cranmer and the Reformation in England,* Edinburgh, T. & T. Clarke, 1900.

———, *England under the Tudors,* London, Methuen, 1905.

Innocentius et Alexander Pontifices, etc., (papal bull against rebels), Westminster, Wynkyn de Worde, 1495, *STC* 14,098.

Jackson, William A., unpublished material for a revised edition of *STC.* See *Short-Title Catalogue.*

Judson, Margaret A., *The Crisis of the Constitution,* New Brunswick, N.J., Rutgers University Press, 1949.

Journals of the House of Commons, 1547–1714, 117 vols. London, 1803–63.

Keir, David L., *Constitutional History of Modern Britain since 1485,* London, Black, 1938.

Kerridge, Eric, "Returns of the Inquisitions of Depopulation," *English Historical Review, 70* (1955), 212–28.

Keynes, John M., *A Treatise on Money,* 2 vols. New York, Harcourt Brace, 1930.

Kidd, Beresford J., *The Counter-Reformation,* 1500–1600, Society for Promoting Christian Knowledge, 1933.

Knappen, Marshall M., *Constitutional and Legal History of England,* New York, Harcourt Brace, 1942.

———, *Tudor Puritanism: A Chapter in the History of Idealism,* Chicago, University of Chicago Press, 1939.

Knowles, David, *The Religious Orders in England:* Vol. 3, *The Tudor Age,* Cambridge, Cambridge University Press, 1959.

Kojouharoff, C. D., "Niccolò Machiavelli: His Contribution to the Social Sciences," *National University Law Review,* 7 (1930), 21–81.

Lambard, William, *The Duties of Constables, Borshoulders, Tything-Men, etc.,* London, R. Warde, 1583, *STC* 15,146.

Lambeth Palace Library, Broadside 432.

Latimer, Hugh, *The Works of Bishop Hugh Latimer,* ed. George E. Corrie, 2 vols. London, 1844–45.

Leadam, Isaac S., *The Domesday of Inclosures,* 1517–18, 2 vols. London, 1897.

———, ed., *Select Cases before the King's Council in the Star Chamber,* London, 1898.

Lee, Sidney, ed., *Dictionary of National Biography,* 21 vols. New York, Macmillan, 1909.

Leland, John, *De Rebus Britannicis Collectanea* (ca. 1537), ed. Thomas Hearne, 6 vols. Oxford, 1715.

Lever, Thomas, *Sermons,* ed. Edward Arber, English Reprints, London, 1869.

Liebermann, Felix, ed., *Die Gesetz der Angelsachsen,* 3 vols. Hall, Niemeyer, 1903–16.

Lily, William, *An Introduction of the Eight Partes of Speche,* London, T. Berthelet, 1543, *STC* 15,605.

———, *De Octo Oratione Partium Constructione Libellus,* London, T. Berthelet, 1540, *STC* 15,604.

Lingard, John, *History of England from the First Invasion by the Romans to the Revolution of 1688,* 8 vols. London, 1819–30.

Lingelback, William E., *The Merchant Adventurers of England,* New York, Longmans, Green, 1902.

London, Corporation of, Journals (MSS), Vols. 10–16 (1493–1553), Corporation of London Records Office.

———, Letter Books (MSS), Vols. L–R (1461–1554), Corporation of London Records Office.

London University, *Catalogue of the Collection of English, Scottish, and Irish Proclamations in the University Library (Goldsmiths' Library of Economic Literature),* London, University of London Press, 1928.

Lopez, R. S., and H. A. Miskimin, "The Economic Depression of the Renaissance," *Economic History Review,* 2d series, *14* (1960–61), 408–26.

Lyon, Bryce, *A Constitutional and Legal History of Medieval England,* New York, Harper and Brothers, 1960.

McArthur, Ellen A., "The Regulation of Wages in the Sixteenth Century," *English Historical Review,* 15 (1900), 445–55.

Machyn, Henry, *Diary, 1550–63,* ed. John G. Nichols, London, Camden Society, 1848.

McIlwain, Charles H., *Constitutionalism, Ancient and Modern,* 2d ed., Ithaca, Cornell University Press, 1947.

———, *The High Court of Parliament and Its Supremacy,* New Haven, Yale University Press, 1910.

Mackie, John D., *The Earlier Tudors, 1485–1558,* Oxford, Clarendon Press, 1952.

Maitland, Frederick W., *Constitutional History of England,* Cambridge, Cambridge University Press, 1908.

———, *English Law and the Renaissance,* Cambridge, Cambridge University Press, 1901.

Malkiewicz, A. J., "An Eyewitness Account of the Coup d'État of October 1549," *English Historical Review,* 70 (1955), 600–09.

Malowist, M., "The Economic and Social Development of the Baltic Countries from the Fifteenth to the Sixteenth Centuries," *Economic History Review,* 2d series, *12* (1958–59), 177–89.

Meinecke, Friedrich, *Die Idee der Staatsräson in der Neueren Geschicte,* 3d ed. München, R. Oldenbourg, 1929.

Merriman, Roger B., *The Life and Letters of Thomas Cromwell,* Oxford, Clarendon Press, 1902.

Milnes, Nora, "Mint Records of Henry VIII," *English Historical Review, 32* (1917), 270–73.

More, St. Thomas, *The Workes of Sir Thomas More, Wrytten by Him in the English Tonge,* London, R. Tottel, 1557, *STC* 18,076.

———, *Utopia* (1516), ed. and trans. Joseph H. Lupton, London, 1895.

Morris, Christopher, *Political Thought in England: Tyndale to Hooker*, London, Oxford University Press, 1953.

———, *The Tudors*, London, Batsford, 1955.

Morrison, H. W., "Silver Coinage of Edward VI," *British Numismatic Journal*, new series, *4* (1916), 137–80.

Mosse, George L., "Changes and Continuity in the Tudor Constitution," *Speculum*, 22 (1947), 18–28.

———, "Sir John Fortescue and the Problem of Papal Power," *Medievalia et Humanistica*, 7 (1952), 89–94.

Mozley, J. F., *William Tyndale*, London, Society for Promoting Christian Knowledge, 1937.

A Necessary Doctrine and Erudition for Any Christen Man, Sette Furthe by the Kinges Maiestie, London, T. Berthelet, 29 May 1543, *STC* 5168.

Nef, John U., *Industry and Government in France and England, 1540–1640*, Philadelphia, American Philosophical Society, 1940.

———, "Prices and Industrial Capitalism in France and England, 1540–1640," *Economic History Review*, original series, 7 (1936–37), 155–85.

New Testament. See Coverdale, Miles; Tyndale, William.

Nichols, John G., ed., *Chronicle of Calais in the Reigns of Henry VII and Henry VIII to the Year 1540*, London, 1846.

———, ed., *Chronicle of the Grey Friars of London*, London, 1852.

———, ed., *The Literary Remains of King Edward VI*, 2 vols. London, 1857.

Nicolas, Nicholas H., ed., *Proceedings and Ordinances of the Privy Council of England, 1386–1542*, 7 vols. London, 1837.

Northampton Record Office, Brudenell (Deene) Collection.

Ogilvie, C., *The King's Government and the Common Law, 1471–1641*, Oxford, Blackwell, 1958.

Old Testament. See Tyndale, William.

Oman, Charles, *The Coinage of England*, Oxford, Clarendon Press, 1931.

Otway-Ruthven, J., *The King's Secretary and the Signet Office in the Fifteenth Century*, Cambridge, Cambridge University Press, 1939.

Perceval, R. W., "Henry VIII and the Origin of Royal Assent by Commission," *Parliamentary Affairs*, *3* (1949–50), 307–15.

Percy, Eustace, *The Privy Council under the Tudors*, Oxford, Blackwell, 1907.

Petit-Dutaillis, Charles, and Georges Lefebvre, *Studies and Notes Supplementary to Stubb's Constitutional History*, Manchester, Manchester University Press, 1929.

Pickthorn, Kenneth W., *Early Tudor Government:* Vol. 1, *Henry VII;* Vol. 2, *Henry VIII*, Cambridge, Cambridge University Press, 1934.

Pocock, Nicholas, "The Conditions of Morals and Religious Beliefs in the Reign of Edward VI," *English Historical Review*, *10* (1894), 417–44.

———, ed., *Records of the Reformation: The Divorce, 1527–1533,* 2 vols. London, 1870.

———, *Troubles Connected with the Book of Common Prayer of 1549,* Westminister, 1884.

Pollard, Albert F., "Council, Star Chamber, and Privy Council under the Tudors," *English Historical Review, 37* (1922), 337–60, 516–39; *38* (1923), 42–60.

———, *England under Protector Somerset,* London, Kegan Paul, 1900.

———, *Henry VIII,* London, Goupil, 1902.

———, *History of England from the Accession of Edward VI to the Death of Elizabeth,* London, Longmans, Green, 1913.

———, ed., *The Reign of Henry VII from Contemporary Sources,* 3 vols. New York, Longmans, Green, 1913–14.

———, *Wolsey,* Longmans, Green, 1929.

Pollard, Alfred W., ed., *Records of the English Bible, the Documents Relating to the Translation and Publication of the Bible in English, 1525–1611,* London, H. Frowde, 1911.

The Primer, Set Foorth by the Kynges Maiestie and His Clergie, to be Taught, Lerned, and Read: and None Other to be Vsed throughout All His Dominions, London, R. Grafton, 29 May 1545, *STC* 16,034.

Privy Council, *A Proclamacion Concernyng the Deuisers of Certain Vile Letters,* London, R. Grafton, 10 October 1549, *STC* 7829.

———, *A Proclamacion Conteinyng the Trouth of the Duke of Somersets Euel Gouernment,* London, R. Grafton, 8 October 1549, *STC* 7828.

Public Record Office of Great Britain, Chancery Warrants.

———, Close Rolls.

———, Exchequer of the Treasury Receipts, Miscellanea.

———, Patent Rolls.

———, State Papers Domestic.

———, Treaty Rolls.

Ramsay, George D., *English Overseas Trade during the Centuries of Emergence,* London, Macmillan, 1957.

Read, Conyers, *The Tudors: Personalities and Practical Politics in Sixteenth Century England,* New York, Henry Holt, 1936.

Ribton-Turner, Charles J., *History of Vagrants and Vagrancy and Beggars and Begging,* London, 1887.

Rich, Edward E., ed., *Ordinance Book of the Merchants of the Staple,* Cambridge, Cambridge University Press, 1937.

Richardson, H. G., and G. Sayles, "The Early Statutes," *Law Quarterly Review, 50* (1934), 201–23, 540–70.

Richardson, Walter C., "The Surveyor of the King's Prerogative," *English Historical Review, 56* (1941), 52–75.

———, *Tudor Chamber Administration, 1485–1547,* Baton Rouge, Louisiana State University Press, 1952.

Robertson, A. J., ed. and trans., *The Laws of the Kings of England from Edmund to Henry I,* Cambridge, Cambridge University Press, 1925.

Ridley, Jasper, *Thomas Cranmer,* Oxford, Clarendon Press, 1962.

Rogers, J. E. Thorold, *Six Centuries of Work and Wages,* Oxford, 1884.

Rose-Troup, Frances, *The Western Rebellion of 1549,* London, Smith, Elder, 1913.

Roy, William, *Rede Me and Be nott Wrothe,* Strasbourg, J. Schott, 1528, *STC* 21,427.

Ruddock, A. A., "The Earliest Records of the High Court of Admiralty, 1515–58," *Bulletin of the Institute of Historical Research,* 22 (1949), 139–49.

Ruding, Rogers, *Annals of the Coinage of Britain* . . . , 3 vols. London, 1819.

Rymer, Thomas, et al., eds., *Foedera, conventiones, literae et cujuscunque generis acta publica* . . . 20 vols. London, 1703–35.

St. Germain, Christopher, *The Dialogue in English between a Doctor of Divinity and a Student* (1531), ed. William Muchall, Cincinnati, 1874.

Schanz, Georg, ed., *Englische Handelspolitik gegen Ende des Mittelalters,* 2 vols. Leipzig, 1881.

Scofield, Cora L., *A Study of the Court of Star Chamber,* Chicago, University of Chicago Press, 1900.

Short-Title Catalogue of Books Printed in England, Scotland, and Ireland, and of English Books Printed Abroad, 1475–1640, ed. Alfred W. Pollard, G. R. Redgrave et al., London, Bibliographical Society, 1926.

Simon, André L., *History of the Wine Trade in England,* 3 vols. London, Wyman and Sons, 1906–09.

Smith, Goldwin, *A Constitutional and Legal History of England,* New York, Charles Scribner's Sons, 1955.

Smith, Lacey B., *Tudor Prelates and Politics, 1536–58,* Princeton, Princeton University Press, 1953.

Smith, Preserved, "Luther and Henry VIII," *English Historical Review, 25* (1910), 656–69.

Society of Antiquaries Library, *Proclamations* (MSS and *STC*), Vols. 1–3 (1464–1558). See also *Tudor Proclamations.*

———, *Lemon Addenda* (MSS and *STC*).

———, MS 116.

Somerset, Edward Seymour, Duke of, *An Epistle or Exhortacion to Vnitie & Peace,* London, R. Grafton, 1548, *STC* 22,268.

State Papers, Henry VIII, 11 vols. London, 1830–52.

Statutes of the Realm, eds. Alexander Luders et al., 11 vols. London, 1810–28.

Staunford, William, *An Exposicion of the Kinges Prerogatiue* (1549), London, R. Tottell, 1567, *STC* 23,213.

Steele, Robert, *A Bibliography of Royal Proclamations of the Tudor and Stuart Sovereigns and of Others Published under Authority, 1485–1714: With an Historical Essay on Their Origin and Use,* Vol. 5, *Bibliotheca Lindesiana,* Oxford, Clarendon Press, 1910.

Stephens, James F., *History of the Criminal Law of England,* 3 vols. London, 1883.

Stephenson, Carl, and Frederick Marcham, eds., *Sources of English Constitutional History,* New York, Harper, 1937.

Stone, Lawrence, "Thomas Cromwell's Political Programme," *Bulletin of the Institute of Historical Research, 24* (1951), 1–18.

———, "State Control in Sixteenth-Century England," *Economic History Review,* original series, *17* (1947), 103–20.

Stow, John, *The Annales of England, From the First Inhabitation Vntil 1592,* London, R. Newberry, 1592, *STC* 23,334.

Strutt, Joseph, *Sports and Pasttimes of the People of England,* 4 vols. London, 1831.

Strype, John, ed., *Annals of the Reformation* (1709–31), 4 vols. Oxford, 1824.

———, *Ecclesiastical Memorials,* 3 vols. London, 1721.

———, *Memorials of the Most Reverend Father in God, Thomas Cranmer* (1694), 3 vols. Oxford, 1848–54.

Stubbs, William, *The Constitutional History of England, in Its Origin and Development,* 3 vols. Oxford, 1874–78.

———, ed., *Select Charters and Other Illustrations of English Constitutional History* (1874), ed. H. W. C. Davis, Oxford, Oxford University Press, 1913.

Tanner, Joseph R., ed., *Tudor Constitutional Documents, A. D. 1485–1603,* 2d ed. Cambridge, Cambridge University Press, 1930.

Tawney, Richard H., *The Agrarian Problem in the Sixteenth Century,* London, Longmans, Green, 1912.

———, *Religion and the Rise of Capitalism,* London, J. Murray, 1926.

———, and Eileen Power, eds., *Tudor Economic Documents: Being Select Documents Illustrating the Economic and Social History of Tudor England,* 3 vols. London, Longmans, Green, 1924.

Tootell, Hugh. See Dodd, Charles.

Tudor Proclamations: Facsimiles of Proclamations of Henry VII, Henry VIII, Edward VI, and Philip and Mary, Now in the Library of the Society of Antiquaries, London, 1897.

Tyndale, William, trans., *The Fyrst Boke of Moses, Called Genesis . . . (The Second . . . The Fifth Boke),* Antwerp, H. Luft, 17 January 1530, *STC* 2350.

———, trans., *New Testament,* 1526, *STC* 2824.

———, *The Obedience of a Christen Man,* Antwerp, H. Luft, 2 October 1528, *STC* 24,446.

———, [The Parable of the Wicked Mammon] *That Fayth the Mother of all Good Workes Iustifieth Vs,* Antwerp, J. Luft, 2 October 1528, *STC* 24,454.

———, *The Practyce of Prelates,* 1530, *STC* 24,465.

Tytler, Patrick F., ed., *England under the Reigns of Edward VI and Mary,* 2 vols. London, 1839.

University Microfilms, *Partial List of Microfilms of Books Printed in England before 1640,* 41 issues, Ann Arbor, 1937–51.

———, *English Books 1475–1640: Consolidated Cross Index by STC Numbers, Years 1–19,* Ann Arbor, 1956.

Vinogradoff, Paul, "Reason and Conscience in Sixteenth Century Jurisprudence," *Law Quarterly Review, 24* (1908), 373–84.

Walker, Patrick C., "Capitalism and the Reformation," *Economic History Review,* original series, *8* (1937–38), 1–19.

Wanley, Humphrey, *A Catalogue of the Harleian Collection of Manuscripts,* 2 vols. London, 1759.

Warbeck, Perkin, *Richard, by the grace of Gode, King of England and of Fraunce, Lord of Ireland, Prince of Walles, To All Thos that Thes Our Present Letters Shall See . . . Greeting . . .* (1497), BM MS Harl 283, 123*v*.

Warmutts, F. D., *The Origins of Modern Constitutionalism,* New York, Harper, 1949.

Weissberger, L. A., "Machiavelli and Tudor England," *Political Science Quarterly, 42* (1927), 589–607.

White, Beatrice, ed., *The Vulgaria of John Stanbridge and the Vulgaria of Robert Whittinton,* Early English Text Society Publications, 187, London, Kegan Paul, 1932.

Wilkins, David, ed., *Concilia Magnae Britanniae et Hiberniae,* 4 vols. London, 1732–37.

Williams, Charles H., *The Making of Tudor Despotism,* London, T. Nelson and Sons, 1935.

———, "The Rebellion of Humphrey Stafford in 1486," *English Historical Review, 43* (1928), 181–89.

Williamson, James A., *Maritime Enterprise, 1485–1558,* Oxford, Clarendon Press, 1913.

Winfield, Percy F., *The Chief Sources of English Legal History,* Cambridge, Cambridge University Press, 1925.

Wolf, Adolf, ed., *A Dialogue between a Christian Father and His Stubborn Son* (1530), Vienna, 1874.

Wriothesley, Charles, *Chronicle of England during the Reigns of the Tudors, 1485–1559,* ed. William D. Hamilton, 2 vols. London, 1875–77.

York House Books (MSS), Vols. 1–6 (1486–1490), City of York Record Office.

Zeeveld, W. Gordon, *The Foundations of Tudor Policy,* Cambridge, Mass., Harvard University Press, 1948.

Indexes

[All index references are to proclamation text numbers, not to page numbers.]

Index of Statutes

Index of Names

Index of Subjects